Artists Who Kill

& Other Essays on Art

Other Books by Alexander Theroux

FICTION
Three Wogs
Darconville's Cat
An Adultery
Laura Warholic; or, The Sexual Intellectual

FABLES
The Schinocephalic Waif
The Great Wheadle Tragedy
Master Snickup's Cloak
Fables

SHORT FICTION
Early Stories
Later Stories

POETRY
The Lollipop Trollops and Other Poems
Collected Poems
Truisms

NONFICTION
The Primary Colors
The Secondary Colors
The Enigma of Al Capp
The Strange Case of Edward Gorey
Estonia: A Ramble Through the Periphery
The Grammar of Rock: Art and Artlessness in 20th Century Pop Lyrics
Einstein's Beets: An Examination of Food Phobias

Alexander Theroux

§

Artists Who Kill
& Other Essays on Art

Tough Poets Press
Arlington, Massachusetts

ISBN 979-8-218-17343-2

Tough Poets Press
Arlington, Massachusetts 02476
U.S.A.

www.toughpoets.com

For Sarah,
Shenandoah, and Shiloh,
my favorite artists

and for Peter Palandjian

Scripta volent, amor manent

Contents

Artists Who Kill

Artists live dangerously. Creation is a risk that can mix perception with obsession, that can open the floodgates to violence. And as Oscar Wilde once reminded us, "There is no essential incongruity between crime and culture." A violent tension can exist, and in my opinion usually does, between the artist and society. Worse, artists always compete with themselves, often fighting against the drive to create as passionately as they do for the chance to do so. A blank and empty canvas, arguably, remains as much an obstacle to art as a challenge or opportunity to fill it with one's dreams. It might also be said that in a very real way, artists are driven to regard part of themselves as an enemy.

The world is a club in and to which many of us feel we do not belong. We suspect half the time we not only succeed, but even exist, through chance or luck or even sham. This might very well point to one of the most basic motives for suicide, the paradoxical attempt, oddly enough, an elemental existence assertion, of trying to offer some desperate proof one exists as worthwhile.

Art intimidates artists, and intensity wounds. An artist may not even feel worthy of creation, may feel, with terror, he can't do it—or do it again—and that further and newer attempts at his craft will only prove his emptiness or reveal him a fraud. The artist's work itself connotes a certain danger. Plato, and many other thinkers after him, have concluded that all art is immoral and all artists a menace to the safety and well-being of the state. Some painters have rejected the style of art that had won favor with their public and brought them money and fame. After several attacks brought on by mental crises, Scottish painter David Wilkie dropped the manner which had made him the most popular painter of his day. The successful illustrator Achille Deveria, dissatisfied with doing chic things for his many clients, threw up his hands and took a job, happily took a job, in the print department of the Bibliothèque Nationale in 1849 in order to make a living in some other way. Antoine-Jean Gros refused to paint the Battle of Jena at the command of the court of Louis Phillippe.

Are painters and writers and musicians any different in their indignation and fury than the average man? If so, then in what way? What characterizes their hatreds? What is the nature of artistic neurosis? Creative passion? Vanity? Revenge? Need? Guilt? ("There is nothing to compare to passion for giving one cold insight," wrote Bertrand Russell. "Most of my best work has been done in the inspiration of remorse.") Are artists any less or more prone to violence than the rest of us? Isn't the very act of creative change often effected through violence? (Film director Werner Fassbinder's play *Katzelmacher* was itself an aggression against the very audience that applauded it.) But if violence is the result of a heightened sensibility, isn't a contradiction involved? How can someone with the talent to create at the same time so readily destroy? Does the strange and intimidating power of the one inherently carry with it the power of the other? What Zoroastrian mystery is at work?

One answer is that artists, supremely men and women of

passion, often live on the edge of the law, no matter how propagandists outside their world try to drag them by the hair into the national morality. They seek kinship, many of them, to a terrible degree of intimacy, with the irrational and the inexplicable, with dedication as idealistic as prayer and invariably a will of iron to succeed as consuming as hellfire. "As men's prayers are a disease of the will, so are their creeds a disease of the intellect," wrote Ralph Waldo Emerson, who could have been thinking of any one of a number of driven writers, painters, and sculptors with an inexorable, unstoppable, irrevocable drive to create.

Friedrich Nietzsche portentously wrote, "Unless you have chaos inside you, you cannot give birth to a dancing star." The artist who reaches into the inner resources of his deepest and darkest dreams in order to *make* would never have been able to become freely creative, daring, or brave unless he was willing to mine that havoc and face that disarray and plumb the depths of that tumult and turmoil necessary to beget his vision.

An artistic need for concealment and for control is often contemporaneous with—cotemporaneous to—the concomitant need to convey. The tension can be merciless. The famously complex grid paintings of Canadian Agnes Martin, for example, which to me represent that duality, were both a screen and a shield, simultaneously. The mental illness suffered by this Abstract Expressionist, what art critic Peter Schjeldahl identified as "oceanic states of mind that she couldn't help experiencing"—Martin was diagnosed with paranoid schizophrenia in early childhood—almost perversely reveal and restrain her visions, both. Perhaps this was the source of her creative madness. She would wait sometimes for weeks on end, rocking in her chair, steadying herself for a glimpse of whatever vision would emerge. Then an exquisite painting would appear—a matrix, a graticule, a lattice, a grating, framework seeded with hundreds of tiny, paired dots—always reserved yet revealing, where everything is relentlessly the same, and yet out of this sort of psychotic sameness emerged visions unlike anything that had gone before. The scaling alone, the fractions, the strictures!

Confrontation is involved in almost all artists do; the testing of emotions, flirting with conflict, asking the unavoidable if sometimes unanswerable questions. Theirs are the dark and lunar paths that must be trod. "There is no passion to be found playing small—in settling for a life that is less than the one you are capable of living," stated the brave and uncompromising Nelson Mandela, who for his dreams spent 27 years in prison. The Athenian painter Parrhasius, for example, having decided to represent Prometheus, bought an old man and tortured him in order to study agony's changing features. Painters during the Renaissance had no access to cadavers because of the theological belief in the literal resurrection of the body (the only human material available to them for study would have been an occasional severed head from a decapitated criminal or a leg or two severed in combat).

So, Leonardo da Vinci once calmly—some say ruthlessly—proceeded to sketch a body hanging from a building of one of the Pazzi conspirators while on the very same sheet disinterestedly making the following note: "Small cap, tan-colored, doublet of black satin, black-lined jerkin, blue coat lined with black and white stripes of velvet. Bernardo di Bendino Baroncelli. Black hose."

Without question, there is a voyeuristic pull toward the ultimate horrors of life—conflict is the beating heart of any play, story, novel, opera, painting—exploiting the invention of even the most pacific of artists and writers. Doesn't Tolstoy liken Hadji Murat's severed head to a beautiful Tartar thistle he uprooted one day from a ditch? There is the thunder and lightning of menace in an artist's daily dreams. Consider William-Adolphe Bouguereau's *Dante and Virgil in Hell* (1850), and simply ask yourself if that shocking canvas as its stands could have been borne a conception—never mind made a painting—by your common salesman or fainthearted CPA or diffident loading clerk? Look at Paul Cézanne's *The Murder* (1867) or Giovanni Bellini's *The Assassination of St. Peter the Martyr* (1507) or Artemisia Gentileschi's *Judith Slaying Holofernes* (1620) or Edward Munch's *The Death of Marat* (1907) or Van Gogh's *Skull of a Skeleton with Burning Cigarette* (1866) or Francis Bacon's triptych *Three Studies for Figures at the Base of a Crucifixion* (1944).

Who is shocked that Francis Bacon painted human screams? "I think probably the best human cry in painting," this strange English painter once remarked, "was made by [Nicolas] Poussin." He was speaking of the hair-raising *The Massacre of the Innocents* (1625-1632), showing a baby put to the sword. Who is surprised at the violence of Frieda Kahlo, whose grim *Suicide of Dorothy Hale* (1938)—the defenestration of that beauty in three successive stages—surely matches in goriness the horror of *A Few Small Nips* (1938), where the artist is shown naked, bloody, having been carved to death by her husband. (Kahlo often warned her lovers to be careful, as her husband Diego Rivera, who always carried a gun, "was perfectly capable of murder.") The idea of "making" almost always involves plumbing one's soul. It has often been said that the origin of art began with tracing an outline around a person's shadow.

We have often been told how art moderates and tempers the emotions; a palliative, the Aristotelian catharsis that purges the viewer of pity and fear. What then of Bacon's painted figures as victims of aggression? His nightmarish distortions of friends, businessmen, ecclesiastics, and animals, all set in ominously confined spaces? His triptychs of grotesque male forms writhing in sequence across panels? Can we assume that his *Head Surrounded by Sides of Beef* (1954), for instance, means that he is not likely to go marauding through the night or shove bamboo splints under a visitor's fingernails? Perhaps. (One of his favorite lines is reportedly, "I give champagne to my real friends. I give real pain to my sham friends.")

A large number of artists can be found whose very work is actually directed against their own attempts at *trying* to work—and not always because of anything very rational, merely often because it seemed actually to comfort them to be dissatisfied. Existential Dread began to be very popular in the 1940s and 50s, but a great deal of slashing and burning has always gone on in the fierce world of art. A magnificent pietà, barely visible in a corner of the Duomo, reveals the battering hammer marks of Michelangelo's frustrated fury. Almost penniless, Claude Monet left a house he rented in Ville d'Avray in 1866—he was 26—after slashing as many as 200 canvases to keep them from creditors.

Paul Cézanne would fly into rages against himself, indiscriminately slashing his own canvases. In fact, Cézanne, according to Alberto Giacometti, never really finished any of his paintings— he merely abandoned the job, in despair. "After Vollard had posed a hundred times the most Cézanne could say was that the shirt front wasn't too bad. And he was right. It's the best part of the picture." Giacometti once confided to his friend James Lord—he was posing for him—that he doubted his own ability to paint Lord as he saw him. Giacometti, in fact, is a prime example of artistic anxiety. The sculptor had elaborate rituals of avoidance when facing a blank canvas and would often become irrational and tear up piles of drawings, feeling that they were all "hopeless." In his youth Piet Mondrian would periodically borrow a friend's automatic pistol and shoot holes in paintings that no longer pleased him. Jasper Johns has been said to burn his work, and there are many reports of a frustrated Winslow Homer carting off his watercolors and burying them in a swamp. I've done it myself—disposing not only drawings, but manuscripts. It feels fabulous.

Violence has often characterized the world of painters. When he was an old man exiled in France, Goya claimed he had not only once been knifed in the back in Madrid but fled Spain and the small town of Fuendetodos, where he grew up, because of a fatal street fight there. The painter Gustave Courbet, a highly passionate republican, did time in prison (and eventually went into exile) for the role that he played in 1871 in tearing down the Colonne Vendôme, a Napoleonic monument in central Paris that was detested by the Communards. Salvator Rosa was a bandit. Thomas Rowlandson was loud, crass, and a fanatical gambler. Paul Gauguin was seriously hurt in a brawl with sailors in Brittany in 1894. And on Christmas Eve, 1888, while he was walking in the street, he heard footsteps behind him and turned with alarm to see an unstrung Van Gogh coming at him menacingly with a razor. Gauguin later reported that he "stared him to a halt" and that Van Gogh retreated. Later that night Van Gogh cut off the lobe of his left ear, put it in an envelope, and gave it to a trollop in a brothel named Rachel with these words, "Guard this object carefully."

Carlo Crivelli was imprisoned in Venice for adultery in 1457. The leading German late Gothic sculptor Veit Stoss, after attempting to exculpate himself from a criminal charge in 1496 by forging a document, was sentenced to be branded on both cheeks and forbidden on pain of death to leave the city of Nuremberg. Fra Filippo Lippi not only went on trial for fraud but once abducted a nun, Lucrezia, the mother, it turns out, of the genius Filippino. And then

Duccio di Buoninsegna, the first great Sienese painter, was heavily fined throughout his entire life, once for refusing military service, and another time for refusing to swear fealty to the Capitano del Populo, a civil official. He was also fined in 1302 for debts incurred; and yet again a few years later for activity connected with sorcery. William Hogarth was rabidly anti-French and xenophobic and constantly pugnacious, delighting, as he did, in scourging the likes of Wilkes, Pitt, Temple, Chandos, and Lord Burlington with his unrelenting pencil. And George Morland was arrested (as a French spy) while on the run from his creditors, after which he spent time in the King's Bench Prison. He died in prison in 1804 after producing an enormous amount of stamped work in order to pay his debts.

Benvenuto Cellini, whose work as a goldsmith took him from Florence to Mantua to Rome, was often obliged to move because of his brawls and intrigues. The Italian goldsmith, sculptor, painter, soldier, and musician had the tongue of a scorpion and the vanity of a child. Cross him, speak ill of his craftsmanship, choose the wrong word in conversation with him, and he became a foaming Mercutio—"And but one word with one of us? Couple it with something; make it a word and a blow." It requires but a quick read of Benvenuto's classic autobiography (1563) to prove how real are those tough Italian street scenes found in Shakespeare. He stole papal jewelry, constantly picked fights, seduced a prostitute's 14-year-old serving girl, and repeatedly spent time in jail. He became notoriously embroiled in a blood feud with the Guasconti family, admitting he was "somewhat hot-blooded by nature." He attacked them "like a raging bull" and stabbed one of them—for which he was sentenced to death in absentia, having already gone on the run. After his brother was murdered, Cellini ran to confront the killer to try "to cut off his head cleanly" before stabbing him with a long, twisted dagger that he "drove down so deeply through the man's shoulder that he could not remove the blade." In another imbroglio, he also shot an innkeeper dead—and he recounts all these crimes in his autobiography. He escaped being executed because he was so admired as an artist. In those days, geniuses really could get away with murder.

An angry Cellini also claimed to have killed a certain Imperial commander named Charles de Bourbon during the Seige of Rome, where, according to his own account, he played a heroic part in the defense of that city. On January 14, 1523, he was sentenced to pay 12 *staia* of flour for relations with a boy named Domenico di ser Giuliano da Ripa. While in Paris, a former model and lover brought charges against him of using her "after the Italian fashion" (i.e. sodomy). In Florence in 1548, Cellini was accused by a woman named Margherita for having engaged in certain familiarities with her son, Vincenzo. On February 26, 1556, his apprentice Fernando di Giovanni di Montepulciano accused his mentor of having sodomized him many times. This time the penalty was the fine of fifty golden *scudi* and a sentence of four years of prison, a punishment that was eventually remitted to four years of house arrest, thanks to the intercession of the influential Medici.

Added to that, Cellini threatened to kill the impresario painter Francesco Prima Ficcio "like a dog." Then there was another person, one Pompeo de' Capitaneis, a jeweler from Milan who had crossed Benvenuto in negotiations over work to be done for Pope Clement VII. Pompeo became insolent with him, then boldly walked away. Waiting for him outside an apothecary shop minutes later, Cellini had satisfaction. "I drew a little dagger with a sharpened edge, and breaking the line of his defenders, laid my hands upon his breast so quickly and coolly, that none of them were able to prevent me," Cellini explained. "Then I aimed to strike him in the face; but fright made him turn his head round; and I stabbed him just beneath the ear. I only gave two blows, for he fell stone dead at the second. I had not meant to kill him; but as the saying goes, blows are not dealt by measure."

Who is surprised that Herman Melville in *Moby-Dick* (chapter 28) compares his contentious and unappeasable character, Ahab, at the captain's first appearance, to a sculpture by wild man Cellini? Melville, who could not have picked a more apt double for his anti-hero, wrote, "His whole high, broad form, seemed made of solid bronze, and shaped in an unalterable mould, like Cellini's cast Perseus."

I am reminded in all this of the poet and apparent ne'er-do-well François Villon, considered by many as the most illustrious and genuine precursor of the "cursed poetry." He was involved in a scuffle in 1455 that resulted in the stabbing death of a rogue priest named Philippe Chermoye (aka Sermaise) who disputed the free favors of a beautiful girl. Villon, who was losing the fight, grabbed the dagger from his belt and struck down his romantic rival and so immediately had to flee Paris. Some say that it was an angry Sermaise who first attacked Villon with a dagger after an exchange of words; Villon defended himself with his own knife, but also managed to strike Sermaise's skull with a rock, killing him. In 1456, Villon obtained a pardon, but later with a group of friends he looted the Collège de Navarre. After being imprisoned many times he confessed to all of his crimes, including the priest's death. He was sentenced to be hanged and strangled. His masterpiece, *"Ballade des pendu,"* was written while awaiting his death. However, fortune smiled on him again and the sentence was commuted to 10 years of exile from Paris. Villon received a pardon on grounds that the homicide was justified, however, after friends and family petitioned on his behalf.

Then of course there was Mexican painter David Alfaro Siqueiros, who had been enlisted as an agent in the 1930s by the Soviet NKVD. He was not only imprisoned and exiled many times during his tempestuous career as a political revolutionary but in 1910 actually led a massive armed assault on the house of Leon Trotsky. (Incidentally, Russian poet Marina Tsvetaeva's husband, the poet Sergei Efron, was also an NKVD hitman, and was implicated in a plot against various White emigres. He was executed in Russia in 1941.) Siqueiros's 50,000 square foot mural, *March of Humanity*, was conceived, in fact, while he was a political prisoner. He only painted scenes of national concern, murals filled with striking colors, massed persons, and raw emotions, the subject matter of which is indicated by such titles as *There Is No Other Road but Ours* and *Third World* and *The Complete Safety of All Mexicans At Work*. Siqueiros, who was really a painter and politician in equal parts, once wrote, "An art without ideological function . . . changes the artist progressively and inevitably into a juggler for the society of 'ladies and gentlemen.'"

It was also the political activities of Adriaen Brouwer, whom Rubens admired—his pictures, apart from a few landscapes, represent sordid tavern scenes, usually of boors carousing—that led to his imprisonment in 1633, where the prison baker, incidentally, was Joos van Craesbeck, who eventually became his pupil and imitator.

As an individual, the American painter James Abbott McNeill Whistler—who published his letters under the title *The Gentle Art of Making Enemies* (1890)—was arrogant and irascible, a compulsive quarreler. His ego was legendary. When someone once told him that the two greatest painters who ever lived were Velázquez and himself, he reportedly replied, "Why drag in Velázquez?" He went bankrupt after suing John Ruskin for libel when Ruskin criticized his work, particularly his *Nocturne in Black and Gold: Falling Rocket* (1874), asserting that Whistler's paintings were "only flinging a pot of paint in the public's face." In fact, at the time of his death in 1903, he was considered so disreputable that no public gallery in England owned one of his works. Of course as far as arrogance goes one cannot forget El Greco who replied, when Pius V proposed to cover the nudities in Michelangelo's *Last Judgment* (a work eventually done by Daniele da Volterra), that if the whole thing were demolished he would paint another as good.

Envy is also violence. Delacroix detested Ingres. Watteau snubbed Nicolas Lancret. Daumier accused Manet of reducing painting to the "faces on playing cards." Algardi despised Bernini. And Cellini hated Baccio Bandinelli, a Florentine sculptor, who enjoyed the favor of the Medici through whom he got the commission for his *Hercules and Cacus*, done in direct emulation of Michelangelo's *David*. Pietro Torrigiani, whose masterpiece is the *Tomb of Henry VII* (1512), not only once broke Michelangelo's nose in a fistfight, but actually starved himself to death from sheer spleen. Leonardo and Michelangelo of course disliked each other intensely, but Michelangelo was also actively hostile to Perugino—he tended to dislike all Umbrians—and his sallies against him were proverbial. It was Michelangelo who also declared that Titian could not draw. Then there was bitter enmity between Giovanni Lanfranco and Domenico Zampieri (a.k.a. Domenichino) at having to share the commission by Pope Gregory XV for the decoration of the choir and pendentives of St. Andrea delle Valle. (Domenichino, so the story goes, weakened part of the scaffolding, hoping that Lanfranco would break his neck.) Gauguin thought Cimabue clumsy, and Cézanne ridiculed Gauguin, saying, "Gauguin isn't a painter, he has only made Chinese images."

André Breton despised Jean Cocteau. Picasso abhorred Juan Gris. William Blake hated the engraver Cromek. John Lirinell's son-in-law Samuel Palmer hated him. There was deep animosity between Baron François Gerard and not only Jacques David, his teacher, but also Antoine Jean Gros, whom he defeated, by political guile mostly, in his efforts to secure the court appointment to the restored Bourbons. Manet remarked that Courbet's ideal was a billiard ball. Writer Wyndham Lewis set out to kill the philosopher T. E. Hulme, who had bested his rival in a love affair with the painter Kate Lechmere and declared he preferred Jacob Epstein's work to Lewis's. He marched in, according to one observer, seizing Hulme by the throat, but the bigger man dragged Lewis out to Soho Sq., where he hung him ignominiously upside down from his trousers on an iron railing there and calmly returned to his soirée.

Raphael Sanzio's altarpiece painting *St. Cecilia* (1516-17), a masterpiece done for a church in Bologna in which the patroness of musicians is portrayed not as heavenly and remote rather but fetchingly depicted as a singing saint who is in a trance, with a musical instrument broken at her feet, was so overwhelming in its power that, so legend goes, it supposedly caused his contemporary, the Italian painter Francisco Francia to die of depression—could that be ruled a suicide?—at his own inferiority. However, as his friendship with Raphael is now well known, this story has been discredited.

And what of Henri Rousseau's death? It was also a suicide of sorts, for the Douanier—an appellation taken from his job as a customs officer—although he had been married twice before, nevertheless died of a broken heart in the Necker Hospital in Paris on September 2, 1910, after having been repeatedly turned down by the woman he wanted to marry and whom he had pressed, always in vain, with increasingly urgent proposals of marriage. Romantic disappointment has caused the death of several other painters. Jean Francois de Troy, after being replaced as Director of the French Academy in Rome, died of grief in 1752 at the thought of leaving a young Roman woman with whom he had just fallen in love. Then there was Pierre-Paul Prud'hon who, after contracting at an early age an unfortunate marriage, which caused him many years of grief, became deeply attached to his pupil and mistress Constance Mayer. It was such a shattering blow to him when she committed suicide that the shock led quickly to his own death.

Artists' suicides abound. Antoine Jean Gros drowned himself. Emanuel de Witte was found hanging from a bridge. (He couldn't bear the thought that his second wife and daughter had been convicted of theft.) Nicolas de Staël threw himself out of his studio window in Antibes. According to Vasari, Giovanni Rosso killed himself. Pietro Testa, also called Lucchesino, drowned himself in the Tiber in 1650—he was only 39—a suicide brought on by bitterness at his failure to secure commissions for his work. "Pascin," the pseudonymn of Julius Pincus, a Bulgarian Jew, strangled himself in 1930 on the opening day of his one-man show at the Georges Petit Gallery. Ernst Ludwig Kirchner, one of the leaders of *Die Brucke* art and a man of a nervous and ultrasensitive temperament, committed suicide at 58 in June 1938. Three French surrealists—Jacques Rigaut, Jacques Vaché, and Rene Crével—each made elaborate preparations for their suicides months and even years prior to the actual events. There was a dedication to it. (Rigaut, who earlier had written, "Suicide is a vocation," shot himself with a revolver; Vaché took an overdose of opium with a friend; Crével, a fervent Marxist, after a falling out with André Breton, attached a cardboard label with his name printed on it to his left wrist and gassed himself.)

Pablo Picasso's closest friend, the lovestruck Carlos Casegemas, shot himself in a café in Paris over his unrequited love for the illegitimate, half-Spanish "model" Germaine Gargallo Pichot, the Catalan artist who had been a roommate of Picasso and then his lover. He had fallen desperately, insanely, in love with her although she was married, but she refused to be his mistress. On February 17, 1901, Casagemas, a morphine addict and alcoholic—he was also said to be impotent—took a shot at her in a Montmartre restaurant, missed (or, rather, had his arm deflected), and then put a bullet through his own temple. His pockets were found to be bulging with suicide notes.

Grieving, Picasso never got over it. "Pondering on Casagemas's death is what started me painting in blue," he told a biographer, the French journalist Pierre Daix. Picasso painted his masterpiece, *La Vie* (1903), the pinnacle of his blue period, in the Barcelona apartment that the two men had once shared.

Other painters who took their own lives were François Lemoyne, Wilhelm Lehmbruck, the haunted German sculptor, and Benjamin Haydon who at 60 found himself so deeply in debt and so crushed by disappointments that he scrawled the line, "Stretch me no longer on this rough world," and put a bullet through his head. Francesco Bassano, of the famous Venetian family of painters (Jacopo, his father, was probably the most considerable artist of the four), died by his own hand at 43 a few months after his father's death. Claude Monet, who saw 200 of his paintings sold by auction in lots of 50 francs each, tried to commit suicide in 1867. In 1898 Paul Gauguin tried the same thing in Tahiti, hospitalized, suffering mentally—his beloved daughter Aline had died the previous year— and afflicted with syphilis. The Marseilles artist Adolphe Monticelli committed suicide by absinthe consumption. And then there was the American artist John Mulvaney, who painted a famous version of *Custer's Last Stand*. After years of uncontrollable drinking, he could take no more and jumped into the East River on May 22, 1906. The *New York Times* reported that he had become "a ragged derelict uncertain of a night's lodging or a day's food."

On Wednesday, May 20, 1931, in a posh apartment on Manhattan's East 57th Street, with a Laurens Khedive cigarette held in his fingers, a revolver in his other hand, and a copy of *Gray's Anatomy* lying open on the bed, Ralph Barton, the leading caricaturist and social satirist of his time and four times married bon vivant—one wife, Anne Minnerly, afterwards married e.e. cummings and another, Carlotta Monterey, later married Eugene O'Neill—was found dead. He bequeathed the world a grim, tortuous suicide note and two decades' worth of highly acclaimed drawings.

And, of course, Vincent Van Gogh, unwilling to continue a life which he thought was becoming a burden to others, committed suicide not during one of his mental attacks—although the reason he had been sent to the asylum at Saint-Rémy on May 7, 1889, was for trying to drink a quart of turpentine—but during a period of depression, borrowing a revolver on the pretext that he wanted to shoot crows. (His depression was probably the result of temporal lobe epilepsy.) He had been living in the Cafe Ravoux, an inn in Auvers-sur-Oise, a village 22 miles north of Paris where his brother Theo had arranged for him to live under the sympathetic eye of Dr. Paul-Ferdinand Gachet.

These were to be the artist's final few months. Incredibly, Van Gogh completed 70 paintings during the 70 frenzied and prolific days he lived in Auvers.) He almost always worked in impatient haste—often on unprimed canvas. The brushstrokes in his last paintings (*Thatched Roofs at Auvers*, for example, which was completed only weeks before he died) are discernible, primitive, unruly, and betray the artist's agitated mental state. It was on July 28, 1890, a Sunday, that Van Gogh went into the countryside, set his easel against a haystack, and shot himself in the side with the revolver. The bullet missed his heart. Somehow, he dragged himself back to the inn and, without a word to anyone, went upstairs to his attic room. The innkeeper discovered him only sometime later. It was Adeline Ravoux, the landlord's 13-year-old daughter, whom Van Gogh had painted a month before his suicide, who was with him when he finally breathed his last. Van Gogh had lived on for several days in indescribable agony before he succumbed. His coffin was placed in a room on the ground floor of the café and was surrounded by canvases he had just painted, including the portrait of Adeline (on the auction block with a $15-million-plus estimate as I write. [1988]) His palette and brushes were arranged at the foot of the coffin.

I have often wondered many times how Van Gogh's final declaration related, if it did, to that very last painting of his, a storm-tossed Auvers cornfield out of which an ominous flight of black crows is rising. But is that not finally the tragic point of it all, that William Blake's *Songs of Experience* is an absolute part—a counterbalancing weight, literally half of the equation—of the *Songs of Innocence*? "Cézanne's anxiety," Picasso had flatly once declared, "that is what interests us."

Arshile Gorky, one of the pioneers of American abstract expressionism, was born Vosdanik Manoog Adoian in Armenia in 1914 and had once watched in horror as his four grandparents, six uncles, and three aunts were massacred by the Turks. In addition, his mother died of starvation in his arms. He immigrated to the

United States at 16 and seeking to hide his Armenian identity—he always suffered from deep insecurities—proceeded to change his full name. Arshile derives from Achilles, the brooding Achaean hero of the *Iliad*, and the name Gorky is Russian for "bitter." He was of course no relation to the famous Russian writer Maxim Gorky, but Arshile was happy to allow people to believe they were cousins. He subjected himself to long apprenticeships, painting in the style of Cézanne, Miro, and Picasso, trying not to imitate, rather assimilate, their aesthetic vision. He labored for years in New York with little recognition, living on donuts and coffee during the Depression. A strong Surrealist influence eventually led to a change of style in his work, paintings that became biomorphic forms suggesting plants or human viscera floating over an indeterminate background of melting colors.

A series of personal catastrophes haunted Gorky's last years—a studio fire, fear of impotence, and an operation for cancer. A colostomy was performed, with the cost borne by his friends and the doctor, who took as his payment two paintings by the artist. All of it exacerbated a tense and often unhappy second marriage. While he often expressed his belief that suffering resulted in the ability to feel more deeply and to perceive more keenly, his burdens only mounted. He had little time left before a crippling auto accident which broke his neck and damaged his painting arm led to his suicide a few weeks later. He was found hanging from a rafter in a woodshed on his farm in Sherman, Connecticut on July 21, 1948. On a wooden picture crate the 44-year-old artist in despair had scrawled in white chalk only three words, "Goodbye My Loveds [sic]."

For several weeks Gorky had been reading and rereading, or having read and reread aloud to him, a short story by Anton Chekhov, "The Black Monk," especially a specific passage on the very last page that went as follows:

> "He saw on the floor close to his face a large pool of blood, and from weakness he could not utter another word, but an inexpressible, a boundless happiness filled his whole being. Below, just under the balcony, they were playing the serenade, and the black monk whispered to him that he was a genius and that he was only dying because his weak human body had lost its balance and could no longer serve as the garb for a genius."

Mark Rothko (*recte* Marcus Rothkovitch), another Abstract Expressionist, in a typical fit of self-loathing and utter despair took his own life in New York City in 1970. His paintings—work that almost always went unnamed (or sold off with non-descriptive titles like *Number 10*, 1950)—he himself once described as showing "a clear preoccupation with death." Personally, I tend to agree. I have always found something monumentally depressing, secular, and logically positivistic about his work—not merely "wistful," as many quietists prefer to describe them. But what about those nameless paintings? What is behind changing one's name, as so many artists and writers and entertainers have done for the public in the show business of art? Doesn't it somehow involve—and terribly—repudiating that name? Isn't a self-loathing involved here that somehow invites correction?

I remember seeing his original name signed on early work at the Rothko Foundation, where all those WPA productions wound up that were used as plumbing insulation and sold for 4 cents a pound. When the paintings came back into his own possession, he would paint out the old name and proceed to paint in the new. To me there was something eerie in it, involving cognition and mixed-up identities. Rothko was born in Latvia after which his family moved to Portland, Oregon. Although his early work consisted mainly of northwestern landscapes, cityscapes, portraits, and nudes, he soon went through a surrealistic phase, where vague, totemistic forms and strange biomorphic apparitions emerged out of shadowy, almost monochromatic tonalities.

In his mature art, he was solely interested in relationships of form and color. He sought to convey basic human emotions—anger, dread, etc.—by isolating the viewer before abstract but powerful images: almost invariably rectangles suspended one above the other, creating the impression of a horizon that recedes. Eyes appear and disappear in his paint. There is something especially unsettling and confessional in his later canvases. His reductive approach was deadly and frank. He pronounced, "We wish to reassert the picture plane. We are for flat forms because they destroy illusion and reveal truth." Toward the end of his life, the vagueness with which his painting always had something to do seemed fully to infect his work. In the 1960s, some of those large dark canvases, purplish-maroon under-takings, very like a bruise, all reflecting a growing despondency and each one of which becoming alarmingly empty. (The color combina-tion of black and red has repeatedly been observed in patients with suicidal tendencies, and it is said that those with acute psychosis often paint in monochrome.) He seemed trapped in a kind of dead subjectivity, his work seemingly contradictory and indecisive. A New York *Herald Tribune* reviewer, as early as April 27, 1955, wrote, "Rothko's pictures get bigger and bigger and say less and less."

Rothko's canvases became bleaker. And sadder. And more abstract. His light, lacking modeling and shadow and paragraphed in rectangles, seemed to have no location, no perspective. Only two rectangles remained in his paintings, the lighter area always below, as if conquered, the darker on top.

Was this then his real vision? Could Antonio Porchia, the Argentine aphorist, be right when he wrote in his strange little book *Voices*, "Truth has very few friends, and those few are suicides"? Rothko's last black paintings are virtually gestureless, blank and frontal and staring, like the Boscoreale wall-paintings and frescoes he habitually used to visit at the Metropolitan. There is a harrowing emptiness in the painter's last work. They are not only vague, but amorphous, famished, worse than neutral, efforts abandoning the very idea of a future and an audience. "It takes an effort to see them," writes critic Brian O'Doherty. "As one approaches a surface, particularly a dark one, areas simply covered with paint, rather than painted, appear. . . . They may shine with unabsorbed oil, or be flecked with knots of canvas and contain 'mistakes'—meaningless strokes . . ."

The "turbulence," to use Rothko's own word, was in him, however, not the paintings. At the end, color utterly evaporated. Grey, then black rectangles, reached like famine or a spreading plague to the very edges of his paintings. The work transmogrified into all mask. His marriage had broken up. He had suffered a heart attack the year before, and his health had badly deteriorated. He was drinking, smoking heavily, and sinking increasingly into depression and paranoia. He was taking anti-depressants. His friends say that he was suffering terrible anxiety and guilt and had become unproductive over the last six months of his life. Worse, he felt he was being ignored by the art world in favor of younger artists aping his style. On February 24, 1970, the day before he was to sell more paintings to a dealer, Rothko's physician told the painter that his health was improving. That evening he had dinner with a woman he had been seeing since he had separated from his wife the year before. It was sometime later that same night, alone in his studio on East Sixty-Ninth Street, after taking an overdose of barbiturates, possibly to dull the pain of the razor blade which he had taken care to wrap partly with a tissue so as not to cut his fingers, that the 66-year-old painter took the razor, slashed the ulnar veins in his arms, and quickly bled to death.

There have been many passive suicides. Maurice Utrillo was an incurable alcoholic. Toulouse-Lautrec's excessive drinking, crippling him further, virtually extinguished his prodigious vitality. Sir Joshua Reynolds, like Turner, possibly succumbed to an alcoholic cirrhosis. George Grosz was a drunkard who choked to death on his own vomit. Ralph Earl, the Massachusetts portrait painter, killed himself from drinking. So did Amadeo Modigliani, who dying at the age of 36, was also addicted to drugs (his mistress, Jeanne Hebuterne, incidentally, distraught and pregnant with their second child, committed suicide on the day of his funeral in 1920 by jumping from a fifth floor window to her death) along with other savage drinkers from the creative world such as Malcolm Lowry, Sinclair Lewis, Ernest Dowson, W. W. Denslow, illustrator of *The Wizard of Oz*, Ambrose Bierce, Brendan Behan, Stephen Crane, Edna St. Vincent Millay, O. Henry, Alfred Jarry, F. Scott Fitzgerald, William Faulkner, Sherwood Anderson, Dylan Thomas, John O'Hara, Grace Metalious, Jack Kerouac, Truman Capote, Robert Lowell, and Elizabeth Bishop, among others.

English novelist Wilkie Collins's addiction became so uncontrollable that he began consuming large quantities of laudanum—opium dissolved in alcohol—all sufficient to kill an ordinary man. And in 1955, when he was 71, the lugubrious actor Bela Lugosi told the Los Angeles County authorities he'd been a narcotics addict for 20 years and pleaded desperately for their help. Edgar Allan Poe, who drank by the bottle, died in the grip of the DTs, and Brancusi suffered them six or seven times himself.

Playwright Eugene O'Neill's favorite drink, according to a contemporary, was "Benedictine by the tumblerful." Blues singer Bessie Smith was addicted to gin. Singer Tommy Edwards, whose last hit was ironically titled "It's Not the End of Everything," sadly died from excessive drinking. Alcoholic Eddie Condon's cure for a headache was, "Take the juice of two bottles of whiskey." Clyde McPhatter also drank himself to death, so did singers Chuck Willis, Dinah Washington, Frankie Lymon, Billie Holiday, and the disc jockey Alan Freed. Lyricist Lorenz Hart supposedly drank to excess both because of sexual frustrations and a "dwarf" complex. And the unstable and alcoholic Bix Beiderbecke, in 1931, died at the pathetically young age of 28—as novelist Frank Harris said of "everything."

Jackson Pollock, the Abstract Expressionist painter, ended a life that was going nowhere in the final years when, filled with rage and disgust, one desperate afternoon he drove his car straight into a tree. All his life Pollock chain-smoked Camels and drank beer after beer, not—as Baudelaire said of Poe—as an epicure, but barbarously, as if he were performing a homicidal function. I suppose it was inevitable that someone who spent a lifetime ripping the headlights off parked cars, crushing drinking glasses in his hands, and punching his fists through panes of glass would end in violent death, and leave a surfeit of contradictions for others to solve. "The artist who destroys himself," notes Brian O'Doherty, "becomes the relic of his genius, that is very like his pictures."

O'Doherty goes on to explain, "The artist is encouraged to cooperate in his own self-destruction, while having an inkling that he is not free to do otherwise, leading to an imperfectly understood resentment that erodes his belief in his own freedom. This in turn he finds intolerable, leading again to further excesses. Only by destroying what the public feels is its vested interest—that is, himself—can the artist exercise the last freedom available to him." Unfortunately, that last freedom available to him allows no other.

While suicides are obviously violent, most of them, I believe, are also potential murderers, capable of further killing. They have merely taken a local life. A suicide has almost always wanted first to kill someone else. Nobody who takes his own life, in my opinion, has not also yearned to take another's as the first cause.

Finally, we should remember those tragic deaths of the spirit, where the mind is killed in a madness sought like a sanctuary from the murderous insistence of life. Seraphine de Senlis, that unique and gifted painter of flowers—self-taught, she was inspired by her religious faith and by stained-glass church windows and other religious art—died friendless and alone in a lunatic asylum and was buried in a common grave. Other depressive alcoholics who ended up in an asylum were the painters Carl Hill, Gino Rossi, Johan Jongkind, Ernst Josephson, Yayoi Kusama, and James Edward Deeds Jr.

Norway's Edvard Munch suffered all of his life from agitationsand powerful inner torments, the kind graphically invoked in his *Self-Portrait by the Wine* (1906). He used his art to express—and surely in part to surmount—the profound personal disturbances that made his streets echo with fear, filled his landscapes with death, turned women into vampires. Munch (his countrymen say "Moonk") was a highly neurotic, misogynistic artist who led the revolt of the 1890s against the formal, detached, analytical approach of the French Impressionists. His first one man Berlin exhibition in 1892 contained a weird collection of 55 screechingly colored, cacophonously designed canvases.

In Norway, when he was still young, he fell in love for the first and last time. In a secluded village where he was painting, it was suddenly reported that his beloved had shot herself and was dying. Rushing to her, he found the report exaggerated. "Hardly had I entered the room," he later wrote, "when she sprang out of bed and said, 'You love me, Edvard. I knew you would come!' We quarreled and finally she produced a revolver and threatened to shoot herself. I did not believe her, but of course I had to be chivalrous and put my hand over the revolver. But don't think the bitch failed to press the trigger.'" Munch emerged minus part of his left index finger and free of any desire to marry. A nervous breakdown in 1908 forced him to undergo electro-shock treatments (his work was never the same) and for a time he was institutionalized, after which he died in lonely seclusion in his house.

John Bushnell, who died in 1701, was mentally unbalanced. French sculptor Jean Baptiste Carpeaux's last years were clouded by persecution mania. Landscapist John Robert Cozens's mind gave way in 1793. Quentin de Latour, the most celebrated pastellist of the 18th century, as a very old man went mad. Sir Edward Land-seer, known for the group of lions at the foot of the Lord Nelson monument in Trafalgar Square, died in 1873 hopelessly insane. Johan Jong-kind, who lived in squalor near Grenoble, ended up in a madhouse. Hugo van der Goes was seized by madness (from a contemporary description, a form of religious melancholia) and died insane, in 1482. Adolf Woelfli spent his entire life in a Swiss mental institution. And Charles Meryon, who ranks with Piranesi as the greatest of architectural etchers, spent the last years of his life in a lunatic asylum, believing himself to be Christ. (There he drew Dr. Gachet, later to befriend van Gogh in his madness.)

Another who died in an asylum was the painter Ralph Albert Blakelock (1847–1919), whose wife and family of nine children lived in poverty, while he was forced to peddle—for pittances—some of the most luminous and haunting forestscapes in American art. He had a fixation for painting trees against a moonlit sky, the reach of their dark, skeletal Hallowe'enish morbid branches looking like desperate forked hands grasping for help, which recall for me lines from Robert Browning's "Bad Dreams III," which go:

> ". . . each oak
> Held on his horns some spoil he broke
> By surreptitiously beneath
> Upthrusting pavements, as with teeth,
> Gripped huge weed widening crack and split
> In squares and circles stone-work erst."

In 1913, in fact, Blakelock's *Moonlight* (1885) sold at auction for $13,900, the highest price ever paid for a work by a living American artist. (And in 1916 his *Brook by Moonlight* [1891] sold privately for $20,000.) Blakelock never realized a penny of his work, if he realized it at all. According to his biographer, Abraham Davidson, Blakelock, who had no dealer, was defeated by his desperate poverty. "Partly because he was small, weighing only about 100 pounds, and partly because he was a poor businessman who wore his anxiety on his sleeve, dealers took particular delight in knocking down his prices."

In the 1880s a disreputable Third Avenue junk dealer named Robert Fullerton paid him $100 for 33 paintings, $3.03 apiece. His family was evicted from their home on 21 different occasions. During one particularly rough winter, the Blakelocks stayed alive by cutting ice out of the Hudson and selling it. By the 1890s, his eccentricities had become pronounced. He wore his hair long and carried an old dagger prominently. "I am sure he wore it only because he thought it artistic," his wife said. "I was never afraid of him."

On September 11, 1899, the day before his ninth child, Douglas, was born, Blakelock brought one of his best pictures to a collector, who offered half his asking price. Blakelock refused and left but then changed his mind and went back. This time the collector offered even less. Blakelock accepted! He took the money home, showed it to his wife, then threw it in the kitchen fire. The next day the normally gentle artist became violent and was committed by his wife to the Long Island Hospital at Kings Park. "He threatens to kill the members of his family," the admitting physician wrote. "He threatens to kill his son because he bought a new coat. Claims he is the Duke of York."

Diagnosed as suffering from dementia praecox, Blakelock was transferred to the State Hospital for the Insane at Middletown, New York. Imagining himself fabulously wealthy, he designed his own money from scraps of paper and torn shirts, signing the bills "A-1" for Albert the First, and giving multi-million-dollar benefactions to collectors and the National Academy of Design. Blakelock lived out his life shuttled between the asylum and the dubious care of a self-appointed and autocratic guardian named Beatrice Van Rensselaer Adams who took over his life. She intruded in his affairs, bullied him, and sequestered him from his family, then living in a two-room cabin in the Catskills for $4 a month. He was a mere skeleton at the end, weighing only 76 pounds. Ironically, on December 23, 1941, Mrs. Adams—once wealthy, finally a homeless vagrant—was diagnosed in a highly bizarre turn of events as suffering from dementia praecox herself at Kings Park Hospital, where she was taken after collapsing on a street near Grand Central Station. Only a few blocks away, an exhibition of paintings by Blakelock was simultaneously being held.

The final turn of the screw came when Blakelock's eldest daughter, Marion, began to earn some money for the straitened family by painting pictures herself when she later found that an unscrupulous dealer was altering her signature and selling her work as her father's. And then in 1915, she, too, was confined to a sanatorium.

Edgar Degas once remarked that a painter paints with the same passion that a criminal commits a crime. And in his essay *Pen Pencil and Poison* Oscar Wilde even went so far as to say of one criminal, in this case the forger and murderer Thomas Wainewright, "His crimes seem to have had an important effect upon his art. They gave a strong personality to his style, a quality that his early work certainly lacked." It is a poetic analogy, even if extravagant one, that raises all sorts of questions about the creative urge touching on terror and desperation and need. There are instances, certainly, when the analogy emerges into bold truth, and the passionate mind that can do one, instead chooses the other—suddenly, the artist becomes a murderer. Conditions vary, circumstances are almost always different, and motives are very rarely the same. But the fact is, many artists have killed.

Andrea del Castagno, one of the most influential Florentine painters of the generation after Masaccio—and a painter, traditionally, of gruesome effigies of rebels hanged by the heels, from which he derived the nickname *"Andreino degli Impiccati"* [of the hanged men]—supposedly murdered the fresco painter Domenico Veneziano.

Caravaggio—whose real name was Michelangelo Merisi (which he took after his birthplace near Milan)—was a man of strange habits. One contemporary called him *"stravagantissimo"* (very eccentric) and said that his excesses cut 10 years off his life. He went about the streets with a sword and dagger ever at the ready and a shaggy black dog called *"Cornacchia"* (Raven) who did sporty tricks. A servant boy carrying a rapier always followed along with Caravaggio.

As a painter he was a technical wizard. After studying under teachers of little originality (he had been a mason's laborer) he struggled in his own work for more dramatic, more realistic effects, and the result was a sort of concrete paganism. He painted religious characters as if they were everyday people. His saints, Biblical characters, his angels—even his portraits of Christ—had an earthiness appalling to the art patrons of the day. A basket of fruit appears in many of his paintings and is almost always either bruised or rotten. He produced an unusual number of severed heads.

Caravaggio had no shortage of personal vendettas—he was known to stalk the streets of Rome carrying any weapon for protection—but one of his most famous feuds involved rival painter Giovanni Baglione. The disagreement began in the early 1600s, when Baglione painted a response to Caravaggio's chiaroscuro masterwork, *Amor Vincit Omnia* (1601). Caravaggio and his circle ridiculed him and claimed plagiarism, so Baglione upped the ante and painted a second version—this time with a caricature of Caravaggio's face on the body of the devil. Never one to let an insult stand, Caravaggio got revenge by distributing a series of vulgar and highly comic poems denouncing Baglione and suggesting he use his paintings as toilet paper. A deeply offended Baglione took Caravaggio to court on libel charges and had him jailed for several days. He would later write a biography of Caravaggio that offers a particularly unflattering portrait of his former rival. When discussing Caravaggio's untimely demise, the book notes, "He died as miserably as he had lived." The volcanically tempered painter also made vicious accusations against the painter Guido Reni (who, incidentally, admired him) for copying his style, and was arrested for libel.

On one occasion, in 1604, at the Osteria del Moro, Caravaggio viciously threw a plate of hot artichokes into a waiter's face and threatened to run him through. In October of that year, authorities seized him after throwing a stone at someone. From 1600 to 1610, he is mentioned constantly as an offender in police records. It seems that the capacity to control a ferocious and unbridled temper was literally beyond him. If it seems strange that pettiness can coexist with such brilliance—he was probably the most important Italian painter of the 17th century—one need only reflect on how slim a hold even the best of us has on his identity. Possibly genius compounds it. Wagner was spiteful, Nabokov hopelessly arrogant, and Robert Frost was a grumpy son-of-bitch.

After 1590, Caravaggio seemed no longer satisfied with mere physical beauty. He turned exclusively to religious themes, no more Bacchuses and still lifes. (The wormy fruit in paintings like *Fruit and Foliage* (1599) now looked less like a touch of reality than a theological complaint.) All that seemed to interest the painter at this point was the form of shadows falling on bodies, as if to veil in darkness the drama going on within. Never had sacred subjects been depicted so entirely in terms of contemporary lowlife. He plunged into atmospheres of ever-increasing gloom, sharpening a style that became more revolutionary and using contrasts of light and shadow laid on with a sort of fury. He began to concentrate on hard clear images and increasingly insistent psychological focus to works that were becoming more and more baroque in the original meaning of that term—contorted and grotesque.

In his *Conversion of St. Paul* (1600), a scene commonly depicted with a vision of Christ descending from heaven, a horse fills up most of the composition. ("You can smell the sweat," said Dali.) In the thick murky atmosphere enveloping the scene, no space is left for the shaft of supernatural light that has struck down the saint. Caravaggio almost willfully gives Paul's servant a varicose vein in his leg. The painter has not merely confined himself to depicting the event without idealization, as it actually happened, he virtually prosecutes in the painting all the possibilities he refuses to be deprived of and simultaneously reveals a personality that, rash and reckless—even pugnacious—revels in shocking confrontation.

He loved backgrounds of nowhere. He was famous for disagreeable facial expressions and accentuated deformity. He often painted the soles of the feet. He had a penchant for depicting goiters, which were common in the mountainous regions of Italy. In his *Death of the Virgin* (1604–6), one of his most controversial paintings, we see a corpse being carried from the morgue, her legs swollen, her face already showing signs of decay. This painting, which was done for St. Maria della Scala, particularly scandalized church fathers because Caravaggio's model for Mary was a drowned woman already bloated by death. To humanize the Virgin was one thing, but to do so with such truculent insistence on reality was another. His paintings soon began causing terrible scandals and were condemned out of hand by Bolognese artists and critics in Rome, and many were roundly and angrily refused by the clergy. Was Caravaggio simply inviting scorn? And what of his anger? Was he intentionally subverting himself? Were his paintings, like his actions, merely desperate attempts to exercise his freedom, the bold refusal to be vanquished by custom or courtesy?

In his later works—*Death of the Virgin* (1604), *The Adoration of the Shepherds* (1609), and *The Resurrection of Lazarus* (1609)—qualities can be found reflecting the misery of his life, his pent-up grief and his bitterness. It was also daring to approach *The Calling of St. Matthew* (1599–1600) the way he did. Such men as Matthew, a publican, someone who dealt with public revenues, were usually social outcasts and classified with "sinners" and other irreligious persons whose flagrant abuses connected with tax-collecting were legend. Matthew would also have been scorned, being a Jew, for working in the employ of hated Romans, specifically under Herod Antipas. The setting for the painting is a dimly-lit gambling den, an airless two-dimensional world where the seated five men, rich and over-decorated and counting money, could be pimps in a brothel. (The delicate, almost indiscernible halo over Christ's head seems a small concession to the religious subject of the painting.)

And in his terrifying and apocalyptic *David with the Head of Goliath* (1610), Caravaggio seems to be making some sort of despairing personal confession by the macabre way he gave his own face to the severed head of Goliath the Philistine, dripping blood, mouth agape, held up by the hair in the left hand of David. It somehow recalls the words of Picasso, "Art is the child of rejection and suffering, and I paint as others write their autobiographies." Meanwhile, Caravaggio was nursing an even deeper grievance. Vain, prone to jealousy, he had been gravely offended that he had not been offered any of the new commissions for the altarpieces that were being given out for the great basilica of St. Peter's. It was an honor hugely to be prized. In those days, cardinals had to be sought out by artists for endorsements the way politicians today are solicited by candidates applying to West Point. Lesser lights like Ludovico Cigoli and Bernardo Castello, and even utter mediocrities, had been preferred.

And while Caravaggio was ignored, his behavior only worsened.

On Sunday evening, May 28, 1606, on the Via della Scrofa in Rome, Caravaggio and some friends were attending a game of *pallacorda*—a kind of court tennis—when he got into a fistfight during the match over a wager he had made with someone. It was Caravaggio who owed the money, a debt of 10 *scudi*, and it was Caravaggio who refused to pay. A contemporary account of the fight records it as a long and furious one, with four companions scuffling on each side. Ultimately, though Caravaggio was badly wounded in the head, it was his opponent, a fellow named Ranucchio Tomassoni of Terni, whom he fatally ran through the heart. Caravaggio immediately fled. He went south, roaming the countryside, and for his crime was hunted intermittently by the Knights of Malta.

During the next three years he was constantly in and out of trouble. He fled to Naples and to Malta, where he was imprisoned for another attempt to avenge a quarrel. He was always as ready with his dagger as with his brush. Escaping to Sicily, he was attacked by a party sent in pursuit of him and severely wounded. Being pardoned, he set out for Rome, but again came in contact with the law. He finally died in a rage, when, after having been taken off a vessel and summarily imprisoned—it was a case of mistaken identity—he went wandering in a fever along a hot beach at Pontercole in July, cursing and howling at the ship that sailed away with all his belongings. He was only 39.

"Only the hand that erases can write the true thing"—so runs a paradoxical apothegm from one of the sermons of Meister Eckart, the shadowy 13th-century German mystic and author of the *Opus Tripartitum*, stressing, even if on the verge of non-conformity—in 1328 this Roman Catholic theologian was brought to trial as a heretic by the Franciscan inquisition under John XXII but who died just before his verdict came down—the dimensions as to how far one is willing to go to realize one's personal vision, in short, to *dare*. It can sound truly insolent and implies a shocking radicalism (murder?), but it represents the kind of extreme desperate, and even unholy, premise a detached mind can push itself to reach a rash conclusion. Detestations figure largely in Eckart's vision—as does ego. "If I myself were not, God would not be either," he declared. "Through nothing I become what I am." Such is the intransigence, the heterodoxy we find in the obstinate creatures underhand here.

The Spanish painter Alonso Cano (1606–1667) also killed someone. An architect and sculptor as well, he claimed to have religious raptures. It somehow never kept him out of duels. A contentious and difficult man, he was forced to leave Seville in 1638 because of a vendetta he had initiated with another painter, Sebastián de Llanos Valdés. He was also said to have risked his life by committing the then-capital offense of smashing a statue of a saint in a rage when its purchaser demanded a discount. He was finally arrested in 1644 when his young wife was found stabbed to death. Cano is generally thought to have done it, though it was never proven (some circumstances pointed to his servant as the culprit, and Cano did not confess though he was tortured).

It is nothing less than remarkable, given his violent life, that Cano's paintings are not only religious but done with such elegance and ease, such classic balance and symmetry that he is still known as the Michelangelo of Spain. One thinks of Yeats's theory of the "anti-self," where the artist is seen as someone always endeavoring to construct by fiction what he lacks in fact, seeking the opposite of what he is.

Voices and visions figure in several cases where an artist has killed someone. The trouble with artists in general is half the time one cannot ascertain whether they are mad or simply impulsive or listening to the Muse.

The story of the "fairy" painter Richard Dadd (1819–1887), is a case in point. It was Dadd who, ironically enough, killed his own father. Richard, a son by his father's first wife, was the fourth of seven children, of whom four were to die insane. (Both of the wives of his father, Robert, a canvas gilder, died young.) A talented painter, Dadd was admitted to the Royal Academy in 1837. His enchanting *Titania Sleeping* in 1841 brought him official acclaim. His paintings, which soon took on an eerie quality, were mostly haunted-looking caves, deserts, and lunescapes, 100 of which he did for Lord Foley, taking his subjects from Byron's *Manfred* and Tasso's *Jerusalem Delivered*.

In 1842 he traveled to Egypt, Italy, Greece, and Asia Minor for a year. In Rome, Dadd in some sort of crazy fugue was overcome with irrational urge to attack the Pope right in the Vatican. On his voyage home, he began to imagine his traveling companion, Sir Thomas Phillips, a solicitor, was playing cards for the captain's soul. He suddenly felt his mind was imprinted with a mission to rid the world of the Devil. It was his physician's judgment that his behavior was due to Egyptian sunstroke.

Soon his lapses of self-control could no longer be ignored. One visitor arrived to find Dadd had cut a birthmark out of his forehead because, as he said, it was put there by the Devil. He was convinced that he was being pursued. He began leaping about for no reason. He started stocking the pantry in his lodgings with vast quantities of eggs and ale, hundreds of the shells later being found in his rooms, along with drawings he had made of many of his friends, portraying them with their throats slit.

On August 28, 1843, Dadd, who was only 22 at the time,

asked his father to take a trip with him to Cobham in Surrey, a childhood haunt of his, where he said he wanted to "unburden his mind." No particular enmity had been recorded between them prior to that night. They took lodgings at a place called The Ship Inn, dined on boiled ham and porter, and then went for a stroll together. Then, with a clasp knife, which he had brought along specifically for the nefarious project, Dadd—after an initial attempt to cut his father's throat with a razor—proceeded to stab him to death, shoving the corpse afterwards into a chalk pit called Paddock Hole. He later explained that he was simply carrying out a supreme command to destroy the Devil. Dadd crossed the English Channel and might have escaped, but was arrested near Fontainebleau after attempting to kill a complete stranger. In 1844, he was extradited to Britain and committed to Bethlehem Hospital (Bedlam) in London without standing trial. Curiously, there was a marked improvement in his painting in the madhouse. He drew cartoons, Easter scenes, caves. (As one critic put it, the paintings he did there were "strongly interesting though marked by a certain disequilibrium.")

Mostly, the work he did was delicate landscapes, peopled with fairy folk—gnomes, particularly, intrigued him. (He always spoke of them as if they were real.) Dadd became a prolific painter and left behind some 232 works, the finest of which are *Contradiction: Oberon and Titania* (1854–58), *The Flight Out of Egypt* (1949), and *The Fairy-Feller's Master Stroke* (1855–64), which is now in the Tate Gallery—you can see the little folk who persecuted him peering through the shrubbery—and *The Crooked Path* (1866). He died of consumption on January 8, 1886, a white-bearded old man.

Where love and (one is sorely tempted to write or) marriage is involved, there is often murder. A full ten years elapsed between the time Pre-Raphaelite painter and poet Dante Gabriel

Rossetti, met and married the shop girl and model, Elizabeth Siddal. The family name originally had two l's; Gabriel later made her change the spelling, apparently because he believed one l looked more refined.

An exquisitely beautiful girl with lustrous red-gold hair, large eyes, and a sensuous mouth—Ruskin said she could have passed for a countess—Lizzie captured everyone's heart, with Rossetti's own family, however, especially his mother and sisters, being the one exception. A model at the time in those censorious days was considered to be barely one step up from a tart. Elizabeth bravely in any case went ahead and became a model anyway, sitting for various painters, Holman Hunt, Madox Brown, Walter Deverell, and even John Everett Millais (notably for *Ophelia*, probably his greatest picture). Rossetti, having met her when she was only 20, became her protector and lover and as time went on forbade her to model for anyone else. They were happy, but it was sporadic. Eventually she moved in with him, a daring and scandalous thing to do in the Victorian Fifties and lived for years in his house in Chatham Place on the river by Blackfriars Bridge.

The relationship was soon fraught with tension. Rossetti, who wanted neither a wife nor children, suffered an almost pathological fear of responsibility. He once told a close friend, "I loathe and despise family life." It was part neurosis, part artistic pose. Although he taught Lizzie how to draw and paint and even write, poems mostly (always about death and loss) he also saw prostitutes and had affairs with other models, one a long-haired temptress named Fanny Cornforth, the *nom de salon* of Sarah Cox, a blacksmith's daughter who coming up to London from the country was something of both. Their strange and interminable engagement, however, finally ended in marriage when Rossetti was 32 and Lizzie 30. No friends and no members of either family were present. There was no trousseau, no wedding feast, and complete strangers signed the register as witnesses. A tragedy followed soon after, one she could never get over, when Lizzie gave birth to a stillborn child.

On the night of February 10, 1862, the Rossettis, after dining at the Hotel Sabloniere in Leicester Sq. with the poet Algernon Swinburne (who adored Lizzie), returned to their home in Chatham Place by 8:00, and around 9:00 Gabriel went out alone. As he would go on to explain later, upon returning at 11:30 p.m., he went up the stairs and found his wife lying on the bed completely unconscious. On the table beside her sat a two-ounce bottle labeled "Laudanum Poison," emptied of its contents. (Two ounces of laudanum, if not watered down by a chemist, was the equivalent of 600 mg. of morphine; 60 mg. is a lethal dose.) There was a note pinned to her nightgown asking Gabriel to take care of Harry, her retarded brother.

Elizabeth lived through the night in a coma but at 7:20 the following morning was pronounced dead. The note was mysteriously burned in the fireplace. An inquest was conducted at Bridewell Hospital the very next day. Hers was judged an accidental death. But rumors about Lizzie Siddal's death had suddenly surfaced overnight. Tales of physical cruelty, of perfidy and adultery, of Gabriel dragging Lizzie across the drawing room by the hair were served up in whispers as corroborating evidence.

It was Oscar Wilde, admittedly not an unimaginative man, who was heard to say that Lizzie had acted silly at dinner and that Rossetti, completely losing patience with her, had shoved her into a cab, taken her home, and pressed the bottle of laudanum into her hands, shrieking, "Take the lot!" After scolding her, he was alleged to have stormed out of the house. What of this scene? Had there been sharp words? Was it a suicide or had she only been trying to frighten her husband? What of Rossetti himself, did he resent her so much? The story that many of his friends chose to believe was that he indeed had gone out to see Fanny and that Lizzie had known where he had gone and emptied the bottle in a fit of despair.

So many unanswered questions have remained to this day, and regarding the case, so much is still unclear. True, Lizzie had been under intense emotional strain for years. Bad health had enervated her. Her endless engagement had taken its toll on her nerves. Gabriel, who married her out of obligation and guilt, did so at a time when she was—and he knew she was—desperately ill; she knew this, and the knowledge must have weighed on her. And, of course, the death of her baby was a crushing blow.

But what of the fact that Rossetti was tormented with guilt about Lizzie's death for the rest of his life? Was it somehow proof he was responsible for her death, or that he did indeed go out to see Fanny that night? William always maintained that his brother had gone out to the Working Man's College, London, but Gabriel had resigned his teaching post there four years earlier! Her husband's behavior after her death even remains mysterious. He immediately left Chatham Place forever, burning every letter he could find that Lizzie had every written to him. (He would also never publish any of her poetry.) Finally, in an act of desperate finality he destroyed every last photograph of her in his possession, wiping out almost every actual image of the poor woman (only two photos of her remain), effectively seizing control of how posterity would know Elizabeth Siddal.

Mary Lamb, the English writer best known for her literary collaborations with her brother Charles with the book *Tales from Shakespeare*—a collection of "junior editions" of the Bard's classic tales—suffered from mental illness and was confined to mental facilities off and on for much of her life. She and Charles presided over a literary circle in London that included the poets William Wordsworth and Samuel Taylor Coleridge, among others. Sadly, both siblings suffered from serious mental illness, all of which culminated in Charles being institutionalized in 1796, as well, leaving the highly unstable Mary to care for their invalid mother, as well as their senile father and elderly aunt. The burdens of these dependents mounted and began to tax Mary, who on September 22, 1796—she was 32 years old at the time—stabbed her mother, Elizabeth, to death with a kitchen knife during a heated argument.

While preparing dinner that night, Mary became irrationally furious and overly aggressive with her apprentice, roughly shoving the little girl out of her way and shoving her into another room. Her mother, Elizabeth, began shouting at her daughter and upbraided her for excessive cruelty. Spiralling into lunacy as her mother continued bellowing, an outraged Mary took the kitchen knife she had been holding, unsheathed it, and, approaching her mother (who was sitting down) then fatally stabbed her full in the chest—in full view of two of her siblings, John and Sarah Lamb, who were standing nearby. (There were seven children in the family.) Charles ran into the house soon after the murder and took the knife out of Mary's hand. Mary would spend time at a mental facility called Fisher House in Islington for her crime—which was basically ruled a by-product of madness—before being released into her brother Charles's care. He continued to look after her for the rest of his life, even as both he and Mary established successful literary careers.

In December 1814 Mary wrote a piece entitled "On Needle-work," which was published in the *New British Lady's Magazine* in 1815 under the pseudonym "Sempronia." The article argued that sewing should be made a recognized profession to give independence to women whose only skill and means of making a living was sewing, which at the time was something they were mostly obliged to do as part of their household duties. Her brother stood loyal to her to the end. She died at 83.

Another strange case of love and murder involved the English pioneering photographer Eadweard Muybridge—he was born Edward Muggeridge in England in 1830 but returned to the Anglo-Saxon form of his name after coming to the U.S.—who was tried and acquitted for the murder of his wife's lover. Muybridge was one of the great photographers of the American West, renowned today mainly for his famous frame-by-frame snapshots of a galloping horse, but he had also invented the "zoopraxiscope," a machine that, reconstructing motion from his photographs, a project on which he collaborated with the painter Thomas Eakins, became a forerunner of cinematography.

Muybridge had been in California busily working on a geodetic survey for the U.S. government at the time that Governor Leland Stanford made a historic bet with two other horse-racing enthusiasts—James R. Keene and Frederick MacCrellish. Stanford wagered $25,000 that a horse sometimes has all four hooves off the ground when galloping. The difficulty was how to settle the argument. Muybridge solved the problem by lining up 24 cameras to take pictures one after the other. The horse used was Stanford's own mare, "Sallie Gardner." After the stop-action photos were taken, and the exposure of each negative was less than the two-thousandth part of a second, they proved uncontestably that Stanford was right.

Indeed, two years after that famous photograph of the galloping horse, Muybridge began to suspect that a drama critic known as Major Harry Larkyns was sleeping with his wife of two years,

23-year-old Flora Shallcross Stone. On October 17, 1874, an out-raged Muybridge, properly incensed—indeed, actually convinced that this military rogue was the father of Flora, his wife's (and his?) seven-month-old boy, Floredo—took a ferry across San Francisco Bay and then a train up into Napa Country to Calistoga and went to the officer's house, stood outside in the darkness, and called for his wife's lover to come out. When the major stepped through the door, Muybridge cried out, "Good evening, Major, my name is Muybridge and here's the answer to the letter you sent my wife," and shot him point-blank. Larkyns died that very same night, and Muybridge was immediately arrested, without protest, and placed in the Napa County jail. At the trial, Muybridge pleaded insanity.

A jury at Napa, California, acquitted Muybridge after he invoked the then-popular "unwritten law" of *crime passionel.* convinced that he was justified in killing the man who seduced his wife. He was acquitted, in short, on grounds of "justifiable homicide" where they disregarded the judge's instructions. Muybridge was only 44 years old at the time of the murder. The episode, needless to say, interrupted all of his photography studies—it was a sensational trial and quite widely covered—but not his relationship with Leland Stanford, who had arranged for his criminal defense. (The American composer Philip Glass would later create an opera, *The Photographer*, with a libretto based in part on court transcripts from the case.) In 1875 the photographer travelled for more than a year on a previously planned nine-month photography trip throughout Central America, as a "working exile." By 1877, he had then returned to San Francisco to resume his work for Stanford.

Later, Flora petitioned for divorce, but was initially unsuc-cessful. Her second petition received a favorable ruling, and an order for alimony was entered in April 1875. Flora died three months later while Muybridge was in Central America. She had placed their son, Florado Helios Muybridge (later nicknamed "Floddie" by friends), with a French couple. In 1876, Muybridge had the boy moved from a Catholic orphanage to a Protestant one and paid for his care. Otherwise he had little to do with him. Photographs of Florado Muybridge as an adult show him to have strongly resembled Muybridge. Put to work on a ranch as a boy, he worked all his life as a ranch hand and gardener. In 1944, Florado was hit by a car in Sacramento and killed, at approximately the age of 70.

Ludwig Bemelmans (1898–1962), the Austria-Hungary-born American writer and illustrator of children's books—he is known best for his seven best-selling *Madeline* picture books—had a violent temper. He was born to the Belgian painter Lambert Bemelmans and the German Frances Fischer in Meran, Austria-Hungary (which is now Merano, Italy). His father owned a hotel. He grew up in Gmunden on the Traunsee in Upper Austria where, growing up, his first language was French, his second German. In 1904, his father left the family for Ludwig's governess, after which his mother angrily removed to her native Regensburg, Germany with Ludwig and his brother. Ludwig had difficulty in school and hated the German style of discipline. He was apprenticed to his uncle Hans Bemelmans at a hotel in Austria, where he reportedly shot and seriously wounded a waiter. Given the choice between reform school and emigration to the United States, he chose the latter.

Edward Hopper, a spoiled, crotchety, short-tempered and irritable reprobate with a scowling disposition—he was bald and moose-tall (6' 5")—was by all accounts verbally and physically abusive to his tiny wife Jo, a relationship that the writer and art critic Kirsty Bell in her essay for the recent Whitney Museum exhibition in New York calls "violent" and "claustrophobic." The Hoppers were childless—one senses a distinct barrenness about them—and in the pages of her diaries, Jo, who had ambitions of her own, makes clear having sacrificed her own career as an artist upon marriage to her husband. Vivien Green Fryd, professor emerita of art history at Vanderbilt, depicts the couple in *ARTnews* as "squawking chickens with ferocious beaks." In the same magazine, art critic Stephen May discusses Hopper's merciless caricatures of his wife, "with Edward portraying himself as the victim of his wife's aggression and alleged failings as a homemaker (she often refused to cook), as well as mocking her artistic efforts." Christopher Benfey quotes Jo in the *New York Review of Books* (Feb. 23, 2023) as saying that she "always found tall men exciting [but] not when they use that extra span of arm length to swat me tho [sic]." Talking to her husband, wrote Jo in her journal, was "like dropping a stone in a well, except that it doesn't thump when it hits bottom."

Wieland Schmied, our best authority on Hopper, lucidly underscores the artist's "deep-seated sense of alienation," and, I must say, nowhere does the bullying artist seem a more self-accusing gasbag than when he has the gall sententiously to write—was Edward Hopper *that* incapacitatedly unable to take a good honest look at himself?—"Great art is the outward expression of an inner life in the artist, and this inner life will result in his personal vision of the world." Confessed the psychologically abusive painter, "Maybe I am not very human—what I wanted to do was paint sunlight on the side of a house." And, hey, why not bop a woman on the head who won't make me an omelet?!

On September 8, 1985, the sculptor Carl Andre, then 49, was accused of pushing his 36-year-old wife, Ana Mendieta, out the window of their 34th-floor Greenwich Village apartment. She was a sculptor herself and in 1980 received a Guggenheim. He is known for outdoor displays of both figurative and symbolic forms, what have been described as "mathematically precise, factory-tooled, a-personal, ground-hugging sculptures." One of the founders of minimalism, Andre, who has a fairly wide reputation, has declared he is not interested in pedestal sculpture but refers to himself as a "post-studio" artist and says his work is atheistic "because it is without transcendent form, without spiritual or intellectual qualities."

One of his more enthusiastic projects involved setting up a 34-foot line of unattached firebricks on the floor of the Jewish Museum. Another consisted of placing 184 bales of hay 500 feet across an open field. And then there was his "situational sculpture" *Reef*, a series of brightly colored, identical styrofoam blocks placed side by side at the Whitney Museum's 1969 exhibition. For Andre's controversial *Stone Field Sculpture*—described by one of the arresting policemen as a "bunch of boulders" (Andre proudly showed it to him in a catalogue the morning of his wife's death)—the artist was paid $87,000.

There is a bogus profundity, an almost laughable kind of *poshlost*, to his projects, which calls to my mind the type of sculptor novelist Vladimir Nabokov vilifyingly describes as building "crankshaft cretins of stainless steel, zen stereos, polystyrene stinkbirds, *objects trouvés* in latrines, cannon balls, canned balls."

Andre, who by the way claimed to be a Marxist—he attended Phillips Andover and at the time asked up to $250,000 for his work—habitually wore overalls, along with an unkempt beard that reached to his chest. His wife, Ana Mendieta, was dark and striking, a tiny, lithe, 93-pound vegetarian and jogger with a loud voice and a fondness for dangling earrings and bracelets. She had been born in Cuba.

There were many anomalies and a good deal of conflicting testimony in this controversial case. According to medical and forensic testimony during the trial, Andre and his wife had been drinking throughout the evening before her death. The amount of alcohol in Ana Mendieta's brain after her death was measured at 0.18 percent, which a toxicologist testified would have caused physical and behavioral changes that were "roughly in the mid-range of the full range of alcoholic effects." It had been a hot summer night. (The temperature at six a.m. was 78 degrees, the humidity 88 percent.) The implication of Andre's own testimony was that he had been in the bedroom when she went out the window, although he would later deny it. In the 911 emergency call that he made that night and recorded verbatim. Andre's voice was characterized as highly distressed: "What happened was we had . . . My wife is an artist and I'm an artist and we had a quarrel about the fact that I was more, ah, exposed to the public than she was, and she went to the bedroom and I went after her, and she went out the window."

The couple had been married for only nine months when the event took place. (It had been his third marriage, her first.) Andre, who has always denied killing her, said they had been watching a lot of television, the U.S. National Tennis Open, a Yankee game, and several films, *Dracula* and *Without Love* with Katharine Hepburn and Spencer Tracy. They had also been drinking. (There were numerous empty wine and champagne bottles found in the kitchen.) He had claimed earlier that they had got into an argument, after which she had gone into the bedroom. This was about 3 a.m. After a few minutes he went into find her, but she was not there. There were signs of struggle in the apartment, however, at least the bedroom was in disarray, and a deep fresh scratch on the suspect's nose. The defense claimed that Ms. Mendieta got up on the sill to open a window and in slamming it open with both hands lost her balance.

A nearby doorman supposedly heard someone screaming, "No, no, no, no!" but it was later revealed that he had often been subject to delusory voices.

Andre's lawyers called Ms. Mendieta's death a "sub-intentional suicide," which a psychiatric witness explained was one in which a person, perhaps under the influence of alcohol or drugs, might take risks he would not ordinarily take. The body was so badly damaged in crashing to the roof of the Delion Grocery 32 floors below that it was impossible to know if Mendieta had been assaulted prior to the fall.

Several of her friends were aware of and testified to the fact that Ana Mendieta's artistic reputation had been surging and that, in spite of their failing marriage—she had angrily and repeatedly accused him of womanizing—she was energetically committed to several new projects in Rome. They also explained, for many of them knew, that she had been mortally afraid of heights all her life. And it was asked over and over again, how could a four-foot-10-inch tall woman who suffered from acrophobia fall out of a window that came up to her breast and had a 20-inch deep radiator cover and sill? "For Ana Mendieta to fall out of the window," according to the prosecution, "she would have had to fall up approximately three feet, and then fall 20 inches forward before she would fall out." Although indicted a third time in March of 1987 by a grand jury after two previous indictments were dismissed, Andre was finally acquitted a year later and all of the charges were dropped.

Would it be worthwhile to track back through Carl Andre's art, searching for the spoor of murderous impulse? It would be at least intriguing. He wrote of his Jewish Museum piece *Lever*: "All I'm doing is putting Brancusi's *Endless Column* [1938] on the ground instead of in the sky." Then he gets deep. "Host sculpture is priapic with the male organ in the air. In my work, Priapus is down on the floor. The engaged position is to run along the earth." What did minimalism really mean to him? Did he feel threatened by his wife? Unmanned? What can we make of the "anaxial symmetry" that he often spoke of in reference to his sculpture, a technique "in which one part can replace any other part"? Did this apply in a cynical way to human beings? To women? To wives? And was defenestration part of what he meant by spatial extension? What of those austere combinations of steel plates, blocks of wood, bricks, and other every-day, ready-made materials he used, aren't they utterly soulless? "I purposely do not glue," he once said, "and I do not join."

But the artist is by no means limited to the familiar homicide, born of sudden anger or madness. There are several hideous cases of mass murder, as well. One of Japan's most horrific crimes occurred at Tokyo's Teikoko (Imperial) Bank on January 26, 1948, when the painter Sadamachi Hirasawa, pretending to be a Dr. Jiro Yamaguchi, entered the bank at closing time and created an instant panic by announcing a dysentery epidemic. He somehow induced the 15 bank employees to swallow a medicine that he dispensed which supposedly prevented dysentery. The "doctor" then fled with 181,400 yen ($600) while the victims all collapsed in pain, writhing on the floor. Three of the potential victims, however, survived. A nationwide manhunt for the killer immediately ensued, and a painstaking police investigation led after almost a year to the arrest of Hirasawa.

It was soon learned he had attempted two robbery-murders earlier, in both instances posing in the guise of a doctor. At a sensational trial, two of the survivors positively identified Hirasawa, who maintained his innocence but was found guilty and sentenced to death. Inexplicably, the warrant for his execution was never signed by the justice minister, and Hirasawa carried on painting in his jail cell. For some reason, the works he produced from then on gained even *greater* favor in the art world!

A curious fact that might be noted in passing is that only *after* killing someone can—or do—certain artists begin to get down to the real business of their creative work, as if finding their focus somehow depended in a bizarre way on a purgation by means of violence, by some ritual or other of bloodletting. There are the cases of Dadd and Hirosawa. Other examples might be ornithologist-murderers Nathan Leopold, who with a partner, murdered a little boy in 1924 and the legendary Robert Stroud, the "Birdman of Alcatraz." Another painter-murderer is Conrad Maass, a German nobleman who immigrated to Oklahoma in 1890 with his wife Martha. In 1898 he killed his wife with a shotgun blast, burying her in his dugout home. Sentenced to life imprisonment, Maass began to paint historical and religious murals he did in his cell at the Oklahoma State Penitentiary in McAlester. He became so extravagantly attached to his art that when he was granted parole in 1920 he refused to leave the penitentiary unless the murals left with him. As this was impossible, Maass chose to stay in jail up until his death in 1936. Though they are bullet-scarred from prison riots over the years, his murals which have remained in place have made him a legend among McAlester's inmates. (The "Lifers' Club" there recently raised funds to buy him a new tombstone.)

A murderer who, like the demented Hirasawa, killed his victims by means of poison was the art critic, forger, and English painter Thomas Griffiths Wainewright (1794–1852). Most of his best efforts in painting were watercolor and monochrome sketches and drawings in crayon. He exhibited once or twice at the Royal Academy. An acquaintance of Lamb's and Hazlitt's, he was a literary dandy, a perfumed and jeweled exquisite, who wrote affected and fussy essays for the *London Magazine* under the pseudonyms "Mr. Egomot Bonmot," "Mr. Janus Weathercock," and "Herr Vinkbooms." He lisped, loved to wear jewelry—especially rings—and collected antiques.

An orphan, Wainewright went to live as a boy of seven with his uncle, George Edward Griffiths, the owner of Linden House and a large surrounding property. He grew to young manhood and joined a regiment, along the way coming in contact with a small, rather financially pressed family from Mortlake, a widow named Mrs. Abercromby who had a son and one daughter—Miss Frances Ward, whom Wainewright would marry—by her first husband, Mr. Ward, and two daughters by her second, Lieutenant Abercromby. In 1828, Wainewright and his wife went to live with his bachelor uncle. Within a year of their going there Mr. Griffiths died—"suddenly"—and the house and property, now considerably reduced in value, were passed on to Wainewright. When his financial situation worsened, he subsequently arranged for his wife's mother and two half-sisters, Helen and Madeleine, to make their home at Linden House. In 1830 he insured Helen's life for several huge sums, which covered, however, only a short period. Mrs. Abercromby thought it callow of him. She objected and promised to stand in the way. As it turned out, she didn't get the chance.

Conveniently enough for Wainewright's purpose, she died "very suddenly" in August 1830. Helen's insurance was then quadrupled. That very December, the poor girl—who was only 21—died in a great agony, the symptoms of her brief illness found to be identical with those of her mother and George Griffiths. "Something more goes to the composition of a fine murder than two blockheads to kill and be killed—a knife—a purse—and a dark lane," wrote Thomas

De Quincey. "Design, gentlemen, grouping, light and shade, poetry, sentiment, are now deemed indispensable to attempts of this nature."

It was soon discovered that Wainewright had poisoned them all, using strychnine in jelly. Someone asked him directly how he could have the cold-blooded barbarity to kill such a fair and innocent creature as Helen (whose portrait he had once done in colored chalks). He reflected a moment or two, then quirkily replied, "Upon my soul, I don't know, unless it was because she had such thick legs."

Wainewright's ruling illusion was of his grandeur. In prison he refused, as a "gentlemen," to sweep or handle a broom. The sight of him in Newgate and what he learned of his history suggested to Charles Dickens his melodramatic novelette *Hunted Down* (1859), a very rare detective story by the author of *Oliver Twist* and *Great Expectations.* In the end, Wainewright was eventually banished to the grim ship hulks of Portsmouth and under sentence of transportation then sent to Van Dieman's Land in Tasmania for life, where after mouldering away for years—his sole living companion was a cat—he died of apoplexy in 1852. No portrait of the murderer is known to exist. As noted earlier, however, it may be observed here that Oscar Wilde wrote an essay about him.

I am reminded in all of that of the death of Lucretius, the Roman Epicurean philosopher and poet. His wife Lucilia, grown bitter over his sexual neglect, deviously gave him a love potion—a toxic aphrodisiac—that drove him mad. During intervals of insanity, he managed to write a number of books, which were later emended by Cicero himself. Supposedly, it was after composing his classic work, *De Rerum Natura* (1st century BC)—*On the Nature of Things*—a poem written in some 7,400 dactylic hexameters divided into six untitled books, which explores Epicurean physics through richly poetic language and metaphors, that he killed himself by his own hand at age 44.

One wonders if artists who kill are not somehow convinced of their power over life and death. Is the compulsion to dominate stronger in them than in others? To feel superior? To mete out some sort of aesthetic justice they alone see, or think they see? Is it, for instance, the impulse to shape a plot in a writer gone awry, merely another way for a painter to scumble a figure? Or is his killing an act of ego, a way of preferring one's own life, destiny, and desires to another's, a sort of satisfaction some artists have felt due them by right? "Every artist's strictly illimitable country is himself," E. E. Cummings once wrote. "An artist who plays that country false has committed suicide." But is an artist alone in having that autonomy? And is an artist's compulsion to kill stronger than it would be for others? More legitimate? Easier to understand? And what about the frequency of the artist doing away with himself? Can we always say that his suicide, like Kirillov's in Dostoevsky's *The Possessed*, is an absolute that he demands in the same way, and with the same power, he creates?

Clearly, many artists kill for the same reasons—anger, greed, jealousy, madness, etc.—that others commonly do. I do not mean to suggest that art is an illness. Many artists are aware that they must live with their devils, their obsessions, and a good many obviously struggle to come to terms with the fact, often by means of their very own art. On the other hand, there are others who come to realize that to rid themselves of their demons would strip them of defenses built up from their earliest years and leave them vulnerable.

Charles Dickens, a public saint today, had an uncanny insight into the criminal mind and liked to joke about his "murderous instincts." "I have a vague sensation," he once said, "of being 'wanted' as I walk about the streets." A. N. Wilson in *The Mystery of*

Charles Dickens has insightfully highlighted the nature of that man's divided self, how he darkly imagined himself as a hunted and covert criminal—he had scandalously kept a secret mistress of 14 years with Nelly Ternan—and so extreme was that novelist's unsparing and publicly abusive hatred for, rages against, and virtually libelous persecution of his wife, Catherine Hogarth, that Wilson cites the ominous words of T. S. Eliot's Sweeney, "Any man has to, needs to, wants to / Once in a lifetime, do a girl in."

Vulnerability, turned inside out, can have another face—viciousness. Dimensions within us are often lost to logic. Poet Sylvia Plath was so plagued, it seems, a young woman who hived off personalities the way a ventriloquist's dummy mimics its owner's many voices, yakking away happily or ranting in endless fits of blue rage. I suspect that when she looked in a mirror in a suffering mode, she saw doubles. Ostensibly her "mother's daughter," a damaged "Sivvy" at age 26 held grudges against Aurelia and in 1958 after one sit-down session with her therapist, savagely wrote in her journal "I lay in my bed when I thought my mind was going blank forever and thought what a luxury it would be to kill her, to strangle her skinny veined throat which could never be big enough to protect me from the world." Lady Macbeth herself had no more a drilling hatred or contempt.

A year later, Plath entered this item in the same journal: "What inner decision, what inner murder or prison-break must I commit if I want to speak from my true voice in writing."

Novelist Patricia Highsmith's relationship with her mother, not unlike Plath's, was a *folie à deux*, as well. They found each other's company unbearable but yet could not leave each other alone. Plath and Highsmith both lived on the cusp of frantic extremes, diligent and prolific but angry writers whose minds were wired with such high-wire tensions of abiding hostility and grievous and murderous hatreds that on a bad day they could become like gibbering ghosts. A lifelong depressive, Plath was morbidly competitive, meeting existence in a survival mode and through all her days demanding perfection of herself. She bit when she kissed and underwent powerful rages. Highsmith had a profound fetish for secrecy, was a compulsive stalker, a virulent anti-Semite, cultivated pet snails, and had a neurotic aversion to being touched, bristling even if anyone shook her hand. Both women were brilliant.

Creation with such figures seemed never far away from Destruction—indeed, one drive seemed to follow the other like buskin upon sock. After a two-year affair but ultimately romantic failure in the 1950s with Marijane Meaker, for example, another but older writer who called herself an "underdog lover"—she is co-credited with launching the lesbian pulp fiction genre, the only accessible novels on that theme in an uptight decade—Patricia Highsmith, suitably called the "balladeer of stalking," sat down and wrote in retaliation a twisted and violent novel of voyeurism called *The Cry of the Owl* (1962), in which a toxic and malicious—and, notably, "unsuccessful artist"—Nickie Forester, a thinly disguised version of Meaker, is at the end in a horrible scene viciously knifed to death.

Henry Evaluardjuk, known as the "Michelangelo of the Eskimos," a rough but ill-tempered genius from the area of Frobisher Bay who had grown up in a rustic hunting camp in the early 1930s—his dramatic pale-green stone carvings of seals, polar bears, and various arctic scenes often sell nowadays for tens of thousands—and served several stretches of prison time. He had killed a man in a drunken brawl. Before that he had tragically killed his son and his third wife when he caught them together.

Chris Burden, a contemporary artist, once nailed himself to

a car, and for a work entitled *Shooting Piece*, in Venice, California in 1971, he asked a friend to shoot him in the left arm—unfortunately, the bullet which he wanted to graze his arm (and shot from 15 feet away) instead blew away a large piece of flesh. Another effort the following year, *Deadman*, was a close encounter with death, until he was arrested for causing a false emergency to be reported. This time he lay wrapped in a canvas bag in the middle of a busy Los Angeles boulevard, defying traffic to run over him. The calculated risks involved, to Burden, were "an energizing factor," his painful exercises meant to transcend physical reality—in his words, "to re-enact certain American classics—like shooting people." With acts presented in such semi-controlled conditions, he hoped they would alter people's perception of violence. My only thought is, how very much more interesting to watch a knife-thrower, which involves real skill, sleight-of-hand, talent, dramatic development, a denouement, and, in short, a sense of artistry that transcends the merely "cerebral," whether in fact it is "death-defying" or not.

This was the kind of performance art (also popular in rock 'n' roll) that recapitulated a movement that flourished in Europe in the 1960s, quasi-artistic in the sense that many of its events took place in art galleries and related to things the practitioners called art, though that is debatable. It was called "actionism," and according to one adherent, it was "not only a form of art, but above all an existential attitude." It related to earlier forms of Viennese Expressionism as filtered through the Dadaists and the horrors of World War II and was mixed with a kind of unhealthy and lugubrious Freudianism.

Arnulf Rainer, for instance, imitated the gestures of the mentally insane. Rudolf Schwarzkogler, an Austrian artist, bled to death after castrating himself in a gallery. And in Paris, an artist named Gina Pane inflicted cuts on her back, face, and hands. She believed that ritualized pain not only had a purifying effect, but felt such work was necessary in order "to reach an anaesthetized society." Using blood, fire, milk, and the recreation of pain as the "elements" of her performance, she succeeded—in her own terms—"in making the public understand right off that my body is my artistic material." A typical work of hers, *The Conditioning* (Part I of "Auto-Portrait[s]") consisted of Pane lying on an iron bed with a few crossbars, underneath which burnt fifteen long candles.

Another example of someone seeking to understand ritualized pain of self-abuse and the disconnectedness that occurs "between the body and the self"—a rather acute distinction—was Marina Abramović, a Serbian conceptual artist who undertook several equally terrifying projects in the name of art. Her strange, daring work explores body art, endurance art, feminist art, the relationship between the performer and audience, the limits of the body, and the possibilities of the mind. In 1971, in a work entitled *Rhythm D*, she willingly permitted a roomful of spectators in a Naples gallery to abuse her at their will for six hours, using instruments of pain and pleasure that had been placed on a table for their convenience. By the third hour, her clothes had been cut from her body with razor blades and her skin had been slashed. A loaded gun that someone held to her head finally caused a fight between her tormentors, bringing the proceedings to an unnerving halt.

While men of average stripe tend to depend upon outside—other's—approval of who they are and what they do, estimates that generally become synonymous with success, at least satisfaction, the artist is often stuck in the lonely position of having to find approval from within, a need for self-acceptance that, desperately bound up with his work, neither praise or blame can alter. It can be a demanding and desperate characteristic, often generating a violence turned against oneself or another.

As in other arts, those tragic excesses can be found in the world of music. At the time he was composing the *Corsaire* Overture, Hector Berlioz was plotting to return to Paris disguised as a chambermaid with the purpose of murdering his former fiancée, her new boyfriend, and her mother. Composer Johann Krumpholz (1745–1790) committed suicide by jumping into the Seine after learning of his wife's infidelity. Robert Schumann went insane in 1854, throwing himself into the Rhine, and although he was rescued, he remained despondent and was finally committed to an asylum. Beethoven's famous letter to his brothers (among whom there was great friction) known as the "Heiligenstadt Testament" is filled with suicidal gloom. Peter Ilyich Tchaikovsky is thought by some to have committed suicide in November 1893 by intentionally drinking un-boiled cholera-tainted water in St. Petersburg.

John Stromberg, the Tin Pan Alley arranger who wrote "Dinah," "Dream On, Dream of Me," as well as Lillian Russell's signature song, "Come Down, Ma' Evenin' Star," died by his own hand in a New York apartment in 1902. Sister Luc Gabriel or Soeur Sourire, "the Singing Nun," born Jeanne-Paule Marie "Jeannine" Deckers, a Belgian singer-songwriter and a member of the Dominican Order in Belgium who had a big hit in 1963 called "Dominique," left the convent, failed as a singer, and proceeded to commit suicide along with her lesbian lover. For that matter, Emperor Nero—lutanist—committed suicide in 68 A.D.

David the Psalmist himself, another musician—and murderer. He slew Uriah and married Bathsheba. He was later confronted by the prophet Nathan with a story (2 Samuel 12:1-4) in which a wealthy man wronged a poor man by taking his one precious possession. The 17th-century Neapolitan composer Don Carlo Gesualdo (c. 1560–1613), a 30-year-old royal prince acclaimed for his chromatic vocal music and a brilliant composer of motets, religious songs, and several books of madrigals—the harmonic complexity of which, incidentally, would later inspire and fascinate Stravinsky—on October 16, 1590, found his adulterous wife, Donna Maria d'Avalos, in bed with her lover, the extremely handsome, cross-dressing Fabrizio Carafa, the Duke of Andria, and murdered them both. The woman's stab wounds were all in her belly and, more particularly, "in those parts which she ought to have kept honest." After Gesualdo slaughtered them both on the spot, he dragged outside the bodies of his wife and her lover, both mutilated and naked, and left them in front of the palace to be exposed for everyone to see. He later fled to his castle at Gesualdo, Campania, to be safe from any relatives of the murdered ones swearing vengeance. In an article on Gesualdo, "The Prince of Darkness" (*The New Yorker*, December 12, 2011) Alex Ross, writes,

> "The final stage of Gesualdo's short life was, in some ways, ghastlier than the beginning. If any readers have found the story insufficiently lurid so far, let them now be satisfied. In 1603, two women of his household were tried for sorcery by local authorities, and, under torture, confessed. One of the alleged witches said that she had given the Prince potions of menstrual blood, and that after sexual intercourse with him she had inserted a piece of bread into her vagina and then served it to him in a sauce. (The trial record contains the phrase "soaked with the seed of them both.") Both women were imprisoned in the castle, which cannot have improved the domestic atmosphere."

Gesualdo ended his days afflicted by an imaginary horde of demons, whose torments only ceased if a dozen young men beat him violently three times a day. While the cause of Gesualdo's death is uncertain, it is believed he was beaten to death during one of these masochistic frenzies. Gesualdo died in isolation, at his castle Gesualdo in Avellino, three weeks after the death of his son, Emanuele, his first son by his marriage to Maria.

One 20th-century biographer has raised the possibility that he was murdered by his second wife. He was buried in the chapel of Saint Ignatius, in the Church of the Gesu Nuovo in Naples. The sepulcher was destroyed in the earthquake of 1688. When the church was rebuilt, the tomb was covered over, and now lies beneath it.

Stephen Foster was an alcoholic. Henry Purcell was reputedly a desperate drinker. Composer Charles Graham who wrote "My Dad's the Engineer," "Two Little Girls in Blue," and "The Picture That Is Turned toward the Wall," etc. died sordidly at Bellevue Hospital in New York, in 1899, after many years of helpless addiction to gambling and alcohol. The great cornetist "Bix" Beiderbecke of course died of excessive drinking and dissipation in 1931. And the Russian composer, Modest Moussorgsky, best remembered for *Night On Bald Mountain*, *Pictures From An Exhibition*, and the opera *Boris Godunov*, drank himself to the point of physical collapse after being rejected by a lover in 1858. Due to his chronic alcoholism, his career soon severely declined. "Friends would often rescue him from some disreputable place, nearly in rags, his hair disheveled, his face swollen with alcohol," wrote a musical contemporary. He died at 42 of "alcoholic epilepsy."

Mikhail Glinka was a wastrel and a libertine. Domenico Scarlatti's penchant for gambling—a passion the great violinist

Paganini also shared—left his family in the grip of dire poverty. Carl Maria von Weber led a corrupt life in Stuttgart, embezzling money from a conscription fund in his early twenties. Michael Wise (1648–1687), an English composer and organist known for his quarrelsome temper, died in a brawl with a night watchman. In 1704 the young Georg Friedrich Handel fought a duel with swords at Hamburg. The immortal author of the *Messiah* had a falling out with another composer, a man named Matheson, over a breach of etiquette—young Handel wouldn't vacate a seat at the harpsichord—during a performance of Matheson's opera *Cleopatra*. Later, during the confrontation Matheson's weapon broke against one of his adversary's brass buttons, which put an end to the combat.

Brilliant Luigi Illica, one of Puccini's greatest librettists—among his most famous opera libretti are those for *La Bohème, Tosca, Madama Butterfly,* and *Andrea Chénier*—would fly into a rage on the slightest provocation, especially when under the influence of alcohol, and lost his ear in a saber duel over a woman. Whenever he was photographed thereafter it was always with his head slightly turned. Conductor Herbert Von Karajan, the brilliant maestro of the Berlin Philharmonic, was also an SS man and surely had a hand in killings. And according to rumor, pianist and composer Louis Gottschalk was assassinated in Rio de Janeiro from getting involved in shady dealings.

There was envy. Salieri hated Mozart. Gluck despised Puccini. Handel felt the same way about Gluck. "He knows no more about counterpoint than my cook," Handel once sneered. Haydn dismissed Beethoven as a mere "pianist." Debussy called Mendelssohn a "facile and elegant notary." He also described Grieg's music as "a pink ribbon filled with snow" and cattily pictured Berlioz as fastening a romantic curl to old wigs, likening his music to leaves that had dried between the pages of a book. Rossini said Weber's music gave him a stomachache. Arrigo Boito referred on one occasion to Leoncavallo's *I Pagliacci* as "that vile spectacle" and on another declared that "the charivari entitled *Salome* [Strauss's opera] is nothing but a clatter of pots and pans which lasts for an hour and fifty minutes." Alfred Catalani accused Puccini of just about every intrigue, including plagiarism. And Strauss, who envied Puccini his popularity, considered his music as nothing but *"Schund"*—trash. Virgil Thompson dismissed George Gershwin's *Porgy and Bess* as "crooked folklore and halfway opera." And Victor Herbert utterly hated singer Madame Emma Trentini.

In 1865, Henry James gave a dreadful review to both Walt Whitman's "Drum-Taps" and to Charles Dickens's novel *Our Mutual Friend,* stating of the latter, "And it is poor with the poverty not of momentary embarrassment, but of permanent exhaustion." He called Dickens "the greatest of superficial novelists." In the review, writing in a hectoring, even catty way, James lectured the popular, the "Inimitable Boz:" "But a community of eccentrics is impossible. Rules alone are consistent with each other, exceptions are inconsistent. Society is maintained by natural sense and natural feelings."

As far as prima donnas went, Renata Tebaldi and Maria Callas had a distinct loathing for each other all their lives. But then Richard Wagner despised Brahms. And Hegel. And Jews. Just about everybody, in fact. For the superior Wagner, no human relationship had any true lasting value—it seemed that as soon as there showed the smallest slip in total subservience to him, love turned to hate or contempt. Wagner no human relationship had any true lasting value—it seemed that as soon as there was the smallest slip in total subservience, love turned to hate or contempt. And for reasons I have still to determine pianist Glenn Gould hated Mozart.

Then there was despair. Anton Bruckner had a nervous breakdown. French composer Juste Lafage died in the madhouse of Charenton in 1862. Librettist Johann Schikander—the original Papageno in Mozart's *Die Zauberflöte*—also went insane. Composer Bedrich Smetana suffered a complete mental breakdown after going stone deaf at 50 and then died of syphilis in an insane asylum at Prague. Gaetano Donizetti who also went mad from syphilis at 47, died at 50. American operatic soprano Pauline L'Allemand (born Pauline Elhasser in 1862)—she created the role of Delibes' *Lakme* with the National Opera Company—after several reversals occupied what was described as little more than a but near Beaver Creek, Illinois, living in direst poverty with her son, and finally died in a mental institution. Trumpeter Buddy Bolden, who wrote and played, among other classics, "Careless Love," "Maple Leaf Rag," and "Make Me a Pallet on the Floor," lost his mind one day in 1907, while performing in a street parade. Until his death in 1931 he lived in an asylum. Arid of course Robert Schumann who attempted suicide by once throwing himself into the Rhine spent the remainder of his days in a private asylum.

Tenor sax player Wardell Gray was shot and killed in Las Vegas. Eddie Jefferson, who is today remembered for his great renditions of "Body and Soul" and "Moody's Mood for Love," was shot. Trumpeter Chet Baker fell out of a window under mysterious circumstances. Mezz Mezzrow spent two years in jail for selling drugs. At the end, Hank Williams, who died at 29—his favorite song was supposedly "Death Is Only a Dream"—was a ruined shell of himself, ravaged by drugs and alcohol. Jazz clarinetist Sidney Bechet, a chronic drunk, was deported from England for taking part in a brawl. (He is said to have thrown his English money overboard, sick of seeing George V's face.)

And then on November 26, 1978, in Van Nuys, California, at 4 o'clock in the morning, Frank Rosolino, one of the best-loved men in jazz, who once played trombone for both Gene Krupa and Stan Kenton with such great euphoria, walked into his children's bedroom and shot and killed his son Justin, who was nine, but only wounded—but permanently blinded and paralyzed—the younger Jason who was then seven. (He would undergo 14 hours of surgery.) Rosolino then turned the gun on himself. Tragically, three years before, Frank's third wife, the mother of his two sons, had gone into the garage, shut the door, turned on the car's engine, and sat there in the fumes until she died. Frank Rosolino had always been widely known for his wise-cracking personality. As a friend Roger Kellaway said later, "When somebody cracks four jokes a minute, we all should have known there was something wrong."

Jazzman Charlie ("Bird") Parker was addicted to drugs, which crippled him. He had no veins left to inject toward the end of his life. He grew loamy and fat. He was rootless, often depressed, always old before his time, and in desperate shape. After his little daughter, Pree, not yet three, died of a congenital heart condition in 1954, Parker swallowed iodine in an attempt at suicide, was twice hospitalized in Bellevue, and died the following year. Sonny Boy Williamson drank himself to death. So did Johnny Thunders, ex-New York Dolls guitarist, at 38, on April 23, 1991, ingesting a lethal mixture of alcohol and methadone. Tenor saxophonist Lester Young died of drunkenness and despair at 49. One of the singers in the pop girl group the Shangri-Las, Mary Ann Ganser, died from a drug overdose. So did actor Peter Lorre. And David Ruffin, lead singer of the Temptations. Singers Chuck Willis, Billie Holiday, Frankie Lymon, Judy Garland, Jim Morrison, Janis Joplin, and Jimi Hendrix all died of drugs or alcohol, as did country singer Hank

Williams, an alcoholic before he was out of his teens and who all his life was also morbidly afraid of the dark.

Singer Johnny Ace (his real name was John Alexander) who in the Fifties recorded his huge hit "Pledging My Love," fatally shot himself through the mouth with a small, cheap .22 pistol (made in Italy) on the eve of December 25, 1954, at a "Negro Christmas Dance" at Houston City Auditorium during a backstage game of Russian roulette specifically to prove he wasn't afraid of guns. He was holding his girlfriend, Olivia Gibbs, on his lap. He had been drinking vodka. He had once served time in a Mississippi jail. Larry Williams, a drug addict who in the late Fifties popularized "Short Fat Fannie," "Bony Moronie," and "Dizzy Miss Lizzie," on January 2, 1980, shot himself through the head. And Dinah Washington (born Ruth Jones in Tuscaloosa), who according to rumor supposedly shot and killed someone at 39 in Detroit—and two of whose killer hits were "Evil Gal Blues" and "Blow Top Blues"—took a lethal overdose of sleeping pills in 1963. Hot-tempered, fiercely jealous, over-bearing, even megalomaniacal. (She took her billing so seriously, she referred to herself as the "Queen of the Blues" even when answering the telephone.) She could never assuage her feelings of inadequacy, not with fur, jewels, a succession of men, alcohol, or the pills that eventually proved fatal. She supposedly would walk in to a recording studio, look at the band or small orchestra, step up to the microphone, and say, "OK, one take, motherfuckers!"

Other notable rock 'n' roll suicides were Donny Hathaway, both Tommy Evans and Pete Ham of Badfinger—Ham, extremely intoxicated, hanged himself in his garage in the middle of the night in 1974—Joe Meek, Phil Ochs, Ian Curtis, Larry Williams, Bobby Fuller, Graham Bond, Dell Shannon of "Runaway" fame, who shot himself, Terry Kath of Chicago, Ron ("Pigpen")

McKernan, Wendy O. Williams, Al Wilson of Canned Heat, Kurt Cobain, Nick Drake, Naomi Judd, Pete Ham, Sid Vicious, Elliott Smith, Paul Williams, one of the (many) lead singers of the Temptations—not the Hollywood songwriting midget of the same name—and although she died of a heart attack, it isa commonly accepted that the Supreme's Florence Ballard actually drank herself to death.

Huddie ("Leadbelly") Ledbetter was a violent man who once had his throat cut in a Texas juke joint and, though he survived, carried ever after an ugly scar that ran almost from ear to ear. Born in Mooringsport, Louisiana, about 1888, Huddie (pronounced "Hew-dee") went from being a poor black field worker to becoming an itinerant singer and blues performer. His music, which was all he knew, had its roots in the folk tradition of the Gulf Coast, and he called himself "the twelve-string champion guitar player of the world." A genuinely mean, anti-social, and unapproachable man, he was committed in 1918 to a Texas prison called Harlem (an all-black unit no longer in existence) for murdering a man and stayed there until 1925. And then in 1930 he tried to kill another man in Louisiana and was sent to Angola for four years.

Dangerous especially when drunk or angry, Leadbelly once even pulled a knife on folk-archivist and friend John Lomax, who avoided him after that. Although he made a series of recordings for the Library of Congress in the Thirties and became something of a legend, he never mellowed, however. In fact, in 1949, the year in which he died, he was jailed in New York on assault charges.

Staff Sergeant Barry Sadler, who co-authored and sang the 1966 #1 hit "The Ballad of the Green Berets"—and who, after leaving the Army upon injuring his leg in a booby trap in Vietnam, died in Tennessee on November 1989 at 48 of a gunshot wound inflicted upon him while he was employed as a mercenary in Guatemala training Nicaraguan Contra rebels—made the news both in 1978 and 1981 when he was accused in two unrelated shootings. No charges were ever filed in the first case and Sadler was found innocent in the second. During that trial Sadler rather bumptiously told the surprised court that, if it were *he* that shot the man who lived, "He'd be dead. I'm a Green Beret."

And then there was that trouble in 1988 when soul singer James Brown—the "Hardest Working Man in Show Business," the "Godfather of Soul," "Mother Popcorn"—in a fit of high antics that exceeded even his extravagant, extroverted camel-walking went careening through the streets of Atlanta, high on PCP, unsuccessfully tried to run down several policemen, failed, was nailed, and got sentenced to six years in the cooler. Sid Vicious ("I hate art") of the punk group the Sex Pistols, always wore a black leather jacket with no shirt underneath and enormous black combat boots. He wore his greasy black hair standing straight up on his head in a spiky stook of true "punk fashion." Sid was a cadaverous 6'2", 135 pounds. One of his eyes drooped, the result, he always claimed, of a fight. His real name was John Simon Ritchie. He was a headbanger. He is credited with having invented pogo dancing, which consisted of hopping up and down in place, arms spastically flailing. He was also an advocate of "squelching," the act of making love without any emotion. An interviewer once asked him why his chest was all slashed. "One night nobody was payin' any attention to me," he told a *Rolling Stone* interviewer, "so I thought I'd commit suicide. I went to the bathroom, broke a glass, and slashed my chest with it. It's a good way to get attention."

Another way, of course, is to kill a person, which is exactly what he proceeded to do, stabbing his wife with a seven-inch hunting knife, a 20-year-old Jewish groupie from Pennsylvania named

Nancy Spungen, and leaving her to bleed to death under a sink in the notorious Chelsea Hotel on October 12, 1978. She was found wearing only black lace panties. Why did he do it, he was asked. His reply, with a shrug, was "Because I'm a dog. A dirty dog." He had been violent with her often, once actually ripping off one of her ears—she had it stitched back on. Sid would die himself the following year in New York City after taking an overdose of heroin. He knew nothing of music, he hadn't the slightest idea of how to play the guitar, and the high point of his career was a caterwauling cover version of Frank Sinatra's hit "My Way." " It had been a strange short life for the marginalized singer. "The Sex Pistols weren't into music," said Malcolm McLaren, their mentor.

During the spring of 1972, after his wife Priscilla had left in a station wagon stuffed with luggage and went to live with Mike Stone, her karate instructor, Elvis Presley, who wouldn't hesitate to whip out a gun and threaten anybody who displeased him, constantly made threats against his wife's lover, oddly enough by calling her week after week. It became his obsession for nearly a year and a half. He owned an 11-16 automatic rifle. The "King" loved guns. Much of his adult life was spent firing at targets, shooting out lights, and blasting TV sets. As one of his closest companions Red West said several times, "Elvis had a need to kill." Soon Elvis's threats became worse. "Doesn't anyone understand?" he once screamed. *"Why can't you all understand this man must die!"* Although at one point Elvis actually went so far as to commission a member of the Mafia to make the hit for $10,000, it ultimately led to nothing, and the matter eventually blew over.

In the world of country music there are all sorts of redneck stories about killings, most of them totally spurious. Hank Williams several times took shots at his first wife, Audrey. The first time he was drunk, thought he killed her, and fled to Los Angeles. Another time, after his gun misfired, she grabbed a knife off a plate and tried to stab him. Johnny Paycheck, a short, grizzled guitarist whose biggest hit was "Take This Job and Shove It" and who swapped his real name—David Lytle—for that of a small-time heavyweight once KO'd by Joe Louis in two rounds back in 1940, was sentenced to nine and a half years in prison for a barroom shooting in Ohio. The country singer, Merle Haggard, although he never killed anyone, certainly grew up a punk and was tending in that direction. Born in Oildale, California, he was arrested for car theft, burglary, and breaking and entering, and not only escaped seven times from reform school—the letters "PSI" remained tattooed on his left wrist until the day he died—but spent his 21st birthday in solitary confinement in San Quentin, just a few cells down from the about-to-be executed rapist Caryl Chessman.

The only "time" country singer Johnny Cash ever did, incidentally, for all that pre-possessing, "tough-guy" Folsom Prison blues persona, was a night or two in a local clink for just plain drunkenness, although he took drugs over the course of much of his life. The scars on his face are the result of something like wart surgery or a cyst removal. But Jerry Lee Lewis, known as "The Killer," was a different story. After 13 years of marriage when his third wife, Myra Gale Brown, filed a divorce suit against him in 1970—his first marriage (to Dorothy Barton) lasted only a year—Lewis swore he would never marry again. The marriage to Myra Gale created a huge scandal in 1957. Myra Gale was not merely his cousin, she was only 13 years old. He was kicked out of England high and headlong on a concert tour because of that scandalous fact. She claimed he once put out a lit cigarette on her arm. He also threatened to hurl her into the river and "throw acid in her face." After their divorce, Lewis proceeded to marry again, and then again, several times.

Some people say Jerry Lee killed two of his wives. In any case, both of them died under mysterious circumstances. Jaren, wife number four, who had several times accused him of threatening her life, drowned in a swimming pool, and in 1983 wife number five, Shawn—barely three months after her marriage to "The Killer"—was found dead of a drug overdose in their house. Another story involved another wife, one of them, whom he left sleeping in a Nashville motel room. He proceeded to wake her in a novel way when he ambled home just before dawn, spraying and shattering the wall above her head with a Thompson machine gun, *blam blam blam blam blam blam.*

He definitely shot his bass player, Norman ("Butch") Owens, a man he suspected of cuckolding him. "Look down the barrel of this," murmured Jerry Lee sitting in his living room and waving a .357 Magnum. He had been drinking. He said, "I'm gonna shoot that Co' Cola bottle over there or my name ain't Jerry Lee Lewis." He took careful aim and pumped two bullets into Owens's chest. Owens lived, and Jerry Lee was merely charged with discharging a firearm inside the city limits, a misdemeanor in his good ol' hometown of Ferriday, Louisiana.

Jerry Lee always suffered major confusions about religion. One of his cousins was the scandalous, yam-in-the-mouth television evangelist Jimmy Lee Swaggart. ("I went to Bible college in Waxahatchie, Texas, and I preached for three years. I was probably one of the best," said Swaggart with characteristic humility. "A lot of people were saved under my missionary.") Somewhere he said he made a Faustian pact with the Devil when growing up, that if he could learn to play the piano, he'd give up his soul. "His church is Church of God Pentecostal, a religion that will give you a hundred quick ways to get to hell," says a happier Myra Gale who later became a real estate agent. Her theory is that Jerry Lee Lewis thought he was too wicked to be saved because of doing "the devil's work" by playing rock and roll, which making him only worse simply confirms it. She adds, significantly, "Everyone that's walked into Jerry Lee's life has either become a tragedy, a fatality, or a disruption." Lewis married wife number six in 1984, and his seventh and final wife in 2012.

We should also include country singer Spade Cooley here. He was born in 1910. During the late 1940s, Spade Cooley and His Orchestra was one of the most popular Western-swing bands in the country. At his first Columbia session in 1945, Spade—his full name was Donnell Clyde Cooley—cut the biggest hit of his entire career, "Shame on You." He was even featured in two musical films, *Spade Cooley, King of Western Swing*, a 10-minute Warner Brothers short subject produced in 1945, and Universal's 1949 *Spade Cooley and His Orchestra*. In December 1945, Cooley married his second wife, Ella Mae, who was 21 years old. (When he had a television program in the 1950s, she played fiddle in his band.) Cooley had three children: a daughter, born in 1947, and two sons, born in 1933 and 1948, by his first wife, Ann). In 1945, the year of his second marriage, Spade Cooley was arrested for rape in California, but was acquitted.

Cooley worked as a stand-in for Roy Rogers in the younger singer's films. he looked almost exactly like him. In any case, on the evening of April 3, 1961, he arrived at his home in Willow Springs, about 85 miles north of Los Angeles. He had been drinking and taking pills. There was an argument. Spade began beating Ella Mae. He forced his daughter to sit. "You're going to watch me kill her," he said. Bobbie Bennett, Cooley's female manager, came to the house. Cooley's wife was naked, bruised and red and dying. Her breasts had been burned with a cigarette. Spade stood there, in shock. There was blood on his fancy cowboy boots. On April 25 in Bakersfield, a murder indictment was returned against Cooley. He was convicted of first-degree murder, ironically enough, largely on the testimony of his 14-year-old daughter. On August 22, Superior Judge William L. Bradshaw sentenced the King of Western swing to life imprisonment. As the verdict was read, Cooley slumped, and in a cracked voice merely said there was nothing he wished to say. He sat in Vacaville, a prison 40 miles northeast of Oakland for many years. In August 1969, it was announced that he had been granted a parole and that he would be released on February 2, 1970. On November 23, he was granted an evening leave to perform in an Oakland show that was sponsored by the Alameda County Deputy Sheriff's Association. Cooley was well received and given a standing ovation. During intermission he collapsed and died of a heart attack.

Ella Mae bragged to many of her acquaintances that she had seduced Roy Rogers. Spade apparently believed that for a time, but before he died, according to Rogers, later tried to apologize for having accepted his wife's story.

There is nothing new in pointing out that the basis of much creativity is dissidence and disruption. (An artist's options resembles a murderer's options: "the art of adding," as John Updike once defined writing, "and the art of taking away.") Yet the unavoidable irony remains that the forces often released are forces about which the artist is not always sure and of which he is not always in control. Destruction often ensues, where repudiation, bitterness, anger—mis-expressing who knows what wish?—lead directly to murder.

It is interesting. The French playwright and novelist Jean Genet, who admits to frankly admiring certain kinds of personal murder and who was no stranger to active crime—both he and the professed anarchist Antonin Artaud, defending mass extermination, identified Adolf Hitler with that tyrant's anarchic freedom of total personal expression which is celebrated in the hero of his prose piece *Héliogabale ou l'Anarchiste couronné* (Heliogabalus or The Anarchist Crowned) (1934)—was once asked in a interview why he had never committed a murder, and he famously replied: "Probably because I have written my books."

We recall the famous injunction to "Exterminate all the brutes!" in Joseph Conrad's *Heart of Darkness*. The words are scrawled in the impulsive unconscious of delirium by a representative of colonial exploitation, a small-scale tyrant by the standards of Nero and Heliogabalus, but one who like them gave himself up to a tyrannous anarchy of total gratification. And yet what is one to make of the alarming reference in a letter to R. B. Cunninghame Graham, which discusses both that novel and some related political matters, when Conrad points out that he respects extreme anarchists who frankly desire a "general extermination"?

The story of writers and violence is endless. Many have come close to murder, missing merely by degrees. Luís Vaz da Camoës, the national poet of Portugal and author of its epic, *The Lusiads*, not only lost an eye fighting in Ceuta, but was once imprisoned for trying to kill a palace retainer. The poet Chiabrera murdered a Roman gentleman in revenge for an insult; the historian Davila killed a man and was himself assassinated. Tasso in his periodic fits of frenzy was wont to attack people with a dagger; Murtola and Marini were in the habit of shooting at each other; and Guiseppe Ortale, a Sicilian poet, was known as the *"Cavaliere sanguinario"* for his bloodthirsty tendencies. Lope de Vega, the Spanish dramatist, at the very time he was writing light comedies, presided with cool fanaticism over a monk's execution for heresy. Swedish playwright August Strindberg often beat women. English writer and poet Walter Savage Landor, the irascible hothead who spent much of his life in legal disputes and contemptuous spats and who famously once said, "The flame of anger, bright and brief, sharpens the barb of love," threw his cook out of a window. Arthur Schopenauer kicked his landlady down the stairs and had to pay damages to her for the rest of his life. A. N. Whitehead, poor man, supposedly shoplifted. And O. Henry as a teller embezzled money from the First National Bank of Austin, fled to Honduras, returned, and in 1898 was sentenced to five years at the Ohio Penitentiary in Columbus.

Sir Thomas Malory, whose great work *Le Morte d'Arthur* was written in prison, led a highly discreditable life. In 1450 he not only tried to ambush and murder the Duke of Buckingham but broke into Coombe Abbey where he robbed and insulted the abbot. He was also charged on two occasions of feloniously ravishing a certain Joan, wife of Henry Smyth of Monks Kirby (it may have meant nothing more than abduction), stealing cattle on a large scale, and highway robbery. For these misdemeanors he served eight periods of imprisonment, and twice escaped—in July 1451, swimming the moat of Coleshill Prison; in October 1454, making an armed breakout from Colchester Castle. In 1468 the king excluded him from a general pardon, whereupon he appears to have been imprisoned at Newgate until his death three years later. Then there was that other pattern of chivalry, John Tiptoft, earl of Worcester. Otherwise known as the "butcher of England," in 1470 it was with great difficulty that he was brought to the scaffold through the London mob thirsting for his blood. His translation of *Controversia de nobilitate* was also published by Caxton.

Was the novelist Miguel de Cervantes a murderer? To this day, reasons that forced the writer to leave Spain still remain uncertain. Possible reasons include that the writer was a "sword-wielding fugitive from justice," fleeing from a royal warrant of arrest for having wounded a certain Antonio de Sigura, a painter, in a duel. On September 15, 1569, the legal authorities in Madrid ordered the arrest of Cervantes for having wounded a certain "*andante*" in court by the name of "Antonio de Sigura." Whether he was the painter in the court of Felipe II cannot be said for certain, and the identity of the true rival has been highly debated. There is no question that the touchy, ill-tempered Cervantes was a fighter. While he was stationed there in the Spanish navy, Cervantes participated in the battle of Lepanto in 1571, in which Juan de Austria fought against the Turks. Cervantes was injured and lost his left hand, giving him the nickname "*El Manco de Lepanto*" (The one-handed man from Lepanto). In his life, Cervantes had fallen afoul the law several times. It was in prison, in fact, in Seville that at the age of 50 he supposedly began writing his masterpiece, *Don Quixote de la Mancha*. After the brawl Cervantes, fleeing justice, ended up in Italy.

Arthur Rimbaud badly wounded the photographer Étienne Carjat one night in January 1872 with a sword cane when a quarrel broke out over dinner, and he cut Paul Verlaine's wrists and thighs while drinking one night in the Café du Rat Mort. The two poets Verlaine and Rimbaud of course were not only weirdly unpredictable but often behaved as utter madmen. When absinthe was percolating through Verlaine's system, he would often behave brutally, frequently taking out his deep-seated anger on his passive wife, Mathilde. He beat her, ridiculed her, set fire to her hair and clothes, and even once slashed her with a knife. Rimbaud, for whom drinking was not a pleasure but a necessary form of flagellation, making his nerves sing like harp-wires, urged him on, persuading him that a "good family man," a true seeker, would never cater to the feeble requirements of domesticity.

On July 10, 1873, in Brussels, when the younger poet tried to break off relations with him, Verlaine in a fit of jealousy shot his young lover in the wrist, although he patched him up. But then as Rimbaud once more prepared to catch a train for Paris, Verlaine again took the pistol and threatened to kill him. This time Rimbaud called the police, and Verlaine was arrested. During the police investigation, their sodomitical relations were revealed, and Verlaine was arrested and sentenced to five years in prison. Years later, around 1888, Rimbaud would be running guns into Abyssinia.

Alphonse Daudet, a womanizer and lust-monger who suffered badly from syphilis, in his mad love affair with Marie Rieu, several times tried to stab the poor woman. F. H. Bradley allegedly skulked around Oxford killing cats. (Henry James—not exactly Trader Horn—once killed a cat with a stick and was sickened by the violent act immediately threw up.) Vittorio Alfieri, the Italian poet and dramatist, who had many affairs in England, got into frequent duels with husbands he had cuckolded. The Swedish novelist Carl Almquist, who wrote books and stories of folk life, his most important work being the 14-volume *The Book of the Rose*, tried to poison one of his creditors and then escaped to America. The genius Robert Oppenheimer, the "Father of the Atomic Bomb," tried to kill his university tutor with a poisoned apple.

George Gissing was imprisoned for stealing money to support his prostitute, Marianne Helen ("Nell") Harrison. Ludwig Bemelmans, writer and illustrator, who was born to Belgian painter Lambert Bemelmans and a German mother Frances Fischer in Meran, Austria—his father also owned a hotel—grew up in Gmunden on the Traunsee in Upper Austria, his first language being French and his second German. In 1904, after his father deserted the family for Ludwig's governess, his mother took Ludwig and his brother to her native city of Regensburg, Germany, where young Bemelmans had difficulty in school and hated the German discipline. He was apprenticed to his uncle Hans Bemelmans at a hotel in Austria, where he apparently shot and seriously wounded a waiter and was in consequence forced to choose between being institutionalized or emigrating to America. He chose the latter and spent the next several years working at hotels and restaurants, when in 1917 joined the U.S. Army, although was not ordered to Europe because of his German heritage. And novelist Norman Mailer in a moment of fury stabbed his second wife in the abdomen and the back. ("He just came at me with a funny look in his eyes," she later explained. "He just looked at me. Then he stabbed me.") Violence is strong in artists. Goethe perhaps may have been speaking for many when said he could imagine himself committing any crime on earth.

Alexander Pope despised Lord Hervey. Lord Byron ridiculed Robert Southey. Ben Jonson, trying to belittle Sir Philip Sidney, claimed he had "an ugly, spotty face." John Dryden said that Edmund Spenser, in imitating the ancients, "writ no language." Molière—the stage name of Jean-Baptiste Poquelin—after several betrayals, never spoke to Jean Racine again. (The infamous actress Catherine Voisin, moreover, accused the intriguing Racine of having poisoned her with a view to giving the part of Phèdre to Mlle. Champmeslé, who eventually became his mistress.) The anti-Christian poet Jacques Gruet, having written the word "Nonsense!" in John Calvin's book, was beheaded in 1547 for blasphemy and treason. Fyodor Dostoevsky vilified Ivan Turgenev. Charles Dickens mocked Leigh Hunt. Anthony Trollope hated Benjamin Disraeli. Poet Robert Browning loathed Edward Fitzgerald for writing scathing things about his wife's poetry. Nathaniel Hawthorne disliked Margaret

Fuller. The anti-Papistical novelist Charles Kingsley, who loathed Cardinal Newman, wrote, "In him and all that school"—he meant Catholics—"there is an element of foppery, even in dress and manner; a fastidious, maundering die-away effeminacy, which is mistaken for purity and refinement; and I confess myself unable to cope with it." H. G. Wells ridiculed Henry James, who in turn referred to both Tolstoy's and Dostoevsky's novels as "fluid puddings." And Janet Duff-Gordon Ross once happily horsewhipped the novelist Ouida, in the middle of London's fashionable Bond Street.

"I greet you at the beginning of a great career," Ralph Waldo Emerson wrote to poet Walt Whitman, saluting him after having just read *Leaves of Grass*, but then, sending the book to his friend Thomas, Emerson shruggingly suggested, not unhypocritically, "And if you find it an auctioneer's inventory of a warehouse you may light your pipe with it." Algernon Swinburne bitterly hated Thomas Carlyle, by the way, who had dismissed him out of hand as a sensualist and sodomite, and Carlyle hated Benjamin Disraeli whom he called "a cursed old Jew not worth his weight in cold bacon."

Edgar Allan Poe hated Longfellow and thought his work a tissue of plagiarisms. Tolstoy Shakespeare the nonpareil and called him a fraud. ("I despise Shakespeare when I measure my mind against his.") So did George Bernard Shaw dislike Shakespeare. He also thought the work of his contemporary, playwright Victorian Sardou, superficial, calling it "Sardoodledom." Baudelaire hated George Sand ("She is stupid, heavy-handed, and a gossip") as well as Voltaire ("the king of squares, prince of superficiality, the anti-artist, the preacher to concierges"). William James detested George Santayana. Willa Cather hated the Boston cigar-smoking poet Amy Lowell. Lord Alfred Douglas never spoke to W. B. Yeats again for having excluded him from *The Oxford Book of Modern Verse*. Baron Corvo turned against Robert Hugh Benson and just about every individual with whom he came in contact. Max Nordau called Emile Zola "a sexual psychopath." Osbert Sitwell mocked D. H. Lawrence. Sean O'Casey described Graham Greene's attitude to life as a "snot-sodden whinge." Evelyn Waugh showed complete loathing for Somerset Maugham. And Virginia Woolf, who contemptuously, invidiously, thought James Joyce a low-born churl with no literary talent whatsoever dared to call *Ulysses* "the book of a self-taught working man . . . of a queasy undergraduate scratching his pimples."

F. Scott Fitzgerald so despised Robert McAlmon, who had an ironclad reputation for bitchiness, that he once said, "God will forgive everybody—even Robert McAlmon." Oscar Wilde contemptuously dismissed the decadent illustrator Aubrey Beardsley (who did many wonderful drawings for him, which, however, included caricatures) for many snobbish reasons, sneering, "He has a face like a silver hatchet adorned with green grass hair." G. K. Chesterton described the American editor and journalist H. L. Mencken as a "bitter Jew." (Mencken was from a German Christian family and grew up speaking German.) Mencken despised Theodore Dreiser, referring to him as "an incurable lout," and Dreiser once slapped the novelist Sinclair Lewis's face at a dinner party in New York because Lewis had accused him of stealing Lewis's wife Dorothy Thompson's book on Russia.

Aldous Huxley derisively called the English Sitwells—Osbert and Edith—the Shufflebottoms. Edith Wharton could not stand the company of Wyndham Lewis. Wyndham Lewis ridiculed Stephen Spender and T.S. Eliot. Vladimir Nabokov mocked the Argentinian Jorge Luis Borges. On February 12, 1976, Peruvian novelist Mario Vargas Llosa knocked the Columbian Gabriel García Márquez unconscious and left him lying flat on the floor in the lobby of a Mexico City auditorium. Spiky Katherine Mansfield, who had an exceptionally nasty talent for hatred, once confessed quite frankly that it was far and away her favorite emotion. Poet (and suicide) Anne Sexton hated poet James Dickey. And J. D. Salinger, according to Norman Mailer, was "the greatest mind ever to stay in prep school."

There was a class of writers who enjoyed the reputation of "fighting authors," people with what John Ruskin called "stage fire," who not only drew swords on reviewers who condemned a play but fiercely challenged any of the audience that hissed it. Duels were fought between Francis Jeffrey and Thomas Moore, the French poet Alphonse de Lamartine and the Neapolitan general Gabriello Pepemilo who took offense at some scurrilous verses impugning the weak and servile nature of Catholic Italy.

Spanish dramatist Pedro Calderón de la Barca, who later became a priest, killed a man in a duel in 1621, as did the Spanish poet Francisco de Quevedo ten years earlier, who then fled to Italy. John Scott, the early 19th-century editor of the *London Magazine* died as the result of a duel, embroiled as he was in the Cockney School controversy. John Gibson Lockhart had been abusing many of Scott's contributors in *Blackwood's Magazine* (under the pseudonym *Z*). In May 1820, Scott began a series of counter-articles, which provoked Lockhart into calling him "a liar and a scoundrel." In February 1820, Lockhart's London agent, Jonathan Henry Christie, made a provocative statement, and Scott challenged him. They met on February 16, 1821, at a farm between Camden Town and Hampstead. Christie did not fire in the first round, but there was a misunderstanding between the seconds, resulting in a second round. Scott was hit in the abdomen and died 11 days later. Christie and his second were tried for willful murder and acquitted; the collection for Scott's family was a notable radical cause.

The playwright Richard Brinsley Sheridan fought a duel—twice—with a certain Captain Thomas Mathews in London, 1722. Matthews, a married man, was persecuting "with dishonorable addresses" a young woman beloved by Sheridan's younger brother, Charles. While acting as her protector, the playwright fell in love with this same woman, eloped with her to Calais, and eventually married her. Upon the couple's return to England, Sheridan (whose own brother was outraged, by the way) was formally challenged to a duel, which proved inconclusive. A second duel followed, at Kingsdown, near Bath. The fight was severe and, according to one account—and the "Wager of Battle Rules"—disgraceful. "Both their swords breaking upon the first lunge, and eventually to murder."

In 1598, the playwright Ben Jonson in a duel killed fellow actor Gabriel Spencer, a pro-tem leader of the Admiral's men, for which Jonson had written several plays. Spencer, a rising star (and shareholder) in the Admiral's Men Players was himself no stranger to violence, having two years before stabbed to death James Feake, who had attacked him brandishing a candlestick. Spencer's fatal encounter with Jonson took place the very month when Johnson's first play for the Chamberlain's Men—*Every Man in His Humour*—was performed. Ironically, at the time of the quarrel Spencer was learning his part in a collaborative (and ironically) titled play for the Admiral's Men, *Hot Anger Soon Cold*.

The duel took place on September 22, 1598, in Hogsden Fields (today part of Hoxton). Philip Henslowe, the Elizabethan theatrical entrepreneur and impresario (and diarist), wrote Spencer's epitaph: "slain in Hogsdon Fields by the hands of Benjamin Jonson, his stepfather had been a bricklayer." The so-called "Wars of the Theaters"—"much throwing about of brains," as Guildenstern in Hamlet describes, regarding the debate over the child actors usurping the London stage—were rife at the time, and although Jonson had been classically educated, his stepfather had been a bricklayer and Jonson's enemies always delighted in reminding him of it. Brought to trial on a charge of manslaughter, Jonson pleaded guilty—he claimed in his defense that his sword was 10 inches shorter—but was released by "benefit of clergy," a legal loophole dating from medieval times through which he gained leniency by reciting a brief Bible verse (the so-called "neck verse") by which a criminal under a detail of ancient English law could be set free if he could demonstrate he was able to read. As a penalty, however, Jonson was forced to forfeit his "goods and chattels" and was branded on his left thumb. As no one was allowed to plead "benefit of clergy" twice, felons who managed to avoid the gallows were stamped with as letter "T"— for Tyburn Hill, the notorious site of execution in London—on the base of the left thumb with a red-hot iron. While in jail, Jonson converted to Roman Catholicism, possibly through the influence of Father Thomas Wright, a Jesuit priest, who was himself being kept a prisoner for his faith.

The ruffian Jonson enjoyed sleeping with other men's wives (but apparently not with single women)—some say that his dramatic interest in adulterous triangles was a product of his own philandering—notoriously sired one or more illegitimate children, was once paraded through the streets of Paris in a drunken stupor, and narrowly escaped having his ears and nose mutilated after collaborating on a play that lampooned King James I. In his thirty-third year, his own mother was supposedly on the verge of trying to kill him and acquired a dram of "lustie strong poison" for that specific purpose. Jonson was, by all accounts, a touchy, quick-tempered fellow who was quick to reach for his sword. The roots of his aggressiveness went back to his childhood and adolescence, culminating in his reckless marriage to Anne Lewis and his conflicted relationships with his children. As I say, gibes about being a bricklayer's son also followed him to the end of his career. A daughter's early death grieved him sorely. In any case, Jonson was imprisoned for the Spencer murder— he had been incarcerated at least two other times—and all of his property was confiscated.

In May 1610, the famous poet and playwright renounced his Catholic faith and became a Protestant—again. (Jonson supposedly gulped down a full chalice of Communion wine to mark his return to the Anglican church.) A persistent question has been raised as to whether Jonson really was a Catholic in his heart. Concerned that he would be executed for his crime, he wanted to receive Catholic absolution for his soul. Jonson judiciously kept his new faith quiet, staying underground for many years. When James was crowned King of England in 1603, Jonson may have been optimistic that a greater toleration of Catholics might have prevailed. Although King James's reign made the situation no better for Catholics, his wife, the Queen Consort Anne, not only a secret Catholic like Jonson himself, but a powerful dignitary who particularly enjoyed the court masque entertainments he wrote—and which she would occasionally star in. She became Jonson's un-official patron.

A dark sea change took place in November 1605, with the "Gunpowder Plot," however, a Catholic conspiracy to kill King James and blow Parliament up sky high. Petrified no doubt that he might be arrested because of his faith Jonson had good reason to fear; the Gunpowder Plot conspirators frequently met at the Mermaid Tavern—the same tavern that Jonson visited the most. Shakespearean sleuth David B. Schajer, pointing to the fact that King Henry IV of France was slain by a Catholic assassin on May 14, 1610, offers it as a legitimate reason for Jonson publicly renouncing his Catholic faith, suggesting that he was afraid that Catholics would be punished in the wake of that murder, just as they had after the Gunpowder Plot. Asks Schajer in the end, "Was his conversion sincere? I don't think so. He probably remained a secret Catholic in his heart."

A famous contemporary of Ben Jonson, by the way, the contentious and outspoken Christopher Marlowe, one of England's greatest playwrights, together with a man named Thomas Watson was arrested and sent to Newgate in 1589 for having murdered a man, although it's commonly believed that Watson did the killing. It was a final irony that in a tavern in the small village of Deptford, after a bout of drinking, he himself was stabbed to death (through the eye) by a serving-man, a rival in a quarrel over a whore. He was buried in an unknown spot beneath the grey towers of St. Nicholas, where in the parish book was laconically written: "Christopher Marlow, slain by ffrancis Archer, the 1 of June 1593."

Apparently Elizabethan artists lived close to the kind of violence they felt obliged to express from intense rivalry. Playwright John Day (1574–1638?), considered a rogue in his day, also killed a man, fatally stabbing fellow dramatist Henry Porter with a rapier in Southwark in 1599. Born at Cawston, Norfolk and educated at Ely, he became a sizar of Caius College in 1592, but was expelled in the next year for stealing a book. He became one of Philip Henslowe's playwrights, collaborating with Henry Chettle, William Haughton, Thomas Dekker, Richard Hathwaye, and Wentworth Smith. Little is known of his life beyond these small details, and disparaging references by Ben Jonson in 1618/19, describing him (with Dekker and Edward Sharpham) as a "rogue" and (with Thomas Middleton and Gervase Markham) as a "base fellow." It may be indicative of his abilities that of all the writers he did a substantial amount of work for Henslowe's companies. Jurors found Day guilty of manslaughter only, and he was eventually released, to resume writing for the Admiral's Men.

Sir Kenelm Digby, the English courtier, diplomat, and highly reputed natural philosopher, known as one of leading Roman Catholic intellectuals in his lifetime, killed a French nobleman in a duel, then when he returned to England by way of Flanders in 1642, he was jailed by the House of Commons. He was eventually released by the intervention of Anne of Austria, again went back to France, and remained there during the remainder of the period of the English Civil War. Parliament declared his property in England forfeit. A large and powerfully built fellow, Digby was, like many if not most gentlemen of his time, a skilled fencer.

What happened was, he attended a banquet in 1641 at which a French nobleman named Mont le Ros openly insulted England's King Charles. Digby challenged him to a duel. He himself wrote that, in the "fourth bout, he ran his rapier into the French Lord's breast till it came out of his throat again," when needless to say he fell dead. Digby was involved in several other affairs of honor that were resolved without bloodshed. According to expert on martial arts Paul Kirchner, author of *The Deadliest Men: The World's Deadliest Combatants throughout the Ages* (Paladin, 2001) in his splendid and well-researched essay about a famous urban attack, "The Extraordinary Street Fight of Sir Kenelm Digby" which can be found in *Arma: The Association of Renaissance Martial Arts*:

> "Digby's most impressive work with the sword was performed not in a duel, but in a street fight in Madrid in the summer of 1623. On the evening of the day he arrived in that city, he dined at the home of his uncle, the Earl

of Bristol, then England's ambassador to Spain. By the time Digby was ready to return to his lodgings the hour was late and the streets were deserted. However, it was a clear night with a full moon, so Digby turned down the offer of an escort of torch-bearing servants in favor of walking with Lord Bristol's son and another friend. As they strolled the streets, enjoying the cool serenity, they heard a woman singing on a balcony. Lord Bristol's son knew her, and as the three of them approached to listen, they were attacked by a party of fifteen armed men. An account of the combat is included in Digby's memoirs."

Quoting from Digby's memoirs, Kirchner provides the long passage in those memoirs of a blow-by-blow description of that fight in Spain, transcribed from the 1827 edition of the memoirs, not excluding idiosyncratic 17th-century spelling, concluding,

"According to reports, Digby awoke the following day to find himself the talk of Madrid, and news of it soon carried back to England. There were no repercussions, and Digby remained in Spain until September. In addition to this account, a note was found among Digby's personal papers which referred to the incident and mentioned that he had been wounded in the hand during the fight. The cut to Digby's hand was on his right which is interesting as the account suggests that neither Digby nor his companions had second-hand weapons. Digby lived until 1668."

Later Digby published a work of apologetics in 1638, *A Conference with a Lady about choice of a Religion*. In it he argued that the Catholic Church, alone in possession of the qualifications of universality, unity of doctrine, and uninterrupted apostolic succession, is the only true church, and that the intrusion of error into it is impossible. Digby was regarded as an eccentric by contemporaries—he wrote a cookbook, was fond of quack nostrums, and, among other things, was supposedly the inventor of the modern wine bottle (he owned a glassworks)—not only because of his rare, effusive personality, but because of his interests in scientific matters. Henry Stubbe called him "the very Pliny of our age for lying." He lived in a time when scientific enquiry had not settled down in any disciplined way. He spent much time and effort in the pursuits of alchemy and astrology, which he studied in the 1630s with van Dyck. Notable among his pursuits was the concept of the "Powder of Sympathy," a remedy—a kind of sympathetic magic—that was applied, not to the wound, but rather to the *weapon* that had caused a wound in the fond hope of healing the injury it had made; it was a salve he wrote a book on that went through 29 editions. Synchronizing the effects of this extraordinary powder, which apparently caused a noticeable effect on the patient when applied, was actually suggested in 1687 as a means of solving the longitude problem!

Another artist who killed someone was the German playwright Heinrich von Kleist. Driven by intense melancholia—discovering the philosophy of Kant in 1801 put him in a state of metaphysical despair by destroying his faith in the value of knowledge—he came to see truth illusory, wisdom deceit. He lost every article of his faith. His writing could be savage. Most of his stories are about dislocated causality. Inexplicable factors intrude. His five-act play *Die Hermannsschlacht* (1808), possibly his greatest achievement, is incredibly bloodthirsty. At one point he became engaged to Wilhelmine von Zenge, then suddenly set off that same year on a journey, finally surfacing in Würzburg where he underwent some kind of unspecified medical or surgical treatment which would make him, as he enigmatically wrote to his fiancée, "worthy" of her. This episode has never been clarified. But it didn't seem to matter. He eventually broke off his engagement, and a certain amount of mystery surrounds his sexual life in general. He led a hapless life. Goethe supposedly hated him. He was once arrested by the French as a spy and kept in solitary confinement for half a year. (He had actually joined the French army in the hope of being killed during Napoleon's planned invasion of England.)

Although Kleist felt miserably that none of us could shape his own destiny, it didn't seem to stop him from trying. It was on the shore of the Wannsee, near Potsdam on November 21, 1811, that Kleist shot a woman Henrietta Vogel at her request in order to cut short her suffering from an incurable disease (probably cancer), and then—at the age of 34—shot himself in the mouth. The two of them had been singing the day before. They had drunk a number of bottles of wine and rum and finally 16 cups of coffee. They had been sitting across from each other. There had been nothing sexual between them. For his literary work Kleist had received no recognition whatsoever during his lifetime. On the morning of his death, he took the time, deliberating, to write several letters, notably to his half-sister, Ulrike, and it was there he expressed his desolation succinctly, when he confessed: *"dass mir auf Erden nicht zu helfen war"* (there was no help for me on earth).

Strangely, in his writing Kleist specialized in happy endings. In "The Duel," a catastrophic story, there is a final and benevolent ending. And Antonio Piachi and Michael Kolhaas on the scaffold are shamelessly jubilant as they wait for trap to be sprung or the axe to fall. As a matter of fact, just before blowing his brains out he said goodbye to his friends and family in what were among the loveliest and most joyous letters he ever wrote.

Mark Twain once killed a man. He never got over it and has left us a full account of the tragedy in his tale "The Private History of a Campaign That Failed" (1892). The killing took place in the first months of the Civil War. It was 1861. There were Union troops in Missouri. He was part of a rag-tag group of soldiers called the "Marion Rangers," teenage boys really. One night from a hidden position in the woods Twain, along with several others—there were six altogether—spotted a man, alone, riding along a forest path. He was a complete stranger, unarmed and wearing no uniform. They confessed later they took him to be a Yankee. In a mixture of high spirits and adventure of the cruel and brainless sort Twain described in reporting the malicious pranks of Tom Sawyer at the end of that book, the boys decided to take action. Twain, briefly, heard the word "Fire!" and shot the man off his horse. They waited, then slowly crept out. The moonlight revealed what they had done. The man lay there on his back, moaning, his white shirtfront splashed with blood. They all stood there helpless. "The thought shot through me that I was a murderer," Twain wrote, "that I had killed a man." Just before he died, the man murmured the names of his wife and child. In despair Twain was overwhelmed with another reflection: "This thing that I have done does not end with him; it falls upon them, too, and they never did me any harm, any more than he."

It turned out that each of the green recruits had fired simultaneously, that Twain had taken the volley for one shot. As he himself had shot to kill, however, he felt no less guilty. "That was the coldest situation that ever went through my marrow," he wrote. The thought preyed on him night after night. He remained forever unpersuaded thereafter about fighting, that night threw down his arms, and never went soldiering again.

In the literary world, there have been some bizarre killings. The author of *The Kabbalah Unveiled*, Liddell Mathers—he decided to take the first name "McGregor" in honor of an ancestor who fought for James IV of Scotland—is said to have been killed in 1927 in a psychic duel (or "mind war") by the pornocrat, cultist, and black magician Alistair Crowley, who called himself "The Wickedest Man Alive," used to file his teeth, and, prior to biting their necks, often asked women, "Would you like to taste a serpent's kiss?" Born in 1875, he was a Satanist and a drug addict. A host of his books were banned—every last copy of one novel, *Snowdrops from a Curate's Garden*, was confiscated by the British government—though his poetry is quite good. He made a practice of homosexuality. He drove two of his wives insane and the third committed suicide. He had a long series of mistresses whom he named after various animals: the Dog, the Camel, the Ape and so on. Mathers once supposedly suborned his wife, then posing naked in Montmartre shows, and sent her to murder Crowley. But Crowley who claimed his magic was blacker, overcame her and threw her out.

In 1905, Crowley left for India on expedition on an expedition to ascend Kanchenjunga, the third highest mountain in the world—he was an expert mountain climber—but the entire affair turned into a disaster. One of three members and several coolies who simply could not bear his abuse turned back but perished in an avalanche; Crowley, when he learned of this, refused to help dig them out. They were "rebels," he claimed, and so deserved their fate. Immediately he went on to Calcutta, when wandering through a bazaar late one night he was attacked by a gang of robbers. Crowley repulsed them, but before they could all get away, he promptly pulled out a Webley .38 and shot two of them dead. A great furor ensued, and a reward of 100 rupees was offered for anyone who could identify him, but he managed to escape. He died at 72. Disciples still worship him as a supernatural being.

George Selwyn, an 18th-century writer famous for the collection of letters he left, written to him by virtually every prominent man of the age, was also an ardent Satanist and avid necrophilist. He loved to witness death and suffering and in fact harbored an odd passion: attending public executions. He had a standing arrangement with undertakers to inspect the corpses brought into them. He took a great deal of trouble to travel to Paris when Damien, a man who had attempted to assassinate Louis XV, was being tortured to death in the public square. There were rumors Selwyn was a eunuch.

On August 9, 1967 in London the pathetic and self-pitying British actor and writer, Kenneth Halliwell—a 41-year-old mentor and long-standing homosexual partner of playwright Joe Orton—so far as anyone can determine, as a result of feeling jealous, insecure, and outcast by the overnight success and sudden fame of his friend and lover, proceeded to bash in Orton's skull as he slept with nine hammer blows to the head. After the murder, Halliwell, who 20 or so years before had witnessed his own father's suicide, then killed himself in a much milder way, overdosing on pentobarbital sleeping pills. It was Halliwell who actually died first! His suicide note made reference to a particular passage in Orton's diary, which, madly infuriating the killer, explained his motive—jealousy—for the savage killing: "If you read his diary, all will be explained. KH PS: Especially the latter part." The reference was presumably to Orton's notes of numerous incidents and descriptions of his promiscuous "cottaging" in public lavatories and other casual sexual encounters.

German political novelist Hans Fallada—in a duel—killed a man. Perhaps best known for his criticisms of Nazism, he wrote many novels of social criticism. His first major success came with his

1932 book, *Little Man, What Now?* which became bestseller in the United States and Great Britain. In 1937, he published another successful novel, *Wolf Among Wolves*, that marked his temporary return to the realist style; and in 1947 he launched yet another bestseller, *Every Man Dies Alone*. It turned out Fallada had led a very troubled life, one marred by depression and addiction. Perhaps most haunting was his accidental murder of friend and lover Hanns Dietrich von Necker. After his parents learned—with outrage—that their teenage son had an intimate relationship with a man, he was sent to an institution for psychiatric evaluation, which led only led to further chaos.

It was then that young Fallada and his best friend, fed up with the homophobic views of society, agreed to make a pact to commit a double suicide, which they chose to mask in the form of a duel in order to make it look more honorable. Things did not go according to plan, however. Both were inexperienced with weapons, to begin with. But the tragic detail is that Dietrich missed his partner, but Fallada's gunshot was right on the mark, killing his friend instantly. Distraught, Fallada then turned the gun on himself, firing into his chest. He survived, however, was arrested for murder, and, although ultimately found not guilty by reason of insanity, was taken to a psychiatric hospital. He spent the rest of his life undergoing multiple stints in and out of institutions. In 1944, he returned to behaving in a violent manner when in an argument with his ex-wife Hans shot off a gun, but his wife, who was not hurt, had him returned to an institution. At the time of Fallada's death in February 1947, aged 53, from a weakened heart from years of addiction to morphine, alcohol, and other drugs, he had completed *Every Man Dies Alone*, his anti-fascist novel based on the true story of a German couple, Otto and Elkise Hampel, who were executed for producing and distributing anti-Nazi material in Berlin during the war.

Dutch crime novelist Richard Klinkhamer was a murderer. He bashed his wife Hanny over the head with a blunt object, killed her, methodically buried her body underneath a shed, and then proceeded to seal up the makeshift grave with concrete. His writing career had soared with the publication of his novel *Obedient as a Dog*, which drew extensively from his experience as a French Legionnaire. Critic Will Woodward observed of the book in an article he wrote for the *Guardian*, "'The first thing they teach you,' [Klinkhamer] said, 'is how to kill somebody; the second, how to dispose of a body properly.'" The author obviously put this knowledge to use in 1991 with the slaying. The couple had a troubled relationship for a while and Klinkhamer, who was both a notorious wife-beater and reported Nazi sympathizer, initially explained to police that Hanny had simply left him and that he had no idea where she had gone. This plot may have worked out just fine, except for the fact that a year later, Klinkhamer came to his publisher with a manuscript entitled *Wednesday, Mince Day* that, again according to Woodward, "was a grisly, detailed exploration of seven ways in which Klinkhamer could conceivably have killed his wife." In one of the scenarios set out in the hellacious book, he actually disposes of his wife's body by pushing her cadaverous flesh through a mincer very like a meat grinder and then blithely feeding the ground meat to pigeons. Klinkahmer's publisher, who felt the novel was too gruesome, rejected it, but the manuscript nevertheless did draw the attention of the police. However, without a body, the authorities could make no arrest—that is, until new tenants of the author's former house decided to raze the old shed in the garden, when they found Hanny's skeleton. In 2000, nine years after the murder, Klinkhamer was arrested. He confessed to the crime shortly thereafter.

A famous killer, Louis Althusser, the French Marxist philosopher, strangled his wife. Born in Algeria, once a student at the École Normale Supérieure in Paris—he eventually became Professor of Philosophy there—the man described in a posthumously published memoir, *The Future Lasts a Long Time*, what was surely the most horrific event of his life—strangling his wife to death. He claimed that he had no memory of doing so, however, saying he blacked out while massaging her neck, only to find her lifeless in his hands moments later. For while he had developed a persecution complex and suicidal thoughts. He would recall later, "I wanted not only to destroy myself physically but to wipe out all trace of my time on earth: in particular, to destroy every last one of my books and all my notes, and burn the École Normale, and also, 'if possible,' suppress Hélène herself while I still could."

This strange murder took place on November 16, 1980, when Althusser strangled Hélène in their ENS room. It was he himself who reported the crime to the doctor in residence, who then contacted psychiatric institutions. The doctor and the director of ENS, before the police arrival, decided to hospitalize Althusser in the Sainte-Anne hospital where a psychiatric examination was conducted on him. Due to his mental state, Althusser was deemed as being unable to understand the charges against him or the process to which he was to be submitted, so he remained at the hospital. The psychiatric assessment concluded he should not be criminally charged, based on article 64 of the French Penal Code, which significantly stated that "there is neither crime nor delict where the suspect was in a state of dementia at the time of the action." The report said Althusser killed Hélène in the course of an acute crisis of melancholy, without even realizing it, and that the "wife-murder by manual strangulation was committed without any additional violence, in the course of [an] iatrogenic hallucinatory episode complicated by melancholic depression."

As a result, the philosopher lost all of his civil rights, entrusted to a representative of the law, and he was forbidden to sign any documents. In February 1981, the court ruled Althusser as having been mentally irresponsible when he committed the murder, therefore he could not be prosecuted and was not charged. A warrant of confinement was subsequently issued by the Paris police prefecture; the Ministry of National Education mandated his retirement from the ENS; and the ENS requested his family and friends to clear out his apartment. In June, he was transferred to the L'Eau-Vive clinic at Soisy-sur-Seine. Authorities took Althusser's depression into account, and he was thus absolved of being tried in court. Althusser instead was committed to a psychiatric hospital. Gilbert Adair and others took issue with this outcome, believing that it was in fact Althusser's fame and influence, and not his mental state, that spared him any jail time.

The bizarre murder of Hélène attracted much media attention, needless to say, and there were several requests both public and private to treat Althusser as a common, ordinary criminal. The newspaper *Minute* journalist Dominique Jamet and Minister of Justice Alain Peyrefitte were among those who accused Althusser of having "privileges" because of the fact he was a Communist.

Althusser was very ugly, almost frog-like in his face. He had known only home, school, and POW camp by the time he met his future wife. In contrast, she was a daring and somewhat intrepid woman. When he first met Hélène in 1946, she was a former member of the French resistance and a Communist activist. After fighting along with Jean Beaufret in the group "Service Périclès", she joined the PCF. However, she was expelled from the party, accused of being a double agent for Gestapo. Althusser confessed in *L'Avenir dure longtemps*, "I had never embraced a woman, and above all I had never been embraced by a woman (at age thirty!). Desire mounted in me, we made love on the bed, it was new, exciting, exalting, and violent. When she [Hélène] had left, an abysm of anguish opened up in me, never again to close."

"Hélène represented the opposite of himself," according to Élisabeth Roudinesco, a French psychoanalyst and historian; "she had been in the Resistance while he was remote from the anti-Nazi combat; she was a Jew who carried the stamp of the Holocaust, whereas despite his conversion to Marxism, he never escaped the formative effect of Roman Catholicism; she suffered from the Stalinism at the very moment when he was joining the party; and, in opposition to his petit-bourgeois background, her childhood was not prosperous—at the age of 13 she became a sexual abuse victim by a family doctor who, in addition, instructed her to give her terminally ill parents a dose of morphine." According to Roudinesco, Hélène embodied for the grotesque and murderously scheming Althusser his "displaced conscience," "pitiless superego," "damned part," "black animality."

Despite many critics, some of his friends, such as Jean Guitton and Regis Debray, defended Althusser, saying the murder was an act of love—as Althusser had argued, as well. Hélène had bouts of melancholy and self-medicated because of this, Guitton said, "I sincerely think that he killed his wife out of love of her. It was a crime of mystical love." Debray actually compared the strangulation to an "altruistic suicide." "He suffocated her under a pillow to save her from the anguish that was suffocating him. A beautiful proof of love . . . that one can save one's skin while sacrificing oneself for the other, only to take upon oneself all the pain of living." Althusser stated that "she matter-of-factly asked me to kill her myself, and this word, unthinkable and intolerable in its horror, caused my whole body to tremble for a long time. It still makes me tremble. . . . We were living shut up in the cloister of our hell, both of us."

The crime seriously tarnished Althusser's reputation on just about every front. As Roudinesco has pointed out, from 1980, he lived his life as a "specter, a dead man walking." A schizophrenic, Althusser forcibly lived in various public and private clinics until 1983, when he became a voluntary patient. He was able to start an untitled manuscript during this time, in 1982; it was later published as "The Underground Current of the Materialism of the Encounter" (*Le courant souterrain du matérialisme de la rencontre*). From 1984 to 1986, he stayed at an apartment in the north of Paris, where he remained confined most of his time, but he also received visits from some friends. In 1987, after Althusser underwent an emergency operation because of the obstruction of the esophagus, he developed a new clinical picture of depression. First brought to the Soisy-sur-Seine clinic, he was transferred to the psychiatric institution MGEN in La Verrière. There, following a pneumonia contracted during the summer, Althusser died of a heart attack on October 22. 1990.

María Carolina-Geel—her real name was Elena Georgina Jimenez Silva—was a respected feminist author and literary critic in Chile. On April 14, 1956, for reasons that are still difficult to ascertain, Geel, age 46 at the time, shot and killed her lover, Roberto Pumarino Valenzuela, who was just 32, while the pair were sitting in the famous and highly luxurious Hotel Crillon in Santiago. She pumped four shots right into his chest, fatally wounding him. Eyewitnesses noted in the newspapers of the time that after committing the murder, the writer threw herself on her victim and then kissed him and hugged him, exclaiming: "He was what I loved most on earth." She was sentenced to three years in prison, a rather short sentence for such a crime. While in prison, she managed to write one of her greatest novels, *Cárcel de mujeres (Women's Prison)*, which surprised the critics because it ranged between testimonial literature and fiction. Thanks to her friend and Nobel Prize winner Gabriela Mistral, she was granted clemency. and she was eventually pardoned by Chilean president Carlos Ibáñez del Campo, and continued to write after her release.

In 1996, Geel died of terrible complications related to dementia and Alzheimer's disease. The Chilean novelist, a woman who was controversial not only in her life but also for the daring and irreverent literature that she compulsively wrote. She wrote her first book in 1946, which was titled *El mundo dormido de Yenia (The Sleeping World of Yenia)*. It was followed by *Extraño estío (Strange Summer)* (1947), which tells the story of a divorced woman, and then *Soñaba y amaba el adolescente Perces (The Teen Perces Dreamed and Loved)* (1949), *El pequeño arquitecto (Little Architect)* (1956), and *Huida (Escape)* (1961). In 1949 she wrote *Siete escritoras chilenas (Seven Chilean Writers)*, a book of literary criticism, an undeveloped field by the Chilean writers of her time.

Science fiction writer Alice Bradley Sheldon, who wrote under the pen name James Tiptree Jr. because she believed she had a better chance at publishing and selling her science fiction work with a male name—she successfully fooled her fans for nearly a decade before anyone figured it out—murdered her husband in cold blood and then shot herself while lying in bed next to him, holding the hand of his corpse. The suicide note she left behind had been composed *years earlier*. Always struggling with her identity—from 1974 to 1977 she also used the pen name Raccoona Sheldon—"Tiptree" was fairly reclusive; she never made any public appearances, for example; but she did correspond regularly with fans and other science fiction authors through the mail. When asked for biographical details, Tiptree/Sheldon was forthcoming in everything but her sex. According to her biographer, Julie Phillips, "No one had ever seen or spoken to the owner of this voice. He wrote letters, warm, frank, funny letters, to other writers, editors, and science fiction fans." In her letters to fellow writers such as Ursula K. Le Guin and Joanna Russ, she would present herself as a feminist man; however, Sheldon did not present herself as male in person.

Writing for her was a way to escape a male-dominated society, themes that Tiptree explored in the short stories later collected in *Her Smoke Rose Up Forever*. One story in particular offers an excellent illustration of these themes. "Houston, Houston, Do You Read?" follows a group of astronauts who discover a future Earth whose male population has been wiped out; the remaining females have learned to get along just fine in their absence. Never a happy person, her depression deepened in her later years. As her husband's health failed, she became his primary caretaker. As early as 1976, when Sheldon was 60 years old, she spoke of wishing to end her life. In 1987, she finally did so, but not after first murdering her husband and taking him along with her to the Great Beyond.

And down in Mexico City in March 1952 the novelist—and "junkie"—William S. Burroughs, author of *Naked Lunch*, shot his wife, Joan Vollmer, through the head. They had been playing a game of "William Tell" with a gun (a Star .380 automatic) in a friend's apartment, and a glass instead of an apple was placed on Joan's head. Both were sitting across from each other, about 10 feet away. Burroughs took one shot, missed the target, and accidentally killed her. They and their friends had been drinking heavily—the floor was strewn around with empty Oso Negro gin bottles—but they always had. Burroughs, who had just returned from traveling, had begun feeling deeply constrained by marriage and hadn't tried to hide it. Joan, who habitually drank from morning to night, had stayed with him even though he was a homosexual and a drug addict. He languished for several weeks in a Mexican prison, according to several accounts, but could afford influential lawyers and was soon out on bail. (He was a scion of the well-known Burroughs Adding Machine family.) Their son was taken to St. Louis to live with his grandparents. He later wrote novels himself and was working on his third when he died in 1981 from liver complications due to heavy drinking. "Anyone who holds a frying pan owns death," Burroughs once wrote in what remains one of his more memorable epigrams.

And at the age of 18, Herman Melville's son Malcolm, after a severe parental reprimand for keeping late hours shot himself in the head. Robert Frost's son Carol also took his own life, and the poet might have been speaking for all artists when he wrote the telling line, "I have been one acquainted with the night."

Another strange murder involving a writer took place in Cape Elizabeth, Maine, in June 1974, when the poet and former English professor James E. Lewisohn—he claims accidentally— shot and killed his wife. The couple had been married for 19 years and had four children. He was found guilty a second time on October 10, 1981, after he had been in prison more than six years. In three days of testimony in 1981, the jury heard Mr. Lewisohn's two daughters recount the events of June 3, 1974. The daughters, Dina, 17, of Hamden, Connecticut, and Debora, 21 and a senior at Brandeis University, said that their father came home about midnight that same day. He was shouting for somebody to help him clean up the kitchen, they said. Their mother got out of bed and went to the kitchen. "She was pretty angry," Debora testified. "After that I heard a shattering of glass and my mother screamed, 'Jimmy, I'm bleeding, call the hospital.'" After the shooting, Dina Lewisohn testified, she found her mother lying on the floor. She said that she saw her father pick up a gun and shoot himself in the throat. He was hospitalized briefly with the wound. Mr. Lewisohn admitted the shooting but said it was accidental. When asked by his attorney, Peter J. Rubin, if he intended to shoot his wife, he replied: "I'm a terrible fool. I've done some very foolish things. I would never have hurt Roslyn or any one knowingly, never." Despairing, he apparently asked an officer to shoot him. Edward J. Tolan, a Cape Elizabeth police sergeant, testified that when he arrived at the Lewisohn home, Mrs. Lewisohn was unconscious. He checked Mr. Lewisohn's wound, and Mr. Lewisohn said to him, "Please take out your gun and finish the job."

Lewisohn's parents, the writer Ludwig Lewisohn and opera singer Thelma Spear, had divorced when he was six, and he admitted to being insecure growing up. It appears there had been some difficulty for him getting jobs. Eventually, Lewisohn did manage to become an associate professor at a state university, but he soon began acting erratically, abusing his colleagues, drinking too much, raving. He also began ominously toying with handguns. "I was under stress, immature, and I didn't face problems," he admitted. "Roz [his wife Rosalyn] accepted it." A long period of depression, coupled with muffled anger, followed. "I was really a miserable, self-indulgent little man." Finally, Lewisohn's anxieties erupted in tragedy. After bidding goodnight to some dinner guests, he went out to a bar, inexplicably, where he had "a drink or two." He remembers returning after midnight and calling for his wife to help clean up the kitchen. "I was back again at the table with my gun, and I was pushing and pulling the mechanism when the gun exploded," he explained. Far too many questions remained for it to be called anything but murder, the children were adopted out of state, and Lewisohn, who was judged guilty, was sent away to the Maine State Prison, where he wrote and taught poetry. His poems were published in magazines, including *The New Yorker*. In 1977, Mr. Lewisohn received a $7,500 grant from the National Endowment for the Arts. *Support your murderers!* The award caused controversy within the Maine State Commission on Arts and Humanities. One of his published books is titled *Roslyn*.

Novelist Michael Peterson was convicted in 2003 of murdering his wife Kathleen, whose body had been found at the bottom of the couple's staircase. Despite Peterson's insistence that Kathleen had fallen down the stairs, authorities suspected foul play. Police then drew connections to a family friend, Elizabeth Ratliff, who died in a strikingly similar fashion, but whose death at the time was ruled an accident (Ratliff's children became Peterson's wards). Peterson maintained his innocence in both cases and appealed his conviction. He was granted a new trial in 2011 after a key witness admitted to falsifying statements on the stand. (His lawyers declined to file a motion based on T. Lawrence Pollard's "Owl Theory," which asserted that Kathleen had been attacked by an owl just prior to falling down the stairs, which would "explain" the amount of blood found). In 2017, Peterson entered an Alford plea, which allowed him to maintain his innocence while also acknowledging prosecutors had enough evidence to convict him.

"Not long ago," Truman Capote once wrote, "my doctor suggested that I adopt some healthier hobby other than wine-tasting and fornication. He asked if I could think of anything. I said, 'Yes, murder.' He laughed, we both did, except I wasn't laughing." He went on to add, "Everybody at one time or another has wanted to kill someone . . . as for me, if desire had ever been transferred into action, I'd be right up there with Jack the Ripper. Anyway, it's amusing to think about: the plotting, the planning, the surprise and regret imprinting the face of the villain-turned-victim. Very relaxing. Better than counting sheep."

"I am desperate to kill a man," wrote Yukio Mishima, the Japanese novelist, in his autobiographical novel *Confessions of a Mask* (1948). It was a serious truth for him. "I want to see red blood. An author writes love stories because he isn't popular with women; I began writing novels so I wouldn't end up with a death sentence." All his life, Mishima—his real name was Kimitake Hiraoka—felt himself a hollow man. He experienced great trouble feeling alive and seriously began to wonder at times if he truly existed. He felt that language (art) was to blame, "eating reality away," as he put it, before he had a chance to experience it. In a bizarre way, the act of writing became for him a sort of warped self-investigation. "I will turn upon myself the scalpel of psychological analysis I have sharpened on fictive characters," he once wrote. "I will attempt to dissect myself alive."

A militant nationalist, a right-wing prophet, a poet, he was, especially to himself, more than just a popular novelist. He was an incorrigible narcissist and almost surely homosexual, although his wife who was interviewed after his death denied it. He had thin legs, lifted weights, rose at 1 p.m., hated orgasms with women, danced poorly, and was obsessive about being punctual. He also had fantasies of swords. Among his more serious compulsions were posing for photographs either in leather or half-naked and dressing up in uniforms of all kinds. He also loved motorcycles.

Along with everything else, he harbored a warped erotic longing for death. Death, first as an aesthetic ideal and then in a very real way, remained his life's aim. He spoke and wrote of it constantly. "Was it death he was now waiting for? Or a wild ecstasy of the senses?" wrote Mishima in "Patriotism," surely the bloodiest short story ever written. "The two seemed to overlap, almost as if the object of this bodily desire was death itself." And in his novel *The Sailor Who Fell from Grace with the Sea*, he wrote, "For Ryuji the kiss was death, the very death in love he always dreamed of. . . . Death roused inside him, stirred." Mishima almost always referred to the artist as "the murderer." He got erections from looking at Guido Reni's famous painting *St. Sebastian*, where the saint, half-naked and dying, is pierced with arrows. This particular painting, as is well known, has for a long time been held as a gay icon. Mishima had his first "ejaculation," his word, while looking at it. Indeed, he himself was several times photographed, his face twisted in agony, while posed as St. Sebastian. "I behave normally," he once confessed to someone, "but I'm sick inside."

Yukio Mishima grew disgusted with the student revolutions in Japan during the Sixties. He was angered that the students were so unwilling to die. He found them soft and selfish. He couldn't understand (and doubtless feared accepting in himself) the cowardice of the untested and the unproven. He loved ritual, and organization, and made a fetish of self-discipline. Toward the end of his life, he founded an ultra-nationalistic group, complete with uniforms, called the Shield Society—a small private army—and encouraged its members, among other things, to die bravely. It was a matter of honor with him. Seppuku, the ritual act of suicide in Japan, involves a person—the victim—knifing himself in the abdomen always specifically cutting left to right and then on signal being beheaded with a long sword by someone standing behind him, slightly to the left, who is then in turn beheaded (a particular act called *kaibaku*) after short-knifing himself in like manner.

After taking over a military complex by force and giving a rambling fanatical speech from a high balcony that almost no one could hear, Mishima shouted *"Tenno Heika banza!"* ("Long live His Imperial Majesty!") then withdrew, knelt down, and taking up a knife, proceeded to rip himself open. (A writing brush and special paper were in readiness: he had intended to write the character for "sword," but the pain he felt overcame him.) So he desperately nodded, and was immediately beheaded, an act dutifully carried out by his devoted, and no doubt homosexual lieutenant, Masakatsu Morita. It should be mentioned, finally, that upon hearing the news of Mishima's death, and deeply feeling the loss, the older and revered Japanese novelist, Yasunari Kawabata, a writer of high repute and winner of a Nobel Prize, brought shame upon his memory after committing suicide at his villa at Kamakura on April 16, 1972 by means of sticking his head into gas oven, which in Japan is considered an ignominious and dishonorable death. There was no farewell note.

Issei Sagawa, a writer born on April 26, 1949, also known as "Pang," is a Japanese writer who, while living in Paris in 1981, killed and cannibalized a Dutchwoman named Renée Hartevelt. After his release from two years of pre-trial detention upon being found legally insane, he became a minor celebrity in Japan and made a living through public interest. On June 11, 1981, Sagawa, then 32, had invited his Sorbonne classmate to dinner at his apartment under the pretext of translating poetry for a school assignment. The demented writer planned to kill and eat her, having selected her for her health and beauty—characteristics that he felt that he himself lacked. Sagawa considered himself weak, ugly, and small (he was 4 feet, 9 inches tall) and explained to the arresting authorities that he wanted to absorb her energy. She was 25 years old and 5 feet 10 inches tall. After she arrived, she began reading poetry at a desk with her back to him. He then shot her in the neck with a rifle. Sagawa said that he fainted after the shock of having shot her but awoke with the realization that he had to carry out his plan. He then proceeded to have sex with Renee's corpse but was unable to bite into her skin, so he left the apartment and purchased a butcher knife. Immediately after killing her, he raped her corpse and began cutting her open. "The first thing I did was cut into her buttock. No matter how deep I cut, all I saw was the fat beneath the skin. It looked like corn, and it took a while to actually reach the red meat. The moment I saw the meat, I tore a chunk off with my fingers and threw it into my mouth. It was truly a historical moment for me."

Ultimately, he madly declared that his only regret was that he hadn't eaten her while she was alive. "What I truly wished was to eat her living flesh," he said. "Nobody believes me, but my ultimate intention was to eat her, not necessarily to kill her." He said that human meat is tender and tastes like tuna.

This took place in actual life, although in its ghoulishness it recapitulates "A Very Original Dinner," a horror story by Fernando Pessoa from 1907 in which Herr Prosit, president of the Gastronomical Society of Berlin, invites all its members to come and enjoy a special meal, a dinner in its uniqueness that none had experienced before. Each guest in a happy frolic is challenged to guess the nature of the food—its originality. Is it the sauce? A new ingredient? The scent? It turns out they are dining on human flesh.

For two days, Sagawa ate various parts of her body, eating most of her breasts and face, saving other parts in his refrigerator. He also took photographs of her at each eating stage. He then attempted to dump the dead, ravaged body in a lake in the Bois de Boulogne, but was seen in the act and arrested by French police. When the police interrogated him, he confessed everything in a calm way. When he was caught, he was carrying two suitcases. Those suitcases contained the dismembered body parts of Renée Hartevelt. "It's simply a fetish," he calmly explained to the police. "For example," Sagawa declared, "if a normal man fancied a girl, he'd naturally feel a desire to see her as often as possible, to be close to her, to smell her and kiss her, right? To me, eating is just an extension of that. Frankly, I can't fathom why everyone doesn't feel this urge to eat, to consume, other people." Two days after killing the poor girl, Sagawa blithely disposed of what remained of her blasphemed body. He had eaten or frozen most of her pelvic region, so he put her legs, torso, and head into two suitcases and hailed a cab. The taxi dropped him off at the Bois de Boulogne, which had a secluded lake inside it. He had planned to drop the suitcases in it unnoticed, though several people noticed the suitcases dripping blood, and notified the French police.

Sagawa's wealthy father provided a lawyer for his defense, and after being held for two years awaiting trial Sagawa was found legally insane and unfit to stand trial by the French judge, Jean-Louis Bruguière, who ordered the mad man held indefinitely in a mental institution. After a visit by the author, Inuhiko Yomota, Sagawa's account of the macabre event was widely published in Japan under the title *In the Fog*. Sagawa's subsequent publicity and macabre celebrity likely contributed to the French authorities' decision to deport him to Japan, where he was immediately committed to Matsuzawa hospital. Examining psychologists there all declared him sane and found sexual perversion was his sole motivation for murder. Because charges in France had been dropped, the French court documents were sealed and were not released to Japanese authorities; consequently, Sagawa could not legally be detained in Japan. He checked himself out of the hospital on August 12, 1986, and remained free until the day of his death in November 2022.

He was an extremely short man and spindly, skinny with legs that "looked like pencils." He blames the media's representation of Western women like Grace Kelly for sparking his cannibalistic fantasies, equating it with what most people would call sexual desire. Where other people dreamed of bedding these beautiful women, Sagawa dreamed of devouring them. He maintained, however, that he never thought of killing them, only "gnaw[ing] on their flesh." "Almost every night I would bring a prostitute home and then try to shoot them from behind . . ." he said. "It became less about wanting to eat them, but more an obsession with the idea that I simply had to carry out this 'ritual.'"

Sagawa's continued freedom was widely criticized. He continued to live in Tokyo and was considered a minor celebrity in his hometown, so he is frequently invited to go on television shows. Besides the books he wrote about the grisly murder that he committed when he was a university student, he has written *Shonen A*, a book about Seito Sakkakibara, a 14-year-old murderer, and the 1997 Kobe child murders. He also wrote restaurant reviews for the Japanese magazine *Spa*. Sagawa could no longer find publishers for his writing, and he struggled to find employment. He was nearly accepted by a French-language school because the manager was impressed by his courage in using his real name, but employees protested, and he was rejected. In 2005, Sagawa's parents died. He was prevented from attending their funeral but repaid their creditors and moved into public housing. This monster actually received welfare benefits for a time. In an interview with *Vice* magazine in 2011, he said that being forced to make a living while being known as a murderer and cannibal was a terrible punishment. In 2013 he was hospitalized from a cerebral infarction, which permanently damaged his nervous system. After being released he was under the full-time care of his brother.

Several other prominent Japanese writers have also come to grisly ends. The poet Zenmei Hasadu, after the Japanese surrender in 1945 shot his commanding officer and then killed himself. Kitamura Tokoku, a 27-year-old poet who was the son of a samurai and an admirer of Byron and Emerson, hanged himself from a tree in his garden on May 16, 1894. Akutagawa Ryunosuke, the author of *Rashomon*, on July 24, 1927, at the age of 35 drank a fatal dose of Veronal. The revolutionary Arishima Takeo and his mistress, the married woman journalist Hatano Akikoi, hanged themselves in his villa in July 1923, a month after he had written a letter expressing his admiration for Chikamatsu's *Double Suicide at Sonozeki*. The writer, Osamu Dazai, a 38-year-old drug addict and alcoholic of anarchist bent—he once threatened to stab Kawabata who had called his writings the soliloquies of a deviant—whose last novel was called, significantly, No Longer Human, tied himself to his mistress with a kimono sash and jumped into the Tamagawa Canal on June 13, 1948. It should be mentioned, finally, that upon hearing the news of Mishima's death, and deeply feeling the loss, the older and revered Japanese novelist, Yasunari Kawabata, a writer of high repute and winner of a Nobel Prize, brought shame upon his memory after committing suicide at his villa at Kamakura on April 16, 1972, by means of sticking his head into gas oven, which in Japan is considered an ignominious and dishonorable death. There was no farewell note.

Violence and tragedy also characterized the life of Eghishe Charents (Ye-ge-shea, or Elijah), an Armenian poet (1897–1937) who in 1915 joined a volunteer battalion in Russia and marched across the border to Van in northeastern Turkey to help liberate his fellow countrymen who were being slaughtered by the thousands. The Turkish government succeeded in terminating virtually all Armenian life in Anatolia by 1918, and Charents's poetry reflected much of the phantasmagoria and horror of that genocide, as in "Dead City":

> "Their dead bodies with blue legs yellow breasts,
> swollen and blood- spattered buttocks,
> danced, staggering before
> my terror-filled eyes
> in the grave-pit dark."

Although he joined the Communist party in 1918, his poetry became too "inward and romantic," as one Soviet critic charged. He traveled, founded the November Union of Armenian Proletarian Writers, and continued writing. And then a tragedy took place. On a clear afternoon one September on the main avenue of Erevan, the capital of Armenia, an aggrieved Charents inexplicably pulled a gun out of his pocket and shot a woman. It was not fatal. The full context of this event is still shrouded in mystery, but the immediate cause seems to have been that the woman spurned Charents's flirtatious advances. He was immediately arrested and sentenced to eight years in solitary confinement. A journalist who covered the trial described him as depressed and disconsolate from the insomnia and alcohol that he had been battling for several years. He also became a morphine addict when, after being briefly let out of prison, he was operated on for kidney stones in Moscow.

Again, Charents was arrested though, like many of Stalin's victims, he was never told why. (His wife Isabella had also been arrested and incarcerated in the same prison, unbeknownst to him.) He spent his last months in a tiny cell, addressing God and writing poems on handkerchiefs. When he died after sustaining head injuries against his cell wall—was it an attempt at suicide?—a poet in a neighboring cell wrote, "it seemed impossible that I should stay sane after hearing his heart-piercing voice, his shout."

The creative mind, intense, it appears can easily become unhinged in times of stress when the delicate sensibility of the person is challenged. In 1924, when Julius Robert Oppenheimer, often called the "father of the atomic bomb" for his role in the Manhattan Project, the World War II program that developed the first nuclear weapons, was informed that he had been accepted into Christ's College, Cambridge, he wrote to Ernest Rutherford to request permission to work at the Cavendish Laboratory. He was recommended by his Harvard professor, Percy Bridgman who conceded that Oppenheimer's clumsiness in the laboratory made it apparent his forte was not experimental but rather theoretical physics. Rutherford was unimpressed, but still Oppenheimer went to Cambridge in the ambitious hope of landing another offer. He was ultimately accepted by J. J. Thomson on condition that he complete a basic laboratory course.

There he developed an antagonistic relationship with his tutor, Patrick Blackett, who was only a few years his senior. While on vacation, as recalled by his friend Francis Ferguson, Oppenheimer, confiding in his mate, confessed that he had once left an apple doused with noxious chemicals on Professor Blackett's desk. Ferguson's account is the only detailed version of this event, but we know that Oppenheimer's parents were alerted by the university authorities who considered placing him on probation, a fate prevented by his parents successfully lobbying the authorities. After protracted negotiations, it was agreed that Robert would be put on probation and have regular sessions with a prominent Harley Street psychiatrist in London.

This Freudian analyst diagnosed in his patient *dementia praecox*, a now archaic label for symptoms associated with schizophrenia. He concluded that Oppenheimer was a hopeless case and that "further analysis would do more harm than good." A tall, thin, solipsistic chain-smoker—he was diagnosed with throat cancer in 1965 and died at his home in Princeton, New Jersey, on February 18, 1967, aged 62—who often neglected to eat during periods of intense thought and concentration, Oppenheimer was a depressive. Despite his evident success as a scholar, he was plagued with doubts. In a letter to a friend, he once concluded A list of his feverish academic pursuits with the abrupt phrase "and wish I were dead." As an adult he recalled that, during his adolescent and college years, nearly everything about him aroused "a very great sense of revulsion and wrong." Many of his friends noticed that he had not only melancholic but self-destructive tendencies.

Another bizarre and indeed violent event occurred when he took a vacation from his studies in Cambridge to meet up with his friend Francis Fergusson in Paris. In a hotel room, Fergusson noticed that his friend was in "one of his ambiguous moods" and in a small attempt to divert him from his depression, showed him some poetry written by his, Fergusson's, girlfriend, Frances Keeley, and announced that he had proposed to Keeley and she had accepted. Robert, inexplicably, was stunned with this news and for some reason snapped and tried to strangle him. "I leaned over to pick up a book," Fergusson recalled, "and he jumped on me from behind with a trunk strap and wound it around my neck. I was quite scared for a little while. We must have made some noise. And then I managed to pull him aside and he fell on the ground weeping."

Although Fergusson easily fended off the attack, the episode convinced him even further of Oppenheimer's deep psychological troubles. Plagued throughout his life by periods of depression, Oppenheimer once told his brother, "I need physics more than friends." Plagued by ethical doubts about the atomic bombs dropped on Hiroshima and Nagasaki, he told President Harry S. Truman, "I feel we have blood on our hands." Truman asked Secretary Patterson to see him out and, filled with rancor, said, "I don't want to see that son of a bitch in this office ever again."

Johann "Jack" Unterweger (August 16, 1950–June 29, 1994), an Austrian writer and serial killer, is believed to have killed more than 12 prostitutes in Europe and Los Angeles. His first murder took place in 1974. The victim was an 18-year-old girl named Margaret Schäfer, whom he strangled with her own bra. Unterweger was sentenced to life in prison, and it was there that he wrote stories, poems, and his autobiography *Fegefeuer oder die Reise ins Zuchthaus (Purgatory or the Trip to Prison—Report of a Guilty Man)*, a book that later would be adapted into a film. Unterweger was born in 1950 to Theresia Unterweger, a Viennese barmaid/waitress, and an unknown American soldier whom she met in Trieste, Italy. Some sources describe his mother as a prostitute. His mother was jailed for fraud while pregnant but was released and travelled to Graz, where he was born. After his wayward mother was arrested again in 1953, Unterweger was sent away to Carinthia to live with his grandfather, a man well known as a "rough fellow," who regularly used his grandson to help him steal farm animals. Unterweger was in and out of prison for much of his youth. He worked as a waiter, but between 1966 and 1974 he was convicted 16 times, mostly for theft and burglary, but also for pimping and sexual assault on a prostitute;

he spent most of those nine years in jail.

After spending 15 years in prison. Unterweger was released in 1990 by request of several intellectuals and Austrian politicians, all of whom briskly claimed that he had undergone a complete rehabilitation. Writers, artists, journalists, and politicians—mostly Socialists—agitated for a pardon, banging the drum for his release, including, among others, the notable author and 2004 Nobel Prize-winner Elfriede Jelinek, Günter Grass, Peter Huemer, and the editor of the magazine *Manuskripte*, Alfred Kolleritsch. Unterweger was released on May 23, 1990, after the required minimum 15 years of his life term. In 1991, Unterweger was hired by an Austrian magazine to write about crime in Los Angeles, and the differences between U.S. and European attitudes to prostitution. Unterweger met with local police, even going so far as to participate in a welcoming ride-alongs around the city's red-light districts. As fate would have it, during Unterweger's time in Los Angeles, three sex workers—Shannon Exley, Irene Rodriguez, and Peggy Booth—were beaten, sexually assaulted with tree branches, and strangled with their own brassieres. The following year the hidebound Unterweger went on to murder about six more prostitutes, He was arrested in Miami, Florida, in February of 1992 and taken to Austria. After the trial he was sentenced to life imprisonment without parole on account of 11 deaths. That night he was found hanging in his cell. He had used his shoelaces and his belt, similar to what he did to execute his victims.

The list of writers and poets who took their own lives probably underscores, more than anything, the complexity that lies deep within the artist whose congested spirit so often seems at odds with all the possibilities otherwise given him to celebrate. Such a life is precarious simply because the act of communication is as difficult as it is urgent, where thought itself can become an impasse, "leaving one still," as Eliot wrote in *Four Quartets*, "with the intolerable wrestle with words and meanings."

Ernest Hemingway blew his head off with a shotgun. John Berryman jumped off a bridge. The French writer Gérard de Nerval at age 42 hanged himself with an apron string. Virginia Woolf walked into the river Ouse. Sylvia Plath stuck her head in an oven. At age 32, on April 27, 1932, Hart Crane leaped off a boat in the Gulf of Mexico. Jack London became severely ill, but rejected the advice of his doctors. The effects of alcohol coupled with a poor diet resulted in chronic pain. In 1916, at the age of 40, he took a lethal dose of stropine with morphine sulfate. The poet Vachel Lindsay made a gruesome exit by drinking a bottle of Lysol. Mandelstam committed suicide with a poem (so did Petronius, although we have lost that list of Neronian atrocities), and Sergei Esenin wrote some final verses in his own blood before proceeding to hang himself. Vladimir Mayakovsky shot himself. Paul Celan drowned himself in the Seine in April 1970. Henry Montherlant, losing his eyesight and fearing impotence, swallowed a cyanide capsule on September 21, 1972, and, to make certain of death, also shot himself with a revolver. Romain Gary, whose suicide farewell was *"Au revoir et merci!"* shot himself in the mouth with a Smith & Wesson at age 66. Ernst Toiler, German dramatist, poet, and left-wing political activist who had emigrated to the United States in early 1933 immediately before Hitler's accession to power, not only separated from his young wife but impoverished and convinced that his expressionist plays like *Masse-Mensch* were passé, hanged himself in the bathroom of his New York City hotel on May 22, 1939. The anti-Nazi German exiles Stefan Zweig and Ernst Weiss both killed themselves from fear of living in a Nazi-dominated Europe, Zweig in

Petropolis, Brazil, with his second wife on February 22, 1942.

The Dadaist Jacques Rigaut, who had once suggested the creation of an Agence Generale du Suicide for helping would-be suicides do it successfully, shot himself at age 30. His fellow Dadaist, the pugilist-poet Arthur Cravan, supposedly drowned himself in the Gulf of Mexico but also is said to have been murdered by the Mexican police. Austrian poet Georg Trakl, a psychiatric patient in a military hospital in Krakow—desperately lonely, a casualty of the war—killed himself with an overdose of cocaine on November 3, 1914. Francis Giauque, who killed himself in a mental institution, in his last days was seen standing around train stations watching the trains leave and muttering to himself with each departure, "One day it will be yourself, with your feet ahead."

Constance Fenimore Woolson, a neurotic novelist and close friend of Henry James, flung herself out of a window in Venice in January of 1894. Anne Sexton gassed herself in a car. Suffering abrupt changes in mood, the photographer Diane Arbus on July 26, 1971, while living at Westbeth Artists Community in New York City, took her own life by ingesting barbiturates and slashing her wrists with a razor. Her body was found in a bathtub. She was 48 years old. Primo Levi, at the age of sixty-seven, hurled himself down a stairwell in Turin in 1987. Jerzy Kosinzki pulled a plastic bag over his head to suffocate himself. The intense but melancholy poet Marina Tsvetaeva, friendless, isolated in the remote town of Yelabuga in the Ural Mountains with her daughter in a prison camp and her estranged husband about to be executed, hanged herself in a bathhouse on August 31, 1941. Simone Weil on August 24, 1943, starved herself to death. So did Nikolai Gogol, shrieking crazily, burning his manuscripts, at the age of 43. The beautiful German poet Ingeborg Bachmann, who lived out her childhood under Nazi rule, died in Rome in 1973 after setting herself on fire. She has since become a cult figure throughout the world, and there is a museum devoted to her in Austria. Speaking of strong women and suicide, the historical Dido, Queen of Carthage, killed herself—not as in Virgil's account on his epic the *Aeneid*—but in order to escape marrying the vile Berber king, Larbas, not out of grief for the flighty Aeneas. Virgil gave us melodrama, but not truth. Missing her dead, murdered husband Acerbas, Dido ascended a funeral pyre, announced that she would go to her husband as she had long desired, and then slew herself with her sword.

And William Cowper, Goethe, Mary Wollstonecraft Godwin, Joseph Conrad, Edgar Allan Poe, Else Metchnikoff, Ludwig Wittgenstein, Isadora Duncan, Evelyn Waugh, Busby Berkeley, Tennessee Williams, Truman Capote, Werner Fassbinder, and Buckminster Fuller all made major attempts at suicide. The temptation to do so bothered Dr. Johnson all his life. F. Scott Fitzgerald actually tried it several times. As a young man, in 1878, after having lost 800 francs in a Monte Carlo gaming room, Joseph Conrad tried to commit suicide. Eugene O'Neill's one-act play *Exorcism* was a rationalization of his attempt to commit suicide in 1919. The bullet left in his body from Maxim Gorky's near suicide troubled him all his life. In 1923, Dorothy Parker (neé Rothschild) slashed her wrists but recovered. In 1959 Michel Leiris, after a desperate love affair had gone awry, attempted to kill himself by means of swallowing a vial of phenobarbital. Novelist William Styron claimed that for many years he had often come very close to doing away with himself, writing of "the grey drizzle of horror induced by depression takes on the quality of physical pain. . . . I watched myself in mingled terror and fascination as I began to make the necessary preparation."

Cesare Pavese, the Italian novelist and poet, suffering from impotence, committed suicide on August 27, 1950, in a Torino hotel. He asked for a room with a telephone, made three or four calls during the night, the last to his sister, and then took an overdose of sleeping pills. His suicide note was only one mordant line, "Not too much gossip, please." Some believe his death was precipitated by the unrequited love for a young American actress named Constance Dowling, whom he had met with her sister in Rome. Returning to America, she had failed to keep her promise to write to him and come back to Italy. (He was even willing to marry her sister Doris.) Upon hearing of his death, the actress commented, "I didn't know he was such a famous writer." His last diary entry—revealingly, poignantly—read, "The thing most feared in secret always happens."

Charles Churchill, clergyman poet and co-founder of *The North Briton*, drank himself to death. Despite his office, he led a secret dissolute life and was actually a member of the infamous Hell-Fire Club, an association in 18th-century London dedicated to orgies and magic, which included, among others, Ben Franklin, the Prime Minister, the Lord Mayor, and several of England's greatest artists and poets. Once while conducting a funeral service, he was jeered at by a man in the congregation who had seen him drunk with some girls the night before. Churchill peeled off his clergyman's coat, jumped out of the pulpit, and beat the man to a pulp. His poems had been so popular that when news of his death in 1764 was announced the British fleet lowered their flags to half-mast.

Somehow each incident seems stranger than the next. At 17, Thomas Chatterton, broken by poverty and neglect—ironically, having tried to pass off his own work as another's!—killed himself by swallowing arsenic. The Russian writer, Mikhail Lermontov, died almost as young, at 27, a death that was virtually a suicide.

Known to have had a sharp tongue, Lermontov fought several duels, the first an inconclusive one in 1840 with Ernest de Barante, the son of the French ambassador. A year later he began to mock a certain Nicholas Martynov and ridicule his native dress and make him look silly in front of some girls he was trying to impress. Martynov challenged him to a duel with pistols. Lermontov obliged him. Inexplicably, during the duel, Lermontov made no attempt to fire—nor did he with Barante—and was shot dead.

One often hears about "negative susceptibility," the self-destructive capacity shared by a number of artists, an almost immolating excessiveness. Hard work surely killed Kierkegaard, who had an almost suicidal energy. Charles Dickens, expressly disobeying the alarmed advice of his doctors, continued traveling widely on reading tours that he knew would kill him and then he dropped dead. The English poet Christopher Smart, whose overzealous addiction to prayer without ceasing left no doubt in the minds of several doctors that he was mad indeed, finished writing his finest poem, the "Song to David," partly with charcoal on the walls and partly with a key on the panels of his cell in Bedlam in 1763. Hungarian poet Nicolaus Lenau was possessed by a blazing romantic spirit fueled in part by a hopeless love for the wife of a friend. In a fit of idealism in 1832, he came to America and settled on a homestead in Ohio for a few months. Disappointed with the New World, he returned to Europe, where, undertaking a poetic drama based on Don Juan, he left the work unfinished under desperate circumstances. In 1844 he lost his mind. And composer Gustav Mahler's last years, spent in an almost suicidal effort to win by storm the economic independence he coveted, are a tragic record of personal futility as well as critical intolerance.

The playwright William Inge, author of *Picnic*, *Bus Stop*, and

Come Back, Little Sheba, sat in his Mercedes automobile in a locked garage, turned on the engine, and gassed himself. He was homosexual, had a strange and complicated childhood, and had been a heavy drinker. He was 60 years old. The manuscript of his final novel, *The Boy from the Circus,* was found on a table in his living room after his suicide. It had been rejected by a New York publisher and returned to him. He had not opened the envelope containing it.

At the age of 51, the poet Randall Jarrell, an expert tennis player, was in excellent physical condition. He neither smoked nor drank. All agree that he had an almost maddening sanity. Many have therefore judged his violent death accidental, although at the time he was separated from his second wife, Mary, he was being treated for depression, and at some point earlier had even cut his wrists in a bungled suicide attempt. In any case, one night in 1965, wearing a dark coat and dark gloves, he stepped onto a highway and, according to the driver who struck and killed him, "lunged into the path of the car." Arthur Nortje, a black poet and one of South Africa's finest young writers, committed suicide at Oxford in 1970—he was 29—not only because he was homesick and "desperately lonely," but because, some say, he dared not return to his native land to oppose apartheid.

On February 20, 2005, gonzo writer Hunter Thompson shot himself in the head, dying immediately from a self-inflicted gunshot wound at Owl Farm in Aspen Colorado, his "fortified compound" at Woody Creek. His son Juan, daughter-in-law Jennifer, and grandson were visiting for the weekend. His wife Anita, who was at the Aspen Club, was on the phone with him as he cocked the gun. According to the *Aspen Daily News,* Thompson asked her to come home to help him write his ESPN column, then set the receiver on the counter. Anita said she mistook the cocking of the gun for the sound of his typewriter keys and hung up as he fired. Will and Jennifer were in the next room when they heard the gunshot, but they mistook the sound for a book falling and did not check on Thompson immediately. Juan Thompson found his father's body. According to the police report and Anita's cell phone records,[he called the sheriff's office half an hour later, then walked outside and fired three shotgun blasts into the air to "mark the passing of his father." The police report stated that in Thompson's typewriter was a piece of paper with the date "Feb. 22 '05" and a single word, "counselor."

Thompson's inner circle told the press that he had been depressed and always found February a "gloomy" month, with football season over and the harsh Colorado winter weather. He was also upset over his advancing age and chronic medical problems, including a hip replacement; he would frequently mutter, "This kid is getting old." *Rolling Stone* published what the writer Douglas Brinkley described as a suicide note written by Thompson to his wife, Anita, entitled "Football Season Is Over" It read:

> "No More Games. No More Bombs. No More Walking. No More Fun. No More Swimming. 67. That is 17 years past 50. 17 more than I needed or wanted. Boring. I am always bitchy. No Fun for anybody. 67. You are getting Greedy. Act your old age. Relax This won't hurt."

A private funeral took place On August 20, 2005. Thompson's ashes were fired from—blasted out of—a cannon. The explosion was accompanied by a medley of red, white, blue and green fireworks, all to the tune of Norman Greenbaum's "Spirit in the Sky" and Bob Dylan's "Mr. Tambourine Man." The cannon was placed atop a 153-foot tower which had the shape of a double-thumbed fist clutching a peyote button, a symbol originally used in his 1970 campaign for Sheriff of Pitkin County, Colorado.

On October 22, 2008, one day after last blogging about the Obama election, writer Carol Anne Burger, age 57, a regular *Huffington Post contributor*, fatally stabbed her estranged gay spouse, Jessica Kalish, 222 (!) times with a Phillips-head screwdriver, "primarily around the back of her head and across her back, arms and face." She was never formally convicted of the murder because Burger committed suicide two days later before any police could question her. Burger and Kalish, a software executive, had been married in Massachusetts in 2005, the *Sun-Sentinel* says. Both were in their 50s. Friends said the breakup a year earlier had been painful for Burger, and that Kalish had in the meantime gotten involved with another woman. Police said that Burger killed Kalish in the garage of the Boynton Beach, Florida, home that they still shared, She then stuffed Kalish's body into her BMW, drove two and a half miles, and, leaving the car behind a medical office, walked home.

She took pains to clean up the murder scene as best she could, but later Luminol tests fluorescing under ultraviolet light revealed a tremendous amount of blood. A chemical agent that makes blood traces fluoresce under ultraviolet light showed a "tremendous amount of blood" in the garage and "Burger's glowing sneaker prints." Under suspicion for the murder, she called to report her old flame missing and then in her backyard she shot herself to death before police could question her. She had been greatly depressed, had recently lost her job, and often talked of moving to Mexico or Panama to start again.

Anne Perry, a successful author of historical detective fiction—perhaps best known for her Thomas Pitt and William Monk series of novels—is a murderer. Born Juliet Hulme, she was convicted, along with her friend Pauline Parker, for murdering Parker's mother, Honorah Rieper, in 1954. (She changed her name after serving her five-year sentence.) Young Hulme seemed to have had strange and compulsive fears of desertion. Her parents were in the process of separating, and she was supposed to be sent away to South Africa to stay with a relative. The two teenage friends, both of whom lived a rich fantasy life populated with famous actors such as James Mason and Orson Welles, did not want to be separated. On June 22, 1954, in consequence, the girls and Honorah Rieper—a woman who advocated their separation—went for a walk in Victoria Park in their hometown of Christchurch. The plan was to kill their obstructor. On an isolated path Hulme dropped an ornamental stone so that Rieper would lean over to retrieve it. Parker had planned to hit her mother with a brick wrapped in a stocking. The girls presumed that one blow would kill her, but it took more than 20.

Only 16 at the time of the murder, Perry and Parker were engaged in what Perry called an "obsessive relationship," although both have denied any romantic feelings for each other (as Jackson suggests in his more lurid film). Their fantasy life ruled much of their behavior. Parker and Hulme eventually stood trial in Christchurch in 1954 and were found guilty on August 29th of that year. As they were too young to be considered for the death penalty under New Zealand law at the time, they were convicted and sentenced to be "detained at Her Majesty's pleasure." In practice they were detained at the discretion of the Minister of Justice. They were released separately five years later. Both women have expressed in interviews remorse for their crime. Concerning her stay in the Mt. Eden women's prison in Auckland, Perry has stated, "I was guilty, and it was the right place for me to be." After being released from prison in November 1959, Hulme changed her name and, returning to England, became a flight attendant For a period she lived in the United States, where in 1968 she became a Mormon, joining The Church of Jesus Christ of Latter-day Saints. She later settled in the Scottish village of Portmahomack where she lived with her mother. Her father had a distinguished scientific career, heading the British hydrogen bomb program.

Taking the name Anne Perry, using her stepfather's surname, she published her first novel, *The Cater Street Hangman*, in 1979. Her works generally fall into one of several categories of genre fiction, including historical murder mysteries and detective fiction. Many of her books feature recurring characters, probably of most significance that of Thomas Pitt, who appeared in her first novel, and that of amnesiac private investigator William Monk, who first appeared in her 1990 novel *The Face of a Stranger*. By 2003 Perry had published 47 novels—as many as Trollope!—and several collections of short stories. Her story "Heroes," which first appeared in the 1999 anthology *Murder and Obsession*, edited by Otto Penzler, won the 2001 Edgar Award for Best Short Story. In 2005, Perry appeared on the *Trisha* show to discuss the crime on a special themed show. A 2009 documentary film, *Anne Perry Interiors*, gave a snapshot of her life and the people close to her.

The poet Ezra Pound, whose own follies and fears eventually proved so self-destructive, was once asked by a reporter when he was an old man, "How is it that you who merited fame as a seer did not see?" More than anything else, the artist's dilemma might be put right there, that, facing the mystery of art, he may see only too well and find upon looking he is a stranger to himself.

A simple but terrible truth was uttered by the despairing Arthur Nortje himself when, turning for help to the very art that at the same time couldn't redeem him, he wrote in despair at the end of one of his final poems:

> "It is not cosmic immensity
> Or catastrophe
> That terrifies me,
> It is solitude . . ."

Destructiveness and fame have long happily co-existed and no more so than in the purlieus of Hollywood. Flamboyant movie director Busby Berkeley killed a person in a motor accident. In September 1935, the highly influential director and choreographer was the driver responsible for an automobile accident in which two people were killed, five seriously injured. Berkeley himself was badly cut and bruised. For the court trial, he was brought to court on a stretcher and during proceedings heard testimony that *Time* magazine said made him wince:

> "Witnesses testified that motorist Berkeley sped down Roosevelt Highway in Los Angeles County one night, changed lanes, crashing headlong into one car, sideswiped another. Some witnesses said they smelled liquor on him."

After the first two trials for second degree murder ended with hung juries, he was acquitted in a third trial. Berkeley died on March 14, 1976, in Palm Springs, California at the age of 80 from natural causes. He is buried in the Desert Memorial Park in Cathedral City, California.

Driving in Manhattan bandleader and clarinetist Artie Shaw killed a man on October 15, 1930, at Broadway and 91st

Street. After running over a 60-year-old yacht chef named George Woods, Shaw with his girlfriend, Betty, fled the scene. Witnesses, however, gave his license plate number to the police who arrested him on Columbus Ave. Shaw lied and said that he thought he had hit a traffic stanchion. He was cleared of criminal charges, but was sued by Woods' family for $80,000.

In 1933, director John Huston, who was something of a wild and reckless playboy, actually struck and killed a young woman while driving on Sunset Boulevard. Walter Huston realized that his son could have had a nascent screenwriting career destroyed just as it was beginning, so he went to Louis B. Mayer and Marion Davies and asked them to keep the story away from Hedda Hopper and Louella Parsons, two of Hollywood's most notorious screen gossips. "Stories swept through the town that MGM and Warner Bros. had kicked in money to keep John out of jail out of their respect for Walter," writes Scott Eyman in *Lion of Hollywood: The Life and Legend of Louis B. Mayer*. The writer and future film director earlier in life had quickly gained a Hollywood reputation as a lusty, hard-drinking libertine. In his autobiography, *An Open Book* (1980), he recalled his life at the time as a "series of misadventures and disappointments." In any case, it culminated in the 1933 automobile accident in which a car he was driving struck and killed a young woman. "The grand jury failed to return an indictment; john had supposedly been sober and the light was with him." It is said that it cost Mayer $400,000 to have the matter hushed up, more than half the budget of any MGM feature film. Although absolved of blame, traumatized, he left Hollywood and spent almost a year living a drifter's life in London and Paris.

On July 11, 1936, a Saturday, Howard Hughes, the eccentric billionaire, movie director, playboy, record-setting aviator, and

Hollywood producer—a man impulsive and compulsively reckless in his habits—roaring down the streets of Los Angeles, California struck and killed a pedestrian by the name of Gabriel S. Meyer. A passenger in his car sat Nancy Belle Bayly, the socialite daughter of a wealthy Pasadena family, according to the book *Howard Hughes: His Life and Madness*. She was young. It was her 25th birthday, and the pair had spent the evening at Trader Vic's, the Polynesian-themed LA hotspot where they'd shared three rounds of the house-specialty cocktail, the Volcano, a vivid blue concoction heavy on rum, per *Howard Hughes: Hell's Angel*. "We got real tipsy," Bayly recalled. From there, the partygoers went to the Cocoanut Grove nightclub to go dancing, and then they were headed to the boardwalk in Santa Monica, so that Hughes, all of his life a determined thrill-seeker and speed freak, could ride the rollercoaster. It was just before 11 p.m., when a thick, heavy fog had set in as Hughes took the corner at Third Street and Lorraine Boulevard where the streetlight was burned out, according to *Hollywood Death and Scandal Sites: Seventeen Driving Tours with Directions and the Full Story*.

Gabe Meyer, a 59-year-old furniture salesman at the May Department Store in downtown LA, was waiting for the streetcar to take him to the home he shared with his sister and brother-in-law a half-mile away on South Lucerne Avenue. Standing in the streetcar stop safety zone there, he was killed instantly when Hughes' 1929 Dusenberg slammed into him. He never knew what hit him. Just prior to the accident, Bayly later reported, the two of them were simply motoring along when suddenly she saw the fast-approaching lights of a streetcar through the thick fog. Hughes swerved to avoid an oncoming car, and then there was a loud thump—"like someone had thrown a sack of potatoes onto our hood," Bayly was reported to say, according to Darwin Porter in *Howard Hughes: Hell's Angel*.

She began screaming when she realized what had happened. They got out of the car and the two of them dragged Meyer's dead body to the sidewalk, where a crowd had gathered. The police arrived, and Hughes was taken to a local hospital and given a sobriety test, but not before he had managed to call his attorney, Neil McCarthy, and gotten Bayly into a streetcar and conveniently out of the way, according to *Howard Hughes: His Life and Madness.*

After the accident, Hughes was taken to the hospital and duly certified as sober. The playboy passed his sobriety test, in spite of the fact that the admitting doctor later claimed he had not been present when Hughes took it, for he frankly believed that the driver of the car had been heavily intoxicated at the time. Hughes was booked on a charge of negligent homicide, the press was informed, and newspaper headlines soon rang with the story, as the full scandal—not Hughes' first—had erupted. It was also reported that Hughes refused to reveal the name of the woman who had been his passenger that nigh. His attorney got him released the next morning on his own recognizance. A witness to the crash informed the police that Hughes had been driving erratically and far too fast and that Meyer had been innocently standing in the safety zone of a streetcar stop. Subsequently, Hughes was booked on suspicion of negligent homicide and held overnight in jail until his attorney obtained a writ of *habeas corpus* for his release pending a coroner's inquest. After the accident, Hughes put out a statement to the press that was anything but contrite and never even included mention of the victim. "This is my first accident," the statement began, according to Darwin Porter in his exposé *Howard Hughes Hell's Angel.* "I've been driving since I was 12 years old and I've never hit a cat or dog," Hughes went on record as saying. "My father owned the first automobile in the state of Texas and taught me to drive 18 years ago. I've had a perfect record. I've never even scratched the paint on my Dusenberg in nearly seven years."

During the ensuing investigation, Hughes' attorney, Neil McCarthy, controlled the narrative that this was nothing more than a tragic accident and rounded up several witnesses that actually alleged that *the victim had been drunk* and staggering into the street while Hughes was driving at a slow speed. "I know the facts, and I am confident there is no blame on Mr. Hughes," McCarthy told the Associated Press. A fixer named Archie MacDonald also helped by bribing an important witness who had told police Meyer had been standing in the streetcar safety zone and that Hughes had been driving erratically and seemed drunk, but later changed his story, per *"Family Secret."* By the time of the coroner's inquiry, however, the witness had changed his story and claimed instead that Meyer had moved directly in front of Hughes' car. What had happened— had he been bribed? Nancy Bayly (Watts) who was in the car with Hughes at the time of the crash, corroborated this version of the story. On July 16, 1936, Hughes was held blameless by a coroner's jury at the inquest into Meyer's death. Hughes told reporters outside the inquiry, "I was driving slowly and a man stepped out of the darkness in front of me."

A coroner's jury determined Hughes was not at fault for the "unavoidable accident" (per the AP, in the *Chicago Tribune*), and the billionaire was not charged with a crime. Hughes paid Meyer's family the equivalent of around $215,000 in today's money, and the scandal soon faded away. Hughes beat the negligent homicide without a scratch and managed to get away completely unscathed. Hughes never again saw the woman who was driving with him that night. Nancy Belle Bayly, the socialite daughter, became a non-person to him, just like many other actresses and models and ingenues he knew. Hughes wouldn't be so lucky almost exactly a decade later. On July 7, 1946, Hughes would suffer devastating injuries of his own in a crash, although it was in an accident didn't involve a car, but rather an experimental airplane that he was piloting when it slammed into two Beverly Hills homes before bursting into flames. He suffered third-degree burns and multiple fractures, and, along with the snooping press once again involved, in increasing sense of paranoia, which led to him becoming a recluse

After a night of heavy drinking in March 1945, Clark Gable got into a terrible car accident at four a.m., and killed a woman pedestrian. He had attended a party celebrating the American victory on Iwo Jima and, driving home, lost control of the car that he was driving passing through Bristol Circle, a dense, tree-filled traffic island on Sunset Boulevard in the residential area of Brentwood in West Los Angeles. MGM publicist Ralph Wheelwright and security chief Whitey Hendry got to the scene of the accident first and saw to it that Gable got taken away privately. He needed 10 stitches as a result of the hit-and-run. Howard Strickling of MGM saw that the car was removed and that the entire story was covered up and kept from the public glare.

Fame protects no one. Artie Shaw, the great bandleader and clarinetist, killed a man. After joining a band in California, Shaw was on tour New York, where an event occurred that almost completely ruined his life After a surprise reunion with a girlfriend from Cleveland, Arthur Jacob Arshawsky (his real name) wanted to show her the town in which he was born in 1919. He was zipping around boastfully in a brand-new red roadster when a yacht chef stepped off the curb in front of Shaw's car and was instantly killed. It was a hit-and-run. Shaw, who was always arrogant and autocratic, a "difficult" man, disgracefully fled the scene. Unfortunately for him, the accident had been reported to the police. Although he was eventually cleared of any charges on the criminal side of things, it turned out that he had to face a civil suit for $80,000. Being under 21, his own mother Sarah (*née* Strauss) Arshawsky, a mere seamstress, was sued too, and financial obligations forced the two of them to share a small apartment and scrimp with every penny of their combined incomes to pay off their obligation. When Shaw's band finished their New York engagement and returned to California, Shaw was basically stranded without a job and had to wait six months to qualify for a New York musician's union card.

Celebrity bad drivers seem always to be in the news. On December 8, 1984, Mötley Crüe lead singer Vince Neil and Hanoi Rocks' drummer Nicholas "Razzle" Dingley, went for a beer run after partying all day at Neil's oceanfront condo. Neil made a high-speed turn onto The Esplanade from Sapphire Street and lost control of his sports car, crashing head-on into a Volkswagen. Dingley was killed instantly and Lisa Hogan, an 18-year-old passenger in the Volkswagen, was critically injured and spent several weeks in a coma. The driver of the Volkswagen was also injured. Neil was not injured and pleaded guilty to manslaughter and drunken driving. He received only 20 days in jail and agreed to pay $2.5 million in restitution to the victims.

On January 4, 1970, Keith Moon, the Who drummer, while drunk, his then-wife Kim, friend "Legs" Larry Smith, and others had been drinking at the opening of a pub outside of London that was owned by the son of one of Moon's neighbors. It was nighttime. Some of the Hatfield, U.K. pub's patrons were young skinheads who resented the rich rock star drinking brandy to their beers at their new local. The scene grew confrontational as Moon and his party left and tried to drive away in his Bentley, which Moon owned but did not drive, being unlicensed. Skinheads surrounded the car and would not allow it to drive away. They were beating on and rocking the car as if they wanted to flip it over. Moon's driver, 24-year-old Cornelius Boland, got out to confront the attackers at the front of the vehicle. Moon, still feeling threatened, attempted to drive his party to safety. In the process Boland was trapped under the car and immediately dragged to his death.

On February 3, 2003, the unbalanced, neurotic, eccentric gun-toting record producer Phil Spector—Harvey Phillip Spector—at his gloomy estate (the Pyrenees Castle) in Alhambra, California, inexplicably shot actress Lana Clarkson in the mouth and killed her. The "Father of the Wall of Sound" was never humble. "I felt obligated to change music to art, the same way that Galileo proved the Earth was round to the world and that the Sun did not stand still," he declared at one time. He also went on to say, "People tell me they idolize me, want to be like me, but I tell them, 'trust me, you don't want my life.' I've been a very tortured soul." Spector was later shown to have suffered from being bipolar. I have always wondered whether it was from arrogance of despair that he said, "I am not a bona fide human being."

Actor Matthew Broderick had just finished filming *Biloxi Blues*. Jennifer Grey had a few free weeks before starting the publicity rounds for her new movie, *Dirty Dancing*. So the busy couple, whose antagonistic brother-sister act in 1986's *Ferris Bueller's Day Off* was apparently the start of a more harmonious off-screen liaison, decided to take a vacation. They flew to Ireland and rented a BMW 316, planning to drive around Northern Ireland. On August 5, 1987, the two of them set out from Irvinestown to Maguiresbridge. This carefree jaunt, however, ended tragically some 80 miles west of Belfast in a car accident that left two people dead. Broderick was driving when, at about 3 o'clock in the afternoon, he and Grey, 27, pulled into a gas station just outside Enniskillen to ask directions.

An off-duty policeman told Broderick his route was "just stupid" and offered to lead them to the right road. But the actor, as one critic sarcastically put it, was "on vacation from stage directions," declined and went his own way. "He wasn't going fast," says the policeman, who followed Broderick for a few miles. "Less than 40 mph." Several miles and a sudden downpour later, the pair stopped at another gas station to get their bearings. It had stopped raining, but the pavement was still wet when they pulled back onto the open country road. Some speculate that Broderick may have started driving on the right out of American habit, instead of the left, the proper side in Ireland.

Less than a mile down the road, which had no curves or obstructed views, Broderick's car recklessly collided head-on with a Volvo driven by Anna Gallagher, 28. She and her mother, Margaret Doherty, 63, were both pronounced dead on arrival at Erne Hospital. Broderick was rushed to the same hospital with face cuts and a badly broken right leg. "We had to cut the side away from the American's car to give him first aid," says Ken Ramsey of the local fire brigade. Although Broderick was in agony, "his main concern was for the people in the other car," Ramsey recalls. "He kept saying 'Did I hurt them? Did I hurt them?'" Grey was only superficially bruised but covered with Broderick's blood.

"Open is broken," wrote Norman O. Brown. "There is no breakthrough without breakage." And so every artist becomes his own scandal. Some might go so far as to say that it is part of the art form, the simple but terrible truth that has the poor creative soul turning for help either to the very art that at the same time cannot redeem him, or away from it to places where the demons can even be worse.

Plaid

Amelia Earhart went down in her plane wearing a short-sleeved plaid shirt on July 2, 1937. Rosanno Brazzi sang "Some Enchanted Evening" wearing a plaid shirt in the film version of *South Pacific*. Curly (Gordon Macrae) wears several different colors and kinds of plaid shirts in the film *Oklahoma!* as it has a stylish ingenuousness to it, plaid does, which in its lack of pretension and general down-to-earthness is somewhat godly if cornballishly endearing,

Cowboy Roy Rogers often wore plaid shirts, either full ones or a sort of wing-type, western style, limited to the upper chest, in many of the hundred or so movies he made, like *Lights of Old Santa Fe*, *Under Western Skies*, and *San Fernando Valley*. Dale Evans, Queen of the Cowgirls, wore lots of plaid. So did cowboy Tom Mix. But wasn't cow-simple plaid, like calico, originally a western thing, at least in America? (No Scot of course could ever possibly expect to find a serious plaid on these shores.) In the comic 1950s western *Red Garters*, for example, loud plaid shirts are worn by virtually everybody and found on everything, including Rosemary Clooney's Highland sash, a nutty a-cultural lunacy. Gene Autry in his film *The Strawberry Roan* (1948) actually wears a plaid double-breasted jacket or mackinaw, Mondrian-patterned and as vividly red as the coat of his whinnying cinema mare.

The word plaid is said to be derived from the Gaelic *peal-laid*, for sheepskin (cf. L. *pellus*, skin), an outer garment consisting of an oblong piece of woolen cloth forming the principal outer part of the Highlanders costume in Scotland, where fellows are often called "plaidmen." A wearer wrapped himself in plaid, the lower portion of which reached to the knees and was belted, forming the kilt. The lower, separate section was called the *philberg*. Plaids are commonly of a checked or tartan (cross-barred) pattern. Worn by both sexes in place of a cloak, plaid can refer, more or less, to any cloth that is made with such a pattern. There are infinite variet-ies. "Shepherd's plaid," a particular cloth with a checked pattern of a black-on-white ground, is very like the Palestinian headgear of today, that tine-toothed maroon-and-white which qualifies as plaid. But the color plaid—let's call it a color—is found everywhere, from the plaid Tretons and Pendleton skirts of book-club matrons to wide, ballooning clown-pants to the multifarious canvases of beach umbrellas. The hatband of Mr. Howell's hat, the million-aire on TV's *Gilligan's Island*, is plaid. It seems to have an ongoing and perpetual life in golfwear. John McPhee in *The Crofter and the Laird*, where he returns to the island of his ancestors, Colonsy, mentions, of all things, tartan candles!

The *Annals of Ulster* makes reference to what we know as Scotland as *Cruitintualt*—*Cruithni* means "the tribe of the designs"— which is a portmanteau of the Irish word for the Picts and people, land or nation. In Britain, the Celtic-speaking Britons variously spelled the Irish name "Cruithni" (Pict) as Pryten, which eventually became Briton in the tongue of the Teutonic invaders. The Tribe of the Designs endures still, of course, as the home of the tartan.

Plaid, more correctly pronounced "plāde," by the way, than "plăd," is the garment; tartan is the peculiar pattern denoting the clan to which the wearer of the plaid belongs. "This word in the Gaelic, or in any other language of which I have knowledge, means anything broad and flat, and when applied to a plaid or blanket signifies simply a plain, unformed piece of cloth," says Eliezer Edwards in his *Dictionary of Words, Facts, and Phrases,* applying the word solely to cloth. In this sense, the word has no reference whatsoever to the chequered pattern which the fabric, as we know it, presently bears.

Shakespeare never used the word *plaid.* (Or tartan, for that matter.) Neither does Chaucer, Milton, or Robbie Burns, for all his Caledonian songs—or even Gerard Manley Hopkins, who, however, does speak of plaits in several places in his poems, the same poet who nevertheless uniquely gave glory to God for dappled things and rows and ripples and pied beauty in general.

I tend to think of plaid as Indiana. In his brilliant but corrosive underground cartoons R. Crumb frequently satirizes normal people by drawing them wearing plaid clothes—hats and ties and jackets. Argyle socks, of course, sported by people like Pat Boone, Dobie Gillis, and the comic-book character Archie Andrews, I have always thought, denote total simplicity and dull, fundamental normalcy, even to the point of high-school conventionality, a particular precinct where the fabric is often worn by the kind or guy Valley Girls with snorting derision call a "mare" or a "poindexter." Like someone who reads a lot of books and stuff? Like "bagged out"? A "beige"? A total "eugene"?

There is a kind of pronounced dopiness to plaid, without question, and it can be irksome. No better example of plaid's melvinization can perhaps be found than by the fact that dwarf-sized felon, thief, and simonist evangelist Jim Bakker proudly wore a plaid tie to his wedding to Tammy Faye La Valley, the cutest little 73-pound coed at Worth Central Bible College in Minnesota, or so she says in her autobiography, *I Gotta Be Me* (1973), not quite the worst book in the world. "We were going to get married in our favorite clothes," proudly writes Tammy Faye. "Jim in his black blazer with a little red emblem on it and a Scottish-plaid tie. My favorite was a red dress, trimmed with a little black velvet. We looked just like Barbie dolls in those clothes. We were so little."

When the secretly lusty Bakker seduced one of his disciples, Jessica Hahn, on December 6, 1980, a scandal that was later made public to became his undoing, he had confided to her confidentially, "When you help the shepherd, you're helping the sheep." Curiously (or should this be consistently?) he appeared on the *Today* Show on November 13, 1997 in what seemed to be an uncharacteristically chastened mood, that is, until he rather heretically and blameshiftedly admitted, "my doctrine was wrong." Still persistently button-cute, he was wearing a plaid button-down shirt.

It has an innocent look. Cornpone. Lack of guile. Unpretentiousness. The very connotations that gormless Lamar Alexander hoped to capitalize on—looking suitably plebeian—when asked by one reporter the cost of a loaf of bread, however, he didn't know during his brief, farcical run for president in 1996 when he and all of his organizers and loyalists galumphed around rural New Hampshire wearing rustic plaid shirts with black-and-red squares, trying to look like real human beings. The same plaid was worn, far more dramatically, not to mention sexily, and with far more panache, by handsome Marlon Brando playing Terry Molloy in *On the Waterfront* (1954), in which the toil-plaid pattern of the working man is also quoted, notice, in many of the woolen hats worn by the dockworkers.

Speaking of Brando, several of his cycle cronies in the film *The Wild One* (1954) wear plaid hats, typical of the 1950s but eye-opening in its innocence with the bully who sports it, the very reason, may I suggest, that the director of *The Bad Seed* (1956) had murderous little blonde Rhoda Penmark appear several times wearing a crisp, daintily sweet plaid frock and patent-leather shoes.

Beaver (Jerry Mathers) on *Leave It to Beaver* loved and always wore plaid shirts, as did Wally, and for years wily *Top Cat*, Saturday morning TV's animated cartoon, wore a plaid jacket. Plaid is goofy to a degree. It was a big Fiftyish thing, when young men with crew-cuts in glen plaid jackets were ubiquitous. Plaidness *is* the Fifties. It can be uncool. At prom time, cummerbunds and bow ties, especially in that dull decade, were often plaid, so much more youthful and clean-cut in formal wear, or so it seemed then, than silky lounge lizard-like black or purple things. The low comic and buffoonish connotations of plaid, *pace* Rob Roy, seem obvious and immediate. The fat, nebbishly comic Lou Costello's hats, like Chico Marx's, were often plaid. Big dumb Jethro on TV's *The Beverly Hillbillies* wore plaid shirts. The Three Stooges, especially Curly, were well-known for the plethora of loud plaid shirts, pants, hats, and vests that they habitually wore. Pinky Lee, the frantic, chipmunk-faced Fifties television comic and children's show host, whose plaid wardrobe induced something of a painful eyestrain, actually wore a combination of mixed-and-matched plaid hats, plaid coats, and plaid trousers as, entertaining row upon row of squealing children, he goatishly cavorted and leapt and gamboled around the set. Easily recognized by his trademark lisp and his high-energy antics, his signature costume was basically a loud plaid suit with baggy checkered pants and an undersized hat—typically sartorial burlesque shtick. During his routines, whenever anybody irritated him, which happened frequently, he would unleash his catchphrase: "Oooooh! You make me so *mad!*"

Almost all of Dobie Gillis's shirts on *The Many Loves of Dobie Gillis* were plaid button-downs with long sleeves. Rubber-faced Darrin Stevens (Dick York) on *Bewitched* and breadcrumby Uncle Joe (Edgar Buchanan) on *Petticoat Junction* constantly wore plaid, as did, unforgettably, Greg, Peter, and Bobby, *The Brady Bunch* dweebs; Mike, Robbie, and Chip on *My Three Sons*; and pert, case-of-the-cutes, coiffure-horned Kathy (Lauren Chapin) on *Father Knows Best*, as plaited a family as a warm potholder.

Dorks of course tend to wear plaid. Les Nessman, the bow-tied nerd on TV's *WKRP in Cincinnati*, not only wore plaid shirts but a plaid muffler, which was more or less his signature tog—even his cross-grained but diffident and somewhat milquetoastian fretfulness came across to the viewer as plaid! Dick Lowden (Bob Newhart) and that earnest, bumpkinlsh, plaid-behatted handyman of his, goofy George (Tom Poston) on the TV sitcom *The Bob Newhart Show* both have a Vermonter's rustic penchant for plaid shirts. It is very New England in a maple syrupy sort of way.

As to bumpkinism, didn't Johnny Carson's nervous, milk-pail-stupid character Floyd R. Turbo, with his red plaid hat-with-flaps, have a Down East accent? And Art Fern, the sleazy, bemustachioed tea-time movie host with the bad toupee (". . . and then you get to the Slauson Cutoff, stop, get out, cut off your Slauson, and drive until you reach the fork in the road" [he holds up a card here showing a fork . . .]) was a runty, carnival barker-like slickster who banged a schoolroom pointer and relentlessly wore plaid jackets. Even Doc Severinsen, the nightly brunt of Carson's sartorial jokes, always seemed to err in matters of excess on the side of loud plaid jackets. And when bumptious Ted Knight and Georgette were married on the November 6, 1975 episode of *The Mary Tyler Moore Show*, Georgette's wedding gown was a short plaid dress. She explained, "It's Ted's favorite color."

Plaid has always had a country aura, a sort of 4-H Club connotation, about it. Andy Griffith as Andy Taylor wears a country plaid shirt when, during the opening credits of *The Andy Griffith Show*, he goes trundling off with his pole, whistling, for an afternoon of fishing. In the Fifties, when there was a spate of *Tammy* movies, that pert, braid-plaited teen from the slicks invariably wore a short plaid shirt. Smokey Bear, of course, wore plaid shirts. And Janet Bouvier (Jackie O's mother), when she went hunting and riding, did so, as well. Gary Cooper as Cole Hardin in *The Westerner* (1940) famously wears the sort of plaid cowboy shirt that for the next half century seemed to set the trend in western wear. Plaid was once, incidentally, called "rodeo flannel"—and even "railroad flannel." In Republic's movie serial *Zorro's Black Whip*—a 12-episode done in the Thirties starring a female Zorro!—all the oafish cowboys, especially outlaws, wear plaid shirts. Jimmy Stewart wore a red plaid hip-length mackinaw in *The Naked Spur* (1953). All the Kansas rednecks in the film *In Cold Blood* (1967), especially Richard Hickock and his ill father, wear similar plaid mackinaws, as does the loony with the rifle who in one scene blunders onto the Clutter property.

The outdoorsy aspect of plaid, its L. L. Beanishness, is well known. There adhibits to plaid, in spite of the starker identification commonly associated with Scotland, the country of tartans and plaids, something particularly rural American. It has always been a popular Grand Ole Opry pattern and virtually the cast uniform on television's rustic satire *Hee Haw*. Roy Acuff, who seems personally to have had closets-full of plaid shirts, almost always appeared with his "Crazy Tennesseeans" with all of them wearing the same plaid outfits, rounding out the seminal country-picker's persona. That, and fabric "checks." Nothing in insistent country music rural-wear beats out "checks" shirt or dress for wide popularity. Jean Shepherd's dresses. Cousin Jody's. Lonzo and Oscar's. Bradley Kincaid's. Minnie Pearl's. Look at the Grand Old Opry *WSM Picture-History Book* sometime. It is virtually a tour of plaid.

In *The Egg and I* (1950), Claudette Colbert in plaid shirt and apron does her level best to try, at least by way of sporting duds, living life in the country with her husband Fred MacMurray, who had got the urge to go in madly for chicken raising. The film is a flat-out rural plaidorama, with that pattern appearing and reappearing on locals riding tractors, jitneys, horses. I have long thought that it is from this very movie that President Richard Nixon, who personally looked like a sort of *smudged* Fred MacMurray, got the idea for calling his wife Pat "Buddy," the particular term of endearment that Bob (Fred) in the movie repeatedly uses when addressing his wife Betty (Claudette).

Style and plaid need not be at loggerheads, however. The interior of Balmoral Castle in Queen Victoria's day was covered in Royal Stuart tartan. Edward VIII, the Duke of Windsor, not only favored loud colorful tweeds and two-tone shoes but tartan trousers, and there were well-circulated rumors at the time of frequent spats between Edward and his father both because of his addiction to jazz and because of the rakish, broadcasting plaids and checks he insisted on wearing. Clifton Webb, playing the murderous dilettante Waldo Lydeker in *Laura* (1944), in one scene actually wears a tartan tuxedo rather smartly. As does Edmond O'Brien in *The Girl Can't Help It* (1956), in which, wearing a plaid tux, I must say, he seems very much at home, while looking rather rakish.

The Burberry trench coat, which introduced gabardine in 1879 and was worn by soldiers on the front lines during WWI, is known not only for its clever flaps and vents but its identifiably plaid lining—it is officially called the "Burberry check"—and has been in use since the 1920s. One thinks of Rick Blaine in *Casablanca* wearing it, but for its strength and water-repellent durability it was worn by many aviators, outdoor enthusiasts, and explorers like Roald Amundsen, the first man to reach the South Pole, and Ernest Shackleton, who led a 1914 expedition to cross Antarctica. A Burberry gabardine jacket was worn by George Mallory his attempt on Mount Everest n 1924.

Without exaggeration, it can even look beautiful. Young Elizabeth Taylor in *Father of the Bride* (1950), for example, looks unexpectedly fetching and fashionable in a plain plaid shirt. Thai silk plaids, by the way, show a spectrum of brilliant colors and are quite fashionable. Those for women are frequently brocaded in rich gold and silver threads and are worn only for significant ceremonies in Thailand, such as weddings and royal receptions. The fabrics were popularized in Western fashion initially as women's stoles, thanks to the importing entrepreneur Jim Thompson, the "Silk King," who, incidentally, mysteriously disappeared in the Cameron Highlands of that country in 1967 and has not been found to this day. Always a popular fashion, plaid lends itself, as has been mentioned, to the heartiness of outdoor life camping styles, general Adirondackiana, Land's End, L. L. Bean, Abercrombie & Fitch, and no solid or serious northern-wear catalog is generally without its seasonal spread of fashionable plaid hats, shirts, and jackets.

Speaking of style, two random figures come to mind. Frank Sinatra's Cavanaugh hats, for example. His favorite was supposedly the one he wore in *Pal Joey*, they say, but a lot of his thicker, heavier ones were often plaid. (A story goes that when the "Chairman of the

Board" boldly placed one of those hats on your head, as frequently he would—to close friends of his, at least—you had to sing a song!) I am also thinking of the great Boston Red Sox left-fielder Ted Williams, who liked to wear plaid jackets, with sports shirts—and no necktie, *never* a necktie. I had the chance once to visit his work studio in Connecticut to see sculptor Armand La Montaigne's classic life-size statue, sculpted from bass wood, of the slugger, Ted Williams the fisherman, called "Home Run," which shows him wearing a white/brown/green outdoor shirt in a rich plaid pattern. Naturalist (and Scot) John Muir also loved plaid. And did naturalist Euell Gibbons ever wear anything else?

I mention John Muir, "Father of the National Parks," the influential Scottish-American naturalist, author, environmental philosopher, botanist, zoologist, glaciologist, and early advocate for the preservation of wilderness in the United States. There was not only a series of John Muir plaid shirts available for sale but Gordon Nicolson Kiltmakers created the "John Muir Way" Tartan as a way of marking the 100th anniversary of Muir's death, and also celebrating the opening of the new coast-to-coast cycling and walking route between Dunbar and Helensburgh. According to Gordon Nicolson Kiltmakers, "Living family life in Dunbar (the birthplace and boyhood home of the influential environmentalist John Muir) while enjoying the beautiful outdoors of East Lothian it seemed natural for Gordon to design a tartan to celebrate the opening of the 133-mile John Muir Way."

It can be cool to wear plaid. Alicia Silverstone in the movie *Clueless* (1996) kicks around in a whole series of flirtatious plaid suits and getups—red and black, yellow and black—and manages, with a sort of provocative young Catholic schoolgirl-like sexpot flair, to look quite coquettish. Leslie Caron in the film musical *Gigi* (1958) cavorts through the first third of the film in a lovely French-collared, red-black plaid outfit. Louis Jordan as Gaston, irked that she substitutes it later for an adult dress, wonders aloud—somewhat inappropriately—as to the whereabouts of her "little Scotch dress." All of it correctly echoes Colette's novel on which the musical is based where, on page one, we see the young girl showing off "the perfect oval shape of her knee caps" when she is wearing a tartan skirt.

What could be more fetchingly beautiful or more memorable or even more trendsetting than Ginger Rogers in the film *Top Hat* (1935) wearing, along with riding breeches and near-derby, a plaid check jacket, as with Fred Astaire she sings and dances the number "Isn't It a Lovely Day?" Alan Ladd in *Two Years Before the Mast* (1946) looks utterly cool, even if slightly anachronistic, in his plaid shirt, especially with his sleeves rolled up. As to coolness in plaid, nothing can match the supreme artist of jazz, on the album cover of the Savoy LP *The Immortal Charlie Parker* (London Records' Jazz Series LT2-C15106), where "Bird" actually wears a long-sleeve plaid shirt!

There is a distinct, longstanding preppiness to plaid, which may be the reason that the anti-social punk group Dead Milkmen recorded the angry "Eat Your Paisley!" in 1986. The publishers of *The Preppie Handbook*, Lisa Birnbach's unctuous bible of preppiedom, knowingly used a plaid frame for the front cover of the book to suggest the look of prep school chic. And didn't the priggish and self-referential Ali McGraw as Jenny Cavilleri walk around the campus of Harvard College in the movie *Love Story* (1970) with just a little too much attitude and a few too many *pleated* plaid skirts?

The carefree pattern, real, unkingly, and demotic, lends itself to the kind of simplicity we see not only in farm movies but in broad comedy. Bing Crosby, with his hat tipped, wears a plaid shirt in the comedy *Riding High* (1950), wonderfully evoking a plain horse-owner down on his luck but hoping for fortune with his nag on the racetrack. In the movie, Bing, who incidentally was color-blind in real life, sings "Anywhere Road," one of my favorite songs, in a plaid shirt. Egbert, the boomist American rustic in Harry Leon Wilson's novel *Ruggles of Red Gap* (1915), actually collects plaid suits—grotesque jacket and pants combos—and he sports one such crass, circus-like production in the hilarious film version when first he goes to take Ruggles, the English butler, back out West with him to the tail grasses of Red Gap in the state of Washington, U.S.A.

There is very little sobriety about the color plaid. In one episode of the television sitcom *Mad About You*, fox-faced Paul Reiser's wife's uncle dies, and, since that man liked plaid, everybody wears it—unsuitably, of course—to the funeral. Dead men *don't* wear plaid. It is not a funeral swatch, plaid, although, incongruity of incongruities, the Beatnik writer and poet Jack Kerouac was both waked and buried in Lowell, Massachusetts, wearing a red plaid jacket, one of the singular reasons, no doubt—the lame bourgeoisification of it all—that the crazy poet Gregory Corso, in sorrowful but manic attendance, badly wanted, as he later reported, to lift the laid-out corpse and hurl it across the room! Regarding beatniks, I once saw Allen Ginsberg, that total fraud, wearing a plaid vest in the 1960s and, with his wisps of horrible scraggly hair blazoning out, thought he resembled a huge scrubbing pad, like Brillo, which by the way is something of a plaid object in and of itself!

Speaking of death and plaid, mobster Charles "Lucky" Luciano died of a heart attack at the Rome airport wearing a pair of checkered plaid slacks.

No, I am afraid, buffoonery loves plaid. The comic Buddy Hackett wears a plaid checked suit while singing "Shipoopi" in *The*

Music Man (1962), the only completely pointless song in the musical, as does child star Mickey Rooney in *Little Lord Fauntleroy* (1936). Tom Ewell in *The Seven Year Itch* (1955) sports a plaid bow tie. Jack Oakie in *Once in a Lifetime* (1932) wears what might be called a "full Augusta"—a golfer's outfit of plaid—plaid plus-fours, plaid armless sweater, and plaid socks, all fully hideous. Brian Donleavy in *The Great McGinty* (1940) wears a frightfully loud checkered-plaid suit in a cab scene with Akim Tamiroff. The cab driver, as McGinty gets in, sarcastically mutters, "Great suit." It can be found in everything from the big hairbow of bratty little Jessie Ralph, comedian W. C. Fields' nemesis in *The Bank Dick* (1940), to Charlie Chaplin's vest in *The Circus* (1928).

It was also the identifiable racetrack fabric of Bert Lahr, as seen in *Burlesque* (1946), as much a part of him as his bald wig, baggy pants, and trademark "*Gnong, gnong, gnong,*" just as it was with other burlesque comedians of patter and pratfall, such as Dave Marion, Phil Silvers, Leon Errol, Billy Hagen, Bobby Clark, Ben Blue, and of course the legendary Abbott and Costello, as well as a lot of other old-time "top bananas" who later appeared in *This Was Burlesque* on Broadway in 1962, like Steve Mills, Jerry Lester, Harry Conley, Charlie Robinson, and Dick Bernie, comics who virtually lived in wide plaid three-button suits and nutty pointed hats, goofballs and wackos in jackets of palm-sized plaid and neckties that ended at the ankles.

It was famously popular with the Ritz Brothers for their shirts in the Twenties. Spike Jones wore nothing but jokey, oversized zoot-shaped plaid suits and jackets, and his orchestra, if you will, followed suit. Ventriloquist Edgar Bergen's dumb little dummy Mortimer Snerd had a penchant for plaid. Desi Arnaz in episode after episode of *I Love Lucy* constantly wore plaid. *Broadway Danny*

Rose (1984), Woody Allen's dark comedy about a small-time theatrical agent, is a fashion-show of bad taste in which show biz agent Allen, along with many of his performers, wears boisterous plaid jackets, plaid pants, plaid shirts, and revoltingly mixed striped and plaid and tartan combos. What about the two hopelessly and totally "square," completely out-of-it Voychek brothers on television's *Saturday Night Live*, two transplanted Czechoslovakians living in the U.S.A. with their blue unfashionable plaid Dacron shirts and stupid 1970s Elton John-type button hats?

In *The Road to Utopia* (1948) Bob Hope and Bing Crosby, as "Sperry" and "McGurk," both wear huge outsized plaid mackinaws and shirts and galluses *all at the same time* throughout this pratfall-filled movie, which is set in ice-cold Alaska. Looking like a lumberjack or carnival barker, cool Crosby does a nice job singing "Welcome to My Dream." In one scene Dorothy Lamour herself wears a plaid skirt. "The only time a rainbow ever covered up a pot," quips jealous Hope to tubby Crosby, who is wearing outlandish plaids. Plaid typically adds poundage without power. The author photo of Andrea Dworkin on the back-jacket of her book *Ice and Fire*—its subject, misandry, I should think would call for her to wear Venus red or Mars black leather—makes her look like a huge, oddly incompetent moon pie. Tasteless plaid seems to inspire autocratic coaches in sports. Bobby Knight, former head basketball coach of Indiana University, a venomous and persistent bully given to throwing chairs and belittling his own players, always wore plaid jackets at courtside before opting for sweaters that were the scolding-red of the school. I have always thought that University of Alabama's legendary football coach Paul "Bear" Bryant's small plaid checked hat misendowed him with an avoidable fatness and gave his cheeks a chubby, chipmunkish look.

Creepitude had been matched with plaid, however, before Dworkin's wacko books. The curtains in the Bates Motel in Alfred Hitchcock's *Psycho* (1960)—as Casey Stengel used to say, "You can look it up"—are actually plaid!

The negative aspects of plaid, regarding malice and obloquy, I mean, are few and far between. Herbert Hoover, who of course regarded Franklin D. Roosevelt as crafty, changing, and unpin-downable, several times disdainfully referred to him as a "chameleon on plaid." The psychopathic narrator in Brett Easton Ellis's bizarre novel *American Psycho*, a clotheshorse as well as a psychoneurotic sex-killer of the worst sort, abhors plaid's lack of urbanity and at one point says, "Powell *and* dinner at Evelyn's? These go together about as well as paisley and plaid." The patterns we prefer articulate to a degree our inner beings. Liberace had a closetful of plaid clothes, but it does not seem, at least to me, to be a gay color. "If I was going to pick a color I would say that straight men are yellow and gay men are green," Andrew Ramer writes in *Gay Soul*. "We have access to internal feminine parts of ourselves and that comes out. Another way of putting it is to say that gay men are plaid and straight men are stripes." There is a lesbian preference, I am told, for lumberjack jackets.

But plaid is not necessarily at loggerheads with macho behavior. In *Tarzan the Magnificent* (1960), Jock Mahoney, a heavy in this film, wears a sober red-and-blue plaid shirt all through the movie, until it is torn off his back and ripped to shreds by Tarzan (Gordon Scott). Ironically, Mahoney himself later went on to play Tarzan.

Spitefully, Joan Crawford took all of her daughter Christina's clothes away and, in order to humiliate her, left the 12-year-old girl at school with only two dresses to wear for four months, to cure what Joan considered her disobedience. What had happened was, Christina, feeling cold, had worn a coat to class, which her mother found in a young girl a usurping, intractable presumption. "The trouble was," Christina later wrote in *Mommie, Dearest,* "the two dresses were exactly alike, except for the color. One was blue plaid, and the other was green plaid. I was so sick of looking at those two dresses!"

Black stereotypes have often worn plaid clothes, pants, the odd doo-dad like Aunt Jemima's bandannas. "Spo-Dee-O-Dee," the Negro stage comedian who was born Sam Theard, always wore a plaid orange jacket for stage appearances. There was a barn-like yowl to plaid, oddly aligned to flash, when worn before the footlights, and it was symptomatic of vaudeville trousers, going way back, such as those worn by Buck and Bubble, George Rowland, ("the Great Tramp Juggler"), and Stepin Fetchit. Sammy Davis Jr. had a real penchant for plaid jackets in the 1970s, which he wore with high seriousness. Richard Prior in the lunatic comedy *Which Way Is Up* (1977)—"I can't wait to get my hands on those big beautiful keys," Prior lecherously tells his pretty piano teacher—wears any number of crazy plaid jackets in each of the many roles he plays in that multi-persona format: Leroy, Charles Goodnight, and Rev. Lenox. It wasn't only young Tom Sawyer's trousers that were plaid in the original American Publishing Company book illustrations of Twain's *Adventures of Tom Sawyer.* It was the very same pattern on poor "Nigger Jim"'s hand-me-down shirt.

Lech Walesa, nerdishly—out of it, in a way—commonly wore plaid shirts. So did assassin James Earl Ray, the Kingston Trio, and Twiggy, the matchstick-thin model from the Sixties who looked cadaverously saucy in it. The Madras craze in the Sixties was in a very real sense a sort of plaid "religion." It is a pattern, plaid, that has always seemed highly becoming, even formally pretty, on the skirt uniforms of almost all Catholic schoolgirls, even their knee-socks. It is everywhere a staple of fashion and in its universality has been worn by everyone from Raggedy Ann and Andy dolls to John Lennon—who wore a plaid shirt on June 21, 1967, on his first professional gig with the Quarrymen—to the grimacing Vietcong prisoner, captured in Eddie Adams's notorious 1960s photograph, who was shot dead in the temple in broad daylight by the savage and revengeful South Vietnamese police chief, Nguyen Ngoc Loan. New York reporter Damon Runyon almost always wore a yellow plaid suit. Plaid is also, paradoxically, solid, in a no-nonsense way. It is interesting to note that novelist James Baldwin, along with folk singer Joan Baez, wore a plaid shirt at the starting point on the March to Selma in 1964. Was it because it seems germane to the outdoors in the way of walking?

Speaking of musicians, rock-and-roll pioneer Bill Haley and His Comets, "hep cats" all, usually regaled themselves in plaid. Bill himself, replete with spit curl, almost always wore plaid—and outlandish—dinner jackets, and he can still be seen so floridly adorned, thanks to videocassette, in the memorable London concert of February 6, 1957. Cornell Borchers wears a plaid red dress, with prim white collar, I might add, tinkling a piano for Rock Hudson in *Never Say Goodbye* (1956), a remake of *This Love of Ours* (1945).

Want a surprise? Bo Diddley wore a plaid tux jacket on several of his album covers! A classic Fifties pattern, it also reached into Seventies and Eighties musical styles. Plaid was the popular trademark, for example, of a once briefly popular group, the Bay City Rollers, just as it is for singer Rod Stewart, who often wears plaid as a sort of national emblem—he is a fanatical supporter of the Celtic F. C. football team. Singer Annie Lennox, another Scot, formerly with the Eurhythmics, during her great *In the Park* TV special in May 1996, wore a red plaid suit. One of my favorite musical moments can be seen in the sprightly Fifties film *By the Light of the Silvery Moon* (1953), the sequel to *On Moonlight Bay* (1951), starring Gordon Macrae and Doris Day, when she sensationally sings "I'll Forget You," wearing a tam and a plaid scarf.

Slugger Mickey Mantle wore a plaid jacket on the day that he was elected to the Baseball Hall of Fame in 1974. Dr. J (Julius Erving), after playing in the ABA with the Virginia Squires, wore a plaid jacket the day he signed with the New York Nets. Do you find that odd? At the start of his career, Elvis Presley, the King himself, was actually decked out in a plaid jacket the first time he appeared on TV's *The Ed Sullivan Show*, and so did the members of his backup quartet, the Jordanaires. And on March 24, 1958, Elvis arrived at the Memphis draft board modeling a loud plaid sports jacket over—yes!—a striped shirt. Big E was carrying nothing more than what the induction notice told aim to bring: a razor, a comb(!), a toothbrush, and only enough money to last two weeks. Meanwhile, Colonel Tom Parker, forever the business whore, was busily handing out to the tens of thousands of fans gathered there balloons stamped "King Creole," Elvis's most recent movie.

An important wing of rock music, by the way, was distinctly plaid-clad, most notably the Seattle "grunge" movement which, by way of a reverse-chic allusion to working class fashions, had become identified with this look, a real contrast to the Howdy Doody of yore, say, in his little faux-western shirts, all criss-crossed and prim. As to the appearance of plaid in the music world, David Bowie appeared looking mighty like a rube on the *Good Morning, America* show on March 30, 1998, heartily pushing his art books, sporting a retro waffle haircut—he looked off-puttingly prune-like, thin, homely—and wearing an open plaid shirt with an exposed white t-shirt.

Who can forget Johnny Rotten (John Lydon) of the Sex Pistols wearing that ludicrous, in-your-face plaid jacket while being interviewed by facile, face-pulling television interviewer Tom Snyder, on one of the most intractable interviews—and stupidest interviewers—in the history of television.

Plaid has had a cinematic history. Gloria Swanson wore a plaid bow on her head in one scene in *Sunset Boulevard* (1950), "a bit like those mother had me wear as a child," she later wrote in her autobiography, "a bit like the ones [Mack] Sennett bathing beauties wore." And yet it can be virile. Rossano Brazzi (because or his success with *South Pacific?*) looks sharp wearing a plaid short-sleeve shirt in *Three Coins in the Fountain* (1953). Steve Cochran as Nick courts Joan Crawford playing Ethel in *The Damned Don't Cry* (1950)—laughably, Crawford is in tears throughout the film—and wears a dorky plaid sports jacket in a club scene which gives him the look of a standup comedian. Even Rick Hudson looks natty in *The Lawless Breed* (1953), sporting a blue plaid shirt. We have mentioned Brian Donleavy and his full plaid shirt in *The Great McGinty*, making him appear a trifle World War II-ish and yet slightly swank and *raffiné*. Speaking of Brians, the Beatles' manager, Brian Epstein, wore plaid jackets all through their first visit to the United States in 1964. William Holden and William Bendix and virtually everybody else in the cast wear plaid in the forgettable film *The Streets of Laredo* (1949). Janet Gaynor wears a plaid blouse in *Ladies in Love* (1936), an amusing story of working-class girls in the grip of jittery romances. Full loud plaid suits and straw hats, along with bow ties and white bucks, are worn by Jack Oakie and John Payne in *Hello Frisco, Hello* (1943), a musical with Alice Faye and June Havoc set on San Francisco's Barbary Coast saloon belt. And as pushy Mama Rose Hovick, Gypsy Rose Lee's mother in the Broadway musical

Gypsy (1959), Ethel Merman looks flash in garish plain overcoats as full and boisterous and irrepressible as that rambunctious stage mother.

In *The Spoilers* (1956) Jeff Chandler and Rory Calhoun, although both wear hideous plaid jackets, manage nevertheless to seem fairly manly and mountainous and macho as they pursue Anne Baxter. Actually, Chandler's weird toilet-shaped head and eerie, almost subhumanly strange brontosonic nasality seem much more anomalous than the skunky brown and white mackinaw he wears all through the picture—not unlike the awful one Gary Cooper wears trying to impress Ruth Roman in the impossibly bad movie *Dallas* (1950), an ill-fitting blue plaid wide-lapeled Chesterfield that matches in repulsiveness his pair of white plaid—can you believe it?—pants, a sartorial horror in which both seem to be cut out of carpetbags, which incidentally is the theme of the movie.

Nick, the bartender in Frank Capra's *It's a Wonderful Life* (1946), memorably played by the suspicious, thuggish, nasal Sheldon Leonard, is wearing a crass plaid shirt in the scene where he angrily throws both George Bailey and Clarence the Angel ("Second Class") out of his bar, formerly "Martini's." In the lugubrious postwar domestic film *The Searching Wind* (1946), starring a mustachioed Robert Young, it seems as though every character in the movie wears a revolting plaid jacket—or clothes with incongruous dots and stripes! In *My Favorite Blonde* (1942), starring Bob Hope and Madeleine Carroll, both wear plaid jackets with abandon. In the scene where, escaping her pursuers, she meets Larry Haines in his green room, both leave the theater wearing howling-out-loud plaid coats. "I'm being followed by two men in black," says beautiful Madeleine, fearfully. With one of his typically predictable (over a lifetime) non-jokes, Hope replies, as if she is crazy, "Are you sure you don't mean two men in white?" Little Billy Barty, wearing a plaid Eton jacket, races around with a gaggle of midgets, all sporting jackets and hats of shouting Oz plaids in the cinematic turkey *Under the Rainbow* (1981), a tasteless tour de force dealing with spies, undercover agents, and dwarfs in a hotel during the filming of *The Wizard of Oz* (1939).

It is famously a young person's pattern, plaid is. Shirley Temple, in her early wonderful film *Bright Eyes* (1934), sings her classic "On the Good Ship Lollipop" wearing a cute little plaid number with matching underwear. And in *Rebecca of Sunnybrook Farm* (1938), the little moppet wears a darling short-sleeve plaid shirt and farmer overalls. Scout, the endearing little tomboy in *To Kill a Mockingbird* (1962), wears a perky short-sleeve plaid shirt that shouts small town. As we have seen, Leslie Caron in the film *Gigi* (1958) wears a red plaid dress as a young girl, which allows her to look elegant and innocent at the same time. Is it Paris that seems to impart to plaid such artistic cachet?

Painters seem to avoid plaid as a texture, as a visual alternative. One infrequently sees it in paintings. Henri Matisse, who in old age wore a plaid blanket over his legs, also kept a mohair plaid blanket on his bed that matched many of his favorite sweaters and cardigans. Although texture was his "thing," in only two of the master's paintings does he suggest plaid: *Interior with Dog/The Magnolia Branch*, where the little dog's blanket is plaid, and *The Dream*, the dreamer's blanket. Regarding art, by the way, in a famous meeting between Brigitte Bardot, France's supreme sex kitten, and Pablo Picasso, the great painter on that occasion ostentatiously wore—the photo is printed in Bardot's autobiography—a plaid shirt. Hard to believe? Not really. Picasso also loved blouses and bad, bold trousers shouting with Woolworthian stripes! He dared any sort of dress, plaid being a favorite.

What versatility in plaid! Edna St. Vincent Millay's poem "The Plaid Dress," an allegory in which the poet decides that she can never fully rid herself of her ingrained bad qualities, strangely turns the pattern of plaid into a kind of labyrinth. Low types and crumb-bums can even get away with it, as is proven in the film musical *Guys and Dolls* (1955), in which the chubby tout "Nicely Nicely" Johnson wears a cat-lap plaid jacket, as does his low-life bosom pal Benny Southstreet, who sports an electric blue one. There is a short story in Will Self's *Grey Area* (1996) entitled "Inclusion" in which a revolutionary new *anti-depressant drug*—yes, you read that correctly—becomes available in such "quality-enhanced" patterns as paisley and Stuart tartan! It is the identifiable pattern on virtually every brand of English shortbread and biscuit tin, toffee box, and Scotch whisky label on this planet. And a Scottish hairdresser named Melvin Wood, according to John May in *Curious Facts*, "created the world's first tartan hairstyle called 'The Kilt,' in twenty hours, using twenty-two colors—at a cost of $220." And remember? In Martin Scorsese's superb film *The King of Comedy* (1983), it is the secret password phrase used over the telephone (and perhaps in real life?) by comic Jerry Lewis, playing Jerry Langford who, tied up and being held captive by blackmailing loonies, tries to let his producer know that it is in fact he who is making the call and no one else. Jerry exasperatedly asks, "What's the second cameraman's favorite color?" The correct answer is of course, "Plaid."

In Welsh the word plaid means party, and the "*Plaid Cymru*" means "the party of Wales" and indicates the political party advocating an independent Wales within the European Union. In his poem "Nr. Oban," L. E. Sissman even uses the word to describe the rumpled, checkerboard fields of Scotland:

"Plaid Argyle fields here peter down and out
To seas replete with humpback hebrides,
Black, blue, slate, grey, steel, grey, French grey,
As they recede toward the falling night off-white
To windward."

I am convinced that even braided fish, which I have eaten at the very expensive restaurant Chanticleer on Nantucket, is plaid. It may very well have been born of the architecture of basketry, when you think about it, as indeed perhaps the original tartans of Scotland were. For all its simplicity and barn-big obviousness, however, plaid as a color is not all that commonly seen nowadays, at least when one is trying to look for examples of it or seeking noteworthy moments. I remember once complaining about the paucity of it in evidence. "The 1964 film *The Umbrellas of Cherbourg* was full of baroque wallpaper," replied Edward Gorey, munching a sandwich. "Does that help?"

Mr. Grumpy in Kiddiebookland
or
A Textbook Case of the Anti-Self

From all that I have read about, of, in, and by the illustrator Maurice Sendak, he is not and seems never to have been a very happy or contented individual, extraordinarily successful though he has been as a children's book artist, a particular denomination—and perhaps even a genre—that he personally disliked, but then again, as we all know, the world is not perfect, is it? Go no further than his somewhat egregious remark—he was referring to the late, lamented Jennie, his Sealyham terrier—"The love of my life is a dog." Much as I love animals, allow me to find that particular comment passingly strange.

"I have no faith in anything. To tell you the truth, I never have, much," Sendak confided to Fantagraphics editor Gary Groth in a 2011 interview. "I don't mind getting the hell out of here [by which he meant death]. I have had a successful life, a successful career. But, you know, it hasn't satisfied me. It's like there is something I did not get, I did not understand." This echoed a remark that Charles Dickens once made to his friend and biographer John

Forster: "I have never been able entirely to divest myself of the slight feeling that there was some person I never met in life, some corner I never turned." Groth temporizingly replied to Sendak, "Well, maybe you're too close to yourself." The artist's melancholy reply was, "Maybe I don't like myself." He paused. "That's as close as you can get."

Did Sendak lack faith? The joy of writing? Confidence that his writing and illustrations go a long way in lifting up the world? Could it be that was the source of his melancholy? Is the nature of his ontological disappointment the result of "nothing to believe in"? Is not the very nature of creation optimistic? Ancillary questions occur to me. Was his childhood miserable? Did he turn to art as a way of coping with an otherwise unhappy life? Does his art reflect his cynicism? What do his books and illustrations say about him? Do they throw light on his lack of faith? Does his art redeem his melancholy outlook or, instead, reflect it in ways that warrant further study? T. S. Eliot in his poem "Gerontion" addresses the hollowness in the modern world where secular or disbelieving people have replaced faith with art, where signs are falsely taken for wonders and the truly spiritual is ignored:

> In depraved May, dogwood and chestnut, flowering judas,
> To be eaten, to be divided, to be drunk
> Among whispers; by Mr. Silvero
> With caressing hands, at Limoges
> Who walked all night in the next room;
>
> By Hakagawa, bowing among the Titians;
> By Madame de Tornquist, in the dark room
> Shifting the candles; Fräulein von Kulp
> Who turned in the hall, one hand on the door.
>   Vacant shuttles

Weave the wind. I have no ghosts,
An old man in a draughty house
Under a windy knob.

After such knowledge, what forgiveness? Think now
History has many cunning passages, contrived corridors
And issues, deceives with whispering ambitions,
Guides us by vanities.

I have to admit that I have always been intrigued by the various dilemmas of disaffected people—their depression, their dark pessimism, the stark causes of their bleakness, their lack of—disbelief in—metaphysical or spiritual support, any hope of something that may provide a coping mechanism. I've always believed that Christopher Hitchens's atheistic fulminations and faithless intransigence was basically a career move. (I knew him and once invited him to go on a Trappist retreat with me, which he said he was willing to do, although it never came about.) In the end, Salman Rushdie's pointless and vulgar blasphemies against the Prophet Muhammed in *The Satanic Verses* turned out indeed to be a career move, the fatwa notwithstanding, and after all that hoopla died down that popular middlebrow writer has since become the darling of the New York City jet set, going to parties, dating socialites, etc.

Pessimism and despondency are connected to a refusal—a personal inability or failure—to take a wider view of humanity. A lack of vision pusillanimously follows the letter of the law, not the spirit. Susan Sontag has written, "Depression is melancholy, minus its charms—the animation, the fits."

Shockingly, even the so-called best of men, *leaders*, could be sour, cruel, and lamentingly bigoted. When the Reverend Billy Graham was asked what he thought about the Reverend Martin

Luther King Jr.'s remark in the "I Have a Dream" speech of August 1963 upon having declared that one day "little white children . . . will walk hand in hand with little Black children," the bloviating, rectitudinous evangelist with the perfect marcel of hair who not only transformed evangelical Christianity into a patriotic corporate entity but also never lost the strong Southern Baptist conviction that Our Lord and Savior favors the Republican Party, cynically replied, "Only when Christ comes again." Mahatma Gandhi, for whom alcohol, tobacco, spices and condiments, even of a vegetable kind, should be shunned—since he felt food should be taken not for its own sake but solely to preserve one's strength—boldly asserted that, as a good practicing Hindu, he would much prefer to see his wife and child starve sooner than give them chicken broth.

"This attitude is perhaps a noble one, but. . . it is inhuman," wrote George Orwell, addressing the subject in his essay, "Reflections on Gandhi" in *Partisan Review* (January 1949), going on to clarify,

> "The essence of being human is that one does not seek perfection, that one is sometimes willing to commit sins for the sake of loyalty, that one does not push asceticism to the point where it makes friendly intercourse impossible, and that one is prepared in the end to be defeated and broken up by life, which is the inevitable price of fastening one's love upon other human individuals. No doubt alcohol, tobacco and so forth are things that a saint must avoid, but . . . Many people genuinely do not wish to be saints, and it is probable that some who achieve or aspire to sainthood have never felt much temptation to be human beings If one could follow it to its psychological roots, one would, I believe, find that the

main motive for 'non-attachment' is a desire to escape from the pain of living, and above all from love, which, sexual or non-sexual, is hard work. But it is not necessary here to argue whether the other-worldly or the humanistic ideal is 'higher.' The point is that they are incompatible. One must choose between God and Man, and all 'radicals' and 'progressives,' from the mildest Liberal to the most extreme Anarchist, have in effect chosen Man."

"I don't want to belong to anything," Sendak has flatly stated. "I don't want to be anybody. I wish I could be disembodied. But it's only a body that's going to die and decay. That's all there is." While I suspect this constitutes a sort of end-of-life gloom, to find such a peevish and frankly despondent fellow illustrating bright, hopeful stories, quaint fables of innocence, even spending time making hand-made toys (as he did) can seem bewildering. I have come to see that Sendak also had a long memory and was frankly something of an injustice-collector. It is surprising, if not downright astonishing, to come to see an old man getting upset about greedy and mendacious uncles and aunts from his long distant past who, when he was a boy visiting, ate a lot of the family food! "I was very selfish as a child," he declared. "Uncles ate our food." How very peculiar! What an unexpected annoyance or grievance for an octogenarian to be airing, one cannot help but think. It burned a hole in his sleep. Anxiety over food in the world of psychiatry is, from all I have read—although I find most of that business quackery—a *topos* of the Great Depression. The crisis does not abate, apparently. I know several other people roughly of Sendak's age who growing up in the late 1920s/early 1930s and having suffered deprivation along those lines have remained chronically food conscious, tend to be penurious, and talk lots about cooking.

It is significant to me indeed that three heroes that Sendak compulsively pointed to in his life were Van Gogh, Blake, and Goya—all three of whom were spiritual people, while they were also artists.

Let me add that I do not find it at all odd that a conflicted or sour, disaffected individual would turn to writing and illustrating colorful fables such as *Where the Wild Things Are, Outside Over There,* or *Higglety Pigglety Pop!* It is, if anything, likely. The poet W. B. Yeats believed that writers strive to—determinedly set out to—find their *complete* selves through art by psychologically presenting an anti-self in their work—a projection of another side of themselves—to achieve full disclosure. They present masks as opposed to their real faces in an attempt to complete the full plenitude of who they are. Yeats logically therefore asserts that the poet Dante who wrote of *spiritual* things was by dint of that a *sensualist*, that John Keats who wrote about *pleasant* and happy things was at bottom a *sad*, suffering young man.

According to Yeats's psychological theory, it would be entirely fitting and not at all paradoxical to find a discontented or disagreeable artist such as Sendak writing endearing children's books, simply because to the poet it is a way of exercising his need in seeking his opposite to be "realized."

They are not children's books, by Sendak's repeatedly grumpy estimates. He was frankly more adamant about what his books are not than what in fact they are. "I have never written a children's book," he grandly if peculiarly pronounced more than once but did so, one gathers, in varying moods. His books, strictly speaking, are moral fables, in my opinion. At the same time, they are also complaints, disquisitions on human disappointment, candid expressions of anger, existential cries about crises, and, indeed, *children's books.* "Why do you write poetry?" T. S. Eliot was once asked. His reply was, "To get the existential burden off my shoulders." Why would that not apply to any artist, the short-tempered Sendak included? If Sendak's objurgations speak of anything, it is surely of his many insufferable burdens. I believe all Sendak's books are phenomenological and point directly to his personal experience.

Remember that the original Geppetto in Carlo Collodi's *Le avventure di Pinocchio* (1883) "had a very bad temper," was a curmudgeon, and "could become a wild as a beast" when the boys of the neighborhood mocked him for the yellow wig he wore, and only wants to transfigure a chunk of wood into a marionette "to go around the world, to earn [his] crust of bread and cup of wine."

Where the Wild Things Are (1963) is a book about rage, among other things, and while I deplore falling prey to what is called the "intentional fallacy," even if to make a point, it would be absurd in the light of Sendak's autobiographical remarks over the years to pretend that this story or any of his stories are unaligned to the artist's own life. I concur with Francis Spufford when he suggests in *The Child That Books Built* (2002) that this book is "one of the very few picture books to make an entirely deliberate, and beautiful, use of the psychoanalytic story of anger." I would like to add parenthetically that it has been my experience in life—and I feel this is apposite to a discussion of *Wild Things*—that no gay man has an uncomplicated relationship with his mother. He may hate her, he may adore her, he may condemn or coddle her, but she always figures in his life in a crucial way. The bonding is never simple, I dare say. I am no psychologist but in this popular fable, which, in the words of Selma G. Lanes in *The Art of Maurice Sendak*, is a "blend of menace and make believe," there is a distinctly graphic subtext of mother love as well as mother hate, box it about though you will. Mischief-making Max, a child of four or five, has been banished to his bedroom with nothing to eat. He is angry. His mother has called him a "wild thing," and he says to her, "I'll eat you up." With closed eyes, he almost inflates, balloon-wise, virtually to will himself to enter a fictive forest where he is delivered by boat to a place *Where the Wild Things Are*, a bunch of bizarre big-headed unblinking saucer-eyed loonies with overbite and menacing horns and claws. It is a fugue-dream, borne of a muffled, displaced fury and surely no small sense of spite, one of the indispensable emotional tools available to children and commonly employed. While the book is quite obviously an escape fantasy, it is also a candid portrayal of the acts of sulking and vindictive acting-out. Children adore stories of the senses. Being deprived of comfort, only to get it at the end—facing cold and alienation, only to be warm again and, lo, as if by magic restored to a semblance of solace and sympathy.

It is often rash and frankly unproductive as far as literary criticism goes to make an oversimplifying one-to-one correspondence with a creative artist and his own creations, and the temptation is trying to do so, but Maurice Sendak was always among the first to go on record as to tell us what informed his books and why. He also never bothered to deny the darkness in or around him or that he was saturnine. "I have to learn to live life, just enjoy it," he ironically remarked to his friend Tony Kushner over the telephone—this account is recorded in Kushner's book *The Art of Maurice Sendak*—but immediately shouted, "I'm screaming at my enlarged prostate [and here he screams in a really unearthly voice] JUST SHUT THE FUCK UP!!!"

Reading through both Lanes and Kushner retrospectives gives us a portrait of an extremely caustic Maurice Sendak. It is there in his books, as well. He was fussy. He was angry. There was much of the crotchety, crabby, irascible Geppetto in the man, let's face it. He was intolerant. He was antisocial. He felt ignored. He goes into excessive tirades about inconsequentialia, fussily registering dislikes for things like noise, the actor Alec Baldwin ("a fat-faced fuck"), and, yes—to a degree—children. "Goys" he seemed to envy and darkly to dislike, both. Kushner tells us that he hated New York at Christmas. "The Rockefeller Center tree summons up in him an empathetic rage," Kushner observes. At one point, Kushner tells the artist that he wants to come up to see him in Connecticut. "Great," replies Sendak, "we can dance a kazatzkah." "What kind of dance is that?" asks Kushner." Sendak explains, "A kazatzkah is the Dance of Death." "Sounds good. Do you know the steps?" "Do I know them?" shouts Sendak. "I know those steps in every notch, every noodle, every nerve cell! Of course I know them! I've been rehearsing them all my life!" Along with much hoopla and delight, one can also find reversals, setbacks, fear, cruel apprehension, and metaphysical fret in Sendak's books. It is in many ways an art of displeasure and distinct discontent.

Childhood plagued Sendak. "Childhood was a nightmare, truly a nightmare," the artist said of his own childhood. "It got better as I was leaving school." He lamented, "I was always, like, a downer. Never heaving with joy." CBS Mike Wallace, the successful television journalist of *60 Minutes*, former game show host, actor and media personality (also, admittedly, a lifelong depressive) felt very much the same. He specifically attended the University of Michigan in order to be as far away as he could from his humorless and domineering mother, Zina, according to Peter Rader's biography *Mike Wallace*. Both were Jews, both scowling children of the Great Depression, and both driven madly to succeed. "Maurice is not an observant Jew," writes Kushner, "but he is deeply Jewish. Like most Jews, he is shadowed always by the Holocaust. Relatives of his who didn't make it to America died in the camps. In much of his work, obeisance is made to these ghosts. Memory is enlisted in the name of putting their unhappy souls at peace, in the name of placating the unquiet dead."

Sendak's hatred for his own childhood is a paradox his illustrating vocation seemed to try to retrieve. He once told the great illustrator Art Spiegelman, who recounts it in his *MetaMaus*, "'People say, "Oh, Mr. Sendak, I wish I were in touch with my childhood self, like you!' As if it were all quaint and succulent, like Peter Pan. Childhood is cannibals and psychotics vomiting in your mouth!" In many sufferers, the hollow echoes of early misery never subside. A concluding stanza in A. E.'s poem "Germinal" goes:

> "In ancient shadows and twilights
> Where childhood had strayed,
> The world's great sorrows were born
> And its heroes made
> In the lost childhood of Judas,
> Christ was betrayed."

After his mother, Klara, disappeared from his life, dying from cancer in December 1908—his truculent and disapproving father Alois had died three years earlier—a morbid, disturbed, and solitary Hitler left for Vienna. In a significant sense, he never had a home again. Sendak faced similarly empty horrors, it seems. A.E.'s poem concludes, "A door opens, a breath, a voice / From the ancient room, Speaks to him now. Be it dark or bright / He is knit with his doom."

An immigrant's child and poor, Sendak did not attend college. His early life was a series of dead ends. He was scarred with reversals and recounted related stories with occasional fury. Kushner writes, "Being a self, alone, committed to one-ness"—Sendak like Kushner was gay—"whether through predilection or through a conviction of the necessity of the condition of aloneness, is a part of what Harold Bloom has termed Jewish interiority." "Jewish interiority." That sounds deep. Is *chutzpah* interior? What group of people, what ethnicity, has no interiority, may I ask? I don't think one has to go very far to find psychological terms for Sendak. He was alone, an *isolato*. He was inverted in more ways than one. He never married. He had no family. There is a pronounced anti-family motif in gay culture and much gay literature.

In virtually every one of his avant garde films, for example—*Female Trouble, Desperate Living, Serial Mom, Hairspray,* etc.— director John Waters, aka "The Pope of Trash," paints a portrait of a dysfunctional family. Same with his books. It is the overwhelming theme of virtually all of his work, efforts middlingly subversive with a small S, not that I feel frankly exercised about it. There is no question, however, that queer family values undermine—or you may prefer the word "rethink," if that softens the blow for you—the nuclear family.

Sendak lived with a partner for 50 years, let me add, which when in the instance he spoke of being alone, which seemed to be often, a complexity—one far beyond me to explain—arises. I can only conclude that there is something of narcissism and a sense of victimization in his claims of being a solitary, but maybe it is rash of me to judge. It has been proven that he had strong opinions that tended to alienate people. He was a complainer—or *kvetcher,* if you insist. He suffered infuriating aloneness. Forget Harold Bloom's rosy existentialism. The long and short of it is that Sendak felt that on many fronts he has been robbed and defiled. To read any interview with Sendak is to have to stare into the face of a wild thing—a true malcontent.

"Kiddiebookland" became Maurice Sendak's recriminational—and reductive—word for where unkind critics place him. In an interview with Walter Lorraine, he complained, "It is next to Neverneverville and Peterpanburg. It's that awful place we've been squeezed into because we're children's book illustrators or children's book writers . . . How infuriating and insulting, when a serious work is considered only a trifle for the nursery!" That is not rage? Misspent fury? I have no doubt that many if not all book "illustrators" feel marginalized to a degree, pinned and wriggling on a wall to a simple-seeming genre, having to suffer the inferior feeling that they are held as mere daubers, Daumiers not Delacroixs. N. C. Wyeth felt that way quite often. So did James Montgomery Flagg and Norman Rockwell.

Maurice Sendak won the Caldecott Medal in 1964 with the claim that he altered the understanding of children's dreams, although I never thought so for a minute—there was no rebellion or threats or grotesquerie in the old fables? It was a great honor, nevertheless. But he was not assuaged, alleviated, or appeased. Was it because he was age 36 and felt fame came to him too late? No, it was his *profession* that so piqued and irritated him. Dr. Suess had already addressed the subject in a *New York Times* piece on November 16, 1952:

"There are many reasons why an intelligent man should never ever write for children. Of all professions for a man, it is socially the most awkward. You go to a party, and how do they introduce you? The hostess says, 'Dr. Seuss, meet Henry J. Bronkman. Mr. Bronkman manufactures automobiles, jet planes, battleships and bridges. Dr. Seuss . . . well, he writes the sweetest, dear, darlingest little whimsies for wee kiddies!'. . . Wherever a juvenile writer goes, he is constantly subjected to humiliating indignities. When asked to take part in a panel discussion along with other members of the writing fraternity, he is given the very end seat at the table . . . always one seat lower than the dusty anthologist who compiled *The Unpublished Letters of Dibble Sneth, Second Assistant Secretary of Something-or-Other under Polk.*"

But for all that Dr. Seuss happily understood and heartily accepted the dimensions of his art. "The thing that's so hard to explain to our friends is that most of us who specialize in writing humor for children have cracked the adult field and, having cracked it, have decided definitely that we prefer to uncrack it. We are writing for the so-called Brat Field by choice. For, despite the fact this brands us as pariahs, despite the fact this turns us into literary untouchables, there is something we get when we write for the young that we can never get in writing for you ancients. . . . Have you ever stopped to consider what has happened to your sense of humor?" What redeemed the time for Dr. Seuss—for what he felt should serve to buoy up all (his phrase) "maverick humorists"—was laughter, the plenitude of joy that he brought in such full abundance to his young readers.

I gather Sendak believed he was something of a thinker, a cultural originator, a philosopher, who knows, maybe another Dostoevsky. At one point, he ruefully told Gary Groth about his feelings on this subject. "I remember a sentence in the *New York Times* years ago. There was a show on Norman Rockwell, and it said, 'Is Norman Rockwell a real artist or *merely* an illustrator?' And I took from that I am merely an illustrator, and I should not look further, that's all I could have."

I am inclined to believe that just as Sendak tended to swing wildly and unpredictably between arrogance and self-hatred, he also veered from pride in his work to a kind of dissatisfaction, even revulsion, for all the "adorable" artwork that he has done over the years—posters, CD covers, book jackets, and colorful illustrations—which embody what the late Truman Capote in another context referred to as a "case of the cutes." I do remember that my friend, the great wood-engraver Fritz Eichenberg, who mocked all those kitschy gnome books that came out in the 1980s, did find some of Sendak's work sugar-coated and desperate to please, all those *endearing* monsters like the pop-eyed one in "New York is Book Country, 10th Anniversary" poster from 1988, more like the plushies a little girl would take to bed to cuddle than a creature jumping into the midst of one of your nightmares.

Kushner is correct when he says Sendak's realm "is a world balanced between sturdy, bourgeois warmth, a summery coziness, and shadow ineffability." He refers to Sendak's "clouds of ambiguity." I discern no real ambiguity—well, yes, in the "songs of innocence" next to the "songs of experience" department, certainly—but if I do I don't really make much of it, simply because that is what curmudgeons are all about, the bittersweet. I do find a good bit of ferocity and a kind of unsparing need for what is called counterhegemony in him, however—that crucial need to challenge the status quo, to dare to go just a bit too far, to subvert the bourgeois way of thinking. (Let the one example of Sendak's refusal to hide Mickey's penis in *In the Night Kitchen* stand for the many.) As I say, I find a predictable sense of self-hatred—call it regret, if you choose—for much of the "quaint" work that he has shoveled out to make a living. I also sense sorrow, wistfulness, much forced magic, a not always credible world of delight, and a lot of confused mythology in almost all of Sendak's drawings and delineations in the same way I do in the work of the lugubrious painter Mark Rothko, whose subtly, melancholic rectangularly regions of color—color fields that so often reveal (conceal?) a hollow sense of despair, even horror—seem to me to be desperate, virtually stains of woe, all redolent of the funerals and victimization.

He had no religious faith. His father's death also led him to sever his ties with religion. After mourning his father's death for a full year at a local synagogue, the painter felt depleted and hopeless, thwarted and angry, and vowed never to set foot in a synagogue again. On February 25, 1970, Oliver Steindecker, Rothko's assistant, found the artist lying dead on the kitchen floor in front of his sink, covered in blood. He had overdosed on barbiturates and cut an artery in his right arm with a razor blade. There was no suicide note. He was 66 years old.

Consider Sendak's *Outside Over There* (1981), which concerns a young girl named Ida, who must rescue her baby sister after the child has been stolen by goblins. It is disclosed that Ida harbors feelings of jealousy and resentment towards this little sibling, for whom she is largely responsible while their father is away. When her little sister is kidnapped through the nursery window by mysteriously robed goblins, Ida resolves to rescue her, embarking on a fantastic adventure. Initially, Ida is easily distracted from her goal, nearly passing by her sister as she becomes absorbed in the magic of the strange quest. Ultimately, she succeeds in rescuing her baby sister, however, and so then returns home, now fully committed to the care of her sister until their father also returns from his absence. Where exactly is the *father*? We are never told. This book, which in its enigmas elicits terror, was written by Sendak 18 years after *Where the Wild Things Are* appeared. It draws heavily and quite specifically on the Lindbergh kidnapping case in 1932, where the famous flyer's baby was stolen from its crib through a window accessed by a ladder, and one of the illustrations of the lost baby is quite specific in being a deliberate portrait of the infant Charles Lindbergh Jr., who was later found murdered. The theme of a protective sister is drawn from Sendak's own childhood, when his older sister was his primary caregiver and devoted playmate.

The encounters that nine-year-old Ida undergoes—the ice baby melting, the shipwrecks in the sea, the haunted night sky, and the underworld—are, as existential face-offs, far and quite vividly and offhandedly different from standard children's book fare, simply because in a very real sense they are too *possible*. Could the same be said of *Rumplestiltskin* or *The 500 Hats of Bartholomew Cubbins* or *The Emperor's New Clothes* or *The Glass Coffin*? The answer is definitely no. While it may be asserted that *Outside Over There* teaches that children can master various feelings—anger, boredom, and fear— and come to grips with reality, is that the point of children's books one may ask? Paradoxically, the more outlandish the story is in children's books, the more palatable it is for them to digest. Modern psychiatry seeks for its patients to recognize reality. That is psychiatry's main goal, I gather.

But is *coping* with life a matter for children? Is that an early and pressing need in the lives of young fairy-tale readers? When playwright Tony Kushner points out in *The Art of Maurice Sendak: 1981 to the Present* that the eerie illustrations "refuse to reassure," how comforting is that? Do children read books for epistemological verities? Doses of reality? The heartbreak of real life? The "dis-ease" Kushner alludes to is very much in these drawings. "Children in danger have always preoccupied Sendak," Kushner observes. The very same can perhaps be said of the ominous books and stories of Edward Gorey, whose whimsy however has a lighter, far more adult touch. The macabre text and illustrations of his notorious parody *The Gashlycrumb Tinies* is surely the *locus classicus* of the truism about children and danger. ("P is for Prue trampled flat in a brawl," "R is Rhoda consumed by a fire," "K is for Kate who was struck with an axe," etc.) but Gorey's books—lurid, morbid, gruesome, and comically dreadful—are like an expensive and superb dry wine, strictly for adults.

I was not surprised to learn that Sendak was gay. It is a tic of gay writers, if not a theme, as I say, to satirize as ridiculous the kind of "model" or nuclear families we once saw in *Ozzie and Harriet* or *Father Knows Best*. I do not mean to generalize but I tend to find a gay subtext in many of their stories where methodically, thematically, the nuclear family is repeatedly subverted, not to sound like the idiotic, tub-thumping right-wing Republican evangelical. It was the case with so many other gay writers: Tennessee Williams, William Burroughs, James Purdy, Gore Vidal, even certainly with Edward Gorey, and, again, John Waters's movies, which are to me only randomly amusing and virtually nothing less than case histories of bunty, dysfunctional mother-father-children families. As I say, to me it is a gay "hobby-horse," satirizing norms. It invests the homosexual world with something like comfort to witness wacky families out of sync, in crisis, illogical, at loggerheads.

Weirdly, Sendak's drawings "seem to menace the very text they're meant to illustrate, illuminating if not igniting the ambiguities of every sentence," as Kushner observes. He is correct, and while the terrors in his pages provide a scary "thrill" to readers, as do the many stories from the age of German romanticism to which this picture book *Outside* culturally refers, no one would deny that many of the turns can be traced to the dark disposition of 50-year-old Sendak.

Higglety Pigglety Pop! or, There Must Be More to Life (1967) Sendak's thaumaturgical dream poem/novel/play/whatever is unclassifiable, although Kushner describes it as belonging to "the select library of essential art about death and grief.," adding that it is a story in which he—Sendak, that is—"mines his psyche and soul for his art." Here the heroine of the book is Jennie, the Sealyham terrier. It is a cute touch, and consequential, for the book is in fact a tribute to that revered dog of his who died back in 1968, an event that for a while badly crushed Sendak's spirit.

"I was desperately in need of a dog," he confessed in 1953 at the age of 25, and this dog served the purpose of becoming his true friend, his—one gets the distinct impression from one's reading—*sole* friend. What can one say of someone whose animal pet plays such a unique role? It is at once a revered condition and yet a mockable one, as I have often thought, for I have neighbors whose pet dogs are the mainstays of their very lives, their virtual offspring. "These are our sons," say a neighbor of mine, who actually makes a chair for the dogs at the table—I am not making this up—and their annual Christmas card features a photograph the animals arrayed with festive red stocking hats! It is devoted, pitiful, caring, insane, merciful, kind, wistful, cheerful, depressing, and crack-pated all at the same time.

I find that all of Sendak's stories come in on a slant, all of them, cobbled together from various odd sources—pop culture, historical sources, music, and long-held childhood memories, and I see a good deal borrowed from Edward Gorey in the Mother Goose Theater production pages of *Higglety*, as well—and it would be foolish to deny that they are often at intellectual variance with what we have normally come to associate with standard children's fables. This particular story is especially strange. We are shown how Jennie becomes nursemaid to a human baby—an angry, unpleasant baby, in fact—that has been abandoned by its parents. The dog saves the baby from the menacing Downstairs Lion and at the end brightly comes to star in the book's grand finale in the Mother Goose Theatre's rendition of an American nursery rhyme by Samuel Griswold Goodrich, "Higglety Pigglety Pop." Jennie has to prove herself in the world of art outside of her master's house and finds fulfillment "by fully utilizing her twin talents for acting and eating," according to Kushner—that is, eating mops made of salami. As I say, Sendak is nothing if not oblique. A milk wagon conveys Jennie to fantasyland. Why a milk wagon? Why a dog heroine, for that matter? Why an abandoned baby? Why an angry, unpleasant baby? Why does the dog never return to her master? Why the title for the book that was another's poem?

"Why is there a dead child in so many of your books? Always a chagrined mother?" Sendak exasperatedly asked, repeating— echoing—questions that he himself was repeatedly asked. He harrumphed with his standard, not particularly elucidating response, "Because that's the way it is." That is the very answer every incompetent if not bullying parent always gave to a questioning child as an excuse for an explanation, and it works no more for me now than when first I heard it.

It is a fitful response, always inadequate.

But grizzling fits Sendak. It accommodates his unsettling books. It fits to a degree the pen-and-ink illustrations which look like steel engravings. Severity applies to Sendak in many instances. It certainly applies to the man who once said—metaphysically wailed in a sense—"I am discontented. I want something I do not have. There must be more to life than having everything." This is close to sentiments felt by Mike Wallace, to whom I have already alluded. As I've said, during much of Wallace's life he suffered depression. There is no shortage of Jewish curmudgeons. Lorenz Hart. Al Goldstein. Lennie Bruce. Bert Lahr. Sandra Bernhard, Bert Lahr, Don Rickles, Bernie Madoff, Stanley Kubrick, Mark Rothko, Stooge Mo Howard, Norman Mailer, Dominic Strauss-Kahn, Jack Warner, Woody Allen, TV's Bill Maher and Jon Stewart—they are all of them in one obvious way or another loud cranks, grouches, sourpusses, crosspatches, noise-making scoffers, skeptics, and pessimists.

Curmudgeons "R" Us! I have read and heard from actor friends of mine that the Hollywood performer Danny Kaye was supposedly cynical and very hard to get along with. The odious singer, comedian, and monstrously arrogant "toastmaster-general" George Jessel as well. Cranks, kvetching grumpuses, crosspatches, old trouts! Savage Jed Harris (born Jacob Horowitz in Lviv, Austria-Hungary), the renowned Austrian-American theater producer and director. Harry Cohn, the pooh-bah of Columbia Pictures. Surly Walter Winchell, the gossip columnist. Lenny Bruce. Phil Ochs. Don Hewitt (born Horowitz). Totie Fields (born Sophie Feldman). The unfunny stand-up Jewish comedians Louis C.K. (born Louis Alfred Székely) and Lewis Black. I don't know, throw in Ebenezer Scrooge and Ms. Clara Peller ("Where's the Beef?"), if you'd like. There was a deep unsympathetic flintiness to the way they saw the world. Many of these may seem to you harmless showbiz carpers or cavillers, but many were (or are) sour, despised, and ruinous cynics.

No, Sendak was not exactly Captain Handshakes. I believe that in his despairing world view he looked to fantasy while secretly trusting that reason—or at least the amount of it he could call upon for solace—was superior to mysticism/religion and that egotism had a truer morality than altruism. But who of us can thrive by what we ignore or hope to live by what we despise?

The artist/writer's lack of faith as a redeeming virtue calls to mind for me the irreconcilable contradictions of the pugnacious writer Ayn Rand. A short, rude, homely, maniacally right-wing endocrine-near-dwarf, born Alisa Zinovyevna Rosenbaum, she cultivated acolytes to praise her only because she was so unwinning a human being. She despised much if not most of the world she saw and there was little beyond her own imperious theories of selfishness-as-a-virtue that she didn't deplore. Teeming with unsophisticated peasant biases, she was notorious for her mean-spirited and turgid harangues, liked to see herself as an ardent custodian of truth, although in her own life she had a hard time abiding too much of her manufactured "reality." She claimed to appeal constantly to reason—"Objectivism"—but was a bundle of hideous emotions. "Emotion," wrote Lisa Duggan in her book on Rand, *Mean Girl and the Culture of Greed*, writes, "had brought down the house of reason." She was a cynical amphetamine addict. A relentless and hectoring abuse was her go-to language, a vocabulary of outrageous spleen. "The unifying threads are meanness and greed," Duggan writes of her subject, "and the spirit of the whole hodgepodge is Ayn Rand." She hated children, the undeserving weak, sex with pregnancies, gay people, immigrants (she was one), family, church, and was a rabid advocate of abortion rights, fetishized the importance of making money and raw capitalism. On March 6, 1982, at her funeral, her floral wreath was shaped like a dollar sign.

When he was only eight years old, the once popular singer Al Jolson (born Asa Yoelson) saw his mother die in childbirth. Biographer Herbert G. Golden in *Jolson: The Legend Comes to Life* believes that the traumatic sight defined Jolson's life, leaving him forever "an emotional child . . . a self-assured braggart who was terrified of being alone, a sentimentalist . . . who made life miserable for most of those around him, and a lothario who chased, conquered, and in turn ignored young women." Jolson was rarely happy. A megalomaniac, he would turn the faucets on in whatever green room he found himself in order to avoid hearing applause for other entertainers.

As I say, Sendak repeatedly went on record as having no faith. The flight into his own private mythologies, by which I mean the subjects of his books—both text and drawings—forces one to speculate as to the whys and wherefores of his seemingly deep unhappiness and to wonder why such a condition exists, especially in an artist who so often enters the world of innocence and guilt.

There is a lack of acceptance in many such angry, unappeasable, unsatisfied people. It makes me wonder about some of the reflections offered by the Russian religious and political philosopher Nicolai Berdyaev (1874–1948) about the spiritual conditions of Jews without faith. I understand there are many Jews with faith, understand me. I am addressing here the subject of Jews without faith, and Sendak—and the man kept repeating this—happened to be one of them. Berdyaev addressed the subject in *The Meaning of History* (1923), notably in chapter six. He sees the Jew as he finds the modern Jewish spirit, in conflict and inner turmoil from the pressure of having to be a success on this earth and in this life, which Berdyaev finds an immanent position as opposed to transcendent. He finds the Jew existentially confined, as it were, having to live within the limits of possible experience or knowledge.

Berdyaev believed that Jews perpetually live with a crisis of faith, that they are necessarily terrestrial in outlook. Where the Jew feels he has to succeed in this world, for Berdyaev the Christian is all along encouraged by Christ in the Gospels to have poverty of spirit, to accept suffering, to have faith in Him, and to hope to be with Him in Paradise. The Jew suffers in ways that the Christian does not, for, according to Berdyaev, the Jew is often at variance with himself, in a secular and earthly prison, where his comfort, never mind his identity, is precarious. To Berdyaev the Jew in the way he interprets the world without the Christian Gospel finds it very difficult to know which way to turn in this world regarding not only faith but the whole nature of redemption. It is Berdyaev's belief that any potential disposition to assume the religion of the majority is countered by the Jew's unbudging, almost inborn, natural, understandable reaction against doing so, all the while meeting prejudice which forces the consequent tendency to cling to his own group for whatever safety it may afford but which in many instances leaves him an isolato.

"After such knowledge, what forgiveness?" T. S. Eliot asks in "Gerontion." "History has many cunning passages,/contrived corridors and issues,/deceives with whispering ambitions,/Guides us by vanities." Indeed, that is what history does, and Sendak not only had that knowledge but knew—had experienced—much of that history and had been burnt by it.

The philosopher Berdyaev believed that man in the modern world has witnessed the process of dehumanization in all phases of culture and of social life, that a savagery and cruelty is characteristic of the age, an amazing fact since it has taken place—World War I, World War II, the Armenian Genocide, the Holocaust, etc.—at the so-called peak of human refinement, at least in terms of history and the advancement of culture. Berdyaev particularly blamed national passion for tearing the world apart and forcing the destruction of European culture. He lamented that the Christian-humanistic process of unifying seemed to be disappearing. Germany's aggression proved to him that nationalism was a kind of polytheism, incompatible with monotheism. Nationalism turns nationality into a supreme and absolute value to which all life is subordinated—this was idolatry for him. Nationalism involves not only love of one's own, but hatred of other nations, and hatred is a stronger motivation than love. Why did Sendak never find the satisfaction he needed in life?

Almost Salieri-like, Sendak told Groth of the younger fellow artist Tomi Ungerer, "He was everything I would have wished I could be as a human being. But I was not." He described Ungerer flatteringly as a "mad man, crazy, and rash from the word go." He was "refreshing" to Sendak, "inspired." "And this goy from Alsace-Lorraine shoots up to the top, marries a girl with a beautiful house, divorces her, marries somebody else, has beautiful children, everybody knows him. How I didn't kill him is amazing, OK?" There is much levity here.

But there is also some truth.

Was Sendak a tormented Jew?

For all the fugues, flights, and fantasy in his books, was he himself immanent? Non-transcendent? Terrestrially bound?

I have every reason to believe that he meant every word of it when he declared, not without enmity, "I used to think if I get through my life without killing somebody, I will be a lucky man."

Magpies
or
"Only Collect"

Collecting, first of all, deals with the assembly mentality. Overreaching. Is it creative? Something can be said for that, surely. Is it done as an end in itself? In instances, no doubt. It is also often pursued out of greed, boredom, monomania, and in a good many cases probably the deep ontological need to multiply oneself. It goes without saying that the element of control is deeply involved. Psychiatrists might add that it is also a substitute—in the face of increasing dehumanization and the loss of new frontiers—for the hunter-gatherer compulsion natural to man. (FDR, for instance could throw nothing away—his library, after he died, was found to contain hundreds of thousands of Christmas cards, every one he ever received.) Isn't there a special link between a costermonger and his pippins, Ford and his cars, Hitler and his phalanxed troops at Nuremberg? There's a type of person who simply likes to see things lined up in a row. Is it neurotic? No question. ("I *have* to have it," said Mr. Grapplewitch, drooling, as he fondled the rare and exquisite piece.) We've all heard at one time or another of the guy who has acres filled with rubber tires, the man with the largest ball of string on Earth, the postman who built a palace entirely out of bottle caps.

Brother Timothy, of the Christian Brothers Vineyards, owned 1,800 corkscrews. The late Boston Celtics president Red Auerbach collected 400 letter openers (Tip O'Neill collected them, too). Ken Kercheval (J. R.'s nemesis on the television show *Dallas*) had 1,000 pieces of pressed glass. Liquor distributor Michael Roux had 2,000 perfume atomizers. Houston house painter Victoria Herberta had 7,000 soda bottles. Stanley Block had 4,000 marbles: cat's eyes, aggies, Akro imperials. Mary and John Mikovisch of Houston had 50,000 beer cans. Dr. Neill Macauley collected 6,000 dental artifacts. Sheriff John F. Nichols of Oakland County, Michigan, had a collection of more than 300 porcine replicas, including a 60-pound concrete pig and a litter of piglets on his desk. Dr. James Beal collected 2 million sea shells. Henry Stiffel, a parking-meter salesman, collected just about all of the parking-meter models ever made. Art Turco from California had more than half a million 45 rpm records. (But Val Shively from Haverton, Pennsylvania, had a collection of the rarest and most valuable.)

Designer Tommy Steele had 5,000 matchbooks. Writer Leon Dixon had 1,000 bicycles. Illinois lawyer Francis Monek had 4,000 canes. Bartender Charles Lang had 501,534 jigsaw-puzzle pieces. San Francisco tattoo artist Lyle Tuttle (who has put his mark on Peter Fonda, Joan Baez, and J. Paul Getty III) collected 400 tattoos—by tattoo artists from all over the world—all over his own body.

As well as paintings by her friends Picasso and Matisse, Gertrude Stein collected buttons (and wrote a book called *Tender Buttons*). Elvis Presley collected sheriff's badges and had "arresting power" in Denver and Memphis. (Since he never returned a gift someone sent him, he also had a huge number of teddy bears.) Oscar Wilde collected blue willow china. James Michener collected Japanese prints (he wrote a book about them). Cartoonist Charles Addams collected medieval armor. Maurice Sendak, writer and illustrator, collected figures of Mickey Mouse from the 1930s, those "rigidly bound," as he says, to the first decade of his life, "with that face, that completely nuts look of fiery intense animation." Woody Allen collects American folk art, and Elton John 45 rpm records. Steve McQueen was a very serious collector of wind-up things: pinball machines, toy cars, mechanical thingamajigs.

Frank Sinatra went in, passionately, for toy trains. Basil Saffer, director of the Museum of Ancient Brick, spent much of his time collecting—guess what? Right. It's a very serious business. Often, an obsession. Sometimes a vice. Vivian Greene, the wife of novelist Graham Greene, was both a collector of, and expert on, dollhouses, which in their case virtually explained the breakup of their marriage.

Child prodigy William Sidis (1898–1944)—a mathematical wizard who entered Harvard University at the tender age of 11 and had an IQ estimated at 50 to 100 points higher than Einstein's, the highest ever recorded or estimated—collected streetcar transfers. He continued to publish transfer-collecting newsletters, to correspond with other enthusiasts, and to run a "transfer deposit bank" called the Transfer-X-Change, whereby collectors could make deposits and withdrawals through the mail. His own collection consisted of over 2,000 items. Several other correspondents claimed collections as large as 5,000 transfers, representing over a thousand cities.

Collecting can frequently give way to serious mania. Charles Lindbergh was so beleaguered by trophy-seekers that he could not send his shirts to the cleaners and expect to get them back. Franz

Liszt's cigar butts were snatched up in the street, and his chair seat on one occasion was cut out and preserved as a relic by an admirer. Many collectors are pilferers—candid thieves who pillage hotels, dining cars, and steamships of linen, soaps, ashtrays, and silver. Depredations. Outlawry without penalty. And it has given way to madness. A 15-year-old high school boy from New York, with otherwise perfect deportment, found his valued stamp collection missing only the rare penny orange Mauritius, worth $20,000, and became so unstrung in the knowledge that he could never possess it that he got a gun, went out and proceeded to hold up the shop. Thwarted in his hope, the average collector usually takes defeat in a reasonable manner. Still, monomania is often a threat.

For *in extremis* it can become sheer obsession, almost a disease. The Bluebeard of bibliophilia was, by all accounts, a Spanish ex-monk named Don Vicente, who killed several of his customers in order to possess their books and famously murdered one particular collector in order to acquire a special "unique" volume. During his trial he remained calm until his lawyer, seeking to prove him innocent, revealed that another copy of one of those books was for sale in Paris. Vicente became hysterical, and up to the moment he mounted the scaffold did nothing but moan "Alas! Alas! My copy is not unique!" A king of Thrace once broke an exquisite vase deliberately so it could not be broken by accident. And Matsunaga Danjo Hisahide, a 16th-century constable, intentionally smashed his favorite teapot to smithereens rather than let it fall into the hands of a rival collector.

What is the nature of those who collect? And why? Is it a hopeless addiction? A preoccupation only for the crack-pated, the antiquarian mind simply schooled in the ways of the census? Some sort of misguided compulsion for finality? (English prime minister and passionate bibliophile Lord Melbourne pronounced upon the death of the poet Crabbe, "I am always happy when one of those fellows dies, for then I know I have the whole of him on my shelf.") The unavoidable fact is that a good many of us collect. The fascination, far older than cabinets and shelves, is as elemental and has universal appeal. As novelist Laurence Sterne observes in *Tristram Shandy*, "Nay, if you come to that, Sir, have not the wisest of men in all ages, not excepting Solomon himself,—have they not had their Hobby-Horses;—their running horses,—their coins and their cockleshells, their drums and their trumpets, their fiddles, their pallets,—their maggots and their butterflies?"

Japanese Emperor Hirohito collected Mickey Mouse watches. Arthur Fiedler, conductor of the Boston Pops, was a "sparky," slang for a person with an inflamed passion for chasing fire trucks racing to a fire, and he collected firemen's helmets. Dustin Hoffman collects figures of Punch. Serge Joyal, Canada's secretary of state, collected Victorian women's clothing. Michel Roux, the president of Absolut Vodka, collected perfume bottles and had thousands of them. Colette was a passionate collector of millefleur paperweights. Alain Delon, who collects Impressionist paintings, has a special collection of Bugatti sculpture. Jimmy Carter is a carpenter—and collects Georgia plain-style furniture. Actor Harrison Ford is also a carpenter—and collects Shaker furniture. Producer Joel Silver (*Lethal Weapon*) loves Fred Flintstone and has cabinets full of Flintstone wind-up toys, etc. Biographer A. J. A. Symons was a passionate collector of music-boxes. ("Of course, for me the musical-box is the only form of music.") Governor James R. Thompson of Illinois also collected toys. Art dealer Ivan Karp collected can openers with animal faces, antique food choppers, and those risqué boot-jacks called "Naughty Nellies." Henry David Thoreau collected

Indian arrowheads.

Jimmie Rodgers, the Singing Brakeman, collected cowboy boots. A fellow named Jack Naylor, unrivaled in his field, managed to collect every single camera known to man. Sylvester Stallone, a quondam painter, also collects paintings. (He hangs his own work next to Monet's.) Mary Martin collected needlepoint. Novelist Allan Gurganus collects masks. Ex-New York Yankee Dave Winfield collects marbles. Roddy McDowall collected silent films. Greta Garbo collected furniture and paintings, among which were some Renoirs and a Bonnard. And of course Edith Wharton collected 18th-century furniture. Shirley Temple Black collected glass and china miniatures. PBS news anchorman Jim Lehrer collected motor bus stuff (signs, ticket punchers, brochures, etc.) John F. Kennedy popularized collecting scrimshaw (his 37-piece set is displayed at the JFK Library in Boston.) Somerset Maugham was a serious collector of paintings. As was Voltaire. Betty Ring collected embroidery. Honoré de Balzac collected canes and walking-sticks. As did Cole Porter, whose exquisite period-piece collection included, among others, canes once belonging to Beau Brummel and Louis XV. Erik Satie collected umbrellas. Actress Debbie Reynolds was an obsessive collector of film memorabilia. Diane Keaton, a photographer, collects photographs. And folk artist Ralph Cahoon collected mermaids of every size, shape, facet, and form.

Geoffrey Chaucer collected books—he had 60, a huge library for the time. Samuel Pepys was a bibliophile and biblioklept, rarely returning what he borrowed. Pope Innocent X, before he gained the triple tiara, was involved in a scandal over a rare book he stole from the famous collection of Montier-en-Der Abbey. Collecting can be dangerous. Harry Elkins Widener, for whom the library at Harvard is named, was on his way to the Robert Hoe rare book auction in New York when he went down on the RMS *Titanic* on April 15, 1912. In his pocket was a small, rare volume of Elizabethan essays. ("I think I'll take that little Bacon with me," he said—his last remembered words, to bookseller Bernard Quaritch, before leaving London. "If I'm shipwrecked it will go down with me.") Harry Houdini owned more than 5,000 books on magic, spiritualism, and the occult (they are now in the Library of Congress). J. Paul Getty collected rare books, as did J. P. Morgan. Actor John Larroquette collects American literature, especially Beat poetry. Bronson Pinchot has a superb collection of French manuscripts, among them a lot of rare Balzac. And Louis Szathemary, owner of The Bakery in Chicago, collected cookbooks. Jerome Kern's book collection was so extensive that it took ten full days to be auctioned. (Any volume today with his bookplate greatly increases its worth.) A not overly enthusiastic reader presumably, Dolly Parton several years ago had an interior decorator literally saw the backs off an entire library full of books that she had purchased, actually cutting them in two and throwing half away, so that they'd fit, as decorations, the shelves of the room.

King Charles I understood the passionate collector's psychology (he never went anywhere without miniature copies of his paintings). When Sir Robert Cotton, a zealous book collector himself, fell into the king's disfavor, Charles forbade him to enter his own library. It was an effective punishment—Cotton died of the deprivation. An interesting sidelight: on the day Cromwell had the king beheaded in what is now Trafalgar Square, sympathizers—collectors, in a manner of speaking—steeped their handkerchiefs in his blood, which are now considered saintly relics. I once saw a painting of the king with a glowing halo set off in the reliquarial niche of an Anglican Church in London's East End.

Speaking of royalty, King Charles III has said he has collected more than a hundred toilet seats! Prince Philip, his late father, had a large collection of contemporary cartoons of himself, many of which were hung in the lavatory at Sandringham. Queen Victoria was known for collecting photographs and sketches of friends who had died (indeed, anyone with whom she was even remotely connected who had died), often *immediately* upon hearing of their death, such was her compulsive "magpieism."

A passage in Evan S. Connell Jr.'s encyclopedic *Points for a Compass Rose* documents a fascinating fact. "High on the wall of a cave in the Dordogne, archaeologists found a prehistoric bison represented with remarkable individuality. A cartoon of this bison on a piece of slate, unmistakably by the same artist, was unearthed in the *département* of Ain. Now what this means is that some man or woman or child of the ice-age admired the preliminary sketch so intensely that he or she either bought the slate or stole it and carried it all the way to Ain, a distance of 188 miles."

Was this the first collector?

There is great, even noble, precedent for collecting, both as a hobby and with a higher purpose. A graveyard excavated in Ur, dating from as long ago as 6th century BC, was found to contain metal coffins, in one of which was discovered a collection of gemstone seals and hundreds of their clay impressions gathered from all over the known world: Babylon, Egypt, Assyria, Greece, Macedonia. And we know that the Sumerian princess Bel-Shalti-Nannar of Ur put together an archaeological collection of small sculptures, which were a thousand years old even in her own time. These were almost surely private museums. Then the wise Solomon, we are told in First Kings, knew three thousand proverbs—surely he had to collect what he memorized. Tutankhamen, a keen hunter, collected boomerangs, canes, fowling-sticks, and whips decorated with gold and lapis lazuli. There were also seven beds found in his tomb, one decorated like a panther that was a folding bed.

Taking advantage of a wheat famine in Greece, Ptolemy I, father of that great dynasty, in order to enhance his collection at the Royal Library in Alexandria, of which he was both founder and patron, cagily swapped grain in exchange for all the original manuscripts of Aeschylus and Sophocles, kept them, and sent Athens back only copies. According to Galen, he posted a security deposit of 15 gold talents, a large sum, and let the Athenians keep the money. (Aulus Gellius tells us that at the height of its fame the Alexandrian Library once housed 700,000 volumes or rolls). There are of course no original Greek plays extant—Aeschylus wrote over 80 (seven copies survive), Sophocles over 100 (seven survive)—as they all went up in flames when the Caliph Omar burnt the library down, denouncing any book that agreed with the Koran as superfluous, any that disagreed, pernicious. Brutus, Cassius, Cicero, Julius Caesar, and Augustus all collected paintings and sculpture. The Roman historian Suetonius wrote in his *Lives* that Caesar would purchase "at any cost gems, carved works, and pictures executed by the eminent masters of antiquity." Among other gem collectors were Mithridate, Pompey, and Mark Antony. The thought of ancient Caesar, keen for antiquity!

But the story of collecting is also about objects going from hand to hand to hand. A statuette of Hercules by Lysippus, for example, was so treasured by Alexander the Great that he died with it in his hands. Hannibal then got hold of it and took it to Bythnia, where he poisoned himself. The king of Bythnia appropriated it, only to lose it to Sulla, who took it with him when he invaded Rome.

Aristotle collected natural history specimens sent back by

his pupil Alexander the Great. German Chancellor Helmut Kohl also had a distinguished rock collection. ("These geological specimens remind me of the permanence of nature," he said.) Hanno, the third-century Carthaginian statesman, collected the skins of female gorillas during his voyages along the west coast of Africa, brought them back to Carthage, and hung them up in the temple of Astarte. The seventh-century Buddhist monk Hsuan-tsang, traveling to Samarkand, Tashkent, and points west, spent 40 years collecting the seeds of thousands of flowers, only to lose them somewhere in the Punjab on his way home. Thomas Jefferson actually rode to his inauguration on horseback with a saddlebag full of fossils he'd collected, having been invited to lecture on them before the American Philosophical Society. (An important part of Lewis and Clark's mission, in fact, was to bring back fossils for him.) John Evelyn, the diarist, collected butterflies that he liked to arrange so that they would look like tapestries. And Vladimir Nabokov, writer and lepidopterist, who had a genus named after him (*Lycaeides sublivens* Nabokov), was also a collector of a group of small butterflies within that family known as "Blues." A dynasty in shell-collecting was established by the Sowerbys (three generations), giving the British supremacy in the field.

Madame de Pompadour had over 50 kinds of orange trees. Liberace had 44 candelabra and 22 pianos. Jeanne Baptiste d'Albert de Luynes, born in 1670 in Paris, owned upwards of 60 urns filled with different kinds of snuff and, as a logical adjunct, 500 dozen handkerchiefs. Speaking of handkerchiefs, Bette Davis was said to have a great many, and to be very persnickety about the way they were ironed. Catherine de Medici had a superb collection of fashion dolls, as does the great Romanian gymnast Nadia Comăneci. Janine Montupet, French novelist and author of *The Lacemaker*, collected heirloom lace. Poetaster and songwriter Rod McKuen collected T-shirts and possessed one of the world's largest record collections. Gangster Mickey Cohen collected—hoarded—socks. In their western-style museum in Victorville, California, can be seen Roy Rogers and Dale Evans's taxidermy collection, housing not only Trigger, Buttermilk, and Bullet—Roy and Dale's famous horses and dogs—but hundreds of other stuffed specimens. (There are also hundreds of guns on view there, two of them captured from the Vietcong, presumably not by Roy.) Country singer Hank Williams also collected guns and lugged them about everywhere. Entrepreneur Scott Bruce collects metal lunch boxes (a 1954 Superman Robot model goes for as much as $2,000) and launched *Flake*, a newsletter for cereal-box collectors. And I've heard Warren Beatty has closets full of bathrobes from Tokyo's Imperial Hotel.

The Secret Archives of the Vatican constitute the world's largest collection of primary sources for 2000 years of history, both religious and secular. Each Pope, from St. Peter onwards, added to them until today they occupy 25 miles of shelves. Among the extraordinary collection of documents are the records of the trials of Giordano Bruno, Galileo, Pico della Mirandola, and the Franciscan friar Savonarola for heresy; Beatrice Cenci's murder of her father; the conversion of Queen Christina of Sweden; and a good deal of the diplomatic gossip of the high Renaissance, reflected in the reports of various papal nuncios. So vast is that vast collection in Rome that many objects remain unindexed or, in some cases, unexamined for centuries.

Relics, incidentally, which constitute the Church's collections, have been maintained in an attempt to assure the continuation of its common life, of the living with the dead. There were 19,013 relics in a 16th-century church in Wittenberg. And a church in Halle (Salle) in central Germany in 1521 supposedly had 21,483. (Among the most famous relics of the church are those of the apostle James, St. Peter's bones, the so-called *sudarium* of St. Veronica, and the bodies of the Three Kings, which were brought from Milan to Cologne in 1164 by the emperor Frederick I.) The sultans in Topkapi Palace in Istanbul have a silver footprint of the Prophet Mohammed and several hairs from his beard. The 2,500-year-old Shwedagon Pagoda, the most sacred Buddhist pagoda in Yangon, Myanmar, is believed to contain relics of the four previous Buddhas of the present kalpa, including the staff of Kakusandha, the water filter of Konāgamana, a piece of the robe of Kassapa, and eight strands of hair from the head of saintly Gautama, among other other holy relics.

Otto Von Bismarck, a compulsive drinker of champagne, squirreled all the empty bottles from which he drank in a vault in his cellar. Carol Vaugn, 65 from Birmingham, UK, has an impressive collection of more than 5,000 bars of soap from all over the world. She's been collecting soap bars since 1991. Thirty-nine-year-old David Andreani from Pesaro, Italy, has started collecting Coca-Cola cans since he was 15. His collection includes special edition and commemorative cans from almost every country except Cuba and North Korea. At 22.1 grams, Graham Barker has the largest collection, started in 1984, of belly button fluff. (It consists of his own fluff, in case you are wondering.) Dutch collector Niek Vermeulen has 6,290 airsick bags from 1,191 different airlines and almost 200 countries.

Novelist H. G. Wells collected tin soldiers. David Byrne of the Talking Heads collects Russian constructivist art. And Ian Anderson of Jethro Tull collects flutes. Singer Paul Simon collects American folk art. Owlish Stanley Baldwin, English Prime

Minister, collected owls. Faye Dunaway collects cameos. TV host Dick Cavett collects Indian arrowheads. Gabby Hayes, the snuffy cowboy sidekick of Roy Rogers, was a sophisticated wine expert and a collector of rare vintages. Mary Travers collected netsukes (and fellow singer Peter Yarrow Art Nouveau glass). Former *New Yorker* editor Robert Gottlieb has over 500 plastic handbags from the 1950s, and has written a book on the subject. I have heard that he is now collecting ladies' high-heeled shoes to match. (Look at them on a plinth sometime. Hard to believe, perhaps, but they are quite artistic.)

Marjorie Meriweather Post, whose husband was once ambassador to Russia, left with a trainload of the fancy detritus of the empire, silver, rare enamels, hand-wrought eggs, cameos, cups and silver kovshi. Ed Meese collected toy police cars. Ballet dancer Rudolph Nureyev collected 19th-century salon paintings. Novelist Stanley Elkin collected hotel soaps, and had over 3,000 of them. George Orwell had an extensive collection of vulgar seaside postcards, a subject on which he'd written an essay. (His collection of political pamphlets, some 1,200 or so, went to the British Museum.)

Photographer Robert Mapplethorpe collected Italian glass from the Fifties, as well as those small mammalian ceramics called "feelies." Jazz composer Jelly Roll Morton collected anything with diamonds—stickpins, buckles, watches, etc.—and, memorably, sported a huge glowing half-carat diamond in one of his front teeth. *Saturday Evening Post* illustrator Norman Rockwell lost his collection of antique guns in a fire. Opera manager Giulio Gatti-Casazza collected anything to do with Napoleon. Colonel Tom Parker, Elvis's manager, had a collection of toy and model elephants. Eccentric English novelist C. H. B. Kitchin was an avid collector of Georgian silver, antique paperweights, and Meissen teapots. Paul

Newman and Joanne Woodward collected American folk art. Allen Funt of the once popular television show *Candid Camera* collected Maxfield Parrish paintings. And Stephen Sondheim, who collected antique games, was given a chess set by Dorothy Hammerstein that once belonged to her husband, Oscar, that was once been owned by Charles II.

The dedicated collector—have you noticed by now that this essay is an example of such a magpie, rather like the duck that drinks what it floats on?—is obsessed by the desire to own complete sets. Nothing annoys such a person more than a collection with *gaps*—those irritable spaces he has little hope of filling. There are fairly marked limits to egg-weighers, Babe Ruthiana, old MTA tokens, Wells Fargo strongboxes, Chimayo rugs, Pez holders, or, say, South Carolina license plates. (Whit Nesbitt of Lynchburg, South Carolina, who built a clubhouse in his yard to house his personal collection, displayed hundreds on a wall outside arranged as an American flag.) Because one can pretty much get them all, the temptation is to try. A curmudgeonly, insistent monomaniacal collector's ongoing frustration is consequently proportionate to what, though available, is still madly missing.

Common objects, however, such as matchbooks or thimbles or flintlocks or playbills or pipes or wooden sleds or wicker chairs or rattles or hand-coolers or mourning memorabilia or rattles or character steins or old toilet bowls or spoons or advertising caps or arrowheads or cedar boxes or beer-can-openers or rare Lincoln (1909-VDB) pennies or pictorial sheet music or snow domes or Tibetan bells—things with such open-ended possibilities—are so infinite that a patient and philosophical mind needn't be brought to the task, only because you're not even asymptotically close to a bullseye.

Admittedly, there is something weirdly meaningful about collecting in an area impossible to exhaust. Like taking π to outlandish decimal places, you can always be found coming home late at night singing mad catalog arias at the top of your lungs for having bagged yet another mechanical bank, another *krumcake* iron, another decoy, another telephone pole insulator, another rare stamp, another brothel token, etc. What a thrill! There's no end to it, but that's the delight. And what possibilities to fix on! Locks, trivets, sheet music, match safes, yarn pictures, redware, hatpins, carousel horses, cigar bands—a collecting craze, especially in Spain, called *vitolfilia*—silk pictures, cap guns, advertising giveaways, postcards, firemen's helmets, sad irons, bells, automobilia. Certain commodities nowadays are even manufactured for the collector. There are hundreds of thousands of collectors of Coca-Cola memorabilia in this country and abroad, for example, and the "Cola Clan" used to send out a monthly pamphlet advertising five or six newly manufactured Coke items each issue. It's sort of Franklin Mint legerdemain. Instant antiques. The activity is guaranteed to become endless.

And last but not least, there is the literally finite but virtually impossible to complete—it is, at least to me, an ugly but somehow unavoidable word—"collectible": beer cans, Melmac dinnerware, jazz records only on the Okeh record label, Colt revolvers, Wurlitzer jukeboxes, baseball cards, etc. The largest institutional collection of baseball cards in the world—200,000 cards—can be found in the Metropolitan Museum of Art in New York City. (Former New York Mets catcher Gary Carter also had one of the largest collections in the country). Hockey legend Wayne Gretzky, #99 of the Edmonton Oilers, paid $451,000 for a 1910 Honus Wagner baseball card at a Sotheby's auction.

The world record for the largest baseball card collection

owned by a person, however, not a company or a business, is that of Paul Jones from Idaho Falls, who has over 3 million cards, over 99,000 of them signed! He spent 22 years as a bat boy and will be spending this season with the Idaho Falls Chukars. His favorite team is the San Francisco Giants. He lives with the hope that his vast collection will one day find its way into the National Baseball Hall of Fame in Cooperstown, New York.

There is no end of things people, in taking up, hope to complete. Moxie-ana, GWTW memorabilia, ice-cream scoops, Tootsietoys, American campaign buttons, state car decals (or every license plate), painted Pairpoint puffies, old candy bar wrappers (among many brand names can be listed Fat Emma, Sour Krout, Chicken Dinner, Snirkles, and, of course, the Idaho Spud, "The Candy Bar That Made Idaho Famous")—the bar is sold at room temperature, but is often frozen before consumption—Lladro porcelain, figurines, stereoscopic cards of Niagara Falls or the Ausible Chasm, etc. It doesn't matter what. Half the time the finding is in the seeking, and to a degree what we seek we possess.

The late comedian and actor Robin Williams collected, and wore, extraordinary shoes. Pointing to a pair of bottle-green footwear, he said, "These are Prada," explaining this to my brother Paul, whose essay on him, "Robin Williams: 'Who's He When He's at Home?'" appears in his *Figures in a Landscape*. "'And these are custom made in Tokyo,' he said of a pair that looked like Eskimo mukluks, a form of hand-sewn clodhoppers that guarantees a silly walk." A fanatical bicyclist, Williams collected bicycles as well, bought "the best bicycles obtainable," according to Paul, "several of them costing ten thousand dollars."

There have been some wonderfully eccentric collections. John Aubrey, England's first serious biographer—and the man who left us the only dirty anecdote about Burbage and Shakespeare—actually collected *gossip*. "What are the English like?" it might be asked. A worse answer might be given than "Read Aubrey's *Lives*." H. L. Mencken collected strange given names, like Minnie Magazine and Dr. Gargle and Justin Tune and Ima Hogg—an actual woman, incidentally, one of Houston's greatest collectors of American furniture. Cardinal Ippolito Medici collected people who spoke different languages—he kept at his court a troupe of barbarians who spoke no less than twenty tongues, "each of them perfect specimens of their races."

Elsa Maxwell, the big-bummed, Iowa-born, loud-voiced, under-strapping party-giver and society gossip-columnist for the *New York Journal-American*—she was born poor—who made it her habit to know, befriend, and cultivate only the wealthiest and most influential people in the world from the 1930s to the 1950s, actually *collected them*, for profit—making suitable introductions. It was a service. She had a peculiar and ingratiating talent for staging games and diversions at parties for the rich and superficial and actually began earning a living devising all sorts of treasure-hunt parties, "come-as-your-opposite" parties, and other frivolous gatherings, including a scavenger hunt in Paris in 1927 that inadvertently created disturbances all over the city. She was in great demand by lackeys for these all-important connections and in her prime charged quite a large fee for doing so.

A New York workman in the 1940s collected distances, donning a pedometer and going on walks he carefully measured. His notebooks contained entries like, "Walked from home to the fire station. 9 miles, 2 hours 16 min." and "Walked to Wall St. 5 miles, 1 hour, 4 min." He took special walks to the oldest tree, the oldest house or statue, the World's Fair, and so forth. He even compulsively kept a detailed record of how many pairs of socks he ruined on the way. And what about the phenomenon of tulipomania in Holland? The crutches and trusses at Lourdes? Limericks? Indian *scalps*? Don't these also qualify?

A behavioral scientist at Brown University, Lewis Lipsitt, collected coincidences, specifically names that just happen to match occupations. Aptonym is the definitive term. Larry Speakes, for example, was a White House spokesperson, Sally Ride an astronaut, James Bugg an exterminator, Felicity Foote a dance teacher, and, indeed, Dan Druff was an actual barber. Some other choice ones: Lionel Tiger and Robin Fox who wrote about animal behavior; Mr. Fish, who founded the University of Rhode Island Graduate School of Oceanography; Mr. Hawkes, head of the Rhode Island Audubon Society; Armand Hammer, a frequent American diplomat to the Soviet Union, etc. There is also himself, "Professor Lips-itt," who studies infant sucking behavior. And photographer Ralph Eugene Meatyard, who had one himself, also kept a looseleaf notebook of thousands of grotesque and absurd names.

A medical student, Joel Silidker, collected condom tins from the Thirties and Forties. The tins, containing usually three or four, were durable (and had to be, since you never knew when you were going to need one). Some brand names were Le Transparent, Royal Knights, Double-Tips, and 3 Merry Widows. A certain Russian countess paid fabulous sums for bedpans that once belonged to historical personages. Louise Nevelson collected used coffee filters, washing them, drying them, filing them away. Lizzie Borden, of 40 whacks fame, collected birdhouses and feeders. A man in Arturo Vivante story's "Of Love and Friendship" collects lichens. There are collections made up of laurel leaves pinpricked with the Sign of the Cross. Jibaro Indians collect shrunken heads as trophy-fetishes. At the New York City morgue, there can be found nose bones that have been salvaged from victims of crimes, plane crashes, and various accidents. Then there is Wilson A. Bentley of Jericho, Vermont, who, when he died in 1952, left a photo collection of more than 5,300 *snowflakes*, no two alike, which are on display in the town there. He took the pictures through a microscope. According to a report, "the flakes, caught on a cold board covered with black velvet, were photographed in Bentley's refrigerated camera room." A Vermont farmer all his life, Bentley is regarded as one of the pioneers of photomicrography.

Is that strange? There was a man in Pittsburgh who collected moist towelettes, a woman in Philadelphia who collected funnels. A man named Hanks in London collected spider webs, pressing them between panes of glass. E. Thomas Hughes of Washington had a passion for potatoes and potatoabilia: potato banks, potato poems, potato peelers. We should not forget, of course, that J. Wellington Wimpy from the *Popeye* comic strip was known not only for mooching hamburgers but also collected college degrees—he had 24. Elizabeth Tashjian collected nuts and ran the Nut Museum in Old Lyme, Connecticut (admission, through the eight-foot nutcracker, is one nut per person). Writer and biographer Barry Paris collects the lids of non-dairy creamer containers. Francis Johnson, a hay-baler from Darwin, Minnesota, had a collection of over 1700 nail aprons, gathered from all 50 states. Old John McSorley, owner of the now famous McSorley's Ale House on East 7th Street in New York City, for many years collected wishbones of holiday turkeys and festively hung them for display on a string over the bar where, I believe, they are still gathering dust.

The late Harold E. Burtt, a professor emeritus at Ohio State, collected and classified moss. Illustrator Durrell Godfrey collected stitched mottoes on linen. Novelist Umberto Eco collected rare books on science and the occult, "as long as they're wrong," he once pointed out. And the late Mr. Owen Evan-Thomas of London owned over 1,000 pieces of treen, which is to say, old wood utensils, once relatively common ware among our ancestors—salt-cellars, mortars, drinking vessels, mazers (bowls), molds, and mills. The most primitive, and the rarest, specimens are the earliest used dinner plates, simple squares of sycamore wood hollowed in the middle. The oval meat platter, with a well for gravy, is along lines that have never been improved upon. *Thinking* involves collecting. Bertrand Russell's "Theory of Types," which postulates a hierarchy of types of objects, gatherings grouped together to form sets (where, say, the first type is individuals, the second, classes of individuals, the third, classes of classes of individuals, etc.), becomes a collection in itself.

Fin-de-siècle dandy and decadent Count Robert de Montesquiou, who was a friend of Marcel Proust—this "prince of aesthetes" appears as Baron de Charlus in Proust's *À la recherche du temps perdu*—collected strange treasures. In one of his residences on the rue Quai d'Orsay, he owned, among other things, the bullet that killed Pushkin, a cigarette partially smoked by George Sand, a tear (dried) once shed by Lamartine, the slippers of Lord Byron's great passion, the Countess Guiccioli, and a birdcage that had once housed the pet canary of Jules Michelet—all of that, along with a jewel box containing a single hair from the beard of the same historian. Montesquiou proudly kept Mme. de Montespan's pink marble tub in his garden, overflowing with rambler roses. One of his favorite objects was a bedpan used by Napoleon after Waterloo. He had also acquired a plaster cast of the knees of Mme. de Castiglione, the femme fatale of the Second Empire Court, who, in her prime, had had herself photographed 190 times. (Proud Montesquiou, not to be outdone, proceeded to have himself photographed 199 times.)

Amenhotep III of Egypt had an uncontrollable passion for things that were colored blue, and found in the ruins of his villa were blue cups, blue bowls, blue ampullae, blue amulets, blue jewels. It is reported that Jonathan Swift, of *Gulliver's Travels* fame, enjoyed going about collecting jokes. A person in Southold, New York, collected nothing but videos of hockey fights. Members of the American Coaster Enthusiasts (ACE), a national club, collect roller-coaster experiences. Sir Richard Burton, the Victorian explorer, collected languages, and toward the end of his adventurous life he was believed to have been able to speak and write no less than 29. (At one stage he lived with 30 monkeys in order to study the noises they made, eventually compiling a short monkey-vocabulary!)

And in his house at Talcottville, literary critic Edmund Wilson collected visitors' autographs on windowpanes, asking famous poets to write verses from their work and sign their names with a diamond pen. (I believe Louisa May Alcott did the same thing.) Then there were the irrepressible Plaster Casters, several girl groupies from the hip Sixties who went around collecting as memorabilia realistic impressions in plaster of their favorite rock stars' phalluses. Their favorite "rig" (sic) was Jimi Hendrix's.

Collecting can be a very mysterious thing. What we need to have often becomes what we do. People collect rainwater in Bermuda by way of special roofs because the soil is so porous that it cannot be held in the soil. It suggests all sorts of metaphors. Fat people collect things by eating. It sounds ludicrous, until you realize the obsession often has little to do with hunger. Eating has become a sport in America—a whopping 40 percent of the people in this country are unhealthily overweight. Why is a compulsion, enthusiasm, a fixed fascination, infatuation, or the drive of a mania not a collection of a kind? Why is a fixed and excessive interest in any one thing not somehow a collection? There is an ocnophilic personality, whereby attachment to objects of interest confers symbolic security. According to some psychoanalysts, it replaces the presence of the parent. What object-clinging definitely can do—and often does—is become a substitute for what's missing elsewhere. And whether it's cheeseburgers or chalkware, Chippendale or chalices, aren't they maybe just friends?

Cannot habits to a degree constitute collections?

Does not art professor Robert Cartmell's compulsion of riding roller-coasters somehow, somewhere, involve collecting? (He rated the Texas Cyclone at Houston's Astrodome "the greatest thrill ride built since the golden age of coasters in the 1920s.") What about all of those drifting loonies who followed the Grateful Dead, giddy middle-aged ladies who never miss Wayne Newton in concert, college-age obsessives who have seen *The Rocky Horror Picture Show* more than a thousand times? Novelist Georges Simenon—who wrote more than 400 books, 76 of them about Inspector Maigret—once said that he had made love to 10,000 women. How about the 7'1" basketball player Wilt ("The Stilt") Chamberlain? He was known for his womanizing and his boasts about it in Robert Cherry *Wilt: Larger Than Life*, where he claimed to have slept with—a euphemism—20,000 women during his life. As his lawyer Seymour "Sy" Goldberg put it: "Some people collect stamps, Wilt collected women." Personal friends of his testified that he once had 23 women in 10 days and that he had no problem organizing orgies. It was the ultimate gasconade he was serious about, apparently doing the math throughout his life and about which he kept track like a diligent accountant on a Day-Timer, an appointment diary or electronic organizer.

Barbed wire is a major collectible. There are over 1,000 members in the Barbed Wire Collectors of America. (According to a Texas adage, a barbed wire fence is of no value unless it is "horse-high, bull-strong, and pig-tight.") I've read of people who collect handbag snaps, called "steals" in the trade. Lord Walter Rothschild collected albino animals. I know a lawyer who collected editions of Dickens's *Bleak House*. Doctors in America are famous for collecting enema tools. There was a big market for unofficial military insignia of the Vietnam War. (*Un*official. Does this make sense?) There are also of course "injustice collectors," people like Baron Corvo and Bobby Kennedy and angry, extreme-unforgiving sorts like assassins or mass murderers who have a long memory for slights. There are prostitutes in the Far East who collect fluff from the navels of their clients.

King Farouk hid the world's greatest collection of erotic objects in the cellars of the Koubbeh Palace. Poet Philip Larkin supposedly collected pornography, too. And persistent rumors say the same of Sophia Loren and even Toscanini. There have been a good many sexual hunter/gatherers down through the years. Turkish sultan Abdul Hamid II, deposed in 1909, collected wives—he had 370. Victor Hugo, who was sexually insatiable, often made love to three or four different women a day. Sarah Bernhardt, who was raised in a convent and died at age 81, had over a thousand affairs in her lifetime. Rubens, Diego Rivera, Modigliani, all slept with thousands of women.* Most of their models sat for them in the nude and before any painting sessions usually made love with them. Satyriasis or nymphomania may be considered a form of collecting, until we stop to realize it's quite the opposite, non-collecting, shedding in

---

*One of those women, in Amadeo Modigliani's case, one Suzanne Thiroux, distantly related to our family, had a child by him.

fact, *repudiation.*

Legend has it that the classic rake Giovanni Casanova, a man tall, dark, and powerfully built, was capable, in his prime of having sex anywhere, with anyone, and in any position, with particular reference to the positions described by 16th-century satirist Pietro Aretino. In 14 years of life in the NBA, with almost 100 different teammates, there was only one man, according to star Wilt Chamberlain, among all those players—Paul Arizin—who was content with his marriage and didn't use road trips to cheat on his wife. So are we talking about collecting here, in any way? Can Casanova's attitude toward sex be described as anything but wastrelism? Or Erroll Flynn's? Or Alma Schindler's, who "collected" celebrity husbands—Gustav Mahler, Franz Werfel, Oskar Kokoschka (she merely lived with him three years), Walter Gropius? No, no, no. Collecting is having to hold. In some instances, desperately so. I knew a billionaire in Boston back in the 1980s—there were only 26 in the country at the time, currently there are more than 700 (we're talking about a *thousand million* dollars)—who collected buildings. He once frankly confided to me that he had always been hungry growing up and that his mother, who ran a boarding house, locked up the food cupboard at night. Lenon H. Hoyte, who had over 5,000 dolls, was forbidden to play with toys when she was little. So it was with the insatiable William Randolph Hearst, the tragic but avaricious newspaper magnate, lord of San Simeon (and prototype of the main character in the film *Citizen Kane,* the locus classicus of acquisition) who started with stamps and went on to collect in 504 separate categories—scarabs, paintings, gold candelabra, coins, marble caryatids, silver *épergnes,* rooms from great houses, sculpture, and no doubt Flexible Flyers.

Stephen Spielberg, who collects movie memorabilia—and

who, incidentally, bought that famous sled "Rosebud" for $55,000 (said to be one of three used in the film, although Welles stated it was a fake)—not only has a great collection of Walt Disney animation cels but also collects American Indian artifacts. The walls on the executive floor of his company building in Los Angeles are studded with facsimile Indian petroglyphs. Collecting is of course not always a way of expressing a passion; it may be nothing more than the upshot of consulting financial hipsters and investment advisers. But who's to say that this too isn't passion, and for real, even in Hollywood? Decades ago, Sylvester Stallone said his idea of art was "paintings of John Wayne on velvet." Now his fascinations are in the line of Francis Bacon, Willem de Kooning, Rodin, and the like. Pop singer Madonna back in her day took up modern painting—Picasso, Kahlo, Léger. Cher is said to go in for Egyptian antiquities. Kirk Douglas, Edward G. Robinson, Ray Stark, David Geffen, Billy Wilder, and Elizabeth Taylor went in for paintings and sculpture, often quite seriously. Apart from large jewels (she had a 69.42 carat diamond and the Peregrina Pearl, one of the jewels Isabella pawned to launch Columbus) Taylor also owned an important Franz Hals. (Incidentally, literary critic Camille Paglia collects photos of Liz Taylor.) Frank Sinatra had a Childe Hassam. Davis Bowie bought a Tintoretto, Kirk Douglas a Rosenquist. Anthony Quinn collected Etruscan art. And John McEnroe is said to have bought furniture at a fabulous pace. When asked what sort of furniture he collects, he replied, "Oh, all kinds. You know, desks, tables, chairs."

Speaking of furniture, John Lennon went in for Art Deco. Tennis player Martina Navratilova still does. Ivan Lendl collects lithographs by the Czech painter Alphonse Mucha. Pam Shriver goes for American, a field once dominated by the creepy comedian Bill Cosby, now a convicted felon. Architect Michael Graves collected Biedermeier. Richard Gere bought arts and crafts furniture to go with his contemporary art. Joan Fontaine liked Chippendale, Bette Midler Omega Workshops. And Oprah Winfrey collects Shaker furniture. Fashion photographer Roger Prigent collected Empire. Olympic runner Carl Lewis collects crystal, Helen Hayes Victorian valentines. Rolling Stones front man Mick Jagger loves Tiffany (and furniture shaped like gigantic sushi, or so I've read).

Henry Fonda cherished a small collection of hats, which included Spencer Tracy's favorite, given to Fonda by Katharine Hepburn after they finished the film *On Golden Pond*. Pianist and singer Michael Feinstein collects sheet music. Writer Richard Bissell collected railroad timetables. Bookseller Andreas Brown collected postcards. Senator Barry Goldwater had a prized collection of Hopi kachinas. Calvin Klein collects Georgia O'Keeffes. John Cage collected Jasper Johns. And Allen Funt collected the paintings of Sir Lawrence Alma-Tadema.

Charles F. Rosenay!!! of Connecticut collects Beatles memorabilia and *legally* added the exclamations to his name ("yeah! yeah! yeah!"). Michael Brooslin of Lincoln, Nebraska, collected antique roller skates ("Old roller skates never die," he said, "they just lose their bearings"). FDR, whose jackdavian streak has already been noted, also collected historical autographs and maritime memorabilia. So did JFK.

Director Mike Nichols collected Post-impressionist paintings, as did CBS's William Paley, who owned what is arguably the most famous of Picasso's *Saltimbanques*. Writer Anatole France had a superb antique collection of early Gothic—his house was generously filled with paintings of the Madonna, saints, ancient altar cloths, and church vessels, a strangely ironic enthusiasm when one calls to mind, as occasionally I do, his bitter anti-clericalism. John Travolta collects cars. As does baseball's Reggie Jackson. As did Elvis, who had motorcycles, Cadillacs, tractors, Ferraris. A small word here on the problem of size: it can obviously complicate, and no doubt, in many instances significantly curtail, certain big-item collections. How many cars can television's Jay Leno garage, for instance?

A friend of mine in Kentucky, Mr. Dinwiddie Lampton, had to make room for one of the greatest collections of carriages in this country, ladies phaetons, "four-in-hands," broughams (a rare roof-seat brake coach where all the seats are on top, the most comfortable way to ride), and his prize, the actual road coach, once "belonging to Mr. King of Bath," that is mentioned (Book X, chapter 6) in Henry Fielding's masterpiece *Tom Jones*.

A man in Allegheny, New York, collects Studebakers. Mr. Hugh Lesley of Oxford, Pennsylvania, owned more Edsels than any living person—he had Edsels in the woods, Edsels in the cornfields, even a rare 1958 Edsel station wagon with the push-button automatic transmission located in the center of the steering wheel. (Only 2,864 were built in the 1960 model year, making it a genuine collector's item.) The Edsel Owners of America is an organization of 1,600 strong. Henry Ford was a passionate collector of violins, as well as firearms, clocks, early Americana, and of course automobiles. Curiously, he also had a complete collection of the *Eclectic Readers* of William Holmes McGuffey (1800–1873). But he not only assembled the books, he made a trip to Washington County, Pennsylvania, bought McGuffey's birthplace, and had it transferred, runners to rafters, all the way to Dearborn, Michigan.

Ford then went on to collect houses. He managed to get the courthouse from Postville, Illinois, where Lincoln practiced law from 1840 to 1847; the birthplace of Stephen Foster; America's oldest windmill from West Yarmouth, Massachusetts; Noah Webster's house; and Thomas A. Edison's Laboratory from Menlo Park, New Jersey. A great admirer and friend of the inventor, Ford in gathering Edison memorabilia took his tendency to collect to an extreme. (He actually went so far as to have Edison's dying breath sealed up in a vial.) In all, more than a hundred historic buildings were gathered by Ford into "Greenfield Village," which is located in Dearborn. It is adjacent to the Henry Ford Museum, which houses the vast array of all of Ford's diverse collections.

One of the most omnivorous collectors of antiquities was the Israeli general Moshe Dayan, who was accused, incidentally, of plundering digs with the help of his troops and thought nothing of using rare pottery as ashtrays. General George S. Patton famously collected guns and greatly enlarged his collection with World War II booty. Other collectors of guns are guitarist Eric Clapton, Brad Pitt, Mel Tormé , Buddy Hackett, Ernest Hemingway, Disney's Fess Parker, and Alton Brown, the celebrity chef, TV personality, and author. The National Firearms Museum in Fairfax, Virginia, is a wonder in this field.

The Duchess of Windsor collected jewelry and pillows in the shape of pugs. Mario Buatta, the once reigning "Prince of Chintz," collected paintings of King Charles Spaniels. Pat Buckley collected porcelain King Charles Spaniels. William F. Buckley Jr. always watched television with King Charles Spaniels sitting on his lap.

Surrealist artist Joseph Cornell compulsively collected stuff related to the women that he became obsessed with, which were many—almost always ballet dancers and opera singers—part of a passion in him that encouraged vision and gave birth to works of art. At one point in 1969, he became obsessed with the ballerina Allegra Kent who, while visiting him one afternoon in his apartment to pick up a creative box he had made especially for her, inadvertently left behind a sweater. Surprisingly, he made a point of returning it a few days later with the note, "Don't think I'm a fetishist."

Artists usually tend not to be collectors. More often than not, they make what they want. Andy Warhol, who in my opinion wasn't really an artist at all, did not so much collect things as *accumulate* them. (But, after all, accumulation is a significant aspect of the habit of collecting, let's face it.) He was a recreational shopper, a rummager, a magpie. He even looked like one. Is it not somehow revealing that Warhol always wore *two* wigs? He had an eye for kitsch and was pathologically greedy and loved to see a lot of things in a row, which is maybe the *ur*-impulse of collecting, although hardly its crowning glory. He desperately needed to have duples, copies, series of things, and he constantly reproduced art in multiple images: soup cans, Marilyn Monroes, black electric chairs, etc. His driving compulsion derived not from a sense of aesthetics, but from a *horror vacui*. ("I am a deeply superficial person," he once confided to a friend.) All those things bought and burrowed away after his thrift-shop perambulations were just that, *things*, and the comic melodrama of trying to clutch them all at once was only a parody of graceful ownership. Many of the things that were auctioned after he died were worth something—10,000 items fetched $25.3 million— only because the artist had once owned them. Like those cookie jars you can still buy, if you poked around a bit, for $25 each. Warhol owned 152 of them. They sold, altogether, for $247,830.

There are of course exceptions. Picasso collected African masks and sculpture. So did Henry Moore and André Derain. Michelangelo, like Peter Paul Rubens and Joshua Reynolds, collected drawings of the old masters. According to Vasari, he used to copy old works, age them with smoke, and then trade them for the originals. Michelangelo also collected antique gems, as did Benvenuto Cellini. Lorenzo Ghiberti collected Greek sculpture and owned a bed said to have belonged to the fifth-century BC Greek sculptor Polycletus. Van Gogh collected Japanese prints (several can be seen in his Père Tanguy painting). Artists Diego Rivera, Rufino Tamayo, and Miguel Covarrubbias all collected pre-Columbian art. So did Zero Mostel and John Huston. It was also a passion of Evan Connell's ("I also like Chupicuaro miniatures and Xochipala Olmecs and Jalisco couples with long noses, and brown Colima dogs polished until they gleam . . . and once in a while a helmeted Nayarit warrior"), as well as the subject of his novel of 1974 on the monomania of collecting, *The Connoisseur*. And artists Josef and Anni Albers became addicted on a trip to Oaxaca in 1934 after purchasing from a peasant boy for a few pesos one of those teeny weeny figurines from the Tlatilco culture of southern Mexico. Josef especially liked examples of Chupicuaro women, of which he owned 283, and particularly delighted in pointing out the "charms of their *derrières*."

Painter Raphael Sawyer collected Impressionist juvenilia, Elie Nadelman American folk art, and Andrew and Betsy Wyeth enjoyed collecting Americana. Jacques Lipschitz and Sir Jacob Epstein collected antiquities, Georgia O'Keeffe bones, and cartoonist Saul Steinberg collected postcards. Jasper Johns collects—and sometimes includes in his paintings—the work of Mississippi potter George Ohr. Frieda Kahlo collected doll furnishings and dolls—as well as books on the subject of parturition! When friends took leave of her, she would often say to them, "Bring me a doll." One may perhaps wonder here if this morbid lady was in some way intentionally echoing the last, dying words of the prima ballerina Anna Pavlova: "Get my swan costume ready."

What about collections, then? Are they only extensions

of ourselves? Existence assertions? The objective correlative of our identity? Do they speak to us of hidden aspirations? There is certainly a case to be made for all of that and more. Choreographer Jerome Robbins, for example, collected costume designs. Dancer Mikhail Baryshnikov collects ballet watercolors. A hunchback, Charles Proteus Steinmetz, the wizard of General Electric, collected ugly things, unlovely entities, nature's odd and outcast creatures like alligators, a Gila monster, two crows, cacti, etc.; the more thorns, prickles, fangs, scales, and claws an animal or plant had, the better he liked it, the more tenderly he cared for it. Poet John Ashbery, author of *Self-Portrait in a Convex Mirror* collected—guess what?—right, convex mirrors! American zealot and billionaire H. Ross Perot use to buy American eagles to go with his Remington bronzes. The swan was, of course, ballerina Anna Pavlova's signature totem. She kept a flock at her London home, danced *Swan Lake* with Nijinsky, and made Fokine's dying bird her swan song. On her deathbed, she said, "Bring me my swan costume." Show business personality Arlene Francis collected heart-shaped jewelry and Jayne Mansfield heart-shaped everything, her outdoor swimming pool being only the largest example. (Her funeral casket, in fact, was draped with 500 roses with a large heart-shaped floral piece in the center).

Adolf Hitler specialized in autographs of Frederick the Great. (Goebbels gave him many as presents.) So did Napoleon Bonaparte, who also liked relics of William the Conqueror and Charlemagne. Jazz singer Bobby Short collected not only canes but also Negro memorabilia, Aunt Jemima figures and the like. Actor and dancer Geoffrey Holder collected Haitian art. Founder of the Southern Comfort Corp., Francis Fowler was a collector of rare and curious drinking vessels. William L. Hewitt, CEO of John Deere

& Co., collected anything with a deer on it. The Welsh poet W. H. Davies collected paintings and sculptures of himself, brazenly having wheedled artists like Jacob Epstein, Walter Sickert, Augustus John, Laura Knight, and others to swap their work for his own thin, rather reedy poems, and then surrounded himself with this great art in his dingy, mice-infested rooms on Great Russell Street. Alfred "Lash" Larue, the popular western motion picture star of the 1940s and 1950s, collected cowboy lobby posters and western memorabilia. Helen Hayes, who lived in Nyack, New York, collected paintings of Hudson River artists. Chef Jean-Robert de Cavel of New York's elegant La Régence collected ceramic cooks, kitchen utensils, and food posters. The late Roy Cohn, that avaricious lawyer with a distinctly saurian appearance, collected frogs. On the other hand, in what dark way do such our collections conjure up our anti-selves?

Ghoulishness has cast its dark shadow across the world of collections. The Japanese samurai of the 16th century collected the noses and ears of Koreans they killed, and there's a mountain in Nara, the Mimidzuka, or "Ear-Mound," where 38,000 pairs of ears and the noses to match are buried. The Iban tribes of Borneo collected trophy heads and wore them as ornaments from their belts. Charles Semsen, a 17th-century Parisian hangman, collected paintings depicting torture and death. William Rossetti, who went after anything "odd, Chinese, or sparkling," was famous for a collection that included, along with the lantern of murderer Eugene Aram, hangmen's nooses and executioner's axes. Artist Jean Dubuffet had a large collection of what he called *art brut* (raw art), much of it produced by psychotics, of which he was one of the leading candidates. Nancy Reagan's pal Jerry Zipkin collected snakelike objects, stuffed snakes, lamps like cobras, etc. Artist Fritz Scholder collected mummies, but what he prized most in his collection his wife gave him was a vial of mummy dust, seriously considered during Victorian times to be the ultimate nostrum. And I went several times to Edward Gorey's cluttered attic and saw his amazing collection of skulls—iron skulls, ivory skulls, beanbag skulls, skull watches, drawings of them, shelf after shelf. He also collected, along with fur coats—and will only wear—iron jewelry.

Excess is all. During the 18th and early 19th centuries many collectors in England were desperate for pieces of rope from hanging victims, and hangmen made fortunes by improvising longer ropes which they cut into souvenir lengths and, after executions, passed out for sale.

To try speculating on what informs the collecting mind is intriguing. In essence, there are two kinds of collectors: those who find the One in the Many, and those who find the Many in the One. (There's a legend that dictator Joseph Stalin had copies of the same room constructed in buildings all over Russia so that no matter what town he was in, he would always feel at home—a weird example both of collecting and refusing to collect at the same time!) Collectors often spend their lives, like Hawthornian protagonists, turning over rocks and looking for absolutes. Many people, for instance, weirdly, grow insensibly attached to what gives them a *great deal of trouble*! The mere challenge of collecting may generate the impulse, the impossibility of success like the inevitability in high-jumping of failure guaranteeing a strange kind of buoyancy, because it is endless.

A certain amount of amateur pedantry is always involved, the collector invariably becoming, like the village explainer, an expert on whatever it is he or she has chosen to gather and gathers to know. Another impulse might be the passionate tropism for order—the compulsion for finding a perfect arrangement. (Ironically, the perfection-seeking of female anorexic bulimics has the opposite effect.) And things, after all, are there. "Objects give both the form to the world and supply its content," as Ludwig Wittgenstein points out in the *Tractatus Logico-Philosophicus* (2.025).

Many psychiatrists agree that there is an extraordinarily large presence of the nonhuman world in mental life. It was said of Ramanujan, the self-taught and seminal Hindu clerk whose centennial was 1987 but whose still mysterious formulas presaged shoestring theory in today's physics, that he saw numbers as living things, as characters in a story. Are the comforts that Geppetto's clocks gave him the same mensurative consolations that soothe the antisocial nerd mind? *Counting is a consolation!* "Not count?" cries Winnie in Samuel Beckett's play *Happy Days*. "One of the last few pleasures left in life?" It is also the major joy of Watt and other characters in Beckett's novel *Watt*, in which the uncanny repetitions of words, phrases, and sentences seem very like an assemblage! Psychotherapist Sándor Ferenczi somewhere describes the ontogenesis of the interest in money as a series of stages from the child's interest in feces through an interest in dirt and sand to an interest in odorless dehydrated pieces of metal made to shine—so why not from there to the whole concept of collecting, with adults in a final morphological stage turning coins into what they can buy?

There are those, nevertheless, who find the whole idea of acquisition, especially to such extremes, not only vulgar, secular, and offensive—even unnecessary (if you can afford to buy it, you can afford not to)—but the very kind of disposition that flies in the face of Matthew 6:19–20. Dr. Samuel Johnson severely criticized in people the "desire of accumulating trifles," charging that it distinguished them by a means "through which no other distinction could ever have been obtained."

Edith Wharton, in her wonderful short story "The Daunt Diana," with amazing insight brilliantly explicates the psychological state of how a collector's passion for a piece of statuary is rewarded, in fact, only when he is *unable* to afford it. There are certain of us who find the meaning of life not by the habit of adding but rather by subtracting. "In Saladin's treasury when he died," Evan S. Connell Jr. writes, "there were 47 Nacerite *dirhems* and a single Syrian gold piece. He owned nothing, left nothing and coveted nothing. He left no houses, furniture, gardens, plowed land or property of any sort, and money floated like a ribbon between his fingers. Whatever chanced to come his way he distributed, gracefully permitting himself to be exploited and swindled. How foreign he sounds."

How foreign indeed. Trappists, anchorites, lilies of the field come to mind. Blessed Benedict Joseph Labre, the "Beggar Saint," a French mendicant, Franciscan tertiary, and Catholic ascetic, wandered the world for his entire life utterly penniless. Coming from a well-to-do family near Arras, France, he became a cloistered monk for awhile. He soon left choosing instead the life of a pilgrim, traveling to most of the major shrines in Europe, subsisting on handouts and calling on passersby for food. As part of his abstemiousness, Nikolai Lenin, the revolutionary, lived intentionally poor in a kitchen in the Kremlin apartments with cracked plates, oilcloth on the tables, and so forth. Perhaps I am distorting my envy, but sometimes—often—collectors, the "100 Top Connoisseurs," drummers of whatever kind, seem pathetic, venal in terrible ways, clinging so desperately to their egos through the small temporal world of found objects. Better to have a collection that fits under a hat. As Goethe said, "All things are metaphors." I tend to believe it.

On the other hand, there is something in us that cannot help but delight in knowing that Colleen Moore, star of *Flaming Youth* and the greatest box-office attraction of the Twenties, spent seven years (and half a million dollars) on a dollhouse devoted to the idea of fantasy. The lightbulbs inside, the size of a grain of wheat, actually worked—the house had its own electrical system and running water. The windows were stained glass, chairs of Battersea enamel, floors of inlaid mother-of-pearl and gold. There were over 2,000 objects inside: a dressing table of carved ivory, a canopied boat-shaped bed of solid gold, jeweled chandeliers, an ivory spinet piano that played. In the library were tiny books handwritten by Willa Cather, Sinclair Lewis, Thornton Wilder, and F. Scott Fitzgerald, and an autograph album signed by Einstein, Churchill, de Gaulle, Wilbur Wright, and five presidents. The Fairy Princess Bedroom had Peter Pan murals painted on pale-pink walls. The dining-room was King Arthur's Court, with a round table and armor and real tapestries on the wall.

And of course Malcolm Forbes, who personally owned more than 800,000 antiques of all kinds, also collected rare Fabergé eggs (the Imperial ones) at two million dollars a pop—he had one more than the Kremlin, something like 12 or 13.

Often, however, the enterprise of collecting is a fairly ordinary one. The Postal Service estimates that over 22 million people collect postage stamps in the United States alone. The late Francis Cardinal Spellman, prelate of New York, had a superb collection. As a kid, physicist Richard Feynman collected triangular postage stamps from Tannu Tuva, a remote mountain-capped fastness in Mongolia. The best collection was likely Queen Elizabeth's, inherited from George V. I like to think of her sitting in Windsor surrounded by glassine envelopes and little tongs. Many of her newer acquisitions must bear her own face, and the world's first stamp, the Penny Black, has her great-great-grandmother Victoria's stately profile. (An old English joke has someone who, upon meeting the Queen, suddenly snaps his fingers and says, "That reminds me. I have to buy a stamp!")

Louis XIV had virtually everything he wanted, but the thing he loved most was his coin collection. He could never be separated from it, and would only handle his coins with special spatulas of gold. Petrarch collected coins, as did Boccaccio. And Darwin, who had large collections of minerals and seashells, began with coins as a young boy. Seashells, by the way, remain the most collected objects in the world.

We should finally distinguish between collecting things and simply having a passion for them, though clearly passion, whether vulgar or not, is the beating heart of the collector. It is always a passion, let it be understood, of the monomaniacal kind. James Joyce, for example, was a great aficionado of fine clothes and virtually collected them. (So did Nora, his wife.) Joyce also loved eating out in fine restaurants, which I suppose comes under the category of a passion. It's not always easy to distinguish between the two. Did his sartorial mania constitute collecting? Well, if it was a *mania*— and various accounts actually suggest this—it probably did. And yet a case could be made for the idea, ironically enough, that there is something vulgar and even philistine in the utilitarian idea of wearing what you feign to collect, *using*, so to speak, art. It mocks the whole enterprise.

Actor Michael Caine has a similar thing about clothes; he wears—and collects—blue dress shirts exclusively; I recall having read that he has something like 500 of them. Rudolph Valentino was a fanatical collector of shoes. So was the great diva Maria Callas, who also had a fetish for matching handbags, with a preference for red. Elvis Presley supposedly had hundreds of pairs of white cotton panties, but let's not discuss it. Instead, take those hideous cream-colored Good Humor suits writer Tom Wolfe affected (unfortunately, pale as poached fish himself). Maybe he was mimicking Mark Twain, another white suit addict, although Twain was taller, ruddier, and did write *Huckleberry Finn*. Hard to match those, indeed. Wolfe must have had racks of these suits, but they mean no more than suits *qua* suits, shirts *qua* shirts. Isn't intention deeply involved in giving meaning to a gathering?

Imelda's shoes. What does what we collect say about us? What's involved, for example, in always going after the same thing? Imelda Marcos didn't collect shoes—she simply hoarded them. (Six thousand pairs of shoes were found in her closet on February 26, 1986.) They weren't art to her, they were commodities, hedges against the horror of running out of them, a hedge against terrible fears of poverty, goods gathered against an imagined catastrophe (which in her case came to pass anyway). And what, it might be asked, most embarrassed her growing up in poverty? You could almost prove one by the other through algebra. Bare feet. It was no different with the brutal and vindictive Romanian political witch Elena Ceaușescu, who with her peasant origins developed a mania for honorary degrees. She also had a raging passion for fur coats, and owned 40 or so. Unlike his wife, Nicolae kept nothing; it is rumored that his clothes and accessories were burned after a single wearing, so that no one could claim the distinction of ever wearing anything worn by him.* But neither was a collector. After all, collecting, in its

---

*A fanatical hunter, however, who shot thousands of animals a year, the dictator did collect hunting trophies. He owned 244 trophies for deer, and 385 for bear. On one hunt he shot at close range 66 black wild mountain goats, a rare and protected species.

best sense, is about art. Aesthetics. (As Philip Larkin once observed, "The impulse to preserve lies at the bottom of all art.") Collecting may derive from a low compulsion to acquire, but surely transcends it. There is something self-consciously useless about it.

Were eerie Elena and idiotic Imelda, greedily snatching up furs and shoes while children in their own countries starved to death, any different, say, than the Collyer brothers, Homer and Langley, who accumulated—*squirreled away*—virtually everything they came across? Both were college graduates. They lived at 2078 Fifth Avenue, their surrealistic residence in Harlem. In 1947 they were found dead amid junk, newspapers, crockery, rags, a forest of furniture, cans, spare parts, rat traps, machines, breadboxes, rocking chairs, and literally walls of newspapers. Their doors were padlocked, the windows boarded up. The gas, water, and electricity had long ago been disconnected. In all, over 140 tons of orts and oddments were carted away.

A raven's nest was found some years ago in England, lined with medieval royal English documents, including one signed by King Richard II, which the plucky little bird, greedy for spoils and with the thrill of the new, had pilfered out of a library attic somewhere. It may have looked like collecting, but it wasn't. It was only dumpy Elena with her furs. It was merely Imelda Marcos with all of her Charles Jourdans, Bruno Maglis, Ferragamos, Cassinis, and rhinestone-studded disco Guccis (size 8½).

We mustn't forget, speaking of clothes, Mrs. Smiling's matchless collection of brassieres in Stella Gibbons's novel *Cold Comfort Farm*. "She was reputed to have the largest and finest collection of these garments in the world. It was hoped that on her death it would be left to the nation." Her search for the perfect one is important. There is something of the Pilgrim of the Absolute in

Mrs. Smiling, especially in her quest for the perfect one, as it is the case with anyone with the mindset of the authentic collector. A metaphysical faith, given sanction by Plato himself in his Theory of Forms, literally informs the search of those looking for the One behind the Many. Stella Gibbons writes of her character, "She was an authority on the cut, fit, colour, construction and proper functioning of brassieres; and her friends had learned that her interest, even in moments of extreme emotional or physical distress, could be aroused and her composure restored by the hasty utterance of the phrase: 'I saw a brassiere today, Mary, that would have interested you.'"

Restored composure.

There is the comfort in collecting of philosophical essence giving meaning to one's existence. Some years ago in France a lot of important paintings began to disappear from the walls of various museums. Police searched everywhere, looking on several continents, feeling quite certain they'd find them fenced. It turned out a year or so later that they were still in Paris, in the apartment of a poor student. He had not really stolen them, he confessed, he had planned to give them back—merely borrowed them out an overwhelming desire, one he couldn't contain, to be surrounded by beauty. The French people voted desperately he not go to jail. They understood the passion of the true collecting mind. It *depends* on beauty. And in this we have one of the essential doctrines of life as lived.

"I am what is around me," wrote Wallace Stevens in the poem "Theory,"

> "Women understand this.
> One is not a duchess
> A hundred yards from a carriage."

The Stendhal Syndrome

When I was a Trappist postulant at 18, we nightly chanted at Compline, in the dark of the abbey just before retiring, the magnificent *Salve Regina*. A soft suffusing light was trained on a stained-glass Virgin Window. And I fell into deep reveries, spiritual ecstasies almost, over the heartbreaking beauty of each night's devotional: spiritual, artistic, romantic, erotic all at once. There was an elemental feeling generated by that deep beauty that welled up inside of me. I felt seized by a primitive force. "I once stood in front of a huge piece of sulfur so yellow I began to cry," wrote Diane Ackerman in *The Natural History of the Senses*. "The intensity of the color affected my nervous system." I remember a friend of mine at the University of Virginia, a young gay professor, being transported—weeping—listening, as he sat on the floor, bowed head, to *Tristan and Isolde*. Is art psychologically subversive? Can moods be induced that compare to the rapt, rushing feelings St. Teresa of Avila underwent in her mystical ravishment? Is it all part of the reason Plato banished poets from his *Republic*?

Ancient treasures can sometimes overwhelm. The city of Florence, for instance, with all its art, claims so many victims being overcome by art, if you can believe it, that is has actually opened a clinic—at the hospital of St. Maria Nuove—for what doctors refer to as the "Stendhal Syndrome," after the 19th-century French novelist, Marie-Henri Beyle (1783–1842), who went by the pseudonym Stendhal. It was he who described the extraordinary phenomenon he experienced during his 1817 visit to Florence when he visited the beautiful Basilica of Santa Croce, where Machiavelli, Michelangelo, and Galileo are buried, and where he was overcome with profound emotion. A key passage in his *Voyages en Italie* (1837–39) makes manifest the state of his overwhelming reaction:

> ". . . finally I arrive at the church of Santa Croce. There on the right, as you enter, is the tomb of Michelangelo. Further inside is the tomb of Alfieri by Canova: I recognize this great Italian. Then I see Machiavelli's tomb, and facing Michelangelo rests Galileo. What men! And Tuscany could add to them Dante, Boccaccio, and Petrarch. What an incredible reunion! My emotion is so deep that it becomes spiritual. The dim and religious light of this church, its simple wooden roof and its unfinished facade, speak powerfully to my soul. Oh, if only I could forget it! A monk approaches . . . and I ask him to open the chapel in the northeast corner for me, the one with the frescoes by Baldassare Franceschini. He brings me there and leaves me alone. In the chapel, sitting on the base of a kneeling bench, my head backwards and leaning on the pulpit to see the ceiling, Baldassare's Sibyls gave me the greatest pleasure that art ever did. Just being in Florence and close to the great men whose tombs I had just seen put me in a kind of ecstasy. Absorbed in the contemplation of this sublime beauty, I could see it close to me, I could almost touch it. I had reached that impassioned state in which one meets

with celestial sensations and with passionate feelings. . . . Everything spoke so vividly to my soul. Ah, if I could only forget. I had palpitations of the heart, what in Berlin they call 'nerves'. Life was drained from me. I walked with the fear of falling. Coming out of Santa Croce, my heart beat fast . . . as if life was over for me."

Stendhal had been seized, so to speak. He passionately records his emotions, his vertiginous indisposition. "I walked fearing that I would fall down," he writes. "I sat on one of the benches in the Santa Croce square and re-read with pleasure those verses of Foscolo that I carried with me. I didn't see their defects: I needed the voice of a friend to share my emotion. The following day the memory of what I had felt gave me a funny idea: for happiness, it is better to have a heart like mine than a Cordon-Bleu cook."*

It is a psychosomatic disorder, or fugue state, which seems to affect certain people in the presence of art, unstringing them, so to speak, as they stand before a work of sublime beauty. Dizziness, a rapid heartbeat, feelings of panic, fainting, confusion, incoherence, fugitive ideation, hallucinations, even visions of angels are among the identifying symptoms in the onset of this curious and extreme indisposition, an inability to function affecting one's feelings. It is predominantly an emotional crisis.

It was Dr. Graziella Magherini, chief of psychiatry at the Santa Maria Nuova Hospital in Florence, who for many years has given her attention over to this exotic syndrome, naming it after the

---

*For proof that not all travelers or art-lovers are susceptible to the syndrome, see Mark Twain's curmudgeonly response in *Innocents Abroad* to this very same church, Santa Croce.

French writer with the German pseudonym, who, as we have shown, lived in Italy and suffered from it. Stendhal was so undone—and, it seems, specifically upended by the Franceschini frescoes, as he confesses in the above passage, that he actually went so far as to write that he felt his life ebbing away! Suddenly in some kind of equally epiphanic way, as he goes on to write, he is saved—cured—by the poetry of Ugo Foscolo. Stricken by art, saved by it: the symmetry shows how impassioned a fellow Stendhal was and how open he was to the kinetic force of art.

Dr. Magherini, in her book *La sindrome di Stendhal* (1989), observes that it is usually the emotional texture of the artwork that sets off reactions, the magnificence of creation, not always the religious themes that they display. She points out the existence of like phenomena occurring, for example, in places like Jerusalem, another city of deep religious significance, and in Ravenna, an artistically rich Italian city on the Adriatic Sea. The problem, however, seems to be most common in Florence, the *locus classicus* of art, filled with Michelangelo's, Raphael's, Caravaggio's, and Brunelleschi's great work.

It is mainly the psychological reaction of tourists, in my opinion, succumbing, so to speak, to a strong inner response rising, rioting at times, to a sort of Dionysian frenzy and at other times leaving victims exhausted, uncertain, and powerless. Magherini makes much of the fact that most are sort of pilgrims far from home, alone, open to the air of unreality that pervades a city such as Florence, where so many are in transit, on corners reading maps, in strange and exotic surroundings. Can it be the overwhelming result of suddenly seeing the original work for the first time, and not mere reproductions?

A fugue of sorts takes place. Patients, we learn, are mostly under 40, unmarried or unattached men and women, sensitive types—you might even say precious types—traveling by themselves or in small groups, earnest people perhaps who do not travel much, who tend to be impressionable, and for whom cultural Italy has become the cynosure of their "tour," the center of their expectations as much as art. The problem is, to a degree, sensory overload. A breakdown of objectivity takes place, with the result a sort of "anguish by art," although the nature of the syndrome varies: some faint, some soar. One delirious patient, after viewing Caravaggio's homoerotic *Bacchus*, screamed that his "head and heart [were] in flames." Another man stripped stark naked, stood next to Donatello's *David*, and began passionately imitating the statue's pose. American girls in their twenties, lovers of art and brimming over with aesthetic emotions, seem as a group especially vulnerable.

Years ago I read in the *New York Times* of a 22-year-old woman who, only a few days after visiting the Uffizi Museum in Florence and touring rooms filled with sacred art (lives of the saints, the Crucifixion, Madonna and child) began to hallucinate. She imagined she saw angels and could hear them sing and even became convinced that she was the incarnation of a nun who had been buried in a town in Umbria. What happens is that in the heady presence of provocative paintings or sculpture, certain people either fall apart or respond hypomaniacally. Some feel euphoric and begin to dream, fantasize, theatrically erupt, feel even omnipotent. Others can become depressed, experience a rapid heartbeat, begin to perspire heavily, feel stomach pains, and even begin to feel the horrible sensation of being persecuted.

Overly sensitive souls such as these have some noble predecessors, all of whom, in the presence of art, have at one point or other, in the paraphrased words of the English art critic Walter Pater in his

Studies of the Renaissance, opened themselves up "to burn always with a hard gem-like flame, to maintain this ecstasy," which, by the way, he declared was nothing less than "success in life"—Proust, James, Goethe, Schiller, and Ruskin. Even the dour Sigmund Freud at the ancient Acropolis in Athens, for example, was so overcome by what he himself called *Entfremdungsgefühl*, or "perplexing unreality," that he fainted. He later remarked, "So all this exists, just like we learned in school."

When Henry James as a young man found himself for the first time in Rome, he might have been seen, by his own account, wandering through the streets in a drunken ecstasy, reeling and moaning in a fever of delight. He had that exquisite kind of sensibility, natural or cultivated one cannot say, that responded intensely to art, whether for weal or woe. At one point on a Tuscan tour, beauty so "discomfited" and so inspired depression in this novelist that he blamed sculpture in general for "placing a certain heaviness on the heart." And the sensitive Marcel Proust, who experienced actual asthma attacks while listening to Claude Debussy's five-act opera *Pelléas and Mélisande*—he claimed that, while listening to it, he was overcome by the overpowering scent of roses—was such an extremely intense and highly excitable person in the presence of beauty that, although in the terminal stages of tuberculosis, he set forth to see the exhibition at the Jeu de Paume of Vermeer's *View of Delft*, a painting he considered "the most beautiful in the world." He had to be dosed with narcotics even to walk. So mesmerized was he by a glorious yellow patch of light in that canvas, in any case (and only for that moment, *for the Flemish style bored him!*) that he suffered a near-fatal stroke, a seizure he would later diagnose as indigestion from potatoes.

Stendhal's, of course, was the classic case. Who exactly was this man and what was behind his syndrome? Marie-Henri Beyle, though he was born (Grenoble) and died (Paris) in France, was one of the most compulsive travelers who ever lived. He was completely peripatetic, never had a settled home, and rarely stayed for six months in one place. He hated his father, suffered from a genuine sense of persecution, and, writing, had upwards of as many as a hundred pseudonyms (including "Junius," "Mr. Love Puff," "Ths. Jefferson," etc.). On every topic except his own soul, and he wrote of much, he was the most amateur of amateurs, a fact that was simultaneously both a major limitation and his crowning glory as a writer, for that is what he became, and in many modes. He tried his hand at journalism, drama, criticism, verse, biography, treatises, political commentary, government reports, novels—*The Charterhouse of Parma* is his masterpiece—short stories, travel sketches, and autobiography. The man was, in fact, a compulsive autobiographer.

Confession fascinated him, especially about intimate and romantic interludes. His love affairs were the major occupation of his life. His relations with women were always at a fever pitch. He was often an unhappy lover, a sulking and wounded one, and it was a favorite persona even in his novels. He liked to make notes of amorous conquests on his suspenders and to scribble the intimate details of his life in random old books, the odd envelope, scraps of paper. He had an excessive, almost feminine sensibility. Emotions meant a lot to him, and for our focus here cannot be stressed enough. "I have always felt rather than perceived, which makes me naive as a child," he wrote in his *Journal*.

He was a pronounced Italophile, falling in love with that country primarily because, to him, all Italians were, like the noble savage of Jean Jacques Rousseau, "noble and natural," a simple people who had access to, and fully trusted, their emotions without hesitation of self-consciousness. "At first sight and without any metaphys-ical reasoning, a statue by Canova will move a young Italian woman to tears," wrote Stendhal in *Promenades dans Rome* (II, 24). Seeing Italy for the very first time, he wrote, *"J'etais absolument ivre, fou de bonheur et de joie"* ("I was absolutely drunk, mad with happiness and joy"). It is a typically undampened *Beylisme*. In fact, he chose to spend the greater part of his life in Italy. When he came back to Milan in September 1811, he experienced feelings full of delight and his heart overflowed with emotion. "I am on the verge of tears," he emoted, almost bursting. Tears, emotion, ecstasy were in vogue in the mid-19th century, just as they were in the late 18th century, the beginning of the Age of Sentiment, as witness Henry Macken-zie's novel *The Man of Feeling* (1771). Waterfalls of tears were shed over the protracted death scene of Little Nell in Dickens's novel *The Old Curiosity Shop*, whereas now there is only snickering.

It was always in states of heightened response that Stendhal fell in love, and the urgent, intense affairs he had with countless women prove it: Angela Pietragrwa, Clementine Beugnot, Victo-rine Mounier, and especially Metilde Dembowski, a woman whose indifference to him generated the work *De l'Amour*. (He wrote it in romantic despair as an alternative to suicide and supposedly wept on the galley sheets.) He loved to distraction, almost always with mar-ried women. It is quite evident that he believed drama, intrigue, and complexity were virtual requirements for real, actual romance and that deep passion was the *sine qua non* of the artistic temperament ("wild eyes, sudden movements, and disheveled dress"). He became obsessed with a now-forgotten operetta by Pierre Caveaux called *Le Traite nul* and its leading actress, Mademoiselle Kubly, and stood for hours outside the theatre poring over notices where the actress's name was written in large letters. Discovery of music, painting, and love occurred almost simultaneously in his life. For Stendhal, the arts were one of the prime means of attaining happiness, or, as he himself effusively wrote in his *De l'Amour*, *"La beaute nest que le promesse du bonheur"* (Beauty is the only promise of happiness). But it was the heady stimuli of beauty that left him so vulnerable and open to emotional flux.

He worshiped Shakespeare, Canova, Correggio. He collected engravings. He had such an abiding fixation about Raphael's *Madonna of the Chair* that in 1814 he actually thought of trying to smuggle the painting out of the Louvre. "In my view," wrote Stendhal, "painting is the art of portraying a passion by the features of a physiognomy and the position of a body, and of moving the spectators . . . by sympathy." The simple mimetic doctrine he held, that art was a matter between the "characters and himself," was to become the entire basis of his art criticism. Stendhal did not claim to judge paintings by formal criteria, color, surface texture, and so on and so forth. The criteria by which he judged paintings—that he used as a pretext for reverie—were what he felt in the impassioned, nervous, moving, and subjective responses within himself, a mirror for his own sensibility, almost a projection of his own needs.

Stendhal actually regarded Correggio's paintings as human beings, embodying his own ideal of happiness and beauty, moods of the same voluptuous qualities he sought in women—and perhaps because women in paintings exist only in a state of potentiality and cannot break promises, unlike a loved object in real life, he was never disappointed by Correggio. (In this, with his fascination for the irreconcilable tension between art and life, he was very Keatsian.) He came to look on art as a kind of substitute for the lost illusions in his own life. And as we've seen he ran in the process the whole gamut of psychic reactions, where, to use Dr. Magherini's phrases, *l'esperienza estetica* led to *la vacanza della mente.*

Briefly, it is a panic disorder—but one that is meaningful (not chemical) in origin. A conflict underneath an unresolved crisis, or a crisis being avoided, may trigger it. It may very well be an attempt, in fact, to evade an incident that threatens us simply by articulating it on a smaller scale, and deliberately, as though settling a bill as cheaply and as quickly as possible, sacrificing the part to be rid of the whole. But it is not contentless over-activation, like most panic attacks. A psychotic break can sometimes disorient, confuse, and appear to be like a delirium—by which term is usually meant a dulling or a clouding of the consciousness—impairing the registration of memory. Often of course hyper-arousal or vigilance is a *defense* against underlying delirium. Psychiatrists seem for now divided on the subject. Some believe that the syndrome is serious, while others judge it a minor and temporary disorder effected from the tapping into deep emotions.

One recalls that Stendhal's passion for Metilde was almost as overwhelming as physical constraint. He never got over her. Even years after they had been together, he once happened to see in the street a little white satin hat very like the kind she used to wear, and, upon seeing that alone, he grew faint and fell against a wall. With love as with art, *spossatezza* results, an exhaustion or powerlessness. Or *inganno*—delusion. Victims of their emotions, whether facing a fetish of love or the *Bacchus* of Caravaggio, are, so to speak, "lost in the Boboli," left wandering in dreams.

In a way, one may align, even assign, the characteristics of such seizures to a sexual spasm, of which one may not even be conscious because of the collapse of so many other faculties, along with inflamed imagination, and because of its character as a momentary return to chaos. And in a way that is what it is, a soul suddenly flooded with darkness or light or maybe even both. Often it is sudden. Unrecognizable in the shocking complexity of its onset. And like any seizure, it can be painful, and even if ethereal, it can also be scary—for one is unexpectedly, weirdly, no longer connected to the real world. Something familiar now appears alien. One can point to Sigmund Freud's notion of "the uncanny," perhaps even the odd and unexpected suggestiveness at the bottom of what Edgar Allan Poe called the "imp of the perverse." It is to have a taste, to paraphrase Allen Ginsburg, of "unreality sandwiches," a dropping away underneath of psychic floorboards. Disorientation.

Disorientation to the point of hallucination (auditory) is often transient and usually not a very grave sign. The old entity called "hysterical psychosis," in which people hallucinate walking talking persons, is certainly well known. Doctors now speak of "brief reactive psychoses." Aesthetes and persons with delicate sensibilities on the schizophrenic spectrum can be overwhelmed by pictures and scenes, like Keats' "negative capability" taken to its extreme. There are 107 case studies of beset art lovers in Dr. Magherini's book, cases quite varied in cause if not in effect. Travelers and *viagattore* and museum-goers who suffer the syndrome are often victims of trying to squeeze too much art into too short a period of time, or of perhaps even trying to find too much meaning in a work. They are sometimes also too lonely, overly religious, not in love, *in* love, blue, symbol-mongering, saturated with unexamined memories, sexually frustrated, or seeking something.

There is something about the unreality of museums on tourists, as well. The eeriness of the places, like confessionals. They are old, dark, labyrinthine, forbidding, and slightly Marienbadesque. "Museums are in the end nameless and continuous," writes John Updike in *Museums and Women*. Monuments can exert on one, not an appeal to beauty, but of one's own relative insignificance. And solitude, often a precondition for emotionally experiencing an aesthetic object, can be intimidating. Museums are also erotic. Empty rooms suggest a certain lubricity. Forgotten corners. Echoing galleries. Stairways. Nudes and beauty. Even the silence, the aeroferic silence. Silence is suggestive. There is apprehension in it. Tension. Foreboding. Promise. "Nothing seems more like a whorehouse to me than a museum," wrote Michel Leiris in *Manhood*. "In both you are in a sense under the sign of beauty, archaeology, the slave-market aspect, a ritual prostitution." As a matter of fact, Leiris was himself once "undone" coming across a work of Cranach's in the Dresden Museum, *Lucrece and Judith*, nudes painted on complementary panels. And even jet lag can lead to odd syndromes akin to mania and depression in the susceptible. How many lapses are forgiven, pardons made, excuses offered for those hours of extended flight?

The rigors of travel, by the way, the toll, cannot be discounted. The victim is already destabilized for being out of normal time and his or her normal element. Stress is often related, especially in tourism, to the physical abuse of simply being shunted about, of having to find food and lodgings, of fatigue, of not being able to communicate or speak the language of the country. There is often alienation and great tension. When traveling, even friends often bicker. Unpredictable aspects even to one's very own personality often surface and must perforce be confronted. (In high school, me and various friends of mine who yearned to travel abroad were thoroughly convinced that girls, I mean American girls, too, behaved more "loosely" in Europe. And it was foreignness itself that seemed to guarantee it.)

More than half of those hospitalized in Magherini's study, to make another point, had previous contact with a psychiatrist or psychologist, which may come as no surprise. Much repression may be involved coming to the fore. Many patients of the syndrome, touched by beauty they had previously withdrawn from or avoided, suddenly confront the self and suffer what Magherini calls "*la mente nel guado.*" The mind at the river, pausing, is about to ford it. A moment of uncertainty. It involves abandonment. Crisis. Unease. Security shuts down. Suddenly there is no one to lean on.

A psychosis often involves intentionally doing what we are afraid of in order to deliver ourselves from it—responding to a painting, say, by the exaggerated sense of allowing ourselves to be overwhelmed, even appropriated by it, and usually in public circumstances—a situation that is often exemplified in suicide, which in many respects derives its sole prestige from the fact that it appears to us, paradoxically, as the only means of escaping death by in fact making use of it, by creating it ourselves. Another point here—an observer of art is often diminished by what he or she witnesses, hugeness and palpability. The Stendhal Syndrome, in many of its manifestations, has more than a hint of desperation about it, of flinging reaction. Doesn't perfection often sadden us? Leave us wistful? ("God, it's terrible to love what you can't have. Maybe that's why you love it," notes Updike.)

May it not also speak to what, regarding beauty, is maybe missing in ourselves? Of what we perhaps can't create ourselves? Don't embody? Can't have? Yearn to join, so to speak? Isn't that what John Keats is getting at when in his famous poem he apostrophizes the cold perfect lines of the Grecian urn, saying, "Thou, silent form, dost tease us out of thought as doth eternity"? I also feel that, for many people, to come into the presence of the famous, the well-known, the recognizable, the powerful, the uncircumscribable, or the exotic is, simply by the very act, too much to take.

Assassins often kill for reasons of what might be called the "envy of admiration." It is fairly well-known now that Lee Harvey Oswald deeply admired, and so perhaps ironically came to dislike, President Kennedy. Same with the nebbish Mark David Chapman, assassin of John Lennon. An overreaction to a work of art is often an "around-the-end" move personally to relate to it, the straining attempt at trying to get closer to what, by failing to do so, only repudiates what we are, leaving us ignominiously unrecognized. When we strike a blow, isn't the shattering only the *contre coup* to (and part of) the strike? Mark Chapman shot Lennon out of the despair of wanting to *be* him—he often in fact *signed the singer's name instead of his own*—and so, coming to hate himself for what he wasn't, enviously killed his double in a kind of suicide. I don't think it goes far to suggest that the Stendhal Syndrome is a way of "seeing" art, dramatic yes, but a valid frame of a specific response, and, who knows, the violent or exaggerated response, dramatizing the self rather than the work, a way of "killing" it.

Reactions characterizing the Stendhal Syndrome are often of the theatrical, exaggerated kind often associated with homosexual frenzy, deep, emotional, almost visceral. There is a participation, mind to art object, that is too exclusive and, in a word, overly precious. In a very real sense, Gustav von Aschenbach in *Death in Venice*, overwhelmed as he is by the Greek beauty of the Polish boy Tadzio, catches the very same virus that symbolically and literally brings him through foppery and foolishness finally to his death. In a figurative sense, he is killed by beauty, as Stendhal fears he himself might be, that same Stendhal who once observed that bad taste leads to crime. (The reverse is also true.) It was the exquisiteness of Aschenbach's taste that was his undoing, that, ironically, led to his forsaking all taste in the end simply for the demented extremes of passion to which he succumbed. For the golden beauty of the boy Tadzio, for beauty itself, nothing is sacrificed, and the tired delirious writer, willingly forsaking reason, becomes almost pathologically passive to his fate. Gustav von Aschenbach is irrecoverably—and profanely—stricken by what, alone, he has repressed for years. Bliss is his agony, beauty his undoing.

"Spiritual enlightenment produces feminization of the male," writes Camille Paglia in *Sexual Personae* in one of her coruscating, if slightly cavalier, observations. "The more intricate biological pattern of the female has become a model for the artist, the mystic, and the saint." She goes on to say that intuition or extra-sensory perception is "a feminine hearkening to the secret voices in and beyond things. [Lewis] Farnell says, 'Many ancient observers noted that women (and effeminate men) were especially prone to orgiastic religious seizure.' Hysteria means womb-madness (from the Greek, *ustera*, womb.)" While Paglia and Farnell go on myth-making with what can sound like outlandish generalities, there is something to be said for the sharpened sensibility veering into the hysterical. Yukio Mishima, for example, got erections from looking at Guido Reni's famous painting *St. Sebastian*, where the saint, half-naked and dying, is pierced with arrows. Mishima had his first *ejaculatio*—his word—while looking at it. Indeed, he himself was several times photographed, his face twisted in agony, tied up, while posing as St. Sebastian.

I know a particular devotee, an often obsessed male acquaintance of mine, who once traveled all over Europe just to see the various Antinouses, lovely male faces with sculpted lips and perfect, flawless bodies: the Farnese Antinous in Naples, the Mondragone Antinous in the Louvre, the exquisite Antinous in the museum of Eleusis, etc. It became such a consuming passion, an urgency, a fixation of such acuteness that when he came into the presence of one, he told me, he'd perspire and feel faint and, feeling a sense of kinship, even ownership, begin gravely to resent *other* people watching it. And I feel that's another aspect common to the syndrome, Aschenbachian in its dimension, the compulsion in the exaggerated response and intensity of fixed devotion of trying by drama to claim the work for oneself, to own as it were the rights to it by fiat.

An issue of *Opera News* in 1944 contains a letter from a fan who wrote about nearly swooning at a Wagner concert he attended with his father. "The music of the second act [of *Tristan*] reacted on my emotion so strongly that I almost fainted and I had to feel my way out to the stairway, not to lose control of my body. After feeling better I returned and my father said to me, 'What's the matter with you, boy?' 'The music' was all I could answer."

It was one of Freud's assumptions, to my mind a fascinating one, that the unconscious is both the creator and the recipient of art. "An Insight into Richard Wagner and His Works," by James Clark Moloney and Laurence A. Rockelein, offers the case history of a patient obsessed with *Tannhäuser.* The theoretical starting point of the authors, Freud's assumption, is that the reactions of patients to works of art contain pointers not only to the problems of the patient but also to the conflicts felt by the artist. A dialogue between the two is always there, and an astonishingly Dionysian response often a result, as can be seen, for example, in Nietzsche's vivid description of certain sections of Wagner's audience. "Just look at these youths—rigid, pale, breathless! These are the Wagnerians: they understand nothing about music—and yet Wagner becomes master over them." It is a view echoed by Max Nordau: "The emotional excitement which the works of their idol made them experience did not proceed from the singers and the orchestra, but in part from the pictorial beauty of the scenic tableaux, and in greater measure from the specific craze each brought with him to the theater, with each worshipping Wagner as the spokesman and champion."

Stendhal wrote in *Memoirs of a Tourist*: "The most insignificant ancient column has an infinite advantage: it projects the soul into a new dimension of feelings." And yet in facing art for many, a tourism of the soul is often involved, and many don't want to go. Or they may want to go, but can't. The moment of passage can become a transformation or lead to a sort of pathological breakdown. Again, *spossatezza* results, sapping powerlessness. Or *inganno*, delusion. One is, so to speak, poking around and about Florence "lost in the Boboli," and wandering. Is it wild? At the end of it all is there only uncertainty? Disorientation? Or can somehow one speak dreamily of expansion of the self?

Thrill is often terror, and pleasure can be as overwhelming as pain. We spend half our time in life drawn to what burdens us, elevated by the deep emotional panic of what, in going missing, leaves us flat and fallen. "Between nothing and grief," wrote Faulkner, "I will take grief." There is surely a delicious and dangerous frisson to such intense feeling. It is clearly a seduction of a kind. "I love the Stendhal Syndrome," wrote David Forrest, a psychiatrist friend of mine, in a letter to me. "That's how I want to go mad."

R. Crumb Goes to Church

One way to judge an artist is whether or not you want to see his work over and over again, and to me Robert Crumb's cartoons have always been and remain endlessly fascinating. I consider him matchless, inimitable, the nonpareil of illustrators, than whom no one is more daring. The explanation for illustrating Genesis, of all books, an opus thought to be inspired by God, he neither offers nor explains, which is only part of what may seem an enigma here.* Another is that this instantly recognizable and daring stylist, whose acidic drawings and amusing scatologies we all know, has chosen to pledge allegiance, inversely, to such a different ideal that many may find it as unlikely a prospect or about-face as Mahatma Gandhi playing the banjo!

I would never presume that illustrating Holy Writ was unlikely for an artist like Crumb, for nothing is unlikely with or frankly beyond him. I have long treasured his range, the twists of his mind. Raised Catholic, he is an unbeliever and vigorously anti-clerical. He boasted to me that he was never an altar boy. In 1998, Crumb sent me a copy of a book his father wrote, Charles V. Crumb's

---

*The Book of Genesis, W. W. Norton, 2009.

Training People . . . Effectively (1970), a militant book title that might have been used by SS-Obergruppenführer Reinhard Heydrich, Deputy Protector of Bohemia and Moravia! "A true believer, the 'Organization Man' of his generation," Crumb described his father to me, adding, "I wonder if this book sold well . . . probably not . . . it's not entertaining enough." A man with 20 years active duty in the U.S. Marines, Crumb Sr.'s book—one of several he wrote and replete with charts and diagrams—sets down laws of control, repetition, instruction for "trainees." I can see he would have been a father who brooked no griping or guff. "My father was an openly preferred atheist," Crumb wrote me on June 5, 1997, when the subject of faith came up, stating, "He sent me to Catholic school, he claimed because he thought the 'discipline' was better than public schools. He attended church on Sundays out of social obligation and conformity. My mother was a 'lukewarm' Catholic—she basically had no belief system, really—she lived on an elemental level, taking each day as it came."

I confess that I have always considered Crumb's victimization tales and rug-chewing reasons for leaving the Catholic Church, at least the explanations he gave to me, puerile and slightly contrived. All of that grousing and handwringing about having been walloped by a few nuns for minor infractions? Total bullshit. As far as any festering wounds go—what, he got yelled at in the confessional for stealing a bag of M&Ms, berated for swearing at his mother, scolded for trying to look underneath a schoolgirl's dress? Come on, man—I would have my martyrs made of sterner stuff. Martin Luther at least had *dogmatic* complaints! Christianity and the requirements to follow it seriously and with honor have, of course, always been a particular bugbear not only to the conveniently faithless but also to bored and idle anti-intellectuals. Crumb has always had a sneaking dislike of complexity, big words, academics selling "wolf tickets."

Whenever Crumb would write to me with all of his tall tales about having to study "Latin and crap like that," remarks always offered with irreverent, agnostic sallies and muttering insinuations about the dark lunacies of "Father McGuire's *Baltimore Catechism* with its diagrammatic milk bottles of sin," I could only laugh out loud. In letters Crumb would bristle at my critical and open dismissal of his respectful, xenophiliac interests in Eastern thought, ayurvedic diets, Theravada suttas, and what to me is the chloroform-in-prose writings of such bloviating nature mystics as Baba Ram Dass, Maharaj Ji, and Swami Ramakrishnananda, work which has always made me want to chew gum and cry. Maybe it is because we are so different in many ways. Crumb loves porkpie hats, sandals, riding on women's backs, France, 78-rpm records. I prefer going hatless, loafers, watching a woman ride a horse, Germany, and 45-rpm records.

So ours has never been a David and Jonathan situation, OK? He thinks I'm a prig, overeducated, dogmatic, and wordy. I find him eccentric, hidebound, priapic, and in some very serious ways stubborn—to me, an aspect of stupidity.

No funnier or hipper correspondent could be found than R. Crumb, but I early found an anti-intellectual component in many of his arguments, a sort of muscular endorsement of populism (which I can't take)—in letters he would paradoxically inveigh against Bruce Springsteen but then go on to puff Charles Bukowski, when they are both of them, let's face it, basically middle of the road—and an earnestness in regard to contradictory positions. People who did not go to college always seem to be those who make a big issue of it, I've noticed, and bristle at systemic intricacy, and always seem to act as if complexity is an indulgence of the formally educated alone. It is surely sociologically diagnostic if not a matter for the psychiatric couch that Crumb in correspondence always puts polysyllabic words in quotation marks. He is a complete original, but there has often been something of the stubbornly doctrinal in the man, so I was not at all flabbergasted when he told me that he was illustrating this sacred book.

I was simply looking for fiercer grace.

I myself would have chosen, had I Crumb's brilliance for illustration and were looking toward Scripture, instead of the first book of the Bible—well, I was going to suggest the *last* book, Revelation or the book of the Apocalypse, a challenging sci-fi option that would highlight his own crazy dreams, pictorial wit, astonishing imagination, and illimitable interpretive genius, in spite of the fact that he has been for while, or at least so it seems to me, to be well past his Gonzo period. Upon reflection, however, I would have to say that the correct choice of biblical book for Crumb to illustrate should have been the book of Job, a tale perfectly suited for his particular fret-patterns, endless griping, sweaty ultra-agitation, execrations, loud misery, false counsel, revenge, and scabrous bitterness—by cursing his birth out loud, Job sets in motion no end of destruction—all of it allowing for R. Crumb's patented sword-to-the-heart satire, delight in sexual foolishness, and the depiction of a howling string-band of weird God-botherers and freakazoids!

While the book of Genesis can be dark, theatrical, and full of moiling and intrigue in places (the Serpent, Lot and his daughters, Abraham and Isaac, the fire and brimstone of Sodom and Gomorrah, etc.) it is mainly the pious if occasionally dramatic account of the Hebrew story with the usual if predictable *contretemps*: anger, jealousy, bitter rivalries, personal failures, love and betrayal and death, standard fare in the annals of human behavior.

There is the phantasmagoria of the Creation and Garden of Eden, which as graphic possibilities do lend itself to fantasia, but in terms of illustration R. Crumb charts familiar territory—a lot of Hebrew visages face to face: big noses, teeth, headbands, *raiment*—and gives us with his amazing succession of drawings a very literal account of the book that recapitulates, on a Scoville scale of non-outlandishness, the sort of Sunday School images I have come across many times. The project is worse than failing to call up Crumb's specific talent—it ignores it. Literalism is the bane of Crumb's big undertaking.

Where is the Gustave Doré here? The dark fantasy? The unexpected corners turned to evoke magic and astonishing surprise? Whither the kind of grotesque elongations that we loved in the savage Crumb of the 1960s and 1970s, the mutilating satire, freaky, outlandish, twisted, bizarre—*fugly!*—of those underground comic books of his that we collected like *Uneeda, Hytone, Bijou, Hup, Weirdo,* and *Dirty Laundry*?

For such coruscating concoctions, for that kind of monstrous whimsy, look somewhere else. Still, this undertaking, nevertheless, is identifiably R. Crumb.

To those who do know his work is to recognize it here. One is able to discover the usual Crumb signifiers in these elaborate 175 or so closely worked pages (they are quirkily not numbered) in *The Book of Genesis Illustrated by R. Crumb* (the production's official title): round, buttocky women; a love of feral, toothy grins; the ongoing gallery of wonderful rubbery faces—the splendid lineage of Ishmael in chapter 25 and the children of Israel who came to Egypt in chapter 46 are two particularly splendid ones—and, repeatedly, acts of sexual congress, always the missionary position ("And Shechem, the son of Hamor, the Hivite, prince of the land, saw her . . . and took her . . . and laid her . . . and defiled her" [chap. 34]), which come as no surprise to any of R. Crumb's loyal fans, and yet those scenes, drawings, an equal surprise, are as tasteful, subdued, and chastely unveering from those of Moses' own brief references to them. In this illustrated *Genesis*, a respectful and obedient Crumb is staying strictly in bounds. "In a few places I ventured to do a little interpretation of my own," writes Crumb in his introduction, "if I thought the words could be made clearer, but I refrained from indulging too often in such 'creativity,' and sometimes let it stand in its convoluted vagueness rather than monkey around with such a venerable text."

Crumb is scrupulous. Having worked so hard on this demanding project for so long is certainly proof of that. He is always graphically accurate. Certain panels show entire landscapes, travel narratives, hectic conflagration, court scenes, full assemblages. There is a stream of facial realizations and reactions so detailed, so specific, running through the panels of Crumb's Genesis as to constitute the creation of an entire people, an actually realized populace!

Many of the Hebrew faces he draws one can observe today on any New York City street and subway. Abraham looks like Ed Asner, Leah Julie Kavner, Laban Mel Brooks, Shechem Adam Sandler, Sarah Molly Goldberg, and there is more than a hint of Norman Podhoretz in Noah! Isaac looks like an aging Victor Borge! Fumble through the pages and you can find in this or that face, panel to panel, the lineaments of Old Testament faces—a grin here, a grimace there—the identifiable mugs of people who resemble Don Rickles, Elie Wiesel, Barbra Streisand, Mandy Patinkin, and other celebrity Jews. There is enough force in Crumb's splendid images for this book, dispensing with the text—high praise for any illustrator of vivid scenes—to be passed around like those old wordless pictorial midget Bibles by missionaries to illiterate but impressionable aborigines in order to convert them. It is the different personalities in Genesis that one remembers more than anything. Crumb manages to bring to even the least celebrated figures on these pages—the smallest supernumeraries—a distinct uniqueness of face.

Let no one think, however, that the master of grotesque cannot draw a tender figure or a soulful one. Consider some of the profoundly realized women's faces and figures Crumb has drawn so well in his series of remarkable *Sketchbooks* or, say, illustrated on a lot of those restaurant menus in his *Waiting for Food*, graphic books which embody great gentleness and are as sweet as any done by Raphael himself. Let me mention here that I have seen in London at the Victoria and Albert Museum the Raphael "cartoons" (that is indeed their correct designation), which were commissions done by the great Italian Renaissance master and planned as full-scale designs for a set of ten tapestries that Pope Leo X had intended to use to cover the lower walls of the Sistine Chapel in the Vatican. The cartoons were sent to Brussels in 1517, where several sets of tapestries were woven—10 now exist—and I can say that Crumb's strong visual gifts, his innate *depictive* sense, the way he can bring out the structure of a face and animate it with both the passion and the dimensional precision we can recognize, are not far behind Raphael Sanzio's.

Fans of "underground comix" know *The Sweeter Side of Crumb*, a 2006 title, which, assembling a potpourri of drawings, states on the dust-jacket flap that it purports "to help him establish a more positive public image with women," compiles many of his softer drawings: pretty girls, former high-school classmates, blues singers, all sorts of amiable sketches, a lovely drawing of his son Jesse as a tyke, even "Women Singers from the Torrid Regions of the World." I do not need to be convinced of R. Crumb's softer side.

His confessions show humility, even if crude, he and he conveys a spiritual sense in the role of seeker.

Crumb, a self-professed "unbeliever," as I say, also gives us in God the Father an imposing Supreme Being, who in white raiment and the long white beard that reaches down to his toes, looks every bit like the conventional high-and-mighty Cecil B. DeMille prototype that we can all identify from our collective unconscious; a big, tall, scolding, electric-eyed aristarch of a Walt Whitman who, with a booming, firmament-loud voice and hair 'til Tuesday—white and wild—appears from on high throughout the book with a dark scowl and a mood blacker than muscular dystrophy to chastise us poor inchlings. Crumb's Satan makes a brief ludicrous appearance as a Creature from the Black Lagoon. I daresay—and I am hardly the first one to say so—that it is inevitably a creative blunder, as well as far too taxing, to attempt to illustrate Satan or the Supreme Being. Writers always fail, even the best of them, like Milton in his *Paradise Regained*, having weakly resorted to jewel imagery to convey the concept of heaven and majesty—and artists are no different. It is always an inartistic mistake to try to delineate the ineffable. I gotta tell ya, when I saw Crumb's conceptions of both God the Father and of Satan—the Jerry Falwell versions, try—I needed quickly to go reread a few of his early *Zap Comix* as a comforting anodyne.

R. Crumb's commitment to the project was unswerving. It had been long in the making. He is a tenacious and dogged man. He wrote to me about it almost five years previous to publication, as early as March of 2006. In a letter of April 19, 2006, he wrote, "I'm up to page 50 on the Genesis Project. I will enclose a few pages with this [letter], to give you some idea . . . Man, it's a lot of work. I get so obsessed with the detail . . . But it's a good challenge for me, and I think my drawing skills have been upgraded in the process . . . I figure I've got about 125 or so pages left to do. . . ." Crumb was unswerving. But was he unsparing?

I have used the phrase "staying in bounds." But let me ask, is that what anyone wants from Crumb—self-editing, damping down, circumspection, being good, balance, sobriety and sense? We tend to want what we are used to from the cantankerous Godfather of Underground comix, the misanthropic, sexually obsessed, madcap creator of Skutch, Fritz the Cat, Whiteman, Angelfood McSpade, and loonies like Snoid, Eggs Ackly, Shuman the Human, and the Mr. Natural we know and love who spent time in a loony bin in the 1970s, along with his thumbfumbling companion Flakey Foont, who in their hysterical and profane madness chase Cheryl Borck, Devil Girl, and twist off her head and violate her in a hundred ways!

So let me ask then, when we picked up Crumb's *Genesis*, was it not with a bit of fear and trembling? R. Crumb—illustrating Genesis? And, as we turned the pages, was it reasonable of us to be asking where is the sabotage, the satire, the spice, the scorn? Fair of us to be looking through his rendering of the first of the Pentateuch, to try to find the same rough-edged, revolutionary irreverence that for half a century now has animated Crumb's astonishing universe, one that is uniquely his? What can we discern in this great anomaly of Crumb illustrating Moses to applaud? Can we honestly accept it as part of the Crumb oeuvre or is it pure apocrypha?

In short, does this book succeed or fail?

An old apothegm goes, "Sinners commit, saints omit." All literature depends on conflict—clashes, battle, antagonism, etc. Stories inherently need a state of opposition in the very same way heat needs blister. Most actors (except Robert Redford, I gather, who repeatedly loves playing the hero) far and away choose to play negative parts: bedlam figures, heavies, rogues, marginals. Iago, Richard the Third, Captain Ahab, Uriah Heep, Dracula. The explanation is simple: such creatures *do* something—act, act up, act out. *Misbehave!* Wussy roles tend passively to do nothing! Take John Milton's *Comus* (1634), a masque presented at Ludlow Castle in honor of chastity. The plot concerns two brothers and their sister, denominated the Lady, lost in a journey though the woods. The Lady becomes fatigued, the brothers wander off in search of sustenance, and then, all alone, she encounters the debauched and devilish Comus who, disguised as a villager, claims he will lead her to her brothers. Deceived by his amiable countenance, the Lady innocently follows him, only to be captured, brought to his pleasure palace, cruelly taunted, and victimized by his necromancy. Comus accosts her; she rebuffs him. With his guile and schemes and magical inventiveness, he uses his wiles, but she refuses, arguing for the virtuousness of temperance. She is too sedate.

In terms of drama—of pure theater—one character commits, the other omits. In short, the Lady is static, while the wily Comus is kinetic. That is why, although the masque's actual full title is quite long and didactic, it is colloquially known as *Comus*, for Comus, as it were, gets all the good lines and hogs the best scenes. *All actors want to play Comus!* It is a theatrical given to want to play the villain and the rogue! It is to be able to *act!*

What is missing for me in Crumb's *Genesis*? Salt. Spite. Satire—specifically, *his* salt, *his* spite, *his satire!* I mean, a *Mad* comics version of the book of Genesis, not a polite Gustave Doré-esque simulacrum of the thing. Much of this work here is splendid. The 70 or so pages on the Joseph story, for example, probably the richest lode to mine in Genesis, at least in terms of narrative, are amazing, almost as dramatic, all things considered, as the wood engravings done by the genius Lynd Ward for his supernal *Madman's Drum, Wild Pilgrimage,* and *God's Man.* Crumb's line never flinches, the detailed root-work and scaling of his pen in these pages are wonderful. The cross-hatching! The guy can draw anything and never fails to get perspective right in backgrounds and settings, the vistas and views. He went to the trouble to be accurate, one can see that. Look at the nap in his drawings of stones, wood, cement, brick. Skies! He knows surfaces! The flow of water. The cast of trees, buildings. The shims, shadows, and graininess of his black-and-white illustrations, the exactitude, never fail to ignite the many scenes.

But the moralist in Crumb having taken over, even an over-reverential timidity, ultimately addresses a subject matter too intimidating even for him—who knows, maybe even his imagination—to dare to test it with the extravagances of revolutionary audacity or coldly satirical boldness or of rude, thumping innovation. I suspect in facing this text, Crumb was—wanted to be—obliging. There is not enough bite in Crumb's *Genesis,* is what I am saying, too much cozy reverence. Consider the brilliance, the untrammeled racy *insolence* of, say, "The Young Crumb Story" or "My Troubles with Women" in *Hup* #1 or *Introducing Kafka* simply to compare genres. I prefer the work of the guy who had been coloring outside the lines since the 1960s!

Truthfully? I would have told Crumb to pass on the job. Not to accept the undertaking. Why did he do it? Did he do it for money? Was he paying penance for all of his lewd and blasphemous comic books of the past? Had this been a childhood goal? Was some kind of epistemological voyage involved, some kind of ethical *rite de passage,* whereby he set himself the task of drawing the images of such a book in order to study such a subject in order to learn something? Who can say? Was it somehow an act of contrition? Of conciliation? Is this an example by way of art of the man throwing himself down on his face with chest-thumping *mea culpas* to the very God he draws? Do I want to keep this book on my shelf? I most certainly do. Can one say that this is R. Crumb's *capolavoro*? It is most definitely not. It is quaint, like those old biscuity colonial handstitched chapbooks with homely drawings of alphabets, animals, farm implements. It is not his A-game, not even close. Was he the perfect choice to manage this vast, four-year-long undertaking, to stay the course? Yes. For the resolve to bring it off? Indeed. For the exactitude required? Absolutely. For staying loyal to the scriptural text? Without question. And why?

In many ways, Crumb is a very literal person. He is literal because at bottom he is—yes—a moralist. Most satirists invariably are. Remember, satire is ridicule in order to *correct*. Oodles of fun satirists are not. Scapegraces, maybe. Scamps, scoundrels. But the fact of he matter is, they all take themselves seriously. Alexander Pope, Jonathan Swift, Mark Twain. Scratch a caricaturist and find a didactician. If one were to choose to illustrate something like the book of Genesis—and such a person would indeed do such a thing—he would rarely try to extrapolate or even innovate with a drawing, for the didactician is unbudgingly stubborn, one of the worse manifestations of the moralist who is of course a compulsive truth-teller.

Who would deny in R. Crumb's rendering of the book of Genesis—and there is no question that it is the major thrust of his work—that autobiography figures largely? I would venture to say that, in the matter of simple unadorned confession, in words alone never mind drawing, no one, not one person, celebrated or not—not St. Augustine, not Jean-Jacques Rousseau, not Thomas Merton— has exceeded Crumb for his addictive frankness, in his willing, brutally impartial, pathologically relentless depth of exposure, self-deprecation, or rudely raw, even humiliating candor. So to find Crumb's slavish adherence to the word, in this case to the Word, does not surprise me in the least. I have seen it before. I once took the initiative to send him, with a view to his illustrating it, a manuscript of mine entitled *Truisms*. I was astonished to find the returned pages annotated by a Luddite, an earnest and flat-footed herbert, immune to irony, a man with neither a sense of humor nor a concept of either the tropological or the figurative. A few of those truisms follow—they are composed in quatrains—with Crumb's comments in brackets:

"A handshake's more than anything a code. [-?huh??]
You rarely see a pretty woman walking. [not true! I seen
        lots of pretty women walking—thousands of them,
        so what are you talking about??]
Dryness never figures as a concept in a toad. [silly]
There's lassitude in every rumpled stocking. [??]
Baseball writers are always sentimental. [—?]
It is vulgar to smear jelly over bread. [snobbism]
Commitment is avoided by a rental. [? not necessarily]
Texans like buckles as big as their heads. [silly]
Eating coffee-grounds will kill a dog. [nah...]
Impotence is common among sports fans. [conjecture,
        snobbism]
The act of voting is like feeding hogs. [who says?]
A ballerina's beauty's in her hands. [No, in her legs!!]
Chaplin was a bore compared to Keaton. [opinion]
Mountains always range from north/south. [??]
A good biscuit's never overbeaten. [you don't beat bis-
        cuits]
Bad teeth slubber a pretty mouth. [slubber?]"

I would hasten to point out that Crumb's lowbrow humorlessness here, certainly not characteristic of him and by no means the essential Crumb, reminded me then and does even now of W. B. Yeats's theory of the "anti-self," by which the poet advances the unique idea that, as a deep, subconscious act of self-completion, the work that we do in art—the nature of the things we make—is inevitably the opposite of what we really are. Yeats convincingly offers that Dante Alighieri, being a sensualist, wrote spiritual poetry, that John Keats, an unhappy fellow, wrote joyous poetry, and so on. It is about paradox, all of it.

The mask, as it were, becomes the face.

"In setting out to illustrate the Book of Genesis," Crumb writes in a final Commentary on the book, "I quickly learned that I had to read the text very carefully and closely in order to render as accurately as possible the words that were actually written there." *Render accurately?* But no artist is bound to any particular set of images when illustrating Scripture, for no such set of images exist. It is just that Crumb being so literal a fellow—and I will hasten to add, in the matter of approaching a sacred text, even slightly obsequious—decided to set aside the Yeatsian mask and show us, for whatever reason, the moralist's face. It is at least in one morph an act of anti-transformation. At the Transfiguration Jesus Christ "illuminated" himself in one dynamic instance. (The deeper and perhaps more notable miracle is that Christ remained otherwise *un*transfigured during his entire ministry on Earth.)

I would guess that this is Crumb's version of such a momentary transfiguration. It is his "coming forth," so to speak, to demonstrate for us, that he is more than just the "comix" creator who in his "fuzzy" acid-taking period back in the wild 1960s gave us so many creeps, inveterate self-loathers or unsavory little peckerheads like

Mr. Snoid, and all those bulb-nosed, gross-booted little zoot-suiters who are keepin' on truckin'. As poet Robert Browning wrote, "Ah, but a man's reach should exceed his grasp, or what's a heaven for?"

The Art of Revenge

I remember—forgive the paradox—an unmemorable girl-friend of mine who in leaving me for someone else left me as well with a previously unfelt and inadmissible emotion, it being for a moment impossible to face the truth, never mind tell it; but as surprise ebbed another urge flowed. My immediate thought was a simple and uncomplicated one: I wanted to kill her.

Revenge, exactly what I felt, is forgiveness's other face. It is an emotion, discounting mercy, neat to the taste and born of a desperate need to rectify a wrong by inflicting harm in return for an injury, a slight, or an insult and to exact satisfaction for that which, at least in the sufferer's eye, blind and stupid fate (never, of course, without its specific agent) not only has allowed but in a way has cruelly fostered. The sole desire in retribution is to equalize: "I'll get even with you!" To revenge is, in fact, to avenge. Simply put, it seeks—it demands—justice.

A popular legend has it that the Italian composer Antonio Salieri, overshadowed by his rival Mozart's glory but, worse, nursing a deep wound at the cosmic inequality of things-as-distributed, at the first-night performance of *Don Giovanni*, alone of all the others, hissed and stormed out of the theater—and then when opportunity arose poisoned his enemy. Caesar was stabbed by senators, Socrates was murdered by judges, and Christ was slapped by lackeys. So envy is always involved in revenge, but that is only the beginning, for the overwhelming and monomaniacal conviction superseding it is the thought on the revenger's part that without his personal intervention, correcting happenstance, the galling want of fairness will forever prevail and the suddenly—and often reasonlessly—despised will go scot-free. It will be remembered that while Salieri toiled desperately over his own mediocre compositions, feeling ever unrewarded, Mozart's work reputedly came easy and fame followed. Salieri couldn't abide this. In *Mozart and Salieri* (1830), Pushkin gives us his complaint:

> "Where, where is justice, when the sacred gilt,
> When deathless genius comes not to reward
> Perfervid love and utter self-denial,
> And toils and strivings and beseeching prayers,
> But puts her halo round a lack-wit's skull,
> A frivolous idler's brow? . . . O Mozart, Mozart!"

Revenge transfigures you. It boils and concocts into poisonous nourishment all the facts and fictions it compounds from the lives of its enemies, and fuels the delight it abhors, for your grief has found the one thing in this life that *causes* it. Alive, it is your plague, instigates against you, throttles all you are. The vigorous if irrational idea is that you alone of all others on earth are left to correct what otherwise must go forever uncorrected. And in spite of the fact that in the process you become a cauldron of pure pain—owned, in fact, by that which you would sell, and are diminished by ("The murderer," writes Nabokov, "is always the victim's inferior")—there is often a crazy comfort in the obsession with whatever must be vindicated by whomever must be abused or punished or killed.

Revenge, like hemorrhoids, seems to have been created to locate in one particular place one particular pain to absolve the body in all other places of all other pains.

Do we fear the Gorgon or simply create it to locate our fears? The retributive aspect of revenge, in any case, whether logical or not—to put things right—is nevertheless its primal scream, what indeed gives it its most commonly applied epithet: "sweet."

Revenge! Where hasn't this shadow reached? It is a poem by Tennyson, the name of Sir Richard Grenville's famous ship, and a tragedy by Edward Young. There is an Iranian drink so named. Fairy tales virtually have no other plot. It is as old as the first murder ("And Cain was very wroth and his countenance fell") and as recent as the summer of 1982, when the Israelis invaded Lebanon and announced that this was in retaliation for the shooting of a diplomat in London. It is the central theme of Elizabethan and Jacobean tragedy, animates every discussion of capital punishment, and is even implied in the Virginia state motto: *Sic semper tyrannis*—Booth, avenging the lost Civil War, shot Lincoln howling those very words. I'd suggest that along with love and war, with which themes, let us say, it has more than passing acquaintance, revenge is the single most informing element of great world literature. And George Orwell, in his essay "Why I Write" (1947), cites it as the first motive for many taking up the profession ("the desire . . . to get your own back on grownups who snubbed you in childhood, etc."). The revengeful personality—it is more often than not an intellectual's, of which Hamlet, a thinker, not a "rash and splenetic" type, is only one example—very often has the power, in fact, to give a significant penetrating quality to literary expression; one thinks of Juvenal on

Roman decadence, Luther on papistical excesses, Milton on Charles I, and Hitler on the Treaty of Versailles. But for the pure, unadulterated masterpiece of contumely very little surpasses Alexander Pope's almost gibbering attack, in his "Epistle to Dr. Arbuthnot" (1735), on the effeminate Lord Hervey ("Sporus"), who had been collaborating with Lady Mary Wortley Montagu on scurrilities against him and so met with this response:

> "Let Sporus tremble—"What? that Thing of silk,
> Sporus, that mere white Curd of Ass's milk?
> Satire or sense alas! can Sporus feel?
> Who breaks a Butterfly upon a Wheel?"
> Yet let me flap this Bug with gilded wings,
> This painted Child of Dirt that stinks and stings . . .
> Whether in florid Impotence he speaks
> And, as the Prompter breathes, the Puppet squeaks;
> Or at the Ear of Eve, familiar Toad,
> Half Froth, half Venom, spits himself abroad . . ."

While black, there is something splendid, almost mythological, in such ramping revenge, the wicked ebullience, the *folie de grandeur* mounted to frame a prose so determined to collaborate with anger, disappointment, and fury. The beating heart of revenge is its excessiveness, and its excesses—the pathological lengths to which it will go—are astonishing. The misandrous Delia Bacon, part critic, part crank, spent her entire life trying to besmirch William Shakespeare. Rufus W. Griswold, who secretly hated Poe but was made his literary executor by wheedling it out of Mrs. Clemm, maliciously proceeded upon Poe's death to blacken his reputation through hundreds of lies and falsifications. Revenge is a feral branch of hatred. The anticlerical historian of philosophy Will Durant (educated by the Jesuits) dismisses all of medieval philosophy in one sentence: "A baffling circuit from faith to reason and back to faith again."

The wound—the insult spawning revenge—is ever open, as the mind gropes to deal with it—but not to cope with it, as if to assuage. Not at all, not a bit of it! Coping with revenge is not to solve but to *cooperate* with it, to see the fiery flame of fury heightened! The longer it lasts, the sharper it feels. "Wrong turns are like tuberculosis," wrote Nicolo Macchiavelli, "hard to detect and easy to cure in the beginning and easy to diagnose but very hard to cure in the end." Expect no genuflections—no suppliant knee—from the infuriated victim bent on revenge. In never submitting, he but echoes Milton's Satan:

> "What though the field be lost?
> All is not lost; the unconquerable will,
> And study of revenge, immortal hate,
> And courage never to submit or yield:
> And what is else not to be overcome?"

There is something intriguing here worth another word. Another sort of pathos seems involved. There is a certain hopeless kind of revenge, never far from insanity, that insists on mounting itself against the abstract, the too vast, the uncircumscribable, a few examples of which might be Nietzsche's opposition to Christianity, Frederick Rolfe's position against the Anglicans, Hitler's vindictiveness toward the Jews. Otto Weininger, riding his hobbyhorse, wrote the dense neo-Kantian *Sex and Character* to prove women had no souls! Such mountainous fury can only consume, wear away, and rot the antagonist, but it is a type of intransigence, even if in a negative way, that in its uncompromising madness approaches genius. The person given over to revenge is never an ordinary man. The New York Yankees played so poorly in a doubleheader against Chicago on the night of August 3, 1982, dropping both games, that owner George Steinbrenner, rancid with fury, publicly declared as a humiliation to his team—"they weren't worth even watching"—that all 34,000 fans attending that night could attend another game free!

It is the lot of such people, if to be opposed, then also to be invigorated by opposition, beholding their enemies in an eternal vigil, like the lifeless cobra in whose eye the murderer's image is forever embedded, and they actually crave to hate that constant hallucination of face—whether smirking through the attack it signals or the absolution it seeks—which becomes, in fact, almost a badge of those enemies for one attributes to them not that state of normal human happiness, shot through with the common moods of mankind, that should move us to entertain for them a feeling of kindly sympathy, but a species of arrogant delight that merely pours oil on the furnace of our rage. One thinks of Richard Nixon and the press, imagined leaks, the enemies list.

In its usual form, revenge is the change in behavior that is classic reaction—a response to a stimulus. For instance, Mr. Abdullah Tariki, the radical Saudi Arabian founder of OPEC, organized the oil-exporting states specifically to strike a blow at the United States, where, because of the treatment he received during six years' engineering study in Texas in the late 1950s—the "Jim Crow" years, when he was considered black and treated vilely—he became embittered for life. The not-to-be-disowned John Hinckley was shown in his trial for shooting President Reagan to be nursing a deep grudge against authority figures (his wealthy father, advised by a psychiatrist, had sent him packing with only $100), who in his confused mind seemed fully unimpressed with his young, impossibly high, certainly megalomaniacal ambitions to be a successful rock star and boyfriend of a famous movie star. And then Peter Sutcliffe, the "Yorkshire Ripper," was a pathetic and cowardly little boy who, bullied at school, grew to take up body-building and was soon snarling at the weak himself. He adored his mother, who, however, had an affair that desolated him, and within months of his marriage (he both hated and feared his wife, Sonia) he began attacking and killing women—prostitutes—who, queerly, were an essential part of both his despair and his marriage. There is something in the dark soul of the mass murderer—J. B. Troppmann, who did away with a woman and her five children, Henri Desire Landru, the French Bluebeard, and Theodore Bundy come immediately to mind—that is never far from revenge, its weird little posture giving destruction added motive in early failure, grievous disappointment, remembered scorn.

The revenger is, by definition, a victim. He is solitary, often in exile, forgoing communion with the society he terrifies. "What dog," asks George Eliot in *Silas Marner*, "likes a figure bent under a heavy bag?" The world has done badly by him. A formula of rupture has taken place; suddenly his consciousness is heightened, for he has spied (a word he'd favor) what he immediately can neither countenance nor forgive, and he fixes upon that one thing that the reductionist mind madly isolates as the only solution to the world's woes. Every former excellence of his enemy becomes every conceivable fault, every promise—expected, if not actually made—an impervestigable lie, and every memory a viper eating through the bowels of his benefits, all to set in motion such a fell and deadly hate that through a sea of sins he'd wade to his revenge. Human feeling curdles. Lenin, visiting Maxim Gorky, once demanded that he shut off a phonograph playing Beethoven's "Appassionata" lest it weaken his anticzarist resolve with feelings of sentiment. Oliver Cromwell sent his soldiers back to Drogheda to slaughter the Irish children they thought to spare, with the remark "Nits will be lice." There are many passions that we are condemned to feel only in a reduced form: never revenge. With it you have come under the shadow. You would countenance black magic. And yet how little is achieved, though other problems be solved! How *mistakenly* can a person have wanted what, taken away, repudiates the meaning of life itself?

Revenge is a restless desire precisely for the *ideal*. The tormented soul, hobbled by denial, by prohibition, sees himself betrayed and so, paradoxically, tries to recover by an act of supreme alienation and anger that which has been taken from him and which, constantly fleering at and ridiculing him by the very nature of its existence, mocks the mind to murder. "I want satisfaction!" cried the duelist in his humiliation. And yet what most generates, most often animates, revenge? Disappointed love, perfidy, dissolved friendship. And why so? The revenger is a person, usually, who has expected eternal unflinching fidelity from family and from friendship, and often in a quite ungainsayable way, but having lost it—he literally suffers a reverse—then employs the most effective and rigorous means of correction and so goes through life fixed on delirious hope in order to pledge allegiance to an inverted form of the same ideal. "Oh," cries Ahab, "now I feel my topmost greatness lies in my topmost grief."

The smoldering aspect of revenge is often in direct proportion to the degree in which the person's right to exist as a human being has been taken away. In his illness—he is literally infected—he has been handed, so to speak, a writ of *ne exeat*. He must be cured. The cure is freedom. Whoever will set the revenger free—and the cry for release is the *sine qua non* of his gnawing vindictiveness—

can be the only one, in fact, able to do so, and so ironically remains, as the singular agent of deliverance, also the sole abettor of his own destruction. It is a marriage, pledged until death do them part. A man in the grip of revenge has not so much lost the ideal as he has transferred the whole concept of one ideal to the furthest extreme of another, and challenging in the process the necessity of injustice that exists—often as the emanation of a punitive or arbitrary God—he writes in his own bitter soul not just a complaint but an entire destructive theology.

Revenge, indeed, has curiously theological implications. The law of talion—an eye for an eye, a tooth for a tooth—cries out to its cognate, "Retaliate!" Blood revenge is actually sanctioned in the Old Testament, the returning of evil for evil, blood for blood, a "justifying"—in the printer's phrase—of an unbalanced line. In Melville's *Moby-Dick*, the rankling Captain Ahab, named after the Old Testament ruler who "did more to provoke the Lord God of Israel to anger than all the Kings of Israel that were before him," becomes the embodiment of revenge itself. He has been wounded ("unmanned") by the whale, inexplicably, and the dismemberment has driven him to such a pitch of anguish—homicidal, suicidal, and deicidal, all at once—that in maniacal pursuit of his nemesis ("the incarnation of all those malicious agencies which some deep men feel eating in them . . .") he has to be confined at times to a strait-jacket in which, mad, he "swung to the rockings of the gales."

Ahab's intellect is enslaved but yet also concentrated by his madness, and, as happens in the matter of revenge, he has lost his humanity in the very act of vindicating it—the essential paradox of revenge—and has become the very image of the thing he hates, a statue of penalty cast in a single mold, a fireman of punishment and egotism. "I'd strike the sun if it insulted me!" he shrieks. Every dilemma has two horns. For Ahab has made himself not just a proud, self-appointed judge like Prometheus, Faust, Manfred, and Lucifer but also, like them, revenge's plaintiff, a tragic scapegoat. He is both victim and executioner—revenge always involves both—who in his compulsion for seeking equality has also elected to accept vengeance as the sole law of existence (the opposite was his intention), and so transmogrifies virtue into vice.

The greater the punishment each revenger feels merited by his action, the greater the value the agent of revenge attributes to the burden of his having to do so. Each constructs his revenge more or less according to the only logic available to him in a world that, however, illogically presents itself, for since he is forced to accept the fact that a positive, lost, is evil, the alternative of a negative, found, must perforce be the only good at hand to address it—and so the breach actually becomes the observance in a desperate attempt to settle a matter of contradiction by means of conflicting evidence. There is no better poacher than an ex-gamekeeper. We have here inversion, a topsyturvification of moral values that in revenge becomes its canon law. The condition is found in, among others, the autobiographer as avenger, the rejected lover, the disaffiliated child who grows up to settle the score.

Shakespeare's *Hamlet*, which takes its cue from Kyd's *The Spanish Tragedy* (1587), the father of all revenge plays, simply cannot be understood except in its theological context. It is, characteristically not just the case of an eye for an eye, for the jaw must be taken, along with the tongue and ears—*and* the victim must, after exquisite torments of both body and mind, go straight to hell. Revenge, to the Elizabethans and Jacobeans, demanded hellfire and everlasting torment.

Excess is all. Extremism in the pursuit of justice—the

revenger's conundrum—is no vice. And it's to be taken as a matter of breviary, this supernatural backdrop before which revenge is enacted—heaven, hell, and purgatory—that only with so much at stake can this terrible emotion be comprehended or, in fact, taken to have in it something akin to the slow grinding of the mills of divine vengeance—slow, yes, for often extreme patience is required.

Revenge is not always blister upon heat. It loiters, it bides its time, it grows. It perhaps alone gives full *meaning* to the full measure of the injury suffered. Months, years, decades may wear away, but not the corrosive and intolerable recollection of an injustice burning a hole in your sleep, if ever sleep there is. The nightmare that prevents, however, eventually *corrects* sleep. The wheel of fortune turns. It is the gift opportunity hands to adversity, a reward crowning pursuit and throwing up the exact set of circumstances that only time can give when, for the victim, it is most inopportune—he has moved away, say, remarried, grown older, changed his name, and, perhaps best of all, *forgotten*—but when, for the executioner, irony is made iron in the delirious turnabout that literally defines serendipity and without which, it may be argued, revenge can never be sufficiently *raffiné*. The revenger is a sinner with patience, a saint without forbearance, a master of what Borges calls the art of the *cachada* (to grab, to take somebody unawares). Delay is in fact only a kind of subtlety. The infernal deity Nemesis, goddess of vengeance—her statue in Rome was in the Capitol—is the daughter of Nox, and under the carapace of night one waits, waits, until all is ready. Revenge a hundred years old still has milk teeth.

Edmond Dantès, left to rot for 14 years as a prisoner in the gloomy Chateau d'If in Dumas's *The Count of Monte Cristo*, finally escapes ("Enough of this prison, let me now seek the antidote . . .") masterfully—and premeditatively—to wreak vengeance on each of his persecutors. "They'll remember my carbuncles," said Karl Marx from obscurity, writing *Das Kapital* in ill health, poverty, and the exile forced on him, as on others, by a corrupt economic system.

This is what's called "revenge in lavender"—revenge reserved—hanging fire, truly, as the years lope over the hill. But the cancer has metastasized. And that's just when the fun begins. "I'm back!" cries the revenger, demanding remembrance. "Look at me! Pay attention!" I read in the papers a few years ago of a man whose son had been hazed to death during an initiation by several fraternity boys, and the aggrieved father chose to take his revenge only after 10 long years had passed when, *pro re nata*, he methodically hunted down each of their sons and killed them in kind. "Thus," says Shakespeare in *Twelfth Night*, "the whirligig of time brings in his revenges." Revenge, as the proverb says, is a dish best served up cold.

There is, finally—and importantly—a penalty in revenge that can never be disregarded, the calm willingness to slay the self in the attempt to free it by those who, in daring personally to mete out justice, even if as only they see it, must also take the medicine they dispense. There was, for example, an uprising in the Sixties on Pulau Senang Prison Island, off the coast of Singapore. The prisoners could have fled. But they lingered to mutilate their guards—they castrated them, put out their eyes, etc.—and because the revenge was such time-consuming cruelty they were quickly caught and hanged, 66 of them, six at a time, on the Singapore gallows.

It is a sensibility, the revenger's, that, if open to the asperity of insult and keen to redress it, is also one equally arranged to feel all the while the criminal denial of true justice his very act contravenes. The tragedy is that he can't do otherwise. Forgiveness to him is the absence of justice, and so he "commits" justice, so to speak, in order to abolish crime—even as he perpetuates it. The crime is the punishment. It's as if he reasons: I am pleased with defeat in what I do because secretly for what I do I know I am guilty and only punishment can redeem me. Revenge has something about it oddly propitiative, an act often spitefully but inexorably united to contrition. Let heaven exist, he seems to say, even though my dwelling place is hell.

Of penalties there are many. There's often an unconscious wish for revenge in alcoholism, an indirect aggression born of anger and resentment against either oneself or others, and the same might be said of impotence and frigidity—a disposition, often, involving a subconscious impulse to thwart—and I have no doubt that this might also apply to failure in school or gluttony or bedwetting.

There's suicide. The Chinese and Chuvashes often hanged themselves on the doors of their enemies. In Hugo's *Les Misérables*, the crafty, inexorable, and ubiquitous Inspector Javert dogs Jean Valjean for 40 years (for stealing a loaf of bread to feed his sister's starving children) and then, robbed of his chance for retribution, commits suicide. His absolute fixation on revenge—*and in the name of law*—alone has given meaning to his sterile life. He has known only one emotion. Crazed with that detail, he cannot understand the whole. Or can he? Perversely, dreadfully, he comes to win *admiration* for the thief he's so long hated and pursued—a galley slave, a convict, who illogically, cruelly, returns pardon for hatred, good for evil! His nemesis in his forgiveness becomes his benefactor. An entire order of unexpected facts, fragmenting all certainty, arises to subjugate him, a moral sun rising only to blind him like an owl. All the axioms that had been the supports of his existence suddenly crumble:

> "He saw before him two roads, both equally straight;
> but he saw two; and that terrified him—him who had

never in his life known but one straight line. And, bitter anguish, these two roads were contradictory. One of these two straight lines excluded the other. Which of the two was the true one? His condition was inexpressible . . . what should he do? Give up Jean Valjean, that was wrong; leave Jean Valiean, that was wrong . . . what then! Such enormities should happen and nobody should be punished?"

But someone must be punished. That is just the *point* of revenge, that which for so long has given to it the battle cry "Somebody's going to pay for this!"

But who? Compelled to recognize all of a sudden the existence of forgiveness, Javert can only conclude—a horror to himself almost as if he had lost his faith (which, in fact, he has)—that *he* has become depraved, and so what should he then do? Call for Pontius Pilate's basin and wash his claws? That is ontologically impossible for him, precisely what the revengeful man is unable to do, for, as we've seen, this emotion—"so durable and obstinate," according to La Bruyère, "that reconciliation on a sickbed is the greatest sign of death"—is fed by the law of balance, equality, and a mania for justice that, even if it turns on itself, must be satisfied. And so, like the pygmy rattlesnake that bites and poisons itself in the convulsions of its fury, the empty Javert—"getting even"—revenges himself on himself and plunges headlong in suicidal despair from a parapet into the murky Seine. This is not victory, but if it is not victory it is yet revenge, and that is perhaps its most terrifying side, that, meeting nothing else, it becomes an end in itself. Who fights with monsters may thereby become one. Let Ahab beware Ahab. It is always ourselves we must fear first.

Dabblers and Dabbling

"I'm not a professional," novelist John Dos Passos once wrote of his artwork, "my sketches are like the penciled notes you jot down in your notebook and forgot to do anything with." The manner is self-conscious, the mode clearly a way of defending one's fragility—or facility—and there is a touch of excusing one's tentativeness. Nevertheless, there is passion. Dabblers need to feel free. In the way that an amateur feels a roomy, uncriticized openness, he *is* free! What more than anything the amateur artist would have you know about him is his need to play over the dire necessity of being judged.

Dabblers are hobbyists—painters *ex propriis*, weekenders, in essence like Porgy's woman, a "sometime thing." A hobby's a holiday, a pastime, arguably a way of getting away from work—because the lighthearted and comfortable fact of the matter is, it is not work. It might even be argued that only by maintaining an amateur status, by a sort of creative insouciance—what W. B. Yeats called "the old nonchalance of the hand"—can certain people achieve anything. Dabbling is in a sense a form of indirection by which many people interested in the arts often feel liberated from the burden of professionalism. It is cultivated inaction to a degree, a tranquil disdain for mere money-getting, a passive openness, "an archaic probity," as Edith Wharton, though in a different context, describes it in *The Custom of the Country*, "that [has] not yet learned to distinguish between private and 'business' honour." Indeed, one way a dabbler gets to work is by calling it fun.

Like many another lad, I myself grew up drawing and painting. My school notebooks were filled with cartoons, faces, and shapes of all kinds. "Drawing and painting were just something we all did, like playing outside in the snow," wrote Carolyn Wyeth, later in life. So it was with us. My mother painted pictures, as did my brother Gene, an international lawyer now, who nevertheless graduated from Pratt Institute after studying industrial design and still keeps an illustrated diary. I remember the text of my brother Paul's first tentative attempt at a novel, *The Fat Bird*, had drawings throughout the text. The desks of my two eight-year-old daughters, Shiloh and Shenandoah—we have no television set—are filled with paper, pencils, pens, and colored pens, and they draw all the time.

We all shared, my brothers and sisters, a common interest in art and could always be found, especially on snowy or rainy days, in one of the small rooms in our house on Webster Street in Medford, Massachusetts, making art. Spread out chaotically over every available table and floor, we worked in every medium, ink, crayons, watercolors, pastels, and in that scrum of paper, brushes, and coffee-can accessories, you heard little squawks of exasperation like "How do you do *shadows*?" or "Your trees are better than mine!" or "Look"—someone pointing to tiny circumflexes in the sky—"I've got birds." It was the kind of spontaneous enterprise our parents constantly encouraged. We were also among the last family in the entire western hemisphere to get a television set in our house.

A Theroux was always drawing a poster or making a sign

or doing a frieze in a classroom. We kept crayons in button-boxes and cookie tins, and our kitchen shelves were filled with art pads and jam jars filled with muddy brushes. I felt that I could draw anything. Writing of Toulouse-Lautrec, Aldous Huxley once wrote, "Up to the age of ten, provided of course that his teachers don't interfere, practically every child paints like a genius. Fifteen years later the chances of his still painting like a genius are about four hundred thousand to one." I was always fascinated with those old India ink bottles, back then shaped like chess pieces. I wrote small books—booklets—but always got C's in handwriting. I blamed the ink. And those sharp steel pens! And the old pour-spouts used to fill the wells! (It was the Age of Blotters. Banks gave them away wholesale—everybody did, law offices, churches. I wonder, have blotters gone out of fashion, like protractors in old school pencil boxes? Did any kid ever actually use a protractor, put one to use in school? Does anyone even know that *word* anymore?) And of course every Christmas—every holiday—we made and sent our own cards, fashioning them from our imagination and whatever materials we had at hand. We entered all sorts of art contests, and for or several years we published a family newspaper which we also wrote and illustrated. We were the Bruegels of Medford, Massachusetts!

There was a time back in the Thirties and Forties, perhaps because radio unlike television didn't usurp one's visual function, when drawing was not only a great diversion for youngsters but among the few to be had. It was also the Golden Age of comic books. Great cartoonists and illustrators who were popular at the time truly took on for us the stature of heroes. Our favorites were Munro Leaf, Rube Goldberg, Howard R. Garis, W. W. Denslow, Virgil Partch, Jimmy Hatlo, Basil Wolverton, Chic Young, Al Capp, and of course a local sports cartoonist, a brilliant one, named Gene Mack, who drew for the *Boston Globe*. Oliphant was a brilliant illustrator and had political courage, and I respected Herblock, who was one of the first to attack that ranting demagogue Joseph McCarthy.

We especially loved Munro Leaf, whose simple drawings in *How to Behave and Why* and *The Story of Ferdinand* we always tried to copy, his and of course the *Goop* books of Gelett Burgess. O. Soglow didn't mean as much to us. Virgil Partch seemed daring. I loved Jimmy Hatlo's cartoons and books and collected them, squirreling away any I found. Dr. Seuss, all of whose early books my mother read to us, was in a special category all his own. I remember being impressed with the words "The Yeomen of the Bowmen," a character in *The 500 Hats of Bartholomew Cubbins*. I also thought that the author had made a terrible spelling mistake on the last page of *Thidwick the Big-Hearted Moose* in the motto at the end of the story when he wrote "Veritas," which I thought should be Very Tasty

Later in life, I wrote a poem about Dr. Seuss' art:

> *Dr. Seuss's Eyes*
>
> Dr. Seuss's eyes were U's,
> Whether painted greens or blues,
> And whereas grammar this defies
> Truly all his U's were eyes.
>
> Dr. Seuss's U's were eyes.
> This the Golden Rule revives
> And Mr. Buber's wish renews!
> Dr. Seuss's eyes were U's.

We understood early the importance of nubs and 4-B pencils and learned about cross-hatching, stippling, and perspective, especially the phenomenon in drawing known as the "vanishing point." We wanted to emulate, not imitate, artists. There was a kid on our corner who could draw Dick Tracy and Ernie Bushmiller's Nancy, all matt-black hair and bristling fire points. For a while, I had little regard for books that were not were illustrated, and in a sense Arthur Rackham and Edmund Dulac were my favorite authors and illustrators, for owing to them I read stories which otherwise I would have ignored. Dulac introduced me to Hans Christian Andersen, Rackham to Rip Van Winkle, and Reginald Birch to Little Lord Fauntleroy, all of which had a profound influence on me.

Storybook illustrations foamed on within me long after I had seen them. Howard Pyle. Maxfield Parrish. N. C. Wyeth. George Cruikshank's drawings in *German Popular Stories*—perhaps his best work—so evoked the grotesque, strange, yet matter-of-fact qualities of witch and goblin, Rapunzel, Rumpelstiltskin, that like some of those old German engravings in early books, they actually had the power to silence me in awe and reverence. Then there was Elmer Rache's *Uncle Wiggily* (a bit better than Lang Campbell's, it seemed to me) and all the other loony characters in that wonderful saga: Skeezicks, Woozy Wolf, Bushy Bear, Skillery Scallery Alligator and the fierce Bobcat, and Nurse Jane Fuzzy Wuzzy. Somehow, Randolph Caldecott's drawings held little magic for me. But I can remember in detail the beautiful drawings by John H. Bacon and Harold Copping in Evelyn Nesbit's *Children's Stories from Shakespeare*. To this day the exquisite drawings of *The Wind in the Willows* move me like a symphony. My deepest conceptions of the world were through the landscapes of nursery stories, cobblestoned streets, storybook skies, illustrated events.

I still take great interest in drawing, sketching, and painting, though like several others in my family I've since become a writer. The amateur by definition works for his own amusement and self-satisfaction, and, as they usually say, the work is its own reward. Sometimes it has to be. I spent a great deal of time back in 1981, for example, painting the jacket for my novel *Darconville's Cat*, which Doubleday publishers proceeded to use, but for which to this day they have never paid me.

"We must not be too ambitious. We cannot aspire to masterpieces," Winston Churchill once wrote about amateur painting in his well-known essay "Painting As a Pastime" (from *Amid These Storms*, 1932). "We may content ourselves with a joy ride in a paint-box. And for this Audacity is the only ticket." One of the world's most famous dabblers, he recommended spontaneity as both a cure for and nostrum against diffidence. "There really is no time for the deliberate approach. Two years of drawing-lessons, three years of copying woodcuts, five years of plaster casts—these are for the very young." Churchill, who called his own paintings his "daubs," actually took up painting in 1915, during the bleak days of the Great War, when one day in the country he began fooling around with his children's paint-box and very soon got the bug of wanting to paint. Ironically, Adolf Hitler, Churchill's nemesis, also fancied himself an artist, and sometimes even went so far as to append the word *Kunstler* to his name. "My dearest wish," the Führer confided to his friends at dinner on July 22, 1941, "would be able to wander about in Italy as an unknown painter." Would that he had done so.

During the 1930s, the wilderness years for Churchill, he painted under the pseudonym Charles Marin, producing canvases that are, more than anything, the record of his aimless wandering: landscapes of the Riviera, the Dutch canals, the Norwegian fjords, several scenes of his friend Bernard Baruch's estate on the Waccamaw River. His close friends thought his finest piece of work of that period a still-life of two glasses alongside a bottle of brandy and a bottle of Scotch. Painting became for Winston Churchill—simply because it is—a complete distraction. Immediately he found something, without exhausting the body, that entirely absorbed his mind. (The prime minister was also an accomplished bricklayer, did you know that? He proudly held a union card, and, not without a keen eye and a major interest, he adorned the grounds of Chartwell with brick walls, terraces, and even a swimming pool.) The icon of the British prime minister sitting on a duck stool before a canvas in brimmed straw hat, a soiled white linen duster, and baggy trousers is as easily remembered now as the curmudgeonly old incarnation of John Bull making the victory sign or waving a cigar. "Whatever the worries of the hour or the threats of the future," he later wrote, "once the picture has begun to flow along, there is no room for them in the mental screen."

It might be pointed out as a matter of fact that Maurice Utrillo only began to paint as a therapeutic distraction between sanatorium confinements—he was a desperate alcoholic, even as a youngster—after copying his many views of Paris streets from picture postcards. The cultivation of a hobby, Churchill felt, is of first importance to a public man. He personally found painting restful. What's almost axiomatic in dabbling beyond that is that the element of variation enter into it, that it be a change, a bit of fun, larking, a pleasant occupation unconnected with—one's almost tempted to say opposed to—one's daily work. A sharp contrast is essential to real relief. Strictly speaking, of course, dabbling is about art. But what about novelists like John Updike, who wrote light verse?

Wasn't that dabbling? Or Daniel Defoe who raised civet cats? Or Albert Camus who grew roses? Or Buckminster Fuller who sailed? Or King Hussein of Jordan who was a ham radio operator? Or Amelia Earhart who wrote poetry and fashionably designed clothes, allowing women shirt-tails for the first time? (Millie also loved to dabble in paint, and in 1906, at the age of 11, gave her Grandmother Otis a lovely watercolor of the Atchison Bridge in Kansas, that being her hometown.) One can understand that a man who drives a bus for his living would be glad to play the crumhorn for his amusement. In a very real way, Thomas Jefferson dabbled in building the house that became his preoccupation for nearly his whole life long. His "castle," Monticello absorbed him more than human relationships, even more than the great offices he held. He drove workmen crazy, overseeing every last detail, from marble entablatures to the perfect nails to the right kind of sash cords on the windows. It was the kind of absorption children have when they are making something.

And it usually works out that way.

But here, dabbling is not only about art.

Emmanuel Swedenborg cultivated flowers. Pearl Buck liked to sculpt. Charles Dickens became a superb amateur actor and conjurer. Oliver Wendell Holmes was a carpenter. Georges Braque boxed. Elliott Richardson made his own Christmas cards. Stan Musial was an amateur magician, soprano Kiri Te Kanawa a fine golfer. Writer Carl Van Vechten cataloged cat literature. Novelist Günter Grass was not only a painter but a gourmet cook, as is writer Len Deighton. So was Irving Berlin, opera singer Tito Gobbi, Claude Monet—his journals on the subject have been published—Alexandre Dumas the elder, who wrote the *Grand Dictionnaire de la Cuisine*, nearly 1000 pages long, and philosopher David Hume, who after retiring from public life in 1769 devoted himself to cooking, as "the science to which I addict the remaining years of my life." And yet, oddly enough, cook James Beard gave acting lessons and the great French chef Auguste Escoffier yearned to become a sculptor. Certain passions predominate. Music, say. And gardening.

Novelist Robert Louis Stevenson played the flageolet, Mussolini the violin, and evangelist Oral Roberts the guitar. (He actually considered becoming a country singer.) Henry David Thoreau played the flute, Malcolm Lowry was an enthusiastic taropatch player, and Ansel Adams played the piano. (While Humphrey Bogart, Harold Lloyd, and Senator Howard Baker were amateur photographers.) Governor Thomas Dewey was a serious baritone, as was the screen actor, Russian-born George Sanders. The *Oz* books creator, L. Frank Baum grew prize dahlias and chrysanthemums. Poet Emily Dickinson was a skilled horticulturist, who grew pomegranates, calla lilies, and other exotica in her Amherst greenhouse. Nero Wolfe, the corpulent detective created by Rex Stout, raised orchids as a hobby. (He owned over 10,000 orchids.) Rudolf Valentino was also an expert gardener. So was gangster and *rosieriste* Bugsy Siegel. And Victor Sorge cultivated grapes on his farm in Portugal.

Is there a lot more involved here? Does dabbling point to deeper concerns? Does true happiness, as Sigmund Freud said, really lie in the fulfillment of childhood wishes? Initial hopes? Early dreams? James Thurber once sat down at a piano at Harry Adler's birthday party. "I love music," he exclaimed, "I've always loved music. I always wanted to be a musician. But what am I?" he shouted as he slapped the piano. "Nothing but a god [slap] damned [slap] humorist!" Interestingly, Charles Dickens's long cherished dream—a lifelong fascination—was to manage and have sole control of a great theater. Edmund Wilson would liked to have been a magician. The brilliant philosopher A. N. Whitehead once confessed he secretly wanted to become the head of a huge department store. Ludwig Wittgenstein speculated about becoming a doctor or carpenter. (He designed furniture, once built a house in Norway, and also sculpted.) Conger Metcalf would rather have been a pianist than a painter. And Cyril Connolly wanted to become the conductor on a wagon-lit.

There are surely as many motives for dabbling as there are people who take it up. Avenging boredom. The need to distract oneself. Simple fun. Seeking a challenge. Developing one's powers of observation. Expressing a creative urge or some deep-down personal need. (Much amateur painting is biographical.) How about showing off? In any case, it is surely not "to lift"—as T. S. Eliot (also a dabbler) once gave as the reason he wrote poetry—"the insufferable burden off one's shoulders." Far too dramatic. Dabblers and daubers walk on much flatter terrain. Parnassus is usually nowhere in sight. Neither is Helicon. "Why do you paint?" goes a bit of E. E. Cummings dialogue from an exhibition catalogue of his own paintings and drawings.

> "For exactly the same reason I breathe."
> "That's not an answer."
> "There isn't any answer."
> "How long hasn't there been any answer."
> "As long as I can remember."

"To paint is to love again," wrote the writer Henry Miller who, taking up painting to exorcize his pain after his wife deserted him, confessed to having seized a brush and done a series of frenzied and vicious portraits of her and her lover on the walls of their basement apartment. Miller would eventually go on to fry bigger fish. "I finally sold a watercolor to the Museum of Modern Art in San Francisco," he wrote to Lawrence Durrell in 1946. The great

Boston Celtic basketball player Tommy Heinsohn, a worthy landscape painter in his own right, grew up a lad of German extraction in tough Union City, New Jersey, during World War II and told me over the telephone he began drawing and painting during those long afternoons when he stayed home to avoid the bullies of the neighborhood. People will take up a brush for a thousand reasons. It was for Churchill, among other things, a way of developing an accurate and retentive memory. He was convinced that memory not only played a large part in painting but believed with the poets Wordsworth and Coleridge that one's best work was done only after one's initial impressions were gathered and suitably reflected on. "All the greatest landscapes," he wrote, "have been painted indoors."

There really isn't a generic dabbler, I think. While the paintings of many, like Victorian novels, tend to be trite, prosy, and heavily pious, suddenly appears an original—poof!—a pupil of no school whose private *deus* comes flashing forth like pure light. I suppose, in a way, composer George Gershwin came close to being such a one. A natural painter, he never studied technique, but there is a bold, vital line to his drawings, a lyricism reminiscent of Matisse. His portraits are among his best work—his father and mother, Jerome Kern, DuBose Heyward, Diego Rivera, Arnold Schoenberg, and many of himself.

Gershwin was of course also a major collector who owned Modiglianis, Utrillos, a Pascin, a Gaugin, and Picasso's *The Absinthe Drinker*, which was donated to the Museum of Modern Art after his death. Singer Enrico Caruso was quite a good caricaturist, though he never took any formal art lessons. Some of his work was published regularly by Marziale Sisca in his Italian-language newspaper *La Follia*, printed in New York. Drawing was his joy. In 1909, Caruso in fact befriended the then young Norman Rockwell who at

15, to supplement his income while he attended the National Academy School, was working as an extra at the Metropolitan Opera House for 50 cents a night. Once when Mark Twain gave a dinner party for all the leading cartoonists of New York, Caruso was hurt at not having been invited. "It seems that he knows me only as a tenor," said Caruso sadly.

Speaking of composers, Francis Poulenc was something of a dabbler. Paul Hindemith in caricatures drew his wife Gertrud as a lion and himself as a little bald man. Felix Mendelssohn courted the beautiful 18-year-old soprano Cécile Jeanrenaud by playing piano and drawing sketches of scenery they had visited together, and after their marriage he continued sketching domestic scenes of his wife and children. Cole Porter also tried his hand at painting—mainly quixotic, angular figures, painted on glass—during 1926 and 1927, before giving it up, presumably to devote more time to his music. Jazz trumpeter Miles Davis, also a dabbler, sold his paintings for between $15,000 to $25,000. John Hendricks, the jazz singer and lyricist of the group Lambert, Hendricks, and Ross, personally studied painting for eight years. Russian opera singer Fyodor Chaliapin, who drew, had a great feeling for line and color. Composer Stephen Foster was also supposedly a creditable watercolorist, though not a single specimen of his work appears to exist. His songs are eminently pictorial.

What perhaps most distinguishes the dabbler from the professional artist is that his need to draw and paint is a generally far less urgent one. His work tends to be more random, not always prolific, less often reworked, and his urge to be exhibited in galleries or shown to art critics is less often pronounced. A spontaneous, highly inventive art can often result, a sort of "Art Brut" freed from the ordinary runs of art. "What's important about drawing is drawing,"

Henry Miller states quite flatly—uttering more or less the Dabbler's Credo—"the doing it right or wrong, good or bad, finished or unfinished. Them as wants perfect horses, perfect nudes, perfect architecture, let them go to those as makes 'em."

There are echoes here of the French novelist Victor Hugo, another dabbler who left a large body of eccentric drawings in his notebooks. It is in his art, unfortunately too little known, where, an early surrealist who experimented with inkblots, he revealed much of his originality. Most of his drawings are caricatures and acerbic pen spurts that probe deep into the human character. Although he cultivated drawing as a marginal activity, he nevertheless strove to give as much of his work as possible an original twist, even resorting to such implements of composition as the feathers of birds, crumpled pieces of paper dipped in ink, candles, burnt matches, red-hot curling irons, a deliberately blunted pen, and several times, taking a cue from "spiritualism," a subject that fascinated him, by tying a pencil to a leg of a chair and recording its movements on a sheet of paper in the manner of automatic writing. He refused, of course, to call any of it art. In 1862 he wrote to his publisher Castel, "I very much fear that these nondescript pen strokes set down on paper more or less awkwardly by a fellow who has other things to do may cease to be drawings from the moment they claim to be such."

The attempt of course is, in the process of understanding, to distinguish what we are not from what we are and happily to accept the difference. "My gifts are small," wrote Max Beerbohm, whose caricatures are brilliant, often framed and found in English offices. "I've used them very well and discreetly, never straining them; and the result is that I've made a charming little reputation." On the other hand, one's vocation is not always discrete from one's avocation. A good example is Samuel F. B. Morse, father of the telegraph and a man who is better known as an inventor. Before 1832, however, he was primarily a painter, and an extremely distinguished one. A student of Washington Allston, he painted landscapes (somewhat derivative) as well as portraits (quite impressive) that included many notable figures of his day. And although he won numerous awards for his work, even founding an organization that would eventually become the National Academy of Design, he left it off for experiments in electricity. Was he therefore simply a dabbler?

It is often difficult to separate the vocation from the avocation. In 1918 the Socialist Party newspaper in Paris, *La Vie Ouvrière*, carried a small classified advertisement, which read: "You who would like a living remembrance of your relatives, have your photos retouched by Nguyen Ai Quoc. Handsome portraits and handsome frames for 45 francs." That poor artisan seeking business, trying to eke out a small living using his own manual on photo retouching, was—you guessed it—Ho Chi Minh.

Dabbling is of course limited to no one group in particular and to no single class, although it goes without saying that the more prominent the person painting, the more highly prized that work, often regardless of its quality. Charles III, who paints under the semi-pseudonym "Arthur Cornwall," would obviously have little trouble selling what to me are etiolated and rather famished watercolors—there's a good deal of self-aggrandizement by association among the best of us—but then why blame him for trying to paint? Or President Eisenhower, who couldn't do a portrait unless someone started it for him by making a nose? Or Lord Baden-Powell who did funny little cartoons? Or Frank Sinatra for his compulsive and less than confident need over and over again to paint clown faces, usually sad and wistful ones? (Did the idea come from the album cover for *Only the Lonely*?)

The world of show business has many famous dabblers. Comedians Red Skelton and Jonathan Winters painted. Winters, who met his wife, Eileen, as a fellow student at the Dayton Art Institute in Ohio, where he enrolled after World War II, once said, "The thing about art, aside from the fact that it's so therapeutic, is that it at least lets you think you're a spokesman." He added, "And it's also a great place to hide. It's like comedy in that." Actor Zero Mostel during summers painted in a studio on Monhegan Island in Maine. And Lenny Bruce for a short cartoon once did a whole series of animated drawings in color. Screen star Tony Curtis painted. As did Elke Sommer, and Anthony Quinn, who sculpted as well and possibly got involved in the whole business by once having played the role of Gauguin in the movie *Lust for Life*. Film director John Huston, who began painting as a teenager ("Nothing has played a more important role in my life"), was so talented he was asked to paint a wine label for the House of Mouton Rothschild. Singer Peggy Lee was an excellent painter. She once did four paintings, commissioned by the Sylvania Co. for an ad campaign, of which 200,000 sold. Composer "Duke" Ellington was also a passionate dabbler. And many agree that actress and former sex-goddess Kim Novak was by far the most talented painter of all in the old Hollywood set.

Actor Lionel Barrymore was far happier, though much less successful, painting, sculpting, and doing etchings than acting. He longed to be an artist. He felt ambivalent about the stage and hated films, which he found demeaning. During one period of depression, he persuaded his uncle, John Drew, to let him enroll in the Art Students League. Later he prevailed upon his actress sister Ethel to support him for as long as three years while he studied art, to little consequence, in Paris. Their younger brother John ("The Great Profile") Barrymore, before taking up acting and the sad, dissolute life it led to, began his career as a cartoonist, signing his work "Jake." It was the same with 19th-century thespian Joseph Jefferson—acting was his trade, painting his enthusiasm. Xavier Cugat, the popular bandleader who popularized such Latin rhythms as the mambo and rhumba, was more than a dabbler and first took a job in California drawing caricatures for the *Los Angeles Times*. In her later years, Clara Bow, the "It" girl, painted in oils in a sanatorium in the Hollywood Hills after her nervous breakdown. And Clifford Odets also took up painting for a time. In 1947, he had an exhibition of 33 of his paintings, of which, incidentally, Boris Aronson, the artist and scene designer, at one point in time took a dim view and sardonically told Odets that he would promise never to write a play if the playwright would promise never to do another painting.

Katharine Hepburn and Spencer Tracy, in between filmmaking, used to paint together—and she worked at it until late in life. Once an art student at Grinnell College, Gary Cooper originally came to Hollywood to draw caricatures. In the film *The Fountainhead*, he actually draws a cartoon; the camera, never swerving, records it all! Working for Famous Players-Laski, Alfred Hitchcock's first cinematic job was drawing scenes for films. Henry Fonda for a time actually studied with Andrew Wyeth. So did Michael Jackson, at least for one day.

Orson Welles did illustrations in 1934 for *The Merchant of Venice* in the Mercury Shakespeare series, little inky semi-defined sketches all up and down the margins. Harry Lauder was an inveterate doodler. The beautiful Linda Darnell was a serious student of painting. Frank Parker, of Arthur Godfrey fame, painted, as did former actress Anita Colby (Mrs. Palen Flagler). Farrah Fawcett's hilltop estate in Bel Air was filled with her own sculptures. And singer Tony Bennett, a highly reputed painter of landscapes and portraits—he signs his canvases with his baptismal name, Anthony Dominick Benedetto—sells in the five figures, and so esteemed is his work that he was commissioned by the United States government to design a postage stamp.

Liberace, who rarely signed an autograph without incorporating a grand piano into the swirling paraph, painted ties and blouses. "For instance," he said, "I did one for the American cabaret singer Hildegarde. It has all her trademarks. The waving arms, the upswept hair, the chiffon handkerchief. I'm doing one now for Dorothy Shay in the hillbilly theme. And I paint personalized ties for men." Sylvester Stallone's *Rocky I* is a collage that includes pieces of the original movie script. Actor Pierce Brosnan paints. As did *M*A*S*H*'s Loretta Swit. ("Painting was always just another form of expression to me.") The actor Van Johnson painted, as well. Gene Hackman, who also paints, said, "When I'm acting, a part of me maintains a wall, a guise. But my paintings are me." Peter Falk was an artist who loved to draw and sold his lithographs for $500. Dancer and actor Buddy Ebsen once said, "What you do on the canvas is either all your fault or all your credit."

Ron Wood, of the Rolling Stones, does portraits. Eric Clapton studied stained-glass design at Kingston Art School until he was thrown out. Bob Dylan actually painted the cover for one album, *Self-Portrait*, and for another, *Music from Big Pink*, did a funky, not overly memorable primitive of six people playing instruments next to an elephant. Singer Joni Mitchell attended the Alberta College of Art in Calgary for a while and in early life planned to concentrate on commercial graphics, then became sidetracked by folk music. Pop singer Cat Stevens (born Steven Georgiou) spent a year at Hammersmith Art College. He has drawn several of his album covers and illustrated a picture book, *Moonshadow*, taken from one of his biggest hit songs. John Mellencamp does oil paintings. And in 1975 David Bowie made a series of posters, or serigraphs, sets of amateur drawings rather muddily conceived although now selling for thousands of dollars—only 50 were made—consisting of five different renditions of the Tarot pack, cards of the earth, moon, death, star, and lovers. He signed, numbered, and dated the sets and handed them out as Christmas gifts to his friends.

Pop singer Donna Summer painted. One of her larger paintings, *Two Sisters*, was valued at $38,000 at the Circle Gallery in Chicago. David Byrne of Talking Heads attended Maryland Institute's College of Art and then transferred to Rhode Island School of Design. Mark Mothersbaugh, co-founder of the rock band Devo, is a graphic artist who often uses fluorescent and phosphorescent paint. And Jerry Garcia, lead guitarist and vocalist of the Grateful Dead, who attended the San Francisco Art Institute, where he studied under Wally Hedrick and Elmer Bischoff, sold his signed and numbered lithographs for $250 to $3000. "I hope that nobody takes them too seriously," he once commented.

Some athletes who dabble are Rocky Graziano; the old marathoner, Johnny Kelly; pitcher Jim Bouton; football's Don Hasselbeck and Ernie Barnes, the 260-pound blocking guard of the 1960 San Diego Chargers, whose paintings of black ghetto life have been hugely successful; and, as I have mentioned, the Boston Celtics' Heinsohn, whose huge-fisted demeanor and great size—he's 6'9"—can't belie the fact that he's a member in good standing of the Copley Society of Boston, the oldest art association in the country.

And of course there are writers. There was a time long ago, especially during the last century, when many writers seemed equally absorbed by the passion to draw and sketch, when dabbling was accepted practice, not so much an alternative as a complement to vision. One thinks of Chesterton, Rossetti, Hardy. The Brontës, Charlotte, Anne, and Emily, often sketched in the drawing room at Haworth. It seemed natural, a co-expression of energy, an adjunct to writing and borne of the same impulse as telling a story. Variously, an entirely opposite strategy may be at work. "Out of trivia often grows the serious," witty James Thurber once observed, "after the serious often comes the trivia, after the labor of writing came the relaxation of my drawings or there wouldn't be any." The Indian poet, philosopher, and Nobel laureate Rabindranath Tagore exhibited his paintings in Moscow and Paris. He became a painter at the age of 67 when he found he could no longer simply cross out a word on a manuscript without the scribble becoming an elaborate design. Who knows, maybe the relaxation of drawing for a writer is in fact merely a way of avoiding what words otherwise have to describe. Maybe it's part of the hand's act, the inevitable movement from letters to larger, loopier lines. "The tools are allied," wrote John Updike on this very subject—citing the need in both professions to strive for vivacity, accuracy, and economy—"the impulse is one."

Alexander Pope was an extremely capable portrait painter. (The poet's uncle on his mother' side was Samuel Cooper, the miniaturist.) Poe did small portraits—brilliant ones—in crayon. In ill health most of his life, Robert Louis Stevenson, a commendable watercolorist, wandered about looking for favorable climates and in his travels, especially in Samoa, found a major source of his art. Rudyard Kipling, who had artistic ability, often illustrated his letters and could do cartoons and caricatures with cruel exactitude, especially of himself. I recall one of him satirizing himself on a bicycle. People like William Blake and John Ruskin of course were artists in their own right. As was novelist George Sand. And Jean

Cocteau, who, according to reports, often dashed off more than 30 or so drawings a day. Kate Perugini, one of Dickens's daughters, became a proficient painter. W. H. Davies drew, poorly, then decided collecting art was more fun. The bird-scratchings which H. G. Wells, insisting on calling cartoons, superadded to the pages of his *Experiment in Autobiography*—he complained that they had to be "reduced and compressed"—to my mind improve neither the flat prose nor venal judgments of that book. García Lorca drew, painted, and made puppets. Antonin Artaud painted in the asylum at Rodez. And Hans Christian Andersen made "scissor fantasies" to illustrate his own tales, often making these paper cutouts while telling stories to audiences of children.

Fyodor Dostoevsky very much enjoyed drawing. While he was writing *Crime and Punishment*, he drew the compelling faces of his characters all over the manuscript pages. I have personally seen them in St. Petersburg, Russia, one of the highlights of my trip there. His favorite painting was Raphael's *Sistine Madonna*, which he raved about. Alexander Pushkin was a highly original artist, the "real thing," expressive, loose, and free form, and the margins of his manuscripts are filled with drawings, which suggest a mind teeming with images, many of them smart doodles, wonderful ones, including a self-portrait. Ivan Turgenev actually took lessons in painting, while Nikolai Gogol originally intended to be a painter and often illustrated the covers of his own books. Vladimir Mayakovsky doodled, as well.

General Lew Wallace, author of *Ben-Hur*, was something of a dabbler and took it upon himself to draw rather rudely elemental likenesses, before they were hanged, of the four main conspirators in Lincoln's assassination—he sat in on their judgment—all except Mary Surratt, whose face was obscured by a veil throughout the trial.

No draftsman, but Oscar Wilde drew well. So did Thomas Hardy, William James, Harriet Beecher Stowe (who left childhood etchings on her windows at the family home, "Apple Slump," in Concord), John Masefield, and, among others, Joyce Cary who several times in print actually referred to himself as a "dabbler" and wrote what is surely the best modern novel on a painter and painting, *The Horse's Mouth*. J. D. Salinger was known to have drawn. "His room on East Fifty-seventh Street was extremely bare," remembers author Leila Hadley. "He used to do rather good sketches, and when I read 'De Daumier Smith's Blue Period,' I was sure he had based the hero on himself."

Poet Sylvia Plath studied art for a time. Many insist that Herman Hesse painted better than he wrote. Among those with first-rate talent as painters and artists—dabblers merely by dint of their comparatively greater worth as writers—might be mentioned Lewis Carroll, G. K. Chesterton, W. B. Yeats, August Strindberg, George Russell (Æ), Max Beerbohm, William Carlos Williams, T. H. White, and Günter Grass, who was trained as a stonemason and studied art in Düsseldorf. A friend of mine once told me how fascinated he became when they were once together during a writing seminar in 1976 simply watching Grass sketching snails—his signature "familiar"—on a napkin. And of course James Agee left a wonderful array of doodles all over his movie script of *The African Queen*.

Booth Tarkington was a wonderful cartoonist. The explorer Richard Burton drew. E. T. A. Hoffmann illustrated his letters. So did playwright Sean O'Casey, usually with sharp-nosed bespectacled caricatures of himself. Eugene Field, beloved poet of childhood who wrote "Little Boy Blue" and "Wynken, Blynken, and Nod," was also a maestro of colored inks and uncial initials. His original manuscripts, written in a fastidious tiny script, are calligraphic mas-terpieces, often illuminated in brilliant inks of red, blue, green, and gold. William Sydney Porter (O. Henry's real name) enjoyed him-self sketching customers who came into his Uncle Clark's drugstore in Greensboro, North Carolina. They were dead accurate cartoons. In the early days he illustrated many of his own stories. "Who was it?" his uncle would ask, coming in from lunch. "I never saw him before," said Will, "but he looks like this," and he would rough out a pencil sketch on wrapping paper. "Damn good. That's Fat Gerry Burke, the drunk," he would reply. "Oh, that's dumb ol' Rick Weeks, with his slope-head and almost Chinese eyes. He owes me $7.85." Hendrik Willem Van Loon turned out history after history and biography after biography (one on Rembrandt was really about his own life!), all illustrated with a plethora of cartoons and brilliantly colored sketches.

There was an exhibition of D. H. Lawrence's erotic paintings held at the Warren Gallery in London in 1929 that was raided and closed down by the police. Most of the offending pictures, which I have seen in Taos, New Mexico, are galumphing orange-colored nudes with fat buttocks and thick lips (almost all the male figures are idealized portraits of Lawrence himself, who in real life was tubercular and unhealthy), which put everyone off not only because they off-puttingly revealed, of all things, pubic hair (the receptacle into which lovers naughtily stuck wildflowers in the unexpurgated *Lady Chatterley's Lover*, published that very same year), all of it being a bit too much for viewers back then.

And of course virtually the full complement of Bloomsbury got paint on its daubing fingers, in the wake of the Post-impression-ist discovery that "art" was easier to fake than "literature." Virginia Woolf, especially in personal letters and notes, showed an unexpected artistic talent. Amateurism, however, was not for everybody. F. Scott Fitzgerald admired Gerald Murphy for deliberately and graciously *giving up* painting when, as he told Scott, he realized he would never be a truly great painter. Sheilah Graham, Scott's lover at the end, protested that it was sad, because Murphy enjoyed painting. Scott snapped, "That was not the point." Fitzgerald obviously did not quite understand dabbling.

Several writers initially set out to be painters. John Ruskin was of course invited to be the first Slade Professor of Fine Arts at Oxford in 1869. And William Thackeray actually studied art in Paris. (His own watercolor illustrations to the original manuscript of *The Rose and the Ring* are quite fine.) E. E. Cummings, even after he began writing—and he often wrote art criticism for *The Dial*—seriously expected one day to be famous as a painter. He was fascinated with Cubism. (He illustrated *The Enormous Room* with 60 on-the-spot drawings of events described in that book.) And Evelyn Waugh, who attended the Ruskin School of Drawing and Fine Arts, confessed art not only to be his first interest, but the preferred one: "My meagre gift had been over-praised at home, at school, and at Oxford. I never imagined myself a Titian or a Velasquez. My ambition was to draw, decorate, design, and illustrate. I worked with the brush and was entirely happy in my employment of it, as I was not when reading or writing." He did very neat black and white drawings.

Rev. Gerard Manley Hopkins, the Jesuit who dreamt very early of being a painter—his brothers Arthur and Everard became professional artists—ultimately gave it up because of certain scruples and confined himself to pen-and-ink sketches for one or two nature poems and several letters, for, as he put it, "parts of the art put a strain upon the passions which I should think it unsafe to encounter." His drawings are small, self-contained sketches of tiny landscapes delicately framed in meticulously drafted trees and of figures, many of whose faces are, inexplicably, never shown.

Writer Stevie Smith made drawings for much of her work. As did Prosper Merimee and Alfred Jarry. Charles Bukowski often drew illustrations in his books of poems for readers instead of simply signing them. The eccentric writer Denton Welch, dead at 33 (his dates are 1915 to 1948), who even did some work for *Vogue* as an illustrator, illustrated his novels *Maiden Voyage* and *In Youth Is Pleasure* and the jacket of *Brave and Cruel*, his first collection of short stories. In the mid Forties, poet Weldon Kees began to paint; he exhibited in one-man shows at the Peridot Gallery, and on at least one occasion his work was shown along with paintings by Hans Hoffmann, de Kooning, and others of the Abstract Expressionist movement, with which his work in this field can be associated.

Poet Richard Wilbur drew cartoons and poet Mark Strand set out to be a painter and pursued both writing and painting at Antioch College in Ohio and as a graduate student at Yale, but he confessed, "I got much more praise for my writing than my painting." And Kurt Vonnegut's novel *Breakfast of Champions* was published—pointlessly, in my opinion—"With Drawings by the Author." Short story writer William Trevor spent long years as a painter and for 16 years, as a sculptor, worked in wood, terra cotta, and metal, before deciding to write his first short story. His dissatisfactions with art led him back to writing. "My sculpture had become increasingly abstract. Some part of me missed people." Annie Dillard, who does a lot of drawing and painting, told me, "I have no style but a sort of manual glibness. I have no color sense, so I use only three colors and white—only four tubes, Pelikan oil paints that clean up with water—in hopes that my colors will at least be related. I hope to trick myself into something harmonious." In her *An American Childhood* there is a wonderfully evocative passage about her drawing a base-ball mitt!

Very few painters and artists, however, ever seem to have written as well as they drew. Hilaire Belloc did. Aubrey Beardsley was a fine writer. James Thurber of course did both superbly. And the extended descriptive passages of Mervyn Peake, also a painter as well as a writer, are quite fine. William Simpson, author of Following the Sun, was probably the best illustrator who ever traveled and wrote, unlike Rockwell Kent, who provided the artwork for several of his travel books but, at least I feel, wasn't much of a writer. (Of course, the brilliant drawings of America's first native-born artist-naturalist, William Bartram, whose famous *Travels* appeared in 1791, were sent to patrons in England and circulated among connoisseurs.) The master, Edward Gorey, did both brilliantly. And the *nonpareil* Edward Lear, who was a master of both, often started watercolors he never completed in paint but oddly enough finished in writing, penciling descriptive notes into reserved blanks and various outlined spaces, in flowery words and phrases as likely as not in Greek.

Ironically, it is for his tidy watercolors that Edward Lear is commonly thought of as a dabbler, though he actually earned his living by executing zoological illustrations and landscapes, was Queen Victoria's drawing master, and doubtless would never have imagined that his later reputation would be based on his "nonsense" books. (An opposite fate fell to Wyndham Lewis, who seems to be valued today more for his paintings than his novels.) Lear did the definitive book on parrots, *Illustrations of the Family of Psittacidae, or Parrots* (1830), and the magnificent *Gleanings from the Menagerie and Aviary at Knowsley Hall*, which was privately printed in 1846. Lear in all likelihood turned to making art for comfort. He was surely one of the loneliest men that ever lived. He himself mocked his bulbous nose. His letters are sprinkled with comic drawings. He also spent years planning to illustrate Tennyson's poems with scenes drawn from his own travels. Late in life he sketched 200 small pen-and-wash designs, mounted them on card, two to a page, and wrote the relevant lines from Tennyson beneath. (He got to know Tennyson well enough to call him Alfred, and to receive from the tribute of a poem, "To E. L., on his Travels to Greece.")

I remember several years ago flipping through a book called *Self-Portrait: Book People Picture Themselves* (1976), a collection of writer's drawings of themselves put together by Burt Britton who had access, while working at the Strand Book Store in New York, to a number of various literary figures who routinely went in and out. There are a hundred or so drawings included in the collection. Awful work for the most part. Much of it is simply childish. Carlos Fuentes left a remarkably good likeness. So did Donald Justice and Brendan Gill. William Styron's was also strong. May I smugly suggest that mine was among the three or four best? Writer Peter Taylor caught his own jutting chin. Woody Allen's was a quarter-inch trapezoidal face. But the rest of the lot were tortured and tormented, not simply unrepresentative, just bad scribble. Robert Lowell did six faces: desperate midgets. Joan Didion left the print of a fingertip. Some simply cheated and

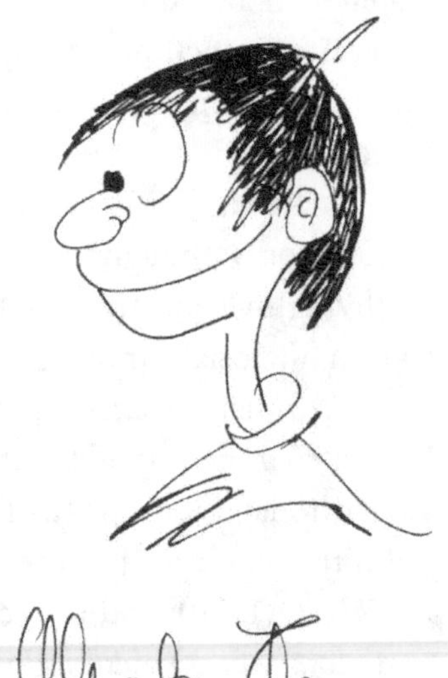

wrote a line of poetry. Or drew a balloon. Or lips. Or made amorphous squiggles. Yevgeny Yevtushenko's was insectile eyes. Arthur Miller's head was an unfortunate knob. And Ann Beattie, who gave herself an Adam's apple, immediately became with a few talentless strokes a freckled hag.

It was surprising to see how fox-footed and incompetent most of them were, given the literary ability of the group, how difficult it can be (*pace* John Updike) for so many in the attempt to show rather than tell merely to realize even a simple shape. In fact, Updike's own self-portrait was oddly unarresting, though he did manage to capture his nose. He spent a year in art school, though to my knowledge has never undertaken to draw or paint the dust-jackets of any of his own books. (He did take the photo for the cover of his *Museums and Women* [1972] and designed the jacket for *Trust Me* [1987].) His cartoons, done mostly for the Harvard *Lampoon* during his undergraduate days—he doesn't seem to have done any since—strike me as stiff and oddly unrealized; like Gary Trudeau's and Jim Davis's, they seem to rely more on ideas than drawing for humor.

But it is obvious in his writing that John Updike knew about art, the way he sees a face and, noticing things, draws such penetrating distinctions of texture and form, even in the way he constructs personalities in his stories and novels. I have always thought Updike was the Great Noticer—no detail in his work is too irrelevant, too out-of-the-way to mention—and should have been enrolled as one of the first traveling non-astronauts sent to the moon to tell us, finally, what that orb really looks like!

A number of other writers began as cartoonists. Max Beerbohm. Flannery O'Connor. Cecil Beaton. Stephen Tennant, "the last professional exquisite," who in decorative reclusion did quite impressive watercolors as well. Alistair Crowley, who dabbled in everything—including black magic—did amateur drawings. Long before he became a monk, Thomas Merton did a lot of cartoons, mostly gamboling nudes, for the Columbia literary magazine, *The Jester*. Gabriel García Márquez, who personally drew a bouquet of flowers in a copy of *One Hundred Years of Solitude* that he gave me, had a like talent. "By drawing," he replied when an interviewer once asked him how he started writing. William Faulkner, who drew cartoons for the Ole Miss yearbooks between 1917 and 1922, planned to earn money in New York City by drawing, advertisements he thought, while trying to establish himself as a writer. S. J. Perelman's cartoons were mediocre, but at least the overlong and witty captions that he used gave him an idea of what it was in his power to become. Television's Alistair Cooke was quite a good cartoonist, as well. Baudelaire drew cartoons. So did Dylan Thomas and Thackeray, whose first independent publication was a series of lithographs.

Ventriloquist Edgar Bergen advertised himself as a cartoonist in his early youth. Giovanni Guareschi drew all the cartoons for his Don Camillo books. As did Thirties writer Will James for his classic western autobiography, *Lone Cowboy*. John Lennon with his Shmooish though rather weak ovoidal line-drawings had a sort of wobbly-handed ability as a cartoonist. Eccentric novelist Frederick Rolfe ("Baron Corvo"), one of my writing heroes who left behind almost as many self-portraits as pseudonyms—and who like Delacroix also loved to take photographs as an aid to painting (though Rolfe's favored subject was naked Italian boys)—not only drew cartoons, friezes, and made oil paintings, although, granted, rather frigid, stiff, and mannered ones, but also painted and designed the jackets for his novel *Don Tarquinio* as well as for his masterpiece, *Hadrian VII*. And then Djuna Barnes, author of *Nightwood* and a woman who studied art both at Pratt and at the Art Students League, was known for her small ink-penned bohemian icons and satirical cookie-cutterish cartoons which, hand-colored and stiff, resembled chromolithographed "juveniles" or turn-of-the-century children's books, and which she hawked for centimes on the streets of Paris.

I think the greatest defense of wonderfulness in dabbling can be found in *The Stones of Venice*. There Ruskin tries to explain a paradox, that rudeness or imperfection in art, instead of calling up reproach, proves in fact one of its most noble characteristics, that men were not intended to work with the accuracy of tools, to be precise and perfect in all their actions. The only real art for him has the human touch, and the human touch is of necessity an art of imperfection, an art of addressing any amateur—"Out comes all his roughness, all his dullness, all his incapability; shame upon shame, failure upon failure, pause after pause: but out comes the whole majesty of him also."

The demand for perfection, he concludes, is always a sign of a misunderstanding of the ends of art. Greater encouragement for any undertaking, whatever it may be, doesn't exist. It leaves you, if nothing else, the courage of your convictions. Dabblers of the world, unite! You have nothing to lose but your doubt!

Simonetta Vespucci

Leonardo da Vinci sketched her. Lorenzo de' Medici threw lavish banquets in her honor. Italian diplomat Luigi Pulci and classical scholar and poet Angelo Poliziano composed poems for the great beauty. Young men fell in love with her on the spot. Many great Renaissance artists painted her, among them Filippo Lippi, Domenico Ghirlandaio, and Piero di Cosimo. She was perfection. It was of Simonetta that the Florentine diplomat, statesman, and patron Lorenzo the Magnificent said, "Her manners were so sweet and attractive that she gave everybody who was familiar with her the absolute certainty that she loved him. It seemed impossible that she was loved by so many men without any jealousy and praised by so many women without envy." Fair Simonetta, a noblewoman from Genoa, was tall, svelte, intellectual, and had a presence almost meltingly beautiful in what it reflected of ideal loveliness: the exquisite face, the wide-set, radiant, yet tender eyes, the full bust and long golden hair, the creamy skin, the high forehead of refined birth and intellect.

But it is, of course, primarily as Sandro Botticelli's inspiration that she is most well known, for it was she the great artist took as the model for his masterpieces, the *Primavera*, the *Birth of Venus*,

Mars and Venus, Pallas and the Centaur, and many others. Her glory blazed even as she lived. And yet her life was brief, for she disappeared in the flush of youth. Much myth and mystery still surrounds her.

I remember, in 1965, searching for the Botticellis in the Uffizi. Upon seeing them, I felt almost immediately overwhelmed by the innocence and almost breathtaking, truly extravagant loveliness of his *Madonna of the Pomegranate* (ca. 1487), her soft pale-blue eyes, the muted flesh tones, the long graceful neck and sloping shoulders, the honeyed torrent of her golden cascading hair about the exquisite body. More than anything, I was struck by the sweet face, that unworldly, compelling faraway look that, for all its heavenly majesty, displayed in its movie-star beauty sensuous, even voluptuous modern good looks. The dimpled chin, the delicate eyebrows, the ripe mouth, as paperback writers say. I wanted secretly to kiss her. Her lapis-lazuli blue cloak, alone, is regally breathtaking, along with the six attending angels (a shock to some—all angels are male!) who stand in adoration. There is something wistful and heartbreakingly feminine about this Madonna. My full heart was flooded with the words of Gabriele D'Annunzio singing of her city and her matchless beauty:

> *O Fiorenza, O Fiorenza,*
> *giglio di potenza,*
> *virgulto primaverile;*
> *e certo non e grazia alcuna*
> *the vinca tua grazia d'aprile*
> *quando la valle e una tuna*
> *di fiori di sogni e di pace*
> *ove Simonetta si giace.*

(O Florence, O Florence,

lily of power,

spring sapling;

certainly no grace

can match your grace in April

when the valley is a cradle

of flowers, of dreams, and of peace

where Simonetta reclines.)

Rumors and falsehoods about Simonetta have persisted down through the centuries. Some claim she was betrothed to Giuliano de Medici, others that they were lovers. Still others insist she was Botticelli's mistress. (In nearly all of Botticelli's paintings of Simonetta, she appears almost completely nude.) She is also said to have despaired of the fact that she was merely the symbol of what she really wanted to be. It has also been alleged that, proud of her astonishing beauty, she once announced to the adoring Botticelli: "I will be your lady Venus. You shall paint me rising from the waves."

Her name was Simonetta Cattaneo. She was born at Porto Venere, near Genoa in 1454—precisely where Italians believe the goddess Venus emerged from the foam after her birth in the Mediterranean—the daughter of a leading family there with Teutonic forbears. The Cattaneos of Genoa, in fact—along with the Pinellos, the Centurione, the Dorias, the DiNegri, the Spinolas, and the Berardis—are listed among the bankers of the explorer Christopher Columbus. Although her own family's wealth was in decline, her mother, Cattocchia di Marco Spinola, was connected by blood to many of the great houses of Tuscany, including that of the ruling Medici. In spite of the fact that she was Genoese by birth, Simonetta spent her early years in Piombino living with her sister Battestina, the wife of the lord of the castle there, the despotic, somewhat infamous Jacopo III d'Appiano, and their daughter.

It was in the castle of the Appiani that the busy and ambitious Piero Vespucci, on his way home to Florence from a voyage to Constantinople, forged the first link in his dream of greatness by arranging the marriage of his son Marco—a cousin of the legendary explorer and cartographer Amerigo Vespucci—with this beautiful woman. The two of them had met in April 1469, when Simonetta was with her parents attending a church service in San Torpete in Genoa, where, it so happened, the doge Piero il Fregoso and much of the Genoese nobility were in attendance. Marco had been sent to Genoa by his father to study at the Banco di San Giorgio. Smitten with Simonetta, Marco was accepted by her parents as their daughter's prospective bridegroom, an advantageous marriage because Marco's family was well connected in Florence, especially to the Medici family.

The wedding took place in Genoa in August 1469. Simonetta was 15 years old, not only beautiful, but now also fairly blossoming with wealth. It was, notably, Lorenzo de' Medici, first among the Medici and richest of Florence's merchant princes, who gave the Vespucci-Cattaneo nuptial feast at Careggi. Jacopo III, Prince of Piombino, gave her as a munificent part of her dowry several of his iron mines located on the island of Elba. It was a good marriage for both of them, and the newlyweds, young and hopeful, both the same age, began their trip south to Florence, home at that time of the greatest painters, sculptors, poets, and humanists in the known world.

She was about 20 when young Marco Vespucci—of whom we have no portrait and know next to nothing—brought her to his home in Florence. It must have been an exciting time for her, as the city in the middle of the 15th century was the artistic center of

Italy, a place swarming with artisans of all trades, weavers, leather workers, painters, and musicians. The Vespucci lived in the northwestern quarter of the city, bordering on the Arno—it was known as the Ognissanti quarter—where each branch of the family had a palace, close to the Porto al Prato, and Simonetta moved into one of the lesser palaces, living with Marco's parents and his sister Bice. The Vespucci ancestral home was in Peretola. They had been among the leading families of Florentine political life and trade since the 14th century, ranking with the Pitti, Strozzi, Pazzi, and Tornobuoni families. Their relationship with the Medici, with whom they were intimate friends and business partners, went back to the founder of that dynasty. Simonetta must have been thought a superb addition to the distinguished family: in the famous Ghirlandaio fresco in the chapel of S. Salvadore d' Ognissanti church—where the Madonna maternally enfolds the entire Vespucci family, grandparents, children, grandchildren—she almost surely without a doubt can be pinpointed as the beautiful young woman with the attractive, pearl-draped coiffure.

Simonetta Vespucci's hair, by the way, in the many portraits and representations of her, was almost always intertwined with strings of pearls. It was a symbol, a characteristic, an ikon almost honorifically extended to her by the likes of Botticelli, Fra Lippo Lippi, and Piero di Cosimo. Curiously, while Amerigo Vespucci, unlike Columbus, neither mentioned nor sought gold in the New World, pearls as gems were another story. In Florence the word "orient" was almost always associated with pearls—"orient" as a term in lapidary-speak, in fact, actually *means* the faint play of colors on a pearl—and during the Renaissance a necklace of pearls was among the greatest pledges of love.

It might be noted here that Amerigo Vespucci, who was

only two years older than Simonetta, was also one of the 13 members represented on a well-known Ghirlandaio fresco, one of the detailed narrative frescoes, which include many portraits of leading citizens in contemporary dress. An agent of the Medici, Vespucci often found himself on business in Seville and Cadiz and eventually became a "private" explorer who, as we know, would one day lend his name to a continent. After three long voyages, he made a fourth and supposedly reached the mainland of the New World on June 16, 1497, a mere eight days before the Venetian sailor John Cabot did.

It was Vespucci's controversial account of that voyage called *Mundus Novus*, a pamphlet first published in Latin in 1503 in which Vespucci purportedly corresponds with his patron, Lorenzo Pietro de Medici, about his voyage to the new world—which many writers and historians down through the years, including naval historian Samuel Eliot Morison, insist was (suspiciously?) predated two years—that led to his name being used as the name for America. He would outlive Simonetta by 34 years.

Sandro Botticelli also lived in the Ognissanti quarter at that time. His full name was Alessandro di Mariano di Filipepi, and he was born around 1445. His family, a large one, owned a tannery on the other side of the river, near the Santa Trinita Bridge, one of those which spanned the Arno. It is thought that his nickname derived from either his burly father or his older brother Giovanni, or both (*botticello* means little barrel), a name, in any case, that eventually stuck to Sandro. He was apprenticed in 1458 to Fra Lippo Lippi, who was to become a major influence on him and in whose workshop he would remain an assistant until 1467. The young Botticelli stood in friendly relations with some of the pupils in Verrocchio's workshop, particularly with Leonard da Vinci.

Most of Botticelli's commissions came from the work he

did for leisure-loving Florentines who had inherited wealth. It was for the Vespucci family, specifically, while taking Simonetta as his model for the reclining Goddess of Love—if not close friends, they would surely have seen each other often—in his allegorical painting *Mars and Venus* (ca. 1485), adding as a symbolic touch for the Vespucci family the swirling "wasps" (*vespe*) above the head of the reclining Mars. The Vespucci were to become for the busy painter an important conduit. It was through them that he was introduced to the even wealthier Medici family, who were eventually to become his important patron.

Sandro's special patron, for whom he executed several of his most important extant works, was not, however, Lorenzo the Magnificent, whose family maintained the great estate on the Via Larga, but his almost as powerful cousin Lorenzo *"il Popolano,"* the son of Pierfrancesco de' Medici, grandson of a natural brother of Cosimo *Pater Patriae*. And it was for the newly purchased country villa of this younger Lorenzo at Castello that in 1478 Botticelli painted the famous *Primavera*, or Spring, and then in 1485—a full nine years after Simonetta's death—that second great masterpiece of fanciful classicism, *The Birth of Venus*, an icon of the Italian Renaissance, often called *Venus Anadyomene*, which depicts the goddess arriving at the shore after her birth, when she emerges from the sea fully grown, the design of which seems to have been inspired chiefly by the *Giostra* of Poliziano (more about which anon) and perhaps also by the *Pervigilium Veneris*. For me, Simonetta, as Venus, is the most beautiful woman ever painted in the history of all art. The movement of all four figures in the painting is a pavanne of heavenly grace.

The Birth of Venus is a glorious detonation wind, mood, beauty. It is a huge imposing canvas, thirteen feet wide, and full of light. There is no better description of the painting than in Camille Paglia's *Sexual Personae*:

> "She scuds to shore on a metallic scallop shell, the heraldic shield of woman's marine origins. On her face is the pensive smile of Donatello's dreamy *David*, and around her winds, as a heavy rope of strawberry-blonde hair, the ruddy wish-stream of Donatello's bleeding Goliath. *The Birth of Venus* . . . is a pagan altarpiece. The goddess's monumentality and proud separatism come from sculpture. In this cultic epiphany, Venus dominates the eye, as she dominates the picture plane. She rises from the star-burst shell (a trumpeting petrifaction of her splashing foam) to stand in Apollonian sunlight. She is sex and love washed clean of mystery and danger. The freshest of breezes skips across the scene, a dewy spume blown from the lips of a libidinous zephyr into a handmaiden's billowing cloak. The shallow composition is Byzantine, as is the sharpness of line. Botticelli's Venus is Kenneth Clarke's Crystalline Aphrodite. She is a springtime goddess, showered with flowers of mathematical calculation. There is no chthonian tangle or brooding pregnancy in this nature. Every tendril and herb has a fine Apollonian identity. The sea itself has no murky depth. . . . Female secrecy and entrapment are abolished in her frank, yet decorous nudity, her perfect visibility. An air-blown or aerated womanliness. . . ."

The death of Lorenzo the Magnificent in 1492, and the accession to power of his worthless son Piero, soon plunged the city of Florence into political troubles. Lorenzo di Pierfrancesco de' Medici, who with his brother Giovanni became political rivals of their cousin Piero, continued his patronage of Botticelli. He was in the confidence and employ of Lorenzo as late as 1497. Their relationship came to an end, possibly following the overthrow and execution in 1498 of the religious preacher and reformer Girolamo Savonarola. A strange and sudden new interest in mystic and religious speculation took hold of Botticelli, and he became an ardent, if belated, disciple of the friar mainly through the influence of his brother Simone, long a declared devotee of Savonarola and the author, incidentally, of a manuscript which has since become one of the best historical sources of the friar and his movement. It has been said that some of the finest paintings of Botticelli grew from the period of his religious preoccupation. Later, there came a division between the two. (When I was a youngster, I hated Savonarola when I had heard that he had stopped Botticelli from painting.)

Botticelli rarely painted on canvas. His favorite support was the panel, usually walnut. He preferred using egg tempera. He was reputedly so sensitive that one of his rivals swore that he had no skin at all. There are supposedly three or four self-portraits of him. Some critics say that he appears as that moody young man of about 30 with the heavy eyes and sensual lips on the far right in the brown cloak—with an Oscar Wilde-looking disdain—in his *Adoration of the Magi* (1475). There is always a delicacy, a musical coherence to Botticelli's paintings; at the same time we almost sense a longing in him, an uncanny suggestion that goes far beyond the reaches of his pale and limpid skies that seems to imply, along with a nostalgia for the immortal, that earthly beauty can only palely reflect the ideal loveliness of a higher sphere. Classicism in the work of other early Florentine painters was largely intellectual, but in Botticelli's day it was becoming more sensuous.

It was through his beautiful young neighbor that Botticelli

came to realize the possibilities of actually realizing such a vision. There were other famous beauties in Florence at the time, of course. We know of several. There was Lucretia Donati, Albiera degli Albizzi, and Maria Maddalena, Lorenzo de Medici's daughter, who died tragically before she could wed her handsome first cousin, Giovanni de 'Medici. And there was lovely Catherine Sforza, whom Giovanni eventually did marry. But it was Simonetta whom Botticelli elevated into the Platonic personification of ideal beauty and goodness, and it was her image that went with him until the end of his days. The question is often asked: Was Simonetta ever Botticelli's mistress? Aside from the fact that Simonetta was married, known for her chastity, an aristocrat, and died at 22, the painter was supposedly ill-at-ease with women. It is reported he was reclusive. He was also the son of a tanner, penniless, and nine years her senior. No woman's name, in fact, other than the great beauty he immortalized in paint, has ever been connected with Botticelli. He never married. Supposedly, when asked why, he said that he dreamt about marriage once and woke so terrified that he walked the city all night.

The idea that they were lovers is less likely than unthinkable. Simonetta was not only the embodiment of moral beauty to him, but a woman of exquisitely high repute. Beyond that, she was married to a man of distinguished family. Added to which, she was probably more than any other woman in Florence the cynosure of all eyes in that city. Finally, not a syllable has ever been written, in a letter or journal, during her lifetime or after her death, that suggests infidelity, and the documents of the period are not only voluminous, but the Florentines, who were inveterate letter-writers, loved gossip.

Proof was given in 1473, about the time she first came to Florence. Simonetta was present at the ball given in honor of Eleonora de Aragon, daughter of the king of Naples, who was passing through Florence on her way to marry Ercole d'Este, Duke of Ferrara. It was a celebration fit for a princess. The most distinguished families of Florence would have been in attendance, the Altoviti, the Pazzi, the Acciaiuoli, the Ruccellai, the Spini, the Soderini, and most notably of course the Medici, richest of the merchant princes. Like all other festivities arranged in Eleonora's honor, the ball must have been an momentous event. The traditional folk festival, a "St. John," was the city's act of public homage to Eleanora: flag races, processions, fireworks, and a sumptuous banquet, which reached its grand finale in a ball.

The ball was held in the open air, on the banks of the Arno in the gardens of the Palazzi Lenzi, close by the houses of the Vespucci. There was singing, dancing, lute music. The three graces of the ball were Eleonora de Aragon, Albiera degli Albizzi, and Simonetta Vespucci. Simonetta's star was rising. From then on she never left Florence. The afternoon of the dance she was seen—and for Simonetta to be seen was to be loved—by all the young men of Florence. Above all, it was the ardent eyes of Giuliano de' Medici, the passionate and headstrong younger brother of Lorenzo and the second son of Piero de' Medici and Lucrezia Tornabuoni, that supposedly followed her every graceful step.

Like Marco, Giuliano was the same age as Simonetta. He was wealthy and dashing and given the good looks his older brother lacked. His friends called him the "Prince of Youth." Botticelli painted his portrait in 1478, just after his death at age 24, around the same time that Andrea del Verrocchio fashioned a terracotta bust of him. He had a clandestine affair with a young woman of Gorini who bore him a son, Giulio, though the existence of this child was revealed only after Giuliano's death. A good deal of political controversy followed, and there rose the inevitable questions about bastardy. The boy, however, had Medici blood in his veins and eventually became Pope Clement VII.

That there was a heartfelt passion between these two beautiful creatures, Simonetta and Giuliano, has often been repeated, along with much romantic speculation that because the chief personages of several of Botticelli's paintings—notably the *Primavera* and *Mars and Venus*—were figured in likenesses of Simonetta and Giuliano, they were lovers, but the web of romance spun about their names, as with Botticelli, remains insubstantial. Idyllic love during the Renaissance, moreover, was very popular. One only has to think of Petrarch and Laura, Dante and Beatrice. And yet Vasari, biographer of Renaissance artists, born more than 30 years later, did go on to identify Simonetta as Giuliano's *inamorata*, an assumption that generations of art historians have continued to repeat. It is almost certain, however, that Giuliano's love for Simonetta, though intense, remained on a purely Platonic plane, though he did worship her, write verses for her, and give illustrious pageants in her honor.

In any case, by a strange fate and romantic fancy they are, inevitably, almost always linked. It is one of those uncanny casualties of legend. Angelo Poliziano memorably conjoined the two in his vernacular *ottava rima* poem *Stanze cominciate per la giostra del Magnifico Giuliano de' Medici*, which was composed between 1475 and 1478 and has become a classic of Italian literature. The poem describes the love of "Julio" (i.e., Giuliano de' Medici) for "Simonetta" (i.e., Simonetta) by means of a poetic transfiguration in which beauty is glorified according to humanist ideals. Stylistically, the *Giostra* is influenced by Latin epics and encomiastic poems and reveals the author's taste for refined poetry. It was interrupted at Book II, stanza 46, possibly because of Giuliano's death in 1478.

For two years after the Aragon ball, the city of Florence

chose to celebrate its alliance, a political and religious one, with Venice and the pontiff. A huge tournament was held on January 28, 1475 in the Piazza Santa Croce, at which 21-year-old Giuliano was to be the central figure. Lorenzo the Magnificent sent out delegates to cities far and wide bearing invitations. Virtually all the nobility of Europe was invited. Each contestant, backed by 20 young men in jeweled armor made by Florence's world-famous goldsmiths, was followed on horse by a full troop of soldiers. According to a chronicle of the event, Giuliano's silver armor and velvet mantle cost 8000 gold florins, the horse he rode having been sent as a gift from Apulia, and the brightness of the sparkling jewels on his tabard and cap dazzled the eye. According to tradition, each cavalier that day was to carry a banner on which had been painted the lady of his dreams. Guiliano called in Botticelli to paint the "La Bella Simonetta" on his banner. The painter obliged, conceiving as his subject Pallas Athena, the fully-armed goddess of wisdom. This was supposedly the only time that Simonetta was ever painted from real life. She was crowned queen of the tournament.

For reasons of a literary nature, this tournament achieved an historic importance far beyond that in which Giuliano contended. Several poetic accounts have come down to us, notably ones by Agnolo, Luigi Pulci, but it was the Poliziano's, by far the greatest, that best memorializes the two, presenting Giuliano as a hunter conventionally fleeing Love but chasing a white dove and then having Cupid suddenly present him in the depths of the forest with a living irresistible vision of nymphlike Simonetta Vespucci:

> "White is the maid and white the robe around her,
> With buds and roses and thin grasses pied;
> Enwreathed folds of golden tresses crowned her

> Shadowing her forehead fair with modest pride:
> The wild wood smiled; the thicket where he found her,
> To ease his anguish, bloomed on every side;
> Serene she sits, with gesture queenly mild
> And with her brow tempers the tempest wild."
> (translated by John Addington Symonds)

A proud brow which is modest, gentle, virtuous—that was how Poliziano has fixed the traits of Simonetta, poetic characteristics that reappear in all the verses and paintings of which she is the elegant subject. Always shining was her beautiful golden hair—*"aurem testa scende in la frente umilmente superba,"* in Poliziano's words. It is generally accepted that Botticelli found in the *Giostra*, the inspiration for his *Primavera*—even to the detail of the dress, which he supposedly took, not from the one she wore the day of the tournament, but from the one she wore the afternoon of Eleonora's ball.

A musical painting, a dance, the *Primavera* is like a tapestry garden, the graceful, swinging arabesques that tie together the various figures as delicate as the transparent fabrics that are as fantastic as they are poetic. Simonetta is not only Venus but the flower-decked spirit of Spring and the Three Graces as well. Her spirit pervades the painting. One cannot tell whether the movement of the figures is defined by their bodies or by their veils, nor whether the veils sway with the movement of the dance or flutter in the breeze. The figures, as usual, cast no shadows. The meaning of the allegory is uncertain.

Many commonly regard it as a moment in the reign of Venus. To the right, Zephyr pursues Flora who, once possessed, becomes the "hour" of Spring and scatters flowers on the world. Venus, in the center, is *Humanitas*, patroness of the Medicean humanists. Then there are the dancing Three Graces (Chastity, Beauty, and Love) and Mercury dissipating the clouds. Others have read much into the symbolic meanings and connotations of the five 500 or so distinctly different flowers, herbs, blooms, and grasses in Botticelli's extravagant meadow, truly a botanical paradise—it is said that of 190 flowering plants that appear in the painting, 138 have been identified, and half of them supposedly still grow in the gardens of the villa at Castello. One critic has suggested that the scene depicts a ball at which Simonetta appeared both as Flora *and* as Grace, and another, Emil Jacobsen, finds in it a provocative "mystery" somehow relating to the death of Simonetta Vespucci, which by then had taken place. Was Botticelli somehow depicting her arrival in the next world? Depicting her in some kind of commemorative way as arriving in Paradise?

Botticelli's *Primavera*, it should be noted, was also the earliest important example of large-scale painting on canvas for indoor decoration. It was painted in the Eighties of the 15th century; from that time on, canvas becomes gradually more significant.

Simonetta was indeed the embodiment of the Renaissance ideal. Light seems to penetrate blonde forms, allowing, as it were, matter and spirit to blend, and no one seems to prove a better subject of such electricity than she does. In the *Primavera*, she is the glorious embodiment of nothing less than Spring itself, as well as the Three Graces. In the *Birth of Venus* she is not only the iridescent Venus, the dream of beauty, but the inspiring zephyrs. She is Botticelli's ravishing *Young Woman* (ca. 1475) in profile and wearing that exquisite scarlet robe, now in the Gemäldegalerie in Berlin. In the version of Botticelli's *Calumny of Apelles* (ca. 1494), she is very likely the possible model for *four* distinct but beautiful women, all superbly golden-haired, which is to say, not only the innocently naked figure of Truth on the far left pointing (and looking) heavenward, but also the woman in the blue cloak, full of malignant passion yet holding high the blazing torch, as well as the superlative beauties, one in a red robe, the other yellow, both said to be, respectively, Fraud and Conspiracy. The amazing takeaway is that Simonetta, in whatever guise, is always impossibly beautiful.

In Botticelli's *Pallas and the Centaur* (1482) she is, of course, the figure of Pallas holding a pike in that filmy, filigree gown, just as she is the supernal Madonna in both the *Madonna of the Pomegranate* and the *Madonna of the Magnificat*, in which the rendering of Simonetta's face, under a silver crown held by two angels, may be said to be even beyond alluring or prepossessing. All of these figures are her emanations, authentic projections, as one critic says, "if not of Simonetta as she saw herself in the mirror, then of Botticelli who saw her mirrored in the eyes of his own longing."

A year after the tournament Simonetta Vespucci was dead— of tuberculosis. (The painted serpent often seen around in her throat symbolized the disease.) The stunning creature was only 22 years old. It was the month of April 1476. All of Florence reportedly followed her to her grave. Edgar Allan Poe wrote that the most poetic subject of all is the death of a young woman. But the death of such a ravishing young woman had to be beyond poignant, indeed. When he received the news, Lorenzo the Magnificent had just seen a star that no one had observed before. "That is Simonetta," he said, and indited the sonnet *"O chiara stella, cha co'raggi tupi"* from which one quatrain goes:

> "Bright shining star! Thy radiance in the sky
> Dost rob the neighboring stars of all their light.

Why art thou with unwonted splendor bright?
Why with great Phoebus does thou dare to vie?"

The lid of the young beauty's coffin was left open as she was carried through the streets of Florence, so that all could see her beauty. Everyone strained to have a last glimpse of her uncovered face. She was the embodiment of the realm of light. Leonardo da Vinci, who formed part of the funeral cortège, sketched her head. The poets Giuliano de' Medici and Luigi Pulci composed stately elegies. Another poet who was present, looking up to the heavens, cried, "Her soul hath passed into a star." Her body was laid to rest in the Vespucci chapel in the Ognissanti church. There too, just outside but close beside hers in the Ortaccio or garden burial ground, the body of Sandro Botticelli was eventually laid to rest in May 1510. And then a final enigma, still not understood. In a characteristically unpredictable gesture sometime after her death, Piero Vespucci inexplicably gave Simonetta's portrait and her personal belongings to Giuliano, not to her own husband, Piero's son Marco.

The portrait in question was most likely the one now known as *The Chantilly Simonetta*, now in the Musée Condé in Chantilly. It is attributed by some to Piero di Cosimo, and by others to the painter Antonio del Pollaiuolo, both members of the Vespucci circle, and remains the most famous—and definitive—portrait of her. It is the complete image of her beauty, and the high Renaissance forehead, which no one felt any need to veil. It shows her in profile, her breasts bared. Her elegantly braided tresses are festooned with pearls. She wears a gold necklace and a simple robe, worn half off shoulder. The city of Florence rises in miniature in the left background. The stormy sky, the stark contrast between the leafless and the leafy trees, the snake coiled around her gold collar, all allude to the young girl's untimely death. Her face is beautiful, but rapt and melancholy, an otherworldly mask. Is the snake, as Vasari suggests, also an allusion to Cleopatra, another archetypal beauty?

Strangely, in the year of her death—as if a lasting link had to be maintained—there was an attempt to arrange a marriage for Giuliano with Simonetta's very own niece, Semiramide, daughter of Battistina and Jacopo III d'Appiano d'Aragona. Through this particular marriage, the Vespucci family would have been linked to the Medici, but for some reason the marriage never took place. It was Giuliano's destiny to die young, at the age 24, as had the beauty of the house of Vespucci. He was violently stabbed to death—as many as 19 times, before Francesco Pazzi struck him on the head with his sword—during a High Mass in the Duomo and left in a pool of blood on the floor during the Pazzi Conspiracy of 1478. Lorenzo was almost killed as well, but managed to escape the scene with severe but not life-threatening wounds. Two years after Lorenzo's death the Florentines, despising Lorenzo's son Piero, sacked the Medici Palace and drove the family into exile.

A final irony to be mentioned was that another Piero, Simonetta's father-in-law, mysteriously connived in the escape of a certain Napoleone Franzeci, a minor one of the cruel Pazzi assassins, and then disappeared himself. Questions were immediately raised as to the reasons why. Had he secretly hated the Medici all along? Was he simply trying to help someone in trouble? Had he his own political agenda? Did he have foreknowledge of the conspiracy? Why did Franzeci turn to him? Was it that Piero Vespucci had finally decided to take satisfaction in the removal from this world of the reputed lover of his daughter-in-law, a man who had dared to write amorous poems about her?

Piero's sudden disappearance, in any case, incensed the Florentines. A massive manhunt was mounted to find and punish the guilty parties. Piero was finally caught, though Franzeci never was, and he was dragged back to Florence where he was tortured for 20 days; his screams, it is said, could be heard for blocks. The extent of the whole conspiracy was soon uncovered, and everyone summarily dealt with. The honor of the Vespucci was deeply compromised, however. In their homes the name of Piero was never spoken again. Most of them fell all over themselves trying to make a public profession of loyalty to Lorenzo de' Medici, the Magnificent. Piero was sentenced to life imprisonment, writing pleading and pathetic letters to Lorenzo's mother, but to no avail.

Young Marco was exiled forever and never heard from again. We know nothing else about him. He had a family of his own no longer. Like so many beauties of legend, the beautiful Simonetta had died without offspring, though her image, needless to say, continues to live on and surely will forever.

Peanuts:
The Sagacity of Common Sense

A skeptic once declared that the most difficult part of success is finding someone who is happy for you, as if such a response were a rather rare and uncommon finding. I daresay it is hardly going out on a limb to make the assertion that the comic strip *Peanuts* made just about everybody happy, above all its prolific creator, although, in something of a disheartening paradox, David Michaelis in his biography, *Schulz and Peanuts* (2007), gives us the image of his subject as an isolated, lonely, solipsistic, and basically melancholy fellow who to create his comic strip drew deeply on his nagging restlessness and disaffection. (One of the cartoonist's children, Monte, described the biography as "preposterous.")

Charles M. Schulz was the embodiment of industry—he single-handedly drew as many as 18,000 *Peanuts* comic strips, flatly refusing to allow assistants to ink or letter his comics—and so if he was prone to depression he certainly cannot have been charged with anything like writer's block.

Who else can be named who has been published every single day for as long as half a century—50 long years? Considered to be "the longest story ever told by a single person," an original *Pea-*

nuts strip was prominently featured on the comic page of over 2,500 newspapers every single day from the series' debut in 1950 to February 13, 2000, just mere few hours after the cartoonist's death. A total of 17,897 *Peanuts* strips had been produced by the time Schulz retired.

During his life, the cartoonist took pains to say that he did not see his cartoons as "serious art." He did not even like the name "Peanuts" when he began to draw. There was no torturous presentation in evidence, no signs of torturous handwringing in the palimpsest. It was a breezy, open-hearted comic strip simple enough in conception, a conduit over half a century covering just about all the timeless subjects of art possible, except the heartbreak of psoriasis—loss, mistrust, obedience, sports, cheerfulness, frustration, affection, friendship, bewilderment, loyalty, annoyance, disappointment, the "blues," bouts of betrayal, love crises—including thumb-sucking, kite-eating trees, the Great Pumpkin who never appeared, and many anomalies of the age. It is difficult to come up with any of the basic verities, no matter how small a scale, that were not covered as the longest running story in the history of mankind ran its tender course.

As to the instructive aspects of the strip, it was all about simple truths. Intellection, no; common sense, yes. Much of *Peanuts* is what I call "soft knowledge," in the way that certain college subjects like sociology and psychology are. To me, the strip is basically about *cognition*; in various ways, all the characters are engaged in trying to figure things out—in a very real sense looking to solve the same crises that we idiotic adults face in our daily lives. Schulz had the "answers to the test"—as a friend of mine would say, making reference to the secret schoolboy key to studies and exams—got to the solid bottom of things. I tend to see *Peanuts* as "civilization by instinct," with kids like cutter-ants encountering and trying to deal with the various, if basic, problems of life. Foibles. Simple hobbles. Irksome reversals.

Vladimir Nabokov, who, granted, was egotistical, snobbish, and dismissive of so many things—he has gone on public record as utterly detesting (one of his favorite verbs) brutes, supermarkets, vulgarity, Marx, swimming pools, Picasso, dishonest art, jazz, music in general, sleeping (he referred to it as "moronic"), advertising, Henry James, literature with too many quotation marks, the German language, certainly Freud, the *Orient*, although not Soviet literature ("There *is* no Soviet literature!" he told a Cornell colleague)—always insisted that great art is never simple or sentimental. For Nabokov, any creative work that sought to convey moral values—"deft social commentary"—was bogus and contemptible.

Racial and gender equality issues? Hints of commentary? Religious themes such as those found in *Charlie Brown's Christmas?* Faith? Security blankets? The whole nondescript Midwestern neighborhood? Psychiatry? *Psychiatry*, Vladimir Nabokov's personal *bête noire?* Psychiatry—remember Lucy's "Psychiatry Booth"?—no, no, no it all would have made Nabokov gag.

No, Schultz was not Nabokov's doppelganger. He was dream eager, had longings and passionate, wide Technicolor dreams.

Cognition has to do with perception, insight. Dreaming, dreaming big, in fact—aspiration—is an ancillary theme of a Schultz comic strip, as well as the need to discern, to aspire, to grow. Are not all of Snoopy's fantasies aspirational? The little beagle is endearing in his dreams to become something, I would suggest, *because* he fails. It is such an inviting trait. What could be more winsome, adorable, attractive, or lovable than blundering failure? ("Bless his heart," a Southerner is often given to say, a remark that is always made warmly but just as always condescendingly, say, when referring to any pitiful loser, a slow learner, a nebbish, a loser, an ineffectual dolt, and the remark is almost always accompanied with the supercilious gesture of a patting of the head.) Snoopy fancies that he can speak, he desires to write books, although his short "novels" are never published, and his trusty little airplane, his Sopwith Camel, is repeatedly shot down by the Red Baron, his imaginary enemy. Schultz once declared of the bravado of his quixotic little dog, "He has to retreat into his fanciful world in order to survive. Otherwise, he leads kind of a dull, miserable life. I don't envy dogs the lives they have to live."

Action in the comic strip is invariably aspirational, which does not exclude fun, needless to say. Consequently, there are lots of tears shed, a great deal of rue, bewailing, lamenting, and bitter regret. Sighs predominate. So do groans and moans. There is a heartiness to the kids' standard engagement. Schulz is big on kite-flying. Football, baseball, and bowling are major activities. Topics—"fixations" is not a misapplied word to describe them—include warm blankets and thumb-sucking, rough weather crises, bubblegum, rivalry. A dissertation will probably one day be written on the use of the hammock in *Peanuts*. I believe it is connected to Schulz's concept of fideistic meditation and the deliberations of brooding reverie.

The edifying and instructional, cozily apothegmatic aspects of *Peanuts* give it a sermonizing quality, as well, one distinctly homiletic, even when Schulz seems to be reaching past a gentle laugh in hopes of making, well, a social "statement," which is one of the reasons the cartoon proved to be just right for lunchboxes, sox, T-shirts, backpacks, tumbler cups, and especially popular greeting cards. I mean, sales on greeting cards for *all* occasions is a cottage industry for the Schulz brand, is it not? Capricious is the word for it. Schulz examines moods and temper, notions and impulse, dispositions and tones, flavors and propensities, desires and dreams. I have been told that over the years many of the cartoons, many of the characters, have become the subject of serious, well-framed, and effective religious sermons, pulpit stuff! Dennis R. Hoover in his essay "Peanuts for Christ" (2000) points out that:

> "Biblical themes and references were a common feature of *Peanuts* throughout its 50-year run; by one estimate, 10 percent of the 18,000 strips involved religion. And then there was Robert Short's 1965 best-seller, *The Gospel According to Peanuts*, which used individual strips as modern-day Christian parables. Thus far the book has sold 10 million copies, a figure that has 'no doubt topped the number of sales of all books in theology-not-associated-with-cartoons published since 1965,' writes [Rev.] Martin Marty in the foreword to a new edition out this year."

There is no question that the warmth of the strip—its easy amiability, its soft-sell congeniality—lends itself to merchandising. Yesterday I discovered in our attic a dusty old 1965 oval red "Splash-and-Play" lawn sprinkler, featuring a cocky-looking Snoopy and his garden assistantWoodstock, both wagging green hoses. It is so quirkily odd and perhaps out-of-date that, upon checking it out, I could not find another one on eBay. There are Snoopy collectors clubs and conventions, hundreds of websites hawking *Peanuts*ware and *Peanuts*goods and *Peanuts*memorabilia!

As everyone knows, *Peanuts* focuses entirely on a miniature society—the whimsical interrelations of a bunch of young children and a zany beagle, without any reference to adult characters.

Grown-ups are never shown. Homely values predominate. The main character, Charlie Brown, is a sweet, gentle underling, a nervous but reflective little boy who lacks self-confidence—a lovable loser who frequently suffers but always tries his level best to figure things out. He is unable to kick a football, win a baseball game, or fly a kite. "I like to have Charlie Brown to be the focal point of almost every story," Schulz said of his quirkily endearing protagonist.

Short squat lovable characters populate *Schulzwelt*. They are all completely innocent, youthful, unimpeachable, irreproachable. It is a simple, uncomplicated, and wholesome Ronald Reagan-idea of a world (Schulz and the president were in fact friends). Guile, when it appears, is fairly harmless. With a lot of emotion in the air, there is a prevailing sense in the strip of a feminine sensibility at work. Double-dealing and trickery appear, but truth, openness, sincerity prevail. There are bullies. Overcoming tormentors is a big theme in the strip—in fact, this may have been Schulz's main go-to subject matter.

The *Peanuts* gang is passingly cerebral, to a degree. Is it the big heads? Round heads are invariably young heads. Moralizing balloonheads describe most of my uncles and aunts, who were sententious to a fault, as well. The art of Schultz is clean, scrubbed of messiness, even of specific locale. The is a good deal of silence and pausing, the caesura of deliberation. That does not mean lack of drama, not at all. "Construction can be put on silence," as Hilary Mantel writes in her novel *The Mirror & the Light*. There is a quality of *standstillness*—or is it predictability?—from panel to panel, strip to strip. Its pauses are a comfort. I mean to say it is a guileless neighborhood, a locale that we return to over and over. The dialogue reminds me of little Ping-Pong matches; there are original "takes" on subjects, it is true. Mainly, however, it is all—or at least much of it—a compendium of bromides, an art that is full of the *"All you need is love. But a little chocolate now and then doesn't hurt"* syndrome.

I see Schulz's comic strip essentially coming out of the world of Mark Twain, specifically *The Adventures of Tom Sawyer* (1876) and *Adventures of Huckleberry Finn* (1885), the latter novel being the one that Ernest Hemingway famously claimed that "all modern American literature comes from." Children have a kind of power, both innocent and willful, that is almost always in conflict with the society, never mind the emotions and personal complexities, they face. Twain's masterpiece, as Andrew Levy notes in *Huck Finn's America*, was written at a time when the country was nervous about reckless youth and "uncivilized" hoydens, and at the time longwinded debates were raging about education. The myth of a carefree childhood is gainsaid in *Peanuts*, in which a winning set of little roughnecks are trapped in the kind of myths the missing adults have left them to face alone. The strip documents the escapades, opinions, and reactions of this small group to that culture, fighting for "freedom"—freedom of self, freedom of identity, freedom of their sense of place.

Human comfort is found in their vitality. Looking back, I see the comic in its relative ease, its repose, as a kind of running condolence and reassurance to readers during a period of some of the most hair-raising horror and war ever seen, the last violent decades of the 20th century, full of social unrest.

The strip, to my mind, fulfills the sense of Aristotle's word *ethic* (*ηθική*) because the character of the patient and resourceful "hero" (and his ilk) is displayed in action guided by reason. Aristotle explained that the dominant *motive of action* in the *Odyssey* is strong on portraiture of character. By the word *reason*, I mean, not so much hard-driving ratiocination, but rather the sagacity of common sense, the brave attempt of decent little people, vital as opposed to self-conscious, devotedly trying hard to coax or persuade some kind of logic out of daily life.

Furthermore, the saga of *Peanuts* follows some amazing templates. There is a primitive, almost prelapsarian intelligence at work in these panels. It was the notion of British classical scholar R. C. Jebb that the capital distinction of Homeric poetry is that it bears in its *habitus* both the freshness and simplicity of a primitive age—evoking a charm that we associate with the "childhood of the world": rudeness of form, the struggle of thought with language, a tendency to grotesque, semi-mangled modes of speech, and, yes, a sort of crude rubric, in Jebb's words "the incapacity for equable maintenance of a high level, which belong to the primitive stage of literature." In fact, its general character is that which the insightful English critic Matthew Arnold defines in his lectures on translating Homer, when he states that Homer's style has four principal qualities—namely, it is (1) rapid; (2) plain in thought; (3) plain in diction; and (4) noble.

My intention is not to overegg the pudding here, but merely to point out that in his graphic labors Schulz created a fantasy world in which a distinct kind of benign ungainliness, a coarseness—a greenness—predominates, one that bears the characteristics of a time-tested style. Was Schulz aware of this? I daresay no. Were his efforts part of what Jung called the "collective unconscious"? Possibly. The austerity of the strip, its plainness, the homeliness of the construction, its rude simplicities, have nobility. The touches of the *hand-made*, remember, can be seen in every facet and feature, surface and strand, of Chartres cathedral. My mother always told us to *make* thank you cards, not buy them, for that they meant more.

Peanuts is minimalistic. There are no detailed backgrounds to the strip panels; they are invariably little clouds, a scrimp land-scape of green, a plain house, a wobbly fence. Consider also the font in the *Peanuts'* balloons—always uniform, always the same. Where is a variation? What, maybe by the emphatic use of a bold alternative when someone is shouting? The kids have small mouths, unfrazzled faces, dots for eyes. Al Capp's *Li'l Abner* was a veritable porcupine of styles, bristling with various typefaces, exclamation marks, no end of crazy words, weird dialects, outlandish and nutty names, and was a profane and cheeky send-up of everything. Schulz's style has been described by art critic John Carlin as forcing "its readers to focus on subtle nuances rather than broad actions or sharp transitions." Schulz held this belief all his life, reaffirming in 1994 the impor-tance of crafting the strip himself: "This is not a crazy business about slinging ink. This is a deadly serious business."

I have always been struck by the unadorned, unembellished nature of *Peanuts*, the sparseness, the austerity, the clean lines, the lack of adornment, the absence of decoration. In our family, we have two children, Shiloh and Shenandoah, both age eight, very bright, responsive girls, and reading to them nightly as we have done over the years, I have often been struck repeatedly going through the various children's books at the often impenetrable, convoluted, and bewildering messes of so many of them. Far too complicated. Bram-bly and tangled. Confusing. Ridiculous for the wrong reasons. A lot of the art-work is also rubbish. May I suggest that great artists themselves even nod?

Look at two of Dr. Seuss's books, for example, *Yertle the Turtle* and *The Lorax*. Much as I love the man—and I grew up with his ingenious books—to me both are failures as children's books, not so much because they are relentlessly coy and almost headachingly didactic, pointlessly clogged up, overarched with didactic strapping, but rather that the little stories unraveling have plots more complicated than Wilkie Collins's *The Moonstone*! To me, Dr. Seuss lost his fastball somewhat as he grew older, peaking with *The Grinch*. I love his earlier books.

Overcontrivance—which Schulz always avoids—can kill. I would cite as a parallel example Ira Gershwin's lyrics to "Let's Call the Whole Thing Off," a song that Fred Astaire sings in the musical *Shall We Dance* (1937), an effort far too wordy, with a tune, by the way, that is itself fairly melody-less, all sharps and flats, and, really to push it, the plot of the film—that entire farce of marriage/ divorce reversals and re-tactic-ing, all maneuvers and strategems—is too confusing for words. You have to know when to stop, understand when the delivery has been made. I would also point to the same noisy complications in Richard Scarry's illustrated children's books, where the graphics, often puzzlingly overprecise, are jammed together. Of 14 major Shirley Temple films, only one of them, *The Blue Bird*, was a commercial failure. Why? It was too damned complicated, an overembellished allegorical quest by way of dream journeys to various realms of fairy, ending with the Kingdom of the Future, where the souls of yet-to-be-born children, awaiting the hour of their birth, prepare various reforms.

I love a remark that the greedy, overly cunning peckerwood Flem Snopes makes when pondering buying an old horse in William Faulkner's *The Hamlet*; deciding against it, his suspicious reflection on the sales explanation is, "It can't be right. It wasn't complicated enough."

From all that I have read on him (not a lot), Schulz was personally and blessedly himself uncomplicated, something of a remote man, a conventional fellow who loved to ice skate, was an avid hockey fan, grew enthusiastic over the U.S. space program, and was a staff sergeant in the U.S. Army with the 20th Armored Division in Europe during World War II as a squad leader on a .50 caliber machine gun team. (Schulz said he had only one opportunity to fire his machine gun but forgot to load it, and that the German soldier he could have fired at willingly surrendered.) I tend to regard the fellow in my mind's eye as a genial Midwestern man, the very kind of 1950s person who *would* be born in Minnesota. (Was it because as I read through decades of *Peanuts* strips, I saw no signs, for example, of the Atlantic ocean, seafood, odd or striking animals, references or allusions to things European allusions, or general exotica?) Randy Kennedy writes in a book review of Michaelis' biography,

> "Looked at simply as a narrative problem, it is not hard to see why any biographer would want a strong framing device in trying to tell the story of Mr. Schulz. He was a homebody workaholic whose passions, other than his strips, were golf and hockey. He was a Sunday school teacher who was not only a teetotaler but disdainful of drinking and those who did it. His favorite ice cream was vanilla. A woman who knew him at the height of his early fame described him as a 'genius at becoming invisible.'"

What about Schulz's artistry—the reach of his designing hand? Could he draw with any calculus of genius, work in the high range? His little hydrocephalics, winsome, never did anything all that much for my eye. Can Charles Schulz be placed in the genius category? Has he flair? Haughty courage? Is he anywhere close to Thomas Nast? Rube Goldberg? Virgil Partch? Edward Lear? Hablot K. Browne? George Cruikshank? John Leech? Winsor McKay? Chuck Jones? Ronald Searle? Max Fleischer? Ub Iwerks? R. Crumb?

Chris Ware? Ernest Shepard? John Tenniel? Hilaire Belloc? Edward Gorey? Gerald Scarfe? George Herriman? Ralph Steadman? E. C. Segar? David Levine? But does he need to be? I suppose the fundamental equation is that if you want to convey Attic simplicity with your characters, in your panels, there cannot be too much linear noise, no ingraining, no fine tuning, nothing along the way with Ben-Day techniques, no zoo-like whipsnadery reaching out to grab the reader.

"Sparky," as his wife called him, loved watercolors but felt it was the most difficult medium. He also enjoyed stretching his artistic muscles by sketching the scenery around him. His *A Change of Scene* presents a travel sketchbook and 13 never-before-exhibited sketches that he created during the several trips he made to England, France, and Yosemite National Park. But his sketches never really pleased him and he was often inclined to rip them up.

I mentioned Edward Lear, a master of watercolor. On January 12, 1871 from San Remo, Italy, the English artist, illustrator, musician, author, and poet, a man who is known predominantly for his exquisite literary nonsense in poetry and prose and especially his limericks, wrote to a friend of his, David Morier:

> "The critics are very silly to see politics in such bosh
> [as my nonsense songs and illustrations]: not that but
> bosh requires a good deal of care, for it is a *sine qua non*
> in writing for children to keep what they have to read
> perfectly clear & bright, & capable of any meaning but
> one of sheer nonsense."

Schulz love nonsense, silly palaver and exchanges passed in the midst of absurdity. He possessed a great sense of space—"framing" his ideas—which is so all-important in piecing out one's ideas. One good example is a strip of January 8, 1961 showing Charlie Brown skiing, with each panel a small athletic maneuver, uphill, downhill, standing: all perfectly timed. The cartoonist loved speed lines; exclamations ("Pow!" "Clunk!" "Bonk!" "Snap!" "Tear!"), and lived on the old vaudeville trope of often having one of his characters turn a deadpan face to the reader for succor. Those oval loops of the gang's big heads, often rendered with a tiny, smarmy curl, even if defining what Truman Capote would call a "case of the cutes," serve as perfect focus for the speaking figures, always with an arrow to the punch line: "You're not listening!" "Abandon ship!" "Run. Run faster!" "Pounce!"

Snoopy, Lucy, Linus, Peppermint Patty, Sally Brown, Schroeder, and of course Charlie Brown (repeatedly using the full name of a character is of course an affectation, one used by Ernest Hemingway in *Islands in the Stream*, where the typically stoic male figure is referred to as "Thomas Hudson" throughout the entire posthumously published novel) talk way above their age and pay-scale, of course. And, as I say, Schulz is very big indeed on the didactic front and often sought the anagogical level. It is a major rubric of the *Peanuts* strip: lessons have to be learned.

The *Peanuts* gang is full of *capability*. Reasoning as such is not their *forte*, nor is it Schulz's. Johann Wolfgang von Goethe, who was a critic of reductionist science in the 18th century, argued that the natural world can only be known through subjective and qualitative experience, and what stands forth as one of his intellectual tenets was his lifelong effort to show that the process of reducing human experiences to mathematical quantities was not empirical, which is one explanation why he developed a theory of color that incorporated the direct sensory experience of different colors. Big on intuition, not reason, *Peanuts* people indeed try logically to justify, explain, and probe their actions, although they are far more at home with the wisdom of hunches, guesses, instinct. The reader is often challenged to see deeper.

Philosopher David Hume emphasized the value of custom and instinct as guides to life. Instinct at work, often trying to halt the pretensions of reason, seeks to put reason in its place. If reason is taken as fundamental, it can lead to confusion, and so, explained Hume, custom, a summary of knowledge, is a better guide. Shultz was very keen to have us all see with fresh eyes. How often did we turn to one of his comic strips, as we did to television's calming, soothingly reductive Fred Rogers in *Mr. Rogers' Neighborhood*, for the simple unpretentious comfort of relief from the cold, dark, nasty, brutishness of real life?

An ongoing scandal to me is how many cartoonists cannot draw—I mean, draw with *compelling magic.* The slim, attenuated line-drawings of Jules Feiffer, Giacomettian sketches mainly, are little more than standing or perambulating dwindles, people in conversation of an arch sort, always touching on an existential struggle. But could the man draw? In a *Playboy* interview, he explained, "I couldn't write well enough to be a writer, or draw well enough to be an artist, and so realized that the best way to succeed would be to combine my limited talents in each of those fields to create something unique."

The cartoonist Gary Trudeau, an insightful writer with a questing, original mind, nevertheless shows a limited sameness in his capacity as a cartoonist, in my opinion. *Saturday Review* once voted Trudeau, foolishly, one of the "Most Overrated People in American Arts and Letters," denouncing his comic strip as "predictable" and "mean-spirited," which is of course far from the truth, but what I would call into question are the cartoons themselves, the predictable graphics, with little variation of face and figure in his characters.

In this dimly lit department, however, no one, at least to me, is worse than Bruce Eric Kaplan, the American cartoonist known as "BEK," whose hideously bad single-panel cartoons appear in the *New Yorker* virtually every week, without fail. To say that his style is simple is to say that summer is warm. I find him such a hack, so desperately lacking in any aspect of the art—drawing, writing, imagination, style—that I have often wondered if he is related to someone at the magazine or whether nepotism is involved. His captions alone—banal, threadbare, humdrum, stupid, vapid, rigid, and unimaginative, right down to his stilted, wooden, *frozen* figures, always in mid-walk—are egregiously meaningless, always humorless, so brutally scalped of any significance, so batshit-awful, that you wonder whether the man does not possess some weird, unsavory, untellable information on those employers of his who are in such thrall to him.

I mean, what is the story here? Consider the *New Yorker* magazine itself: so many of the cartoonists simply cannot draw well or even draw at all. I find it less scandalous than corrupt. OK, Caravaggio had problems with perspective, Michelangelo with his Mannerist paintings placed women's heads on male bodies, El Greco comes in at a slant, Mark Rothko could not even draw a simple cat. Could Kenneth Noland draw? No. Richard Hamilton? Peter Blake? Keith Haring (who claimed to be influenced by Charles Schulz) with his quaquaversal grammar school squiggles and itchy, twitchy, neonized jumping-jackiana? Doubtful. A lot of this psycho-gyrational legerdemain is described as "alternate art," but for me much of it comes under the aegis of τέχνη, the Greek word for craft—technologized mechanics—if it has to come under the aegis of anything.

I am convinced that it was surely one of the waking dreams of Charles Schulz to have passionate, dedicated readers snip out strips and send them to friends or tape them to refrigerators as a kind of reinforcement of the fuzzy-warm verities that he was selling. I know that this happened all the time, which is invariably the case with sentimental art, akin somewhat—but far, far better—to hopeless Rod McKuen's putrid doggerel in books like *Listen to the Warm*, or that mawkish and often cloying posturing junk that Maya Angelou was always selling, asinine crapola.

Still, to deny tenderness, grace, and soft affection to Charlie Brown *et cie* is unquestionably in itself a vice. Schulz was surely an innovative cartoonist and caught the dreams and dynamic of watching, reading America in a very real way. I have read that the comic helped cement the four-panel gag strip as the standard in the United States, and together with its merchandise earned Schulz more than $1 billion. Reprints of the comic strip, syndicated to this day, still run in almost every U.S. newspaper. The world adores *Peanuts*. It seems that the barking cynic (cited above) who declared that the condition of finding someone who is happy for you remained the most difficult part of success has to eat crow in the career of Charles M. Schulz.

"High seriousness" can be the bane of comics—and comedians. In the end the late stand-up comedian George Carlin, as far as I am concerned, became little more than a fulminating professor, scolding *Wortmeister*, unsparing in his polemics, and that half the time he ended up rebuking someone with laborious etymologies, humdrum and monotonous, although there were times when he did show genius. Couldn't the same thing be said of 1960s Mort Sahl, a stand-up version of a news anchor, except he was a far less intelligible and painfully moralistic and sanctimonious?

Lenny Bruce was a boor, a talentless and embarrassing curmudgeon who never let up demanding all sorts of license while trying to make easy money by the laughable but unworthy pretense of insisting that he was a pioneer of freedom and First Amendment rights. He was worse than an obscene, out-of-control drug addict—he was a cheapjack. It can often come across as lame to be too righteous. Still, it can be said that Schulz had his own sense of daring and did not hesitate to satirize any number of issues when he chose to do so. Over the years he tackled everything from school dress codes to the so-called "New Math."

But in *Peanuts* Schultz kept his homilies mainly out of the way or in the background, although he was not at all shy in raising many issues of the day, thorny subjects like gun control, health care, the environment. Although he was pretty much a centrist, determined to let readers interpret his strips in their own way, he gently communicated the issues of the changing world around him through his characters and their innocent wit. He touched on psychiatry, illiteracy, the civil rights advancement on women in sports. Lucy embraced feminist philosophies, Linus grew weirdly anxious when he mistook snow for nuclear fallout, and Sally wondered about praying in school. There is in the strip a lot of "out-of-the-mouths-of-babes" astuteness, shrewdness.

On the other hand, I still do not see how Schulz could have sat by through Vietnam, Nixon, Watergate, the assassinations, the political demos and seething unrest, etc. without feeling compelled to throw major darts—innocent perspective, the naïf, has always provided a perfect vehicle for a satirist—so I don't feel that Schulz had fire in his belly or was daring or very brave.

Loneliness, the personal lack of a sense of place, and the

state of an indifferent and "bitter" world predominate largely in the strips. Schulz gave us a unique character named 5 whose sisters were named 3 and 4—their father had changed their family name to their Zip Code—making an Orwellian comment on the way numbers could take over people's identities. (A big Dr. Seuss theme, as well.) Charles Schulz was patriotic. There are panels in which he made reference to the Cold War. One strip published on May 20, 1962 even had an icon that declared "Defend Freedom, Buy U.S. Savings Bonds." Racial equality was, to a degree, a running topic that Schulz broached over the course of the half-century that the strip ran. On July 31, 1968 he introduced Franklin Armstrong, a black character, into the predominately white cast, just months after Rev. Dr. Martin Luther King Jr. was assassinated in Memphis, Tennessee. In his first appearance, Franklin met his friend Charlie Brown when they were both at the beach. Franklin's father was a soldier fighting in Vietnam. Schulz said, "The two never met before because they went to different schools."

As I say, the strip is satirical. Satire, by definition is a genre that is meant—often sharply—to *correct*. Whimsy unquestionably often takes a backseat to preachiness in the *Peanuts* strips. Other cartoonists could be preachy, polemical, but for the most part it was done with irreverence, intentional disrespect, anger, even lewdness. Al Capp had more grit, Dickensian brilliance, and far less respect for tradition. Virgil Partch had far more boldness, even approaching the rude and the terrifying. "I-don't-give-a-damn" James Thurber, who drew his cartoon figures with the same simple lines as Schulz did, was nevertheless nastily misogynistic—I find those to be his funniest bits—although it was dry and cagily understated. R. Crumb has always been feral, undomesticated, mad with innovation and cruel abandon, zapping anyone and anything at all. By the way, have we yet mentioned the word "cute"?

Small children evoke sentimental appreciation for the charming, the adorable, and the diminutive, especially those imitating adults, from "Our Gang" and "Little Rascals" to early Jackie Coogan. John F. Kasson, in *The Little Girl Who Fought the Great Depression* explains the cuteness (the word originally meant "shrewd") by way of Shirley Temple, its paragon:

> "Cuteness invited the beholder's responses on various levels: aesthetic delight, moral protection, and possessive desire. It powerfully combined elements of sentimental reform and the rise of modern commercial culture, especially as they conjoined in admiration and indulgence of childhood's innocence and wonder. . . . Benign parents and other protectors could cherish children's eager imitations of adult life, even their play of work, marriage, and child rearing, safe in the belief in the boundary separating the realms of childhood and adulthood."

There is invariably something of the pet in cuteness. Schulz had a gift for the dainty detail. The rule seemed to be, go for individuation. How about Linus's blue blankie? Schroder's fluffy top-knob? Pig Pen's aura of fleas? Charlie Brown's captivating hair-comb, that one swirl of hair over his forehead, which was a favorite coiffure in 1944? Said the American fashion designer Cynthia Crowley, "Everything looks cute when it's small."

A syndicate editor chose the name "Peanuts," despite Schulz's own protests. As I say, he confessed to have frankly disliked the title of his famous comic strip. In a 1987 interview, his surprising comment about the name was, "It's totally ridiculous, has no meaning, is simply confusing, and has no dignity—and I think my humor has dignity." (Does it not give you some idea of Schulz's blessed naïveté, however, that he had wanted to call the dog "Sniffy"?)

Still, there is an intrepid, somewhat literary side to Schulz. Consider the fact, for example, the waggish, droll, and even fantastical side to him—it was the direct opposite of his more conventional side—when it came to inventing names for many of the satellite characters he chose to add to the main roster of his strip, witty devisings such as Truffles, a female character named by her grandfather after the rare fungus that grows underground; Tapioca Pudding, who has a small crush on Linus, which annoys Sally, who is jealous of the friendship; Shut Up and Leave Me Alone, Charlie's bunkmate at the summer camp where Marcie was introduced in 1971; Morag, Charlie Brown's pen pal. (When asked by Lucy what they write about, Charlie Brown replies, "He tells me about his country, and I tell him about ours"); and other captivating characters such as Miss Othmar, Molly Volly, Lila, Heather ("the Little Red-haired Girl"), Cormac, Eudora, Faron, and, among others, Joe Shlabotnik, a minor-league baseball player who is greatly admired by Charlie Brown. This character never does appear in the strip, but he is occasionally mentioned by Charlie Brown as his hero and in fact becomes part of several plots involving the protagonist.

Indeed, Charles Schulz, like Laurence Sterne, Charles Dickens, and, say, acerbic Evelyn Waugh, did occasionally opt for the outré name, but for the most part he was basically cautious and unadventurous in this department. In contrast, compare the names of the many zany characters in *Li'l Abner* to the common and unaggressively workaday names in *Peanuts* like Charlie Brown, Lucy, Sally, Violet, Franklin, Snoopy, and Linus (actually a name of one of the early popes!). Woodstock is sometimes accompanied by as many as seven other almost identical yellow birds named Bill, Harriet, Olivier, Raymond, Fred, Roy, Wilson and Conrad, who together are known as "Snoopy's Beagle Scouts," or simply the "Beagle Scouts."

Schulz wanted to reach a good many readers. So simplicity went down well in the *Peanuts* comic strip. When people referred to the strip as "refreshing," they invariably mean to convey that it was "simple" and "unpretentious" and "endearing." Girls, young women, all through the 1960s, loved *Peanuts* and used to cut out strips to tape on their walls or—yes—hand them around, with soft smiles. Who was it said that guys gave girls copies of Kahlil Gibran's *The Prophet* in order to get laid? I think young girls in handing out selected panels were in the main trying to flirt with guys, to make manifest their best side as being warm, worthwhile, motherly. A deep aspect of love is need. Boys, men love to feel warmly protected. There is a good deal of the allegory in the *Peanuts* strip, I feel, somehow a saga of Schultz's personal life " Everyman's life is an allegory. God knows it, the saints live it, the poets write it," said the Irish writer," Frank O' Connor, and I think he's right.

In a book review in an English paper, Pamela Travers, author of *Mary Poppins* and its sequels, said that anyone who writes for children successfully is probably writing for one child—namely, the child that is himself." Lewis Carroll, A.A. Milne, Roald Dahl come immediately to mind as examples. I believe this comes close to the truth with "Sparky." Much of the man was a boy.

The remarkable oeuvre that Charles M. Schulz left us becomes a sort of apology for human behavior. Not a single character seemed to have escaped him, as John Dryden said of Chaucer. I will echo Dryden again in saying, "It is sufficient to say, according to the proverb, that here is God's plenty."

Vermeer's Secret

To the Orangerie, in the Tuileries Gardens, the writer Bergotte in Proust's masterpiece, *À la recherche du temps perdu*, suffering from an attack of uremia, goes to see Vermeer's *View of Delft* (1660), on loan from the Hague Museum. A critic had written that a fragment of yellow wall in the painting could be considered a thing of perfect beauty, and against the advice of doctors, Bergotte, ill, still yearns to see it. "His giddiness increased; he fixed his eyes, like a child upon a yellow butterfly . . . upon the precious little patch of wall. 'That is how I ought to have written. My last books are too dry, I ought to have gone over them with several coats of paint, made my language exquisite in itself, like this little patch of yellow wall'. . . he sank down upon a circular divan . . . he rolled from the divan to the floor, as visitors and attendants came hurrying to his assistance. He was dead."

This scene closely parallels one in Proust's own life. Although mortally ill, Proust left his fifth-floor apartment at 44 rue Hamelin (he moved there in 1919) for the last time, on the arm of his friend Jean-Louis Vaudoyer, to see this very painting of Vermeer's, which he considered "the most beautiful in the world." The exhibit opened in May 1921; Proust died in November of the following year, just after completing his massive novel. There is a Vermeer "motif" running through *Remembrance of Things Past*. Swann is writing an essay on Vermeer. Charlus compares Gustave Jacquet with Vermeer. In keeping with her entire approach to life and art, the vain Odette drops all interest in Vermeer as soon as she learns that nothing is known of the romantic part of his life. She simultaneously loses interest in her lover, Swann, and begins to deceive him. What's interesting is that the Vermeer motif in the novel is almost always associated with death (and, to a degree, transfiguration)—with Bergotte's death, with Swann's death, and with the death of Marcel Proust himself, whose very last thoughts appear to have been directed toward the paintings of Vermeer.

Proust in his adolescence frequently visited the Louvre. At age 13 or 14 he was already expressing preferences in art. Young Proust's very first book, *Portraits de Peintres* (1896), dealt with the subject dearest to his heart. He had the reputation as he got older of being something of a connoisseur in art, in fact. ("A guide to the galleries," as someone described him.) Some have gone so far as to say that his experience of painting molded his writing style. He was attracted to both old and modern masters. He has been criticized for paying more attention to society painters, invariably his friends, lesser artists, for example, like Helleu and Boldini and Forain, than to greater figures of art, but he has gone on record as adoring Leonardo, Rembrandt, and El Greco as well as newer masters like Monticelli and Whistler.

Above all, Proust adored Claude Monet (who partially comprised his portrait of the fictional character Elstir), but it was to the Dutch Baroque Johannes Vermeer, as early as 1910, that he gave his highest praise. ("*Vous savez que Vermeer est mon peintre prefere depuis j'age de vingt ans. . . .*")

Due to his secluded life and various other of his many crotchets that kept him from going out anywhere, Marcel Proust rarely visited galleries outside of Paris. In fact, for the last 20 years of his life, with the one exception in 1921 of going to see the Vermeer exhibit, he never went to a museum. It was while traveling abroad in Holland, however, that on October 18, 1902 he visited the Mauritshuis and saw for the first time Vermeer's incomparable masterpiece *View of Delft*. (He had seen Vermeer's *The Lacemaker* in the Louvre many times before, of course.) Seeing this work became an ineffable experience for him. "As soon as I first set eyes on *View of Delft* I knew that I had seen the loveliest picture in the world," he wrote to Vaudoyer. And it excited him in terms of his fiction. "In *Du côté de chez Swann* I could not resist the temptation to make Swann plan a study of Vermeer. . . . This artist who keeps his back to us, who set no store upon being seen by posterity, and who will never know what posterity thinks of him, moves me profoundly."

Although it seems hard to believe, Vermeer's paintings—his art in general—had been overlooked for almost 200 years. After all, what could critics do with an oeuvre of just 30-odd pictures that had no clearly identifiable subject matter, no "content," only an effect of color and light? Not only were his categories different—mythological, historical, political, and religious subjects were barely in evidence—but here was a Dutch genre painter who never painted children or flowers or even animals, with the single exception of the dog in the very early *Diana and Her Companions* (ca. 1655), which, incidentally, some critics insist was painted by his father in the first place.

Vermeer commanded very little attention even when he was alive. The facts of his life can be very briefly told. For the most part, he led a quiet existence in Delft. The dates of his birth and death (1632–1675) are recorded, and there are no records that he ever lived or worked in any other town or visited any other country. His father ran an inn called the Flying Fox and occasionally dealt in pictures, though he was a poor accountant and seems to have often been deeply in debt (15 years after his death in 1652, his heirs were still paying off interest in loans that he had contracted). We know so little about Vermeer and actually nothing about the painter's own formative years. Since at the age of 21 he registered with the painter's guild, he must have served an apprenticeship with a recognized artist for at least six years. Some critics believe that, because of certain similarities in their handling of color and light, he must have studied with Carel Fabritius, a pupil of Rembrandt and a member of the Delft School. (Let it be noted that among Fabritius's works, strikingly, are *A View of Delft*!) Other critics feel that strong documentary evidence makes the more likely candidates on Vermeer in the pedagogical and influential departments to be Evert van Aelst (a still-life painter who knew Vermeer's father), Gerard ter Borch (who specialized miniature portraits in 1640 and who also witnessed Vermeer's marriage), Abraham Bloemaert (to whom he was distantly related by marriage), and/or Leonart Bramer (a local celebrity), all part of his life.

He was married in 1653 at the age of 21 to a certain Catharina Bolnes of Gouda (art historian André Malraux believed her to be the beautifully serene and seemingly modest figure delicately portrayed in his *Woman Holding a Balance* [1662], a Roman Catholic—converting to the faith, Vermeer became one in consequence) and went to live in his mother-in-law's well-appointed house in the area called "Papist's' Corner." It is thought that only by marrying above himself, as he did, was he able to move to that grander part of Delft. (The cupboards, paintings, rugs, and sunlit corners of this house are those that have long become familiar to us through Vermeer's work.) The fact of his wife and children being Catholics may explain the relative obscurity of his life. In its long and bitter war of independence, Holland had thrown off the Catholic rule of domineering Spain, but there was a lingering resentment and memories of atrocities that would not soon die.

Vermeer fathered 15 children with Catharina, four of whom died in infancy. Until 1672, when Louis XIV invaded the Netherlands in the Franco-Dutch War of 1672–1678, the second war of conquest by a king whose aim in the conflict was to establish French possession of the Spanish Netherlands, Holland's economy collapsed. Vermeer managed to support his family with the help of his mother-in-law and a few small legacies, including selling two or three of his own paintings a year and also dealing in other artists' work. In 1672, however, the art market collapsed. Three years later, Vermeer died at the age of 43, leaving not only a widow but 11 children and many debts, including 726 guilders owed to the baker to whom Catharina gave two of her husband's pictures on account. (His paintings were then worth between 60 and 150 guilders). She still owned *The Art of Painting* (1666) and *Woman with a Pearl Necklace* (1664). The other paintings had surely all been sold.

In an ironic juxtaposition, the following year Anton van Leeuwenhoek was appointed to administer Catharina's estate on behalf of her creditors. The great biologist and student of optics—he invented the microscope and was the first to describe the lens of the eye, capillaries, and spermatozoa—was Vermeer's exact contemporary. Despite their common interests, there is no evidence, however, that they ever knew each other. Vermeer's name next appears in 1696, when 21 of his paintings, "extraordinarily vigorously and delightfully painted," were auctioned off in Amsterdam. *The Lace-*

maker, which Proust saw in the Louvre, fetched only 28 guilders. *View of Delft* brought 200.

Today, only 36 paintings are generally accepted to be by Vermeer's hand, of which three are in the Frick Collection. Queen Elizabeth II owned a rare Vermeer, the quietly beautiful *Music Lesson* (1662), showing the woman seated at the virginal—and that gorgeous draped carpet, matchless for rugs in all world painting!—in addition to two Rembrandts and works by Titian and Van Dyck. Many paintings in the Royal Collection were acquired by King George IV (1762–1830), who had a keen eye for art. They are, all of them, hung in Buckingham Palace. Of the 36 paintings attributed to Vermeer, 12 reside in American public collections.

This excludes *The Concert* (1664), acquired in an 1892 auction in Paris for $5,000 and formerly in the Isabella Stewart Gardner Museum in the The Fenway in Boston, which was stolen along with a dozen other paintings in a heist on March 8, 1990, by thieves disguised as policemen, a crime that to this day has never been solved. Nor has that rare painting ever resurfaced. It is thought to be the most valuable work currently unrecovered, with a value generally estimated to at $250 million.

It was not until the mid-19th century that an extraordinary French polymath—aristocrat, journalist, photographer, critic, politician, and revolutionary—named Théophile Thoré-Bürger, who also went by the pen name William Burger (German for "citizen"), rescued the painter from obscurity. He founded in Paris, in 1848, a journal called *The True Republic* and as a reward the following year was exiled from France by Louis Napoleon. It was immediately after seeing *View of Delft* hanging in the Mauritshuis, among scores of other 17th-century painters—this included Carel Fabritius, by the way, as well as Frans Hals (Thoré-Bürger was the first to describe his wonderful portrait of that cackling mythic witch-figure with the owl, *Malle Babbe*) that Thoré-Bürger's interest in Vermeer began, and it became his life's work. He looked everywhere, spending much of his exile haunting museums, rummaging among old catalogues, and sifting through archives in search of more works by Vermeer, whom he referred to as "the Sphinx of Delft." He had no money himself, though he constantly urged his wealthy friends to buy one of the rare paintings whenever they could. At one time he himself owned at least five Vermeers—today, only four Vermeers are privately owned—but many more passed through Thoré-Bürger's hands.

With his knowledge of photography, Thoré-Bürger was the first to use techniques in this field as an aid to documenting the works of Vermeer. He turned up 70 paintings altogether, although many eventually proved to be the work of other artists, including landscapes by a certain "Jan Vermeer of Haarlem." Of the undoubted Vermeers, there are 31 assured paintings; an additional four are problematic; eight more, sold in the 1696 sale, are lost today. Two-thirds were identified by Thoré-Bürger.

In 1866 he presented his opinions and findings in a series of articles and a book communicating his enthusiasms. This was followed in 1888 by Henry Hovard's *Van der Meer de Delft*. It was not long afterwards that Proust, always eager to gather information on Vermeer and who read these and other accounts passionately, unreservedly judged the Dutch artist to be the greatest of all painters, an opinion enthusiastically, and not surprisingly, shared by "Marcel," the narrator of his great novel.

Twenty years later then, Proust again had to see the Vermeers. (In the novel, Albertine mistakenly thinks "the Vermeers" are living people!) In order to attend the exhibit of Dutch painting at the Jeu de Paume in 1921—it included two major works of Vermeer, *Head of a Girl*, or as the painting is more often called, *Girl with a Pearl Earring* (the painting is a *tronie*, the Dutch 17th-century description of a "head" that was not ever intended to be a portrait), and *View of Delft*—he had to forgo his sleep for the day. At 9:15 a.m. he sent his chauffeur Odilon Albaret to fetch his good friend Vaudoyer to escort him, and off they went to the museum.

By dint of large doses of narcotics, Proust was able to admire the immortal pictures by leaning on the arm of his companion. Suddenly, Proust became dizzy and began to sway. And then he was seized by such a severe stroke that he nearly died. (He at first thought that it was a case of indigestion from potatoes.) He returned home, still shaken, and said to his housekeeper Celeste, "I don't know whether I shall ever be able to go out again." Ever the artist, however, as we have seen Proust found in this incident the inspiration for the celebrated description in the novel of Bergotte's death—he constantly followed the method of composition by insertion—and dictated the revisions of this episode (in *La prisonnière*), almost to the letter, when he got home, literally the day before he died.

"Celeste," hoarsely whispered the fading writer, always keen for accuracy, "I think that it is quite good what I have just dictated to you. Don't forget to see that it is put in its correct place. I count upon you. Do not fail to add it to my manuscript where it is to follow in the text. I must stop, I feel quite done."

What was it that struck Proust as he looked at the painting? Was he genuinely ill? Feverish? Or had he a dark glimpse somehow of his own insufficiency, his own impending death? Was it a yearning to *enter* that sunlight? Proust's sensitivity, his *sensibility*, was legend. In 1910, to take merely one example, he was among the first to subscribe to a new telephone invention, a sort of *fin-de-siècle* modem, that carried theater and opera performances over the telephone into the home of subscribers. Proust was living at the time at 102 Boulevard Haussmann (the flat of his recently dead uncle, Georges Weil) in the now famous cork-lined room where, a chronic invalid, he wrote in small, cramped notebooks nearly the entire body of his masterpiece. It was by means of this telephone contraption, consequently, that the novelist heard for the first time Claude Debussy's illustrious opera *Pelléas et Mélisande*, propped up in bed with the earpiece clamped to his head. So moved was Proust, so refined and delicate were his responses, that at the critically dramatic moment when Pélleas emerges from the caves into the sea air, Proust claimed to have experienced, in a moment of exuberance, no doubt, such an overpowering scent of roses that it gave him an asthma attack.

Proust often took "fumigations" for this asthma, breathing Legras powder in saucers in his rooms. He wasn't only, of course, a hypochondriac. He was witty, often sarcastic, and a voluble talker, coiling his legs together when sitting and holding his hand to his chin. He was reputedly to be a superb mimic. Fashionably dressed but never tidy, slim, pale, with black hair that was never turned grey, large dark eyes, heavy-lidded and of an incredible gentleness and melancholy languor of expression, he dared to see how abject and threadbare the lives of the well-fed and the well-to-do often are, how flabby and un-daring their imaginations, how dim and timid their tastes and desires. He loved to ask questions and was a pitiless observer—a saboteur of those very salons, of the *faubourg* itself, of which most think him the advocate. A longing to show himself affectionate, nevertheless, always breathed through his remarks, and his talk by all accounts was permeated with compliments. Dining out he loved, before he became too ill to do so, and his guests always ate the same meal he ordered for them—always wearing white gloves—the one he himself would have preferred if he had been able to eat it. He never failed to send gifts to his guests, flowers to women, cigarettes to men, the following day. He loved gossip, adored Russian music, and wrote incessantly.

He was a lonely and neurotic man. None of his sexual relationships lasted for more than a year or so. He developed intense crushes, many that soon faded. "Desire, reaching out always to what is most opposite oneself, forces one to love what will make one suffer. . . . It is a mistake to speak of a bad choice in love since as soon as there is a choice, it can only be a bad one," he wrote. His only long-lasting love was surely for his mother; their relationship remained abnormally close for 34 years. She treated him all his life as the child he constantly remained for her.

After two imperfect but remarkable false starts, Proust had settled down about 1909 to write a long first-person story that addressed the idea of self-discovery by a writer very much like himself. The first volume of *À la recherche du temps perdu* was published in 1913. (*Contre Sainte-Beuve* was actually the first version of the novel rather than an aborted literary essay; in fact, the novel begins in the earliest stages of *Les Plaisirs et les jours* and only ends with *Le Temps retrouvé*.) World War I—what Henry James always referred to as "the Great Interruption"—and other delays in Proust's own life permitted or required the original 500 pages he put down to grow to about 3000 by the time he died in 1922, sadly enough, just at the very moment when a great measure of success was beginning to come to him. His grief on account of the terrible war, incidentally, was almost an obsession, the slaughters a perpetual anguish. After decades of puffing on medicated anti-asthma cigarettes and doping himself with Trional and morphine, he would finally salvage 34 years of wasted time with a masterpiece.

The sickly novelist was word-perfect as to knowing about the range of contemporary treatments for his asthma. Over many years, he had been prescribed all sorts of strategies, from powders to inhalants to pulls, including opium, caffeine, iodine, and morphine (which had once been injected by his father, Dr. Adrien Proust) to ease his pain and discomfort. He inhaled smoke, his nose had been cauterized numerous times, he had adopted a milk diet, and he had occasionally attempted to relieve both his asthma and his hay fever by visiting health resorts, such as Evian-les-Bains, on the shores of Lake Geneva.*

Legends abound telling us how Marcel Proust worked all night in bed, writing although feverish and disheveled, calling for coffee, reshuffling, dictating, and endlessly revising his wonderful sentences until the manuscripts took the form of three-foot collage scrolls and the manuscript proofs were maniacally crisscrossed with all sorts of additional and emendations. The legends are generally all too true.

His bedroom became his study. He adopted an eccentric lifestyle, sleeping during the day and staying awake at night, when, strangely enough, he found it easier to breathe. He awoke at 5:00 p.m. generally and had a cup of café au lait with three crescent rolls, which was often the only food he took all day. (The bathtub, in his last years at Rue Hamelin, served as a storage for potatoes.) His linen and underclothes were always kept warm in the oven. He was very

---

*Mark Jackson in his essay "Divine Stramonium: The Rise and Fall of Smoking for Asthma" has given us an amazingly detailed account of Proust and the use of smoking stramonium and other strategies to breathe. It is a masterpiece in itself.

particular about the softness of materials. He habitually drank cups of coffee, the hotter the better. He would then proceed to work in bed in his nightshirt, wearing a cardigan (sometimes two or three) of natural Pyrenean wool over that. He often wore woolly waistcoats even under a loose dinner jacket. Sometimes he had a dish of stewed beef or a small chicken sent to him from a restaurant. Of course he could not go out; night air was death to him. At the very end he was drinking iced beer brought over from the Ritz Hotel while he was correcting proofs of *Albertine Disparue.* At one point in the evening, Celeste, who had been cook and maid to his mother, his aunt, and his grandmother, would place at his bedside a tray with a cup, a bottle of Evian water, sugar, a kettle, and a box of lime blossom.

Although the doctor had insisted on his giving up all idea of work, Proust went on with his proofs and, to propitiate the doctor, as he thought, sent him expensive bouquets of roses to make up for defying his orders. He acclimatized himself to working in bed because there was nowhere else he could spread his papers. He could not afford to rent a flat of his own, so always lived with his "Mamma" whose indefatigable efforts to dominate his life and possessive hold over him continued into his adult life. (He was terrified she might one day find out about his homosexuality. It is hard to believe that she did not know.) Sometimes he would proudly offer to pay rent, but, earning almost nothing from his writing, he would only have been paying back the generous allowance given to him.

Suspecting that he was dying, Proust tried to impress on Celeste that under no circumstances should she send for his younger brother Robert, a physician. He wanted to die by himself. At the approach of death he called for that part of his manuscript depicting the passing of his grandmother, alias mother, observing *"J'ai quelques retouches a y faire."* He was fond of Robert, as far as it went, although the two brothers frankly had little in common. Nor does one cherish at one's deathbed the presence of relatives with whom one has been out of touch. Now that he began to choke and struggle, a concerned Celeste, badly frightened, quickly forgot all of her promises and ran downstairs to a shop in order to put in a telephone call to his brother, who as it turned out soon arrived and began administering injections to relieve Marcel's terrible pain, though he succeeded only in prolonging it.

As they lifted the writer to a sitting position to try to enable him to breathe better, an abscess on his lung burst, throwing Proust into a welter of mortal agony, gasping with the strain and long struggle to take a breath began. When Robert understood that it was all over, heartbroken, he said *"Mon pauvre frère,* I'm afraid I have caused you a great deal of needless pain." Marcel Proust, opening his eyes just before he closed them forever, murmured, *"Mon pauvre Robert,* I'm afraid you have."

In his novel, Proust had written of Bergotte:

"He was dead. But for ever? Who can say? It is certain that neither spiritualist experiments, nor religious dogmas, bring us proof of the survival of the soul. What one can say is that everything happens in our life as though we had entered upon it with a burden of obligations contracted in an anterior existence; there is nothing in the conditions of life on this earth to make us think ourselves obliged to be good, to be sensitive, even polite; nor for the artist to feel himself compelled to begin a passage twenty times over again when the praise it evokes will matter little to the body devoured by worms. . . . All these obligations, which have no sanction in our present life, seem to belong to a different world, a world founded on goodness, on scruple, on sacrifice, a world entirely different from ours, and whence we come to be born on this earth, perhaps to return there and live under the rule of the unknown laws which we have obeyed here because we carried their principles within ourselves, without knowing who decreed that they should be; those laws to which every deep intellectual labor draws us nearer, and which are invisible only—and not even!—to fools." (Moncrieff translation)

So that (Proust concludes) the idea that Bergotte was not forever dead was not without verisimilitude. Next morning his friends came to look at the dead Proust. In death, the relatively young man of 51 seemed to have regained his youth. There was another redemption. Piled in two rows, on either side of him, as in his own description of the lying-in-state of Bergotte, were copies of his works.

There is, needless to say, much of Proust in the character Bergotte. He is a stand-in, a surrogate, a virtual double of his creator. Hence, Proust's recurringly uneasy relationship to him, the symbiotic link of author to character. Bergotte is a writer—he was supposedly modeled on Anatole France—who, like the early Proust, labors under the charge of "preciousness," and Proust shifted to him his literary guilt, with its nexus of doubt, self-searchings, and anxieties. The parallels are important and all quite obvious. He is also unwell. In this he bears a marked resemblance to descriptions of Proust himself in his last days. (We have noted that he dies of uremia, as did both Proust's mother and uncle). Bergotte never went out of doors, and when he did get out of bed for an hour in his room, he would be smothered in shawls. He is also "socially ambitious" and selfish. And like Proust, Bergotte—significantly for us—goes to look at the *View of Delft* in order to contemplate its *"petit pan de mur si bien peint en jaune"* before he is struck down forever by death. In Vermeer's art, yellow is his crowning color—"a color," as van Gogh once remarked, "capable of charming God."

What in Johannes Vermeer charmed the always febrile and highly sensitive Vincent van Gogh may also have been the intriguing sublimations and tensions in his paintings, enhanced by color and light, that constitute the human moments into which he has chosen to draw us in further and further. In *The Lacemaker*, for example, which Renoir considered one of the best pictures in the world, the subject is tranquility itself, and yet as the tightly coiffured woman bends to her task in whisper-quiet concentration, her delicate fingers plying her bobbins, completely engrossed—surely she tatted her own collar—Vermeer gives us an antithesis in that springing curl. Here is a woman so intent on her task that the rest of the world has fallen away. Like all of Vermeer's paintings, it captures a world breathlessly poised. We suspect she's working in one of those small Dutch houses typical of the times—often in his interiors Vermeer sometimes withholds the magic of color—but in *The Milkmaid* (1657), one woman, a strong domestic, stands in a nimbus of light. Vermeer has composed here in a calm, meditative moment an entire still-life from loaves of bread, a basket, an earthenware jug and bowl, and a milk jug. It is also a good example of how in Vermeer's paintings light becomes an unerring record, here revealing wicker, texture of cloth, even nail holes in the whitewashed walls. Both are examples in their self-absorbed way of women in the workaday world, moments of female inwardness that inviting us so far are only half open, half not.

The main figure in *Woman Standing at a Virginal* frankly acknowledges us. Vermeer's light, which is here uncharacteristically unselective, seems to show by way of mocking comment that Cupid's gaze behind her is very like the woman's—in an incongruity of which she is unaware. Or is there a knowing look in her eyes? What the irony indicates, if there is any, between the treatment the painter conveys in her rich satin dress and Cupid's nakedness is anybody's guess.

Meaning is never expressed in Vermeer. It is suggested. *The Art of Painting*, a masterpiece of Vermeer's mature period, has been described as a "realistic allegory." (Adolf Hitler himself actually acquired this painting in 1940 at a price of several hundred thousand dollars, buying it for the grand museum that he megalomaniacally dreamed of establishing after the victory of the Reich in his mother's honor in the Austrian town of Linz.) Does the girl in the laurel wreath holding the golden book and trumpet represent Fame, as some think? Or is it Clio, the Muse of History? Why does her Dr. Suess-ish expression suggest to me a model having fun? Is there something in her figure, that lovely insouciant face, outlined against the map of the "Seven Provinces" of Holland, that makes a nationalistic boast of some sort? Or is irony involved as well? The problem of the identity of the artist, planted firmly on the stool, his back turned on us, is insoluble. There is no motion: the model, of course, is holding her pose; the hand of the artist, painting her laurel wreath, is still—he has turned his eyes for this instant to Nature before he will place the next stroke. It is for us, the onlooker standing on the threshold of the studio, to judge, to try to discern what can be said and why. There is always mystery. Strangely, it is always part of a familiar world.

"You told me that you had seen some pictures by Vermeer," Proust wrote in "*La prisonnière*," the section of *À la recherche du temps perdu* which picks up where *Sodome et Gomorrhe* leaves off,

"You realize, of course, that they are fragments of the same world: a world that is always—with whatever genius it is recreated—made up of the same table, the same rug, the same woman, the same fresh and unique beauty. He is an enigma in an epoch in which nothing resembled nor explained him; and he can only be explained if you do not try to connect him to the others. . . ."

There are no known preliminary drawings by Vermeer, and infrared photography does not reveal any black underdrawing on the ground layer beneath the paint surface. There is, however, convincing and circumstantial evidence that he frequently made clever use of a *camera obscura* and other optical devices in order to gain a better insight into the thorny construction of pictorial space. A camera obscura was a 16th-century invention that consisted of a darkened box containing an arrangement of lenses and mirrors. These would project a reduced image, similar to that of a modern reflex camera, onto a flat surface from which an artist could trace a precise and detailed drawing. (In conversation years ago, John Updike told me one of the first people he would like to greet in heaven is Vermeer, adding that he particularly wanted to ask the artist specifically how he used this machine.)

Haunted like Bergotte by approaching death, then, Proust, who deeply believed in the redemptive quality of art—redemption by means of art, in fact, may be said to be the most important theme of his work as a whole—made his own visit to the museum, committed once again despite ill health to see the *"saphires de Vermeer,"* to stand one last time before the ideal perfection of a work that seemed to him the very manifestation of immortality, to imbibe so to speak all of its well-known passages.

View of Delft—an oil on canvas (38" x 46"), signed IVM and datable to about 1660—is generally taken to be part of a grouping including *The Milkmaid*, *The Lacemaker*, and *The Little Street* (1657), the latter a small painting, only 21.4 inches high by 17.3 inches wide, but one of my favorites, on which he employed a relatively limited number of pigments, red ochre and madder lake for the reddish-brown brick wall, the blue in the sky containing lead white and natural ultramarine, with the green shutters and foliage painted with an azurite mixed with lead-tin yellow.

Turning to *View of Delft* we witness the quaint and angular city seen from across the Rotterdam Canal: the wide Schliedam Gate is in the center, the medieval Rotterdam Gate on the right. In the background on the right is the bright tower of the Nieuwe Kerk, the church in which Vermeer was baptized; on the left the spire of the Oude Kerk, where he was buried, can be seen above the colored slate roofs. It was in the Prensehof opposite the Oude Kerk that William of Orange, known as the "Taciturn," the founder of Dutch independence, was assassinated by a mad Burgundian in 1584. (The cities of Holland have changed very little during the past few hundred years. If you study a reproduction of Vermeer's painting well and then go visit Delft, perhaps you will feel at home!) P. T. A. Swillens, an art historian, is convinced that Vermeer painted his view of the city directly from the rear upper window of his father's house. Rockwell Kent believed the same. This would have been an unusual practice in the 17th century. Most Dutch landscape painters took a walk and first made drawings and sketches of their scene, then did the actual painting in their studios.

A male figure in the far left foreground, critics note, has been painted out. Due to the absorption of the yellows, the trees have faded somewhat and turned decidedly bluish over the course of time: the yellow pigment Vermeer laid on top of blue to make green has oxidized. And due to the dirty yellow varnish the picture now appears considerably altered. The brushwork is comparatively broad and free. I have frankly never seen an accurate reproduction of the painting. Prints rendered it either gloomy and flat, washed of color, or overbright with resonations that are not there. There is an inexplicable forked, two-angled—digonous—quality to the work. All in all, it is an eerie, extremely mysterious painting.

The city, floating on water, almost like a still-life, is silhouetted against the great arc of the sky; the sun breaks through and illuminates the center and right side of the composition, while the left remains partly in shadow. The painting is bright with color. Blue, red and yellow in varying graduations harmonize with one another. The rendering of the brickwork alone I find densely beautiful. The red tile roofs glisten in the sunshine. It was perhaps this that made Proust liken it to "some specimen of Chinese art, of a beauty that was sufficient in itself." The light pours down out of the towering sky: real light, particularly Dutch in its liquid character. A fraction of a second later the clouds would have shifted; the central flood of light would be gone. Many artists have been drawn to light as the source of their vision, making light itself the subject of their paintings.

It is a strange coincidence that Vermeer and Claude Monet, Proust's favorites, are the two artists who have best realized in their paintings what Goethe called "the deeds and sufferings of light." And yet the painting also catches a mood more subdued, a muteness, a motionlessness that while creating a calm, devoted attitude before still, silent objects is not unrelated to brooding, an atmosphere that might be called pensive, but "too refined," as another writer says, "to be described as melancholy." It seems the very manifestation of immortality. Is it the world's greatest landscape painting?

The small grouping of ordinary people on both sides of the

canal induce so quiet a contemplation of beauty, of timeworn structures and vessels in diffused light and moisture-laden air, that it seems that all life itself is held for a moment in a sweet, gentle, almost elegiac clarity. The area Vermeer painted was usually a bustling harbor; this quiet moment thus has something of the sadness of memory. The stillness is wistful. (Many times watching this view, I have often strangely felt that I have actually been there—in person.) There is a darkness to the boats that evokes the shadowy water docks of Charles Dickens's *Our Mutual Friend*. We sense the tenuousness of human presence, feel an almost ominous slippage of the moment that holds it all in suspension. The view is only half-open to the viewer, visible and hidden all at once. The tonal values are exquisitely adjusted. Vermeer has not allowed any one point in the full scene to over-engage his—or our—interest; rather he has set it all down with a complete evenness of focus, a strategy that endows the work with an amazing and widely incorporating lift. The rendering of atmosphere reaches a point of perfection. We seem almost able to experience the warm red of the old bricks and tiles with our own eyes. Even the clouds in the vast rolling firmament above, dark and light, have a sultriness and weight that few of the professional landscapists of the 17th century could ever quite capture. The climax of the picture, it has often been said, is the sudden stab of light on the distant church spire.

There is everywhere a pattern of strangely reconcilable opposites in *View of Delft*. A series of tensions, subtly conveyed, are found in the resistance and penetration between things distant and near, horizontal and upright, open and closed, heavy and light, suspended and at rest. It is riveting in that, palpably there but equally impersonal and disembodied, it manages to connote stability and evanescence at the same time. No resolution of these contradictory impressions beyond the painting's mode of organizing them, in fact, seems possible. It is, as it were, all intimation. Vermeer seems instinctively to have avoided synthesis—that impression of closed completeness—in favor of a fleeting yet focused image.

It is, as Edgar Snow wrote, "the impression of a world delicately, breathlessly poised, held as if in the palm of a hand. Images of full presence double as evocations of absence and aloneness; openness upon the here and now yields to the impression of a remote, already encapsulated world of the perfect tense." Snow perhaps sees what may have been so compelling to Proust, as it remains for so many: "Completeness of being resonates with intimations of death and impending loss; an atmosphere of timelessness evokes thoughts of evanescence, of the momentary, of life passing, and passing by."

What was the precise nature of that compelling momentousness? What, apart from the realization of immortality, conditioned it? Proust surely found in this painting what was confirmed in the theory and study of his very own work: in those rare moments, those entirely fortuitous moments which the conscious will can do nothing to evoke, our being, momentarily released from the one-dimensional Time to which in actual life it is tied, becomes real without being actual, ideal without being abstract

Proust had experienced nothing less than a glimpse of himself in eternity. He had touched a point in the fifth dimension. He had re-lived an isolated moment in its crystal purity, free from the strain of anxiety and the blight of habit which in real life can so often sully experience and make it nebulously unreal. He had re-lived it, this time, with insouciance because he had recognized it as both real and ideal. Utterly real, with nothing in it to abstract from simultaneous realization, the moment also caught the ideal of contemplation. Man no longer stood in his own shadow. The duality had been bridged.

We imbibe these essences—states of being—as from vials filled with a special perfume, its own climate, suspended in the vortex of memory, there sheltered and withdrawn from Time, perpetuated in eternity. At a sound, a secret touch, we involuntarily tap these vials which release their fragrance to make us breathe a new air. The air of paradise it is, new only because we had already breathed it in years we have forgotten. Forgotten, eternity had preserved it for us in its pristine purity, no longer cloyed or distorted by our fears, habits, or intentions, in the full beauty of its infallible proportions of light and shade, which vouchsafe its authenticity. These involuntary bursts of memory that assail us, so seldom but so powerfully, are like sudden raids into the treasure house of the resurrected life. That is why, for Proust, art was vividly more urgent than life, since it not only amazingly revealed life to itself, but resurrected its very essence, translating intimations of immortality into the facts of the dynamic medium which for him was words, and for Vermeer, paint.

Vermeer is the great artist of silence. He settled on the pause, the close viewpoint, the moment of hanging fire—what Wallace Stevens meant by "the world as meditation." (All but three of Vermeer's paintings represent interiors). It is fascinating to realize in this regard that Proust himself, like Vermeer, also looked for the small detail—the transcendent moment—that like the "little patch of yellow wall"* so often becomes in his novel the quintessential fix

---

*George Painter, Proust's masterful biographer—*Marcel Proust* in two volumes (1959, 1965)—was the first to bring attention to the *"petit pan de mur jaune."* He believed that it was to be located at the extreme right of the painting, stating, "in reality, where the *'petit pan de mur jaune'* is found, or rather the pieces, because there were more than one, on the extreme right, one cannot see a roof but the upper part of a drawbridge with parts of parallel wooden beam."

and focus, through involuntary memory, informing whole characters and entire scenes. The uneven step in the baptistery, for instance. The shock of the madeleine. The belfries of Martinville. The tinkling of a spoon against a plate. The *"petite phrase"* of Vinteuil's Sonata is another good example, the first movement of the Sonata for Violin and Piano in D minor by Saint-Saëns, as Proust identified it for Reynaldo Hahn—his lover, and one of the very few friends he would allow to read the opening chapter of *Remembrance of Things Past* and whose favorable reaction encouraged the author to continue with it—along with the favorite song of Odette's, *"Pauvres Fous"* (in *Swann's Way*) and the guessing game, *La Furet du Bois*, played by Albertine and her friends (in *Within a Budding Grove).*

The *View of Delft* in many ways takes on the character of portraiture—or more precisely, still-life—rather than topography. It shapes the city into a mood, transmogrifies it into a specific temper, the very same way that Venice is brilliantly caught by Tintoretto. In his *Contre Saint-Beuve*, posthumously published in 1954—is this not a scandalous revelation of the dilatory aspect of Proust studies?—Proust compared the faces of famous people with historic buildings, only to conclude that in both "what we see . . . is less than what we imagined." Like Proust, Vermeer doesn't distort reality; instead, he transfigures it, in a sense transubstantiates it, and finds in it a patch of yellow wall, a tiled roof, a pearl, or a girl's yellow turban the means of expressing the highest poetry. Significantly, André Maurois wrote, "Vermeer's colors have the velvety softness of Proust's adjectives." Proust may have been attracted to Vermeer because of his affinity with the Impressionists, in fact.

As we have mentioned, Proust was very fond of the painter Claude Monet. With the generation of 1890 rediscovering the quattrocento, people began to seek in old masters sources for the most modern art, and it was with the ascendancy of the luminous vision of the Impressionists that Vermeer rose from oblivion to the glory we know him for today. Many critics choose to see in the "Sphinx of Delft" a luminous painter, a forerunner of Monet. It is fascinating to realize that a few centuries before Monet, Vermeer had specifically touched on the challenging artistic problem of light in the open air, departing from the 17th-century Dutch painters who had never quite dared to paint a landscape of light background without adding dark shadows in the foreground to balance it.

Proust, of course, well understood Vermeer's method, which renders things neither photographically nor too imaginatively—and, especially for that, he felt secret affinities to him, for Proust always extolled the art of hiding art. It was Proust, after all, who taught us that art by no means represents a copy of reality, rather that it creates a truer, a nobler, a more poetic reality. Vermeer and Proust shared this same vision. They were men determined to get the last ounce of what Ruskin called "fact" into their work, but who, to secure that end, had no fear of the transforming imagination.

The Calumny of Apelles

Apelles's works—his paintings—are all lost. We have nothing. There is not a single work preserved of this renowned painter of fourth century BC Greece, nor have we a copy of any known painting directly from his hand. All his efforts have completely disappeared and not a trace remains. A treatise that he wrote on the principles of art, reputedly a masterpiece on the subject, has utterly vanished, and its specific focus has never been identified. Nothing remains that can conclusively be said to reflect his work. His reputation rests solely on literary references. There is not a single card on him in any of the Yale University libraries. We are entirely dependent on verbal descriptions of everything. Was John Keats right when he wrote, "Heard melodies are sweet, those unheard are sweeter"?

Pliny the Elder, to whom much of our knowledge of this artist is owed (*Naturalis Historia*, book 35), rated him superior to all preceding and subsequent artists, an extravagant claim. According to scholar John Bostock, Pliny dated Apelles back to the 112th Olympiad (332–329 BC), on the evidence that he had produced a portrait of Alexander the Great.

His legendary fame, vouched for all through antiquity, continued throughout the Renaissance. The attributive phrase "After Apelles," indicating the enormous influence of the painter, describes several beautiful works of antiquity, among them the Zeus fresco in the House of the Vettii at Pompeii and the exquisite sculpture of Venus wringing her hair (ca. 350 BC), to be seen at the Penn Museum. He was to painting what Homer was to song. It would become a commonplace to compliment an artist by comparing him to Apelles, as an admiring Boccaccio said of Giotto, and Petrarch of Simone Martini.

We know something of the man. He was probably born at Colophon in Ionia about 370 BC, the son of Pytheas and brother of the painter Ktesiochos. He studied at nearby Ephesos, where he was given citizenship, and for this reason was sometimes called an Ephesian. He flourished between 332 and 329 B.C. He became court painter to Alexander the Great, whose portrait he alone was permitted to paint. A disciple of Pamphilius, he was doubtless from a distinguished family, as no student of mean birth was admitted into the school of that master. It was to a student of his, Perseus, to whom it's thought he dedicated that lost treatise on art. A much-traveled artist, he studied at Sikyon, painted at Kos, and visited Protogenes at Rhodes.

No painter ever applied to the study of his art with greater perseverance than Apelles. He never permitted a day to pass without practicing some branch of his art. It became his watchword, hence his legendary proverb, *"Nulle dies sine linea"* (Not a day without a line drawn), a statement Pliny attributed to Apelles, which of course refers to the painter's diligence at practicing his art every day:

Apelles tried new techniques. He proved to be daring. He not only excelled in composition, design, and coloring, but also possessed an amazing capacity for invention. Like his contemporaries, he used only the four traditional colors—white, black, yellow, red—all of which were already in use two centuries earlier on Attic black-figured vases. What Apelles so ingeniously managed to do that was so unique, however, was successfully to blend them. The curious boast that he made stating he was better than his great rival Protogenes (none of whose work survives, either)—he was known for the minute detail in his paintings—was based on the fact that he knew when to *cease* painting, a capacity to see when a painting is finished, lest further niggling detail destroy its grace. His works were executed on panels in the tempera technique. Plutarch says that Apelles did not paint the flesh of Alexander in its natural color, but rather darker and browner, which suggests he employed chiaroscuro much in the manner as Rembrandt would later. He was known for a dark transparent glaze he used on his paintings, something he also shared with Protogenes, a secret varnish called "elephantine," which he supposedly obtained from burnt ivory, which he diluted with a certain black and used to tone down the excessive brightness of his colors.

In their paintings, the ancient Greeks traditionally used only three colors—black, white, red—to which yellow was later added, according to Polygnotus, a fourth century BC Thracian famed, especially in Athens, for his monumental wall paintings— Aristotle praised his art, calling him a "fine portrayer of ethos" (the characteristic spirit of a culture)—but many other pigments and dyes were in fact available and used. (Aristotle, incidentally, believed that the rainbow had only three essential colors: red, green, and blue.) Painters at the time were not given to careful discrimination of color. They were far more concerned with saturation and brightness than with hue, and it is probable that fairly violent colors were used lavishly, and without much reference to naturalism, on most of the statuary. The Parthenon, Athens's 2,400-year-old temple, portrayed white on every postcard, was originally daubed with red, blue and green, as were many of its sculptures. Time, however, is inexorable. No original paintings of the great period (fifth and fourth centuries BC) have survived, and it was not until the Augustan period that variations and moderation in the use of colors was achieved.

Among the more legendary of Apelles's works, variously cited and described by classical writers such as Ovid, Strabo, Cicero, Lucian, and especially Pliny, were *Herakles*, which, although seen in back view, Pliny states, "seemed not only to suggest but actually to give the face"—Apelles was known for a distinct predilection for "unpaintable subjects," such as one of a powerful thunderstorm, showing *astrapé* (lightning), *bronté* (thunder), and *keraunobolia* (thunderbolts); personifications, many female, such as *Pankaspe*, concubine of Alexander, shown in the nude;* *Alexander in Triumph*, showing War personified sensationally bound in fetters behind his back; and another, *Alexander as Zeus*, depicting the king wielding a thunderbolt, which he painted on the walls of the Temple of Diana at Ephesus. It was so admirably executed that Plutarch reports that it used to be said at the time that there were two Alexanders, one the invincible, the son of Philip, and the other, inimitable, the work of Apelles.

According to lore, one of Apelles's most celebrated works was a rendering of Venus called *Venus Anadyomene* (Venus Rising from the Sea) which was painted for the temple of Asklepios at Kos

---

*In 1720, the Italian artist Francesco Trevisani (1656–1746) did a splendid multi-figured oil-on-canvas painting, *Apelles Painting Campaspe.*

and which Ovid has celebrated in his verses:

"Si Venerem Cois nunquam pinxisset Apelles
Mersa sub aequoreis illa lateret aquis."

Pliny, to whom, as has been pointed out, we owe more than anybody what little we know of Apelles, tells us that Alexander permitted his favorite mistress, the beautiful Campaspe, to sit for this Venus, adding that the painter became so enamored of his model that the conqueror resigned her to him. Some writers say the seductress Phryne served him as the model for Venus. Others say it was the beautiful Lais, who was nicknamed *ευκίνητη σαν χέλι*: "agile as an eel. In any case, most agree that it was living model who gave him inspiration. Although the purple waves and sea-foam from her dripping hair were highly commended, it was the flesh tones of the lovely nude and the beauty of the resplendent figure of Venus that received the highest accolades. According to Greek mythology, Venus Aphrodite was mythically born as an adult woman from the sea off coastal Paphos in southwest Cyprus, a birth which also perpetually renewed her virginity. A scallop shell, seen in it and other historical renderings of that painting, is a symbol of the female vulva.

This much-admired painting of Apelles, now lost, but described in Pliny's *Natural History*, was eventually brought by Augustus to Rome and placed in the Temple of the Divine Julius in the Roman Forum. Tradition has it that Apelles was in the process of making a second Aphrodite of Kos at the time of his death but that it was left unfinished because no artist could be found with the skill to complete it. A room-long mural later discovered in the ruins of Pompeii is believed to have been based on Apelles's *Venus*: in that Roman painting we see a seductive, dark-eyed recumbent nude on a half shell, hair perfectly coiffured, wearing only a bracelet, a neck-lace, and anklets, attended by two winged cherubs.

It is Apelles's birth of Venus that was the prototype of so many other births of Venus, most notably by Titian, the Spanish Romanticist Antonio María Esquivel, the Swiss symbolist Arnold Böcklin, the French Neoclassical Jean-Auguste-Dominique Ingres, and, of course, the inimitable one by Botticelli. The subject, revived greatly in the Italian Renaissance, never fully disappeared in West-ern art.

It was customary with Apelles to exhibit his pictures pub-licly, not so much to profit by the money as to benefit by the criti-cism. He usually concealed himself behind a panel so that the public might better be at liberty to express its views more freely, afraid that his presence would constrain the expression of their sentiments. On one such occasion, a cobbler found fault with with some incorrect-ness in the representation of a slipper, and Apelles, convinced of the judicious observation of the artisan, made the necessary change in the painting. The work being again offered to public view in its improved state, the cobbler, proud of the success of his first criticism, ventured to find fault with the leg. At this point, according to Pliny, Apelles, upset, dismissed him, making the dismissive remark that has since become proverbial: *Ne supra crepidam sutor* (Let the shoe-maker stick to his last).

The portraits of Apelles were ranked especially high among the ancients. We are told by Claudius Aelianus, commonly called Aelian (175–235 AD), the Roman author and teacher of rhetoric—his *On the Characteristics of Animals* is a collection of facts and beliefs drawn from Greek authors—that, after painting an equestrian por-trait of Alexander, which proved less than pleasing to the monarch, or so we are told, but whose horse (or so goes the whimsical account) found the charger in the picture so realistically rendered that he neighed at it, at which point the court artist—he had attained that position by his skill—turned to the great Macedonian conqueror with the haughty comment, "Sir, it is plain that your horse is a better judge of painting than your Majesty."

In another instance, one of the painter's disciples showed him a picture of Helen, which he had loaded with gold. "Young man," said the painter, "not being able to make Helen beautiful, you have resolved to make her rich." The ability to render the perfect resemblance of a person went a long way in proving Apelles's competency and in extricating him from a perilous dilemma into which he was thrown at the court of Ptolemy.

What happened was this. Antiphilus, a Greek painter of reputation and, although a rival, somewhat inferior to Apelles, and who painted both in the court of Philip of Macedon and Ptolemy I of Egypt, accused Apelles of joining in a plot against the Egyptian king, all of this according to Lucian (ca. 125–after 180 AD), a Hellenized Roman satirist, wit, and rhetorician. The accusation was totally groundless. Ptolemy, however, at the height of his resentment, without fully examining the affair, judged Apelles guilty and would have put him to death had not an accomplice of the conspirators declared him innocent, proving that the charges originated with his jealous rival, Antiphilus. Remorseful for having listened to the slander, Ptolemy restored Apelles to his favor, presented him with a hundred talents to compensate for the injury he had sustained, and condemned Antiphilus to become his slave. It perhaps should be noted that as a painter, for his lighting effects, an interest in genre painting, and for various new methods and illusionistic techniques, Antiphilus was brilliant in his own right and was recognized as such. Pliny tells us that he was especially commended for a painting of a boy blowing a fire and for the reflection cast by the fire on the room and on the boy's face.

On his return to Greece, Apelles wanted to avenge himself on his enemies. He decided to paint a picture as a memorial of the persecution he went through, and, exerting all of his inventive energies, he chose to create an allegory. It is for the work that he eventually produced, *Calumny*, perhaps the most famous painting in antiquity, that he is most well-known.

A brilliant *ekphrasis*, or verbal description, of that painting by this same poet Lucian in his very famous essay on calumny entitled "On Not Believing Rashly in Slander" (*για να μην πιστεύοντας απερίσκεπτα σε συκοφαντίες*)—there were as many as four translations of Lucian's Greek into Latin or Italian during the 15th century—goes as follows:

> "On the right sits a man with very large ears, almost like those of Midas, extending his hand to Slander while she is still at some distance from him. Near him, on one side, stand two women—Ignorance, I think, and Suspicion. On the other side, Slander is coming up, a woman beautiful beyond measure, but full of passion and excitement, evincing as she does fury and wrath by carrying in her left hand a blazing torch and with the other dragging by the hair a young man who stretches out his hand to heaven and calls the gods to witness his innocence. She is conducted by a pale ugly man who has a piercing eye and looks as if he had wasted away in long illness; he may be supposed to be Envy. Besides, there are two women in attendance on Slander, egging her on, tiring her, and tricking her out. According to the interpretation of them given me by the guide to the picture, one

was Treachery, the other Deceit. They were followed by a woman dressed in deep mourning, with black clothes all in tatters—Repentance, I think her name was. At all events, she was turning back with tears in her eyes and casting a stealthy glance, full of shame at Truth, who was approaching." (trans. A. M. Harmon)

Such was the ingenious fiction which composed the vengeance of Apelles, and which may be regarded as one of the most admirable examples of emblematical painting that the history of art affords. A good part of the reason for its success went beyond the fame of Apelles. Calumny was a topic of consuming interest in the Renaissance. It is a vice that is the result, specifically, of envy, and that demonic vice to Renaissance moralists was not only a serious sin, a mortal sin, but one of the very worst, *invidia*, one of the Seven Deadly Sins, coming from *invidere*, "to look against, to look in a hostile manner"—it involves the "evil eye"—and is even considered by some, such as the Venetian humanist Lauro Quirini, to be the source of *all* the ills that afflict Man.

If ignorance can be seen as a deficiency of intelligence, the vice of envy is a failure of humanity. It is an abuse of fellowship, or as Plutarch put it, a "theft" of friendship. It is not only an unfulfilling emotion—the feeling of envy gives no satisfaction whatsoever to the envious, which eats him up—but the only vice that attacks virtue alone. It is at once small, morally indefensible, cruel, and embarrassing, a self-inflicting hatred. No, Lucian on slander is one of literature's great polemics!

"Art as revenge" is a distinct genre. One might cite as examples the lampoons that Michelangelo Buonarroti made of his enemies, and those of so many other artists like Federico Zuccaro,

Diego Rivera, Henry Fuseli. In literature we have had outstanding examples: Alexander Pope's venomous attack on Lord Hervey, Robert Browning's furious attack on Edward Fitzgerald for the tasteless ridicule he heaped on his wife Elizabeth's poems after her death—in his furious indignation Fitzgerald writes that spitting on him is too good—and James Joyce's satirical portrait of Oliver St. Jean Gogarty, to name but a few.

It is not surprising, for any number of reasons, that Apelles's *Calumny* seized the imagination of many Renaissance painters. It was so universal a vice, so open-ended, left so much room for abstract possibility, narrative fascination. But the description that Lucian gave of the work intrigued them every bit as much as the work it declaimed did, for flaming rhetoric—especially, during the noble Renaissance, in Greek—was considered an art in and of itself. More than 20 paraphrases of Lucian's account have come down to us over the years, many notable ones, including those of Guglielmo Manzo, Hans Sachs, Philip Melanchthon, Christoph Wieland, Denis Diderot, and Jean-Baptiste Rousseau. In 1408, Guarino da Verona made a very popular translation of it. Leonbattista Alberti wrote an account of it. Bartolommeo della Fonte decorated a manuscript with an illustrated miniature of it.

Sandro Botticelli himself did a painting of the famous allegory, one full of rich detail. His *Calumny of Apelles*, which was done for a certain Antonio Segni, a friend of Leonardo's, is set in the great Basilica of Maxentius in the Roman Forum, the colonnade of which is covered with classical scenes, decorations, and reliefs. The figures are all there as described by Lucian—each painter delighted in adding his own variations and embellishments and themes to the basic *donneé* provided by Lucian (David, Judith, and several other Biblical figures are cleverly added to the cast)—the long-eared king;

the whispering women, Ignorance and Suspicion allegorized; Calumny in the form of a beautiful maiden, carrying her burning torch and dragging the young man. Behind her can be seen Artifice and Deceit, and Truth in the distance, pointing toward heaven, all three of whom, curiously, seem to resemble Botticelli's angelic model, the beautiful Simonetta Vespucci. Consider alone the motion in this painting—there is a full ballet of body positions, a whorl, a whirling, and look at the differently colored raiments on the many figures! *Is any color left out?*

Andrea Mantegna's version is a drawing of nine figures in three shades of brown ink, with white highlighting—it is one of several of his and, in fact, was once owned by none other than an admiring Rembrandt*—and the composition is arranged as though a running sculpture, a bas-relief, the figures all contained in a linear movement within a narrow box-set of a stage. (It is thought that, because of his specific arrangement, Mantegna had used not Alberti's description of Apelles's work.) His figures, identified by caption—each identified in Mantegna's handwriting, run right to left, not left to right, and whereas Lucian had made Envy a male, here she is a female, the traditional *Invidia*, holding a torch in one hand to symbolize her blazing fury, and with the other hand she drags the young person by his hair as he stretches out his hands to heaven begging the gods to witness his innocence. Renaissance artists admired antiquity, but the drama of sinners made exquisite subjects!

Envy, a thin, pale, cadaverous man, beckons bold Calumny forward, while two obsequious servants, Treachery and Deceit,

---

*Rembrandt made a copy of Mantegna's drawing when it may have been in his own collection, and his copy can now be found in The British Museum.

slavishly adjust her hair and dress. The last two figures in the procession are Repentance, a mourning woman who wrings her hands, and finally Truth, pointing to heaven and with tears in her eyes. The allegory was well known in the Renaissance to both artists and scholars scholars. There is sexual variation in Mantegna's drawing that can be seen in the sad little victim being dragged along as if she were a piece of baggage, for here, as pointed out the figure becomes a female and is called *Innocentia*. Two further changes can be noted. Ignorance, who stands by the king, is a fat, dopey looking—and blind—figure, notice, while Truth, originally naked, leaning forward, proving she cares, is not only clothed but wears laurel in her hair.

A tradition of taking up the subject of this painting, with thematic variations, was spearheaded in Italy—in Venice by Girolamo Mocetto; in Siena, by Luca Signorelli; in Pesaro, by the architect and sculptor Girolamo Genga; and in Rome by Raphael Sanzio, who lent it such credibility. Raphael's original is lost; only several reputable copies remain, the most celebrated of which is an unsigned drawing in the Louvre, a much simplified, less ambitious version of Botticelli's *Calumny* (which he very well may have seen as a young man in Florence). Calumny and Innocence here predominate. All the other figures, Envy, Ignorance, Fraud, and Suspicion, and Truth appears to be set off in a nimbus of light.

Mocetto's bold engraving, set in Venice—St. Mark's and Colleoni on horseback are visible—is a perfunctory rendering, fairly uninspired. Signorelli's and Genga's designs on the subject were part of a decorative scheme carried out in 1509 for eight wall and ceiling frescoes in the now despoiled Palazzo del Magnifico. This *Calumny*, cramped between painted pilasters, has the usual compliment of allegories but in this case, along with half-draped

Envy and youthful Innocence, an indescribably tubby variation—like Mantegna's—of blind baleful Ignorance, covering the king's eyes with a veil.

There are so many variations. A stately design by Baldassare Peruzzi. A fragmentary drawing by Perino del Vaga. Another group, influenced by Raphael, comes from France and includes the rather scrimp and tentative drawings by Nicolo dell' Abate, Francesco Primaticcio, and Antoine Caron, along with the magnificent richly-detailed engraving by Luca Penni of the *Calumny* showing Deceit with a net, a cadaverous Envy, Truth ascendant on a cloud, and a fey effeminate Midas-eared king. Almost all of these drawings, set in royal courts, reflect the moral confines and potential evils in which Apelles, a victim to calumny and no doubt petrified, first found himself in danger.

In the 1520s, Albrecht Dürer left on the walls of the main chamber of the Great Rathaus in Nuremberg—Germany's Athens, a town Martin Luther called "a kind of Paradise"—a set of classical designs (since destroyed), one of which was the *Calumny of Apelles,* establishing in the process a tradition for the subject in his homeland. Dürer's version, probably done by his associate Georg Pencz, stressing Justice, was a traditional rendering. His Envy is a woman, and Truth carries both a sword for protection, with the sun as an attribute. There are added symbolic figures: Punishment (*Poena*), Mistake (*Error*), and Haste (*Festinatio*), all crowd in with Envy. In front of the king reads Dürer's innovative inscription—found in Lucian's essay, by the way—*Nemo unquam sententiam ferat priusquam cuncta ad amussim perpenderit* (Let nobody come to a decision before considering both sides).

Peter Flötner (or Flatner), the 16th-century German designer, sculptor, and printmaker, then followed with a strange, wonderful woodcut. Ambrosius Holbein's small woodcut of 1523 is rather formal and static. Anton Wetz's engraving, which shows Truth with a halo, energetically introduces several new allegorical figures, Sadness, Adulation, Credulity, and Vindictiveness. Johann Wolf's is the usual tableau of figures, including himself drawing them. And Pieter Bruegel's drawing of 1565, indubitably his—Envy's face resembles that of *Dulle Griet*—was probably based on Philip Melanchthon's Lucian translation. The influence of Raphael's version is also strong. There are the usual familiar actors here in the small cabinet picture, with the curious detail of Truth being seated, and stark naked, the only example of such in the surviving work of Bruegel.

According to the contemporary account of his son Ottaviano, the brilliant but cantankerous artist Federico Zuccaro's vivid but bitter and apparently libelous version of the *Calumny of Apelles* was a response to what he saw as poor and unworthy treatment meted out to him by his patron, Cardinal Alessandro Farnese, for whom he worked at the villa of Caprarola. It was said to satirize various Bolognese artists, a debt paid for various attacks on him by the envious and ignorant. That was the thing about a Calumny painting or drawing—you could lampoon subjectively allegorize, and make any kind of savage sport with any hated subject you choose to, in a real sense, calumniate anybody!

Accusations were made against Zuccaro, a trial was held, and the painter was banished from Rome, although he was later pardoned. In the painting, the figure of Innocence is portrayed as an artist—he sports an ivy wreath—being protected by Mercury and Minerva against conspirators who seem even more threatening than usual: a bald ugly king, Calumny portrayed as a hideous scaly half-serpent, Violence clanking chains, a winged Gorgon, and all around the frame of the composition a tableau of classical allusions that provide comment on the meaning of the allegory.

Finally, the great Mantuan artist Lorenzo Leonbruno's masterful version (ca. 1525)—and my favorite—shows Envy as a vicious, accusatory old crone, a ferocious, cold-blooded, and ruthless Sycorax, whose horrid sagging breasts are barely indistinguishable from the pouches strung around her neck filled with demonic curses and filthy cash. A mad dog, in keeping with popular iconography, accompanies her, a procession of allegorical figures dragging maligned Innocence toward a doomed audience with a corrupt king. The painting with its balance and wit is a terrifying picture of human foibles, masks and madmen and merciless poltroons. It is a sort of goat dance of pointing fingers, blame-shifting, and angry accusation. Repentance is in leg irons, Dissimulation holds a mask, and, above them all, stands Fortune dispensing jewels scepters and crowns from a loggia filled with goats and masturbating satyrs.

No one who loses himself in the rich details of these paintings, drawings, and engravings can fail to see that the profound central idea was to the artists not a pale abstraction but a forceful reality. It is more than a painting. Apelles's work was a moral fable, offering meaning, charm, fancy, and a basic epistemology all at once.

As a subject, the calumny of Apelles is a meditation that seems never to end. Examples proliferate. There are versions done by Joachim von Sandrart, Pieter de Grebber, Gerard de Lairesse, and—a small powerful drawing—by Peter Paul Rubens himself. It is ironic that an artist whose works have completely disappeared would became virtually synonymous down through antiquity with excellence in art, although Charles Baudelaire, for one, thought the attitude a hollow convention and, as such, empty and valueless. It is an even greater irony, as well as proof positive, that the imagination is both timeless and enduring, that a painting which has never been seen, which in fact doesn't exist, would establish a tradition in art so strong that it would be followed for 2,000 years.

Paint It Black:
Artists Spelunking the Dark Experience

Looking into the color black is often to find what psychologist William James called, in another context, "unexplored experience." Everything in a sense that feeds into a full-blown portrait of the color black serves to remind us of its odd, anchored, immovable, unbudging unreality—of its all too often piteous antihuman glower—which lays bare, as no abstract analysis can, that one fat-black and unadorned chroma so reductively close to us that with its smoking underground terror and almost implacable despotism so often reaches into our hearts to sabotage the order of common understanding. As Marcel Duchamp told us, any work of art is an act of perception. It is the viewer who must bring the art to completion. We ponder. We concoct for our senses. Frappés could be frescoes. Did I not read once somewhere that Claes Oldenburg painted pictures he could eat?

There are many notable "black" painters, various artists whose use of the bold color is expressed in some of their best work, notably Rembrandt, Goya, Cranach, Manet, and Monet. We have the irrepressible Michelangelo Merisi's—Caravaggio was the name of his home town—shadowy canvases. It is said that the Dutch painter Franz Hals enjoyed using at least 27 different kinds of black. His *Laughing Cavalier* (1624) alone presents a fund of them to examine. We should not forget Joan Miró, Emil Schumacher, Mark Rothko, or Jackson Pollock. And what about Jean-Baptists Camille Corot's genius for the color in some of his black and white pencil portraits? Or Eugène Delacroix's charcoals and crayon studies? Van Gogh could never get a truly *black* black and experimented with soot and even goose grease. Carbon black is probably the most intense in color and tinctured power, and no paint is more elemental. It was manganese oxides, naturally occurring, that provided the black paint for our far-flung forbears—applied probably with horsehair, sticks, or moss, directly onto unprepared walls—for all those bulls, stags, horses, and bison at play in prehistoric cave paintings, like those found in Lascaux, Altamira, the Paleolithic cave near Avignon, and the Chauvet cave.

A contemporary, Pierre Soulages, the French painter, printmaker, and sculptor who died as recently as 2022, was widely known as "the painter of black," owing to his interest in the color that he enigmatically described as both a color and a non-color. "When light is reflected on black, it transforms and transmutes it," he declared. "It opens a mental field all its own." He saw brightness as a work material, with the striations of the black surface of his stark paintings enabling him, paradoxically, to reflect light, allowing the black to come out of darkness and into brightness, thus becoming a luminous color.

On his ship *Joshua*, the intrepid French sailor and ocean adventurer Bernard Moitessier, most notable for his participation in the 1968 *Sunday Times* Golden Globe Race, the first non-stop, singlehanded, round-the-world yacht race, and one of my true heroes in life, painted black all cleats, stanchions, handrails, mooring bits, and the inside of her bulwark. Also, he had black flags replace the usual telltales, or wind indicators. Why black? Because at sea at night, black is much easier to see than white. "Hard to believe," he wrote, "but true."

Since ancient times, black has been closely linked to melancholy, cynicism, and madness. While it carries mainly sad, dark, and funereal connotations in our culture, the history of this color in more nuanced ways has also shown it to embody style, elegance, sophistication, and grace. In the narratives of famous myths, after the experience of night comes the dazzling clarity of truth. Painters' fascination with black is a common theme throughout the history of art, and many artists have obsessed over it.

Black with its undeniable force is as much a property as it is a quality. As to density, it is a color heavier than any of the others, creating larger volume and holding itself in a more compressed field. A density adhibits to it, including bulk, weight, and compactness. In a real sense, it is comparable to forging color. Since black is the densest color material, it absorbs and dissipates light to a maximum and thereby changes the artificial as well as the natural light in a given room. A black shape can hold its space and place in relation to a larger volume and alter the mass of that volume readily.

It may be asked, does black on canvas, in a sense, put a stop to color, in the way the heavy black outlines did of the Fauves, Matisse, Derain, Vlaminck? It seemed so to me years ago when I was using my Crayolas. The first Crayola was black, by the way, developed from carbon black in the Binney & Smith factory, that is, before Alice Binney in 1903 decided to ask her husband Edwin to create them in colors. Their first boxes appeared in that year. Today, there are only eight Crayolas—blue, green, red, orange, yellow, purple, brown, and of course black—out of the hundreds that could be manufactured.

The black Crayola was my *main* crayon; no other one served me as well for foundational use! When I was a kid, I always thought of it as the king crayon, or the knight that did all the brave and elemental work. It was Alice Binney who came up with the name Crayola: "Cray" from Old French *craie*, meaning chalk, and "ola" for oleaginous, containing oil.

"Without doubt, colours exist in nature so as to be seen," observes critic John Berger. "But if you are a painter, colours as such are your enemy. Not because you choose to dominate them, but because you have to get away from them. When you arrange them along the edge of your palette, you take their measure and you keep your distance. Colours are superficial, artificial and lifeless. You can even begin to hate them for their hideous innocence. They look as fresh as new-bought shirts with cardboard yokes under their collars and their sleeves perfectly pinned and folded." It is an idea that replicates, to a degree, Sergei Eisenstein's argument in his work *The Film Sense*, where he convincingly argues that by avoiding the perhaps more seductive but superficial attractions of color, a director is able to attain a greater attention to form. Berger asserts, "As a painter your struggle is to make [colours] disappear, so bodies can take their place. By a body I mean here anything that has substance. When a colour gains substance and becomes a thing it ceases to be a colour. It loses its innocence and its easy describability and becomes heavy with inevitability . . . a colour which has been chosen becomes a fatality. A fatality there's no way round. . . . And there's the happiness."

What is perhaps noteworthy here is that unique concern among many modernists of avoiding easy describability. The black paintings of Robert Rauschenberg, with their craggy, rumpled lunar surfaces of crumpled newspaper slathered in workaday black house paint, work in which, as the painter himself once put it, "there was much to see but not much showing," were described by critic Calvin Tompkins as "remarkably uningratiating—darkly reticent." But that was the job. Reticence never *wants* to be inevitable.

"Color," said the passionate Paul Gauguin, "what a deep and mysterious language, the language of dreams." The Impressionist painters, however, theatrically banished pure white and black from their palettes, asserting, somewhat hyperbolically, that these extreme colors did not exist in nature (outdoors). "They replaced white with pale blue in the morning," said the insightful and very talented painter Françoise Gilot, best known for her relationship with Pablo Picasso, whom she met when she was only 21 and with whom she had two children, "and with mauve, salmon pink, or orange through the warm hours of the afternoon. Instead of black they used ultramarine or purple."

Camille Pissarro, for one, enthused about the "new" landscape painting in the early 1870s, for he himself felt and was never too bashful to declare that there were no boundary lines in nature— color simply merged into color—with no black shadows, either, shadow being but a pale reflection of the object that casts it.

In Pierre-Auguste Renoir's quirkily rigid *Les Parapluies*, the use of the color black can be seen as a definite rejection of Impressionism, but he himself preferred the word "sharp" (*aigu*) to describe it. He refused to resort to the black naphtha commonly defined as and by shadow. Any shadow cast on snow was, for him, a shadowy area colored as much by the atmosphere as by the object that barred the light. It was axiomatic for Renoir, as well, that objects or surroundings exposed to light influenced those parts of the objects or surroundings remaining in the shade. It was about contrast. Dissolving outlines—a constraint with him as much as a necessity that was beautifully effected by the use of thinly brushed color—can be seen both in his earlier and later work.

He once abruptly criticized a certain work submitted by a young artist, pointing to various penumbra with the complaint that its cliché shadows were much too dark. "That tree, for example," said Renoir, "has the *same* local color on the side where the sun shines as on the side where the shadow sits. But you paint it as if it were two different objects, one light and one dark. Yet the color of the object is the same, only with a veil thrown over it. Sometimes that veil is thin," he declared, "sometimes thick, but always it remains a veil. You should paint it that way. Paint the object and then throw a veil over it. Look at Titian, look at Rubens—see how thin their shadows are, so thin that you can look through them."

And then memorably came out with his singular if not immortal pronouncement, "Shadows are not black." It was an emphatic declaration. "No shadow is black. It always has a color. Nature knows only colors . . . white and black are not colors." It was only fully constrictive and occlusive black in rude painting that bothered him, as we shall see. He would later be able to say of Manet's picture of Maximilian's execution, "The beauty of the black tones in it makes up for the brutality of subject."

Black is *indeed* a color, at least for Henri Matisse, as it was especially for Joan Miró, Robert Motherwell, and others later. It is found in various guises throughout his work, even in the late cut-out gouaches, where it arguably reaches full expression in late compositions such as *La Tristesse du Roi* (1952). In fact, the title of his exhibition at the Galerie Maeght in December 1946 was "Black Is a Color," when he remarked, "Before, when I didn't know what color to put down, I put down black. Black is a force: I depend on black to simplify the construction." Was this unique? Not at all. Matisse generously denied that his use of the color black was innovative, pointing out that in Asia, notably with the Japanese in their prints, it was quite commonly used.

He went on rhetorically to ask, "Doesn't my painting of the Marocains"—the painting in question is *The Moroccans* (1915)—"use a grand black, which is as luminous as the other colors in the painting?" The powerful black background to be seen in this Cubist oil on canvas allows every object in it to shine forth. "Like all evolution, that of black in painting has been made in jumps. But since the Impressionists, it seems to have made continuous progress, taking a more and more important part in color orchestration." Consider the daring in the caricatural black outline Picasso employed for his *Portrait of Petrus Manach* (1901). There is bravery to that.

Françoise Gilot insists in her book *Matisse and Picasso* (1990) on the importance of black, where she eloquently sings its beauty almost by way of chant. "Black was a color," she declares, "it was the color, it was the pitch to which all else was tuned. Black was at the beginning; all else proceeded from it. After the night wore out, at daybreak, light invaded the immensity of the sky. Light was blue, and Matisse allowed that color to suffuse his universe." She proceeds to cite "the solid, ominous black areas, usually vertical" as examples of Matisse's chromatic daring with black in his paintings *The Dark Door* (1942) and *The Joy of Life* (1905). We may recall that abysmal darkness, a world of disarray and disorder, stirring chaotically in the universe, carried in it an instinctive urge for transmutation, yearning, as it were, for necessary vision. The book of Genesis recounts the spectral kinesis inexorably driving from dark to light. And was not lead or black earth in the alchemical process the elemental raw material invariably used to initiate the first phase of physical transformation? Evan S. Connell, in fact, reinforces this idea in *The Alchymist's Journal* (1991) when he writes, "And he that fails to read blackness at the beginning shall fail at his magistery."

According to Gilot, Picasso not only praised Manet for disengaging pure painting from subject matter but gave him great credit for seeing the importance of using black as a color, It became a color that the early Picasso seemed to find indispensable. I am thinking here of such pictures of his as *The Man in the Spanish Cloak* (1900), *Still Life* (1901), *Mother and Child* (1901), *The Glass of Beer (Portrait of the Poet Sabartés* (1901)—Jaume Sabartés was a close friend who later became his secretary/administrator—*La Celestina* (1904), half-blind in her cope and mantilla, and the magnificent *Self-Portrait* (1901), showing the mustachioed Picasso in his full black overcoat. His *Moulin de la Galette* (1900) is a pavanne of "lighted black." It seems that at the turn of the century, specifically then in his life, Picasso took a worshipful delight in employing black paint in his canvases!

Regarding Édouard Manet, Matisse particularly singled out the "blunt luminous black" of the velvet jacket in his *Portrait of Zacharie Astruc* (1866) as innovative. I love to think that the powerful *Portrait of Édouard Manet*, painted a year later by Henri Fantin-Latour with its stark background and its subject holding a cane in a Tophet-black top hat, black jacket, and black vest—and throw in the dark beard, if you will—is evocative in tribute to Manet's own paintings, as well as many photographic portraits of the time. Camille Pissarro, the pure Impressionist, has constantly confessed that Manet exceeded them all in strength and power, simply because he could so magically render light by way black. Is this perhaps an aesthetic variation of Leonardo's famous pronouncement, "A grey day provides the best light"?

Henri Matisse, the incontestable master of color, through

using black found a method of expression that was consistent with his constant search for simplicity and purity, so characteristic of his work. Black and its multiple nuances offered him the necessary range in order to depict a face, a nude, a tree, dead leaves. Famous for being a painter and a sculptor, this great master is lesser known as a draughtsman, even though he engraved nearly 900 prints and illustrated more than 90 books. The whole universe of Henri Matisse appears to us in black on white, white on black.

Throughout his life, Matisse loved to tell various friends and acquaintances of how, when he was a young man, he traveled to Les Collettes in the hills close to Cagnes in France to talk to and visit with Auguste Renoir. This was toward the end of the First World War. Renoir, who was then quite old, after showing some of his own paintings, had asked to see the young painter's work, and when Matisse showed him several of his canvases, the old man, after a somewhat perplexed silence, decided to come right to the point and say, "To tell you the truth, this is not at all up my alley. It goes against all my beliefs, all my achievements, even against my personal sensitivity. But I hold that you are a real painter, because you do something I could never do: use pure ivory black in large areas and make it stand on its plane as a given local tone. In your pictures, black is a color, black does not recede, it does not create a hole in the surface of the canvas, it is solid. I can't understand how you manage this effect, but I do understand that it implies real talent" (trans. Gilot).

As a matter of fact, though as he said failing with it, Renoir loved ivory black. It was his favorite color. He called it the "queen of colors." "The more I work, the more I love black," he once declared when speaking of Velázquez, whom he singled out for praise for his knowledge of that color. "You work yourself up in seeking, you put in a little point of ivory black. How beautiful that is." Renoir's well-known declaration "Nature abhors 'pure' colors" never stopped him from remarking how much black there was indeed to be found in nature. The mistake the academic painters made, he felt, however, was in seeing *only* the black and in its pure state. In *Renoir, My Father*, his son Jean writes,

> "While training horses at Bordeaux and Tarbes, my father had learned that in the eyes of true horsemen a horse is never black or white. It is only foot soldiers who use such expressions. Horses which look black are brown bays; and the white ones are light gray. The hair of their coats is mixed. It is the combination of tones, seen as a whole, that gives the impression of the horse's coat being all black. And among the countless hairs in it, even the black come in different pigments. 'We too should use black, but in a mixture as it is in nature.' Renoir was to use pure black later on, though sparingly, knowing pretty well what he was doing, 'because one learns every day.'" (trans. Randolph and Dorothy Weaver)

It is perhaps not surprising to learn that the rooms in Henri Matisse's home were generally kept quite dark, maybe for the very same reason that, for women, the black dress as the seminal or *ur*-accessory has remained so basic. Matisse, who in his late forties genuinely feared that he might go blind—he went so far as to take up the violin as a potentially alternative art—maintained that dimness of the rooms essentially to rest his eyes, and yet Gilot points out that, rather than fearing darkness, he used it, even embraced it, just as Picasso did—she affectionately called both painters "Black Belt Initiates," on account of their shared interest in Japanese art—as "the maternal and primordial source of all creation." She believed that Matisse, like Pierre Bonnard and the early Manet, creatively saw the color black as "a solid non-receding local tone," adding that "a local tone holds its plane in space," as an adjunct and accompaniment to blue, his favorite color. "Colors have a way of developing in the dark," she writes, "because all one's senses are attentive and focused, and objects begin to glow in chiaroscuro."

French painter Georges Rouault, for whom bold black lines, which created the forms in his paintings, were filled with the color, was all black fingers. For him black and white *were* colors. The eight oils and 32 watercolors and crude pastels which he had exhibited in the Salon d'Automne of 1904—bewildered clowns, nudes, mountebanks, bowl-headed rustics, pitchman, and scowling moose-sized prostitutes with piled-up hair, all naked but for their sleazy stockings—"had created," as James Thrall Soby points out, "an impressionistic stir among critics and gallery owners, chiefly because of their blackness of tone. One critic inquired whether his paintings of prostitutes were intended to represent *Negresses in a tunnel*" (my italics).

In *Miserere*, Rouault's profoundly Christian and compassionate cycle completed in 1948, black-and-white becomes color. It is impossible to do its justice to the power of this graphic inspiration in mere words. The series depicts the political turmoil, human devastation, spiritual desolation, and deep longing felt in the burnt ground of Europe during World War I and leading up to World War II. The title *Miserere* ("Have mercy" in Latin) refers to the opening of Psalm 51: "Have mercy on me, O God, according to thy lovingkindness . . ." while *guerre* of course means war. Rouault began the project in 1916, although it was not completed until 34 years later. The prints present an overwhelming and persistent concern for the poor and marginalized, searing criticism of the ruling class, and unapologetic religious devotion.

A deep and abiding Catholic faith informed his work in his search for inspiration and marked out Rouault as perhaps the most passionate Christian artist of the 20th century. Born in a basement, where his mother had sought refuge from shelling during the Franco-Prussian War, the artist remained forever haunted and influenced by his difficult childhood, one marked by poverty, deprivation, terror, suffering, and hardship. Suffering remained an integral part of his life. Much of his focus in painting centered on—took spiritual comfort in—the face of the tortured, tormented Jesus, and the cries of the women at the feet of the cross are symbols of the pain of the world, which for Rouault was relieved by belief in resurrection, "Painting is a way to forget life," Rouault once said, "a cry in the night." And in another context: "I believe in suffering. It is not feigned in me."

I mention photography in the context of black and white. Lest it be forgot, the photographic camera, with its perpetual carousel of lights and shades, allowed for a new way of seeing back in the mid to late 19th century and Delacroix, for one, enthusiastically espoused photography as a proper aid for painters. According to Émile Bernard, as quoted in Van Deren Coke's *The Painter and the Photographer*, Cezanne "did not object to a painter's use of photography," quickly adding, however, that "he must interpret this exact reproduction"—which is the only way that the Impressionists saw camera art—"as one interprets nature."

Gauguin painted a portrait of his mother from a photograph. James Ensor employed photographs for self-portraits. André Derain—we have actual photographs of him—and Edvard Munch used them for accuracy in painting nudes. I love the testy and unrelenting black power in Derain's canvases *Paysage à Cassis* (1907), *Le Samedi* (1913), and *Portrait of a Man with a Newspaper* (1914). Henri Rousseau, having also found inspiration in snapshots, quite freely borrowed a number of his composites or parts of them from photographs. So did James Tissot, Thomas Eakins, and Picasso, to name but three. And there can be seen in the Tate Gallery in London a portrait of the Austrian socialite Princesse Pauline de Metternich (ca. 1865) that was copied by Edgar Degas from a *carte de visite* photograph taken by Adolphe-Eugène Disdéri of this woman, a significant promoter of the work of the German composer Richard Wagner and Czech composer Bedřich Smetana. She was also instrumental to the creation of the *haute couture* industry.

"What I seek in effect is a motionless movement, something that would have been the equivalent of what is called the eloquence of silence, of what St. John of the Cross designated by the words 'silent music,'" Joan Miró said in the 1940s, having spoken a decade earlier of "assassinating" his own paintings. Angry and upset at the fussy preciosity and badly over-intellectualized trends in the very Surrealism he had helped to promote, he began to go into the dark, so to speak. "In several of the dark paintings of 1938," wrote Carolyn Lanchner, curator in the Department of Painting and Sculpture the Museum of Modern Art, "some of the old mastery reasserts itself but in others the blacks now go inert, even dead."

Miró was said to be missing his old French poet friends who had, in the final analysis, given him more than his painter companions, and his own titles become more self-consciously poetic and less telling. His highly mobile and indeed almost frantic painting *Dancer Listening to the Organ in a Gothic Cathedral* (1945) and *The Red Sun Gnaws at the Spider* (1948) are poor substitutes for *Photo: Ceci est la couleur de mes rêves*, or *Étoiles en des sexes d'escargots* (both of 1925).

The latter, known as *peinture-poésie* (painting-poetry), combine text with enigmatic symbols and reflect Miró's interest in dreams and the subconscious. (Only three elements float on the empty, spare white canvas: the word "Photo," the patch of blue, and the phrase *"ceci est la couleur de mes rêves"* (this is the color of my dreams), while the black letters sit on barely visible pencil lines that serve as guides for their size, as in a child's writing primer. British artist John Golding describes them as "cries of protest, angry, ugly threats in the face of death." The last painting in the exhibition, untitled, a vast black canvas begun around 1970 and finished in 1980, is another masterpiece. It is also the most tragic and violent picture Miró ever produced. He had become intransigent in the Thirties, choosing to short-circuit himself with various self-assaults. At the very end, it was something else that informed those inert, dead masterpieces. "I am working very hard trying to make things worse and worse and create difficulties for myself and flee from good taste."

The great underground cartoonist R. Crumb, who in the Terry Zwigoff film *Crumb* (1996) approvingly told his teenage son Jesse, apropos his illustrations, "You're learning to use black," once confided to me, "I've always been attracted to art that has what I call 'black holes' in it. . . Deep, dark places . . . Depth. . . . The mysterious depth of dark places, places hidden in dark shadows." Crumb offered as a classic example of a drawing that featured what he considered "black holes" Bruegel the Elder's *Der Alchemist* (ca. 1560), mentioning how much he particularly liked it. "It pulls me in," he said. "I try to put it [the use of black] in my own work." Crumb's brilliant sketchbook drawings, and his artwork in general, are of course filled with apposite examples of the use of creative black.

Black can be as boxy or sexy as a Versace skirt. More than anything, it is an entity which is unavoidable and must be acknowledged. "Black, in large areas, tends to read as a flat area, more so than other colors," writes Lawrence Alloway, the English art critic and curator, "and it has, when used in linear forms, an ineradicable connection with message-making, either writing or drawing." It is also an elemental truth that, while bold, even obvious, it can also be as deeply subtle as Renoir's legitimate pedantries. Because of its inscrutability, its cold reticence, it is a color that must be faced. And why'? To forfend falseness. To prevent illusion. To engage physical reality in the waking world more palpable than it is on a canvas. Even to welcome what in its relentless presence is unalterably *there*.

Black is inevitable. The imagination is always distorted and warped when it divorces itself from "seeing" what actually exists. Wallace Stevens in his poem, "Thirteen Ways of Looking at a Blackbird," significantly asks

> "O thin men of Haddam,
> Why do you imagine golden birds?
> Do you not see how the blackbird
> Walks around the feet
> Of the women about you?"

Stevens's blackbird, like its color, is a crucial and insistent part of the world. In the reality both inhabit, involving polarities as well as death, is what the poet calls a "fluent mundo," in which we are implicated, whether we like it or not, and without which nothing can be frankly encountered with validity. ("The blackbird is involved / In what I know.") Just as the poet reminds us that the "ultimate value is reality," the blackbird embodies that demanding, cawing reality of whatever that intransigent value is: "The blackbird sat / in the cedar limbs."

"Black mortality," as poetry critic Ed Kessler points out, "is inextricably a part of life's evergreens; it sits 'in' not 'on' them." Black is the essential shadow, the prime, the elemental response to life by both poet and painter. It is by way of this explanation that one may say black dominates, what Gilot means when she refers to it as "the pitch to which all else is tuned," for while black is the ultimate negation toward which all colors deepen, we must also understand that it is from that solid depth that color takes its cue, the darkness, as Kessler puts it, "which must be acknowledged before earth's colors can be appreciated and affirmed. Like 'nothingness' it exists to be opposed, and like death it is the 'mother of beauty.'" Artists may conventionally aspire to the paradigm of white but should be mindful that in the last analysis white is a fiction that the fact of black mortality contradicts. The realization of black is the actualization of fact. The fact of black is never the *tact* of black.

The Spanish romantic painter Goya—Francisco José de Goya y Lucientes—a perfect example, is master of the black canvas. His legendary so-called "black paintings," now housed in the Prado Museum, are nothing less than astonishing paradigms of the focus, most of them grim fantasies done in the 1820s after his terrible illness. Very few paintings can match the pounding irrational brilliant force of these works.

Goya never flinches, and if any painter can be said to be unsparing it is him. In his *Pilgrimage to San Isidro*, painted between 1819 and 1823, a choir of pilgrims singing with twisted faces are all wearing black cloaks and hats. I can say without hesitation that my favorite by far is the uncanny *Burial of the Sardine*, an oil-on-panel painting dating from the 1810s. It portrays a wild and frantic Dionysian whirling parade of mad mummers in masks, gamboling under a devil-black carnival banner depicting a large, smiling, pumpkin-headed goblin. *The Bewitched Man*, also called *The Devil's Lamp* (1798) shows a cleric all in black and covering his mouth, as if to regurgitate, with three elevated donkeys in the background, communing with Satan. And the *Procession of Flagellants* (between 1812 and 1819), its groups of horn-blowing *penitentes* and flagellants and weepers in conical hats wearing black-and-white masks in front of a futuroidally weird black church surrealistically taking up half the picture, reveals an atmosphere of true nightmare. It is as if all these paintings were part of one vast hellish black panorama.

There are also his bravura portraits of stately, elegant, almost preening *Dona Isabel de Parcel* (1805); the vivdly black *Duchess of Alba* (1797)—a woman with whom, it is said, that Goya was intimate—and of course the exquisitely beautiful *Antonia Zarate* (1805), surely his portrait masterpiece, each wearing the black costume of a *maja*, elegant lines matching the lace mantilla, which adorned fashionable Spaniards in the early 19th century. Black predominates in virtually all of Goya's portraits. "Black might be called the third Spanish national color" wrote the artist and writer Wyndham Lewis in *The World of Goya*. "What Velazquez, to whom Goya obviously owed something, could express with it all the world knows. The favour still accorded it by the Spanish of both sexes derives undoubtedly from the High Renaissance, Spanish and Italian, at which period [Baldassare] Castiglione in his classic manual of manners [*Il Cortegiano*, or Book of the Courtier, 1528] at the court of Urbino observes, like Prince Hamlet, 'methinks a black colour hath a better grace in garments than any other.'" Incidentally, one of the world's greatest art treasures is Raphael's brilliant portrait painting *Baldassare Castiglione* (1514), the diplomat, humanist, and the painter's close friend, the quintessential example of the High Renaissance gentleman, a masterpiece in black.

There are some wonderful examples of, or highlighted moments in, what may generally be referred to as "black" paintings. Some of my favorites are Juan Gris's splendid *Self-Portrait* (1912) and Picasso's gouache and India ink *Minotaur Carrying a Dying Horse* (1936). In Henri Toulouse-Lautrec's lithograph *Yvette Guilbert* (1894), Yvette's jet-black funereal gloves match, in a sense, the telling black of the black stockings of the woman in his famous painting *Seated Clown* (1896); two plain subjects are given a distinguished air by the striving boldness of black. I find compelling René Magritte's eerily surrealistic and highly mysterious *Le Drapeau noir* (1937)— five mysterious flying objects—and have always been transfixed by the dark dells and sleepy hollows and shadowy glens in Giorgione's pictures—his *Mose alla prova del fuoco* (1502) in the Uffizi, for example—and to a degree can sympathize with Jan Morris who, in perhaps a slightly hysterical moment suggesting she had a possible bout of the "Stendhal Syndrome," remarked in *Pleasures of a Tangled Life* (1989), "Through Giorgione I am in touch with God."

I also find much to admire in the black velvet dress and hair and eyes of George Sand in Auguste Charpentier's portrait of her (1837–39); the popular French novelist—born Amantine Lucile Aurore Dupin de Francueil—never looked more darkly beautiful, and I always felt greatly moved by the slashing black outlines in Max Beckmann's paintings, particularly the web work of heavy, dominant lines showing the solidity of the struts or mullions of medieval stained glass in his violent triptychs *Departure* (1932–33) and *Beginning* (1946–49). The almost impossibly dark ink-black hair of the Alexandrian prostitute Mary in Emil Nolde's triptych *Mary in Egypt* (1912)—people, confusing Marys, mistakenly believe that she is the Blessed Virgin—is a black cascade, as is Christ's in Nolde's *Entombment* (1915). Nolde had no qualms about the use of drilling black paint. Look at that low-lying black cloud in *Sultry Evening* (1930), which shrouds the farmhouse like a cosmic nightmare.

What about Franz Kline's angular black swipes, especially in *Monitor*? Willem de Kooning's early black and white paintings, like the slightly dyspeptic *Excavation* (1950)? (Upon being asked why he painted in black and white during that period, he replied that those colors were the cheapest house paints!) What about Jackson Pollock's black "drip" paintings—created on raw canvas—especially the black, which predominates in *Autumn Rhythm (Number 30)*? Or Pollock's "poured" painting *Lucifer* (1947), which, with its web of nervous rhythms, is essentially a black and white picture? Or the last black paintings by Mark Rothko for Houston's Chapel of Death? "Black runs like a leitmotif through much abstract expressionist painting," writes William Fleming in *Arts and Ideas*. "Scientifically, black is the total absorption of light, which is the medium of color. Thus, by reducing pigmentation to basic simplicity, black could be seen as a contribution to the quality of abstraction and as a speeding up of the painting process."

Catalan painter Antoni Tapies's *Black with Two Lozenges* (1963) is skull-basic, while Jack Youngman's *Totem Black* (1967), a flat field showing a totemistic cutout becomes almost a phantom head. Then there is the matt black of Robert Motherwell's *Elegy to the Spanish Republic No. 126* (1965). He divined in the color black much that Rouault did and conceived all of his *Elegies to the Spanish Republic* as majestic commemorations of human suffering and as abstract, poetic symbols for the inexorable cycle of life and death. What of Clyfford Still's lightning-bolts of black? That man knew how to apply black, and I like to think that I am a connoisseur of black paint. Picasso's *Guernica* (1937), humans turned by sorrow and horror into gargoyles, is painted entirely in grey, black, and white.

I love Braque's *Black and White Bird* (1960), as well as the tiny black native, undetailed, a faceless doll almost as if stamped from an ink-pad, being mauled in the maw of that lush jungle declivity in Henri Rousseau's brilliant *Negro Attacked by a Jaguar* (1907).

Look at the harrowing beauty—the casualness in the horror is disarming—of the black tones in Édouard Monet's great picture of the execution of Maximilian. He created the series of paintings between 1867 and 1869, depicting the dramatic shooting by firing squad of Emperor Maximilian I, he of the short-lived Second Mexican Empire. Monet produced three large oil paintings, a smaller oil sketch, and a lithograph of the same subject. All five works were brought together for an exhibition in London and Mannheim in 1992–1993 and at the Museum of Modern Art in New York in 2006.

James McNeill Whistler's *Nocturne in Black and Gold: Rag Shop, Chelsea* (1878) is almost completely black, except for the faint-est image in the center of a small girl seen through a lighted doorway and several people seen through a many-paned window. Whistler was deeply fascinated with mists, fog, the odd and challenging effects of light and atmosphere and how these tend to shroud, mystify, alter and transform what is seen. He once remarked, "As the light fades and the shadows deepen, all the petty and exacting details vanish, everything trivial disappears, and I see things as they are, in great strong masses."

This brings us back again to the Frenchman Pierre Soulages, who in stating, "My instrument is not black but the light reflected from the black," describes his paradoxical passion of playing with light in an ironic way. He produced 104 stained-glass windows for the Abbey of Sainte-Foy in Conques in southern France from 1987 to 1994, studying the way that light would not pass through the stained glass, but would be fractionally fragmented, exploding as it were through the stained panes. He invented his own word "*outre-noir*" (beyond black) to define—and explain—the canvases he produced that are known for their endless black depth, always by way of playing with the light reflected off the texture of the paint. In a 2014 interview, he explained the definition of the term, pointing out that the word "outrenoir does not exist in English; the closest is 'beyond black.' In French, you say *'outre-Manche,'* "beyond the Channel," to mean England or *'outre-Rhin,'* 'beyond the Rhine,' to mean Germany. In other words, 'beyond black' is a different country from black."

The fascination—or "infatuation" as Ben Davis in his *Pierre Soulages: Happy to Stay in the Dark* calls it—Soulages had with black began long before his investigations with *outrenoir* at the age of 60. Much of his inspiration came from an early interest in the ancient, antediluvian world and the prehistoric, growing out of which was an elemental desire in him to find something pure and primal, an art profound and almost allegorically dark and deliberately stripped of any other connotations. Soulages declared of his fascination with the color, "during thousands of years, men went underground, in the absolute black of grottoes, to paint with black," as Davis notes. "I made these because I found that the light reflected by the black surface elicits certain emotions in me. These aren't monochromes. The fact that light can come from the colour which is supposedly the absence of light is already quite moving, and it is interesting to see how this happens."

Applying his paint in thick, stocky, and profuse layers, Soulages employed all sorts of objects such as knives, spoons, and rakes to scratch away at the painting, often making scraping, digging, or etching marks in them, depending on whether he wanted to create a smooth or a rough surface, according to Claire Rosemberg in her

"Black Is the New Black for Pierre Soulages, France's Best Known Living Artist." She explains how his textures then either absorbed or rejected light, as he broke up the surface of the painting by disrupting the uniformity of the colors there. Jean-Max Albert, in his *Pierre Soulages, Mouvement sans emplacement* (1975), explains how striational cuts along vertical and horizontal lines, making crevasses and forms, created geometrical angles and contours that were amazingly and darkly bold, all scored like scrapes, scuffs, and sweeps, harrow-like, artistic lacerations in their grazes and abrasions, many almost unsettling excoriations, some like neatly ploughed fields, and others like rudely combed, even brutal roughened chafes and rasping.

In the work that he did from 2013 to 2014, Soulages began explicitly to vary the pigment used in the paint, creatively mixing both matte and glossy types of black, as well as hardened densities of black pigment, according to Robert C. Morgan in his *Pierre Soulages: Painter of Black and Light*. The painter, eccentric to a degree, devised quirky if compulsive exhibiting techniques, preferring to suspend his paintings by wires, to be hung in the middle of a rooms. "I always liked paintings to be walls rather than windows," Soulages has gone on record as saying. "When we see a painting on a wall, it's a window, so I often put my paintings in the middle of the space to make a wall. A window looks outside, but a painting should do the opposite—it should look inside of us."

I have always thought of the moody and often allegorical American Albert Pinkham Ryder as a "black" painter. As a true matter of fact, there is actually not much black in his general work, and yet so many of his paintings seem to look black, or dark—he once said, "Most color is too clean"—like his eerie *Macbeth and the Witches* (mid-1890s); *The Lorelei* (ca.1896–1917), linking love and death, with its haunting bluish black valley and full moon—it seems to evoke everybody's elemental dream, excerpted right out of the universal collective unconscious; his *Siegfried and the Rhine Maidens*, women figures under a massive gnarled oak; and, among others, *The Toilers of the Sea*, a small lone sailboat with two huddled sailors in a wide empty sea silhouetted under a full moon. There is dark genius here.

Then there is Ryder's *The Tempest*, in which we see Prospero and his beautiful daughter Miranda—Caliban, creepily pale, looks on—in a dark scene of exile. This painting combines two of his favorite themes: his love for the sea and his fascination with Shakespeare. According to legend, the eccentric recluse from New Bedford, Massachusetts, who rarely signed and never dated his paintings, reworked this strange painting for more than 20 long years and at one point—out of anger? inspiration?—took a blazing hot poker to the almost eye-killing canvas and dragged it through the thickest part of the sky. The painting remained in the artist's possession until his death.

"Now my experience is that even more rare among painters than a sense of color as hue is a sense of black as hue," declared Robert Motherwell, in many of whose paintings, prints, and collages such as *The Black Sun* (1959), *Iberia No. 2* (1958), *Bull No. 4* (1958), *The Endless Instant* (1959), and the *Soot-Black Stone* series (1973), for example, his black colors glisten, sing, and glow, to a degree scold, and arrest us in their vehemence and challenging, almost spiritual force. Stephanie Terenzio in her *Robert Motherwell & Black* (1992) observed, "Black defines Motherwell's uniqueness . . . the color is his touchstone, the point to which everything he makes has reference. Motherwell's relationship to black engages his art in all media, from the epic forms in his best-known 'Elegies,' through the torn edges of his collages, to the immediacy of his gestures and the black bite of his etchings." She concludes, "Black is Motherwell's gesture, his autograph, his monumental drawing, his protagonist—his consciousness."

Ad Reinhardt, a New York painter, once commented with considered polemical seriousness that he yearned to produce a painting that is "simply a black painting and nothing more." He began almost as if lampooning our sobriety with *Ultimate Black Paintings* (1960), a series of pictures each with a life of its own, independent of the artist, subject matter, color, even shape and form. It may be said that he virtually *defined* the essential black painting when he wrote, "The one object of fifty years of abstract art is to present art-as-art and as nothing else, to make it into the one thing it is only, separating and defining it more and more, making it purer and emptier, more absolute and more exclusive, non-objective, non-representational, non-figurative, non-imagist, non-expressionist, non-subjective." What could possibly be added that is a more primary, fundamental, radical—even more primitive—statement than this of *anything*?

"Mapping the furthest point from reality that art could reach," James Park perspicaciously noted in his *Cultural Icons*, "Reinhardt presented the viewer with square canvases formally divided into nine smaller squares of black, so subtly distinguished as to appear imperceptible. Taking his cue from oriental art and Western minimalism, these works were devoid of any meaning other than that suggested by their presence."

In Reinhardt's last extreme phase, colors have become so dark and so close in value to one another that it seems as if the door has fully slammed. A black square is a black square is a black square: there is a strange hypnotic game of geometry and blackness employed by Reinhardt here. Stand back from one of his canvases and start walking towards it—you will notice a sort of vertigo takes over. You actually begin to feel as if you are going to fall in. Kay Larson, nevertheless, insightfully wrote, "The nature of the Reinhardt experience goes beyond color—it's an immersion in luminosity. Even the dark paintings, the very blackest ones, are about luminosity—but in its last ghostly absence, the way deepest night is still faintly defined by what you see out of the corners of your eyes."

"I once organized a talk on black," Reinhardt wrote in *Artscanada* in 1967, making some elemental distinctions about the color, "and I started with black as a symbol, black as a colour, and the connotations of black in our culture, where our whole system is imposed on us in terms of darkness, lightness, blackness, whiteness. Goodness and badness are associated with black. As an artist and painter I would eliminate the symbolic pretty much, for black is interesting not as a colour but as a non-colour and as the absence of colour. I'd like them to talk about black in art—monochrome, monotone, and the art of painting versus the art of colour." A color. A non-color. Box it about. You judge.

Reinhardt's dream was to make art about nothing but art, uncompromisingly, reducing everything to essentials, creating virtually renunciation itself, which is as dark a paradox as his own non-rational shades of black. Most famous for his "black" or "ultimate" paintings, he claimed to be painting the "last paintings" that anyone can paint. I have to say that I have always found something madly Ahabian about that, a terrifying absolute that brought him in his quest ultimately to an irretrievable dead end.

Novelist Ronald Firbank with his comic, subversive decadence would however have loved those Reinhardts, if only for their utilitarian value. "The habit of putting glass over an oil painting always makes such a good reflection, particularly when the picture's *dark,*" he wrote. "Many is the time I've run into the National Gallery on my way to the Savoy and tidied myself before *The Virgin of the Rocks.*'"

Francis Bacon loved solid black backgrounds. Wyndham Lewis, who saw the 1949 exhibition of the Irish-born British figurative painter at the Hanover Gallery in London, wrote favorably in his regular column in *The Listener* that he was reminded of Velázquez, adding, "and like that master he is fond of blacks. Liquid whitish accents are delicately dropped on sable ground, like blobs of mucus—or else there is the cold white glitter of an eyeball, or of an eye distended with despairing insult behind a shouting moth, distended also to hurl insults. . . . But black is his pictorial element. These faces come out of the blackness to glare or shout."

At the end of his life, Rothko's painting took on an almost self-immolating pathos. Color utterly evaporated from his work. Grey, then black rectangles, appearing, began reaching like a spreading plague or famine to the edges of his paintings. His work became all mask. At 66, alone in his studio, in the midst of unrelenting despair, he slashed his arms and bled to death.

Louise Nevelson, scavenger artist, painted found objects—furniture parts, spindles, barrel tops, etc.—always one color each, black or white or gold. She once referred to this—inexplicably—as "total totality." "When I fell in love with black, it contained all color," said Nevelson. "It wasn't a negation of color. It was an acceptance. Because black encompasses all colors. Black is the most aristocratic color of all. . . .You can be quiet, and it contains the whole thing." She painted wooden objects black (or white) in order to remove, as I believe she wanted to do, all connotations of their former use. Indeed, her large-scale sculptures were meant, or so she intended, to create an aesthetic environment of their own, although I happen to find them as dull as a Formalist's monologue, always monomaniacally confined solely to color and line. She negated things she wanted to assert. ("I'm really always teased and intrigued by the sense that it doesn't matter what poems say," poet Robert Creeley once preposterously declared, presumably believing that what he was saying didn't matter.)

According to site-specific sculptor Richard Serra, who said that he felt the idea of the infinite was implied in Brancusi's module extension—see Serra's large black drawing *Abstract Slavery* (1974)—the black pictures of Frank Stella are indebted to Brancusi's *The Endless Column*. Serra did a lot of black drawings in the early Seventies. "To use black is the clearest way of marking against a white field," he observed, "no matter whether you use lead or charcoal or paint stick." He then goes on unequivocally to state what seems to be the central comment of painters—of thinkers, in general—on black. "It is also the clearest way of marking without creating associative meanings," he said. "You can cover a surface with black without risking metaphorical and other mis-readings. A canvas covered with black remains an extension of drawing in that it is an extension of marking. The use of any other color would be the extension of coloration, with its unavoidable allusions to nature. From Gutenberg on, black has been synonymous with a graphic or print procedure. I am interested in the mechanization of the graphic procedure. I am not interested in the paint-illusion gesture."

Although Picasso introduced color into modern sculpture, Serra does not like it and did not agree with it. The San Francisco-born sculptor of large-scale sculptures declared, "The color of the material is the color of my work. I am not interested in embellishing surfaces by polishing or painting them. If you paint a material, you deny the intrinsic quality of the material. It you paint steel, you prevent the oxidation, which is an inherent property of steel. Applying paint to sculpture is suspect to me."

"Why is the trapezoid black?" asked American filmmaker Lizzie Borden of Serra during a conversation with him in the Stedelijk Museum catalogue in 1977. Black here seems to have deep ontological implications!

Serra: "I don't know if I made it black to make it trapezoidal. I think blackness is a property, not a quality. I made it black to divorce it from being a quality."

Borden: "In other words, the black is not on the drawing, it is in the drawing?"

Serra: "That seems to be correct."

There is no doubt that thee color black appears virtually everywhere: in the paintings of Hieronymus Bosch and Egon Schiele, in photos by the German surrealist Hans Belimer with his totally unnerving images of dismembered dolls and in R. Crumb's wild drawings of vulture demonesses. Robert Rauschenberg did a series of all-black paintings, which became a source of inspiration for John Cage. There are the black-and-white chicken scratches of Franz Klein. Maxine Hong Kingston in *The Woman Warrior*, constituting memoirs of her girlhood, recounts how in first grade, greatly alarming her teachers who found it neurasthenic and saved them to show her parents, her first drawings were all done scarily in black. ("So black and full of possibilities," she said.) She goes on to say, "My silence was thickest—total—during the three years that I covered my school paintings with black paint. I painted layers of black over houses and flowers and suns." She explains it was done for a stage curtain, masking the infinite possibilities of drama, any drama, to begin.

I wonder in my amateur way if Kingston's drawings were

not somehow darkly and disconsolately aligned to the fact that when she was a baby her deranged mother, so that her little daughter, as she later explained to her, would not be tongue-tied—this actually happened—quite insanely sliced the frenum of her tongue. In her early years at school, perhaps predictably, the nervous, self-conscious, little girl who in physiological terms was actually able to talk, nevertheless kept entirely mute, silent in class and silent in the playground and silent at lunch, communicating only by motions.

Should we not perhaps here acknowledge the "black" brush of Lydia Popova, the greatest woman painter? Or would you place that laurel on the head of Natalia Goncharova, both of the post-revolutionary Russian avant-garde?

A contemporary young Spanish artist, Marina Níñez, uses backdrops of solid black on linen which recapitulate the drama of a theatrical stage. The engulfing black expanses with figures, which reveal an absent presence, seem expressly to recall Paul Klee's *Painting on Black Background* (1940), an abstract still-life in which there is no lighted or darkened side on any of the presented shapes, which cast no shadow. And German artist Katharina Fritsch makes sculptures of huge black knots, giant black rats, and demonic black dogs—*Baby with Poodles* (1996) is a circle of 139 solid black life-size polyester poodles threatening a (white) baby in the center, and *The Rat King* (1993) is a sculpture of 16 enormous polyester-resin black rats, each one 10 inches tall and 5 feet wide, all holding each others' tails. Several have drawn conclusions about this Düsseldorfer making comments on the reechiness of the Nazis. Fritsch, however, will have none of it. "I'm not really somebody who's working about political things," she responded. "I really don't belong to these people who are politically correct. I think that is totalitarian now."

I daresay that no real discussion of art and the color black would be complete without mention of the American painter Edward Leeteg, the first modern artist to master the technical problems of oil painting on velvet. (For all of the tackiness now associated with such a thing, it is actually an art centuries old.) Leeteg lived with his mother at the Villa Velour, his private village on Moorea in Tahiti in French Oceania, and painted naked women in sarongs, flowers, leis, etc., all in all an estimated 1,694 paintings over the course of 15 years, mostly in the early 1950s, many of them selling from $7000 to $10,000. At the height of his career, according to Charles Krafft in his article "Leeteg of Tahiti" in *Cad: A Handbook for Heels*, Leeteg managed to produce a painting every four days. Mainly it took him up to three weeks to finish each velvet, carrying forward as many as a half dozen at once to keep up with the demand. The pioneering technique that launched an army of imitators was no fluke. (He once said his idols were Rolfe Armstrong and Norman Rockwell.) After seeing some badly faded and cracked samples of Renaissance and Victorian velvet painting in a St. Louis museum, according to Krafft he set about to learn how to heighten the illusion of light and dimensionality by keeping each thin strand of the pile from caking to its neighbor. Using a limited palette of white and seven colors, which he mixed directly onto the velvet in layers meticulously built up over a period of days, he began to achieve his chosen effects. The luminosity of his style, notes Krafft, has been attributed to Stoffine Wood, an additive patented in France.

And should we not mention as a type of artist the great mathematician, engineer, and surveyor from the Republic of Venice, Niccolò Fontana (1500–1557), nicknamed "Tartaglia" because of his bad stammer—he solved a new type of cubic equation, $x + mx = n$—who, raised in grinding poverty and lacking ordinary drawing and writing materials but was still obsessively determined to learn, took himself into outlying cemeteries and used black tombstones as slates? Could he not in doing so he have presaged the work of the artists Cy Twombly, perhaps the most influential painter of the post-Abstract Expressionist generation, whose "blackboard" paintings—chalklike drawing on black grounds—found in New York such appreciative audiences? What we can assert perhaps is that in the long run, black incorporates all.

"Black is modest and arrogant at the same time," says the 79-year-old Japanese fashion designer Yohji Yamamoto. "Black is lazy and easy—but mysterious. But above all, black says this: I don't bother you—don't bother me." The strange dreamscape of black is the ultimate backdrop to life's quiddities. We come from the dark in the beginning and re-enter dark at the end. The reductive element of the color in a real sense answers every question we can ask that appears insolvable. Black is the one strange world we can all enter equally—and, in the final analysis, must do so, saying goodbye to light. As Voltaire said, "History is after all only a pack of tricks we play on the dead."

Raphael's Lost Madonna

When Baldassare Castiglione first saw Raphael's nymph in *The Triumph of Galatea* (1512) in the Villa Farnesina, which the painter had recently finished for the rich banker Agostino Chigo, the famous courtier was so overwhelmed by the astounding beauty of the captured beauty that he asked the artist where in all the world he had found a model who possessed such harmony. Who, Castiglione wanted to know, had been the source of such irresistible grace? Such breathtaking completeness of vision?

By way of reply, Raphael wrote back to his friend in 1514, addressing the essential problem of painting a beautiful woman—or, as he put it, "the famine" of beautiful women. He explained that he based his *Galatea* on no specific model, making the now famous remark, "I use a certain idea that had formed in my mind." This was of course a direct reference to the standard Renaissance theory that painting should be based on idealization, not realism, a matter implicit in all theories of Ideal Art, where the artist searches for and finds the Platonic Idea of any object in his mind, implanted by God. The perfect idea of a human figure exists, that is, in the painter's own conceptions of what alone he has to realize. Consequently, he need not content himself with merely copying a figure or model that he happens to have in front of him. Raphael Sanzio sought beauty in the purely simple. His paintings embody what is called *gratia*, a harmonious blending of colors combined with the pleasing arrangement of figures. Nothing ingenious. No trumpeting virtuosity or discrepancies of scale. Nothing forced or overemphasized or unclear. No harsh innovative coloring or icy obscenity or rude torso-twisting. Here was pure beauty, the serenity and calm classicism of the High Renaissance done by a painter whose hand created, but seemed as if it caressed.

I remember a tour guide at the Pitti Palace, once when I was visiting Florence, pointing out the symmetries of a Madonna a younger, more academic Raphael did at 21, compared to one he did at 25, and judging the former with a negative pip. *"Frigido,"* he said, meaning of course that the painting was too academic, too symmetrical. The later, more mature Raphael recognized that his figures did not strictly correspond to the canons of beauty based solely on proportion, laws founded strictly upon symmetry, that is, upon a mathematical system of proportions. Since he was conscious of his inability to reconcile his own ideal of beauty with those laws, it is clear that he trusted to what is today called intuition or sensibility, an indefinable, incommensurable quality, which in the eyes of the ancients—for the Greeks were less slaves to ratiocination than is generally alleged—was more esteemed than the meticulous observance of academic rules. It is such bookish laws that often make the academician a pedant, a eunuch, compared to the true creative artist.

Raphael, like his teacher Perugino, had abandoned to some extent the faithful portrayal of nature, which had been the ambition of so many *quattrocento* artists. If we look back to the time of Praxiteles, we may see what was once referred to as "ideal" beauty grew out of a slow approximation of schematic forms to nature. Now the whole process was simply reversed. Artists tried to approximate nature to the idea of beauty they had formed when looking at classical statues—they "idealized" the model. I am convinced that the very same idea was behind Albert Einstein's remark that each of his theories was the result not of a grinding and overly specific scientific application but of months and years of stubbornly pursuing what he called "*idealized* experiments."

The story, told by Pliny, which served for centuries as the basis for Ideal Art, tells how Zeuxis had to paint a *Venus*, and, after inspecting all the most beautiful girls in Crotona, he selected five, painting the mouth of one, the legs of another, and so on. "There is no excellent beauty that hath not some strangeness in the proportion," wrote Francis Bacon in his essay *On Beauty*. "A man cannot tell whether Apelles or Albrecht Dürer were the more trifler: whereof the one would make a personage by geometrical proportions: the other, by taking the best parts out of divers faces to make one excellent."

But despite Raphael's explanation to Castiglione, it is entirely possible that real flesh and blood may well lie behind the ideal image of his Galatea, which may inform many other of his creations as well. There is a certain delicate face, guileless but unmistakably vulnerable, her eyes dark, Italian, and only hesitantly trustful, that appears too often in Raphael's works to be assigned to either coincidence or the realm of idealized conception. The suspicious instinct of men and women over five centuries—to search his pictures for the inspiration of, if not ideal perfection, perhaps a perfect lover—may be correct.

Raphael never married. As with Titian and Shakespeare, we know very little of certainty about his personal life. Nonetheless,

Platonic ideals aside, it seems clear that there was one woman the artist bequeathed to posterity. Was there such a woman and, if so, exactly who was this person immortalized over and over again, not only as the Virgin but also in less exalted incarnations? The clues that are left point to a tantalizing mystery that may conceal a tragic love story. But more of that anon.

Young Raphael—but who dying at 37 could ever be called old?—was not only extraordinarily handsome but a fellow widely known for his sweet disposition, a particular charm, courtesy, and *sprezzatura* that made him a favorite all his life wherever he went. There are several self-portraits we have of this lovely youth. He was not only talented but lucky in health and personal beauty, unlike, say, his contemporary Federico Barocci, the Italian Renaissance painter and printmaker, also from Urbino, who was crippled and could only work two hours a day. His original name was Federico Fiori, but he was nicknamed *Il Baroccio*. There were those who envied Raphael's grace. He would be described later by Michelangelo, somewhat grumpily it is thought, as walking about Rome "like a prince." So solid a body were he and his friends that they could be sneered at by Sebastiano del Piombo as the "Synagogue." Several passionate love sonnets found scribbled on the sheets of some of Raphael's drawings (some examples of which poetic effusions can be seen at the British Museum) lend color to Vasari's assertion, especially for their ardent tone, that Raphael was extremely susceptible to the charms of the fair sex and much given to the society of women.

Although later ages constantly credited him with an illustrious ancestry, his family could not boast a drop of noble blood. His full name was Rafael Johannis Santis de Urbino. The name di Sante or Santi became Latinised as *Sanctius,* thus returning to Italian as Sanzio. There is no evidence that he was known during his lifetime by any name other than "Raphael of Urbino." His father, Giovanni, was a painter and a goldsmith, perhaps also a trader, but he is important to us for two reasons alone, neither connected to his pictures: he wrote a rhymed chronicle which mentions a number of 15th-century artists, and he was the father of Raphael.

The boy was left on his own at a fairly early age. An elder sister and brother of his had died, and his mother soon followed them to the grave before Raphael was eight. His father remarried a goldsmith's daughter named Bernadina Parte but soon died himself from a fever contracted in the malarial air of the Mantuan marshland when his son was only 11. His uncle Simone Ciarla became his guardian. Much of the first 21 years of Raphael's life is a blank, although we do know that at age 17, in 1500, he was living in Perugia and working in the workshop of Pietro Perugino, born Pietro Vannucci, an Italian Renaissance painter of the Umbrian school, who developed some of the qualities that found classic expression in the High Renaissance. Raphael was his most famous pupil. (The speculations regarding composite works in art is fascinating. How many Peruginos, for example, did Raphael paint? How many Rubens, van Dyck?) It was here that he began to learn harmony of composition, how to achieve depth, how to handle Leonardo's *sfumato* technique so as to avoid giving his figures a harsh and rigid appearance. At the time, Leonardo was 48, Michelangelo 25. Within 10 years Raphael was admitted to be their equal.

But in 1504, when Raphael first went to Florence—he would remain in the city for about four years—he was neither the companion nor friend of these giants. For the greater part of his stay, in fact, neither of the great masters were present. Vasari mentions only two painters as being Raphael's close friends there. One was Ridolfo Ghirlandaio, the other Fra Bartolommeo, a painter of religious subjects who was 12 years older. The modest position which Raphael held during his Florentine period is apparent from the fact that a contemporary historian, Mariotto Albertini, another painter—born Mariotto di Bindo di Biagio Albertinelli—omits all mention of Raphael in his account of the paintings then to be found in Florence. But even if Raphael had become famous, it is doubtful whether the city of Florence at that time could have enabled him to show his power as an artist. There were no public edifices to decorate, no large commissions being offered. Private citizens either could not afford, or hadn't the taste, to order the large historical or allegorical decorations which the Medici had commissioned and popularized just a few years before.

The only opportunities available lay in painting the Madonna and Child or groups of saints, work that, during those comparatively more latitudinarian times, was often painted, made—*fatto*, as if like spoons, tables, or chairs—and bought over the counter more or less like domestic furniture, elegantly to enhance a room, and not, as before, painted solely as devotional imagery for a church or chapel. There were at the time many anonymous *madonnieri* in Florence, dibble-dabbling out off-the-rack holy pictures, paintings, and devotional images that tended to be dull, empty, and conventional.

Raphael was far greater than these, of course, but it was with such lucrative commissions that he began to get busy. The recorded list of his patrons is not particularly long. He painted two pictures for his friend Taddeo Taddei, one of which was the lovely *Madonna in the Meadow* (oil on wood, 1505–6), also called the "Madonna Belvedere." The scene shows the Virgin with Christ and St. John the Baptist in a highly serene and tender moment against a landscape backdrop which places the scene in a Tuscan setting. In addition to being the cousin of Christ, St. John the Baptist was the patron of Florence, making his presence here in a Florentine setting very appropriate. For another friend, one Lorenzo Nasi, Raphael painted for his marriage the *Madonna del Cardellino*, or "Madonna of the Goldfinch" (oil on wood, ca. 1505–6) and now in Florence.

A third was for a supposedly tightfisted patrician named Angelo Doni, who owned, among other works, Michelangelo's *Holy Family*, the so-called "Doni Tondo" or "Doni Madonna," the only finished panel painting by the mature Michelangelo to survive. It is a picture that fascinated Raphael and which he closely studied. Raphael painted both Doni's portrait and that of his wife, Maddalena. Other notable patrons for Raphael at this period were members of the Canigiani and Dei families, for whom respectively Raphael painted a *Holy Family* (1518), which is identified with a picture at Munich that he began but never finished, and the large altar-piece called the *Madonna del Baldacchino* (1508), Raphael's first major commission in Florence, produced for the cappella Dei in Santo Spirito, which remained incomplete on the artist's return to Rome in 1508 after being summoned by Pope Julius.

Raphael's Madonnas, curiously, are almost never posed in the same form or the same composition. Some are sitting, others standing. Eyes look forward or are cast downward. A hundred techniques occur in draperies and curtains. There is clever lighting of the Madonna's left arm in the *Terranuova Madonna* (1504), painted with a Leonardo-like delicacy of hand. The lighting in the *Madonna del Granduca* (1505)—the painting belonged to Ferdinand III, Grand Duke of Tuscany, from whom it got its name—is utterly simple, with all affectation gone from the pose, and the Madonna's hands, somewhat large and coarse, are displayed not to exhibit their grace but to perform their business, supporting the holy infant, bum in hand.* Some Madonnas are older than others. In the *Madonna del Granduca*, as in the *Terranuova Madonna*, a moment's comparison of the Virgin's head with that of the *Madonna Ansidei* (1505–7) shows how far the artist had advanced in his power of treating the surface so as to reproduce the texture of the skin and the structure of the features. Here, the Virgin sits formally on a high golden throne inscribed above with "Hail, Mother of Christ," with an adult John the Baptist on the left, and Saint Nicholas of Bari to the right—the latter being an early Christian bishop of Greek descent from the maritime city of Myra in Asia Minor during the time of the Roman Empire. Because of the many miracles attributed to his intercession, he is also known as Nicholas the Wonderworker.

There is in Raphael's *Madonna of Foligno* (1511) a playful and trivial sweetness in Mary with a touch of unemphasized naturalism in the right hand, shown just tenderly supporting the infant's back, a charming stylish characteristic in Raphael that will recur several times. The painting is a *sacra conversazione*, where holy figures, seen in conversation, draw the audience into their discussion. Rather than sitting under a canopy, as the Umbrian or Florentine style would have it, the Virgin is seated on clouds, embracing Jesus, surrounded by angels, and looking down upon Sigismondo de' Conti, kneeling in a red, fur-lined cape. Conti is presented by St. Jerome on the

---

*The Madonna supporting her baby's bottom—look at the *Cowper Madonna*, the *Madonna del Granduca*, the *Colonna Madonna*, the *Madonna del Impannata*, etc.—was a standard pictorial convention with Raphael and many other artists of the Italian Renaissance. (My dear wife Sarah, daughter of a Presbyterian minister, when our kids were small did not like to see me holding our baby daughters that way, out of a scrupulosity born of an idea that it seemed to her "inappropriate." I heartily disagreed.)

right with his lion, appealing for the Virgin's protection, along with St. Francis of Assisi and St. John the Baptist. In 1799, this was one of many paintings that Napoleon ordered transported to Paris. Of noble birth and educated in Foligno, it is Sigismondo (1432–1512) who gave the painting its title.

Much of the quiet dignity of his Perugian Madonnas, the simple flowing lines, the cool, incurious color and the thoughtful repose of the head and hands, can be seen, say, in Raphael's *Cowper Madonna* (1504), depicting the Virgin and Child in a typical scene of the Italian countryside. That Madonna, pensive, is older than others, her face more fully modelled, her form, uncovered by the mantle, shown with more life, more amplitude. The child is also more playful. Raphael was not only making an effort to adapt to the more lively conception of the Florentines, whose Virgins throughout the century were, with loss of neither mystery nor grace, primarily women and not imposing Mothers of God, but he was also trying to surpass them, as well, to break from his old master Perugino with his spare, scrimp, small-figured Northern European style and bring warmth and beauty back to the procreative female, the Christmas-card fullness of the Madonna, a simple peasant girl of open face and arms. He owed a lot to the influence of both Michelangelo and Leonardo in this.

And of course the *Sistine Madonna* (1512)—redeemed though it is by her supernatural beauty—is extremely human, although depicting a vision appearing to saints in the clouds. It is one of the world's most famous Renaissance masterpieces. Only essential elements can be found in the painting, with no elaborate scaffolding or false accessory or wasted detail. The gestures and expressions of the saints adoring the Blessed Mother create a chain of circular movements which enclose her and the spectator, with each participating together in the reverent moment. Heaven and Earth are linked with a theatrical touch by the curtains and the balustrade on which the papal tiara is placed. But the Madonna herself appears humbly barefoot, without a halo or any adornment on her gown. A spirituality can certainly be felt, but the matchless glow of color, a half-liquid envelope of feminine emotion and feeling, warms that glory. And so little does her daring, half-standing, half-walking posture conform to idealized conceptions that, according to several critics, a basis can be found on Raphael's part for "a reminiscence of some peasant maiden from the Campagna."

Raphael was by no means the first painter to humanize the Madonna. The Umbrian quattrocentists tended to do so, as did Florentine painting and sculpture in general. But it was Raphael who managed to strike perfect classical balance and grace in his Madonnas by accentuating their human, emotional side and discarding much of the hieroglyphic symbolism found elsewhere and so often repeated by rote by lesser talents.

A maiden from the Campagna. What a revealing insight that is, at least to me. I have always thought her delicate eyes, hesitating a bit, were so human, very Italian. She is young, very serious, not at all superior, with her role as mother of Jesus, almost rigid with the responsibility of what she has been called upon to be and to do.

Who might this "peasant maiden" have been? Stories of Raphael with women are sparse, though dramatic. To begin with, there was a nameless girl in Urbino whom his uncle Ciarla had selected to be his wife, and it is well recorded that Cardinal Bibbiena of Santa Maria in Portico wished for him to marry his niece. Neither plan succeeded, however. The village maiden remained obscure, and the cardinal's niece died, unhappily it is said, an "unclaimed blessing." Of further history in either affair there is not so much as a trace. There were several other women, one of whom had a dowry of 5,000 *scudi* and a house worth more than 100 ducats.

It could be argued legitimately that Raphael never married because he was too busy, too involved in his work. Marriage, as he later wrote to his uncle, would only have retarded his career. Leonardo and Michelangelo for whatever reasons were both unmarried, and in an age when the most prominent men were clerics, a celibate life, or at least an unmarried one, was more or less the rule rather than the exception.

But it is another woman entirely, the subject of much critical speculation, who remains the center of Raphael's mysterious romance. Her name was Margherita Luti. It has been the judgment of many an art expert that it was this Margherita whom Raphael passionately loved for the 12 years he lived and worked exclusively in Rome—and then proceeded to (have to?) repudiate, like a good churchman (or pusillanimous lover?) on his deathbed. Was it from guilt? Or cowardice? Was it pride? Or was it somehow to save her reputation? It is impossible to say what Raphael's motives were or even whether or not the story is true. (It might be mentioned here that of the many portraits of women that Raphael had painted, none, according to Vasari, has been officially identified for certain except that of a single woman named Joanna of Aragon.) The identification of the mysterious woman in his life with Margherita rests, in fact, on the slenderest bit of evidence. A single anonymous manuscript annotation on the margin of a 16th-century edition of Vasari's *Lives* is its only source, and while there are a hundred different reasons why a woman's name may be placed in the margin of a book, the fondest one—the most scandalous, that is—is always chosen.

The paintings tell their own story. It is simple enough to make the comparison—and so see the likeness—between the individualized beauty of the Madonna reigning above Saints Elizabeth and Catherine in the *Madonna of the Linen Window (dell' Impannata)* (1513–14) and the *Donna Velata* (1516) in which more than a passing resemblance to a portrait persists. It was for the form of this painting that Raphael, varying only the gestures and the lighting, adopted that of Leonardo's *Mona Lisa*, with its stable triangular base. (How delicately the "Lady with the Veil," vulnerable, wide-eyed, romantically expectant, gestures to her heart!) One is posed in a dark costume in front of a light background, while the creamy robes of Donna Velata—also called *The Lady with a Veil*—are balanced against a dark background. Her armlet bears, in large lettering, the proud signature "Raphael Urbinas." It is almost a proclamation, one made all the more prominent by the pointing index finger of the right hand on the breast of the woman.

The subject of *Donna Velata* significantly appears in another portrait of Raphael's *The Portrait of a Young Woman*, a painting that is also known as *La Fornarina*, painted between 1518 and 1519. *La Fornarina* is traditionally identified as the *fornarina* (bakeress) Margherita Luti, Raphael's Roman mistress. There has been some doubt cast on Raphael's authorship of this painting, which hangs in the Palazzo Barberini of the National Gallery in Rome. It is sometimes criticized as being graceless, the eyes too shifty and intense. "For the theoretician of religious art of the nineteenth century," critic and Raphael expert Jean-Pierre Cuzin writes, "*La Fornarina* was a hated symbol of the artist's degeneration and 'moral damnation,' and for art historians of the twentieth century, equally a symbol of a Raphael attempting a tenderness and suavité of which he was no longer capable, or of a Raphael so overcome by his own glory that he no longer had the time to paint his pictures." There is an amazing array of responses to *La Fornaria*, in short.

Several observers, nevertheless, immediately noted the resemblance of *La Fornarina* to the Virgin in Raphael's masterpiece—the classic *maesta*—*The Sistine Madonna.* The distinguished 19th-century critic Giovanni Morelli quickly agreed that the subject, indeed, was the *Fornarina.* The similarity of the Sistine Madonna's head to the type Raphael chose for the *Donna Velata*, to the *Portrait of a Young Woman*, and to the central figure of the St. Cecilia is far too close—too symmetrical—to ignore. The resemblance between that of *The Sistine Madonna* and such heads of the Virgin as those in the *Madonna of Foligno* and Raphael's *Madonna of the Fish* (1513) is nothing less than astonishing.

Morelli's theory that Raphael painted the *Sistine Madonna* "for the black nuns of the Convent of San Sisto in Piacenza" is probably true, confirmed especially by the presence of the two saints particularly venerated by that convent: St. Barbara, who brings comfort in the hour of death, and St. Sixtus, the protector of the house of della Rovere and of the putti who were used on sarcophagi.

Another theory, however, has it that the *Sistine Madonna* was acquired by the nuns of Piacenza only after the collection of Pope Julius II was dispersed. According to some interpreters of that painting, St. Sixtus supposedly displays the features of Pope Julius; St. Barbara, those of lovely Guilia Orsini, niece of the Pope (her, or another of His Holiness's nieces, Lucrezia della Rovere); and the beautiful Madonna, the features, again, of the model who repeatedly seems to have inspired Raphael the way Simonetta Vespucci did Botticelli and the beautiful blonde French model Marie-Thérèse Walter, the illegitimate child of a French woman and a Swedish businessman, did Picasso.

Many have questioned the province of this work. It is considered by some scholars to be strange and perhaps telling for

Raphael to have gone to such trouble on a painting for a small religious community in Piacenza. Why did he do it? For whom did he make the brilliant effort? Did he have an extra interest to declare? Was it for a woman? Was he in love? And if so, with whom?

And who was the Fornarina?

She was a baker's girl, first of all, thus the logical name *Fornarina*. It was the critic Achille Astolfi who identified her as a Sienese girl, Margherita Luti, daughter of Francesco, a baker in the Santa Dorotea quarter in Rome. She was referred to first by Vasari, and then, in 1665, by Fabio Chigi, of the famous Sienese banking family, although she has been treated as mere invention by many modern critics. The evidence collected by the scholar Rodolfo Lanciani (1845–1929), however, underscores the truth of Vasari's story, and furthermore establishes the name and ultimate fate of the Fornarina.* According to local tradition, three houses in Rome are today still pointed out as the successive homes of Raphael's *inamorata*, and each of these houses stands in fact in close and curious proximity to buildings of which the master was successively employed, doing decorations, for whatever that may tell us. The first of these, in the Via

---

*I have personally discerned the face of La Fornarina—sweet, gentle, questioning, hesitant—in young Italian girls many times. I am not only of French extraction but also by heritage proudly half Italian, have briefly lived in Italy, and grew up in a city in Massachusetts with many Italian families living there. My maternal grandfather, Alessandro Dittami, for whom I was named, was born in Ferrara, Emiglio Romagna, Italy. His mother left him in the hospital, where as a foundling he was raised by Carmelite nuns and later priests in the "orphanage" across the street until he was 12 to 14 years old. He then served an apprenticeship to a tailor in the village of Cento. His wife, my grandmother (*nonna*) Ermengilda Buongiorni Calesa, was born in San Pietro d' Agazzano, Piacenza, also

di St. Dorotea, is still occupied by a bakery known as *il forno della Fornarina*; the second is in the Vicolo del Cedro near St. Egidio in Trastevere; and the third is the Palazetto Sassi, which has a tablet in its wall with an inscription to the effect that "Tradition says that the one who became so dear to Raphael, and whom he raised to fame, lived in this house."

According to a census return made under Leo X in 1513, one of the houses of the Sassi family was occupied by the baker Francesco from Siena, a fact that completely tallies with the tradition that *"Margherita, donna di Raffaello,"* as she is described in that contemporary marginal note in a copy of the 1568 Giunta edition of Vasari, was the daughter of a baker from Siena. But even more decisive is the entry found in 1897 in the ledger of the Congregation of Sant' Apollonia in Trastevere, a kind of home for fallen and repentant women. Dated August 18, 1520, a little over four months after Raphael's death, the entry runs as follows: *"A di 18 Augusti 1520 Hoggi e stata recenta nel nro Conservatorio ma Margarita vedoa, figliola del quondam Francescho Luti da Siena"* (August 18, 1520. Today has been received into our establishment the widow Margarita, daughter

---

Emiglio Romagna. She lived there until she was about nine years old, when her family planned to emigrate to Argentina. As there was an illness there, they deferred for about a year and changed their minds, deciding to emigrate by way of New York City in order to visit with the oldest married daughter, Genoveffa (Jennifer), and her husband, Giovanni (John) Ceruti, prior to travelling on to Argentina. But she found enough to like in Manhattan to decide not to travel on to Argentina. Her husband, my great grandfather, (*bisnonno*) Francesco Bonifacio Calesa, headstrong, who absolutely hated the city, picked up, turned right around, and returned to Italy to live with his mother-in-law, Maria Rosa Silva Buongiorni, who died in Val Tidone, Italy.

of the late Francesco Luti of Siena).

The remarkable coincidence of dates and names leaves little doubt that this "widow" was the *la bella Fornarina* herself, the dark bewitching creature who served and sat for Raphael, if for no others, at least as the model for the *Donna Velata*, the *Sistine Madonna*, the *Barberini Portrait*, and for the beautiful face of *St. Cecilia*, the astonishing picture that supposedly caused Baldassare Castiglione to goggle and the Bolognese goldsmith and painter Francisco Francia to die of depression over his own inferiority after seeing it.

The story goes that Raphael's attachment to Margherita lasted up to the very day of his death, when at the pious insistence of the Pope's messenger who was to bring the dying man the penitential "Extreme Unction"—Last Rites—she was removed from the room. There is a legend that she could only be induced to let go of the coffin on Pope Leo's promise to have the artist beatified. Was this merely classic soap opera? The girl from the wrong side of the tracks? A person loved but repudiated? Not good enough to marry? And who was at fault? Vasari relates that in his will, Raphael "left her a sufficient provision wherewith she might live in decency." And so what do we make of this? Did it constitute dismissal? Or hint at something like eternal solicitude? To have stood by her so long? There is strong proof that Raphael loved her, and that Margherita loved him. His long infatuation with the baker's daughter surely explains his unwillingness to enter into the bonds of matrimony, even with as desirable and noble a partner as Maria Bibbiena, to whom he was practically formally engaged in 1514, and who after years of postponement is supposed to to have died of a broken heart. On principle, Raphael would have had so much to gain by marrying Maria.

Vasari's statement that Raphael's reluctance to marry was

due to the prospect of a cardinal's hat being bestowed on him sounds not only bogus but contrary to reason. It is possible that the Pope thought of extending this as a courtesy for owing the painter money or, even more likely, that Raphael considered it merely a diplomatic option to humor a man as powerful as Cardinal Bibbiena.

Raphael was already famous. He had wealth, and he had glory. With Pope Leo's accession, he found himself a prince among artists in Rome. He even bought a vineyard in Rome in 1518. He had triumphantly decorated various walls and ceilings in the Vatican, now known as the *stanze* (rooms) for Pope Julius II. Leo commissioned him to buy all ancient stones in Rome for the building of St. Peter's. He was therefore not only a painter and architect-in-chief but also the first official to preside over the discovery of antiques. The palace in which Raphael lived in a princely state was built by Bramante and bought by Raphael on October 7, 1517, when he was just 34 years old. In very much altered form, it still stands in the piazza di Scossacavalli at the corner of the via di Borgo Nuovo. It was surely in this studio that he painted the greatest and most deservedly popular of his altarpieces: the *Sistine Madonna* and the *Transfiguration*, a painting (now at the Vatican Gallery) that was found on his easel on the day he died. In any case, by anyone's account, Raphael was a very accomplished man.

And then, tragedy. He was suddenly attacked by a fever, one which he had probably contracted in superintending some excavations. The rest happened quickly. He made his last will on April 4, 1520, and died on the sixth. That he repented of his neglectful treatment of Maria Bibbiena is fairly evident from the epitaph that, by his wish, was placed upon her tomb: "We, Baldassare Turini da Pescia and Gianbattista Branconi dall'Aquila, testamentary executors and recipients of the last wishes of Raphael, have raised this memorial to his affianced wife, Maria, daughter of Antonio da Bibbiena, whom death deprived of a happy marriage."

After providing for the Fornarina so that she might "live in decency," he left his fortune of 16,000 ducats to his relatives, and his drawings and sketches to his favorite pupils, Guilio Romano and Gianfrancesco Penni. An enormous funeral procession bore Raphael to the Pantheon, where he was buried in close proximity—a formality, no doubt—to Maria Bibbiena.

Exequies followed. Raphael's solemn epitaph was written by Cardinal Bembo, and Castiglione expressed his grief in the form of a beautiful sonnet. "The death of Raphael," says Vasari, "was bitterly deplored by all the Papal Court, not only because he had formed part thereof, since he had held the office of chamberlain to the Pontiff, but also because Leo X had esteemed him so highly, that his loss occasioned that sovereign the bitterest grief." The Pope's grief may have been bitter, indeed. Grief was everywhere bitter. On the day that Raphael died, April 6, 1520, according to legend, a crack even appeared in the walls of the Vatican. But the deepest loss was surely felt in much lowlier lodgings, in the Palazetto Sassi. And later on, who knows how deeply in the Congregation of Sant' Apollonia in Trastevere, that home for fallen and repentant women.

Chasing Mermaids

"Naïveté in art," wrote Henry James in his novella *The Lesson of the Master* (1888), "is like a zero in a number: its importance depends on the figure it is united with." And while the genre has been taken up by countless painters down through the years, leaving us an important American folk art, it is not uncommon to see, on wood, canvas, or brooch, too many examples in this area where the word "naïvist" more accurately describes the dauber's own slim talent than the mode in which he or she has chosen to work: hydrocephalic infants with middle-aged faces, first-grade land-and-seascapes, and a plethora of poorly executed "busy" narratives somehow always set on frozen New England ponds.

Then there is Ralph Cahoon, master of the sophisticated "primitive," whose paintings combine dignity with irreverence and quaint decorum with sweet ribaldry, a painter whose style suggests, all at once, the color and comicality of Jan Balet, the whimsy and line of Roland Topor, and the imagination of Henri Rousseau.

One day sometime back in 1980, going through the back room of a jumble shop in the seaside town of West Yarmouth, Massachusetts, I happened on an extraordinary print. Done in bright, bold primary colors, it depicted a panoply of ascending hot-air balloons; standing in and hanging from the gondolas affecting little lollipop-faced creatures wearing sailor suits were at play. I was struck by the picture's blithe whimsy, reminiscent of Gilbert and Sullivan's *H.M.S. Pinafore*, but also by the brilliant, accomplished but unpretentious way in which the artist, whose signature on the painting read simply "R. Cahoon," had successively created a third dimension without light, shade, or the blending of colors. Assuming that the painter had worked in Victorian times, I approached the proprietor of the shop and asked him what he could tell me of the painter R. Cahoon. I was happily surprised to learn that Cahoon was an old Cape Codder, quite alive, still productive, and living over in nearby Santuit. I wanted to see more of Cahoon's work and decided to drop him a note with a view to writing something about him. The following week I received a cheerful postcard, which read:

> "Dear Alexander,
>   Next Saturday the 12th 1 p.m. is fine with us. Warning: Cahoons are dull company.
>   Sincerely, Ralph"

That Saturday, in this little crossroads of Santuit, I met both Ralph, his wife Martha, whom I discovered also painted, and their cat, Blackie Rose. Though I was not the first to have found them, that initial visit led to a friendship with the two painters who were anything but dull, with much, I soon discovered, left to learn.

Ralph Cahoon was born of Scottish ancestry (dialect: "Colquoun") in 1910 in Chatham, Massachusetts, on the very elbow of Cape Cod, having descended from a long line of regional oysters, whalers, and farmers. Old William Cahoon, a direct descendant and one of Chatham's founding fathers, settled there in 1664.

It's an old and quite common name on the Cape—more than 60 Cahoons can be found in the local telephone book, and there is the Cahoon Hollow in Wellfleet. This is a salty old part of the world. And the fanciful satires and nautical themes of Ralph's lively paintings—the Lorelei-like beauties and sailors in red-and-white striped pants gamboling at lovely tea parties, picnics, and boat races under blueberry skies—embody this particular region to perfection.

As a boy Ralph showed an early interest in drawing and after high school went off to study for two years at the School of Practical Arts in Boston. Soon afterward he met his future wife—a girl named Martha Farham, the daughter of Swedish parents, Axel and Elma—at a local dance. Martha was working at the time in the family shop in West Harwich, where her father (originally named Farm), having emigrated from Tumalila, near Malmö, Sweden, began restoring furniture and, like many of his countrymen, decorating it as well, using a Scandinavian technique called *rosemäling*, combining scrollwork and flowered design on cabinets, chests, and rockers. "I used to sand, scrape, paint, and refinish furniture all day," Martha told me. Much of her work was done with the old Hitchcock stencils.

The Cahoons were married in 1931 and moved to the "old Bennet House" in Osterville. There, in 1935, they opened a small antiques shop. But both continued to practice Axel Farham's craft, and went on painting bureaus and blanket chests, lamps and trays, chairs and headboards in the folk-art tradition. They followed their own instincts, not complicating the matter, using strong reds, blues, greens, and yellows. Theirs was an original and beautifully spare embellishment on boxes, cabinets, ladder-back chairs, washstands, spool bureaus, and desks, characterized, much of it, by figures of unicorns, thistles, seashells, schooners, whales, and notably—this would become Ralph's colophon—mermaids.

Ralph, incidentally, who once said in reference to the maritime occupations of his ancestors, "I like to think that in all their grim trade they themselves chased the mermaids from time to time," began collecting them as objects, and soon they could be found all over the house—iron mermaids, marble mermaids, stone mermaids, mermaid ashtrays, mermaids made of wood, mermaid weathervanes, and mermaid sculptures! The spell of the legendary Nereides at the Cahoons was in evidence everywhere.

"We made $99 that first year in business," Martha told me. Soon, however, local interest in their work grew. The small shop developed the sort of quaint reputation that made Cape Cod hosts bring guests there to look at their art. People even began to cart over their own small cupboards and chairs to have them painted by the Cahoons, feeling no qualms at all about asking for the two artists to drop what they were doing and decorate a chunk of furniture. Many of these pieces remain today in summer cottages on the Cape, but others were carried away by lovers of naïve art to various parts of the world.

In 1945 Ralph and Martha moved their home and shop to nearby Santuit, into their 18th-century house, once an inn, built in 1750 by blacksmith Ezra Crocker, a descendant of one of the founders of that village. The move effected a sea change in the Cahoon's craft, which evolved—and became "serious art." By then both had grown tired of flowers and leaves and had turned to figures and landscapes, which they both began painting on any flat surface that came to hand. Their quaint New England villages began to appear atop coffee tables, whaling encounters on commodes, mermaid marriages on old wooden secretaries and blanket chests. Generally, they both preferred working on Swedish Masonite of various sizes. Ralph often bought it in batches of large sheets and cut it to different speci-fications. Sizes of their paintings range from porthole to wall dimen-sion. Over several seasons, I began receiving handdrawn Christmas cards from him, some on board, of many sizes and shapes,

Although over the years they had come to share much of the same subject matter, Ralph and Martha now began to culti-vate separate styles. The smoky hues, delicate turns, and generally soft romanticism of Martha's work was more rustic. Ralph's work was more whimsical and sophisticated, with a sly humor that verges on satire. His paintings, with their famous motifs of sailors, bal-loons, and Barchester-like towns and trains—and always, of course somewhere, a signature mermaid or two, bedecked with seaweed or pearls, frisking and flirting—were, according to Martha, "more robust."

There is an effortlessness to their work, a magic in those brightly enameled surfaces, cheerfully, intentionally ignorant of reality, and whether a "sampler" type or period-type painting, each has the distinctive touch or *habitus* of a Cahoon.

It was only a question of time before their work found public acclaim. Joan Whitney Payson, who owned an art gallery in Old Westbury, Long Island, saw some of the Cahoon's fantasies and sug-gested they try framing a few, which they did. Only a few days after they shipped these paintings to New York, Mrs. Payson called to say that they'd been sold. Could she have some more? The running orders that soon flowed in eventually became a torrent; by 1959, the Cahoons were reportedly filling over 200 orders a year. "That put an end to our furniture decorating," Martha told me, adding emphat-ically, "thank goodness." Before long they were able to give up the antiques business entirely, although, until one particular show in Nantucket in 1959, they were still fairly unknown as artists on the

Cape itself. That show—in the Lobster Pot Gallery—sold out in a record four hours.

Since that time, their paintings have found homes as far away as Africa, Europe, and the Far East, and several have even crossed the auction block at Christie's in London at high prices. A few years later at Robert Eldred's, an Cape Cod auction house in East Dennis, Ralph's *Nantucket Incident* sold for $32,000. Among the prominent collectors of their work were the Lilly, DuPont, and Mellon families, and even Jacqueline Onassis, who, when she was first lady, bought several Cahoons as gifts for the president.

Most pictures by Ralph, as I have mentioned, bear the simple signature "R. Cahoon." A decade ago, attending an auction in Rhode Island, however, I had the occasion to come across a beautifully painted blanket chest that had gone for an extraordinary price, on the lid of which, trumping the possibility of any complaint as to its stated value, the small accompanying tag simply read: "Reputed to be a Cahoon." An original Thomas Sully, standing against a wall not far away, commanded less attention.

Over the years I often visited the Cahoons in Santuit. Their old house is painted a barnlike ox-blood. Along the walls of the central stairway inside is stenciling original to the house, with handcut stencils also covering the walls and floors in the upstairs rooms. I never saw more immaculate rooms. Martha kept everything shipshape shining, but I often wondered if Ralph, who was always a bit rumpled, really wanted it that way. I loved his gruff persona. He often grew restless and seemed to need to get outside, anywhere, and the two of us often trundled off to a now defunct restaurant in Mashpee called The Flume to eat fried clams. Seafood was a favorite with him, especially salt cod.

The two of them always painted in the same room, a small

well-lit studio next to the kitchen. I stopped by once or twice when they were working, but it didn't seem to bother them. They insisted that I come in where they continued to paint—Martha at her table, and Ralph, who used an upside-down stool for an easel, chatting away. The two could be peppery, even competitive. Ralph had a curmudgeon's love for Martha, but liked to bait her. In front of me he once claimed that he had married her for her money. "I had $2000 when we got married," said Ralph. Martha later whispered to me, "It was $70."

Ralph loved to talk, and I encouraged his stories, although he always seemed secretly amused at my interest in him. There's an eye-to-eye directness in the way old Cape Codders speak. Conversation made him animated. A witty self-deprecating man with sparkling eyes and a brush mustache, he bore a striking likeness to the actor Gale Gordon, the principal in the *Our Miss Brooks* show on radio and television. He had no poses. He had not the slightest vanity. He cared not a whit about wealth or fame. I think it embarrassed him. He told me about his growing up in Chatham, his Indian arrowhead collection, various of his many childhood enterprises. He mentioned a cartoon strip that he done as a boy and recounted wonderful tales of having once caddied on the golf course for the regional novelist Joseph Lincoln, a great fat man and poor tipper whom he described as a "cheapskate." Ralph's father, also named Ralph, was a disabled World War I veteran who had worked for the town, and the family never had much money. Ralph made his pocket money by fishing, clamming, oyster digging, and diving off Chatham in hope of coming up with a lucrative cache of the whiskey dumped overboard by local rum-runners pursued by the Coast Guard.

I remember his complaints at the time about quitting smoking. It was a habit that he loved and hated to walk away from. As compensation, he enjoyed sucking crystallized ginger and kept a bag of it in his pocket. He enjoyed reading mysteries. He spoke of changing times. He told me oak furniture was once so unpopular they used to leave it outside the antique shop in Osterville, with an attached sign, "Free." He hated overbuilding, commercialism, and the exploitation of the Cape. He could become wistful at times. I sometimes felt a sadness creep in. There were hints he might have once had a drinking problem.

Ralph died of cancer in 1982 when he was 71, by which time he had completed, according to his own report, some 2,500 to 3,000 paintings with his trademark sirens and raffish tars wearing straw Bretons, characters full of life, hornpiping about to beat the band, thematic somehow all at once of the South Seas, Gilbert and Sullivan's *Pinafore*, and a Dion Boucicault play on dress-parade at Broadstairs.

The Santuit house has since become the Cahoon Museum of American Art, a project of Keith and Rosemary Rapp, longtime friends of the Cahoons. It contains an eclectic collection of 19th- and 20th-century American paintings, ranging from the glowing Hudson River School pictures of Alvin Fisher to the luminist marine works of James Butterworth to the landscapes of Dwight Tryon and John J. Enneking, a friend of Martha's father, incidentally, whom she knew when she was growing up.

Everywhere are Ralph and Martha's own magical paintings, sparkling box-sets of skating tableau, ships-in-harbor, dune scenes, browsing animals, the colonial church spires of Martha's Vineyard. Whether the subject is the Great Fire of 1846 or a bevy of mermaids sailing by in flag-bedecked balloons or a toy-like locomotive puffing through a story-book valley, whether it's a group of Edwardians waving flags or a pacific Garden of Eden with a tiny but forbidding serpent in a corner or Julia Child swotting up a bouillabaisse with the help of three mermaid assistants and a bowl of Cotuit Oysters, each somehow manages to combine dignity with irreverence, quaint decorum with sweet ribaldry.

After Ralph died, Martha lived alone in a small wing of the museum, and I visited her in 1986 when she was 81. She did not paint anymore. "I draw with crayons now," she told me, smiling and showing me one of her works, *Back to My Childhood*. We talked about many things, including Ralph. She mentioned how much she missed him. "Even now," she said, "I shut my bedroom door quietly because I think I'm going to wake him up." She paused a moment, looking back at the past. "He wasn't well. He had to go to the hospital. I remember fussing, calling for the ambulance. I asked him, 'Shall I come with you?'"

I waited. Martha paused, shrugged, and had to smile when she echoed—grumpily, in his voice—his reply, "No, I've seen enough of you."

Those were his last words, sweet ones as only the long, durably married know only all too well.

We then walked together through the rooms next door and up the creaking stairs, where, with the help of light and good wall space, their many paintings displayed so delighted the eye. But in fact they did much more, offering us the chance to witness, in their supreme innocence and beauty, those gradations of sense and virtue which are too often lost in what William Wordsworth in his "Ode: Intimations of Immortality" lamented he too easily lost of youth and hope in middle age, allowing us then to regain something not blunted or coarsened by a heavy hand, but rather made light, made joyous, made ineffable.

I felt as if I was being reminded that in the fruitful land of fancy there can be found the dispensation of some grace, which, like holy water, disperses dark contagion, leaving, not naïveté, but rather what in the coming out of shadows can only be called sunlight.

Cigar Box Art

I recall reading somewhere that W. C. Fields, the young unknown Claude Dukenfield this was, living at the time in Pennsylvania, prided himself on having learned to juggle and smoke at the same time. What he first practiced juggling with, 10 at a time, were cigar boxes. (Doubtless he smoked the contents.) In the movie *It's the Old Army Game* (1926) with Louise Brooks, Fields, all gummy fingers and double-takes, mistakenly sets a cigar box alight, along with its full supply, when the fire brigade comes racing in. His horrified reaction gave me my first idea of how valuable its contents were. I saved a lot of empty cigar boxes growing up, mostly Dexter and El Producto brands, in which to keep all my "stuff," things like jackknives, baseball cards, ballpoint pens.

I also tried smoking cigars, much to my great grief later, with the neighborhood boys in a nearby field, getting sick. Gone, like knife-grinders, I'm sure, is the habit of keeping one's goods in cigar boxes. Smoking is unpopular nowadays, especially cigars. And the boxes don't mean much anymore.

It was a prestigious club, that of the cigar smoker: Rudyard Kipling, Franz Liszt, Adolph Zukor, Maurice Ravel (who confessed that it inspired his composing), Alfred de Musset, Ulysses S. Grant,

Mark Twain, Aristotle Onassis, Prince Rainier, Virginia Woolf, Edward G. Robinson, Orson Welles, H. L. Mencken, Amy Lowell, movie director Mike Todd, and Thomas Marshall, Woodrow Wilson's vice president, who once said, "What this country needs is a really good five-cent cigar," surely one of the most misquoted lines in history. A great cigar to be had in the 1920s for five cents was a handmade, rum-cured Sherlock Holmes "crook"—the great detective was once a very popular face on cigar boxes—that cigar box reproducing the lithographed face made famous by Sidney Paget's drawing of Holmes for the 1890s stories in *The Strand* magazine. Incidentally, in their very first scene together in the story "A Scandal in Bohemia," welcoming him back from his wedding, the very first thing we see Holmes do is flip a "case of cigars" on the sofa for his friend, Dr. Watson.

Cigar aficionados, a term they love—the word implies both knowledge of as well as enthusiasm for—proliferate. Connoisseurship is implied, they feel, something like expertise or a sort of savvy proficiency, which applies even to the dimmest dunces and dolts who smoke them. Rush Limbaugh, the fat right-wing radio slob who had the IQ of a pro golf score, thought it made him look cool. Earlier in his life, Ronald Reagan was such an advocate for smoking cigars that he appeared in magazine advertisements promoting the habit. Sigmund Freud, who smoked up to the very last day of his life, preferred getting cancer of the jaw rather than quitting smoking cigars. He died of oral cancer in 1939, at the age of 83. The last 15 years of his life were an extended agony of nicotine withdrawal, heart palpitations, painful, dangerous surgeries, and the replacement of most of his jaw with painful, dumb, inefficient substitutes. Zealous, Frank Sinatra could say, "Fresh air makes me throw up. I can't handle it. I'd rather be around three cigars blowing in my face all night."

Red Sox pitcher Luis Tiant used to smoke cigars taking a shower. Cigars are commonly sported as symbols of wealth. Success. Comfort. Serenity. And it is often a far deeper matter than the mere satisfaction of a good smoke. Cigars, culturally, tend to show strength and impart an air of authority. They "boast," as it were—top off a great success, like having had a baby! Boston Celtics coach Arnold "Red" Auerbach always lit up a fat Hoyo de Monterrey as a victory sign in the waning minutes of his team's basketball victory, not a humble gesture and always a proof of his smugness to opposing teams and their hostile fans.

Winston Churchill, who smoked 15 cigars a day, made them part of his victory sign. Comedian Groucho Marx loved them enough to get himself in trouble. Once, his third wife Eden objected to his "stinky old cigar" and ordered him to extinguish it or get a new wife. Novelist Anthony Trollope loved smoking cigars and did so all his life. He often got "buys" on large amounts of them, probably by way of his postal travels, and sold them at four pence a pop to his friends, notably George Lewes, husband of Maryanne Evans, aka George Eliot. By 1876, he was down from six cigars a day to a single one, which he said was like giving a horse a single straw a day.

Captain James Hook in *Peter Pan*, along with many other exaggerations about him, like the X-shaped scar on his cheek, kept "a holder of his own contrivance in his mouth, enabling him to smoke two cigars at once." Colonel Tom Parker, Elvis Presley's ostentatious manager, a fat, Dutch-born fraud of a musical entrepreneur with a carnival worker background, born Andreas Cornelis van Kuijk who immigrated illegally to the United States at the age of 20, believed that a cigar in his mouth gave him a look of effective pugnacity. (It also compensated for his much less than heroic jawline.) Sammy Glick, the ruthless opportunist in Budd Schulberg's novel *What Makes Sammy Run?* (1941), goes through life with his cigar "stuck out in front of him like a cannon leveled at the world." Short cigars, clenched between the teeth, supposedly connote grit and determination. Boxing managers usually smoke them in movies. Clint Eastwood in his spaghetti westerns thought they gave him a look of grit. Union organizers always wander around with a fat one in tow.

As props, cigars have served many Jewish comedians— Henry Youngman, George Burns, Milton Berle (who favored H. Upmanns), George Jessel, Ken Murray, Alan King, and, among others, the Great Gildersleeve. Comedian Ernie Kovacs spent $13,000 a year on cigars. They scorched the moustaches of Mark Twain, a heavy cigar smoker. Cigars are splendid props, used for timing and style, gesture, and punctuation. It became a dramatic prop at least once. Policeman Sam Crowley, standing in front of the Biograph Theatre, threw his cigar on the ground as soon as John Dillinger passed him, a prearranged sign that this was indeed their man, and the gangster, exiting the theater, was instantly gunned down.

During his 1931 interview he noted Capone repeatedly lighting his Hav-A-Tampa cigar, so we know Capone smoked that brand. Hav-A-Tampa was a cigar manufactured in Florida. The tobacco was imported from Havana and or mixed with other tobaccos. Until he gave up the smoking habit in 1985, Fidel Castro, the dictator who ruled his country with an iron fist for 50 years, was synonymous with cigars. Only a rising national concern over the health risks of smoking would lead to Castro's ultimately unequivocal decision to quit smoking cigars, even in private, to set an example for his people. Just because he abandoned a pastime that he had relished for 44 years did not mean that he didn't still think about cigars. He said he occasionally dreamt that he was smoking a cigar, although he would admonish himself for doing so. "Even in my dreams I used to think that I was doing something wrong," he told an interviewer in *Cigar Aficionado* magazine in 1994.

Fanatical about their "sticks" were many if not most mobsters and thugs, feeling the need to exude power. Remember Johnny Friendly, the dock boss in the film *On the Waterfront* who stormed about always with a cigar in his fist? Carmine "The Cigar" Galante, from Queens, the boss of the Bonanno crime family—also called "Lilo," a Sicilian term for cigar—was a psychopath rarely seen without a cigar hanging from his mouth. He was shot-gunned to death in 1979 by three masked men while dining on an open patio at Joe and Mary's Italian American restaurant in Bushwick, Brooklyn. A newspaper photo of the murdered Galante, splattered in blood on the floor, showed a cigar still stuck in his mouth.

Mobster Michael J. Coppola, a captain in the Genovese crime family (the New Jersey faction), was known as "Mikey Cigars" and Rhode Island mob capo Robert DeLuca as "Bobby the Cigar," to name but a few. Tony Montana's cigar in Brian De Palma's 1983 film *Scarface* was almost bigger than himself.

Cigars give a gangster *grip*. They love the florid action of slowly taking one out of their mouths to talk. It is a prop, a motioning device—giving added threat to a gesture—and a grown-up "binkie" to suck. And who would deny it has phallic implications? Winston Churchill has gone on record as saying he was actually attracted to a cigar's shape. Other hoodlums, mad killers, hit men, and bully boys who loved their "sticks" were Alphonse "Scarface" Capone, Benjamin "Bugsy" Siegel, Charles "Lucky" Luciano, Joseph "Joe Bananas" Bonanno, Anthony "Fat Tony" Salerno, Anthony "Tony Pro" Provenzano, John "Dapper Don" Gotti, Paul "Big Paulie" Castellano, Carlo "Don Carlo" Gambino, Frank Costello—born Francesco Castiglia in 1891—Arthur "The Dutchman" Schultz, and Sam "Momo" Giancana, who also happened to be known as "Sam the Cigar."

And of course cigar smokers are also a fussy and fiercely loyal group. The cigar has long stood as a male perquisite—proof of a certain freedom, the good life, one's cordiality and clubbability. There are domains where it is used with authority, as well. The card room in the old London club Brooks's, founded in 1764, for example, has a smooth, venerable patina of mellow orange caused by generations of cigar smokers. It is the cigar one smokes in such places, furthermore, not its pale or papery adjuncts. There is a story of the crusty old member of the elegant Savage Club (1857) in London who, when offered a Turkish cigarette, would snort, "I don't smoke stationery!"

General Ulysses S. Grant generally smoked a pipe, but after his victory at the Battle of Fort Donelson, people sent him so many boxes of cigars that he felt obliged to smoke them. Cigars were popular throughout the 19th century, especially during the Civil War. After the relatively small *Monitor* defeated the huge threatening *Merrimack* on March 9, 1862, and sent it sagging back to Norfolk, gents in the north were soon smoking cigars named "El Monitor." Twenty-year-old Robert Gould Shaw, leader of the famous black 54th Massachusetts regiment, which was sent down to reduce the forts and batteries on Morris Island in Charleston harbor, as he fell with a bullet in his heart leading the attack, had a cigar clenched in his teeth. In 1916, during his Boston Red Sox years, slugger Babe Ruth, a pitcher at the time, invested money in a small Boston cigar factory that put out a cigar named after him, a nickel number with his picture on every wrapper—"and I smoked them until I was blue in the face," the Bambino added by way of a footnote in his autobiography, *The Babe Ruth Story* (1948). "They sold like hotcakes and some of the critics swore they were." Supposedly one of the reasons he was reluctant to leave Beantown was because of those cigars. But his real taste was for larger cigars. "A super long 60-cent cigar protruded from his lips most of the time," said pitcher Waite Hoyt, a teammate who claimed that Ruth for all the world liked the Admiration Cigar trademark.

Appetite was the "Sultan of Swat"'s middle name! Hot dogs, beer and wine, women, food of any kind were in his bailiwick. "He had the constant need to placate his mouth with food, drink, a cigar, chewing gum, anything," writes his biographer Robert Creamer. He also smoked tobacco pipes, snorted snuff, and even puffed cigarettes, "Twice he went to Cuba to bring back Havanas," notes Baseball Hall of Fame researcher Bill Jenkinson. Photographs without number can be found showing the Bambino puffing a cigar, in his car, wearing a tuxedo, even hitting a baseball ball with a stogie clenched in his teeth. Whatever the cigars he smoked, different shapes and sizes, mattered little to a player who could swing a 54-ounce bat—easily the biggest in the major leagues—but he preferred the biggest cigars. Anecdotes have it that the Babe lit up a big beauty after every sexual congress.

A heavy smoker, Sigmund Freud continued to smoke four cigars a day, even with cancer of the jaw. He also had 36 grim operations to have bone removed and had to wear upper and lower prostheses inside his mouth. Leave it to Freud to have discerned the sexual element linked to ego gratification in the oral activity of smoking! He saw it as a sign—in males—of the "constitutional intensification of the erotogenic significance of the labial region" in the proto-narcissistic, autoerotic child. "'It's a pity I can't kiss myself,' [the aggressively sucking child] seems to be saying," wrote

Freud in his *Essays on the Theory of Sexuality* (1905). On that note, one may innocently ask, can tobacco can possibly be regarded as an aphrodisiac? In *Journal des Goncourts*—a diary written in collaboration by the brothers Edmond and Jules de Goncourt from 1850 up to Jules's death in 1870—they wrote, "There is an antagonism between tobacco and women. The taste for one diminishes the taste for the other. So true is this that passionate Lotharios usually give up smoking, because they feel . . . that tobacco diminishes the sexual appetite and powers." Such a paean to men in the throes of a passionate love of tobacco—or is it hyperbole? Many find the scent of cigars sweet and lovely. Jorge Luis Borges in his 1929 poem "The Mythical Founding of Buenos Aires" wrote: *"Una cigarreria sahumo como una rosa el desierto"* [A cigar store perfumed the desert like a rose]."

Thousands would disagree. Queen Victoria, for example, forbade cigars from being smoked in her presence. So did Pope Urban VIII, who, around 1610, issued a papal bull against Spanish priests smoking the profane things. Queen Elizabeth II could not bear the smell of cigars. "He smoked awful cigars," actress Elsa Lanchester declared of the German playwright Bertolt Brecht, who at one time collaborated with her husband Charles Laughton in the play *Galileo.* She went on to say, "Or perhaps the passing through Brecht made the smoke come out with the sourest, bitterest smell. . . . He hadn't many teeth and his mouth opened in a complete circle, so you'd see one or two little tombstones sticking out of this black hole. A very unpleasant sight." Back in his day, Brecht insisted on the need for what he called a "smokers' theatre," where an audience could puff away at cigars as if watching a boxing match, thus calmly developing a more detached and critical outlook. Mourners, friends, and fans still often leave a cigar on the grave of he playwright at the

Dorotheenstaed Cemetery in the Berlin district of Mitte in Germany.

To many, indeed, cigars were and remain noxious. They have been cited in support of complainants in many a divorce case. The querulous speaker in Rudyard Kipling's famous poem "The Betrothed" ("Open the old cigar-box, get me a Cuba stout / For things are running crossways, and Maggie and I are out") must choose between his fianceé and the "mild Manillas" of which she vigorously disapproves, lines that seem to support the dichotomy, divisive in all its rivalry, of which the Goncourts speak. Kipling's oft-quoted punch line in the same poem, "And a woman is only a woman, but a good Cigar is a Smoke," has offended many an earnest female, particularly those who have never bothered to read the poem, which was first published in book form in his *Departmental Ditties* (1886), where the quip is offered by the waggish, if whimsical young bachelor Kipling, pompously affecting to be worldly-wise. The poem of couplets takes as its epigraph the report of evidence in a breach of promise case, "You must choose between me and your cigar." In the poem a guileless unnamed narrator weighs up the difference between his fiancée Maggie and his habit of smoking cigars:

> For Maggie has written a letter to give me my choice between
> The wee little whimpering Love and the great god Nick o' Teen

Evaluating Maggie's very pretty looks, he projects what she will look like at 50 and the limitations of monogamy against "a harem of dusky beauties" and the relatively unknown woman against the pleasures of his tried and tested "Cuba stouts" and "mild

Havanas," 50 in a string, "perfect and ripe and brown," as well as the taste of a good cheroot and the sweet puffs of tobacco cloud. His conclusion is:

> A million surplus Maggies are willing to bear the yoke;
> And a woman is only a woman, but a good Cigar is a
> Smoke.
>
> Light me another Cuba—I hold to my first-sworn vows.
> If Maggie will have no rival, I'll have no Maggie for
> Spouse!

The boxes for cigars, nevertheless, were perfect receptacles—famous that way—small enough to be hidden away, large enough to house things. Years ago young ladies rubbed the boxes down and waxed or bound them with colorful cotton prints, using them to hold gloves, handkerchiefs, knick-knacks, personal treasures. Sometimes they were covered with red plush and placed on Victorian bureaus. A cigar box is perfectly stackable, solid as tile, neat, aromatic, and quaintly bejeweled. Over the years they have efficiently served both genders. Boys of my generation characteristically kept their marbles in them, or baseball cards, coins, chestnuts. Men kept old medals in them, knives, unsorted stamps, fishing flies and lures. Women famously used them as receptacles for thimbles, sewing needles, love letters. There are cigar boxes of three dimensions, sculpted boxes shaped like log cabins, beer steins, bottles, mailboxes, railroad cars, made of all sorts of unusual materials like inlaid wood, serpentine, pressed glass, and tin. Many people even collect them. Tony Hyman of Elmira, New York, for example, surely among leaders in the field, owned 4,000 of them, of all kinds.

A beautiful box of rich Havanas is truly a work of art. The

rich lettering, Araby-like evocations, bold allegories reveal the kind of imagination that somehow transcends mere labels (originally "stickers"). Each maker had his own symbol, decoration, exterior and interior colors. They were as exotic and beguiling as—in fact, even seemed to combine and magnificently display—travel ads, circus posters, movie announcements. There was enchantment even in the signatures, often in baroque lettering, of the proprietors of the plantation and the more modest stamps of the importer. On the boxes of Rafael González, one of the better brands, you can read the following profession of faith written in antiquated English script: "These cigars have been made from a secret blend of pure tobaccos from the Vuelta Abajo, selected by the Marques Rafael González, grandee of Spain."

A true cigar box is a small elegant mosque. The interior of the classic box was generally made of Cuban cedar, an aromatic material from a tropical American timber tree (*Cedrela odorata*), with both a protective and preservative quality that has never been matched. The Cuban revolution changed things. Much of the cedar that is used today, when cardboard has not replaced it as a saving alternative—as, alas, nowadays it too frequently has—comes from forests deep in Honduras. Cedar is conducive to aging. "A Havana conserves itself in its box," writes Zeno Davidoff in *The Connoisseur's Book of the Cigar.* "Some people have advised opening it and, after taking out one cigar, allowing the others to 'breathe more easily.' This is wrong. On the contrary, I completely trust the expert who wrote, 'The best Havanas ought to live together. Their maturation stays even and they compensate each other.'"

As a matter of fact, the smallest "humidor" is frequently the box itself. A cigar is often taken out and replaced with a glass tube, open at each end furnished with a tiny sponge that you dampen regularly. There are pedigrees. A box of Havanas has a noble history, and by reading the facts on the labels one can ascertain the worth of the beauties inside. The date of shipment can sometimes be found.

Before the revolution, the famous "green" band, the proud seal of the Cuban government, was the assurance of proper manufacture, brand, and authenticity:

Republica de Cuba
Sello de garantia nacional de procedencia
Para Tabacos
torcidas y picadoro

It is the only country in the world that can provide the matchless leaf for the cigar. It was as early as 1698 that Spain established a monopoly in Cuba for making cigars, and it was in Cuba that they beautifully flourished. Cuba with its anthem *"La Bayamesa"* and its national motto *"Patria o Muerte, Venceremos!"* (Homeland or Death, We Shall Overcome!); Cuba, the land of black tobacco, the flower of the Antilles, with its magic areas, Bahia, Candelaria, San Luis Padrona, Alquizar, Orojo, Atoquia, and the celebrated Vuelta Abajo [meaning "return down," as it is the southern slope of the San Juan valley] that sacred square of ochre-red earth.

"Spanish" cigars began being made for domestic consumption as early as 1810 but Cuban cigars quickly replaced them as a regular article of trade. The phonetically spelt word *"segar"* officially (Webster's *Dictionary*, 1859) became "cigar." Stogies, visible in the mouths of so many Civil War soldiers on both sides, became the smoke of the century. Stogies, as such, are longer than cigars, have no binders, usually have a strong molasses flavor, and can even be broken and chewed—President John F. Kennedy loved a stogie—

whereas cheroots are a thin long cigar, its tobacco bound in the same leaf, and not blended.

Cuba may provide the best filler tobacco, but the very best cigar wrappers, it should be noted—the thin, virtually non-aromatic leaves that encase the filler and internal binder leaf of a cigar—come from such unpredictably diverse places as Connecticut, Sumatra, and even the Cameroons. They come in boxes of 100 cigars, 50, 25, and 10. Twenty-four boxes—500 cigars—constitute a "royal supply." (Milton Berle always bought his cigars in such a volume, concerned that they might one day be unavailable.) Certain cigars benefit from individual boxes. A special tool with short flat blade, which exerts strong pressure without endangering the cigars inside, is recommended to open the box.

It was the Cubans who originated the art of decorating their cigar boxes, as well as creating cigar bands. When the box was ready to be embellished, in came the specialist to dress the container. He was called a *fileteador*, whose delicate craft, an art, of pasting up required the patience of a true, dedicated miniaturist, working as he did inside a tiny box. Cigar label art was a lithographer's delight. Boxes were gilded and embossed in all sorts of luxurious fashions with no end of original designs. Some were masterpieces of inlay. *Cromos*, or chromolithographs, were glued not only on the sides and on the lid, but also in the interior of the cigar box. The multicolored lithograph on the reverse of the cover, called the *vista*, or "view," was conventionally matched by the chromos on the sides of the box. All the chromos were printed on high relief, except the *vista*, otherwise the embossed design would be imprinted on the upper tier of cigars lying in the box when the lid is finally nailed shut.

"The chromo, or lithograph, is one of the two art forms native to Cuba—the other is Afro-Cuban music," writes G. Cabrera

Infante in his informative book *Holy Smoke*, a history of the cigar. It is a visual art that originated in the 19th century, when many European artists went visiting that exotic little island. Together with local craftsmen, they made possible a quiet revolution in the art of commercial lithography. It was often an eclectic and uneasy union between classical forms and modern taste, but its purpose was to confer dignity, authority, and visibility to whatever was being purveyed, as the Golden Age would put it. Cabrera Infante quotes Samuel Feijoo, a peasant turned poet, speaking of chromos: "Nobody knows that the cigar has created a style in lithography, a true new art expression." Chromolithography combined fine-art imagery with new industrial products.

The artist draws his subject on the surface of the limestone—or specially prepared zinc or aluminum plates—with greasy crayons, pens, or pencils. When the drawing is completed, a solution of gum arabic and dilute nitric acid is washed across the stone, which fixes the grease against spreading during the painting. The entire surface of the stone is then washed with water, and the stone then rolled with printing ink. Since grease and water quite naturally repel each other, the ink adheres to only the greasy image without sticking to the clean portions of the stone. After the inking, print paper is thereupon laid across the stone, and together they are sent through a special printing press. When the paper is removed from the stone, a mirror image has been transferred from the stone to the paper. It might be noted that John James Audubon, John LaFarge, Winslow Homer, and William Morris Hunt all drew on stone, but their forays into this medium rarely matured into real efforts.

Some cigar-box designs were actually woodcuts, hand-carved directly, each curve, line variation, and bit of shading, into type-high boxwood by skilled craftsman of the day. A less refined medium of reproduction, top brand dies made of heavy brass, were also used to emboss the tops of the old cedar cigar boxes. In any case, much of the work constituted an outstanding contribution to early American art, including cigar bands, a popular collectible—supposedly invented by Gustave Bock, a Dutchman who was one of the first Europeans to cultivate a tobacco plantation in Cuba—as well as cigar-store Indians (in 17th-century London originally known as "Black Boys"), which, decorating tobacco shops in America and dating from about the 1840s in this country, took their name from their headdresses of tobacco leaves that strangely resembled the feathers of full-fledged chieftains who stood sentinel in many a smoke or cigar or cigarette shop in olden days.

America's culture was dramatically changed by chromolithography. It was a new method of producing and disseminating art, displaying accurate registration and faithful color. Printed by the millions in up to 20 colors, these lithographs—illustrating broadsides, trading cards, posters, wall-hangings, stamp albums, billheads (sometimes called "biliheads"), wine labels, menus, promotional giveaways, lyceum tickets, game bird albums, bonds, and letterheads, etc.—were extremely popular. They made their way into every household, were bought by every class of person, and portrayed every subject imaginable, from soup labels to hair oil, still lifes to landscapes. In short, lithography became a giant industry. A notable part of that industry were fruit crate labels—once a popular item and now a collectible—cigarette folios (the old W. Duke and Sons of Durham, North Carolina, cornered this market), and of course cigar-box stickers. Always brand names had to be printed in letters and styles that were big, brassy, rich and distinctive enough to catch a customer's attention.

It was soon realized that decorative cigar bands and box

labels could be used to great advantage. Artists were commissioned by competing manufacturers to come up with florid, imaginative, eye-catching designs of lush tobacco plants, romantic moonlight scenes, dramatic mandalas, famous men, and beautiful women. (Printers' names can be found in tiny type on the miniscule margins of the lid labels.) Some of the labels of the 1800s, before embossing became common, used as many as 22 different stones, and as many different printing inks to achieve their colorful effects. It was, much of it, turn-of-the-century Art Nouveau, tricked out with imaginary Oriental touches and ornamental curlicues.

Perhaps none of the work was as delicately fine or as subtly colored as the fashion plates of those beautifully graphic *Peterson's Magazine*s or *Godey's Lady's Book*s, but they were still remarkable. A magnificent label became a lasting trademark. When a cigar-box label was created, it was reproduced for a length of 40 or more years, therefore good basic art work was put into them. Bronzing powder, fancy silk or satin-finished papers, and elaborate embossing gussied up many examples. An 1808 *New York Sun* article remarked that the "label is often better than the cigar."

There was always in cigar-label art a strong mid-Victorian love of hodgepodge in evidence, much of it reflecting the furniture and fretwork of the day. Butterflies, leaves, and ribbons were popular, as were leafy decorations, eagles, bold men wearing fezes, camels and pyramids. Gold crowns always had snob appeal. The Victorians discovered pulchritude as an aid to advertising, and many of the florid labels of the period emphasized the generous, well-rounded charms and Lillian Russell-like amplitude in women that were so appealing to the man's world of the day. Lovely figures, with shapely calves, appeared in theatrical costume tights. Slightly out-of-date, Carmen-looking women and sexy senoritas with combs in their hair evoked passion. They all looked dark and smoldering, like the international European queens La Belle Otero, Liane de Pougy, and various "grand horizontals" from La Belle Epoque. In his scandalous novel *La Femme et le Pantin*, Pierre Louÿs portrayed that sort of archetype in his main character, one Conchita Perez, who has much in common with Prosper Mérimée's wild and seductive Carmen, who was much lewder in the novel than in Georges Bizet's opera, and who incidentally also works in a famous *fabrica*, one of the many cigar factories of Seville. Correct extracurricular pastimes of men also made for popular themes, and of course such masculine trappings as fly-rods, mallets, guns, and gumboots were exploited. Fancy lettering added style, as did letters drawn with respectable solidity. Label sizes varied. Four-inch squares are rarer than the six-inch rectangles which were also used on box lids.

Artists couldn't go on forever repeatedly turning out pictures of cigars, leaves, Havana harbor with the inevitable Morro Castle in the distance. Imagination was needed. Faraway places and strange-sounding names were adopted, such as "La Pluma," "Armas Reales," "La Española," etc. "Almeda" was named after the wife or daughter of a factory owner. The name "Croquet" reflected a popular sport at the time. "Red Line" and "The Traveler Cigar" took advantage of the great popularity of the railroad. "Iroquois" was a famous racehorse at the time, "Great Eagle" appealed to patriotism. Other names were Hambone, Yellow Cab, and Call Again. A man named Fonseca, a friend of the famous Federico García Lorca, put the noted playwright's picture above his own name on every box he made, Fonseca y Cia. Many names used were found with a short reach. The ontological origins of "Hav-A-Tampa" do not go too deep, let's face it. And "El Producto" is a sort of Marxbrothersesque name that was coined by Jacob A. Voice, born in Romania in 1884, a founder of the Consolidated Lithography Corp. of Brooklyn, the largest United States maker of cigar bands.

Then there were La Palina cigars, a word fabricated from the name Paley. It was simply that Sam Paley, father of the late William S. Paley of Philadelphia, president of the Columbia Broadcasting Co. and who made his entire fortune in cigars, originated that particular brand. (It was the formidable advertising on CBS, notably, that doubled his business.) A picture of Mrs. Sam Paley—Goldie (née Drell), the family was Jewish—in Spanish costume adorned the inside of all La Palina boxes. A Ukrainian Jewish immigrant in a Spanish costume was as imaginative as anything in pushing cigars.

The fact is, there was a lot of fluff in that business.

Those smooth, flat, rectangular cigar box tops were ideal not only for the display of attractive trademark images but especially made for celebrity faces. Of all types of label images, portraits of beautiful women like the entertainer Lotta Crabtree during the Gold Rush days, in the 1880s the highest paid actress in America, were the most popular choice to adorn cigar boxes. Idealized depictions of women, romantic scenes, floral decoration, even cute street urchins, and gold accents all flourished on cigar box labels.

Virtually every great statesman was enrolled in the cigar lexicon, as can be seen in popular brands named after Henry Clay, Daniel Webster, Emperor Wilhelm II, Honest Abe, etc. Civil War heroes like General T.S. Grant and William Tecumseh Sherman graced many a box, as did even the Mexican Army General Ignacio Zaragoza, the wealthy philanthropist James Lick, and the Haverly Club baseball team, California League champions in the year 1887! The most popular name, huge back in 1898 and still going strong, is probably Commodore George Dewey, hero of the Battle of Manila Bay. Celebrated names like William Blackstone and John Ruskin merely illustrated the value of a good name, even though most smokers had no idea who the originals were. (One particular dealer was overheard telling customers that John Ruskin was the fellow who "invented" evolution.) There was a lot of fluff, indeed. "Robert Burns" was a name chosen not because the poet smoked, but because the word "burns" seemed to go well with a cigar. Walt Whitman appeared on a cigar-box label although the poet did not smoke, and as the son of an alcoholic father, he argued on behalf of Temperance causes. Presumably, Whitman ate apple sauce—indeed, Poet Brand applesauce showed his face on the label—but marketers never asked his permission to sell stuff when he was alive, nor was Whitman ever compensated for the use of his good name.

Other notables who prominently graced the cover of cigar boxes were Napoleon, King Edward VII, Pittsburgh Pirates baseball star Honus Wagner, inventor Thomas Alva Edison, and actresses Lotta Crabtree and Ethel Barrymore. Patriotism—highlighting the Spanish-American War, especially—was a dominant cigar box theme from about 1870 to 1920, which was more or less the cigar's heyday, when something like over 1.5 million cigar brands existed. The Civil War mattered greatly in sales and cigar popularity, and President Lincoln, taking advantage of the potential revenue, was astute in levying taxes and duties on cigar imports and purchases. (It was these same strict cigar tariffs, the high import duties that the United States imposed on cigars and tobacco, that drove wily entrepreneur Lazarus Morgenthau [1815–1897], father of the famous banking family, and his cigar-making business into bankruptcy. He and his brother Max made various attempts to find other markets and businesses but found no success.) Dominant themes of the day included American Indians depicted as noble savages, the early days of the automobile, and the rising opulence of the Industrial Age.

One popular cigar-box label showed the portrait of a serious smoker, namely Mark Twain, with the flattering legend "Known to everyone, Liked by all." He is flanked by two boys, one carrying a bucket, the other fishing. Ten guesses as to who those two represented? Twain, who suffered from ill health in his final years and spent much of his time in bed, smoked as many as 40 cigars a day for most of his life—although as a sop to temperance the unrepentant smoker, who is said to have smoked the cheapest cigars he could buy, often declared, "I've made it a rule to never enjoy more than one cigar at a time." He proudly called cigars "the best of all inspirations," despite the fact that, apparently, puffing all day, he smoked ferocious ones, "long, black, deadly-looking cigars," as someone put it. "As he walked of course he talked, and of course he smoked," his friend William Dean Howells wrote in his biography *My Mark Twain*. "Whenever he had been a few days with us, the whole house had to be aired, for he smoked all over it from breakfast to bedtime. He always went to bed with a cigar in his mouth, and sometimes, mindful of my fire insurance, I went up and took it away, still burning, after he had fallen asleep. I do not know how much a man may smoke and live, but apparently he smoked as much as a man could, for he smoked incessantly."

Spanish words like *La Flor de Muria, La Carolina, Aquila de Oro, La Intimidad, Flor del Fumar, La Rosa de Santiago, La Luna de Cuba* were used to suggest Havana leaf. The twin attributes of royalty and Spanishness were combined in a brand name which for years led the 10-cent field, *El Roi-Tan*, although the Roi derived from a man named Roy and the Tan from his partner named Tannenbaum! The spoof brands, "El Ropo," "Creemo," etc., common in the comic books and cartoons of my youth, were no less authentic!

Have I mention there was a lot of fluff in this business?

Every tobacco plant on the face of the globe, whether it grows in the United States, Syria, Sumatra, Russia, Turkestan, Borneo, the Philippines, or China—it was the Portuguese, having reached its shores in the 15th and 16th centuries, who introduced tobacco there—is a direct descendant of the tobacco plants which Columbus found in 1492. On November 6th of that memorable year, according to his journals, two members of his crew saw the natives of San Salvador inhaling smoke from what the awed sailors termed "firebrands." They were smoking rolls of tobacco wrapped in a leaf of the plant itself or in a strip of maize—the red man's cigar. It was the first type of smoking ever to be observed by white men.

Cigar smoking began in America in the 1830s. During the antebellum days, women smoked pipes or chewed, just as men did. Mrs. Andrew Jackson and Mrs. Zachary Taylor both smoked pipes while they inhabited the White House without being thought bumpkins. Singer Nellie Melba, who had a Havana before every performance—she loved to blow smoke rings—claimed she actually got her vocal strength *from* smoking. She was sent boxes of choice *torcidos* everywhere she went by the owner of La Africana, a cigar factory in Havana where, incidentally, the first woman—a white woman—rolled a cigar in 1878. (In Cuba in the days of the Spanish Empire, it was fashionable for rich and titled women to smoke cigars. It was women, in fact, who started the custom of wrapping narrow paper bands around the cigars to protect their delicate fingers from nicotine stains.) Eventually, however, genteel tradition prevailed, establishing the romantic (and frail) notion of womankind, and women's pipes went out of fashion. There were still nevertheless holdouts as to cigars. Georges Sand enjoyed smoking cigars as she wrote, as did both Virginia Woolf and poet Amy Lowell, and in 1915 the latter bought 10,000 of her favorite Manila stogies in a fit of acquisition.

Marlene Dietrich, another famous female cigar smoker, is known to have favored full-bodied Cuban cigars. The singer/actress who appears in the Orson Welles film *A Touch of Evil*, smoking a cigar, is quoted as once saying, "Cigarette is a neurosis, cigar is a friend."

George Sand, whom poet Elizabeth Barrett Browning affectionately addressed as "thou large-brained woman and large-hearted man," smoked hookahs, puffed cigarettes, but mostly preferred to smoke—and manfully chew—cigars. Classified by French society as a cigar-toting sexual outlaw, she said, "The cigar numbs sorrow and fills the solitary hours with a million gracious images." There is a George Sand Society in Santa Monica, where gatherings of women cigar smokers outnumber men three to one.

All the while, there were differences in taste and terminology in American smoking. While John Quincy Adams was president (1825–29), Connecticut seed leaf, rich, was known as—and called—"American tobacco," and cigars made from it were broadly known as "American cigars." Wrappers of cinnamon red color were preferred in the United States, the choicest being a white-speckled leaf known as "cinnamon blotch." Unlike the Spanish cigar, this New England product was packed in chestnut containers. Meanwhile, there was growing hostility to the slow increase of cigarette smoking, and cigar manufacturers engaged in "national advertising" of a covert sort, whispering that these new cigarettes contained opium, were rolled with tobacco from discarded butts, and their thin paper made by Chinese lepers. Soon, cigars replaced chewing tobacco. It was a phenomenon of industrialization, cutting down, at least to some degree, on all the national "chewing, spitting, and drooling" that so disgusted Charles Dickens, among many others, on his two visits to this country.

Speaking of Chinese, in 1875 Samuel Gompers, future

founder of the American Federation of Labor, got a consortium of California cigar manufacturers to apply to their product the first specific union label—one, incredibly, that proclaimed the cigar to have been untouched by Chinese labor. By the way, the Chinese Exclusion Act, which went into effect in 1896 and was not lifted until it became strategically advisable for the United States to do so in 1942, was one good reason why there were not more Chinese running cigar stores in this country, for up to 1898 there were proportionately quite a few.

It took 50 years for the cigar to develop momentum as an accepted form, peaking in the 1870s, when the smoking-car became a fixture on the nation's railroads where even women, "enjoying her rights," had no qualms about lighting up a Havana (a name that became more widely known than the word *Cuba*). It was an addiction. In 1880, New York City alone had 14,500 people working in its cigar factories. Oscar Hammerstein (1847–1919), the father of the famous musical librettist, arrived in New York City in 1863, for example, and, like countless other Jews, first found work in a cigar factory. His son, in fact, same name, before his successful ventures in show business, made millions of dollars from a cigar-cutting machine and from a trade journal devoted to the tobacco industry. And in the late Eighties so many different brands were issued, according to authority A. D. Faber, that in a town of 10,000 people anywhere from 150 to 250 brands could be found. Cuban firms began moving to Tampa, and entrepreneurs were shunted between Cuba and Florida.

Before long, cigars became the gay batons of a civilization on the march toward comfort, style, and wealth—the veritable symbol, in fact, of private affluence, success, and worth. J. Pierpont Morgan had his mighty cigars, eight-inch Kohinoors that cost $1.25

apiece, all specially rolled for his own use. A nonstop smoker, Rudyard Kipling had "R.K." embossed on his box labels (and bands), as did many private clubs, restaurants, and cigar stores. The famously wealthy Rothschild banking family would order from Cuban warehouses 40,000 *Henri Clay Sobranos* at a time, carefully packaged in huge inlaid cedar cabinets. The cigars even had a private shape, *Excepcionales de Rothschilds.* Such high-class restaurants as Rector's and Delmonico's in New York City kept for their clientele giant humidors that held hundreds of boxes of private brand cigars.

An irony as to the kingliness of cigars should be pointed out. Cigar rollers actually formed the militant avant garde of the worker's movement in many countries for years, especially in Cuba. In Germany, for example, they organized the first and most radical union. Thus it is a curious twist in its symbolic history that the cigar should later come to be the status symbol for capitalist entrepreneurs—a paradoxical inversion of its original meaning. "In the Germany of 1815 to 1848, cigars came to serve as a sort of revolutionary emblem," observes Wolfgang Schivelbusch in *Tastes of Paradise.*" Karl Marx smoked them, so did so did the communist playwright Bertolt Brecht, as we have seen, both of whom would have cringed to see the cigar the icon of lordly capitalism.

Experts insist that the Montecristo and H. Upmann brands, both made in Havana, are the very best. Preferences naturally vary. The 19th-century French writer Stendhal, who smoked Italian cigars (Toscani's), and who wrote that those who have known the feeling of happiness even only four or five times in their lives should be grateful, listed smoking cigars among his most pleasurable activities. "On a cold morning in winter," he wrote, "a Tosca cigar fortifies the soul." President John F. Kennedy smoked Upmann's. Aristotle Onassis smoked only Dunhills. Winston Churchill, who owned a gold three-cigar case, smoked select Romeo y Julietas. In Mikhail Bulgakov's novel *The Master and Margarita*, a cat smokes cigars. The prankster Krazy Kat in that wonderful old comic strip of George Herriman, a black man, smoked an "eligint Hawanna cigar." We have mentioned Fidel Castro. He always favored smoking the aromatic Cohiba, a brand that, according to legend and common report, must be hand-rolled against the thighs of beautiful girls no older than 14.

The most famous cigar of them all was probably La Corona, the "Cigar of Kings." It was rolled in Havana, of course—the act of hand-rolling used to be the *law* in Cuba—within the walls of the old Aldama Palace from 1882 to 1932, and even in 1932 cost 60 cents each (around $30 today)! Various strikes, the high cost of labor— the Federation Nacional de Torcedores was an extremely powerful union—and the production costs always kept the price high and the manufacture unpredictable. Then on June 1, 1932, George W. Hill, an American entrepreneur, brought the entire rolling operation up to Trenton, New Jersey. The new name of the company, the main factory of which was built on the lines of Cuban architecture, was International Cigar Brands. Hill even "imported" Don Emilio Rivas, the supervising director of Havana's La Corona, whose personal blending of the Corona made it in the early 1900s the world's finest leading cigar, signaled by England's King Edward VII who chose it for his personal smoke. Now American woman (who didn't smoke up the profits) supplanted male Cuban rollers (who smoked an average each of 10 a day) and were soon making a cheaper, better quality cigar, giving Hill the opportunity before long to sell his La Corona Coronas at three for a dollar. Soon he was turning out Lonsdales, Panatellas, the lot.

It was the old story, of course, half good business, half

exploitation, a matter, creating tension, that would later be exacerbated by the political standoff between the United States and Cuba. It has long been a shameless and unscrupulous convention for manufacturers in selling cigars falsely to appropriate the name Havana, using the word as a come-on in every possible way. Traditionally, manufacturers have used home-grown filler tobaccos combined with Cuban leaf, for the Havana wrapper. Fidel Castro, after rising to power in the late Fifties, in spite of tradition and authority decided that the epoch of great cigars was over and that the baroque decor of the packaging (gold and purple) was an anomaly. Such rare cigars would no longer be manufactured. A single popular cigar, the "Siboney," in three or four varieties at the maximum, would eventually replace them.

Americans have always loved cigars, and we'll probably go on smoking them. We as a nation tend to like the lighter, or *claro*, tobaccos. (Davidoff* dismissed the bland, colorless cigars that we prefer as "candy.") We are close to the island of Cuba, for one thing,

---

*After the Second World War, Zino Davidoff decided to acquire a license to produce his own series of cigars. As he had discerning international customers, he named the various formats of this "Château" cigar series after famous Bordeaux vineyard estates. The first in the series was the "Château Latour" in 1946. In 1967, Zino Davidoff was approached by Cubatabaco, Cuba's state tobacco monopoly, about creating a line of cigars carrying the "Davidoff" name. The cigars were rolled in the newly established El Laguito factory in Havana, which had been established to roll Cuban President Fidel Castro's own personal cigars, named Cohíba. In 1968, the first cigars carrying the name "Davidoff" were released. The first formats were the No. 1, the No. 2 and the Ambassadrice. In 1970, Oettinger AG, located in Basel, Switzerland, acquired the rights to the Davidoff trademark.

and probably inhale its heady aromas. (José Marti, the liberator of Cuba, exiled in Florida, used to send messages rolled in cigars to his compatriots.) Some have gone so far as to say we fought for Cuba in order to maintain our supply of cigars. Hollywood director Darryl Zanuck, under the dictator Fulgencio Battista, literally owned his own Cuban plantation. So did pianist Artur Rubenstein, who distributed cigars to his friends banded with his own effigy. The cigars remain, but the boxes they came in, at least in the way of the great styles by which they once were known, have long gone.

It is a lost art, those strong, often eccentric, but fascinating procedures. When, around the turn of the 20th century, printers started using photolithography, which broke the traditional images into tiny dots of colors, not unlike dot matrix printers today, the end was sadly near and it put the kibosh on cigar box art. With the advent of the camera and the half-tone screen came a sad degeneracy of the art.

The camera could not lie. Gone were the glamorous multi-colored visions dreams once created. Today's four-color process cannot match the superb efforts created by those old lithographers on stone. What examples we have of lithographic and embossed wood printing are worthy of preservation in our museums, libraries, local historical societies.

Boys now keep their stuff in wide, narrow little plastic tubs, which, with convenient snap-on lids, can be had at Home Deport, cheap.

Blind Painters:
The Mystery of Vision-Impaired Artists

A blind painter is a concept almost too paradoxical to conceive. It is virtually an oxymoron. An artist does not choose what he is going to see, however, or really the way he sees it. His unique vision is given to him in perhaps the same mysterious way that his particular painting style and techniques evolve. Who can say how or why? Approaches to what is seen do not always jibe with what is conceived. A *veduta* (Italian for "view") is a painting or drawing of a place, usually a town. A *veduta ideate* is an imaginary view. A *capriccio* in painting or any other work of art represents a fantasy or mixture of the real and imaginary, a drawing often architecturally accurate but fantastic in its many juxtapositions. There are all sorts of ways of seeing, of course.

Seeing well is not necessarily seeing exactly, nor does sight, perhaps, always sufficiently provide what an artist needs in order to say. The accuracy of delineation varies greatly, if accuracy indeed matters at all. What after all is "accurate," if reality is impressionistic? All painting depends on the visual, however, no matter its source or the painter's intention. How strange it seems then even to speak of a painter as sightless.

"Reality is a very subjective affair," novelist Vladimir Nabokov has written. "I can only define it as a kind of gradual accumulation of information; and as specialization." One of course recalls the author's indelible remark in the Afterword to *Lolita* that "reality" is "one of the few words which mean nothing without quotes."

Being unable to see is not a fully inhibitory factor. Some even feel that blindness may provide the basis of a specific and unique creativeness. In it there is not only a distinct difference from visual art expression but also a specific approach to creative art, an approach resulting from the need of building up whole images from partial perceptions. "Lord, grant me weak eyes for things that are of no account and strong eyes for all thy truth," wrote Søren Kierkegaard, addressing the relativity of it. What the blind individual cannot always, or seldom, achieve in life, he may do in art: out of the many partial impressions, he builds up a "whole" and arrives thus at a synthesis of his image.

As the German perceptual psychologist Rudolf Arnheim has declared, in any case, "The least touchable object in the world is the eye." And if the eye makes up what the light leaves out, as has been observed, cannot the mind make up what remains when both are gone? "All perceiving is also thinking," Arnheim has pointed out, "all reasoning is also intuition, all observation is also invention."

No, blindness is an affliction that has rarely put an end to creativity. The epic poet Homer, along with the legendary (and fictional) Ossian, the greatest of the old Celtic bards, were blind. So were James Joyce, James Thurber, Jorge Luis Borges, all went on to prove that their vision exceeded their eyesight. In 1943, at 70, W. C. Handy, composer of the song "St. Louis Blues," referred to by some as the "jazzman's *Hamlet*," having fallen from a subway platform, suffered a fractured skull that resulted in total blindness, but he continued to compose music until he died in 1958. Nor is there any accounting for its various forms of affliction. Victorian poet Robert Browning, curiously, was nearsighted in one eye, farsighted in the other. Gabriele D'Annunzio was blind in one eye. So were General Grigory Potemkin, President Woodrow Wilson, and all-time great jazz pianist Art Tatum. English novelist Aldous Huxley suffered from keratitis, inflammation of the cornea. Astronomer Galileo Galilei went blind when he was imprisoned. Guglielmo Marconi was half-blind, probably from hemianopsia, blindness of one-half the field of vision in one or both eyes. And the English poet and story teller Rudyard Kipling had only partial sight. As early as 1825, Ralph Waldo Emerson, who later wrote, "The only thing worse than being blind, is having sight with no vision," began to lose his sight, a vision impairment that made reading and long study for him very difficult.

Marcel Proust's eyesight badly deteriorated, and although he never found time to visit the famous oculist of whom he spoke so frequently, he worked on his vast manuscript virtually until the day of his death. Jean-Paul Sartre suffered from exophoria, where the eye turns oddly outward. (With exophoria, the eye turns inward.) American historian William H. Prescott had a severe eye injury through an accident in his junior year of college, causing nearly total blindness, and he abandoned the study of law. Booth Tarkington had a series of eye operations from 1928 to 1932, which partially restored his failing sight, and he continued to write during summers in Kennebunkport, Maine. Novelist Anthony Burgess, who was myopic, happened also to be color blind, in his words, "totally without a chromatic glossary." Charles Meryon, the 19th-century artist famous for his etchings of Paris, was color blind. So was "Mr. Rogers"—TV's Fred Rogers—Pablo Picasso, Microsoft's Bill Gates,

CBS anchorman Walter Cronkite, and the Canadian rock musician Neil Young. Painter Claude Monet, who suffered from cataracts, eventually lost his ability to tell colors apart.

Emily Dickinson had trouble with her eyes but was undaunted. The indisposition from which she suffered in her mid-thirties was probably iritis, an inflammation of of the fine muscles of the eye. The onset of it took place during one of her most prolific periods in writing her poems. We read in notes from the Emily Dickinson Museum regarding her health,

> "Her doctor's orders for confinement in dim light, no reading, and writing only with a pencil explain why she called her first Cambridge siege "eight months of Siberia" (Sewall, *Lyman Letters*, p. 76). Yet she managed to write letters (in pencil) and confessed that despite the deprivations, 'I work in my prison, and make Guests [poems] for myself' (L290) . . . By her own account [her eye problems] began in the fall of 1863 (L290), and in February 1864 she consulted the eminent Boston ophthalmologist Dr. Henry Willard Williams. Then for eight months, from April to December 1864, she lived with her Norcross cousins in Cambridgeport to be near that physician for treatment. The next year, with her eyes still painful and sensitive to light, she repeated the treatment from April to October 1865. By then she was apparently cured."

St. Paul had poor eyesight. (I have always wondered if he recognized the high priest Ananias when he insulted him [Acts 23:5]?) And of course Jacob and Isaac went blind. Isaac is the only patriarch who was weak in his old age and could not tell lamb's wool from human hair, goat meat from venison, one son from another. Cicero's master Diodatus taught geometry after he had lost his sight. Sir John Soane, owing to blindness in 1833, retired from architectural practice at 70 but vigorously set up his home as a permanent museum for his collection of paintings and drawings. Golfer Tommy Armour, a superb athlete, had no sight in one eye. The probable cause of "Wild Bill" Hickok's failing eyesight was most likely a side effect of *Spirocheta pallida*, gonorrheal ophthalmia.

As to music, Johann Sebastian Bach, when old, could not see at all. Like his fellow composer George Frederick Handel, who was forced by blindness to stop composing music at the age of 67, his declining vision for the last decade of his life was probably caused by failed cataract surgery. Bach, who possibly had a detached retina, died a few months after his surgery. After 1918, the English composer Frederick Delius began to suffer the effects of syphilis contracted during his earlier years in Paris in the 1890s. He took treatment at various clinics across Europe, but in the early Twenties he was walking with two sticks. By 1928 he was paralyzed and blind. He died at Grez in France at age 72 on June 9, 1934. The American soprano Minnie Hauk (1851–1929), who made her debut in *La Somnambula* and was later world-renown for her fiery interpretation of the flamboyant heroine of *Carmen*, died poverty-stricken and blind. Composer Hoagy Carmichael also suffered from cataracts.

As to music, Louis Braille himself was an organist. The French educator and inventor of a reading and writing system for visually impaired people, at the age of three wounded his right eye with a cobbler's tool while playing in his father's workshop. No medical knowledge could save his eyesight at that time. Louis's left eye became inflamed, apparently due to subsequent sympathetic ophthalmia, and he eventually lost the sight in that eye. Braille's driving interest in punctiform writing—originally devised and developed by Charles Barbier and called *écriture nocturnelle*—grew out of the possibility he immediately saw in it for the formation of a musical notation for the blind. The tactile code was given this name "night writing" at a time when it was valued as a cryptic means for soldiers to communicate silently at night without a light source.

Again, blindness in many strange ways seems almost less a handicap than an aid, although that is obviously a fanciful hyperbole. But think of singers Ray Charles, Stevie Wonder, José Feliciano, and country singer Ronnie Lee Milsap who, blind from birth from a congenital disorder, was abandoned by his mother as an infant and raised in poverty by his grandparents in the Smoky Mountains until he was sent to the Governor Morehead School for the Blind in Raleigh, North Carolina, at the age of five.

There was pianist George Shearing, and consider the many blind blues singers from the South, an almost limitless but astonishing onrush of talent, singers, and musicians like "Blind Willie" McTell, "Blind Willie" Johnson, Sonny Terry, guitarist Blind Boy Fuller, "Blind Blake"—Arthur Blake from Jacksonville, Florida, Reverend Gary Davis, blind as an infant, the gospel singer who was also proficient on the banjo, guitar and harmonica, McKinley Morganfield, aka "Muddy Waters," "Blind Lemon" Jefferson, and the amazing Sonny Terry—Sanders Terrell of Greensboro, Georgia— who was brought up on a farm where he lost the sight of each eye in separate accidents before he was 16 and, unable to do regular work, learned to play the harmonica. Daunting as were these serious and completely life-changing afflictions, coping with them in these cases made art.

Andrea Bocelli, the operatic Italian tenor and multi-instru-mentalist, although born visually impaired with congenital glaucoma—at the age of 12, he became completely blind, following a brain hemorrhage resulting from a football accident—went on to achieve a knighthood, an Order of Merit of the Italian Republic.

At the same time, no one could possibly deny the terrible burdens associated with the condition of blindness, its drawbacks, its requirements. The architects of the great Campanile in Venice were blinded by the doges, lest they try to build a duplicate tower for anyone else. The artificial beggars and unfortunates of the painter Pieter Bruegel the Elder, depending on the charity to live—as can be seen in his unsettling canvas *The Blind Leading the Blind* (1568)—had to grope to move, never mind to live. Masseurs in ancient Japan were required by law to be totally blind in order to work. I was more petrified of the character "Blind Pew" in Robert Louis Stevenson's *Treasure Island* than any of the other characters, made even more terrifying by N. C. Wyeth's powerful illustration in my edition, and, when as a child I had to wear glasses at one point, not strong ones, 0.75 diopter, left and right—I was nearsighted, blinking, kind of cute—I feared in my heart going blind.

According to British eye-surgeon Patrick Trevor-Roper in *The World Through Blunted Sight: Inquiry into the Influence of Defective Vision on Art and Character* (1971), the various vision problems of painters and poets, a sort of myopic personality, is often shared by artists, sculptors, and creative people who have "an interior life different from others," a distinct personality, as Trevor-Roper goes on to say, simply because only the close-up world is visually available to them. It is a way of seeing unique to them alone, making such creative artists reflective and introverted in singular and even uncanny ways that those who are sighted never quite master. Their work reflects the kind of imagery that "can be viewed at very close range."

Of all professions, artists would seem the least likely candidates for eye trouble. But as Bertrand Russell philosophically put it, "It seems to be the fate of idealists to obtain what they have struggled for in a form which destroys their ideals."

John Constable was partially red-green color blind and needed to use additional red in building up his green watches. He saw greens as pale or fawn-colored, because they lacked the extra dose of red that he himself would have inserted. Painter Henry Fuseli once remarked, "I like the landscapes of Constable, but he always makes me call for my greatcoat and umbrella." Paul Henry was also partially color blind. J. M. W. Turner's color style, incidentally, has been widely attributed to his having a reddish cataract. And the eccentric Francis Bacon, who suffered from horizontal astigmatism, once described how, before the war, he used to paint without glasses, but when he subsequently examined his various paintings with his corrective lenses, the vertical backstrokes "seemed too coarse and broken up."

The central European artists Austrian Oskar Kokoschka, German Impressionist Max Slevogt—who, according to one critic "could not see details at all"—and Czech painter Emil Orlik are all recorded as having poor vision. The lack of perspective and depth of the Polish painter Jan Matejko can quite reasonably be attributed to myopia. (His spectacles, with 4 D. and -6 D. lenses, have been preserved in the Krakow Museum.) Others to whom myopia has been imputed include Raoul Dufy, André Derain, Georges Braque, Maurice de Vlaminck, and André Dunoyer de Segonzac. A similar kind of blindness may be ascribed to the Swiss-Italian sculptor and painter Alberto Giacometti, whose reduced monochrome paintings and grim, extraordinarily attenuated, narrow, thin-as-nails sculptured figures—described as "dead men walking" by art critic Laurie

Wilson—may be seen less as a new way of viewing the world or a comment on our existentially barren society than visible proof he had bloodshot eyes and badly needed glasses, both of which were the case.

Resolve will be shown to have been a crucial factor among artists in overcoming this problem of impaired sight. "I will seize fate by the throat; it shall certainly never wholly overcome me," proclaimed composer Ludwig van Beethoven, gone deaf. After a cataract operation, Edward Ardizzone, the English painter, printmaker, and illustrator of children's books, said, "Through my operated eye I see a much colder, brighter world in which reds become pink, greens greener, and blue more intense."

Sculptor and painter Michelangelo Buonarroti became nearly blind in old age, a condition wrongly attributed to "strain" from his exacting work, one of the more common clichés. His was an infirmity that was probably the result of incipient presbyopia, an indisposition due to old age when small details become muddled, as when, say, one fails to see the more minute lines on a canvas, which become vague and ill-defined. The 16th-century musician Miguel de Fuenllana was blind, yet he became a well-known artist in the court of Philip II of Spain. It was supposedly because of failing sight that Leonardo da Vinci's later drawings became much less detailed, when he had to relinquish his fine pencil in favor of red and blue crayon, which he was able to see more readily.

Gian Paolo Lomazzo, a Milanese painter trained under Gaudenzio Ferrari, had his career cut short in 1571 at the age of 33 by blindness, although he would live another 30 years. He devoted his later years to writing mainly on the theory of art, and his treatise *Trattato della Pittura*, published in Milan in 1584, a treatise on artists and art theories written when he was stone blind and focusing on Mannerism, is still recognized as one of the most important works of the period, one of the Renaissance's most scholarly and ambitious undertakings, especially for his discussion on Leonardo.

What of Mannerism? May many instances of it, in its idiosyncrasies, be the result of skewed vision? Is it possible that, initially, in its creative distortions and torquated bodies and elongations, it was the result of a *mistake* of seeing? Can artistic vision ever be called a *mistake* of seeing? Few would be surprised to learn that El Greco, with his lengthened figures and those vertical elongations in his canvases, was astigmatic. Notice how in his painting of St. Peter and St. Paul, the figures have a tendency to lean or "glide." And the elongations and distortions are there, as well, along with acid, brilliant, unconventional colors in, say, *Christ Driving the Money Changers from the Temple* (1568). Trevor-Roper points out that the mechanism that causes the elongated eye (short-sightedness) affects perception of color as well—reds will appear more starkly defined, for example. Francesco Parmigianino had a similar tendency in his paintings—see his *Madonna with the Long Neck* (1535–40), his *Mystic Marriage of Saint Catherine* (1529), and other of his canvases. His kinetic, drawn-out characters with their tall and slender builds, disproportionately long arms, legs, and fingers, and things like breastbones protruding outward or dipping inward, call to mind the build of President Abraham Lincoln who supposedly suffered from Marfan syndrome, an inherited disorder that affects connected tissue, a painful condition related to having an elongated body.

Hans Holbein, the German-Swiss painter and printmaker who worked in a Northern Renaissance style, was a different case. His portrait of Henry VIII—quite the direct opposite of El Greco's lengthened figures—had a broadened look to it. His popular *Portrait of Georg Giese* (1532) seems somewhat flattened and distended and seems to move laterally. "It can be reduced to more normal human proportions by being photographed through the -1.0 D astigmatic lens," notes Trevor-Roper, who also suggests that Holbein was actually astigmatic, with a vertically compressed eye. He attributes Auguste Rodin's squarely built *Burghers of Calais* to a similar astigmatism. Astigmatism is a refractive error that prevents light rays from coming to a single focus on the retina. In extreme cases of the malady, do lissome figures generally become to stumpy ones? Or are elongations in a purely vertical meridian common because of astigmatism? The latter may indeed be the case. Many artists down through the years have been lightly categorized, and sometimes forthrightly, as astigmatic, such as Lucas Cranach the Elder—consider *The Suicide of Lucretia* (1529)—and even Botticelli and Titian, not to mention the even more striking elongations to be found in, for example, Amadeo Modigliani's *Reclining Nude with Raised Arms* (1916).

The problem of aniseikonia is unequal retinal images, a rivalry between retinas, that is, where they cannot be fused. Unequal magnification strangely alters the received image. Walter Humphrey, the American artist/illustrator from Wisconsin who, by wearing an aniseikonic lens, found that his paintings took on a distortion in the manner of El Greco and Cézanne, with faces becoming asymmetrical and the contours drawn towards that side where the images were magnified. With El Greco, the stretching of the contours lean in a fairly constant direction, but, according to Trevor-Roper, "one must resist the temptation to impute this curious ocular anomaly to either of these masters."

Painter Piero della Francesca became blind "through an attack of catarrh" at the age of 60. The sight of Antonio Verrio, the 17th-century muralist who worked in England for the Royal Court, began to fail, as well. He had not finished painting the famous allegory, the *King's Stairs* at Hampton Court Palace, when William III died in March 1702. Queen Anne let him carry on and, eventually, paid him. Soon afterward the self-portrait that he painted (1705)—showing him bald, looking querulous, wearing a showy yellow and white robe while in the act of painting—now hangs in the National Portrait Gallery, London. It is said to have been completed (possibly by a friend) with the pathetic inscription: "*Cieco Antonio, il povero Verrio.*" Two years later, in 1707, he was dead. Then there was also Giovanni Francesco Barbieri, for physical reasons also called—mocked—as Guercino ("the Squinter"), another intense cataractous painter, born at Cento in 1590, whose works include *The Death of Dido* (1631), *Santa Petronilla* (1623), and *Aurora* (1621), and whose self-portrait makes no attempt to conceal that divergent and presumably poor-sighted eye that badly drifted.

Giuseppe Crespi, an Italian late Baroque painter of the Bolognese School who was called *Lo Spagnuolo*, a name given to him by his fellow-students on account of the finery of his dress, died blind at Bologna in 1747. A painter and etcher, born in Bologna in 1665, he developed a vivid genre style, dark shadows and very strong lights, strong contrasts that, at least to me, seem personally to plead for an insistence on stark vision. Desirous of discovering and establishing a new mode of working, he adopted a flimsy method of coloring, one without solidity that consisted chiefly of glazing and which has occasioned many of his works to lose color, become almost obliterated. He had a particular talent for caricature and compositions, full of humor and eccentricity.

Despite failing eyesight, Sir Joshua Reynolds, arguably the most important figure in British painting, historically at least, painted perhaps the finest portraits of his life—simple, comparatively direct paintings (although the use of bitumen he sometimes employed for warm tones was often disastrous), such as *Lord Heathfield of Gibraltar* (1787), *Duchess of Devonshire and Her Daughter* (1776), *Joshua Sharpe* (1786), etc. Still preserved are a pair of Reynolds's actual silver spectacles, wiry, diminutive round goggles that lent him a distinctly pedantic flair, probably the pair he is seen wearing in his well-known 1788 self-portrait—florid cheeks, white hair, a blunt "here-take-a-good-look" expression—specs now in Royal Collection Trust. Reynolds was of short stature with a broad face and cleft chin and a craggy, flushed, red-faced complexion. The bridge of his nose was slightly dented, his skin was badly scarred by smallpox, and his upper lip somewhat disfigured as a result of his having fallen from a horse as a young man. He bore unpleasant features that the diarist James Boswell thought were "rather too largely and strongly limned."

At first, he was merely short-sighted, of an equal amount in each eye (-4.0 dioptres). But it worsened. His handwriting deteriorated. On July 13, 1789, Reynolds made the terrible disclosure that he was forced to stop painting, being, as he wrote, "prevented by my Eye beginning to be obscured," leaving him with a feeling as if a curtain had fallen over his left eye. He eventually lost that eye, along with the extrapolatingly deep and continual dread of soon losing the other. He wore a bandage over the one good eye—writer Fanny Burney, visiting him, has described it—and kept the other "shaded by a green half-bonnet." He would occasionally clean or mend a picture. Towards the end of his life, he grew irascible, like many another blind artist, becoming involved in a series of public quarrels in which—or so go common reports—he was invariably in the wrong.

It was well-known in his day that Reynolds disliked the

British portrait painter George Romney, whom he disdainfully referred to as "the man in Cavendish Square" and whom in rather a petty way he prevented from becoming a member of the Royal Academy. He also disliked Thomas Gainsborough, a contemporary and his main rival—I wonder, was Reynolds being cruelly sarcastic when he announced that Gainsborough's *Girl with Pigs* (1781) was "the best picture he ever painted or perhaps ever will"?—yet in his Gainsborough obituary he said that appreciated his achievements.

No, the two men had their irreconcilable differences—and probably delighted in it. Remember the old story? When Reynolds taught in one of his "discourses" that a good painter should never amass too much of the color blue in the foreground of an image, Gainsborough was immediately prompted to paint his famous *Blue Boy* (1770), not merely a head-and-shoulder take, a but a fill-length portrait in oil!

Reynold's sight failed utterly at the end. As we know, the brilliant man was not only a painter, but thoroughly enjoyed a flourishing literary career, as well. He wrote essays for periodicals, books such as *Discourses on Art* and *A Journey to Flanders and Holland*, and so forth, and in a full lifetime left behind something like 2000 manuscript pages. His literary efforts cost him infinite pains, as he worked into the night, closely by candlelight. His malady was not, as has often been thought, amaurosis or *gutta serena*, a common result of overwork and the Latin medical term for all blindness in which the eye retains a normal appearance. (It is also known as the "drop serene," the same type of affliction suffered by the epic poet John Milton, totally blind for 22 years, whose proud boast, nevertheless, was that he never lost his looks, as witness in his "Sonnet XXII: To Cyriack Skinner":

Cyriack, this three years' day these eyes, though clear
To outward view of blemish or of spot,
Bereft of light, their seeing have forgot;
Nor to their idle orbs doth sight appear
Of sun or moon or star throughout the year,
Or man or woman. Yet I argue not
Against Heav'n's hand or will, not bate a jot
Of heart or hope, but still bear up and steer
Right onward. What supports me, dost thou ask?
The conscience, friend, to have lost them overplied
In liberty's defence, my noble task,
Of which all Europe talks from side to side.
This thought might lead me through the world's vain mask
Content, though blind, had I no better guide.

No, what probably lay behind Reynolds's particular problem was a malignant tumor, from which illness indeed he died, one caused by a disease of the liver. A postmortem showed the painter's liver, in the words of his attending physicians, "somewhat scirrhous" and to have weighed 11 pounds.

Silvestro Lega, born in 1826, was an Italian realist painter and involved with the Mazzini movement. He was a leading member of the Macchiaioli group, painters who, straying from straitened conventions taught by the Italian art academies, began to paint outdoors in order to capture natural light, shade, and color. His political opposition to the French caused him to despise French art. Nevertheless, his masterpiece, *The Pergola* (1868), a rustic afternoon family tea party so splendidly evocative of sun and shade, is unthinkable without the example of Corot and the beginnings of Impressionism. His *La Fienaiola* (1893), depicting a beautiful peasant girl holding a pile of hay on her head—she splendidly evokes Raphael's *La Forna rina*—is one of my favorite paintings. Lega suffered badly, maddeningly, from eye trouble from 1880 and was desperately poor—and stone blind for many years before his death in 1895 in Florence.

Man is a heliotropic creature. He loves light, illumination, shine, brightness. We are not hosta plants, hating sun, seeking shade. Light is associated with well-being, while darkness of course is quite the reverse. We fear the dark, suspect the need for movement in it, where hazards and baffles are compounded and falls are terrifying. By the eye alone can distance be measured. Sound gives very inadequate ideas of extension. Our only physical conception of limitless infinity is derived from the longing of the eye to see farther than the farthest star. The old axiom of Terence that nothing human is alien to him has a popular exception in the nature of life under blindness. It can be, in what it deprives us of, the very definition of misery. Hell in our imagination is inky, coal-black, and gruesome, lit by cruel fires that only accentuate the dark. We are lost in cataclysmic darkness. Our dreams in the *Umwelt* of utter blackness have made menace and monsters of it. It is another word for chaos.

The notion that under blindness there is a constant awareness of the absence of light, and so an awareness of darkness, can nevertheless be contested, although it is surely a paradox that needs some concentration. One need not cause the other. Philosophically speaking, the ability to feel deprivation may even be a fully unsustainable state. The feeling of being in the dark after a brief time—close your eyes merely for 10 minutes—is replaced by photisms of the imagination. Blind people do not sense the color black, nor do most see black, but what I am told is a "greyscale," or dim brown. The unsighted can still tell the difference between light and dark. Jorge Luis Borges called his own blindness "modest, because it is total blindness in one eye, but only partial in the other." The Argentinian writer could still see blue, green, and yellow, but not red or black. Indeed, black. Shakespeare was wrong, Borges explained, when he wrote, "Looking on darkness which the blind do see."

A blind person's "view"—his or her vista or prospect—is not necessarily, then, a sense-field uniformly filled with blackness. Often, it is neutral grey, maybe with constant or intermittent displays of what sighted people term "fireworks," small pyrotechnic explosions or illuminations, moving grey clouds, darkness streaked with light, patches of color, in an endless variety of permutations and combinations.

People whose visual functioning is abnormal have untapped abilities in depiction, according to psychologist John M. Kennedy, who also believes that haptics, the sense of touch, involves an intuitive sense of perspective and that depiction is perceptual, not just visual, and is based on graphic elements as well as pictorial configurations. "The real voyage of discovery consists not in seeking new landscapes but in having new eyes," as Marcel Proust observed, the fistfight visually impaired artists use to cope.

Sunlight can be manufactured of an inner life. Touch thrills a blind person as it cannot, fully, those in possession of their faculties. An old idea has it that the blind desire less because they see less and thus they have a greater cheerfulness. "A blind person's face is often watched steadily," a smiling young woman explained to me at the Perkins School for the Blind in Watertown, Massachusetts, an institute started in by Dr. John Dix Fisher in 1833. "We are extra cherished," she told me. "There is love in strongly felt support." The blind can be artists of their own images. Immediate perception can occur. It begins at inception, being built up step by step. Whatever the blind may register in space with pencil or brush can register mentally. A whole literature exists on those who can feel color. A noted pioneer named George D. Wally, a fellow interested in visual knowledge and the blind, did much seminal work on the subject. His pre-eminent discovery of a micropoint for the sightless for delineation and perception took place in Puerto Rico in 1953. The micropoint is an invisible point in space by which the blind can learn to draw in perspective. It is akin to the vanishing point which one sees when two track rails appear to meet at a point on the horizon. The Wally Method is all mental.

There is a noteworthy observation in Svetlana Alper's *Rembrandt's Enterprise: The Studio and the Market* (1988), where, reminding us that Rembrandt often took blindness as his subject—cf. *Angel Leaving Tobias' Family* (1637), *Anna and Blind Tobit* (c. 1630), and others—she draws a significant distinction for us as to his intent:

> "Blindness is not invoked with reference to a high spiritual insight, but to call attention to the activity of touch in our experience of the world. Rembrandt represents touch as the embodiment of sight. . . . And it is relevant to recall that the analogy between sight and touch had its technical counterpart in Rembrandt's handling of paint: his exploitation of the reflection of natural light off high relief to intensify highlights and cast shadows unites the visible and the substantial."

Artists with eye problems include Leonardo da Vinci (intermittent exotropia), Rembrandt (stereoblindness), Edgar Degas (iridochoroiditis), Auguste Renoir (myopia), Camille Pissarro (dacryocystitis and ipsilateral conjunctive chemosis), Mary Cassatt (diabetic retonopathy with cataracts), Georgia O'Keeffe (macular degeneration)—as that woman's vision perceptibly declined, she manfully marshalled a bunch of willing assistants to help her in her painting and her work, although, stubbornly, she flatly refused give them credit with the egotistic claim that their contributions were "equivalent of a palette knife"—Pablo Picasso (strabismus), the English painter Francis Bacon (dysmorphopsia), and, neither last nor least, Claude Monet (cataracts), whose vaunted eyes in the 1910s came under threat when he developed cataracts and, painfully, slowly, began going blind.

To counteract this, he began to label his tubes of paint, keeping a strict order on his palette. He began to wear a straw hat to lessen *glare*. Slowly becoming insensitive to the "finer shades of tonalities and colors seen close up," as he said, he now began formulating ideas and features in his mind, taking the "motif in large masses" and transcribing them through memory and imagination. In 1922, a prescription of mydriatics—a type of medicine that, focusing the muscles of the eyes, makes the pupils dilate or open up—but it also tended to relax them, which perversely occasioned blurred vision.

In 1923, Monet eventually underwent cataract surgery Persistent cyanopsia, a case of seeing everything tinted blue, was one result—the lovely violet-blue water lilies, for which he was famous, were now off-puttingly bluer than before, he noticed, as he began fussily touching up and restoring some of his pre-operative works— and, being far-sighted, he was given aphakic spectacles (a practice no longer used), thick convex lenses prescribed after cataract surgery. There were no intraocular lenses inserted into his eyes, but now "able to see the real colors," perversely, he began to destroy canvases from his pre-operative period. Upon receiving tinted Zeiss lenses, he felt he was provided short-lived relief, although his left eye soon had to be entirely covered by a black lens.

As he worked, Monet slowly began to discover that layouts began to muddle for him, Tones under his heretofore expert brush turned muddy, with colors turning sour, sallow, and tow-colored. Paint and pigmentation became unreliable, which he found highly frustrating. Many of his paintings appeared slightly blurry as a result of his failing vision, since that is how he perceived the world around him. His perception of color suffered, and his broad strokes, of which he was always in control, were noticeably becoming broader, while his paintings were becoming increasingly darker. With the issue worsening, since he feared his impaired sight would grow worse, he refused to get surgical treatment, even while frankly admitting to friends he would likely have to quit painting soon, the thought of which crushed him. For Monet, life without painting was no life at all.

Many of the Impressionists suffered from myopia, eye problems, and outright blindness. They were the last painters to look directly at the light. Was it more important for them to look to the interior? Was it more than coincidence? What perverse fate was this for a visual artist to go blind? Was some sort of ontology finally declared, before looking *within* came next in art? It is arguable that the most primitive creative work born in the mind of a blind person and produced with his own hands is of greater value than the most effective imitation. The impressionist world is the world of our feelings, of subjective processes. John Singer Sargent wrote to a friend, "Impressionism was the name given to a certain form of observation when Monet, not content with using his eyes to see what things were or what they looked like as everyone else had done before him, turned his attention to noting what took place on his own retina (as an oculist would test his vision)." To paint what impinges on the retina, "in here," as Sargent pointed out, tapping his temple, constituted a very different task from depicting the vibrating field "out there."

A sort of inner transmogrification takes place. To put it another way, a more philosophical way, we keep substituting for the qualitative impression, as Henri Bergson pointed out in *The Immediate Given of Consciousness* (1889), as consciousness receives the quantitative interpretation our intelligence gives of it. Art consists of depicting the relations of the artist to the world of his experiences. What is of final importance is the kind of experience. That is what decisively determines the products of the artist.

In the end, Claude Monet went partly blind. From 1917, the cataracts on his eyes had become constantly worse, and he was obliged to wear heavy glasses. "I see much less well," he complained to Monsieur Gimpel—René Albert Gimpel, the prominent French art dealer of Alsatian Jewish descent who died in 1945 in Neuengamme concentration camp near Hamburg—"I am half blind and deaf." His color vision was also affected. Undaunted, stubbornly self-demanding, he began working in a broader style, on larger canvases, with very long, flexible brushes. He looked for light. Anything except a north light was forbidden in the Impressionist canon, as varying too much with the position of the sun. Light from slightly east of true north varies less than any other light.

Somehow, while working in his studio, Monet was able to maintain his color scheme by a determined familiarity with a controlled range already established, but painting outdoors he was forced to rely on a vision he knew to be distorted. It became a problem of cognition now wherever he sat and whatever he observed. "How do you see that?" he would snap at the table, fiercely indicating his dinner plate; "I see it yellow." How ironic! In 1885, Jules Laforgue, with Monet and Pissarro in mind, wrote that the "Impressionist eye" was the "most advanced eye in human evolution." And yet how false it would be to approach the landscape of Monet without stressing that bright, that visual emphasis.

Even the most cursory survey, from Monet's great *Seine at Bougival* (1869) to the engulfing jungle of the last versions of the *Japanese Footbridge* series painted just before his cataract operation in 1923, reveals a diversity arising from the artist's psyche, as well as from nature and his personal vision. It should be observed that cataracts, especially, inevitably affect color, blurring, and reddening in a drawing simultaneously. Consider J. M. W. Turner, whose later paintings Mark Twain once described as "like a ginger cat having a fit in a bowl of tomatoes." Or Renoir's increasing fascination for fretful reds.

In 1922, during summer, almost blind from double cataracts, Monet began working outdoors in desperation on strangely colored landscapes, trying "to paint everything," as he said, "before I can no longer see anything at all." He had to have his tubes of paint specially marked and had to arrange colors carefully on his palette. He remained faithful to his visual sensations. "Only one eye," famously exclaimed Paul Cézanne, describing Claude Monet, "but my God what an eye." And then he couldn't see at all. He was painting until he was 86—Monet died at Giverny on December 5, 1926, after being virtually unable during the last three dark years of his life to discern a single soul.

Cézanne himself is recorded as being myopic. "Take those vulgar things away," he is said to have replied when being offered a pair of spectacles. Was he losing his sight? Consider the example of his portrait *Man with Crossed Arms Folded* (1900), which shows significant distortion in the subject's skewed visage. The man's features are out of normal line with the the vertical axis of the head. The man's right eye and eyebrow are arched, furthermore, as if seen from below, but his left eye is drawn as if seen from above. I don't even trust the geometry of his hair! At the bottom, that brown wall, notice, is unprofessionally split into two subjective planes, and the lines of the wainscoting badly fail to meet. Cézanne of course also suffered from diabetes, which may have caused some retinal damage as well, and he eventually developed cataracts, suffering a case of partial vision.* In his essay on Cézanne in *Sense and Non-Sense* (1947) Maurice Merleau-Ponty observed, "As he grew old, he wondered whether the novelty of his painting might not come from trouble with his eyes, whether his whole life had not been based upon an accident of the body." Novelist Joris-Karl Huysmans once wittily, and insightfully, described Cézanne as an artist "with a diseased retina, who, exasperated by a defective vision, discovered the basis of a new art."

At 67, Cézanne looked and felt much older than his years. Diabetes had bowed his shoulders and robbed his movements of their former elasticity. The painter badly suffered from almost constant headaches, he had a pain in his back, and his right foot badly hurt him. In myopes especially, posture tends to be bad. This may be directly due in some cases to short-sightedness, which encourages stooping and a hanging of the head. On the other hand, myopia may be due in part at least to the bad posture. His very posture toward the world was antagonistic. He did not enjoy the company of people, was easily upset, especially when he was working, and he was abnormally sensitive to noise—even a dog's barking could send the

---

*Partial blindness is usually defined as "the visual acuity between 20/70 and 20/200 (that is, an object normally perceived at a distance of 200 feet must be brought up to 20 feet in order to be discerned) in the better eye or in both eyes after all medical and optical help has been provided."

painter into a frenzy. Cézanne always went to bed immediately after supper. He had an uncanny horror of even the slightest physical contact, which sent him into a perfect cyclone of frenzy. Townspeople considered him a "lunatic," and he was known as a loner. Worse, he hated his family, calling them "the nastiest people in the world."

Contrary to the lovely, optimistic blind girl I met at the Perkins School for the Blind, someone who encouraged any support one offered, physically or emotionally, Cézanne hated being fussed over generally and had no patience for it. Many blind people come to resent the over-attention of someone making a commotion over them. A critical name even exists for that fussy fascination—*typhlophily*, basically over-affection for someone who is blind, which includes the "noble feeling" one has in helping an unsighted person. Some see it as overweening condescension. The bias may come from being overprotective through guilt, or a feeling of rejection, as it were, due to the *impossibility* of identifying oneself with a blind person: *My body is a jail in which the other's looks keep me prisoner.* The sentimental attitude of the normal-sighted adult toward the blind can indeed be damaging. In a utopia where the blind live only with the blind, some theorists insist, it would be possible that the blind with their peculiar spatial concepts would not feel their handicap at all, just as we do not feel any disadvantage in our inability to see ultraviolet rays.

In his crotchets, Cézanne also had something of a tropism for order. One thing he did not like about Impressionism was an incipient lack of "structure" in it. He hated messiness and wanted form and order, a quality missing in the movement. He is called a Post-Impressionist, as we know, an art movement that developed roughly between 1886 and 1905, from the last Impressionist exhibition to the birth of Fauvism.

Vincent van Gogh himself might have had eye problems. Some critics now feel that a few of his stylistic quirks, such as wavy foliage, for example, nimbuses around stars, or rippling halo effects and coronas around streetlamps, may have been the result of illness and not intentional distortions at all. Could he possibly have damaged his eyes, as has been suggested, from the reductive toxic poisons of paint thinners and resins that he used? At one time, pigments were composed of heavy metals like copper, cadmium, and mercury. "Fumes and poisons could easily get into food, since painters frequently worked and lived in the same rooms," observes the American author, poet, and naturalist Diane Ackerman, writing of impaired vision and painters in her *Natural History of the Senses* (1990), adding, "When Renoir chose his bright reds, oranges and blues, he was also choosing big doses of aluminum, mercury, and cobalt. In fact, up to 60 percent of the colors Renoir preferred contained dangerous metals." Along with some of his bizarre religious hallucinations, remember, it is said that van Gogh drank kerosene and ingested leaded oil paint. It is a myth that he ate yellow paint to become more cheerful, as rumor has long had it, but during his certification at the institution in Saint-Rémy, he wrote in a letter to Theo, "It appears that I pick up filthy things and eat them, although my memories of these bad moments are vague."

Speculation has it—and of this Dutch artist, there is no want of it—suggested that he may have been over-treated with a medication called digitalis. In toxic yet nonlethal doses, digitalis is in fact known to cause xanthopsia, a vision deficiency that causes the sufferer to see more yellow. The extensive list of disorders treated with the medication during that period include headaches, mental illness, nausea, melancholy and inflammation of the eyes. It is also said that he suffered from "visual snow." Explaining some of the possible diagnoses for van Gogh's stark depressions, Trevor-Roper lists, along with cerebral tumors, syphilis, magnesium deficiency, and temporal lobe epilepsy, a case of poisoning by digitalis, which was given as a treatment for epilepsy, as possibly provoking van Gogh's yellow vision, or glaucoma, for, of course, along with painting haloes around lights, he depicted himself in many of his self-portraits as having a dilated right pupil.

French painter Honoré Daumier gave up drawing when he was 69, sightless as a mole. One eye was closed due to the weakness of one eyelid. Soon, he was forced to undergo an operation for cataracts on both eyes, greatly limiting his artistic life. He drew his last lithograph on September 21, 1872, for *Le Charivari*, an illustrated magazine of caricatures, political cartoons, and reviews published in Paris from 1832 to 1937. He had seven years to live, telling his editor, Pierre Veron, "I can't see anymore. Today I drew a figure whose lines wandered so that I couldn't bring them together." It was the announcement of the end of a career, and Veron records that the great caricaturist could not prevent a tear from rolling down his cheek. It was waking to each new day that he felt his blindness most. He couldn't share the general emerging from darkness of the night and sleep. Presbyopia, an ailment from which Daumier suffered, is commonly regarded as one of the inevitable results of old age. "Like the bones of the skeleton," wrote Aldous Huxley, who for decades was nearly bat-blind and read by Braille, in *The Art of Seeing: An Adventure in Re-education* (1942), "the lens of the eye hardens with age." In that book he details his experience with and states his views on the now discredited Bates Method—in 1920 Dr. W. H. Bates of New York had written *Perfect Sight without Glasses*, in which, along with providing corrective exercises designed to relax the eyes, he explained his theory that poor eyesight was due to stress-related bad visual habits. The method which was all about "sunning," exposing one's eyes to the sun, a questionable practice that, according to the English author, not only improved his eyesight but saved him from wearing spectacles.

Could that have been a major reason why the Englishman Huxley moved to southern California in 1937, where he lived until his death in 1963? Another successful benefit the Bates Method claimed for itself was the "exclusion of mental strain" by covering the eyes with the palms, and then uncovering them to focus on a target, whereupon any optically-defective eyes should note a flash of visual clarity.

It has been observed that with age one is more likely to become farsighted, that in an old person nearsightedness tends to decrease, that crisp razor-sharpness goes. Trolleys seem constantly derailing. A world of blurring and haze results. A good description of nearsightedness can be found in Patrick Süskind's novella *The Pigeon* (1987):

> "Every time his eyelid batted, his gaze broke from
> the confounded edge and sprang to some other thing. . . .
> It was as if the air were wavering in heat today, the way
> it does only on the hottest July afternoons. Transparent
> veils fluttered before things. The outlined contours of
> buildings, eaves, were glittering and garish, and at the
> same time indistinct, frazzled. The edges of curbs and
> the cracks between the stone squares of the sidewalk—
> normally as if drawn with a straightedge—meandered
> along in glistening curves. . . . Nothing was left clearly
> delineated. Nothing was left to be precisely fixed. Every-
> thing quivered."

So many difficult eye problems cannot be cured by simple eyeglasses: a cataract, glaucoma, a torn retina, cancer of the eye, retinoblastomas or intraocular tumors in the brain pressing down on the optic nerve. Rather curiously, up until the last century, glasses or spectacles were a luxury normally chosen by trial and error from an itinerant vendor's tray. Early spectacles were often sea-green in color, being sometimes made from the gem beryl, from which, some say, we get the German word for spectacles, *Grille.* Among the pictures of Belgian painter Mattheus Brill (1550–83) can be found several captiously signed with a pair of spectacles.

Most 19th-century oculists frowned on spectacles, holding them to be damaging to the eyes. Renoir, on being fitted with a new pair of eyeglasses to correct his myopia—he would later go partly blind—threw them on the floor, crying, *"Bon Dieu, je vois comme Bougereau!"* It was the painter Adolphe Bougereau (1825–1905), we may recall, who in a rather cloying way painted Renaissance-type nudes, religious subjects, and portraits of photographic verisimilitude, which probably explains Renoir's explosive remark of dismay.

I still love those old photographs of Matisse in his old age, wearing an old cap, hugging his cat, and blinking out from his wire-rim spectacles. He looks so scholarly and so determined to *know.* As the proverb goes, "Many a wise face would look foolish without spectacles." Henry James in one of his less familiar short stories, "Glasses" (1896), referred to them as "straighteners." That tale's intrepid little heroine, Flora Saunt, with her "goggles"—or "nippers," as James also refers to them—is almost comically described as an "exquisite creature, blushing, glaring, exposed, with a pair of big black-rimmed eye-glasses defacing her by their position, crookedly astride of her beautiful nose." The narrator of the story often conveys the awkwardness, the stigma, that she feels wearing them. "She made a grab at them with her free hand while I turned confusedly away."

Edward Degas first described his loss of sight in 1871. He had iridochoroiditis, and his right eye was permanently damaged. It was later attributed to his travails during the siege of Paris, although he had already been refused for the army because of poor sight. He knew he was losing his race with blindness. Zoë, his maid, often read aloud to him. "Ah, sight! Sight! Sight!" the painter would loudly lament, "My mind feels heavier than before in the studio and the difficulty of seeing makes me feel numb." Desperately, he tried taking up pastels and the alternate use of charcoal to draw, limning figures, vague ballerinas, Russian dancers, nudes drying their long hair, almost always automatically starting from the head on paper, then adding strips of tracing paper above and then below, as the drawing expanded, tacking them on to fit the configurations at hand.

"Of the great Impressionists," wrote novelist John Updike, "Degas had the worst eyes. His myopia was severe enough to excuse him from infantry duty; by his forties he was virtually blind in his right eye; and by the 1890s he periodically donned corrective spectacles blacked-out except for a small slit in the left lens. Complaints about '*la vue*' recur in his letters, and late in life he wrote to a friend, 'I'll soon be a blind man.'" Degas tried sculpting. It was a new, complex, and no doubt sobering experience for him. A blind individual can perceive objects that are larger than his hand only by moving his hand over the object. Thus he can only receive partial impressions which he has to unify into a simultaneous whole.

From 1885 on, imminent blindness hung over poor Degas. It was like snow blindness, his indisposition. Snow blindness, which gives the sensation of having sand thrown in one's eyes, is a disagreeable burning of the cornea, which comes on with little warning and has no cure other than time. (The Tarakots of Nepal blow through cloth into each other's eyes to relieve the pain.) He tried ignoring and defying it. He kept on with his sculpture, as if getting back to basics. "I confess myself to be a great admirer of tradition," as Churchill, another artist, once pointed out. "The further you can look back, the further you can see forward. Any oculist will tell you this is true." Degas worked long and diligently. He did an extraordinary portrait bust of Mary Cassatt. Groping in the dark, he was also able to make enchanting wax figurines by touch, and it was after he was blind that he said, as with his fingertips he caressed the portrait of *Mme. de Seronnes* in a retrospective exhibition of Ingres, "Look how pretty the detail is."

Almost fully blind, the crusty Degas grew to become an ill-tempered old man, a ferocious anti-Dreyfusard, full of anti-Semitism and unbridled spleen. He could not maintain proportions as his eyesight failed. By 1908, he wrote, "Soon one will be a blind man. Where there are no fish, one should not try to fish." The artist in his shabby hat and coat nevertheless held his head high, with "the air of an old Homer." He had joined the ranks of the mythic blind. His biographer Pierre Cabanne described him as "Oedipus with a white beard" as the old, hobbling octogenarian felt his way along streets familiar to him from a lifetime spent in the same quarter of Paris, the Ninth Arrondissement. Degas died at 83, in 1917, at number 6 Boulevard de Clichy, although his eyesight had begun to deteriorate a full 30 years before. He sort of embodied at the end the Carlylean view that toil itself might be genius. One thinks of him in terms of Yeats's memorable lines:

> "Grant me an old man's frenzy,
> Myself I must remake

Till I am Timon and Lear
Or that William Blake
Who beat upon the wall
Till truth obeyed his call."

Mary Cassatt, born in Pittsburgh in 1844, the daughter of a banker who offered little encouragement to her early desire to be a painter. In 1868, after traveling widely in Europe, she settled in Paris to study under Charles Joshua Chaplin, a typical academic French painter, but she was far more interested in and attracted to Courbet, Manet, and the Impressionists. In 1877 she met Degas, who invited her to exhibit with the Impressionists. In 1911 a blinding flash struck across Cassatt's vision. She was partly blind by 1912, and totally stone-blind at her death. She was operated on both eyes for cataracts in 1917. She had also been given radium treatments for diabetes, radium being a new discovery at the time, a panacea that could supposedly cure psoriasis, gonorrhea, sciatica, pruritis vulvae, lichenification—a disease of the tongue—and gastritis. It was an age of nostrums. Today, roentgenologists agree—weirdly!—that radium treatments can actually *cause* cataracts!

Cassatt was dead set against modern art, impatient with the times as her eyes deteriorated rapidly. In a letter to her friend Louise Havemeyer, she wrote, "My sight is so enfeebled I cannot read even large print." She saw oculists, who called it conjunctivitis, iritis with adhesions. There are those who find the American-French artist's work, due to this want of perspective, even distorted. In her *Mother and Child* (1890), many feel that the face of the child seen reflected in the mirror is not agreeably sized, as contrasted to, say, the treatment of a mirrored face done by Velázquez (*Venus and Cupid*) or Titian (*Venus with a Mirror*). The same might be said of her *Child's*

Bath (1893).

No one from Philadelphia had come over to see a show she and Degas had effortfully put together, not even Cassatt's own family, and the snub badly nettled her. She became difficult, at times impossibly petulant. Her handwriting changed, became crude, angular, violently shaky. She fired her chauffeur, snapped at people. She had a loud voice, which was raised often in anger. (She once petulantly referred to President Woodrow Wilson as "a syphilitic son-of-a-bitch.") During World War I she spent most of her time in Grasse on the Riviera, where she often visited the aging Renoir. She who constantly drew and painted scenes of mothers with children—perhaps *not* surprisingly—never married or had children and chose instead to pursue a career as an artist, a seeming embrace of traditional values as curiously antithetical as a blind artist insistently trying to draw and paint!

After Cassatt went totally blind, in 1921, the sculptor Augustus Saint-Gaudens, visiting, found her salon "*sombre.*" Her rooms in fact were crepuscular and closed off. The old lady, vaguely waving her hand, often urged visitors to help themselves to jam, adding "if there is any jam on the table." She bent over her flowers in front of Beaufresne even after she could no longer see them. Twenty-seven blurry, generally uninspired, fumbling pastels, executed during 1913 and 1914, mostly of mothers and babies—in her pain was she calling on the former as the latter?—reveal only that the Impressionist light had failed. "Oh Louie dear, my eye has another cataract growing, after all [the doctor's] assurance! Oh dear, do wish for my end. I am so tired," she wrote in 1921. She would live on for five more years. The shadows closed in on her. Her apartment at the end was virtually pitch dark.

Camille Pissarro's central vision was impaired from the

scars of corneal ulcers. Born in St. Thomas in the West Indies, the son of a Creole mother and a father of Portuguese-Jewish descent, he was influenced by Corot and Manet, whom he met in 1859. From 1866 on he worked at Pontoise on landscapes painted entirely out in the open, but he could sell nothing, in consequence of which he and his family were driven to dire poverty. In 1874, he took part in the first Impressionist exhibition: he was the only one who was doggedly exhibited in all eight Paris Impressionist exhibitions, from 1874 to 1886. And it was Pissarro who first introduced Paul Gauguin, then Pointillists Georges Seurat and Paul Signac into these exhibitions. In 1889, this dean of Impressionism began to suffer from an extreme chronic eye infection in his left eye, diagnosed as dacryocystitis and ipsilateral conjunctive chemosis. It became fully and completely impossible for him to work outdoors.

Back in those days, treatment consisted of incision and drainage of the lachrymal sac, followed by cauterization. Is it not significant to note—and one wonders with which how much stress—that generally in Pissarro's work there is revealed very little of color? *A Portrait of Pissarro* (1868) by French Impressionist painter and lithographer Armand Guillaumin depicts Camille standing, be-hatted, in dung-drab brown clothes amid a bunch of muted, washed-out, watery, lusterless, colorless canvases. Two *Self-Portraits* that Pissarro executed (and there is yet another later one showing him sleepy-eyed, dolefully sitting quizzically at his palette), one in 1900 and another in 1903, showing an elfin, diffident, heavily gray-bearded, Hebrew *alter kaker* in floppy hats and wearing half-glasses. From 1895 the aggravated condition that he suffered from—variations of blepharitis or cellulitis—forced the man completely to give up working outdoors. He had a special studio built in his garden in Erogny and, both there and in Paris, frequently worked from behind windows.

Pissarro often overpainted, overloaded his canvases, complaining frequently that his work lacked visual clarity and were often dull or muddy in coloring, especially those from the late 1870s and early 1880s. At first, in 1887, he suffered an inflamed tear gland, but then came bigger trouble, for it turned out that a growth of bone was discovered obstructing the lachrymal canal. He then proceeded to take aurum, a homeopathic medicine that supposedly helped in treating chronic headache and congestion in the head. He was then advised to avoid wind and dust. He tried to work with one eye, like Degas. In the 1890s, he would stroll through Paris with his sons and friends, a small strange-looking, almost garden-gnome of a man, sporting a full snowy beard, wearing a soft black felt hat, a black Inverness cape, and a narrow bandage of black silk over that one ailing eye.

His physician, Daniel Parenteau, in an attempt to relieve him of his pain, began injecting oil with silver nitrate into the tear duct to provoke an inflammation and accelerate the healing process. But it progressively grew worse. A staunch believer in homeopathy, Pissarro submitted to Parenteau who did everything to save his patient without an operation. It became impossible, however. Complications followed after an abscess of the prostate. No sooner would one abscess form, break, and heal, then another would develop. Pissarro succumbed to blood poisoning, dying on November 13, 1903, at the age of 71.

Aristide Maillol (1861–1944), with Rodin a pioneer of modern sculpture, did not actually begin fully to concentrate on sculpture until his sight began to fail at the age of 40. As a painter, he had been initially attracted to Impressionism, but he returned to classical idealism, depicting only the human figure, especially the female nude. His figures appear placid, self-contained, earthy, as if untouched by time or pressure. His sculptures are well-modeled, and it is the bold solidity of his work that is to be noticed. Consider his *Three Nymphs* (1937)—Maillol insisted they were the three nymphs of the "flowery meadows," commenting that they were too powerful to represent the Graces—and *Torso of Chained Action* (1906) as well as *Torso of the Monument to Blanqui* (1905), an aggressively striding female nude, strong and solid-breasted, like all his nudes, sculpted in honor of Louis Blanqui, a socialist who spent half his life in prison, defending his principles. "Nature is deception," said Maillol. "If I looked at her less, I would produce not the real, but the true. Art is complex, I said to Rodin, who smiled because he felt that I was struggling with nature. I was trying to simplify, whereas he noted all the profiles, all the details; it was a matter of conscience."

Most blind or sight-compromised sculptors, incidentally, do not model in the usual way, with the sculpture facing them. They stand parallel to the statue or behind it, their faces parallel to the sculpture's face. Accordingly, the sculpture is formed in the same direction, as though the sculptor were embracing it from behind. The reason for this is that impressions of the outer world do not reach the blind in a mirror-like projection, which is the way these impressions reach the normal eye. The experience of the totally blind is primarily derived from the forms they observe and feel on themselves.

In 1889 Maillol began to design tapestries—Gauguin loved them—an interest inspired by medieval examples that he had seen at the Musée de Cluny in Paris, and in fact he did return to Banyuls-sur-Mer to set up a small tapestry factory and hired some local women to assist him. Supervising his factory, his eyes began to fail. There was still creative work possible with his hands. The tips of fingers possess, like the rest of the body, an outer and an inner skin: the outer, called the cuticle, protects and guards the inner, the true skin. And when attention is in full exercise, much can be had in the way of comprehension there. But with greater insecurity Maillol felt the burden of his handicap. As compared with visual impressions, tactile experiences are much more limited, and he soon felt a lack of confidence in the "fixed representations" of his art he could no longer approve.

Damaged vision prevented the eccentric American painter Albert Pinkham Ryder from proceeding further than grammar school. An important part of his originality was his affinity with night, nocturnal visions receding at times into Stygian obscurity. He left his native New Bedford, Massachusetts, at 23 to go to New York. He proposed once to a woman—a complete stranger—who was playing a violin in the same building; he went to her chamber and without so much as an introduction made the rashest declaration of a lifetime. A loner, a rebel, a wayfarer in a frayed frock coat, he was an itinerant drifter and eventually a recluse. He made no attempt to acquire money. He liked to stroll around New York at night, under the moon. He brewed perfume for children at Christmas and gave it to them in little jars. He refused to paint his studio or meet new friends. Ryder completed fewer than 200 paintings, nearly all of which were created before 1900.

Wyndham Lewis, the British painter who was born in Canada, went blind in 1950, at the age of 70, gradually losing his field of vision as the result of a pituitary tumor that placed pressure on his optic nerve, which in the end—in 1957—also proved to be fatal. It ended his artistic career. A novelist and art critic as well as a painter, he ceased to write regular art criticism in 1951 because he had become blind. This experience is described in a final article he wrote, "The Sea-Mists of the Winter," for what Lewis thought was mist in the streets of London's Notting Hill proved only to be an illusion caused by his declining eyesight. Although his handwriting went out of control, he would not give up and continued writing until his death. He published several autobiographical and critical works: *Rude Assignment* (1950), *Rotting Hill* (1951), a collection of allegorical short stories about his life in "the capital of a dying empire"; *The Writer and the Absolute* (1952), a book of essays on writers including George Orwell, Jean-Paul Sartre, and André Malraux; as well as the semi-autobiographical novel *Self Condemned* (1954). Refusing to go under, he tried working on a drawing, *Walpurgisnacht*, with a magnifying glass. He was just able to finish his painting of T. S. Eliot, now in Magadalene College, by sitting about six inches away from the canvas, before the "sea-mist," as he described it, rolled over his eyes, for good.

Norwegian artist Edward Munch in 1930, at age 66, suffered from poor vision in his left eye, which may have resulted from amblyopia or injuries that he had sustained in a fight in 1904. In any case, for a while the weakness of the left eye did not interfere with his painting, until the onslaught of a right vitreous hemorrhage in his better eye, utterly confounding him. The blood in his eye coagulated, leading to shapes, spots and smudges superimposed on to everything he saw. As one critic observed, "The resulting opacity that cast its shadow on the retina, and which had the shape of a bird with a long beak, began to insinuate itself into his paintings as the dominant subject of the world he depicted, a strange palimpsest, a sort of variation on the theme of the 'Tiberias phenomenon.'" This disorder or infirmity affected not only Munch's work but his mental state

This so-called "Tiberias phenomenon" is the syndrome of

the rarely-heard-of phantom eye, a vision without light or even direct eyesight, where certain patients whose eyes are bandaged claim to see clear visual images through the back of their heads. The eyes of the Roman emperor Tiberius (42 BC–37 AD), according to Suetonius in *The Lives of the Caesars*, were unusually large and, strange to say, had the power of seeing even at night and in the dark, but only for a short time. Ancient Roman busts of this emperor show him to have had bulbous, scarily futuroidal eyes.

The semi-abstract watercolors in the paintings of Munch were executed, or so claims one American professor of ophthalmology, while he was suffering from his disease and reveal the symptoms of his illness. Michael Marmor, of Stanford University School of Medicine, has noted that the painter was deeply frightened by his ocular hemorrhage, which is evident in a drawing of his where he is portrayed with a skull-like visage, his hands are held to his head a pose of fear and anguish, not unlike the agonized face of the that famous subject of his, *The Scream* (1893). Apparently, the effects of the coagulated blood in his eye created bird-like shapes and concentric circles in vivid colors, which Marmor likens to the aura emitted around bright lights on a foggy day. He writes,

> "It is possible that these [circles] represent a view through his resolving haemorrhage as he looked towards an electric light or the sun. He annotated many of his drawings 'electric light' or 'sunshine' to indicate the conditions under which they were made. Other sketches show the presence of a dense blind spot, or scotoma, near the center of his visual field. Sometimes it was simply an opaque shape, but in one striking watercolor it became a skull covering the foot of the artist's bed. In that picture he portrayed himself with a hand covering his left eye,

the better to observe the nature of the scotoma on the right."

Marmor goes on to say that Munch was so fearful of being unable to paint that he spent his convalescence pursuing photography. "However, by 1931 he was again painting, and the strange images disappeared for ever from his work."

At 84, in 1971, Georgia O'Keeffe, who had always been proud of her acute eyesight—one need only look at the knife-sharp edges in her paintings—lost her central vision and had only peripheral sight, an irreversible eye degeneration found among the elderly. She began using a magnifying glass that she sardonically referred to as "my eye," and, like Aldous Huxley, for some time she followed the Bates eye-training method. Ultimately we see what life brings us, and one of the legacies life does bring, is blindness.

The great painter is blind only in the way we are not and sees exactly everything we do not. "No man becomes blind by merely shutting his eyes nor does the fool always see by opening them," goes the proverb. It is an affliction that, in the curious, almost supernatural mode by which we somehow increase in relation to what we are deprived of or are prevented from having—the way the humble are exalted and the last become first—always leaves something in its stead of inner beauty and transcendence. One thinks of the magnificent lines from John Milton's epic poem, *Paradise Lost*:

> "So much the rather thou Celestial Light
> Shine inward, and the mind through all her powers
> Irradiate, there plant eyes, all mist from thence
> Purge and disperse, that I may see and tell
> Of things invisible to mortal sight."
>
> (III, 51–55)

The Vision of Fritz Eichenberg

Illustration has always been an important influence in the understanding and enjoyment of literature. From the manuscript books of the medieval period, with their exquisite illuminations and brilliant miniature paintings, to the contemporary varieties of illustration technique, there is bounty to survey. Although the printing of illustrations from wooden blocks was known to have been used by the Chinese over 600 years before the development of printing from movable metal type by Gutenberg around 1440, it was this singular event that exercised such a forceful impetus upon the art of the woodcut as a means of illustrating books.

The first examples of "carved" graphics on wood appeared in the 6th century in China, and later they spread to Japan. European artists mastered the technique in the 14th century, with the development of book printing, since there had been no paper in the Old World before. For five centuries, the art of engraving has provided the poor with access to art and literature.

The woodcut, which requires the use of the knife on the side-grain of the wood, with designs carved into the block with chisels and carving knives and rolled in ink, was brought to supreme perfection by such masters as Albrecht Dürer, Hans Holbein, Ernst

Barlach, Thomas Bewick, and Hans Burgkmair, with the help of skillful "form cutters." From 1470 on, woodcut illustration was practiced with continued success, and some of the most remarkable, illustrated books came from the established presses in Germany, France, Italy, and the Netherlands during this period of the High Renaissance. The beauty of book decoration, printing as an art, attained to perfection and elegance.

By the early 16th century, the development of copperplate engraving brought a new era to book illustration. The natural transition from the linear woodcut to engraving upon metal was to afford greater flexibility of line and tone, with shadow and cross-hatching, and a more refined technique and texture. But in the 18th century, Thomas Bewick of Newcastle, England, revolutionized book illustration with a simple yet remarkable discovery. He ingeniously adopted metal-engraving tools to cut hard boxwood across the grain, producing printing blocks that could be integrated with metal type, but were much more durable than traditional woodcuts. The result was high-quality illustration at a low price.

By engraving the subject with a burin or graver, as in intaglio work, but on the cross-section of a hard boxwood block, he found that a distinct richness was secured by the contrast of the "white line" against the black background, along with a pronounced sharpness of tone and color achieved by varying the width or variety of those lines. This simple innovation made it possible to maintain the qualities of the copperplate process, but, in terms of relief, the block could be printed with the type in letterpress. The ingenuity of Bewick, best seen in his engravings for *A General History of Quadrupeds* (1790) and *A History of British Birds* (1797), brought a rich new life to wood-engraving illustration, one, thankfully, that was never destroyed by the development of photography in the 1850s.

By looking at the great German-American illustrator and wood engraver Fritz Eichenberg's curriculum vitae we might find some clues to his place in the history of the art of the print, the book, and illustration. He was born on October 24, 1901, and grew up in the venerable city of Cologne, a city 2000 years old, with its ancient wood carvings of saints and sinners and its heritage of great printers and wood cutters.

It was not all one great picture book for him. He remembered being a "painfully reluctant student," or so he told me back in the late 1970s, where, when he was matriculating at a severe and demanding militaristic high school once in class for no reason at all being brutally slapped by a form-master there, a scorching experience that became for him a synecdoche of his early years, which were characterized as much by bewilderment as severity.

At the age of 17, while attending night classes at an art school, he began working as a lithographer's apprentice drawing wine labels on stone at the house of Dumont Schauberg, after which he took a job doing windows in the art department of a big department store before eventually moving on to Leipzig, where he studied at the State Academy of Graphic Arts under Hugo Steiner-Prag. He proved to be the best student of this well-known book artist whose own fertile and dramatic imagination, meticulous craftsmanship, and thorough proficiency in a variety of media, particularly in etching and lithography, was soon matched by young Eichenberg. With borrowed tools, while still a student, he taught himself to work on boxwood. He finished 17 wood engravings for *Till Eulenspiegel* in 1922, along with 32 lithographs for *Lemuel Gullivers Reisen* (1922) in one prolific year, followed by the first of many illustrations he would do for a Fyodor Dostoevsky novel, in this case for his *Schuld und Sühne* (1923). "I always felt the urge to sum up the human predicament in a print" he told me. The great 19th-century Russian novelist would become a lodestone for Fritz for his entire life, a model not only of his art but his spirituality.

Moving to Berlin, he was still very young and searching. A period of 10 years followed when he traveled as an artist-correspondent for various magazines and newspapers, working as a cartoonist, satirist, and illustrator. This experience, influenced somewhat by his interest in the work of Goya and Daumier, developed in him a strong and remarkable facility not only for human characterization but a continued urge now to express himself in various print media.

In 1933, during the rise of Hitler—Eichenberg frequently lampooned him in cartoons—he grew disgusted, left Europe for the United States by way of Mexico, and moved to New York, where his first important commissions were done for the Limited Editions Club, which was then under the entrepreneurship of George Macy. The artist's interpretive genius was swiftly brought to bear upon such classics as *Uncle Remus, Jane Eyre, Wuthering Heights, The Tales of Edgar Allan Poe,* and *Fathers and Sons,* along with much of the writing of Wilkie Collins, Pushkin, and Tolstoy. Many of these prints can now be found in the Metropolitan Museum in New York, the Library of Congress, in the art collections of the Vatican, and the University of Jerusalem, the Bibliothèque Nationale in Paris, and the Hermitage in Leningrad.

At the invitation of Nikita Khrushchev himself, followed by a cultural exchange exhibition of graphic arts in Alma Ata, USSR, Eichenberg found an instant rapport for and recognition of his work by the Russian people. Fritz Eichenberg—it can come as no surprise to those who know his work—had in his woodcuts penetrated to the very depths of the Russian soul, from Pushkin's *Tales* to Tolstoy's *Resurrection* to Dostoevsky's *A Raw Youth.*

His work on Dostoevsky, the confessed "spiritual companion" of his life, began when Eichenberg first read him as a boy, and it endured with him until he died, for both shared, almost symbiotically, the same dramatic power and narrative richness of scene along with a deep and abiding fixedness on the agony of man—the human equation is never simple, as both men had learned firsthand—his deep, psychological complexity, his supernatural preoccupations, and the continuing need of religion, social justice, fair play, nonviolence, and even an abiding sense of mysticism, something Fritz shared with all of the great, caring, truly *committed* souls of the world and its laborers like Clara Barton, Simone Weil, Mother Jones (born Mary Harris), Eugene V. Debs, Thomas Merton, Dr. Benjamin Spock, Peter Maurin, and Dorothy Day, a good friend of Fritz whom he revered and admired and for whose newspaper, *The Catholic Worker*, he carved the headline logo that is still used, one virtually identified with him, and to which he contributed many powerful illustrations.

The personal obligation of looking after the needs of our brothers and sisters was deep-seated in the soul of Fritz Eichenberg. Raised in a non-religious family, by his own account he was attracted to Taoism when he was a young boy. Following his wife's unexpected death in 1937, he turned briefly to the practice of Zen Buddhist meditation and eventually joined the Quakers in 1940, an affiliation that he maintained until the day of his death on November 30, 1990. I attended worship with him at the Friends Meeting House on Fair Street in Nantucket many times. It was at a Quaker conference on religion and publishing in 1949, in fact, that he first met Dorothy Day, after which he became associated with Catholic charity. The people's cause was always his cause. Eichenberg was a long-time contributor to *The Nation*, his illustrations appearing in that magazine at various times between 1930 and 1980.

There is, to my mind, no greater interpreter in any medium of the tortured magnificence of the great Russian novelist than Fritz Eichenberg, and he has without a doubt left us in the sequence of wood engravings for *Crime and Punishment, The Possessed, The Idiot, The Brothers Karamazov,* and *A Raw Youth* his *magnum opus*—a gallery, in immortal grain, of some of the starkest moments in all literature: fat capitalists nobbling the poor; peasant's hovels and gnarled trees; sly Slavic faces with stringy hair; clowns and cripples; Christ-haunted ikons; poor muzhiks' cheeks and bouncing jowls; enchanted troikas flashing through the snow; frozen wastes in the moonlight; political gremlins, be-mustachioed Metropolitans, grotesque inspector generals; and, forever, the fatal melodrama of Raskolnikov at the sudden shock of murder, Prince Myshkin utterly mad, the Karamazovs with their thousand devils, Stavrogin and Kirilov and their supreme self-will! "I have my own view of art," Eichenberg might have said echoing Dostoevsky in a letter to Strakhov in 1869, "and that which the majority call fantastic and exceptional is for me the very essence of reality."

To have in your possession the books with Fritz Eichenberg's engravings of Dostoevsky is to own, for the classic dignity and pictorial distinction, some of the most powerful artwork of the 20th century.

His own artistic development and growth Fritz allows us to trace in his unique chronological "autobiography," *The Wood and the Graver* (1977), superadding for us in a chapter at the end a reverent and loving disquisition on the method of the wood engraver, the value of wood, and the correct use of the various tools involved: the burin (or spitsticker); the straightline tool; the square (or round) scorper; and other gravers of different sizes and shapes. We learn in the course of this frank and beautifully written anthology—a representative tour of this work reaching from the Runyonesque prints of the Thirties ("The Steps," "City Lights," "The Subway," etc.) to the shadow-world of the Brontës in the Forties to the breathtakingly stark and thundering Old Testament wood engravings ("Jonah," "Noah," "Lot's Wife," etc.) of the Fifties to the extravagant 18 woodblocks in the Seventies of *The Adventurous Simplicissimus* and the "Dance of Death" sequence. He worked for the WPA, the Federal Arts Project, in 1935. In 1947, he began teaching at Pratt Institute in Brooklyn, becoming chairman of the art department in 1956, and in 1961 he started publication of *Artist's Proof,* a periodical solely devoted to contemporary printmaking.

"I don't want to be claimed," Fritz Eichenberg once told me in reference to a question on "schools" and academic departmentalization. "I want to be an instrument of God, not a collection of assets." And in spite of the fact that in 1973 he was singled out as one of the "outstanding Educators of America," acclaimed with four honorary degrees within the short course of six years, and was selected by the Smithsonian Institution for its traveling exhibition of American prints during America's Bicentennial in 1976, he was never more nor less than himself—a visionary living in Thoreauvian simplicity only for his craft, a xylophile daily facing in his wood blocks "an emptiness," as Wallace Stevens puts it, "that would be filled."

He would not work on metal, linoleum, or synthetic surfaces. The woodblock, for him, was supreme, the quality of age and grain, even its own imperfections, and whether it was boxwood, slowly aged and cured, carefully planed and polished, or well-seasoned Swiss pearwood, side grain, he was a Druid priest who handled it as reverently as if it were a relic, for he saw not only the holiness of it as it is, but the sacramental, as well, of what's to be. His surname in a wonderful coincidence—or was it fate?—*means* "oak mountain."

The Eichenberg wood engraving, when completed, is recognized, understood—and *felt*—immediately. His personal favorite, for instance, "Nightwatch" (1962)—twelve glowering birds, the owl perched on a skull—reveals instantly that control of form and texture that is the hallmark of his style, a kind of blocking, in theatrical terms, which arranges the figures, brings them out of a tightly grained hardwood tapestry of the finest and tiniest cuts, each one a separate stroke, and throws them into comparative relief of strong light and darkness as if they were on stage. "The illustrator casts himself in the role of stage director," he once said, "working also as a scenic and costume designer and as a lighting expert."

He knew whereof he spoke, not only for having written the brilliantly exhaustive *Art of the Print: Masterpieces, History, Techniques* (1976)—the *locus classicus* on the subject, a seminal work—but also for the masterful contributions he himself has made to that art. His was a hand, never flinching, shaped all at once to the delicacy of Virgil Solis, the technical excellence and imagination of Albrecht Dürer, the wit of Cruikshank, the simplicity of medievalist Gunther Zainer, the chiaroscuro touch of Rowlandson and Doré, and the vitality of—but, then, who in the history of wood engraving *can* match the vitality of Fritz Eichenberg? Who has better done the muscle, the thews, the sudden dramatic power of face and fire flashing out of the wood? The suffering that animates? The passion that enthralls?

There is no irony that Fritz Eichenberg is also the gentlest of men. "Do you not see," asked the poet John Keats, "how necessary a world of pains and troubles is to school an intelligence and make it a soul?"

The artist lived in Peace Dale, Rhode Island, vacationing (to work, naturally) as he had done for 30 summers on the island of Nantucket. A deeply sensitive man, he had a perfectly sculpted face, one ramified by an Old World mustache, which can be found in several of his autobiographical prints, notably "The Artist and the Seven Deadly Sins" (1975); he was courtly, very soft-spoken—although he loved words and language and was proficient in several—and his conversation was full of anecdote, observation, and irony, much of it self-mocking.

Fritz was always beautifully dressed, a vest, golden leather shoes. He was tidy, elegant, and had perfect taste. He was a terrible driver. He was short of stature, could barely perch up to a car's windshield to see over the console and his picking me up at the Nantucket docks or driving me back to catch the Cape Cod ferry was truly a hair-raising experience. We used to wake up early and sit outside on a bench at his house at Quidnet, inhaling the scent of the onshore ocean breezes—his second wife, Toni (Antonia, about 70 or so years old, German-born, of *Vogue* model beauty) usually stayed inside—and enjoy a summer breakfast in the fresh air of multi-grain bread, Stilton cheese—sometimes *gougères*—cold green grapes, and hot coffee. We drank wine later, outside. He was kind, infinitely so, and about wine Fritz had no snobbery or bush-league elitism, but it was always the best of bottles, a quiet wine with Burgundian elegance, chewy and bold. He never showed off. In his innocence, he could find anything and everything amusing. As we talked, he would gently swirl the wine in his glass and, as it descended slowly along the sides—wine experts refer to it as "legs"—he would call it *"Kirchenfenster,"* or church windows, as the wine seemed to form a Gothic arch.

He was a very gentle man, and what I hesitate to go on about was how Toni, his second wife, a bit of a dabbler in watercolors, was very competitive with him, and, to be honestly frank, it was a miracle when Fritz and I would be left alone to talk (he was also a very passionate listener) at those early breakfasts of ours. When she would interrupt, which constantly she did, he would simply hang his head and go silent. I believe that it was painful for her—and why shouldn't it have been?—to have her husband the sole object of almost every visitor.

Amused, Fritz who loved language thought it insightful of me to have once pointed out that almost every American, with a grotesque verbal tic, obsessively answers every question starting with the word *well*. "Well, I guess" *blah blah blah . . .*" He had seen Adolf Hitler in person, in high spirits impersonated runty Dr. Josef Goebbels as a glowering sourball, jokingly showed me how fat Hermann Goering would gluttonously spoon his soup and bow and smile with *taarof*, a Middle Eastern word for overweening, insincere ritual politeness—Fritz with merriment loved doing "bits"—and I recall once or twice he even sang for my delight snippets of *"Blutrote Rosen"* (Blood Red Roses) said to be Hitler and Eva Braun's favorite song, one which Eva played over and over in those last days in the Bunker in April 1945.

I remember one day sitting on our bench and speaking with Fritz about Dostoevsky's *A Writer's Diary* and the moral, social, and political issues raised in its pages. We were discussing the right-wing Russian military officer and journalist Fyodor Vinberg, a fanatical Russian monarchist who with an aristocratic contempt for the masses had been much influenced by the anti-Semitic speculations in the *Diary*, specifically how Jews, controlling capital, were masters of credit and international politics and ruled the stock-exchanges. Dostoevsky seemed formidably if uncharacteristically brutal here—he had a true Slavic, almost blind passion on the subject of Messianism—especially in the controversial chapter, entitled "The Jewish Question," where an incipient anti-Semitism begins to grow flagrant and obvious.

A rabid racist and trumpeting demagogue, Vinberg had called for "Aryan peoples" to unite against the "Jewish plan for world domination." For Russia, he had advocated a return to the muscular authority of the Tsar, which he hoped to reinforce, with German help. He also yearned for Orthodoxy to unite with Catholicism and to learn from its methods in waging ideological war against the enemy, by anathematizing the Freemasonry and all of Satan's servants "at Easter Week in all the churches and all the cathedrals of our homeland."

In the *House of the Dead*, Dostoevsky depicts a deceitful, opportunistic money-lender in the jeweler Isay Fomitch Bumstein, a Jew. In probably his most famous novel, *Crime and Punishment*, the topic of anti-Semitism is hardly mentioned, but still a Jewish character featured in the novel is described in an anti-Semitic way, specifically in the scene where the nefarious pedophile, Svidrigailov, commits suicide by shooting himself in the head, an act committed in front of a Jewish watchman, who is described as having a "look of eternal peevish affliction that is so sourly imprinted on all the faces of the Jewish tribe without exception."

I knew well and loved my Dostoevsky, just as I valued my association with my cherished engraver friend. I had also long pondered the many paradoxes and irreconcilable opposites in the Russian novelist. "One can name Dostoevsky as the genius of contamination. I read him and shudder," wrote the late Harold Bloom, the great professor at Yale University, in his book, *Genius*. Bloom goes on to observe,

> "His obscurantism, which he calls Russian Christianity, embraces a worship of tyranny, a hatred of the United States and of all democracy, and a profound and vicious anti-Semitism. He loathes nihilistic terrorism but endorses the state terrorism of the Russian empire and the church. And yet Dostoevsky is indispensable: he is the satirist who joins Jonathan Swift in exposing our egoism, our cruelty, our hypocrisies, above all our crippling self-consciousness. We are not the same after recognizing the Underground Man in ourselves."

A full listing of writers who had expressed hostility toward Jews and Judaism, extending from Shakespeare to Pushkin, Martin Luther to T. S. Eliot, Louis-Ferdinand Céline to Boris Pasternak, Wyndham Lewis to Ezra Pound, Agatha Christie to Roald Dahl, etc. includes large part of the canon of Western literature. I had long found it to be a strange and perplexing aspect of Dostoevsky's passionate extreme in following Christ to decide to follow in this tradition?

"It was behavior uncharacteristic of him," said Fritz—always that soft voice, the considered opinion—"a dark side."

"By dividing him, don't we excuse him?" I asked.

Looking far way, Fritz kept silent. He knew well the way of the world, far, far better than I did—understood its complexity, its agonies. I brought up the subject of Dostoevsky's *Notebook* of 1880 and one or two of his anti-Semitic rants. ("The Yid and his bank are now reigning over everything; over Europe, education, civilization, socialism—especially socialism, for he will use it to uproot Christianity and destroy its civilization.") I mentioned there was also an entry in the March 1877 volume of *A Writer's Diary* where its author vehemently and explicitly denied being an anti-Semite. Fritz listened. He told me that when he was a small boy he would wander, hatless, into Cologne's magnificent cathedral, the largest, most matchless Gothic church in eastern Europe, the tallest twin-spired church in the world, Germany's most visited landmark, and say prayers that after forty centuries Christians and Jews might get along.

Fritz told me that the Three Kings of Cologne—the blessed Magi or the Three Wise Men mentioned in Matthew's Gospel—are buried in Cologne Cathedral, their bodies having been found in Constantinople in 1158, brought to Milan in an ox cart, and eventually conveyed to Germany by a fiat of the Holy Roman Emperor Frederick Barbarossa. A shrine to the holy men was erected as a large, gilded, and decorated triple sarcophagus placed above and behind the high altar, now a place of pilgrimage. It was among those visited by the Wife of Bath in Chaucer's *Canterbury Tales*.

"'Salvation is from the Jews,'" I said, "as we read in John 4:22 regarding the mystery of your people's salvation." I mentioned that Roy Schoeman, a Jewish scholar who converted to Catholicism, believed that Christianity was the *completion* of Judaism. I met the devoted Schoeman once at MIT. Any Jew who does not accept Jesus, according to Schoeman, has not understood the true role of Judaism in the history of salvation. It is also his belief—his most heartfelt conviction—that what the victims suffered during the Holocaust was an expiation in preparation for the coming return of Christ.

Fritz shook his head in doubt.

But he smiled.

"Or is Mr. Schoeman a showman?"

"*Touché!*"

We sat and looked out at the sea.

"Alyosha, my good scholar, you know your Scripture."

But I only wanted to assure dear Fritz. "It is solid Roman Catholic doctrine that the Jews, in praying for and preparing the way for the Messiah," I said, "actually brought about the incarnation of God as man. Why *else* was Christ born as a Jew? Schoeman's idea is that that Judaism and Christianity can be fully understood only in relation to each other, the very thing you prayed for in Cologne's cathedral. He sees that the role of the Jews, our 'elder brothers' in the faith, so to speak, did not necessarily end with the first coming of Christ. The Church is nothing else but 'post Messianic' Judaism."

My friend replied, "When I grew up, Jews believed that Christianity taught contempt for Jews—despite the fact that 'their' God himself was one—and that if a Jew recognized Jesus as the Messiah, he or she ceased to be a Jew. There are many theories. I have read of course that the prophet Zechariah saw in a vision the first coming of the Messiah. He also prophesied the rejection of Him by His people."

"In a subsequent vision," I said, "Zechariah also saw the Messiah's Second Coming, when He will return to the earth and deliver His people from the nations gathered to fight them. At this time, the Jews will recognize Jesus Christ as the Messiah and worship Him. We know from St. Paul that Jews will exist—persist—as a people until the time of the Second Coming and that the widespread conversion of the Jews at that time will somehow be related to the Second Coming in Zechariah 9–11. Romans 11:25–26 states,

> "For I would not, brethren, that ye should be ignorant of this mystery, lest ye should be wise in your own

conceits; that blindness in part is happened to Israel, until the fulness of the Gentiles be come in.

And so, all Israel shall be saved: as it is written, there shall come out of Sion the Deliverer, and shall turn away ungodliness from Jacob."

The Eichenbergs owned an original Rouault, a black head of Christ, severe, outlined in brutal black lines, which hung in a special place in their living room back in quiet Peace Dale. Fritz loved the book of Isaiah. I remember the fondness he also had for the Epistle to the Philippians, considered to be the most joyful book in all Scripture—the apostle references joy over 16 times in this letter alone all in only 104 verses—expressing how he was struck by the fact that, while it was written by St. Paul the Apostle to the Christian congregation that he had established in a fledgling church Philippi, it was also penned while he was in prison, probably at Rome or Ephesus, about the year 62 A.D.—he was arrested three times in all, the last time in Rome where he was beheaded—where he was jailed for an exorcism that he performed over a slave girl. This is also where the well-known Philippian jailor professed faith in Christ, because he was so moved by Paul's compassion for him.

One afternoon Fritz and I went together to take a look at the Nantucket Whaling Museum, where we enjoyed seeing so many historical objects on display from that dangerous, hard-driving industry that made Nantucket an internationally recognized name in the 18th and 19th centuries—the last whaling ship sailed from Nantucket in 1869—and where in one of the galleries a 46-foot-long sperm whale skeleton is suspended from the ceiling. It was a memorable day.

Why so? Also exhibited there was a splendid collection of

scrimshaw, the real thing, no reproductions, significant objects creatively carved during lulls and various interims at sea by sailors and whalers from the by-product of whales, such as the bones and teeth of sperm whales, the baleen of other whales. Scrimshaw—some think the word derived from a Dutch nautical expression meaning to waste time, for a good piece would require much attention during a sailor's idle hours—was first done by sailors working on whaling ships out of the coast of old New England between 1745 and 1759, until the moratorium of commercial whaling in 1986. Scrimshanders, again, were all amateurs, yet planning a good design required cleverness.

"It is amazing work, isn't it—the detail?" I exclaimed to Fritz, seemingly less enthused. A slight silence held, followed by his gentle laugh. After a delay, smacking my forehead with an anguished palm, I suddenly realized, stupidly, I was standing next to a man, a genius engraver, who could have knocked one off in an hour!

At yet another time I invited him to give a talk and slideshow at the distinguished Phillips Academy* in Andover, Massachusetts, where, having come from Harvard, I was both writer-in-residence and a teacher of English literature from 1978 to 1982. It went over

---

*I have since been banned from the grounds of that school on the basis of a trumped-up accusation against me of a sexual misdemeanor with a female student that was said to have taken place more than 40 years ago, a calumny attributed to me with the craven and overreaching legal ambition of exploiting the deep pockets of that wealthy academy (the #MeToo social movement, praiseworthy in general, also is and was, in many instances, a fishing expedition) but which of course I never committed—or, during my more than 25 years of college teaching, ever thought of committing. To have gone on to fight the charge in court would have cost me and my family a crippling $300,000 or more.

well. I recall Fritz remarking not only on the spaciousness and elegance of the academy but, upon observation, his portentous suggestion that privileges for the young people there was a double-edged sword, not always helpful as they grew.

Fritz had personally known tough-talking Otto Dix, a painter noted for his ruthless and harshly realistic depictions of German society during the Weimar Republic; the Nazis regarded Dix as a "degenerate artist," in spite of he fact that he had fought bravely on western front in World War I and earned the Iron Cross. Fritz also knew Max Beckmann from Leipzig, the German Expressionist painter, a badly wounded and highly disillusioned veteran also plagued by traumatic experiences from The Great War. He also moved to the United States in 1933.

The scandalous contemporary of Fritz, the satirical, irrepressible, "take-no-prisoners" artist George Grosz, he also knew, a fellow whose caricatural and profane drawings Fritz found crude. Grosz was actually prosecuted for blasphemy in 1928 after publishing anticlerical drawings, such as one depicting prisoners under assault from a minister who vomits grenades and weapons onto them, and another showing Christ being coerced into military service! He died in Berlin on July 6, 1959, after crashing down a flight of stairs after a night of drinking. Another of Fritz's friends was Käthe Kollwitz, a committed socialist and pacifist—she later become a Communist—who also worked on wood engraving and lithography, and I well recall Fritz telling me of the anxiety that woman suffered during her childhood due to the death of her son Peter, killed on the battlefield in October 1914.

His sparkling eyes were wise and tender, his smile infectious. He was ever drawn to and fascinated with people and ideas and was easily one of the two or three most widely read men I have ever met, his penchant for long hours of reading not fully unrelated to a life-long disposition to attacks of insomnia ("worrying about the things I plan to do")—his thirst for activity, no doubt, reaching a certain feverish, irrepressible impatience with himself for not doing more. He loved walking along the ocean beach, picking up and later transforming sea stones into strange creatures, faces and animals, and discussing his favorite writers, Shakespeare, Turgenev, Tolstoy, Dostoevsky of course, and Erasmus, whom he personally revered as much as did Hans Holbein the Younger, whose artistry the humanist personally engaged for the first illustrations of the *Praise of Folly*, one of Fritz Eichenberg's favorite books and one for which in 1972 he himself made 10 wood engravings called "In Praise of Folly." He does not paint. "I am not," he smiles, "a colorist."

Those wonderful beach walks! Ambling along a strand of Nantucket or Sandy Neck Beach when he was visiting me at West Barnstable, he would be constantly peering down, searching, only to stop about every 10 feet or so to pick up another stone to examine. "A rabbit," he would say. "A drunken kulak: look at the chin." He'd discard one or two, then snap up another. "That's Neils Bohr!" he'd say. "Why, here is Emil Jannings—the actor? The poor old clown from *The Blue Angel* movie, screeching like a rooster '*keekeereekee*'"? He would laugh. "No, no, no, Alyosha [his name for me]. You're too young to know him."

Fritz had a genius to be astonished. "Look, see the popped eyes on this reddish-yellow stone—I detect a bit of Goethe in the pop eyes!" He would then recite some lines from *Faust*: "*Das Alter macht nicht kindisch, wie man spricht, Es findet uns nur noch als wahre Kinder*" (Age is no second childhood—age makes plain, Children we were, true children we remain). Fritz knew virtually all of the poet's work by heart. He once told me, "I was very proud to be German, Alyosha, I felt it as strongly as part of my face."

A few stones he'd discard after a quick examination. Most he delighted in, turning it for an angle to find a face. Here was Hindenburg, there was a cow. "Look, there is Rasputin! Here, save that one—it's Charlie Chaplin! Charlot!" At one point Fritz bent to pick up a ruddy beach stone with a prominent rail or ridge. "Kaiser Wilhelm II!"

I saw a rude lump with a complicated rictus.

"A mouth?"

"*Schnurrbart!*"

Fritz twirled his own mustache, jokingly.

"The imperial mustache style was called '*Es ist erreicht*'—'it is reached'—and was the brainchild of the German court barber François Haby. He devised a special patented wax on which he also made a tidy profit selling to his elegant and fussy clientele as the 'Kaiser's wax.' See? It was perfumed and turned up at the end. The points stick up with bayonet-like precision. A beard bandage he devised—the 'Haby face strap'—was worn overnight, which had to be fastened behind the ears, like a mask! Haby's barber shop was located in the glamorous quarter of Berlin right near elegant Unter den Linden and became a fashionable meeting place of gossip."

Fritz shook his head negatively and ruefully quoted the Kaiser (*in that madman's raspy demagogic voice!*): "'I trust in God and in my unsheathed sword, and I piss on all resolutions of international conferences!'" In his dramatic personification, so accurate, my friend could have been wearing a Pickelhaube helmet with its distinctive spike on top! "Said the malformed Teutonic dictator whose afflicted left arm, remember, had been badly torn during an arduous birth"—Fritz, his eye for detail ever perfect, draped a hand sideways to duplicate exactly the maimed shape—"'A descendant of Frederick the Great does not abdicate!' No, Alyosha, his descendant just skips town." Fritz smiled to himself, closing his eyes. After slaughtering countless millions, the Kaiser took a train to the neutral Netherlands, at 63 married a German princess, Hermine, 30 years younger than himself, took up chopping down trees and hunting as well as killing thousands of animals as a form of exercise. At night he stimulated his mind by reading, primarily in English, and always aloud—from all reports he never took the tone of the officers' mess out of his voice—the novels of P. G. Wodehouse, his favorite author. He loved candy—Swiss suckets. He passed away calmly tucked in a warm bed in 1941, after having heartily and personally applauding and complimenting Hitler by telegram for capturing the city of Paris, enthusiastically writing, "My Führer, I congratulate you and hope that under your marvelous leadership the German monarchy will be restored completely." Fritz could only add wistfully. "Unimpressed, Adolf Hitler supposedly remarked to Heinz Linge, his valet, 'What an idiot!'"

How Fritz loved to mimic faces, especially the odd types of characters he'd be working on, simply imitating—impersonating—the funny facets and foolishness of subjects he was carving into wood, scrunching up nose and chin and making nutty eyes. Fritz could do every Karamazov face. He was always testing when he worked what facial muscles would go best. (Charles Dickens, who kept a mirror by his writing desk at his chalet at Gad's Hill, also did the same.)

On a long shelf on the porch at Fritz and Toni's house at Quidnet sat a splendid array of various beach stones with the faces of humans and animals he had drawn and colored that had come alive—old men, jut-jawed grumps, foxes, drunks, pirates, witches with seagull-eyes, bears—all of Fritz Eichenberg's ingenious additions in paint following the exact contours of the stones, ribs, hollows, striations, and indentations—and any of their guests upon leaving was allowed to select a stone as a parting gift. I still have and treasure many of mine.

Having become a Quaker, he ascribed to its tenets of integrity, equality, simplicity, community, stewardship of the Earth, and peace. The pacific strain in both the man and his work could be felt instantly upon meeting him. His wood engravings gave proof of that, especially in some of his more renowned single prints such as "Gandhi, Great Soul" (1942), "Black Crucifixion" (1963), "Lao-Tse" (1966), whose *Tao Te Ching* he venerated, and the trilogy on St. Francis, his favorite saint.

Peace is impossible without justice. Fritz believed with Mahatma Gandhi, who always reminded us, "There is a higher court than courts of justice and that is the court of conscience. It supercedes all other courts." Fritz Eichenberg held justice supreme and as an artist could be found to be even didactic—certainly outraged—in the direct, almost Tolstoyan scolding in certain of his prints, animadversions generally against exploitation, social cruelty, and the moronism of war. He was no roundhead, booming evangelical, or vice-spanker but simply a man extremely impatient with injustice, obfuscation, neutral people, and the fakery that is too often the quiddity of subjective art. "My affliction," he once told me, "is perspective."

The affliction—a paramount one, whether literal or figurative—is always the artist's. It haunts his dreams. It haunts his waking hours.

Fritz saw and valued each man as a member of a group, as in a Quaker meeting, with authority remaining essentially mutual between people, not above them, correlating consideration being born of a strong faith in humanity with no loud, brutal, overbearing leaders, cumulative harmony being the inexorable power. Consensus ruled. Love and decency determined consensus.

Toward the end, making decisions, suffering from Parkinson's disease, Fritz offered to donate his entire work to Harvard University, the full *oeuvre*, a gathering of hundreds of his original woodblocks that were all carefully stacked and catalogued in a special room, gathered over decades. "How will we get them here?" he was asked in an official letter by one of the penny-pinching halfwits there in charge of collections, one of the lazy—and, needless to say, almost preternaturally improvident—dumbbells in that university's acquisitions department, surely one of the laziest bastards on earth. With a shrug, Fritz donated the entire collection to Yale.

I could never help but reflect whenever I had the chance to look at one of his original wood engravings—the original completed pearwood blocks, where each delicate stroke had been perfectly gouged, seeing up close the white indented cuts in wood that literally took your breath away, all pristine in finished perfection, a few battered like the failed pietàs of Michelangelo, with each presentation, nevertheless, plausible and containing details so subtle, unexpected, yet artistically consonant with everything else in the framed block—that the affliction for that perspective, pursuing the mystery and magic, the entire endless splendid illustrated almanac of mankind, was born not from common observation, nor solely of the fancy of the Romantic imagination, but rather grew with the long nights of insomnia that had haunted the little boy back in Cologne no less than they had the venerable artist, having grown old, in Peace Dale, Rhode Island, the relentless awareness of the "watchman of the night" who, at constant vigil, to give us the second chance art offers from what life too often steals, must wait out the long terrible hours Dostoevsky writes of—

> "Sometimes whole nights pass in indescribable delights; often in a few hours one lives through a paradise of love or a whole enormous life, gigantic, unheard-of, marvelous as a dream grandly beautiful. By some unknown whim the pulse speeds up, tears spurt, the pale moist cheeks burn with feverish fires, and when the dawn with its rosy light flashes in the window of the dreamer, he is pale, sick, tormented, and happy."

—so that in the morning he can tell those of us who slept just what he saw.

The Barnstable Bat Company

Baseball has a solid Cape Cod tradition. On its many semi-professional ball fields, the Cape Cod Baseball League—one of the nation's premier collegiate summer leagues boasting over one thousand former players (15 percent of Big Leaguers have played in the Cape League and eleven have been all-stars)—has included such notables as Carlton Fisk, Thurman Munson, Nomar Garciaparra, John Valentin, Mo Vaughn, Albert Belle, Frank Thomas, Chuck Knoblauch, and Jeff Bagwell, Ron darling, Jason Varitek, Jackie Bradley Jr., and one of the greatest home run sluggers of all time, the peerless New York Yankee Aaron Judge who played with the Brewster Whitecaps in 2012.

It became the idea of baseball fan Tom Bednark, who was born in Hyannis and who has been a lifelong woodworker—interestingly, the surname Bednark means "cooper" or barrel-maker—to start up the Barnstable Bat Company. In 1992, with the help of his wife Christine, both of whom live in Centerville, Massachusetts, the dream was realized. Bednark's elegant bats are "approved for game play," an accreditation he formally received several years ago. Look closely next time your at the ballpark or watching a game on television. Many batters will be swinging a bat with the trademark cod logo.

It comes as no surprise to anyone that the kings of the base-ball bat industry are, and have long been, the Hillerich & Bradsby Company in Louisville, Kentucky, a firm that turns out about 2½ million wooden bats a year, along with its smaller but dogged rival, Rawlings, Inc. in St. Louis, Missouri, which produces about 600,000 bats a year. In the pre-aluminum bat days, which basically goes back some 50 years—wooden bats are officially required in Major League Baseball—Hillerich was turning out as many as 7½ million wooden bats a year. "I can do about fifty a day," Tom tells me as I watch him, earphones and gloves, sanding down a bat on his impressive Delta DL40 lathe. He slides the form carefully out of the lathe.

"Notice how the knob shape happens to coincide by way of ergonomics with the index finger and thumb," he says, holding the bat upside-down and grasping the handle. Each bat is hewn from a 38-inch ash billet, which is initially cut into an octagon. "It is less wear and tear on the lathe," says Tom, who then sets it into a semi-automatic hydraulic copy lathe, pre-set from a pattern bat, which is cut to shape within minutes, trimmed with exactitude like a perfectly peeled apple, identifiable and ready for use. Bednark with speedy calipers constantly checks the three main parts of every bat—barrel, handle, and knob. Bats are sanded, branded with the company logo by means of a hot branding iron, another small machine, and then in a room upstairs in the shop dipped with two separate coats in a waterborne lacquer. The elegant asymmetries of a baseball bat, with its aerial, rocket-like, biomorphic shape, Bednark with no small authority compares to the fluting of a Doric column, which, as good classical students remember, all imperceptibly bulge for grace.

Tom hands me a smooth, just-finished copy, which feels in

the grip like part of my hand, its smooth parabolic length virtually inviting a swing, the marriage of fat barrel and slender handle whip-tantalizing.

"Ash is best," Tom points out, "because it's a lightweight, flexible wood and has good shock resistance. The material is such, notice, that the fibrous quality is very long." He asks me to squint and eye the grain. "A bundle of straws, you might say, whereas a piece of pine, which would not be good, might be compared to a bundle of rice." One could not miss walking into his shop an array of huge pallets in which were piled square ash slugs. "The key to this business is getting good material," Tom tells me. "I use several suppliers. Most of my wood comes from mills in and around Pennsylvania. Strictly ash." Locust wood, as durable as rocks, he explains, is far too heavy. Apple wood is too scarce, chestnut generally not available. Hickory was often used in Major League Baseball in the Twenties and Thirties but proved to be far too heavy, especially as pitching improved. I asked Tom what wood would make the handsomest commemorative bat. "Brazilian rosewood," he said, "beautiful for its dark super quality. But for flexibility and power, the great workaday wood is ash. Arid not only for bats. The same goes for skis, toboggans, lacrosse sticks, snowshoes, hockey sticks, of course, even ash-split baskets."

Both the American and National Leagues now use Barnstable bats. The Minnesota Twins, Kansas City Royals, and Boston Red Sox also mostly used BBC bats in game play. The Oakland Athletics are particularly good customers, Tom tells me. The front cover of the *A's Magazine* (volume 2, no.2) shows a smiling, muscular José Canseco, in bright color, confidently leaning on a Barnstable Bat. Powerful Geronimo Berroa, the former A's hitter, later with the Cleveland Indians, once hit eight home runs in 24 at-bats swinging a Barnstable Bat, just as he used one back in 1996 hitting 31 of 36 home runs. Going back some, such ballplayers as David Segul, Scott Spiezio, John Valentin, Mark Grace, and Joe Vitiello, among others, often leave model pattern bats for Tom and Christine, the efficient company business manager, to keep on file. The Barnstable Bat Company, incidentally, also makes stick-ball bats, training bats, fungoes—even fish-billies to thwack a big bass—which are given as gifts for graduation, Christmas, birthdays, etc. all over the country and for all ages.

All bats presently used in the Major Leagues have to be regulation brown, neutral, or black. White bats are not allowed, simply because they cannot be seen well against white shirts, get lost in checked swings, etc. Nor are colored bats allowed, striped bats, or any imaginative variations thereof. Tom Bednark suspects, and I agree, that macho guys tend to like black bats. Babe Ruth, who wielded the first black baseball bat of renown, loved his "Black Betsy," which also happened to be the nickname that Shoeless Joe Jackson gave to his own bat. Reggie Jackson in his day was always boastfully wagging and waving a favorite black bat of his. At a spring training news conference in 1977, he had just signed a five-year contract for $3.75 million, to which was added the gift of a brand-new Rolls Royce; Jackson with typical grace and self-effacement told reporters, "You see this? This is the Dues Collector. This now helps the Yankees intimidate every other team in baseball. That is what I do, man, just by walking into this clubhouse! Nobody will embarrass the Yankees in the World Series as long as I am carrying the Dues Collector." Just for the record, the great Jackson struck out 129 times that formidable season, a Major League record for one year.

Cupped bats, a Japanese invention of the late 1970s—actually a legal way to cork a bat—is now commonly used. "Cupping out" the knob of a bat, for lightness, involves dishing out a two-inch in diameter, one-inch deep cut from the top of the barrel, in a sense, Edselizing it. Light bats, unlike in former times, are favored nowadays. A 40-ounce bat today is fairly rare, whereas in the 1920s it was just the thing. Players often used 6-ouncers in the 1970s, but, again, such a bat today is accounted heavy. Ken Griffey Jr. used a 34-ounce, 31-inch bat, Nomar Garciaparra a 33-ounce, 31-inch. All bat measurements, like men's trousers, come in twos. Even Reggie Jackson used a 34-ounce, 35-inch, although Mo Vaughan and Kevin Mitchell, big men, used 36-36 potwallopers, while Tony Gwynne prefers a 32-inch, 31-ounce bat, which nowadays is about as light as it gets.

"Aluminum bats trampoline the ball," Bednark says, explaining how swiftly a ball can fly off metal, say, back to the pitcher, which makes me recall the Herb Score tragedy. On May 7, 1957, during the first inning of a night game against the New York Yankees at Municipal Stadium in Cleveland, Herb Score threw a low fastball to Gil McDougald with Jim Hegan catching. McDougald lined the pitch to the mound and struck Score in the face, breaking Score's facial bones and injuring his eye. "Anything hit back to a pitcher under 4/10ths of a second can be fatal to the guy. Think of someone with José Canseco's or Aaron Judge's or Vladimir Guerrero Jr.'s bat-speed, maybe the fastest today. Using an aluminum bat today, he might kill someone." If that is not a good enough reason why metal bats are prohibited in Major League Baseball, then think of tradition in the sport. Wood being supplanted by metal is like replacing leather gloves by plastic ones.

I asked Tom if a really great hitter could use any size bat and succeed. His answer seemed perfect. "It depends on who is pitching," he said, which I thought was right to the point. Most hitters are, not surprisingly, highly fastidious about their bats—their primary tool, after all. (Note: that is, unless merchandising is involved. Mo Vaughn earned $25,000 a year for wearing a brand batting glove. That's not a lot? Tiger Woods got $40 million a year for wearing Nike apparel.) A big barrel or small? A thin handle or thickish? Whereas the average bat handle goes about .46 in diameter, about 15/16th, John Valentin likes a bat handle almost scarily thin—.826 inch in diameter—coupled with a big barrel. I wondered about "boning" bats, the way sluggers like Ted Williams and Rod Carew used to do.

"I always worked with my bats, boning them down, putting a shine on them, forcing the fibers together," wrote Ted Williams, the greatest hitter in baseball, in his autobiography, *My Turn at Bat* (1969). "Not just the handle, the whole bat. I treated them like babies. Weight tolerance got to be a big thing with me. The weight can change. Early in the season it's cold and damp and the bats lying around on the ground pick up moisture and get heavier. I used to take them down to the post office to have them weighed. Eventually, with the Red Sox, we got a little set of scales put in the locker room. I'll never forget Mr. Hillerich of Hillerich & Bradsby, the Louisville Slugger Company, put six bats on a bed in Boston. One was a half ounce heavier than the others. He had me close my eyes and pick out the heavier bat. I picked it out twice in a row."

After early experimentation, vintage Williams, oddly enough, always chose lighter bats, usually 33 or 34 ounces, never more than 34, once in a while a 31. He tended to use heavier ones in spring. "You're stronger then, the pitchers are still working to get their stuff down, to get their control."

In Tom's opinion, boning a bat or cooking it ("flame-tempering") does not accomplish much. Even if you do compress the bat a bit by boning it, he feels that it is basically done to pass the time, personalizing it somehow, but he does explain that small dings can be corrected by leaving water on them for a while and letting the wood expand.

On almost any new bat, varicolored wood can be seen, darker and lighter striations in the ash grain. All wood of course documents both the tree's growth and the moisture content within it. Summer wood on a bat is the darker strain which is less dense, while spring wood, much lighter, is also more dense. Hitting the ball on the edge grain will always give a better feel upon contact and reduce bat breakage. (A good oak floor always has a vertical or quarter sawn grain.) With the label in the 12 o'clock position, the ball should be hit—"sweetly"—at the 3 or 9 o'clock points or positions, and you may have to rotate the bat in your hand in order to make contact at these sweet areas.

A bat is a hitter's tool, it should be treated as such. Keep the label in the up position. Do not hit objects other than those for which it has been made. Do not leave your bat in the rain or on wet grass, where it will pick up moisture. Keep your bat free of dirt, oils, waxes, and all other foreign materials. It is your weapon and your friend. These simple rules increase bat life. Good luck and great hitting!

I have to add a coda, which speaks directly to American ingenuity. There is something about work done in such small tidy businesses, especially one pursued with passion, invariably having as much to do with dreams as dollars. It could be making spaghetti sauce, tin airplanes, or carnauba wax. Whatever, it involves ritual, becomes almost commemorative and involves in its commitment and its sense of accomplishment a very literal kind of ceremony. A fascination by way of hobby somehow prevails. Preoccupation in such cases marries profession. And how very American is the grand idea or making the perfect baseball bat! Surely the comfort in this age of major technology and soulless major franchises is that, as in the Baseball Bat Company, we find something, so elegantly created, we can not only admire but treasure that is as traditional as baseball and as elemental as good plain wood.

Santa Fé Trails

Santa Fé is a perfumed city, affectionately dubbed—not by me—the "City Different." (I personally find the lumbering pretention of Wallace Nutting-like inversions like *Massachusetts Beautiful* a bit too quaint by half.) No city on earth is pervaded by such lovely scents, the headiest being piñon wood, burned in corner fireplaces all over the city. Small details fix themselves in one's mind: the shades of the hollyhocks in every yard, the graceful branches (and in Gene Autry's' case, of course, the "murmur") of the cottonwood trees, the Indian, the rare colors of the soil, the solid bolts of blue sky, the open expanses of space. The name is properly accented on the first word, at least it is done so there, and in my opinion it is thoughtless, and passingly ignorant, to leave off the accent mark on the second word. Granted, mine is not the argument from authority. Prior to my landing in Santa Fé in March of 1991, I had never traveled west of the Mississippi.

The place is still, as Willa Cather noted in 1927, "A thin, wavering adobe town . . . a green plaza . . . at the end a church with two earthen towers that rose high above the flatness."

The oldest seat of government in America, Santa Fé ("Holy Faith") was founded by Don Pedro de Peralta in about 1610—

10 years before the Pilgrims landed at Plymouth Rock, although New Mexico did not officially become a state until 1912. (Is that strange? Native Americans were not recognized as U.S. citizens until 1924!) During the Spanish Period, pueblo people were not even allowed to have *horses*, which were necessary at the time for threshing wheat, which they in turn consequently had to buy! A century later, the city developed a thriving trade with the Chihuahua in Mexico and with the Plains Indians.

After 1821, the famous Santa Fé Trail, commencing in Independence, Missouri, became an international trade route, with traders coming to deal with Mexican soldiers and Indians and many shipments continuing down to Albur*q*uerque (as it was spelled then) and on to California. (The city's original spelling was lost when an Anglo stationmaster dropped the first *r* on the railroad sign.) By 1824, according to historian R. V. Vine, one caravan along the trail returned with furs and silver worth $190,000. Traders were turning profits of 600 percent. East swapped with west. In return for the goods they desired, clothing, cotton cloth, lace, jewelry, furniture, china, musical instruments, tobacco, and spices, New Mexicans, as for convenience we called people living out there then, exchanged gold, silver, horses, woolen goods—sheep were everywhere out west—furs, cowhides and mules.

It has been famous for some time, along with Taos, an artist's haven, the third largest art market in the United States. As Arrell Horgan Gibson points out in his comprehensive study *The Santa Fé and Taos Colonies*, "By 1920 the Santa Fe and Taos colonies were well established. Intensive application by pioneers to northern New Mexico's hauntingly rich natural and social environments had yielded paintings of considerable quality . . . And the increasing number of tourists visiting northern New Mexico, many of them purchasers of paintings by local artists, and several national newspaper and magazine articles featuring the colonies and painters further popularized the region."

Both strongly contemporary and almost definitively Native American, the Santa Fé market represents less a series of movements or periods than a continuum, what W. B. Yeats called in a different context "unity of culture." The same paintings that originally drew collectors to the Southwest remain the foundation of the lively art market flourishing in that city today. A long, dramatic history connects the old Spanish and Native American traditions with what in pottery, painting, and various crafts is happening today, a common thread that runs through the surrounding land and its people. It is ludicrous to think of Santa Fé only as exporting to the rest of the country what is called the "Santa Fé look" and its iterations, that staple of so many decorating magazines (terracotta tiles, bleached pine furniture, and, on the wall, the strategically placed bleached cow skull). Conveniently, the majority of art galleries in this small western city are concentrated on three streets: Old Santa Fé Trail, East Palace Avenue, and Canyon Road, sort of the "royal mile" of art.

I walked up along Canyon Road, where with something over 60 galleries you wish you were being carted along in a rickshaw. There is an endlessness to it, but it is worth the trek. I saw amulets from Africa, Haitian voodoo banners, and 50 or so bronze and copper Guatemalan masks at Economos Works of Art, along with some superb pre-Columbian art and Mexican Colonial furniture. I also stopped in at and poked around in the Canfield Gallery and at Zaplin-Lampert to look at Native American pottery, intricate beadwork, and coiled baskets. I also saw a Couse, a Gaspard, a Bispham, some beautiful hand-colored George Catlin lithographs, and a superb William Victor Higgins called *By the River's Edge* for $75,000. (A later member of the Taos Society, Higgins, with his bold silhouettes and dramatic color, admirably managed to avoid romanticizing the Indian.)

The Fenn Gallery, owned for the last three years by Nedra and Richard Matteucci, has one of the finest collections of historical and contemporary art in the country. It houses some of western painting's biggest names. C. M. Russell. Randall Davey. Georgia O'Keeffe. Henriette Wyeth Hurd. Nikolai Fechin. Leon Gaspard. There is a wonderful spectrum, as well, of contemporary artists, such as Wilson Hurley, Gary Niblett, Dan Ostermiller, George Lundeen, and Doug Higgins. One can see everything there, shrunken heads, old toys, African sculpture, 18th-century signs, all sorts of Americana. I found, typical with me, one painting I wanted to buy, a lovely Childe Hassam, *Fithian Farm*, selling for $300,000. I walked through the sculpture garden where there is much ornamental art for sale, especially good work by Native Americans Doug Hyde and Francisco Zuñiga. I was shown around the private house. I saw the room where Mrs. Onassis slept on her visits there, also the "shepherd's fireplace," a compound white adobe arrangement where one can sleep on top of the hearth heating you, rather like a duck who can drink what it also floats on, and, among other things, an entire wall hung with collected artists' palettes and a small white bathroom on one of the walls of which Eric Sloan painted a country scene.

There are some wonderful smaller galleries on Canyon Road, as well, like Bella Artes with its Coptic and pre-Columbian art, ancient textiles, and contemporary clay and the Ernesto Mayans Gallery, where you can see, as I did, not only a superb selection of old Afghan war rugs but a 30-year retrospective of oil paintings by Ralph Leon, who, at the time, lived in Santa Fé. At the Munson

Gallery, although its stress is basically contemporary, I saw examples of 100-year-old Lacateros furniture, chairs and doors made from mesquite and ancient rock-hard sabino wood, with its blond and silky sharp grain. Sabino, a family of cypress, is now virtually extinct. A New Mexican law, it was explained to me, forbids anyone from cutting down a Sabino tree. There are many unexpected things to be seen in the galleries and shops on Canyon Road, everything from abstract paintings to contemporary gold-leaf fiber to $10,000 tomahawks to Tarahumara stools, dough bowls, and heavy hand-made stone *matates*, Indian mortar and pestles used for grinding corn.

The Morning Star Gallery, located in an adobe hacienda, is particularly remarkable, with art and artifacts from more than fifty North American Indian tribes. I saw a Sioux beaded baby cra-dles, Nez Percé horse martingales, a Zuni polychrome storage jar, Blackfoot rifle scabbards, and a unique display of 100-year-old col-ored pencil drawings by Arapaho, Kiowa, and Cheyenne children from primitive notebooks done on lined ledger paper, the only paper available to Plains Indians at the time. I was particularly struck by the baskets. I looked into baskets dating back to the Anasazi period. Anasazi (a Navajo word meaning the "ancient ones") refers to the basket makers of about 2000 years ago. The Apache baskets were brilliantly woven. I especially admired a Hopi First Mesa wicker-work cradle, an archer's bow of green wood with a tight foundation of the tough twigs of sumac sterns tied across it with yucca and buckskin thongs. I also managed to learn something about "twin-ing," an old method in basketry which is rarely done anymore, where two strands at a time are woven in and out through a set of founda-tion strands, one passing over and one under, then twisted together each time they meet') For some reason, horrible to relate, I always sneeze around baskets. Or could it have been from the juniper trees or the chamisa, the low saw-green bushes with yellow blossoms that flourish around Santa Fé? And there is no end of breathtaking pottery.

Santa Fé is the *locus classicus* of Native American art. There can be found no end of yucca ring baskets, Hopi throwing sticks, Cochiti drums, Zuni turquoise-and-silver rings, Zapotec rugs, clay luminaries, wedding shawls and sashes, plaited Jemez winnowing trays, tortoise rattles, antique pump drills for making holes in turquoise, Apache bows, arrows, and wrist-guards, stone mauls, Navajo mud rugs, huge Mogollon storage jars, Papago and Anasazi fiber sandals. To my dismay, there was literally nothing whatsoever in the diverse and widely representative collections I saw—and I inquired—done by Indians from the area where I lived, Cape Cod and environs, and the explanation seemed sound; Indians from the east, like Seminoles from Florida and Wampanoags from Massachusetts, disappeared very early, with many killed, thanks to white settlers.

I also saw a lot of kachinas, dolls initially made for Hopi children and originally used to explain to them the mysteries of religion. They represent spirits and supernatural beings, not unlike the saints in Christianity to whom we turn for help and intercession. There are as many as 250 to 500 distinct kachinas—for example, Tawa, the sun kachina, Chaveyo, the ogre (or disciplinarian), Koyemsi, the mudhead clown, Eototo, chief of the kachinas, and so forth—and are said to live, from July to the winter solstice, in the mountains of the San Francisco Peaks near Flagstaff, Arizona, and then dwell for rest of the year as invited guests among the Hopi. Carved from soft wood, sometimes the pith of a yucca plant, most often from the roots of the water-seeking cottonwood tree, which is considered sacred, the dolls are spiritually linked to Mother Earth, source of the *Wuya* or spirit power.

Today the dolls, or *tihus* as the Hopi refer to them, have found their way into galleries and homes and have become a popular collectible. (Senator Barry Goldwater apparently owned a vast collection.) Did you know that the Heheya kachinas are always found in pairs? That there is a male kachina dressed in women's clothes? That the Angwushahai-i kachina is green, has wings, and carries a whip?

I spent next day around the Plaza, visiting more galleries. I went to the Wyeth Hurd Gallery on San Francisco Street. Found there are mostly posters, books, reproductions of the illustrious Wyeth family and Peter Hurd, who resigned from West Point to pursue his interest in painting—nevertheless, he did serve with the Fifth Army in Italy and was on B-17-E bombers in 1942—and whose work is strongly associated with the people and landscapes of San Patricio, New Mexico, where he lived in the1930s. I saw many signed limited editions of his wife since 1921, Henriette Wyeth Hurd, the matriarch of the family, sister of Andrew, aunt of Jamie, mother of Michael, who continued to paint at the Hurd Ranch where, although raised at Chadds Ford, Pennsylvania, having studied with her father, the renowned painter N. C. Wyeth, she lived for more than 40 years until her death in 1997. Many insist that she was the strongest portrait painter in the family, in spite of a crippled right hand caused by a childhood bout with polio.

The silverwork at James Reid, Ltd. was impressive, buckle sets, heaps of remarkable concho belts of countless different designs, ranger belts made of alligator and lizard, and Native American weaving. I was surprised to learn on my trip that there was no Indian silver fashioned before 1050 or so. And even then their material was coin silver, generally Mexican pesos, which were melted in home-made crucibles and hammered in tiny forges. (Did you know, as the Navajo were never converted to Christianity, no silver crosses were done by them?) There is much to learn in Santa Fé. Paradoxically, the closer I looked, and as my interests grew, the more ignorant I felt. Imagine a Bostonian who had never traveled east of Akron, Ohio, and being in Santa Fé for less than a day suddenly hearing, "What you're holding is a classic Second Phase Navajo chief's wearing blanket, circa 1055, in white and brown undyed homespun with accents of cochineal lac and indigo. Are you interested in herringbone yergas? Or plainweave sabanillas? What about Colchas?"

There were at the Gerald Peters Gallery, an especially intriguing place back on Canyon Road, many traditional American paintings, quite a few landscapes by Joseph Sharp and others who in 1915, all having come west later in life, formed the Taos Society of Artists, Oskar Berninghaus, W. Herbert Dunton, E. Irving Couse, and of course Ernest Blumenschein, noted for paintings of Native Americans, New Mexico, and the American Southwest and whose house I later saw in Taos. "We all drifted into Taos," wrote Blumenschein somewhat later, "like skilled hands looking for a steady job. We found it, and it grew into an urge that pushed us to our limits, a joyous inspiration . . .we lived only to paint." I was greatly attracted to one particular Blumenschein, *My Sister Anna*, which cost $135,000. The Taos Society essentially wanted to exhibit its members work through traveling exhibitions. The Santa Fé railroad, actively engaged from 1914 to 1936 in promoting regional tourism and artistic interest in the Southwest, was soon giving artists free passage out West and commissioning pictures for advertisements in popular magazines, which over a very short time were soon decorating the walls of train stations and affiliates, and the pioneering Fred

Harvey restaurants and hotels, the Ho-Jos—dare I say McDonalds—of their day, poking up all along the train routes.

At the Joshua Baer Gallery on East Palace Avenue, I wet through piles of brilliantly colored Navajo wearing blankets, Zapotec rugs, which are Mexican of course and not Native American, chiefs' blankets, and children's serapes of indeterminate age, although almost all are 19th-century—most American Indian art is neither signed nor dated—some of the most beautiful colors and craft work I have seen in any art. I saw at the Baer pieces of Mimbres pictorial pottery from Southern New Mexico and their thousand-year-old "kill pots," prehistoric bowls with ritual holes and dramatic intentional punctures punched into their bases, unearthed long ago from many Indian burial sites.

Making pots was to the Pueblo Indians what masks and woodcarving were to the Indians of the Northwest and beadwork to those living on the Plains. Historically, it was always Native American women who made pots, just as they did baskets, and every woman made her own. An inveterate Indian rule was that the person who was going to use a tool should make it, and pots were women's tools. Flaking stone tools, bows, arrows, and knives were men's work. I saw in Santa Fé some delicate pots done by the celebrated Nampeyo of Hano on Hopi First Mesa and even some of the famous matte black on polished black originals done by Maria Martinez of the San Ildefonso Pueblo who, with her husband, Julian (he applied designs)—one of the few men connected with pottery making—revived pottery in 1910, going through all the steps, grinding the clay, coiling it, shaping it, baking it, painting it, and in her case, even making adaptations of various old styles. Their son, Popovi Da, worked with his parents on pots, as well

The works of Maria Martinez, and especially her black

ware pottery, survive in many museums, including the Smithsonian, the Metropolitan Museum of Art, The Denver Art Museum, and more. The Penn Museum in Philadelphia holds eight vessels—three plates and five jars—signed either "Marie" or "Marie & Julian."

A true expert can recognize pots of different pueblos by whether the clay is fine or coarse, mixed with sand or mica, even by the color and nature of the "slip," layers of soft wet un-tempered clay, usually white or red. He or she can immediately distinguish a Pojoaque Polychrome jar from a Kiua pot from Santo Domingo and Cochitit and so on. As with any work of art, each pot has its specific history, whether it be a three-colored Santa Ana or a Tesuque black on cream or Hopi black on mottled orange. Many of these pots cannot be had for less than tens of thousands of dollars.

They can have come from any one of five periods, early Pueblo (700–1100), for instance, or Spanish (1520–1670). There are of course distinct shapes (Acoma pottery is recognized by its thinness, for example, Santa Clara often for its double-necked spouts, which are almost always wedding vases, etc.) and specific designs (the Zuni specialized in owls, San Ildefonso had its plumed serpents, and the San Juan, Taos, and Picuris Pueblos often decorated their pots with bumps, raised projections, and bas-relief instead of painting them.) Modern pottery-makers, compromising their art, or so many seem to feel, now often use pottery wheels and commercial paint. Many artists even fire their pots in modern kilns. And they look perfect. Symmetrical. But traditional pottery, like Henry Adams's Chartres, dramatically fashioned by the human hand, is not about perfection.

I sat down on a wooden bench for respite in the center of the Plaza—*the* Plaza—and while munching two *sopapillas* took a moment to check out the famous gaffes on the Civil War obelisk there, probably the only monument to Union forces south of the Mason-Dixon line, and the only one publicly bearing the pejorative word "rebels." On the south side, "febuary" is misspelled that way. The deleted word on the north side was originally "savage," in reference to the Indians. In Santa Fé, the plaza has for hundreds of years been the main local meeting area, a smaller version of the Boston Common in my neck of the woods, the square a central hitching-post spot for riding travelers who would cover their burro's eyes with a coat and then go to spend three or four hours in a local cantina.

On the north side of the Plaza stands the Palace of the Governors, where General Lew Wallace, governor of New Mexico from 1878 to 1831, completed writing his novel *Ben-Hur: A Tale of the Christ* (1880, considered "the most influential Christian book of the nineteenth century"). I was lodging during stay at the historic La Fonda Hotel, just off the Plaza, at 65 feet the maximum allowable building height in Santa Fé, where the killer Billy the Kid—a psychopathic teenager named Henry McCarthy, born of Irish parents in the New York slums and whose mother married a miner in 1873 in Santa Fé—supposedly once worked in the kitchen. I finished my lunch, took out my map, found the street, and ran up to Artist Road, pausing for several minutes on a height there to view the lovely rust-pink Sangre de Cristo mountains, an exquisite view during the day but dark and angry in the rain I would later see, in order to leave a note for Evan S. Connell Jr., a novelist I had long admired, asking him to have a drink with me sometime before I left the environs of beautiful Santa Fé.

On my way back I took some time along the walkway, in front of the old venerable Palace of Governors—where incidentally Indians, alone, are by law allowed to sell their wares—to look at the silver jewelry and pawn usually spread out there on rugs. One night I talked to a man just around the corner from the Plaza selling *paño* or "confinement" art, a genre I had not previously heard of, paintings on handkerchiefs (*paños*) that had been done in prisons. There are seven or eight prisons near Santa Fé, including the Penitentiary of New Mexico. Misery exists there, do not doubt it. The drop-out rate in schools in New Mexico then was as high as 27 percent. And I was reminded of the many poor, luckless, downtrodden, and disenfranchised who live in and around that lovely, but in many ways, very preppy, capital, an anomaly to a degree in a state that is often ranked around 44th in per capita income. Most, needless to say, cannot afford to buy paintings. For many people Bingo nights held at various pueblos is their only entertainment. Pueblos have exemptions for gambling, so a game on a reservation—or "rez," as the Native Americans call it—can have high stakes.

Although I roamed the galleries for days, let me assure you, lest you think I swallowed Santa Fé whole, there is some awful art. Horrible stuff! A lot of the camping-under-the-stars variety. Bronze Louis L'Amour cowboys on rearing broncos. Cross-eyed and mojoless kachinas that looked like they had been cobbled together on an assembly line in Perth Amboy, New Jersey. Overly enthusiastic paintings of Indians, showing only the multicolored serapes on their backs, the equivalent in paint, to my mind, of certain regional *jeu de mots* ("Chili today, hot tamale"), the kind of thing found on bumper stickers, thought cute in so many circles. Ersatz pottery. A lot of nickel. Bad turquoise. Ropes of goofily made concha belts and crapola silver. Reproductions of pre-Columbian statues resembling droogs. Almost *anything* with an eagle on it! All bolo ties. Beanbags in the shape of tacos and chili peppers. Appliqued Western wear and coyote humor in all its incarnations. Cow skulls probably mailed in crates from stockyards in Chicago. An entire dunciad, carved in wood, of sagacious Indian chiefs with noses like can-openers staring out of witless whittledom!

I found myself daydreaming about the Blumenschein painting. I stopped for a beer on East De Vargas Street, sipping it at a table in front of the "Oldest House in the U.S.A.," the last remnant, supposedly, from the year 1200 of the Pueblo of Analco. Recent excavations under the Oldest Church, the San Miguel Mission standing nearby, revealed pottery fragments from the period before those ancient people were driven west across the Rio Grande to the cliff dwellings of Puyé and Frijoles. The place was said to be haunted by witches who once lived here with bunches of owl feathers hanging from the *vigas*. My mind was only for the Blumenschein. I was in the grip of the Oldest Vice, greed, haggling in my mind with a stubborn if imaginary clerk at the Peters Gallery. I made various offers in my waking dreams, fair ones, desperate ones. I pleaded, I cajoled. At the actual negotiation, he was intransigent. I remember the final ignominy of our exchange, when he said, "OK, for you— $184,000."

What now, I thought. I had spent too much time in too many galleries, libraries, bookshops checking facts. I wanted to see more of the outlying countryside, the pueblos, the land, the native Americans, the outlying churches, the various cultures that gave us the artists who made those galleries run. It is quite remarkable how, leaving Santa Fé in any direction, you can feel the healing openness of desert spaces suddenly revealed. I climbed the Puyé cliffs, visited soulless Los Alamos—it seems to be 1953 there, perpetually—and one afternoon drove to outlying Abiquiu, to see Georgia O'Keeffe's Ghost Ranch. The location, disappointingly, is now used as a Presbyterian retreat center of some sort, and no one there would tell me of the many houses which of the ones she once inhabited.

On another drive I went south for a while down the bumpy Cerrillos road out to tiny little Madrid, a dusty western town—a name pronounced in those parts on the first syllable—of unprepossessing shotgun shacks, listing houses, and abandoned mines. It seemed like the sort of desolate refuge for not only loners but disaffected marginals from society. (Claire Quilty's profane dude ranch in Vladimir Nabokov's novel *Lolita* was located near Santa Fé!) I noticed a lot of old hippies wearing pigtails.

I walked through the deserted Old Coal Mine Museum. (That new, secret, and cobbled-together city called Los Alamos, high on a lonely mesa northwest of Santa Fé, once needed coal, and lots of it). I stopped to have a beer in the Jail Bar, where standing next to me was a man in black pointed hat who pointed outside. "Madrid has no town drunk," he told me, wheezing with laughter "We all take turns." I was told that back in the 1800s there had been 21 saloons and four hotels in Cerrillos and that a Disney movie (*The Nine Lives of Elfego Baca*) had been shot there in 1958. An old cemented-up opera house still stands there. But where were the turquoise mines I had heard about? Well, there was one, but it turned out it was closed or shut down or something. An old fellow in a general store, where I stopped to inquire and to buy some jerky (*cherque* is Spanish for dried beef), took a moment, slipping off his necklace and nearsightedly fingering a few nuggets, to give me a disquisition on turquoise. I got little out of it, I'm afraid, save the general impression there are as many kinds of turquoises on earth, what with the varieties of color, quality, and weight, as there are, too vast to taxonomize, things like ants or cockroaches or other creepy crawlies. I believe the old dodger's main advice was, frankly, *don't trust any*.

Back in Santa Fé I went to the Channing Dale Throckmorton Gallery to see some African and Oceanic stuff. There was an exceptional selection of 12th-century Anasazi work here, along with Acoma, Zia, and Picuris pueblo pottery. The gallery specialized in tribal arts of ancient peoples from all over the world. I met Ted Dale, who showed me a fascinating array of Senufo helmuts and masks, Luba stools, and knives. He himself collected shields and tapa cloth. The colonial religious art there is remarkable. But my eye was for the carved retablos, the New Mexican crucifixes, with bloody corpses, those dramatic figures called *santos* brilliantly carved by various *santeros*, artists who cut and whittled with a sense of faith and who collected pitch and gypsum and gathered pigments from clays and vegetation growing near their homes to paint *santos* that glowed with the color of earth.

I was especially fascinated, though slightly repelled by, a grim menacing figure called *La Muerta* (Death), often called Doña Sebastiana, a skeletal hag almost always portrayed seated in a rough cart, clutching in a vise-fingered grip a bow and arrow to harvests souls. (Ironically, the faithful appeal to dear Doña for a long life!) I also had the good luck to meet at the Channing Gallery one Pam Mitchell, an authority on retablos—her collection focuses primarily on black and white ones—who was very helpful to me. We got to talking about the legendary Los Penitentes—*Los Hermanos de la Fraternidad Piadosa de Nuestro Padre Jesús Nazareno* (The Brothers of the Pious Fraternity of Our Father Jesus the Nazarene)—a lay confraternity of Spanish-American Catholic men active in northern and central New Mexico and southern Colorado whom I had only heard about. I asked her where I could find them, see them, maybe even talk to them.

My Blumenschein I suddenly forgot. Now I wanted a retablo. I didn't buy one, not yet, but they had became my new passion. Religious paintings, usually depicting saints and sacred scenes meaningful to the devout Catholics of Mexico, they became highly popular in the early 19th century. In Mexico, they were made as far back as the 17th century. Small, produced for individual devotion, done on tin (the "silver of the poor" in the 19th century) or pine panels, covered with gesso, mostly done in oils, occasionally homemade watercolors, they were mostly painted anonymously, a vigorous expression of popular belief, yet a genre of no small artistic significance, for it later proved to be of major importance to some of Mexico's most well-known early 20th-century painters, including Frida Kahlo, Diego Rivera, and Roberto Montenegro. I saw almost too many beautiful ones to buy only one.

But where were most of them found? How had they been sold? Had they been peddled? Stolen? I pictured wily, in-the-know American sharpies making sweeps through the outbacks of Mexico, bilking the poor of their *retablos*, not unlike the way all those Gadsden Purchasers with their fast talk and "annexations" impoverished the entire country. It would have been easy. Willa Cather once wrote, I think admiringly, "Thrift is such a rare quality among Mexicans that they find it very amusing."

There are two basic kinds of retablos (*retro tabula*, behind the [altar] table): the *santo* and the *ex-voto* or *milagro*, primarily votive paintings produced as gifts to God or the Virgin in thanks for an answered prayer. In her classic *The Art of Private Devotion: Retablo Painting of Mexico*, Gloria Fraser Giffords traces the ancestry of the genre, an artistic tradition, imported to the colonies with the Spanish conquests, culminating in a cultural marriage of ancient faith meeting the New World. A retablo in the United States is commonly understood to be a small New Mexican religious painting on a wooden tablet. They were sometimes painted on scrap tin or on discarded metal oil or food containers, thus giving rise to the occasional reference to *santos sobre hoja de lata*, "saints painted on tin cans." We know from a multitude of various colors, techniques, and styles that the best of them were produced between the 1820s and early 1920s by copyists in the *santo* tradition fascinated with what Giffords cites as the four main subjects: Jesus, archangels, saints, and of course Mary ("Marian figures . . . account for about a third of the images produced").

The ex-voto retablos are more anecdotal. There is often a verse, sometimes a letter, occasionally a story, written or printed in longhand along the lower third of the retablo. These testimonies of faith or object lessons, didactic and often moving, accompany scenes of vivid, dramatic color, genre paintings, often from the Bible, stories of the saints, and frequently people's own lives. "In most of them a scene appears," observes Giffords, "in which the victim is in the throes of a situation that has no earthly remedy."

I also wanted to know more about the Penitentes. I was given the name of an expert in North American Indian art and New Mexican Spanish colonial art who had lived up in Arroyo Hondo for 30 years in a small house that had once been a Penitente *morada*, a lodge or meeting-house of the Brotherhood. Many of the Penitentes lived in areas around Trompas and Truchas, Abiquiu and Talpa, Mora and Alcaoda. Sometimes you may see the Calvaria, an area around the *morada*, or see a cross in a field, around which they gathered singing hymns and dirges or chanting *alabados* (from the opening words *alabado sea*, praise be).

You can rarely tell a morada from a distance. There are telltale signs inside, but from the outside, close up, nothing remarkable. Over doors is often written "Dios." The *vigas*—or overhead transverse beams inside—are stark and often speckled with dried blood, for the upward whipping movement of the two- or three-foot-long whips made of braided *amole* or yucca fibers (sometimes dipped in water to increase their weight), as the Pentitentes flagellate themselves, spatters the blood centrifugally. (It should be noted that most of the scourging and bloody suffering among *La Hermandad* is done in the seclusion of the morada.) A *cielo*, a white muslin cloth stretched from wall to wall, is sometimes used to hide the vigas. Such primitive penances have led some critics to believe that Indians, with their fascination for self-torture, have influenced Penitente rites, most notably the Mexican Aztecs and various New Mexican tribes with their "death worship."

It is all done out of love of God, motivated by the sacrificial need to want to suffer as proof of—and by—that adoration.

Rituals, granted, can become extreme. The habit of binding thorny cacti to bodies with horsehair ropes. Painfully kneeling for hours on end in silent meditation on a floor strewn with maize-grains or fine flinty pebbles gathered from ant hills. Taking sage brush tea, bitter as gall. Tying heavy timbers to arms stretched out straight from the shoulders, palms or boughs blessed on Palm Sunday are often burned and their ashes, used as filler, rubbed into the design of a cross pricked into the skin, most often the forehead. Then there are the bloody *obligaciones* of the Brotherhood, ritual gashes representing the Holy Trinity (three longitudinal strokes on either side of the spinal column) are inflicted by obsidian or flint knives on either postulants or full-fledged Brethren wishing to do penance. "The gashes, which do not affect the musculature," observes authority Marta Weigle in *The Penitentes of the Southwest*, "assure a free flow of blood so scourgings do not cause welts or bruises." There is finally the dragging of those heavy wooden crosses, called *maderos*. Even the enactment of a simulated crucifixion is still part of the rites of the Brotherhood in some localities, where the chosen member is bound to the cross until restricted circulation causes him to lose consciousness.

Relentless morbidity, perhaps. But the Spanish have always played up the more tortuous aspects of Jesus Christ's agonies because of its inherent drama. With their simple faith, the Penitentes feel that by emulating Christ's suffering, His torture and Passion, they are *relieving* Him in a sense of some of His burden. Moreover, the Penitentes have always preferred to be left alone to carry out their penitential rites. They have never boastfully intended their penances to be considered part a public spectacle or exhibition.

The Penitentes, *La Cofradía de Nuestro Padre Jesus Nazareno*—commonly called *Los Hermann Penitentes* or *Los Hermanos*—is, after all, a penitential confraternity. They administer to the spiritual and physical needs of villagers in the absence of priests. As a group, they provide lay religious and welfare services for remote villages. They also copy hymnbooks, and maintain the upkeep of various local religious objects, very like neighborhood sacristans. Such religious, fraternities, sodalities, or *gremios* (trade guilds) have long characterized a part of Spanish Catholicism. The movement began sometime in the late 18th century, during what is known as the Secular Period (ca. 1790–1850), when in the far west there were simply not enough priests or friars to go around.

Almost all early missionaries in those western outposts were Franciscans. (I myself back in 1960 was a Franciscan novice, studying for the priesthood.) It was Franciscans in 1598, remember, who spearheaded the Spanish colonial effort in the New World to convert the Puebloans. As a matter of fact, the official name of the city of Santa Fé—*La Villa Real de la Santa Fé de San Francisco de Assisi* (The Royal City of the Holy Faith of St. Francis of Assisi)—memorializes its patron saint. Way back in 1539, New Mexico itself was first called "The Kingdom of Francis." Loose morals over time eventually led to corruption. Certain priests then living in those remote regions soon felt they had to answer to no one, began amassing wealth, charging ridiculous fees to perform the sacraments, and running, as it were, little fiefdoms, like the villainous Antonio José Martínez, a womanizing priest who had illegitimate children and a rogue cleric who presided over "the old order" and went so far as to resist change to the point of armed rebellion in Nebraska-born Willa Cather's duly famous novel of 1927, *Death Comes for the Archbishop*, much of which is located in the town and surroundings of Santa Fé—the old city was named the center of a Southwestern diocese by Pope Pius IX in 1850—whom she describes in her book as a "dictator to all the parishes in northern New Mexico," adding that "the native priests at Santa Fé were all under his thumb."

It was not long before Bishop Zubiria, in 1831, denounced the extreme practices of the Brotherhood, when it was forced to withdraw into its own chapter houses or *moradas*. A French Benedictine priest, Jean-Baptiste Lamy (model for Jean Marie Latour, Cather's fictional archbishop), sent by some in 1851 to the southwest to impose order, steadfastly frowned on, and soon came to discipline the Brotherhood for all its secrecy, overly rigorous penances, and political involvement—even today, it is popularly believed that the Republican party controls most Penitente votes—as a group of recalcitrant and dangerously unorthodox extremists. The movement spread rapidly, however, and, after some local *moradas* were organized into larger councils in 1861, certain compromises were eventually made. On January 28, 1947, Archbishop Byrne formally recognized the Brothers of Jesus of Nazareth as a pious association subject to the guidance and protection of the Catholic Church.

Now as before, the Penitentes flourish in a small society out west of deeply devout Spanish Americans. It is estimated that there are presently about 3000 members, associated with about 150 *moradas*. They tend to exclude the simply curious, strangers in general, and "Anglos," a word that might broadly be defined as everything they aren't. (In Santa Fé the ethnic population breaks down to about 64 percent Hispanic, 34 percent Anglo, and 2 percent Indian.) They live in a grange society, for the most part. The *moradas* are exclusively male. Theirs are local confraternities, of the kind found today in Spain, particularly in the region of Seville, though they have no general meetings. They are more often than not simple farmers, individuals within their own communities, with a hierarchy of officers in the organization that reaches from the highest, *Hermano Mayor*, through various degrees, such as the *Sangrador*, or *Picador*, who inflicts the seal of the Brotherhood, the *Coadjutor* who washes the whips to various attendants, and so on. They communally build barns, sponsor local dances, run orphanages, even determine who can do business and sometimes even help in arranging marriages. It is male world, fore the most part. The meeting places are secret, closed, especially in the *kiva* during Holy Week, a gathering from which women are excluded. They fulfill the community's need for spiritual guidance in times of death especially, and during Lenten and Holy Week services. The Brotherhood is a strong cultural force, preserving language, lore, customs, and faith.

After lunch one afternoon—two fistburgers at Burt's Burger Bowl ("One Location Worldwide") on Guadalupe Street, a conventional repast I tried to improve on later by eating a couple of *nopales*, prickly pear pods, stripped of spines and fried—I spent several hours at the Santa Fé Library reading about the artists called *santeros* (saint-carvers, or those who create *santos*), virtually all guild people who, with their rude and vivid carvings and visionary paintings, filled in a gap for local religious paraphernalia. Missionaries had accompanied the first Spanish military expeditions to Santa Fé in 1598, carrying with them various religious articles used in celebrating Mass. Soon in those distant mountains and plains, because now as then it is predominantly a land of faith, more sacramentals were necessary to use for religious services, for feast days, and for the faithful of the church to keep in the sacred niches of their homes. And so the *santeros*, fashioning retablos of tin or pine and *reredos*, large panels with columns and niches placed behind altars and *bultos* of cottonwood root or native timbers, often on commission, met the requirements.

It was a spare living. Most of the inspiration was drawn from canonized saints and their stories, various legends ascribed to them. Although most early *santeros* remained anonymous due to the old prejudice against an artist signing his name to a religious image, we do know of Father Andrés García (1748–1778), the very first known *santero* making images in New Mexico. It was widely accepted, in fact thought to be necessary, that *santeros* had to be morally good people. Some were well paid, some even famous, like José Aragón; Pedro Fresquis; a stranger simply known as the *Santa Nino Santero*; and of course the legendary Molleno, widely known as the "chili" *santero*, for that recurrent symbol seen in his work. Speaking of chili, if I may digress a moment, I came to love it, even depend on it, as once in Ireland I loved and began to drink too many pints of Guinness a day. It is a commonplace to observe, no doubt, but surely true that travelers literally feed their imagination. From wonder drug to miracle cure, "red or green" chili was even years ago a main staple in Pueblo and Spanish colonists' diet. High in vitamin C, it is also touted to cure the common hangover. While red chili ages on the *ristra* and green on the vine, locals say green is hotter and red is smoother. I also came to love *posole*. All *real posole* calls for a pig's head, incidentally.

In any case, the *santeros* were soon being called upon to do special work for the Penitentes, who had a greater need in their religious services for more than household *santos*. It was a liturgy that relied on art. They wanted special types of figures, larger *bultos*, proclaiming saints, outsized symbols of suffering. They wanted Madonnas, invariably weeping sorrowful ones—a "Dolores," always symbolically clasping her hands, was a popular manifestation of the Virgin—statues of St. Isidro, the patron saint of farmers, to be carried in the spring through the fields to bless the crops and encourage fertility, life-sized, articulated Christos, often with real hair, seated or standing and wearing crowns of thorns, holding crosses, showing deeper pain, shedding of course more blood.

Certain artists, famous Penintente *santeros*, like Miguel Herrera, José Benito Ortega, and a legendary figure known only as "Velasquez" tried in the work they provided on much larger scale (and more gruesome detail) to match the faith, the passion, the religious melodrama these devotees lived out daily in discipline and now asked for in the figures they wanted to raise in witness to the world.

I had my drink with Evan Connell, a tall, wiry adventurer, in the bar at the Inn at Loretto. He told me how he got fed up with California and, after selling or giving away many of his personal goods in Sausalito, including much of his library, he had simply picked up and come to Santa Fé, which he found more peaceful. We talked about writing. I admired his quiet resolve, gentle intelligence. He was handsome, laconic, with something of a real cowboy about him. He encouraged my wandering and gave me a few tips on what to see. I wanted to head north. See Taos. Possibly find a *morada*. Maybe buy a retablo. I wanted to look at more of these paintings and wondered where they were. It was good to get out of the city again, not because of anything to do with Santa Fé, which—tiny, immaculate, brown as hazel wood—is easily one of the most beautiful places in the country, but just to smell the air, park the car, kick around through the greasewood, wander through those unearthly hills and valleys, all green with piñon trees and gray cottonwoods as far as the eye can see. One afternoon I wanted to take a raft shuttle up the Rio Grande, out of Pilar and into the Taos mountains, but the weather was too bad. So I just got into my car and headed for the hills.

I drove to Taos along the "high road," up through the Truchas peaks, the Carson National Forest—the legendary guide and mountain man is buried in nearby Kit Carson Park—through Los Trampas. The road goes from the outskirts of Santa Fé north to Taos through old villages founded by early Spanish settlers and missionaries, places like Nambé, Cundiyo, Chimayó, Truchas, Chamisa, Penasco, and others. The arid, eroded New Mexican landscape of mesas, arroyos, and distinct snow-capped mountains added to the spell. The road winds up, up, up, a storybook ribbon, like the single road into Tibet, through weathered sandstone and scrub-covered hills to wide, overwhelming views from peaks of sky and land that dwarf human beings. The mountains soar. Turning to look at a peak, you could send your car into a clear unimpeded fall of a thousand feet. There are no barriers.

I was rolling along in a rainstorm, which turned to hail, then snow—the temperature in Santa Fé the previous day had been a sunny 65 degrees—listening to oldies on KBOM ("K-Bomb, Your Cool Gold Station"). Another station, KOLT, played of course only country and western music. Springs in the cliffs flow down arroyos and gullies, some precipitous, bearing old Spanish names such as Arroyo de la Cueva, Arroyo de la Morada, etc. I stopped at the Picuris Pueblo, paid the $2.50 fee (most pueblos require a permit), and walked around in a silence almost prehistoric in its solemnity and, I felt, emptiness. The Picuris is one of the smaller pueblos. It was little more than a tiny brown dorp, a few hunched mud and plaster adobes, with nobody in sight. It only made me sad. I said a prayer at a burial mound and left. The present Pueblo population is about 32,000, divided among 19 pueblos, eight of which are in Northern New Mexico within easy reach of Santa Fé. Oklahoma, Arizona, and New Mexico contain nearly half the entire Native American population in the United States.

I had wanted to see a *sipapu*, which I had read about. The Pueblos believe that their ancestors emerged from the great earth womb through a deep hole, a passageway, called a *sipapu*, from the Earth's interior to the surface, an icon as it were, an archetype that has been discussed in many places and in many ways from the Incas to Dante to Charlie Manson with his Dune Buggy Patrol. Every Pueblo *kiva*, or sacred ceremonial chamber, has within it a symbolic hole signifying a *sipapu*, along with a ceiling hole above symbolizing the passageway to the supernatural world. Escape holes are big with Native Americans. Freedom—air, space, land—means everything to them. I later wrote a poem about it:

Sipapu

An Indian badly needs a hole
as faith of course requires needful flight,
the soul to rise and over rise.

A hole that's bored of hope becomes
a distinct cosmology of roundness and of circles,
recapitulating what it can of skies.

Cenotes are sinkholes, kill-hole pots.
The Maya held that water covered openings
into other unwet, worthier worlds.

Leaving home defamiliarizes us
with exactly what we need by exploration
to see what has to be sought.

Riverless Yucatan has neither lakes,
but a soul needing puddles to argue holes
prays, as an Indian's faith unfurls.

A Native American cannot abide confinement in any form. The very nature of closed captivity for him is unbearable. The neck on Zuni three-colored pottery is separated from the body by a band, often a double black line, which must always be broken at one point, as a "spirit path" or exit. Otherwise, the belief is, the maker's soul would be imprisoned and she might die. (Incidentally, all "kill" holes in Mimbres pots are, in fact, *sipapus*.) Later, at another Pueblo, I asked for and met a *cacique*, the spiritual guardian of the place, whereupon I asked him about the passageway. I was told brusquely that *kivas* are out of bounds to visitors. So I drove off, going higher into the mountains, keeping to my route.

The terrain of most of New Mexican changes abruptly, as plains end giving way to primordial cliffs of crimson, chocolate, and ochre, then suddenly mountains loom, all in stark contrast to a turquoise sky. It is an unexpected landscape of mutable colors and changing shapes. A sense of walking through time holds. I find no such quiet in the East. New England mountains murmur. The Midwest seems to hum, even sizzle in the heat. In New Mexico I often felt I was the only person on the face of the Earth. It's the enchanting quiet that makes the thought possible. And the thought always leaves a feeling of infinite grace.

I twice parked my car, somewhere between Las Trampas and Angel Fire, allegorical towns on a pilgrim's progress that made me feel like John Bunyan's wanderer Christian, and I climbed up into the dark mouths of several caves, now hideously filled with bats. I myself was looking for petroglyphs—horned kings! antlered avatars! centipedes and cranes! Kokopelli, the humpbacked fluteplayer!—puzzles from a thousand or more years ago when bands of Indians, later called the Fremont and Anasazi, hunted and farmed in the canyons. Ancient artists delighted in the sandstone of these alcoves, caves, and sheltered spots, cutting as they did into the dark. mineral wash called "desert varnish" to reveal the color of the underlying stone. "Researchers who have tried to duplicate this method," writes Ruth Cashman, "estimate that 25 to 100 strikes were required to make a one-inch line."

I sat on a ledge, staring down at the many winding trails below, and thought of the daring Christopher "Kit" Carson, whose thumbnail biography I remembered reading as a boy in a biscuity old Grosset & Dunlap edition called *Fifty Famous Americans*. I knew that Carson, the guide in the popular cheap dime novels of the 1880s, not only had an exquisite sensibility—"A delicacy which never allowed him to use a profane word, to indulge in intoxicating drinks, to be guilty of an impure action," as one midcentury thriller put it—but was also portrayed as tall, dark, and handsome. A Taos fur trader, he was, in fact, short, bowlegged, illiterate, and had a leathery, squinched-up face. (He had also butchered Indians, a detail I later learned that bothered me.) Still, I was energized by being in his neck of the woods and on the move. The crystal air in New Mexico endows a person with fantastic energy. I am not at all surprised that the roadrunner—*meep! meep!*—is the New Mexico state bird!

It turned out the owner of the La Fonda Hotel in the Plaza was away so I decided to use the late morning to drive up north to San Cristobal and take a look at the D. H. Lawrence Chapel. It was snowing the day I climbed up to it, a sparkling day, and the woods were full of turkeys running about through the flakes. The shrine is really nothing more than a small secular white-stucco temple, perpetually open, at the end of a five-mile-long unpaved road off the main highway. A ceramic phoenix sits on a rude altar there like a monstrance. (Someone had left a scribbled note: "*The Phoenix has risen.*")

The writer Lawrence was actually cremated in St. Paul de Vence—the official certificate ("*proces-verbal d'incineration*," dated 13 March 1935) hangs in the memorial—but Frieda, his wife, had the ashes brought here. This was the site of the Kiowa Ranch, which the wealthy Mabel Dodge Luhan gave to the English couple in the early 1920s. (The heroine of Lawrence's novel *The Plumed Serpent* is modeled on Luhan.) For a short time, Lawrence worked at the ranch, baking bread, making chairs and tables, digging irrigation channels, and milking Susan the cow, one of his chores he did growing up as a small boy in Nottingham, England. He also painted oils here, keeping his brushes in what he called "little casseroles." Lawrence, in fact, did a 23" x 47" painting of the place, *Kiowa Ranch, New Mexico*, in 1925. I had heard a good deal about these controversial paintings of his and wanted to have a look at them. Driving the

18 miles back to Taos, I had the uneasy reflection that DHL in that wide, wild part of the world must have had some grim trips.

Or did Mabel also buy him a car? Her munificence reached to such extremes. She once gave a new LaSalle to her chauffeur, a burly (and extremely handsome) Taos Indian named Tony Lujan, and went so far as to marry him, her fourth husband, preferring, however, to spell *her* married name Luhan, with an h. Tony kept his hair in long black braids, always wore a red, black, and white blanket, and had a haughty demeanor. He had jilted his Indian wife for Mabel, and the Puebloan was angered. (Wealthy Mabel shrugged and settled $75 a month for life on his former wife.) The particular car that Mabel munificently gave Tony for his birthday, according to photographer Ansel Adams, another close member of the Taos community in those days—back in 1929 he gave us many great photos of the area, including that memorable one of the back of St. Francis Church in Rancho de Taos—but Adams was a febrile person whom Tony drove nuts performing on his drum and gutturally chanting tribal songs. Once he was supposed to drive from Denver to Taos. After a long delay, Tony finally arrived, looking quite disheveled. "Tony," cried Mabel, anxiously, "what happened?" He replied, slowly and very convincingly, "I hit cow. She right there. So was me. Boom!"

There were many artists and writers drifting through the wilds of New Mexico at the time. Fremont Ellis. Thornton Wilder. Robinson Jeffers. Aldous Huxley. And John Reed, not only the passionate love of Mabel's life but the person who, in setting out to interview Pancho Villa, first stimulated her interest in the region. Among the intelligentsia in Santa Fé also lived Witter Bynner. "Hal," as he was called, threw wild parties. His friends affectionately called him—to his face!—"America's greatest living minor poet."

Finally, I met Saki Karavas, the energetic hotelier of the Taos La Fonda. He looked like the actor Gale Gordon. He let me into the tiny, crowded office where all of the Lawrence paintings hung *ex utraque parte*. Lawrence was in Taos from 1922 to 1925. He wrote *Mornings in Mexico* there and also finished *Lady Chatterley's Lover*. The office "with the dirty pictures" was a jumble of photographs, odds and sorts, a lot of pictures of Lord Byron—Saki is of Greek descent—photos of boxers Marcel Cerdan and Jack Dempsey, one of actor Dennis Hopper, a signed letter to Saki's father, James, from Albert Einstein, and a portrait of D. H. Lawrence himself done by Canute Merrill in 1922, along with the so-called "infamous" paintings.

Lawrence did about 25 of them—13 were removed from Dorothy Warren's Gallery in London in the summer of 1929 for being "gross, coarse, hideous, unlovely, obscene." The blue-nosed Detective Inspector Gordon Hester arrived with six, count them, six policemen, and impounded the works on the spot. (Technically, these paintings are still banned in England—I checked—under Section 42 of the Customs Consolidation Act of 1876!) The "corrupt thirteen" eventually found their way to Taos with Frieda and her new husband, her third, Angelo Ravagli, and it was Angelo who sold the lot of them to Saki Karavas in whose office they now hang in all their muddy, mildly smutty glory.

There were 10 of them displayed. (One of the paintings, *Boccaccio's Story*, supposedly a savage satire of something or other, has disappeared.) *The Holy Family*, given to Saki by Aldous Huxley's wife, was executed in house paints. *Closeup Kiss*, a homely blubber-lipped couple kissing, was inspired by an Italian movie, the name of which I never learned. There is *Red Willow Trees, Fauns and Nymphs, Dance Sketch, Rape of the Sabine Women*, and the very weird

Flight Back into Paradise, a picture revealing a beefy, stark-naked, huge-titted woman pulling against restraining leashes, symbolizing, I gather, her materialistic baggage, but which to me recalled the grotesque anti-clerical dragging scene in Buñuel's film *Le Chien Andalou*. The paintings altogether are neither good nor bad, merely thick-fisted, overboiled amateur efforts, full of color and vitality and prurience.

They are all signed "Lorenzo." Lusty orange fleshapods and almost cartoon-like mustachioed charmers, often clothed, grope naked women, most of them giantesses. There is a lot of wrestling, bathing, and humping. In one picture, a writhing sex pile, I counted 11 figures. A lot of moon-faced men with tans and satyr-like grins and goatees, idealized self-portraits of what the vain but tubercular Lawrence perhaps hoped he resembled, are lapping women's ears. "I paint no pictures that won't shock castrated public spirituality," Lawrence once wrote. I recall he said somewhere else, "We cannot bear connection. That is our malady." He wanted to do something about that in paint. It is of passing interest, however, to reflect on how dated the sensibility the period was to find such daubs shocking.

I was invited by Saki up to his private rooms where there are many first editions of Lawrence's books and the walls filled with even more photographs and paintings, among them several rare Gaspards given to him by Leon himself, who painted Saki's mother, Noula, a painter herself and a friend of Frieda, Huxley, Stephen Spender, Leopold Stokowski, and the Hollywood crowd. "Tennessee Williams used to come to the hotel," Saki told me. "I didn't know why. It turned out a clerk was his lover." There Saki showed me a rarely seen Lawrence painting, a lovely 8" by 20" watercolor—a landscape—signed in full. I also saw several magnificent retablos (be still, my heart!) and was shown a rare privately printed 1929 edition, one of 510 copies "printed for the Mandrake Press at the Botolph Painting Works, Kingsway," of all of D. H. Lawrence's paintings, including *The Lizard, Fire-Dance, Yawning, The Mango Tree, Accident in a Mine*, and *Fairy on a Verandah*. I said goodbye to Saki and drove back down to Santa Fé. After seeing all that flesh, I was just as happy to be moving. There was so much else to see. And tomorrow would be Ash Wednesday.

Passing into the Chimayó hills, I got lost in the impenetrable dark trying to find the Santuario, the remarkable Church of the "Holy Mud," but soon gave up. After a good night's sleep back in Santa Fé, I woke up early and drove back the 25 or so miles the next morning. I wanted to avoid the teeming crowds of people, some from as far away as Texas and Mexico, who would be coming to this very spot on pilgrimage this holy day, as they did year after year on Holy Week, some hobbling with rice in their shoes, some even carrying crosses, chosen penances, and a good many of them walking barefoot. All that week I saw pious people threading their way toward the church.

But the poor in New Mexico, unlike those, say, in Massachusetts, for instance, walk everywhere. The common highway signs in New Mexico, "Roadside Activity" is, I am sure, a quaint euphemism for barefoot pilgrims. Could it be they are also referring in the wet mountains to falling boulders, many of them, visible from the highway, precariously piled up along the high mesas? I soon found the old church made famous by the pit of healing earth, a small hole, miraculous some say, found in the floor of an anteroom just to the left of the main altar. Pilgrims, tourists, local people kneel and pray there, venerating the crucifix. Crutches and trusses and walking canes are left behind, along with personal notes, medals, candles, and various *ex voto* objects of thanks. Although priests periodically refill the hole with dirt from outside the church, legend continues to maintain that this hole, *El Posito*, replenishes itself.

There is, let it be said, an ancient tradition, modern cosmetology aside, for the belief that mud, even without any religious connotation, has curative power. Have not people worldwide used it as an anodyne for centuries? Is it not the ubiquitous salve for bee-stings? Ant-bite? Even sunburn? Surely the idea of *tierra bendita* is as old as time.* In Oraibi, the Hopi used to rub damp clay on their bodies in a war ritual. There is also of course a sacramental connection to it in the liturgy of Ash Wednesday. Always the Church in

----

*The digestive functions of man in his rudest state, incredible as it may seem, are capable of deriving a species of nutriment from the soil. "There are dirt-eaters among men, who subsist chiefly from. . . so-called *"edible earths"* and *"infusorial earths"* [which] are made up largely of, and owe their nutritive qualities to, the remains of microscopic animals," notes William S. Bernard, "Micro-Organisms and their Effects in Nature" (*Popular Science Monthly*, October, 1879). Such geophagists also subsist on the bark of trees. We read in *Salad for the Solitary and the Social* by an Epicure (1872) that not only in New Guinea, but even in some of our own Southern States, such earth-eaters are to be found. The anonymous author of this century-old but informative book goes on to point out. "We learn from [Alexander] Humboldt that the Ottomaques, on the banks of the Meta and the Orinoco, feed on a fat, unctuous earth, tinged with a little oxide of iron. They collect this clay very carefully, distinguishing it by the taste; they knead it into balls of four or five inches in diameter, which they bake slightly before a slow fire. These balls are soaked in water when about to be used, and each individual eats about a pound of the material every day."

A kind of fuller's earth called *bytoon* was regularly sold in the streets of Aleppo, according to Alexander Russell in *The Natural History of Aleppo*. A

the early Southwest, as in Haiti, say, was constantly trying to contect, validly, ways and beliefs of local culture with its own age-old traditions. "After the Conquest," writes Elizabeth Kay in *Chimayo Valley Traditions*, "Spanish priests realized that linking pagan rites to Christian beliefs would help them convert the Indians to Catholicism, a method of incorporation referred to colloquially as 'baptizing the customs.'"

This religious connection with soil was no abstract or perfunctory faith. In the Southwest as in other places, from time immemorial, people even ate dirt—indeed, consumed it. Geophagy, of course, practiced by Zunis, Hopis, and Navajos, is hardly new or original. The famous San Ildefonso potter Maria Martinez, who

---

species of oolite is used as a foodstuff by the natives of New Caledonia, and in parts of Peru a calcareous earth is reduced to a fine powder and actually mixed with cocoa. *Ampo* is the name of little balls of reddish clay which are bought in the markets of Java and eaten by the fair Japanese, who wish to become thin and graceful. Workmen in the freestone quarries of Kiffhausen, a hill range in Central Germany, southeast of he Harz mountains, habitually spread on their bread, instead of butter, a very fine clay called "stein-butter." Bernard goes on to explain, "These earths are eaten in times of need by the Lapps and Tungusians. They are likewise used in South America, in New Caledonia, Kurdistan, in China, and in some of our own Southern States. The 'bread-stone' of China belongs to this kind of food. On the shores of a lake near Uranea, in Sweden, there is a large deposit of infusorial powder called *Bergmehl* (mountain-meal), which is mixed with flour and eaten. It consists almost entirely of microscopic shells." One last bit of geophagy—some Quechua Indians of Peru smear kaolin clay on their potatoes which masks the bitterness and also detoxifies the alkaloids in the spuds, making them much tastier and even more nutritious (cf. Frederick W. Hackwood's *Good Cheer*, 1911).

made such magnificent use of the earth in her own special craft and creations, left us an account of her mother's instruction to take the sacred Chimayo earth mixed with water: "This is good earth. The Indians knew about it and how to use it a long time ago. Then the padres came and learned about its power, and the Santo Nino came and told them what to do, so they built the church here. Everybody knows that the earth is good. It makes everyone well who drinks it, for the rest of his life."

I myself took the time to scoop up some earth from the hole in the Santuario, put it in a vial, said a prayer, lit a votive candle to the Santo Nino de Atocha, the Holy Child ("Infant of a Thousand Wonders") who, greatly revered by the Hispanics of northern New Mexico, wears out his shoes roaming the countryside at night helping those in trouble, and, still hoping to buy a retablo, on tin or wood, it didn't matter—it was now the only keepsake I wanted to bring back home from Santa Fé—I dodged over to a little gift shop across the parking lot. Gloomily, I found only commercial items, nothing at all memorable, except for *un cuarderno*, a small copybook of the Penitentes, filled with prayers, services, and various rules of that brotherhood of which I was determined to learn more. It was too expensive a book, although I knew it was rare. Instead I walked across the street, bought a package of blue corn flour, simply because I had never seen it before, and drove back to the city.

Finally, I got the rare opportunity through a connection to go with George Villa to a *morada*, on the sacred day of Good Friday, it turned out, a day more significant than any other for at the *Tenebrae* service, known there as *Las Tinieblas* (literally darkness; hell, night), the Penitente rites commemorating the flight of the Apostles and the death of Christ. (It struck me as ironic that on either that particular day in late March, or the one before it, the reactionary Archbishop Marcel Lefebvre had died in Paris, a reform-hating French prelate, more Catholic than the Pope, who had once declared, "Our future is the past.") Late at night, I met George, a woodcarver from Cordova, patiently waiting for me on a road at Truchas. The *morada* was an unprepossessing and remote house situated off a weedy meadow. As we very quietly entered we were not introduced to anybody, which I figured was just as well. We then proceeded to join a small group of people outside that had gathered in the dusty square, and we all walked silently toward an old adobe church around 11 p.m. The air was crisp, the strong breezes blowing out of the high dark mountains bringing the salt-bush smell of *chamiso* with it. I would have been more nervous if it hadn't been for the kind, almost eerily soft-spoken men and women—and several very pretty girls—gathered there.

We, all of us, entered the church.

The service I will never forget. As we knelt and prayed the rosary, I thought things seemed to recapitulate part of the common Lenten service that I knew. I expected little more. The Good Friday liturgy of the Church, the one day in the calendar where the small gilt doors of the tabernacle are left open. All is emptiness and desolate. Here, immediately after the *rosario*, the Brothers silently filed out, returned to the *morada*, but then reappeared in penitential procession. Several were carrying heavy wooden crosses. I also saw flagellants, unbelievably, right out of one of those early grim medieval Bergman movies. Three or four men walked with torturous bundles of cactus strapped to their spines. Others were loaded down, Marley-like, with heavy chains around their ankles, wrists, and waists, arranged so as to hinder their movements and chafe their bodies. Three or four flagellants flung themselves face down in front of the main door, a pre-John XXIII monastic practice, mute invitation to the worshipper to tread on their unmoving bodies. Once inside, the doors had been banged shut. There was shuffling of feet. The Brethren all knelt in front of the altar, inside the rail. The partly clothed penitents, wearing long drawers called *calzones*, lay prostrate before the altar through the entire ceremony with their whips, or *disciplinas*, lying beside them, like props in a drama. Was it true of these people, as Willa Cather once observed of our neighbors to the south who influenced them: "The Mexicans were children who played with their religion"?

Flutes were blown. The congregation stayed deathly silent. The villagers had all been kneeling in segregated groups around the floor, with women and girls mostly in the middle. A solitary singer from the *morada* began to chant, standing near one end of a row of about 10 candles along the front of the altar. They were the only lights in the room. As he concluded each keening verse, he reached over and with finger and thumb pinched out one candle flame after another. There was an instinctive move towards one's neighbor, for everybody knew that the candles, as I soon saw in the descending darkness, were all to be progressively snuffed out. A last candle was put out. The singer, I noticed, fumbled about with a tiny lantern under the folds of his coat, by which he could follow the lines of his song book. Having extinguished the last candle, he made for the low door of the room, which opened off the altar space to the left. We were now in total darkness. Cave black. I remembered Ambrose Bierce's definition of a ghost: *"an outward and visible sign of an inward fear"* (my italics). I could literally see nothing, as if, horrible to relate, darkness was palpably *there.*

Suddenly, a voice cried out *"Ave Maria,"* followed by a deafening thunder. It was at first the clapping of hands, but then in that utter and appalling blackness, Gustave Doré-black, the Brethren began to clack wooden noisemakers called *maltracas*. I almost jumped out of my skin. When Christ is gone in His absence, or so they feel, all is chaos, and chaos is *noise*! Now logging chains were being unrelievedly pounded in the darkness on the floor, along with wooden clubs in a pandemonius cacophony. For a single moment my one thought in the midst of that nightmare noise was: *here I am in the darkness of my mind inside a mysterious* morada *at midnight in a completely unknown village in the middle of nowhere in the hinterlands of New Mexico, alone.* The racket died down briefly, as a woman with a sobbing tremulousness of voice mournfully called out the name of someone, obviously a deceased member of her family or village, maybe her husband or child. Prayers were murmured in response. Then more noise. More and more names were called, as in a litany, and the reverberant, almost chthonian hand-clapping resumed each time, followed by the uncanny, deafening *maltracas* and clanging chains beaten on the floor. The service seemed much, much longer in the sightless dark. This might have been Machu Picchu, in the valley of the Urubamba. A sacred virgin of the sun might have been being sacrificed. We could have been painted Incas!

In the Roman Catholic Church, the office of matins and lauds of the last three days of Holy Week is known as "Tenebrae" and the words are sung. The name means "darkness" and comes from the very old ceremony of extinguishing the lights in the church, one by one in the course of the observance. The ritual is darkly medieval but entirely reverential, as sober as death. It is characterized by gradual extinguishing of candles, and by a *strepitus* or loud noise taking place in total darkness near the end of the service. A single candle is left burning, which is placed behind the bare altar to symbolize the laying of Christ in the tomb. This candle is not put out, since death has no dominion over Him. I felt goosebumps, as my scalp tightened, and I could not help but think of Gerard Manley Hopkins's lines:

> I wake and feel the fell of dark, not day.
> What hours, O what black hours we have spent
> This night! what sights you, heart, saw; ways you went!
> And more must, in yet longer light's delay.
> With witness I speak this. But where I say
> Hours I mean years, mean life. And my lament
> Is cries countless, cries like dead letters sent
> To dearest him that lives alas! away.
>
> I am gall, I am heartburn. God's most deep decree
> Bitter would have me taste: my taste was me;
> Bones built in me, flesh filled, blood brimmed the curse.
> Selfyeast of spirit a dull dough sours. I see
> The lost are like this, and their scourge to be
> As I am mine, their sweating selves; but worse.

What astonished me was that there were no priests, no vestments, no church rubrics, nothing from the Ordo, virtually nothing borne of or identifiable with the prescribed Good Friday liturgy of the Catholic Church. It was profoundly mythic, almost theater, a vision fashioned not only from deep and unswervable faith but the fertile regional dreams of an entire people, *sans voir*, sightless to the secular world coming down around their ears, but refusing to turn from the strange God of their fathers.

Finally, the Brethren formed a line and shuffled backward toward the door, with the huddled, blood-caked penitents. Genuflections were made toward the altar, and the Brethren began to file out, only to take up the heavy crosses—I was later told that some of them, six to ten feet tall, weigh several hundred pounds—and started to walk, dragging their long wooden burdens. The scourging began again, the traditional three steps forward with the rhythmic swing of the lash, *slap, slap, slap*, to the wail of the *pitos*, or hand-made flutes. These crude flutes, long rods of cottonwood trees, were solo instruments played to accompany Penitente services, never for pleasure, for certain, and were said to symbolize Mary's weeping. (It is always a question how much the Spanish were influenced by Indians, for the Zuni used flutes in a corn grinding ceremony, when girls ground corn in unison while a young man played to them.) Several penitents were wearing ominous black hoods and blindfolds.

Whereas before I had visions of Hieronymus Bosch in mind, cartoon menace and traipsing parades, there now seemed something true and honest about it all, and then before I knew it the service was over.

We stood at night outside the church. And there was a great congenial but muted shaking of hands all around. I said goodbye to my host, George, and driving back through the night felt a great sense of well-being, of *agapē*, of what, no matter how primitive, faith in its most dramatic morphs could be.

The Spanish had come to New Mexico searching for the wealth of the Seven Cities of Cibola and to convert Indians to Christianity. In a way, I was like them, but even luckier. I had found a response in my own faith and more wealth in Santa Fé in its many shapes and ways than when before I had come I could have ever imagined. I knew I could only approximate what I felt of all I had seen. In the mystery of its mandala, dreams and religion, tradition and nature, history and adventure, beauty and truth mingled in ways too profound for mere words and far too deep for any explanation. I could accept that for having been given so much. And I felt grateful. It was art I had experienced. I had my retablo, at last.

Gaffes in Painting

Gaffes, in a sense, do not exist in paintings in the same way that they do in literature or perhaps in real life. (I am still bothered, however, whenever embarking or disembarking in Grand Central Station in New York City, to look up at the ceiling of that sky and be reminded, once again, that the locations of the constellations are completely wrong!) The fact of the matter is, anachronisms, incongruities, anomalies, inconsistencies, and so forth may all in fact be part of a painting's irony, never mind point of view. Indeed, the understanding of a picture may even depend on—even thrive on—such a thing. An entire aesthetic, understandably, often comes out of such juxtapositions.

A howler is always a source of amusement, a refreshing alternative to the facts of reality that we invariably meet with a bit of *schadenfreude*, often involving, when not scorn and blame, something like secret delight. Poet William Blake thought that an animal produced wax. Confucius believed the larger the bait, the larger the fish. Victor Hugo thought that the English Inns of Court were churches. Laughably, the savvy woodsman Natty Bumppo in James Fenimore Cooper's novel *The Pathfinder* (1840) is dexterous enough to shoot a bullet through another bullet-hole from a distance of a hundred yards! Thomas Carlyle in his essay "Occasional Discourse on the Negro Question" for *Fraser's Magazine* (1849) laughably referred to Indonesians or Malays, who in fact look like Thais or Chinese, as "the Dutch Blacks of Java." Robert Browning in his play *Pippa Passes* (1841) grotesquely misuses the vile word "twats," in English literature surely one of the more memorable gaffes, actually believing them to be part of a nun's religious habit:

> "Then, owls and bats,
> Cowls and twats,
> Monks and nuns, in a cloister's moods,
> Adjourn to the oak-stump pantry!"

Poor innocent Browning explained afterwards that he believed a "twat" was the knot on the end of a nun's girdle. He had been deceived by a 17th-century poem called "Vanity of Vanities," where the cheeky couplet occurs:

> "They talk't of his having a
> Cardinalls Hat.
> They'd send his as soon an
> Old Nun's Twat."

It should be noted, regarding Browning by the way, that the two words "latest" and "last" are not—and never were—synonyms. (Remember the legendarily unkind jibe: Q. "Have you read my latest book?" A. "I hope so.")

The employment of Piggy's spectacles in William Golding's *Lord of the Flies* (1954) as an effective magnifying glass is totally bogus. Piggy is nearsighted, and the eyeglasses prescribed for his condition, no matter how they were held, would have been quite unable to make the rays of the sun converge. The fact is nearsightedness is corrected by means of negative (diverging) lenses, but a positive (converging) lens is necessary to focus sunlight. A burning or magnifying glass, in consequence, must be positive. Golding failed to realize that Piggy's negative eyeglass lenses would never have worked as a burning-glass.

Speaking of scientific asininities, the visionary novelist H. G. Wells once confidently proclaimed, "I do not think it at all probable that aeronautics will ever come into play as a serious modification of transport and communication"—this from the man who made a fortune writing such astroneopsychedelic sci-fi as *The Time Machine* and *The War of the Worlds*. At another time Wells also refused to see the submarine "doing anything but suffocate its crew and founder at sea." (This has occasionally, tragically, happened.)

But no subs? No planes?

There are, nevertheless, notable exceptions in the world of art, where in various paintings and engravings and sculptures gaffes of a kind do in fact appear, proving nothing more than artists are mortal, too. Peter Paul Rubens was obviously aware that the woman who appears in his famous portrait *Le Chapeau de Faille* (ca. 1625) was *not* wearing a straw hat. In earlier iterations of their portrayal, the Holy Family generally were dressed in whatever the painter's models daily wore. A mural in Venice shows 16th-century Italians busy laying siege to Troy. Dauntless George Washington, the "Father of Our Country," is often placed on high pediments, emperor-like, sporting a Roman tunic. Still, the fact remains Michelangelo's *David*, in his battle pose, does bravely stand forth uncircumcised.

The iconic work of Emanuel Gottlieb Leutze's *Washington Crossing the Delaware* (1851), for example, a romantic rendition painted 75 years after that historic event—a 20' by 12' canvas that

William Sloane Coffin, president of the Metropolitan Museum of Art, once pronounced was "neither history nor art"—has come in for much criticism. The earnest Leutze's ambition was to create a work of art that deliberately glorified General Washington as well as the young Colonial American cause, but his effort here is replete with unhistorical inaccuracies. The flag seen whipping in the wind was not adopted until six months after that particular Christmas night crossing in 1776. (A more historically accurate flag would have been the Grand Union Flag hoisted by George Washington on January 1, 1776, at Somerville, Massachusetts as the standard of the Continental Army and the first national flag.)

The general, instead of being seated, is heroically portrayed standing at the prow of a *rowboat*, a stance, especially during the choppy conditions of a crossing, that would have risked capsizing such a diminutive boat in a matter of mere seconds!* There can actually be seen in other boats in the background defiant, *bucking horses*! When questioned about the boats, a defensive Leutze claimed that research had shown him that, although all types of boats had been used during that historic crossing, many of which were extremely durable Durham boats, ordinarily used to haul pig iron, about 60 feet long by 8 feet wide, of canal-barge strength, able to transport 30 men.

What about the size of the ice? Were Washington and his brave men crossing the Antarctic Shelf? Negotiating the straits of

---

*However, historian David Hackett Fischer has argued that everyone would have been standing up to avoid the icy water in the bottom of the boat, as the actual Durham boats used were much larger, had a flat bottom, higher sides, a broad beam (width) of some eight feet and a draft of 24–30 inches.

Baffinland? As dawn breaks, the crossing is taken in an overwhelming busy ice field, major glaciation, the large chunks of which, the size of giant boulders, make that waters in the state of New Jersey look like winter in northern Labrador or Greenland. In what is a perfect profile, Washington, one foot forward, strikes a pose as if a model to be sculpted, or, as we used to say snidely as kids, "posing for Animal Crackers." (I do not believe, furthermore, that even his sword—hind-side-to—hangs at the right angle.)

There were even complaining rumors and snipes that Leutze, who had been born in Württemberg, Germany, had not only used the Rhine as his model for the Delaware River and German soldiers for models of the Americans, but had actually used a *German laundress* as the model for Washington's head. His daughter Euphemia insisted that her father had worked from the famous Houdon bust. A young James Monroe, the future president of the United States— or so art critics claim—can be seen sitting beside Washington. But had there been in the same boat that night a fur-hatted frontiersman? A New England seaman in a wet slicker? A woman—or what appears to be a woman—pulling an oar? The men in the boat—the frontiersman at the bow is about to have his left foot broken on a floe—clearly represent a political cross-section of all Americans, including, to underwrite the democratic cause, the requisite presence of black man in front of the standing general, pictured next to a fellow in a Scottish tam or bonnet, both facing backward, but sitting amicably next to each other. Two farmers in broad-brimmed hats are crouched near the back (one with a bandaged head and a cockade), both holding rifles, and one at the stern wearing what appears to be Native American clothing to symbolize that all people in the fledgling nation are given full value and attention.

What is presented in the "heroically standing" general/

president reminds me how a bumptious and splay-faced George W. Bush—a National Guard "weekend warrior" who never went to fight in the war in Vietnam while 60,000 men were being killed—after the pointless, vile, and imperialistic U.S. invasion of Iraq, having donned an airplane fighter's uniform and helmet, farcically landed by jet on the aircraft carrier USS *Abraham Lincoln* under the banner "*Mission Accomplished*" off the coast of California as if he had just single-handedly defeated the Spartan armies in the Peloponnese! Six years later, U.S. soldiers were still being killed in Iraq! Talk about gaffes!

Just for the record, by the way, General and later President Dwight D. Eisenhower, the noble D-Day Commander of "Operation Overlord" and the Supreme Commander of all, *all*, European Forces for World War II, never once—not a single time—ever felt the need to appear in his military uniform during his presidency.

Accuracy of detail, in fact, may be questioned in many a painting. British Admiral George Mundy, for example, once reprimanded the painter George Chambers, demanding of his dramatic oil on canvas *The Capture of Bagur* (1831–32), "Why is the foretopsail not set? No man of war loosens her foretopsail as a signal for sailing, unless she is in charge of a convoy and at anchor!" The Duke of Clarence (later William IV), another fellow who claimed to know ships and sailing, after a careful study of J. M. W. Turner's painting of the *Battle of Trafalgar* (1822)—it had been commissioned by his predecessor King George IV as part of a series of works to decorate three state reception rooms in St. James Palace—severely criticized the work, and received in kind, it is so reported, a less than deferential response from the artist. Turner's generally Romantic compulsion for fiery sunsets, shipwrecks, storms at sea, the entire early 19th-century pursuit of the sublime, would not have jibed with the duke's sense of realism, nor perhaps have tempered his frankness. As Clarence, fulminating, angrily put it, "I have been at sea the greater part of my life, Sir . . . and I'll be damned if you know what you are talking about."

In Carlo Crivelli's *The Madonna of the Swallow* (1490), a heavily bearded St. Jerome, almost always portrayed in art as an anchorite, appears on the left holding books and a tiny model of a chapel, stripped to do penance but incongruously robed in a splendid red cappa and cardinal's hat, although the sacred office of cardinal did not exist when Jerome was alive. And in the same painting St. Sebastian on the right is, highly unusually, clothed in the elegant courtly attire of a fashion-conscious knight of the day. Traditionally, iconographically, that saint is portrayed half-naked and fully pierced with arrows. (He has become a gay icon.) The only allusions to him as a plague saint is the single arrow that he holds in his right hand and the bow lying behind his feet, which is rendered there in this painting, as critics point out, to show that he can deal with the arrows of the plague should they begin to fly.

The painting was commissioned by Ranuzio Ottoni and Giorgio di Giacomo for the church of San Francesco in March 1490. Ottoni was Lord of Matelica and Giacomo was guardian of the local Franciscan monastery. St. Sebastian was also a soldier. Clearly, the Ottoni wanted him shown as a knight who might frequent their own court. He is their representative in Heaven. At the very bottom, we see their coat of arms carved on the step, which tells you that this is their take on Heaven.

Where are the strings of the five angels' lutes in Piero della Francesca's *The Nativity* (ca. 1470)? Some critics insist the painting is unfinished. It has certainly been damaged, possibly by the botched work of a 19th-century restorer. Notice Piero has added touches from his native region—his Bethlehem itself has a distinctly Tuscan feel. The flat land on top of the hill where the figures stand evokes Tuscany, as does the winding valley to the left. Meanwhile the sky-line on the right, dominated by the basilica, could almost be the outskirts of Piero's hometown of Borgo Santo Sepolcro. Was Piero experimenting with perspective during the composition? One asks because it is the only one of his works that depicts a building askew from the rest of the composition—specifically here, the simple shed, which is there to remind the viewer of Christ's humble beginnings.

More gaffes? What of the ludicrous visual anomaly of Michelangelo's *Cumaean Sibyl* (1508), where an old woman's wiz-ened face is superimposed on a Herculean body, its arms and shoul-ders very like a pipe-fitter's? Although the edible Galilean fishes in the first century AD would be principally chromids and barbels, in Raphael's *The Miraculous Draught of Fishes* (1515) we find among several semi-vague fish forms of the young painter's fancy two spec-imens which obviously belong to the skate family, fish *never* found in fresh water.

As to the matter of food, consider Fra Angelico's *The Last Supper* (1395), the scene which so many Western painters down through the years have picked as a subject. It is the judgment of many art scholars that this last sacred supper, celebrated on what we now call Holy Thursday and possibly celebrated in Mark's house, was—as depicted by Fra Angelico—*not* the canonical Passover meal. Was there a repast? And if so, what was the fare? The usual traditional ceremony of the Paschal meal was constituted of cups of ritual wine, unleavened bread, wild herbs, and perhaps roast lamb, although not all of these are mentioned by the Evangelists. Tintoretto provided a plate of almonds. Murillo wisely ignored the question of food alto-gether. It was an obscure Italian named Bartolomeo Schidone who provided a square meal for the Lord and His disciples, giving them a barbecued lamb. Is there a particular reason why some of the figures are kneeling and others not? What governs who would do one or the other? All are receiving the bread of communion. Is it not an anomaly that Judas the betrayer, configured with the black halo, can be kneeling in line? And who is the female figure present? Some say Mary Magdalene, but it is clearly the Virgin, portrayed as haloed, who, however, was never recorded to be present there. In answer to the first, I assumed that he was emphasizing that the Last Supper is the Mass; I don't know if there is any tradition that governs who knelt and who sat.

In his mural painting *The Last Supper* (1495–98), Leonardo da Vinci placed an overturned salt cellar in front of Judas Iscariot as a symbol of treachery, although it is doubtless an anachronism. And then Christ in Leonardo's painting would never have been sitting at a rectangular table in the way people dined in common in medieval Italy. Jews commonly reclined while eating their Passover dinner, and Our Lord would have been most likely sitting with his bidden guests, the Twelve Apostles, at a *lectus tricliniarius*, a dining-bed (cf. Luke 14), where most probably he would have taken, not one of the "chief places," but rather, out of humility one of the lesser ones, probably in one of the *imus* locations.

Vladimir Nabokov in his novel *Bend Sinister* (1947) smugly alludes to this famous painting as "the Da Vinci miracle," describing it with dry mockery and his typically secular and dismissive condescension: "thirteen persons at such a narrow table (crockery lent by the Dominican monks)." Unfortunately, with that trenchant little witticism, the pompous Nabokov, a man who generally thought of himself as being above such tawdry errors, flagrantly commits a gaffe of his own. There is no such thing as a Dominican "monk." As most people know, never mind reputable scholars, Dominicans are a religious order of *friars*.

The great Diego Velázquez's only surviving nude is *The Rokeby Venus* (1651), hung in the Rokeby Chapel and painted in emulation of Titian's *Venus of Urbino* (1538). Nudes were extremely rare in 17th-century Spanish art, which was policed actively by members of the Spanish Inquisition The beautiful subject is invariably described as looking at herself in the mirror, although, as any observer can see, this is physically impossible since, as any viewer can see, her face reflected in their direction. This phenomenon is known as the "Venus effect." If you look closely you will see that the mirror held by the winged cherub is actually held in the wrong place—and it ought to reflect the model's stomach. In a number of ways the painting represents a pictorial departure, showing the body of Venus chastely turned away from the observer of the painting. What a irresistible back and glorious buttocks! Women tend to forget that their back, the shapely slope of it, is one of their greatest attractions. Speaking of mirrors, the face of the child seen reflected in the handheld mirror in Mary Cassatt's popular dry-point *Mother and Child* (1905) is clearly of an incorrect size.

Eugène Delacroix, of course, painted battles without ever having seen one. And in Henry Sargent's well-known *Landing of the Pilgrims* (1818–23)—he was a Massachusetts native and should have known better—there was no meeting with any Indian: at the time of the landing, there was no warrant for such a grouping as the artist's picture, and Captain Myles Standish, pictured as a tall, booted, red-vested, gasconading soldier was, from all written reports, a sadly undersized shrimp "scarcely manly in appearance." Nor can one recognize in the crouching pose of the Indian (and such a craven and beholden one!) "the erect and dauntless Samoset" as portrayed in contemporary written accounts by such solid authorities as George Morton (sometimes referred to "George Mourt"), William Bradford, governor of the Plymouth colony for 30 years, and his compatriot Edward Winslow, one of several senior leaders on the ship (and also later at Plymouth Colony). Both Winslow and his brother Gilbert signed the Mayflower Compact. Still, it must be said that Sargent's painting is a distinct improvement over another feeble painting of the same subject that is now housed in the collection of the Historic Genealogical Society of Boston, which represents a boat approaching the shore filled with soldiers in red coats!

In his oil painting *Israelites Gathering Manna in the Wilderness* (1592), Jacopo Tintoretto armed the men of the patriarch Moses with shotguns. (The earliest known gun, as such, unfortunately for Tintoretto, did not appear until 1326, not exactly contemporaneous with the exodus of the Hebrews.) In the mid 1660s, Anthony van Dyck painted several portraits of his patron, the eventually doomed king, Charles I of England, in full armor with two gauntlets (or medieval gloves), both for the right hand. And in one of the 3000 portraits he did, Sir Joshua Reynolds painted one of his subjects with a hat on his head—and a hat under his arm.

Like many of his contemporaries, in 1853 the French painter Theodore Chasseriau bowed to the fashion for the antique with his almost six-foot tall painting rather amply titled *Tepidarium: The Room Where the Women of Pompeii Came to Relax and Dry Themselves after Bathing*. However, the large gathering of bathing women are actually shown to be occupying the tepidarium (warm steam room)—with its elaborate stucco decoration, bronze brazier, and seats decorated with calves' heads—of the *men's bath* at the Forum Baths! The Stabian Baths had a section where women were separated from men, but Chasseriau, who came to study Pompeii in order to reproduce the archaeological details of the doomed city with considerable accuracy, nevertheless confused the two bathing sites!

Paul Revere's over-imaginative and frankly propagandistic engraving *The Boston Massacre* (1770), officially entitled *The Bloody Massacre in King-Street*—showing seven sleek, brutal British Redcoats, or "Lobsterbacks," directed by an angry officer with raised sword, shooting down a large, gathered group of hungry, helpless, peaceful Boston citizens, day laborers, apprentices, and merchant-sailors in black tricorne hats (and a woman in a shawl also appears in the crowd)—is as inaccurate a picture of what happened on that fateful day of March 5, 1770, as could possibly be. (It was based on a drawing by young Henry Pelham, an American painter, engraver, and cartographer who later became well-known both for his *Plan of Boston*, which was engraved in aquatint in London in 1777, and for his illuminating personal letters that shed great light on major events of the American Revolution.)

There were 4,000 British soldiers in Boston at the outset of 1770, a city with 15,000 inhabitants—it was a city occupied—and tensions by then had long been running high. On the evening of March 5, an intemperate crowd that had gathered by what nowadays is called the Old State House begin pelting British regulars with snowballs and rocks, crowding them into a doorway, as tempers flared. The soldiers panicked and did not know how to react. A shot rang out, and other several soldiers fired their weapons. When it was over, five civilians lay dead or dying, including Crispus Attucks, an African American merchant sailor who had escaped from slavery more than 20 years earlier.

It is of historical importance that as a result of his death in the Boston Massacre, Crispus Attucks would emerge as the most famous of all the black men to fight in the cause of the Revolution, becoming its first martyr, in fact, and yet the key man that is visible in the lower left-hand corner of the famous engraving and print is not portrayed as African American, which makes a farce out of the entire story as it happened. There can be found very few towns in Massachusetts where there is not a Crispus Attucks Street. The curious fact, however, is no one knows if Attucks was black, an Indian, or a mulatto. Nor is it known why he joined in the fray. We don't even know if he was the first to be killed. That aspect of the story was from the start all glorious, pro-Colonial propaganda.

Of the engraving, and the print, hardly a detail is correct. There was no such place as "Butcher's Hall," as a sign in the engraving reads. Seven British soldiers are shown with rifles; there were actually eight. Then in actuality the volleys were sporadic, not fired all at once. So much is wrong in the engraving. History *is* bunk! The presence of red-coated British troops in Boston had long been a very sore point among Boston's radical politicians, so Revere wasted no time in capitalizing on the "massacre" to highlight British tyranny and stir up anti-British sentiment among his fellow colonists. Stealing Pelham's drawing also put a good bit of money in Paul Revere's purse.

Documentation that has come to light over recent years, specifically a letter of Pelham's, proves without a doubt that the opportunistic Revere copied Pelham's drawing, hustled quickly to produce his own engraving, for three weeks after the occurrence, advertising went out and his prints went up for sale in several of Boston's newspapers. By the time Pelham's prints hit the street, Revere's print of 200 had flooded the market.

As is clear, Revere's historic engraving is long on political propaganda and short on accuracy or aesthetics. The political bias is almost comic. Notice how the British Grenadiers are shown standing in a straight line shooting their rifles in a regular volley; despite the fact that, when the melee erupted, the gathering of colonists involved were belligerent, provoking, and even wildly riotous. Revere's engraving delineates a blue sky, while, oddly, a wisp of a moon can be detected—the sky is illustrated in such a way that it seems to cast light on the British "atrocity"—although the riot occurred after nine o'clock on a cold winter night in March. There is a noticeable absence of snow and ice on the street, and yet this so-called massacre was caused not only by an exchange of insults, but, as pointed out, by an angry bunch of viciously throwing snowballs, rocks, and anything at hand.

Notice, finally, how the faces of the British regulars are sharp and angular in contrast to the softer, more innocent features of the Yankees, which is contrived to make the British look more menacing. The British soldiers appear to be enjoying the violence, particularly the soldier at the far end. The colonists, who were mostly laborers, are farcically dressed as gentlemen, for elevating their status could affect the way the rest of the colonies, indeed the world, perceived them. A smoking musket barrel actually points out of the State House, for local color and to enhance the specific threat. The distressed woman in the rear of the crowd plays on 18th-century notions of chivalry. There also appears to be a sniper in the window beneath the Butcher's Hall sign, adding to the one-sided intrigue. It is a bloody mess—the the top of one man's head has been shot off.

It may be pointed out, by the way, that the trial of the British soldiers was the first time a judge used the phrase "reasonable doubt." An interesting sidelight to be noted of this famous, or notorious, engraving, is that one of the British soldiers named Pierce Butler left the army and became a South Carolina plantation owner.

In 1787, he was appointed as a delegate to the Constitutional Convention. Who was the lawyer who defended the British soldiers in court and what was nis nationality? It was John Adams, American.

Speaking of engravings, on the United States five-dollar bill can be seen—discerned, for you have to peer—a peculiar shadow. You can see it on the left stair-guard on the Lincoln Memorial steps; you will notice that its torch-like ornament seems much longer than it should be. The angle of sunlight can be judged from the shadow of the top of the Memorial, behind the left-most columns. If a line parallel to this line of shadow is drawn from the top of the bowl or torch on the left stair guard, it intersects the steps much closer than the far end of the engraved shadow. Furthermore, the right stair-guard doesn't cast any shadow on the bushes. My question is, why not? There is no reason that explains it, except that it is a gaffe. Incidentally, the famous Matthew Brady photograph reproduced on the five-dollar bill was taken from the 1864 sitting that Lincoln allowed, except that on the currency it is reversed—thus Lincoln's mole appears, unlike in real life, on the wrong (left) cheek! Another gaffe.

In John Trumbull's historical paintings *Surrender of Lord Cornwallis* (1820) and *The Surrender of General Burgoyne at Saratoga* (1821), to take just two examples—there are several others—you can see Old Glory flying in the breeze. These are gaffes, large ones. The unavoidable fact is not a single land battle of the Revolutionary War was fought under the Stars and Stripes. There was no American flag flown at Bunker Hill, or at Trenton, or even at Yorktown. Indeed, not until the Mexican War did American soldiers fight under the American flag. It is no different with Archibald Willard's famous and often reproduced *The Spirit of '76*—it commemoratively depicts three battle-tested patriots marching with fife and drum—which was exhibited at the Centennial Exposition in Philadelphia in 1876. Myth has it that onlookers were so inspired by it that Willard was invited to show his painting everywhere and that even President Grant gave it praise. The flag under which they march is an historical anachronism, hands down. Sentimental, but false. Although the painting was initially called *Yankee Doodle* in 1875, the name was changed while the picture was on exhibition in Boston because one of that town's notoriously well-known mental cases was also nicknamed—derisively, of course, and cruelly—"Yankee Doodle."

Curiously, Willard's painting did *not* have any initial popularity. It was placed in the Art Annex to make room for a large number of applications and it was scarcely advertised. Nor was it hailed by critics, with one calling it "oppressive." The success of the painting was largely due to the entrepreneurial James F. Ryder's marketing of its chromolithographs, sold first at five dollars apiece and for less as the exhibition progressed that gave it such impetus. After the Philadelphia exhibition, the painting garnered such a groundswell of popularity that it toured the country to large crowds.

This is perhaps the place to note that July 2, 1776, was the day that the Continental Congress actually voted for independence. And that was the day that independence was declared, that is the day it should be celebrated! John Adams, in his writings, even noted that July 2 would be remembered in the annals of American history to be marked with fireworks and memorable celebrations. The written Declaration of Independence was dated July 4 but was not actually signed until August 2! Fifty-six delegates eventually signed the document, although all were not present on that day in August. Nothing happened on the Fourth of July except the *approval* of the Declaration of Independence

Another highly controversial engraving had to do with

Thomas Hyde Page, a British aide-de camp to General Howe, who fought at the Battle of Breed's Hill in what is now Charlestown on June 17, 1775, and who in fact lost a leg due to a severe wound sustained there. It is Page who was responsible for the famous error concerning the site of that bloody engagement, which was later referred to as the Battle of Bunker Hill. He confused the topography when making up a map after returning to England. A third error is found in the spelling of Copp's Hill as Corpse Hill, from which the British artillery fired across Boston Harbor at the American troops in Charlestown. The long and the short of it, in any case, is that the engraving was a bollocks from the first, and so, alas, remains.

A well-known Currier & Ives engraving, published just after Abraham Lincoln was assassinated on the night of April 14, 1865, shows the dying president lying out and attended by nine men, two of them weeping with handkerchiefs, a group including his wife Mary Todd and, among the men, the new chief justice of the United States, Salmon P. Chase. As as it turned out, Chase never even showed up that evening. In another of their prints, subtitled "The Nation's Martyr," while his son Robert Lincoln weeps, Tad, *who was not present*, buries his face in his mother's skirts. Finally, in *The Death of Lincoln* (1868), an oil painting by Alonzo Chappel, the 9 foot by 14 foot room in the Petersen House across from Ford's Theater where the president died now holds exactly *47 mourners*, including Vice President Andrew Johnson keeping vigil, who was in the room only a few minutes before he was removed, for Mrs. Lincoln, hysterical, had hated him.

But with painting, however, one has to be careful. What do you do with El Greco's elongations of face? Are they gaffes? William Blake's dragons with tails? Edvard Munch's futuroidal *Bathing Man* (1918)? Fernando Botero's balloonheads? Francis Bacon's unseemly parade or mouths, carcasses, and meat, to say nothing of his hysterical and brutal explosions—swipes, smears, smudges, brushwhips, bulbous exaggerations—on some of his subjects' "likenesses," like George Dyer, Lucian Freud, John Edwards, Frank Auerbach, Henrietta Moraes, Isabel Rawsthorne, Michael Leiris, or *his own self-portrait?* "I have never had any love in the whole of my life," he told Sonia, George Orwell's wife, "and what's more I don't want any. All I do is cast my rod into the sewers of despair and see what I come up with this time."

For that matter, what about the ancient Egyptian pretense that everything and everyone is always in profile? Aren't we always confessing to our own needs? Shaped to have to see? Edgar Degas once revealingly said, "Paint what I see? No, I paint what would help others to see what I see."

Paintings, drawings, and lithographs have repeatedly shown thousands of French prisoners being freed when the Bastille fell on July 4, 1789, a continual oddity, since there were only seven persons confined there at the time! Nineteenth-century art was also quite often loose with the facts. Idealized paintings are virtually all hysterical with errors. Let us consider the famous chromograph *Custer's Last Fight*, the gory fictionalized picture painted by Otto Becker, for example. Becker made a 20" by 40" lithograph in 1896 of the original diorama painting which was marketed as prints in the tens of thousands as a point-of-sale item (like jackknives, wall mountings, shot glasses, etc.) by the Anheuser Busch beer company to barrooms throughout the length and breadth of the United States, eventually becoming a painting so widely distributed that in time, according to one critic, it has been "gazed upon by more lowbrows and fewer art critics than any other painting in this country."

Considered one of the most reproduced lithographs in our

country's history, with over 150,000 copies distributed to saloons, bars, restaurants, and clubs, it was this print that was used as an advertising promotion for Budweiser Beer. This chromolithograph on paper was based on the Cassilly Adams's 1885 painting, which was inspired by the narrative of the battle by an extremely handsome—we have his photograph—Native American scout named Ashishishe (c. 1856–1923), also known both as Curly (or Curley) and Bull Half White, a Crow Indian the United States Army during the Sioux Wars, best known for having been one of the few survivors on the United States side at the Battle of Little Bighorn.

The original painting by Adams was sold to one John Ferber, who owned a saloon in St Louis, Missouri. Back in 1892, the beer entrepreneur Adolphus Busch acquired the painting along with the saloon when the owner could not pay a bill for the sum of $35,000. Eager to have the original copied for valuable advertising, Busch commissioned the Milwaukee Lithographic Engraving Company to do it, and it was their house artist, Otto F. Becker, who produced a painting that was then divided into six sections and finally given to other artists to create the color plates used to produce the 1896 advertising prints. The restored Becker painting hangs in the St. Louis boardroom of Anheuser-Busch, Incorporated. The original Adams painting was destroyed by fire on June 13, 1946.

Although nobody knows precisely what happened at the Battle of Little Bighorn, we can ascertain certain facts. Until the very end, there were no heavily mounted charges against the surrounded 7th Cavalry by the Native Americans led by Chiefs Gall, Crazy Horse, and Rain-in-the-Face, for the braves were so numerous they did not need to make a full head-on attack—they were shooting arrows and rifles from covert spots, arroyos, and blinds. When the smoke cleared that day, Custer's body was left unmutilated (except that some people say an Indian woman jammed two sticks into his ears, because he "never listened"); in all likelihood the braves probably did not know who he was.

The brash young general had his hair close-cropped that day, quite contrary to the image commonly held of General George Armstrong Custer: no "golden ringlets," thank you. In one of the many films on the subject, *Custer of the West* (1967), directed by Robert Siodmak—the movie is farcically filled with errors—one feverish, exaggerated scene just prior to the battle shows an intractable Custer, played by Robert Shaw, in a over-ritualized one-on-one verbal confrontation with Chief Crazy Horse, who addresses his enemy as "Yellow Hair." The film of this very American story was shot entirely in Spain!

No sabers were used that day, in spite of Otto Becker's extravagant imagination. A rumor also persists to this day that Rain-in-the-Face cut out Custer's heart, a myth that poet Henry Wadsworth Longfellow perpetuated in his poem "The Revenge of Rain-in-the-Face," one stanza of which goes

> "But the foeman fled in the night
> And Rain-in-the-Face, in his flight,
>   Uplifted high in air
> As a ghostly trophy, bore
> The brave heart that beat no more
>   Of the White Chief with yellow hair."

Becker also shows far too many war bonnets in the picture, several of the braves are dressed like Apaches—the attacking Indians were all Sioux and Northern Cheyenne—and one or two of them, in the words of Evan S. Connell, author of *Son of the Morning Star*, "looked like Aztecs carrying Zulu shields." Furthermore, none of the soldiers would have worn gauntlets during that hot day—after all, the battle took place on June 25th. The original work, which was hung in the Kansas State House, was later chopped in two by a furious axe-wielding female prohibitionist named Blanche Boies, who resented its barroom connections.

Thomas Hovenden's painting *The Last Moments of John Brown* (1884), which depicts the brave but intransigent—some say insane—bearded abolitionist stepping down the small jail steps in Virginia on the morning of his hanging—he is wearing pink slippers—and avuncularly kissing the forehead of a black pickaninny lifted up to the firebrand by the child's adoring mother, who wears a bright red bandanna, is completely apocryphal. Although the work was often reproduced as a popular Currier & Ives lithograph, another money grab, the story was fabricated, based on secondhand sources reported as true by Edward F. Underhill of the *New-York Tribune.* "Captain [John] Avis, who was by Brown's side to the very end, denied its truth," states David S. Reynolds in his classic biography, *John Brown, Abolitionist.* "Andrew Hunter, also present the whole time, averred, 'That whole story about his kissing a negro child . . . is utterly and absolutely false . . . Nothing of the kind occurred . . . He was surrounded by soldiers, and no negro could get access to him.'"

There are many considerations regarding gaffes in the domain of art. As a result of a wandering spell in America, François-René de Chateaubriand, considered the founder of Romanticism in French literature, wrote his dramatic romance *Atala* (1801), the improbable story of a Christianized Indian maiden who takes poison rather than violate her vows of chastity. The painter Anne-Louis Girodet, whose ideas as to how Indians looked were rather odd, made this the subject of his painting *The Burial of Atala* (1808)—

yes, he was a he—which shows a Native American beauty, *very* beautiful, wearing what appears to be a soft white filmy Greek tunic (!) being interred by her Indian lover, Chactas, with whom she has escaped into what Chateaubriand describes as an Allegheny "desert" (!), and by Father Aubrey, obviously a Franciscan friar from the look of his habit, a hermit living there.

Gaffes abound! Incidentally, someday take a look at Girodet's celebrated portrait of Chateaubriand. With his greasy dark pompadour, extended cool sideburns, sexy spit-curl over his forehead, and open-necked white collar, that young politician, diplomat, writer, and historian of the Romantic period looks the exact archetype of all rock-and-rollers—especially rockabilly icons Elvis Presley, Carl Perkins, Gene Vincent, etc.—and 150 years or so before those rockabilly singer ever made an appearance! When Napoleon first saw that portrait, he remarked, "He looks like a conspirator who has just come down the chimney." It was an allusion, no question about it, to juvenile delinquency!

The German painter Albrecht Dürer, in his painting *Four Apostles* (1526), portrays St. Paul, looking older, reticent, and introspective, along with Saints John, Peter, and Mark, shown young and with piercing eyes. Unfortunately, from a historical point of view, neither St. Paul nor the evangelist Mark were among of the traditional twelve apostles, which included Peter Andrew, James John, Philip, Matthias, Thomas, Bartholomew, Simon, Matthias, James the less, and Thaddeus. (Judas the betrayer is, of course, never included.)

William Blake's strange illustration—graphite, ink and watercolor on paper—of *Dante and Virgil at the Gates of Hell* (1808) is unforgettable. We see Dante describing the "dim" colors which contribute to his terror. Blake's dark shadows of pure black pigment next to areas of unpainted white paper contribute to the powerful subject. Blake used Prussian blue for the blue areas, and indigo blue mixed with yellow for the green foliage, so that they contrast. The blue, green, and vermilion red do not overlap. Convention and correctness, however, meant little or nothing to the eccentric Blake, who always listened to his own music, so to speak, as often he and his wife Catherine sat naked in the garden reading. He was often careless with facts, as when inscribing the most famous single line of Dante above his drawing, as to garble the Italian and so actually misquote it; the English poet should have written *"Lasciate ogni speranze, voi ch'entrate."* Curiously enough, the name of Blake's illustration, compounding the blunder, is *The Inscription over the Gate* (1824–27).

Actually the full inscription on the Gate of Hell in Canto III of *The Inferno* is: *"Per me si va ne la città dolente, / Per me si va ne l'etterno dolore, / Per me si va tra perduta gente,"* which translates into English as "Through me the way is to the city dolent; / Through me the way is to eternal dole; ' Through me the way among the people lost."

In William Powell Frith's painting of holiday makers, *Ramsgate Sands* (1854), showing an immensely crowded beach—a truly amazing painterly undertaking of color and faces and types and activities—there are over 100 figures, men, women, children, but not a single one of them is eating or drinking. Could any beach photographer today find anywhere a group equally large and equally abstemious?

John James Audubon's exceptional bird painting of the Mocking Bird, Plate XXI of the very first volume of *The Birds of America* (1827–38), rendered with a playfully creative bit of theatric juxtaposition, shows that American songbird as the object of a scary assault in a tree by an open-mouthed rattlesnake, just about to strike. The plate caused a scandal, for it was charged by naturalists that rattlesnakes do not and cannot climb trees and that no rattlesnake has recurved fangs such as are shown in the picture. Audubon had also gone on record in the *Franklin Journal* as giving a description of the rattler's method of constricting prey. A major controversy ensued at the time. In the end, however, specimens of a southern species of rattlesnake were produced showing teeth exactly the way Audubon had represented them. It was also abundantly proved that the rattlesnake *could* climb trees. As to the capacity of the rattlesnake to constrict its victim, Audubon did in fact overreach himself.

As to the outdoors, did you know that Sophie Thoreau, the naturalist Henry's sister, along with being a gardener, naturalist, and teacher, was an amateur artist, as well? Unfortunately, she drew firs, not pines, around her rustic illustration of the cabin—along with a few deciduous trees that did not grow in Massachusetts—for the 1854 edition of *Walden*, a frontispiece that her brother wistfully complained of and which his Concord friend, Ellery Channing, called a "feeble caricature."

W. G. Reed's painting of Teddy Roosevelt's hell-for-leather charge up San Juan Hill—which now resides in the Library of Congress—portrays all of the "Rough Riders" mounted on horses and facing bravely into fusillades of Spanish gunfire. The painting is all wrong when compared to the actual facts of the event. The only man mounted on horseback was Colonel Roosevelt who, however, had to dismount when stopped by a wire fence but who then led his men to the summit on foot. So much for the "rough riders." It is commonly believed by historians that the group of soldiers involved—the 3rd, the 6th, the 10th, the 1st, and the black 9th cavalry—were too eager and too rash in the assault in which many were killed. It was not a rout, to be sure, and slaughter was indeed heavy.

Regarding anomalies in horse paintings, in the well-known painting *Bronco Buster* (ca. 1905), which portrays an annual spring event on the range, William H. Denton (1878–1936), a romantic like the brilliant painter Frederic Remington, reveals in that action-packed moment a singular gaffe—a cowboy would traditionally never wear his gun while breaking a horse, as indeed his cowboy does.

Thomas Hill's official (idealized) painting of the famous driving of the Golden Spike is memorable in several ways. It purports to depict the actual historical ceremony commemorating the completion of the cross-country railroad that took place near the slapped-up tent city of Promontory, Utah, on May 10, 1869. Predictably, the thousands of drunks, gamblers, and whores who attended the occasion are nowhere to be seen in the pious and inflated canvas, an assemblage portrayed as though watching Christ's Transfiguration! California Governor Leland Stanford, who commissioned the painting is, not surprisingly, standing forth prominently for all to see like some glorious white knight, posing with the Reverend John Todd, when the fact of the matter is, at that "august" celebration neither of the two men ever showed up. And then, to add insult to injury, the actual spike of gold in real life was quickly removed before some rascal or thieving renegade from Tent City—surely one of those derelicts omitted from the painting—could steal it and run away!

Let me mention here that Flemish artist Roelandt Savery, the only painter believed to have ever sketched a live dodo bird—the species became extinct in 1681—painted two right legs on the creature! Typically, it became the model for generation after generation of dolt-headed copyists, who simply repeated the same structural error. The Museum of Modern Art in New York City moronically hung upside-down Matisse's paper-cut picture *Le Bateau* (1953) for as long as 47 days before it discovered its blundering mistake. Was that geometrical confusion of space not somehow related to the same goofy misreading of size that we find in the accommodating magazine illustrator Norman Rockwell's perpetual calendar favorite, the warm, kitschy *Freedom from Want* (1943), where in that saccharine Thanksgiving dinner scene we see not only a family at a table, including grammy and grampy, but being served a holiday turkey so gigantic, so unthinkably oversized and glistening with fat, that it resembles a small hippo—way out of proportion to the realistic diners!

It is astonishing to see in how many directions a gaffe can go. Is not the following a gaffe? On the famous golden painting *Daybreak* (1922), Maxfield Parrish's most famous painting, an oil on panel 26½" by 45½", can be seen the artist's *actual fingerprints*—they appear in the mountains where Parrish patted a glaze to achieve just the right density! But then again possibly (a) that inartistic blunder was intentional and surely (b) as a sort of eccentric and unique autograph it made the painting more valuable!

William Makepeace Thackeray's own drawings for *Vanity Fair* (1848), an historical novel, you will recall—the battle of Waterloo takes place in the middle of it—are hopelessly inaccurate, with the latest fashions of 1847 (trousers, lower waists, less exiguous skirts) trying to cover the dowdier fashions of 1815. Thackeray was a serious artist, and quite a good one. So too with Du Maurier's illustrations for *Trilby* (1894), where instead of evoking midcentury styles, he outfitted Trilby not with the fetching crinolines of the 1850s, but rather with the updated fashions of the 1890s.

By the way, Thackeray's novel *The Newcomes* (1854–55) is riddled with errors. Newcome Senior is both colonel and major at one and the same time. Jack Belsize becomes Charles on another page. And Mrs. Raymond Gray, introduced as Emily, is suddenly, amazingly, rechristened Fanny.

Should we really and truly depart this subject of gaffes in art and painting without mentioning, at least one time, the bamboozling fraud so often perpetrated in the name of much Abstract Expressionism, a good deal of it pure bollocks and codswollop being passed off in the art world, especially in New York City, by some of the boldest and shameless hucksters on the planet without so much as a smidgen of talent? Zigzagging configurations by men and women who couldn't even draw a kindergarten cat? Loopy loops and mad meanderings and nutty notions and unhinged upchucks? *Pleeeease!*

It was in his very first column on September 6, 1959, that John Canaday, a leading art critic for the *New York Times* as well as an intrepid and insightful art historian who, by his willingness to tell the emperor he is naked, inflamed the art establishment by proclaiming that Abstract Expressionism, the dominant style of the period, allowed "exceptional tolerance for incompetence and deception." Although he acknowledged the talent of its best exponents, he noted that "we have been had" by the "freaks, the charlatans, and the misled who surround this handful of serious and talented artists."

As to gaffes in art, let me conclude that the Académie Française, that august body created by Cardinal Richelieu in 1635 as the official agency of linguistic formalism, always firmly believed that strange poet Charles Baudelaire was dotty because he had once been observed in the Louvre fussily taking measurements of the

Greek centaur and muttering to himself, "There's no getting around it, he can't wipe himself."

He was never elected to be a member, incidentally.

Soft Art: A Consideration

Nothing an artist brings to his work is not soft in terms of tender focus and force. Patience and tolerance, cooperating with vision, is the challenge of art and its countersign, and creation surely calls for a careful and considered birth, no more poignantly than in the matter of soft sculpture, which is fashioned with the ductility of materials such as yarn, foam, acrylic, latex, leather, vinyl, kapok, polypropylene fur, felt, wool, hair, cloth, rubber, paper, even liquid polyester, and other unconventional materials, substances, and composites with a seemingly endless number of applications. Work can be fashioned out of natural materials if combined to make a nonrigid object. Materials of this sort evoke certain sensations but somehow all retain the "memory"—the *habitus*—of forms, which almost by definition implies softness itself when we consider the plastic arts.

The creative efforts of soft sculpturists are not only a challenge to art but a direct confrontation of softness itself. Artists are literally seeking the definition of its being. Back in 1969, the Swedish-born American sculptor Claes Oldenburg, among those who, along with Yayoi Kusama, popularized it—his Art Pop creation, the large-scale *Floor Burger* (1962), an installation primarily made out of canvas filled with rubber foam and cardboard, is, as someone has said "large enough to serve as a Poconos honeymoon bed"—stated quite emphatically, "The main reason for making a soft version of a known hard object may be (I think more and more it is) to dramatize or isolate the condition of softness. And other conditions such as the response to 'gravity'—this condition under which objects appear to exist, and we as objects, as matter, appear to exist." What is striking about that oversized maroon hamburger patty of his, nestled in the middle of two tan or khaki buns with a green pickle on top, is the *nap* of the thing, the texture and pile that so comically mimics its yummy original.

Another splendid soft sculpture of a matching type, at least conceptually, is Yayoi Kusama's *Pumpkin* (1994), a solid yellow with a clear spot pattern—"Round, soft, colorful, senseless and unknowing, polka-dots become movement," the artist has proclaimed of the trademark of her work. "Polka dots are a way to infinity"—which is located on Naoshima Island, an island in the Seto Inland Sea that is known for its contemporary art museums, architecture, and sculptures, where it sits as a bright, enigmatic icon contrasting with but beautifully enhancing the natural environment. It is located close to water, and the reflection makes this sculpture stand out even more.

A precursor of pop art and an influence on many artists such as Donald Judd, Joseph Cornell, and Andy Warhol, Kusama's work is associated with feminism, minimalism, surrealism, and Art Brut. Kusama, who has created many soft-sculpture pumpkins, began drawing them as a child in pre-war Japan, where her family owned a plant nursery that farmed kabocha squash. "I love pumpkins," the artist explained in a 2015 interview, "because of their humorous form, warm feeling, and a human-like quality and form." One of her most popular soft sculpture works is entitled *Accumulation*

No. 1 (1965), where she sewed by hand painted projections she called "phalluses," and placed them on an armchair. Soft sculpture was also a key feature during the 1970s in Post-Minimalist art, where creations were inspired by nothing more than common items and materials artists found all around them. Another pioneering innovator during this time was Eva Hesse, a German-born American sculptor who fabricated works composed of latex, string, fiberglass, and rope and wire suspended from the ceiling, as can be seen in her *Untitled (Rope Piece)* (1966) and *One More Than One* (1967).

Softness, above all, is obliging. Nap *yields*. The concept allows for accommodating and complaisant agreeability. Conveniently, humorously, everyday items virtually ask to be re-seen in the way of a malleable double which can be reproduced and admired for its suppleness and yielding transformability. Comfort, certainly in terms of handling, applies to the very word "softness" in terms of positive connotations. It denotes impressibility and featheriness and the resilience of being moved in a leisurely manner, rising gradually, having curved or rounded outlines (not harsh or jagged). Compliance is perhaps its first beauty, and that in the arts under consideration here its ductility allows for no end of possibilities. Softness is the ploughshare compared to which hardness is the sword. It is amenable and looks to reconciliation. In softness remains the ancient sense of causing little hardship or suffering. "God has a brown voice, as soft and full as beer," wrote Anne Sexton.

Soft power. There is such a thing as soft power, the "soft sell," unstructured, where structure in its sharpness and angles can offend and put one off. Irish composer, painter, and novelist Samuel Lover—he was also the grandfather of Victor Herbert, the king of glittering operettas—once declared, "Too little is it considered, while we gaze on aristocratic beauty, how much good food, soft lying, warm wrapping, ease of mind, have to do with the attractions which command our admiration."

Not all are fully aboard, of course. Count on the prickly novelist Vladimir Nabokov, not a big advocate of gentle considerations, to blow a contentious note across the pond of soft serenity, who proclaimed outright, "My loathings are simple: stupidity, oppression, crime, cruelty, soft music." American author John Jay Chapman would have agreed with him, who declared, "People who love soft methods and hate iniquity forget this; that reform consists in taking a bone from a dog. Philosophy will not do it."

The morphology of softness is all about amiable adaptation, something about the compromise of settlement—and fabric is its language, its frame, its formation. There is a distinct concession in the subject that also extends to compassion, empathy, and commiseration, at least in the way of the patient ease by which it stems grief and anxiety, as for example with, at least musicologically, compositions like Samuel Barber's heartbreakingly sorrowful Adagio for Strings, Op. 11* or the finale of Gustave Mahler's Ninth Symphony

---

*In January 1938, Barber sent an orchestrated version of the Adagio for Strings to the great conductor Arturo Toscanini, who, strangely, returned the score without a single comment, a fact that greatly annoyed Barber. Toscanini, however, sent word through Gian Carlo Menotti that he was planning to perform the piece and simply had returned the work because he had already *memorized* it! So adaptable, so warmly powerful was this music in its malleability that Toscanini (or so it was reported) felt no need to look at it again until the very day before the premiere! So gently lenient—so *considerate*—is this music that it was broadcast over radio at the announcement of FDR's death (1945), played at the funeral of Albert Einstein in 1955, and performed by the National Symphony Orchestra in a national radio broadcast following the funeral of President John F. Kennedy in 1963.

or the Adagietto of his Fifth Symphony. At least conceptually, I can discern the lineaments of the patience and tolerance in the resilience of such obliging music Antonín Dvořák's mournfully nostalgic Symphony No. 9 is softly mellifluous. Edward Elgar's poignant Cello Concerto, arguably his greatest work, evokes a special softness to me, and shares along with his Violin Sonata, String Quartet, and his Piano Quintet a valedictory, autumnal mood. How complementary to such music, how creatively parallel, for example, would be Yayoi Kusama's *Narcissus Garden* (1966), an iconic project, both a show and an installation, comprised of 1500 mirror orbs made from plastic and laid on the ground. Wearing a golden kimono, Kusama stood amongst the orbs during the show and sold them to any enthralled buyers—or a simple two dollars apiece, visitors would walk away with a piece of Kusama's art.

We rely on the resilience and docility of softness as balm to the troubled heart. "But soft, what do I hear?" whispers love-stricken Romeo in Shakespeare's tragedy; it means simply, "Pause, be calm."

"But, soft! what light through yonder window breaks?
It is the east, and Juliet is the sun.
Arise, fair sun, and kill the envious moon,
Who is already sick and pale with grief . . ."

As it is the antonym of hardness, harshness, the intractable and unmovable, softness is equally the opposite of blasting and booming, ringing and roaring, the clamorous and the clangerous. In that, as on a bed, we are consoled by softness, for emotions—feeling and sentiment—are involved. Reason, I suspect, is also soft. It may be difficult to reason as an activity but the dimensions of its outflow suggests to me in its settling conclusions Sigmund Freud stated, "The voice of the intellect is a soft one, but it does not rest until it has gained a hearing."

The ground is soft after a heavy rain. (Allow for its peevish detractors to call it also squishy, doughy, mushy sloppy, and gloopy). There is the soft glow of the moon. A nursery is painted in soft pink. Softness is marked by mildness, the unassuming, the settled, the secure, and is low key. When a fellow is in love with a girl, he is "soft" on her. The mere welcoming aspect of softness is inarguable. It epitomizes in its fetching attraction the nature of wind, willows, women. Computer software is workable—it fits the form, is the soul of accord, acclimation, and compromise. One thinks of softness, invariably, as having a light and integrating color, not one that is strong or bright in color and tone. Pillow-softness is famously white. Clouds enfold us. Waterfalls and their frothy spume soothe us. G. K. Chesterton begins his poem "Lepanto" with "White founts falling in the courts of the sun, / And the Soldan of Byzantium is smiling as they run."

White is to softness what paprika is to a Hungarian. It may not always be the case, but it seems that little is not soft that is not also white as cotton, as steam, as sheets, as pillows, as aprons, as goose down, as gauze, as linen, as napkins, as shampoos, as light in its airiness and as puff-empty as a scudding cloud or fluffy new-fallen snow. And such kinds of light! Caravaggio. Maxfield Parrish. Claude Monet. Andrew Wyeth. J. M. W. Turner. His *The Lungernsee by Moonlight, Switzerland* (ca. 1848) reveals the perfect marriage of softness and light. Lord Byron's poem "The Bride of Abydos" goes in part: "The light of love, the purity of grace, / The mind, the Music breathing from her face, / The heart whose softness harmonised the whole— / And, oh! that eye was in itself a Soul!"

Who could paint soft, pale light, supporting purity or design and clarity of form, better than Piero della Francesca, whose work was as white moonlight? Elinor Wylie in her "Velvet Shoes" encourages us to enter such a wonderland:

> "Let us walk in the white snow
> In a soundless space;
> with footsteps quiet and slow
> At a tranquil pace
> Under veils of white lace.
> I shall go shod in silk,
> And you in wool,
> White as a white cow's milk
> More beautiful
> Than the breast of a gull.
> We shall walk through the still town
> In a windless peace;
> We shall step upon white down,
> Upon silver fleece,
> Upon softer than these.
> We shall walk in velvet shoes:
> Wherever we go
> Silence will fall like dews
> On white silence below.
> We shall walk in the snow"

In F. Scott Fitzgerald's novel *The Great Gatsby* (1925), when Daisy, sobbing with loving admiration, says to Gatsby, "They're such beautiful shirts!" it is clearly not only the colors, beauty, or the masculinity of the objects, but their softness which makes the dramatically romantic act of his heedlessly throwing them around the room with such casual bravado so beguiling:

"He took out a pile of shirts and began throwing them, one by one, before us, shirts of sheer linen and thick silk and fine flannel, which lost their folds as they fell and covered the table in many-colored disarray. While we admired, he brought more and the soft rich heap mounted higher—shirts with stripes and scrolls and plaids in coral and apple-green and lavender and faint orange, and monograms of Indian blue. Suddenly, with a strained sound, Daisy bent her head into the shirts and began to cry stormily."

Regarding the world of soft art, the drapery that artists delineate may be among my favorite pictorial moments, with their uncanny renderings of folds, swirls, wrinkles, tucks, gathers, pleats creases, sculpted or painted with such airy, delicate, feathery and creatively insubstantial beauty and natural conviction that it takes your breath away. (I can never think of Princess Diana's wedding dress in any other way.) I remember one visiting the Tate Gallery in London around 1969 and seeing an amazing display of art drapery. It is actually a genre, and one can see it in such classic paintings as Leonardo da Vinci's study for the angel's drapery in the second version of the *Virgin of the Rocks* (1508), now in London's National Gallery, Vermeer's *Girl Reading a Letter at an Open Window* (1657), El Greco's *Saint Peter and Saint Paul* (between 1590 and 1600), Peter Tom's *Lady Elizabeth Keppel* (1748), Arthur Devis's *A Lady in Blue* (1757), George Romney's *Margaret Messenger, Mrs. Walter Strickland* (1788) or his *Emma Hart, Lady Hamilton as Circe* (1782), William-Adolphe Bouguereau's *Modesty* (1902), John Singer Sargent's *Mrs. Joseph E. Widener* (1903), Georgia O'Keeffe's *Abstraction* (1915), and Andrew Wyeth's *Pentecost* (1989) and *Wind from the Sea* (1947), among others.

Drapery is often found, of course, also in funerary statuary both in cemeteries and in museums, doleful but elegantly symbolic but beautiful female figures face-veiled in alabaster or hard rock which ingenious sculptors have made to look like thin, gauzy fabric. There is the astonishing alabaster figure of the mourner from the tomb of Philip the Bold, Duke of Burgundy (1364–1404), made between 1404 and 1410, and *The Veiled Virgin*, a Carrara marble statue carved in Rome by Italian sculptor Giovanni Strazza, depicting the bust of the Virgin Mary. And in how many first-century Aphrodites do we not find thrilling folds? Little can match for drapery the elegant work on Michelangelo's matchless *Pietà*.

For utter perfection in drapery, however—almost beyond compare, unparalleled—consider Gian Lorenzo Bernini's *Ecstasy of Saint Teresa* (also known as the *Transverberation of Saint Teresa*), the sculptural group in white marble that is set in an elevated aedicule in the Cornaro Chapel of the church of Santa Maria della Vittoria in Rome. The fully transported saint, enraptured, shown lying in a cloud, one illuminated by natural light which filters through a hidden window in the dome of the surrounding aedicule and underscored by gilded stucco rays, is made all the more transcendingly beatific by the shafts of heavenly grace revealed in her holy acceptance as, overpoweringly penetrated, she yields, the falling backward of her exquisite surrendering shown not only by way of her transfigured face but by the unfolding looseness of her habiliments, a drapery of many mantles rendered in the utter delicacy of her compliant submission to Christ.

On the other hand, is this to say softness and the whole idea of it has nothing in it of menace, of the cow-hearted, the feeble, the unmanly? With the materials we have mentioned arguably lacking in firmness or strength of character—common connotations of softness—they present for those very reasons intractable difficulties for artists not only to handle but to master, to regulate, to rule, finding in softness as much an obstacle to art as an occasion. The utter *impressionable* aspect of softness, its almost unscrupulous manipulativeness, may be its most damning quality, the embodiment of weakness.

Softness in art? I remember at Yale University once taking the time to examine near-at-hand the original painting of Edward Hopper's popular *Rooms by the Sea* (1951) and to discover, to my shock, surprise, and disappointment, frankly, that the sharp, crisp lines of sunlight, shadow, floor, and sea that I had so often admired in prints, up close sadly proved to be loose—fragile, friable, frangible—which ruined it for me.

Consider for a moment the *other* face of softness: weakness, flaccidity, limpness (remember the flaccid hair of Geoffrey Chaucer's Pardoner was off-puttingly limp?), unathletic pusillanimity, the lame aspect—literally—of being out of shape. There is also the negative idea in softness of having or producing little contrast or a relatively short range of tones in art (cf. the "soft" photographic print). We have already noted the attendant connotations of its cushioned, squishy, faint, out-of-condition state, or in food, say, having a bland or mellow rather than a sharp or acid taste. Soft-serve ice cream, tasted, seems merely to dissolve, no? Isn't almost all soft food more or less to be *mumped*?

Let it be noted that softness is subdued, too compliant, unduly susceptible to influence, emotionally suggestible, and in being too responsive *not being responsive at all.* "Soft" news, remember, is relatively less serious or significant, just as "soft" currency is not readily convertible, nor is a soft loan secured by collateral. A soft stock market is sluggish. What worse can be said of a person than that he or she is of a consistency that may be shaped or molded, capable of being spread about like cheap margarine? The fluidity of anything—its kinesis—gives it instability, no? "Propaganda is a soft weapon; hold it in your hands too long, and it will move about like a snake, and strike the other way," wrote Jean Anouilh. Christ's robe—or chiton, without seam, woven whole from the top down—was not soft, nor was it silky, supple, velvety, doughy, cushiony, downy, ductile, formless, fleecy, impressible, balmy, smooth, soothing, loose-fitting, relaxed, cuddly, caressable, snugglesome, or warm. Just as the choice of the materials of soft-sculpture artists emphasize natural forces, such as gravity or heat, power or fragility, and in many cases have metaphorical or metaphysical implications, so to with softness as symbol elsewhere. Cistercian (Trappist) monks, for example, who follow the Rule of St. Benedict, always avoid soft garments, as they are an occasion of sin. The Nazi Party national youth leader Baldur von Schirach—he was convicted of crimes against humanity—insisted that Nazi youth play *harshly*. Softness seduces!

What of a flaccid or slack handshake? A muscleless man? The woeful entropic interactions, rarely subtle, in senior citizens? The vectors of an old man's skin? The flabby shiver of a fat or old woman's thighs or what are called her "bingo wings"? Yugoslavian politician and writer Milovan Djilas described the merciless and inhuman Soviet NKVD director Lavrenti P. Beria as a short man, "somewhat plump, greenish pale, and with soft damp hands." John Steinbeck's intellectually disabled character Lennie in *Of Mice and Men* (1937) is soft of brain, hair, thought. True, softness gives us a baby's cheek, the quack of a duck, rabbit's fur, singer Peggy Lee's soft, laid-back jazz style, slippers, soft drinks, but what about an infirm bed, an overripe peach, a timorous hug? Weak opinions? Lackluster commitment? Sagging bums? Uninspiring sermons?

Lax law?

There is a tepidness to softness—offhandedness, impassivity, room temperature *chambré*. Do we not read in Revelation 3:15–16: "I know thy works, that thou art neither cold nor hot: I would thou wert cold or hot. So then because thou art lukewarm, and neither cold nor hot, I will spew thee out of my mouth"? By the way, now you know where to go if you are ever asked if regurgitation is mentioned in the Bible.

"Soft knowledge" itself—I am thinking of subjects like sociology and psychology, graduate degrees in "education," popular science books, self-help books, and all the bogus and invalid subjects of study they offer, all of it of slippery provenance and value—embodies perhaps softness among its worst forms. I recall an education course being offered one summer at the University of Virginia way back when in which, for serious credits, *graduate* students were taught how to run a movie projector and interactive discussions were held about just how far down window-shades should be pulled!

To me, broadcasting on NPR (National Public Radio) embodies the very idea of soft knowledge, all those bubble-headed segments and "conversational" programs with that tiring and inane chatter and faux-patrician twaddle that always goes on far too long, not to mention the lead journalists there with their self-cherishing voices and huge salaries—Scott Simon earns $477,914 a year and he can't even pronounce the word *news* correctly! (the salary of the president of the United States in the year 2023 is $400,000)—all of them chuntering on with almost always marginal matter trying to give it life. It is all perishing and powdery, fragile and frail. NPR receives funds from the U.S. Government, corporate sponsors (*yes, they do run commercials!*), *and* public contributions—all three! These scandalous facts, a secret to listeners, are all kept mum, not a whisper. Softness. A further softness? You don't hear them tip-toing out of the studio to the bank, gingerly walking in felt shoes!

There can be found, in any case, a strange or irrational—even illogical, unsound, and pointlessly nonsensical—side to soft art. May it therefore not be said of the genre in its most extreme iterations that it undercuts right reason by the very nature of its provocative, outrageous, and not infrequent lunatic modifiability? Fluxion? Gassiness? Transience? Is there not something of the bitterly barbed, thorny, and subversive in the very anti-formal, often antagonistic goading tendencies of many of the works we find being produced? Nothing anti-socially disturbing in Les Kossatz's *Sheep on a Couch* (1973)? Or in Claes Oldenburg's *Soft Fur Good Humors* (1963)? Or Louise Bourgeois's *Seven in Bed* (2001), six pink Yojo-like clay figures lying down in a row and all sexually intertwined? Or her *Soft Landscape* (1963), an oyster-shaped blob that seems to be looking for a shape? Or Bourgeois's *A Girl* (1968), a hanging black figure shaped exactly like a male "package"? Or her gigantic, terrifying urban arachnids (late 1990s), spiders perched on spindly metal legs that all end in points, raised so that viewers can walk beneath them and marvel (or recoil in horror) at their form? Or minimalist artist Carl Andre's lunatic tile patterns, an abstract work, basically floor displays running along in repetitive sets made of repetitive blocks, repetitive bricks, and repetitive metal plates arranged directly on the floor? Or Marjorie Strider's site-specific installations of unbridled polyurethane blue foam that tumbles out of a black purse, like *Rosemary's Bag* (1973) or yellow foam out of *Nestle's Box* (1973) or ooze glopping down a spiral staircase in *Blue Sky* (1974)?

Repetition, not surprisingly, is a soft sculpture *topos*. There is in the fact of repetition—restatement, asseveration, importuning—less of litany than a presumptive if playful rudeness that borders marginally on the hostility of insistence and witty rancor, if such a thing exists. Take Eva Hesse's *Repetition Nineteen III* (1968), for example, a composition of 19 translucent, handmade empty tumblers that in their presentation all sit in an arbitrary arrangement on a gallery floor. They are made of fiberglass and polyester resin, each about 20 inches tall and similar to one another in size and shape with none of them exactly alike. (Hesse did not give specific instructions about how they are to be arranged, so the overall shape varies with each installation). But what it says is simply what it is, like that dopey American phrase that has been popular for far too long, "It is what it is!"—nobody has a clue to what he or she means when making that harebrained remark!

Art, even the best art, I suppose, remains in the final analysis essentially ambiguous in what it conveys. Softness acts in that way, casting different spangles of light on different days, very like the people you value for their silence and custody of self who, when you need to *speak* to them are not there—and vice versa.

Our virtues in a changing light are invariably our vices.

Drudge Work:
The Need for Getting By for Artists

Artists, to be productive, have often had to take jobs in a non-altruistic way as a means to raise cash, effortfully turning to workable and practical ends, even if half-heartedly, to keep the wolf from the door. (Could that have been what Wallace Stevens meant when he said, "Poetry is money"?) Dreams drive us on, nevertheless. Didn't Axel Munthe, the Swedish-born medical doctor and psychiatrist, although fairly solvent, write *The Story of San Michele* (1929) in order to get money for a bird sanctuary? It was not an easy go for him, for he had developed an eye condition that eventually made him virtually blind and unable to tolerate the bright Italian sunlight. Didn't Dr. Sam Johnson write his play *Irene* to raise money in order to pay for his mother's funeral? With many artists, there has been no money at all—often quite the reverse—merely useless jobs as dogsbodies, with little pay, and only a hole in the potter's field at the end awaiting them. Despair has often followed insolvency.

Trying to eke out a living by means of one's art has been a problem over the years for some of the greatest artists in history. Think merely of Mozart. Often it has been necessary to do hard menial work, plodding work, drudge work—grinding toil—

in order to survive. In 1887, having left France, Gauguin had run out of money and was forced to work as a sandhog laboring on the French construction of the Panama Canal. During this dark time, discouraged, he sent off letters to his wife Mette lamenting the miserable conditions he endured: "I have to dig . . . from five-thirty in the morning to six in the evening, under the tropical sun and rain," he wrote. "At night I am devoured by mosquitoes."

Brilliant painters, writers, and thinkers, simply to get by, have often been driven to take the lowliest, most derisive jobs. German scientist Charles Proteus Steinmetz, for instance, this genius in mathematics and electronics—later widely praised as the "Forger of Thunderbolts" and "The Wizard of Schenectady"—was reduced when he emigrated to the United States in 1889 to sweeping floors at General Electric. British novelist Barbara Pym wasted much of her creative time as a research assistant with the International African Institute for 28 years. In order to survive, Herman Melville, America's greatest novelist, spent the last wasteful years of his life stamping crates of bananas in the custom house in New York. Novelist Henry Green toiled away as a factory manager. Philip Larkin worked as a librarian at the University of Hull all of his life. Amelia Earhart worked in Denison House in Boston as a social worker. Julia Child was a file-clerk for the OSS in Ceylon.

Meanwhile, in poorest London, Karl Marx, a man almost never viewed as the socially concerned and uncompromising if intransigent humanitarian that he was, no matter how bad circumstances got, adamantly refused to take a bourgeois job. His children died, he became ill, and yet still he wouldn't compromise. "They'll remember my carbuncles," said the unbudging philosopher from obscurity, writing *Das Kapital,* in ill health, poverty, suffering the exile forced on him by a corrupt economic system.

Small insignificant jobs were often as necessary for an artist to keep on painting, even if in his or her stolen hours, as for the need for money to keep the household together. Self-respect—hope—required it. Roman poet Virgil, author of the *Georgics* (ca. 37–29 BC), his long dactylic hexameter poem on the methods of running a farm, kept, raised, and sold, bees. His detractors often taunted him with his rustic origins.

Ho Chi Minh in 1911, at age 23, was toiling in the kitchens of the Carlton Hotel, London, under the legendary French chef, Auguste Escoffier. Herman Hesse, who underwent serious depression as early as his first year at school, worked as a mechanic and bookseller. In 1892, he made an attempt at suicide and was placed in a mental institution. Film director Werner Fassbinder put up wallpaper and decorated rooms in Cologne. Chuck Berry was a hairdresser, singer Perry Como a barber, the Russian writer Maxim Gorky a baker. From 1898 to 1908 Sigrid Undset, the Nobel Prize-winning Norwegian novelist and author of the masterpiece *Kristin Lavansdatter* (1921–22) slaved away as a humble secretary. Our nation's own work of art, the Declaration of Independence, was signed by many diligent fellows who well knew the meaning of common jobs, although most of the signers were lawyers. Samuel Adams listed himself as a brewer, Benjamin Franklin a printer, and Robert Paine as a preacher. Philip Hart of New Jersey was a dirt farmer with virtually no education.

Sidney Lanier was fortunate enough to obtain a position as flautist with the Peabody Symphony orchestra in Baltimore in 1873. Alfred Kreymborg, poetaster of staccato whimsies, taught chess for money. Poet Madison Cawein wrote virtually all of his poetry during the 19 years he was employed as a cashier in a Kentucky gambling house. Poet James Dickey wrote jingles for Coca-

Cola. Robert Frost was a farmer in Derry, New Hampshire, for 11 years. Poet L. E. Sissman wrote advertising copy. Kurt Vonnegut opened up a Saab car dealership in a stone building on Route 6A on Cape Cod, operating as sole proprietor with one mechanic on-hand. Poetry anthologist Louis Untermeyer for almost 20 years commuted to Newark, where he worked in his father's jewelry manufacturing establishment. (In his case, being a fairly artless drone in his work, it might have been a small blessing had he stayed there!) Down through the years, many poets have scraped and saved, doing anything to survive short of selling their bottoms to randy clergymen.

What about painters? It went as hard for them as with others. Remarkably few painters in the mid-17th century were able to turn a significant penny in the Netherlands solely by means of their craft. At one raffle at the time, a painting by Abraham van Bayeren sold for no more than 12 guilders. (A municipal physician earned about 1500 guilders a year, a ship's carpenter might make as much as 500 guilders a year, and even a minister who lived rent-free got more than 300 guilders for living expenses.) Jan Vermeer, who managed his father's tavern, had to deal in pictures on the side (as did poor Rembrandt) and still died broke and in debt to his baker. Jan van Goyen, who had an ancillary business in real estate and tulip bulbs, died penniless. Jan Steen, son of a brewer, ran an inn. Jacob Ruisdael worked as a barber-surgeon. Karel van der Pluym was appointed municipal plumber in Leyden. Franz Hals, Jacob van Ruysdael, and Meindert Hobbema all ended up in charitable institutions. Ferdinand Bol, on the other hand, married a rich widow and promptly quit painting.

The dire need of making a living plagued many an artist. All sorts of schemes for self-help were devised. Some painters held exhibits for their work and charged admission, a method of selling that began in England. Luckless Benjamin Haydon had to put up for raffle his large *Xenophon's First Sight of the Sea* (1832). Later, imprisoned for debt, he committed suicide, first in an attempt at shooting himself—the bullet failed to kill him—and then by cutting his throat. He left a widow and three surviving children. Jacques David, whose pictures earned him little or no income from before the Revolution 1789 to 1799—although the large income of his wealthy wife ultimately saved him from financial misery—resorted to the more humbling work of portraiture, two notable masterpieces of which, well-designed and realistic, were of two martyrs of the Revolution, both painted in 1793, *The Death of Lepeletier de Saint-Fargeau* and *The Death of Marat.*

Artists over the years often turned for quick income to portrait painting, in fact. It was a genre that especially took strong root in England, where the Protestant religion excluded many other types of subjects commonly enjoyed in France. In 1712, *The Spectator* had commented: "No nation in the world delights so much in having their own, or Friends' or Relatives' pictures; whether from their own National good-nature or having a love to Painting, and not being encouraged in the great article of Religious Pictures, which the Purity of our worship refuses the free use of, or from whatever causes."

It was a particular focus of interest that had comparatively little dignity, however, and many painters had a strong aversion to it. Portraits in the Netherlands 350 years ago were ordered *by size.* And the fees matched. So much for a head, so much for a half-length, so much for a full figure—that commonly for 500 guilders—or a three-quarter length, which was just about the same price. To have your head done by a good painter in Rembrandt's day cost 50 guilders. A group portrait cost as much as 100 guilders per person. Rembrandt's *Night Watch* (1642) aroused a storm of indignation, for each sitter, who had subscribed, ponying up equally to the cost, insisted on having equal prominence in the canvas—and Rembrandt had dared, presumptuously, to *compose* the picture!

Although the genre of portrait-painting had the sanction of no less an authority than the legendary Apelles, antiquity's greatest painter, and was pursued down through the ages by such masters as Titian, Velázquez, and even Raphael, who willingly obliged with a portrait of his first papal patron, the warlike *Guiliano della Rovere* (1511) who later became Julius II, the Vicar of Christ as Pope, portraitists have often come in for attack as lackeys, trundlers, or at least journeymen for hire, like George Romney, the brilliant colorist John Hoppner, G. F. Watts, and Thomas Lawrence. (John Opie, his rival, once said, "Lawrence made coxcombs of his sitters, and his sitters made a coxcomb of Lawrence.")

Many portraitists were merely "face painters," itinerant Ichabod Cranes with palette and brush, who went from town to town like drummers to find and flatter their sitters with generic concepts of who they were and how they appeared. Very often early portraits done in America were typically two-dimensional, with subjects wearing clothing of broad, simplified, and clearly defined patterns and all done in virtually unmodeled color and shape. Poses, postures, and proportions are found to be often similar, canvas to canvas, without small detail and little delineation of face. As old Frank Hagen, late mayor of Jersey City was so fond of saying, "Every time a politician gets specific, he loses votes."

Painters of the itinerant sort generally had not the slightest interest in inventing public personalities for their subjects. Some say that the painter Thomas Eakins, wounded by his lack of recognition and the humiliating need to earn a living that way, projected his sense of failure onto the wistful, dispirited features of his sitters.

Wayfaring and peripatetic painters were taken as bootlicks, prat boys to the idle rich, accommodating tradesmen and paid-by-the-pound yahoos, bowing and scraping for money to wealthy patrons of little or no merit, daubers executing standard portraits as a means to the end of making a living. It was embarrassing, the artist being subjected to the whims and vanities of his customers' vainglorious whims. It was wounding to the ego and led to little in the way of a commodious purse. The necessity of subjecting oneself, eye to eye, to the will of any patron—the artists were literally patronized—often involved the sort of subordination that took away the self-esteem that is needed to paint well. It became something like assembly-line work in many instances. Hyacinthe Rigaud, for example, official painter to the 18th-century court of Louis XIV, painted an astonishing average of 35 portraits a year for sixty-two years! Of Romney's prosaic portraits (and hundreds of execrable drawings) John Wesley noted in his *Journal* (January 5, 1789)—it seems more indictment than praise—that "he struck off an exact likeness at once and did more in one hour than Sir Joshua did in ten."

Sir Godfrey Kneller, the leading portrait painter in England during the late 17th and early 18th centuries, court painter to British monarchs from Charles II and George I, gave us—"knocked off"—a full 15 years of Kit Cats, a series of standard 36" x 28" portraits of Whig politicians and writers showing only the head and one hand—standard head to hip with subject wearing finery—a mini-genre actually named for and after members of the Whig dining club, to be hung in their meeting place at Barn Elms. (A "kit-cat," then, is slang is for a particular size, less than half-length portrait, but including the hands.*) It seemed for its repetition to be donkey work. Glance at them in a row—it looks like one big wealthy family. Kneller painted over 44 portraits of club members.

It was worse than a job. It was drudgework. After every portrait, Jean-Auguste-Dominique Ingres declared that he would do no more, that he was "a history painter" and not a draughtsman of the bourgeois." Thomas Lawrence, a notable portraitist to high society, felt he had prostituted his gifts. All his life Thomas Gainsborough regarded landscape as his real bent, although he painted portraits for a living. To many it was nothing less than a compromise, despicable commercialism, the kind of activity that the visionary, God-drenched William Blake, to take a classic example, condemned out of hand. Artists in 18th-century London, scrabbling for work, generally painted what they were told to paint by rich patrons and peers. Portraitists were especially subject to such pressures. (In Martinique Gauguin preferred to dig in malaria-infested canals rather than support himself as a portraitist.)

Always very much his own man, the passionate Blake grew furious whenever he thought of anyone who, betraying his talent, his vision, compromised his ideals and painted nothing but simpering sitters like Sir Joshua Reynolds:

----

*The special Kit-cat portrait size is said to have been determined because the dining-room ceiling of the Kit-cat Club was too low for half-length portraits of the members. Slightly larger than the traditional head and shoulders format, it allows enough space to include one or both hands. So, while the poses in the Kit-cat portraits may look similar, none is actually repeated. When hung together, the overall effect is of a unified club of equals, though each man retains his individuality through distinct gestures, props and costumes.

"When Sir Joshua Reynolds died
All nature was degraded;
The King dropped a tear into the Queen's ear,
And all his pictures faded."

William Blake, a Dissenter, flatly refused to paint portraits. He left the protection of his patron William Hayley who, he wrote to his brother James in 1803, "thinks to turn me into a Portrait Painter as he did poor Romney, but this he nor all the devils in hell will never do . . . I now defy the worst & fear not while I am true to myself which I will be." James Barry, an Irish painter who was expelled from the Royal Academy in 1799 for his own bitter attacks on the sacred memory of Sir Joshua Reynolds—and who incidentally died in great poverty and squalor—could rarely be persuaded to demean himself to paint portraits, although the portraits we have done by him are very fine. Blake's projected poem "Barry" (which exists only as a fragment) was written, incidentally, in celebration of that painter whose views both of Reynolds and portrait-painting he so strongly shared.

"The enquiry in England," Blake wrote down angrily in the margin of one of his books, "is not whether a man has talents and genius, but whether he is passive and polite and a virtuous ass and obedient to Noblemen's opinions in art and science. If he is, he is a good man. If not, he must be starved." No one of course could buy or hire Blake. As a consequence, while he didn't starve, he was always very poor, content nevertheless to live quietly as an etcher, journeyman engraver and print-seller, sitting at home hand-coloring his poems. On his deathbed, the visionary Blake, while working on his illustrations for Dante's *Divine Comedy*, stopped suddenly, turned to his wife who was in tears by his bedside, and is said to have cried,

"Stay Kate! Keep just as you are—I will draw your portrait—for you have ever been an angel to me." The man who was considered mad by many completed this loving sketch (which is, alas, lost), laid down his tool and began to sing hymns and verses.

At six that evening, after promising his wife that he would be with her always, Blake died on August 12, 1827. Alexander Gilchrist, his biographer, later offered the report that a female lodger in the house who was present as he sighed and passed away, said, "I have been at the death, not of a man, but of a blessed angel."

Few if any artists, of course, are creators all the time. Look at the lives of the poets. Caedmon kept pigs. Chaucer was a diplomat, Villon a burglar, Shakespeare an actor, Marlowe a spy, Vaughan a country doctor, Milton a civil servant, John Clare a laborer, Christina Rossetti a governess, and Matthew Arnold an inspector of schools. At 60, Giacomo Casanova, who had made a living throughout Europe by being an expert on the new financial institution of the lottery, took up employment as a librarian in an obscure central European castle, where to relieve his frustration he wrote his memoirs.

Creativity of any sort needs time, patience, the freedom to work in peace, and to have time takes the leisure that money requires. Nathaniel Hawthorne worked in a customs house, and his wife Sophia decorated lampshades, books, and screens to make extra money while he scratched to write. Thomas Hardy was an architect, and Gerard Manley Hopkins was a priest, as was Philip Hermogenes Calderon. Walt Whitman edited newspapers. Almost all of Greek poet Constantine Cavafy's efforts were written while he was employed in the Egyptian Irrigation Service, from the age of 29 until he was 60 years old. He sent out his poetry, which was never formally published, to various friends at his own expense. (At 47, he wrote "The City," his sad but persuasive poem on the impossibility of changing one's life.) And W. H. Davies was apprenticed as a youth in the picture-frame trade.

During his youthful seagoing years, the great novelist Joseph Conrad hoped to earn an income outside of the merchant service, which paid little, by way of whaling ventures, piloting in the Suez Canal, dabbling in Australian pearl fisheries, even doing work of some sort for an American politician. (As a young man, in 1878, after having lost 800 francs in a Monte Carlo gaming room, Conrad in despair tried to commit suicide.) One thinks of Joris-Karl Huysmans, author of the brilliant novel *À rebours* (1884), spending most of his life—30 long years!—as a bureaucrat in the French Ministry of the Interior, where in the end his chief job was chasing after penny ante anarchists and expelling undesirable atheists. The playwright Eugene O'Neill, at age 21, after a long sea voyage to Buenos Aires and places south, could only find a lowly job there with the Singer Sewing Machine Company, smashing, hacking at, and breaking up old machines with a sledgehammer.

William Sidney Porter ("O. Henry") was a bank teller and registered pharmacist. Vernon Watkins worked all his life in a bank. W. H. Auden was a schoolmaster. Louise Imogen Guiney had for a time a frustratingly awful job as postmistress in Auburndale, Massachusetts, which was her hometown. Her salary depended on the amount of business she transacted, and the bigoted retired Protestant clergymen in her neighborhood, who took exception both to her St. Bernard dogs and her Catholicism, got together and boycotted her, impelling her to go abroad to write her brilliant poems and prose.

T. S. Eliot worked in a bank and then became a publisher. Samuel Beckett held a job as an agricultural laborer in France during

World War II. Playwright Frank Wedekind had a spate of unusual jobs, among them writing jingles for Maggi soup and as a publicist for a circus. Colin Wilson worked in a plastics factory. Allen Ginsburg, before writing "Howl" was working in his twenties as a market researcher. Wallace Stevens was in the employ of an insurance office all his life, and poet Charles Bukowski toiled in a post office for more than 10 years. James Branch Cabell tried to run a coal mine for several years. Ralph Meatyard fretted away grinding lenses in an optician's shop. Arthur Rimbaud shipped guns. And the writer Primo Levi was manager of a Turin chemical factory for 50 years.

"Getting by." How difficult it could be, and often was. After even the death of such a successful writer as Nathaniel Hawthorne, family expenses continued to exceed the royalty income from his books. His wife Sophia was obliged to follow the genteel pretensions of Hepzibah Pyncheon, "hucksteress of a cent shop," as Hawthorne described that scowling old maid of a character in *The House of the Seven Gables* (1851), and practice desperate economies of a rather humiliating kind, dismissing all of her servants, hiring out one of her daughters (Una) as a gymnastic instructor at a female seminary, and selling the amateur watercolors of the other daughter (Rose) at a curiosity shop in the neighborhood.

And it has been much the same with musicians. Dvořák's father wanted him to become a butcher. English composer Frederick Delius in 1884, although resisting the mercantile life of his prosperous family, at age 22 was sent off to Florida in the United States in 1884 to manage an orange plantation, to grow oranges, managing (or neglecting to manage) a plantation at Solano Grove, near Jacksonville. Arnold Dolmetsch, who spent much of his working life in England and established an instrument-making workshop in Haslemere, Surrey, in spite of his successful concerts, could not manage to eke out a substantial living, so in 1905 he moved to Boston to make harpsichords.

It was never easy—or rewarding, or anything even close to romantic—taking up servile work when inspiration beckoned. Italian violinist Guiseppe Cambini spent the last ten years of his life in the Bicetre almshouses of Paris. Luigi Boccherini died in poverty. So did Béla Bartók in 1945. Composer Ferruccio Busoni, when working as the director of the Bologna Conservatory, bitterly claimed that his sole success there was the installation of new lavatories. On the other hand, Giovanni Palestrina, the brilliant Italian composer, took to running, and quite successfully, his second wife's burgeoning leather and fur business. And Wolfgang Amadeus Mozart, never mind the genius we know today, but even then the most creative composer of his time, was reduced in 1788 to making arrangements of other composers' music, especially by Bach and Handel, in order to survive.

Composer Charles Ives sold life insurance. Johannes Brahms played piano in a bordello in Hamburg, just as Puccini did in a similar cathouse in the Via della Dogana, as well in the fashionable resorts of Bagni di Lucca and Lerici in order to eke out the meagre pension of 75 lire a month on which his widowed mother had to maintain her large family. And at age 22, Sir Edward Elgar became bandmaster at the Powick Lunatic Asylum, near Worcester, England, a grim job in music therapy that occupied the man one day a week and augmented the income that he earned from also working in his father's music shop. Sixty years after Wolfgang Mozart died, the German composer Gustav Lortzing, without a patron (or any copyright protection), literally starved to death, having been forced to sell his hugely successful operas to a publisher for a pitifully small sum, an outright fee. On January 20, 1851, the night his musical comedy *Die Opernprobe* premiered in Frankfurt, Lortzing suffered a stroke at his home in Berlin and died without medical treatment on the morning of the following day, under huge stress, deeply in debt, completely impoverished. Franz Schubert was tragically forced to sell half a dozen of his "Winterreise" songs to the greedy publisher Haslinger for a gulden apiece (20 cents, that is). All the music publishers at the time—Naegeli in Zurich and in Vienna Diabelli and Pennauer and Sauer and Leidesdorf—bilked the man.

In the end, it was chemistry that took the lion's share of Alexander Borodin's divided attention, since as a medical man and professor of chemistry, he was constantly distracted with his busy professional life. He rarely wrote his musical compositions "except," as he once said, "during my summer holiday, or when some ailment compels me to keep to my rooms." It was done mostly in his spare time—generally, as he said, in the little leisure afforded him by a bad cold in the head. Both his magnum opus, the opera *Prince Igor* (1887), and his *Third Symphony* (1882) were left unfinished at his death.

On the other hand, Modest Mussorgsky, who had a constitutional reluctance to finish anything, was ridiculed by his friends for resigning his commission in the dashing and exclusive Preobrazhensky Guards regiment in order to write music. Vladimir Stassov called him "a perfect idiot." Even Alexander Borodin had to admit, "I was incredulous when he told me he intended to devote himself to serious music." And in the case of Hector Berlioz, when both of his grand operas proved to be failures, he was forced to earn his living by writing criticism for various newspapers, a job he detested.

In a drudge-like job, the ill-starred Steven Foster, who was poor for most of his life, worked as a bookkeeper in his brother's wholesale grocery in Cincinnati. Jazzman Duke Belaire owned a liquor store in Cranston, Rhode Island. Trumpet player Red Lenox had an insurance agency in Woonsocket. William ("Count") Basie played in a silent movie theater. Folksinger Blind Lemon Jefferson worked as a wrestler in Dallas. In 1941 guitarist Chuck Wayne fumbled along as an elevator operator. Willie Nelson, for a while, was a pig farmer. Singer Nina Simone taught piano to make ends meet. Country singer Tammy Wynette worked as a hairdresser, Lacy J. Dalton as a topless dancer. Luciano Pavarotti for a spell had to earn money as a schoolteacher, as was the case with philosopher Ludwig Wittgenstein. Jazz soprano sax player Sidney Bechet opened up a tailor shop in New York City. Composer Lovie Austin was an inspector in a war plant. And Duke Ellington, who turned down a scholarship to Pratt Institute in Brooklyn, turned a hand painting commercial signs.

There is no "art uniform" by which one can recognize artists. Their peculiarity lies inside them, their inspired, quixotic souls their mandala, their genius in the dances of their dreams. But their needs are no different than ours.

So many painters have been driven to work, desperately, in order to eat. What distinguishes the artist from the common run of men, however, is that he must work not only at a job to put bread on the table but at his craft to see through the realization of dreams that can be fulfilled in no other way. Many lives reflect struggle only in the early years. In other instances, whole lifetimes were lost to grinding poverty and the misery of neglect. Half the time Paul couldn't be paid simply because there was no Peter to rob. The itinerant Bartolomé Murillo is a prime example. As a young man in Seville, extremely poor, he started as a painter of the kind of pictures that are sold at fun fairs and food markets. He had a prayer life, traveled and executed paintings for Franciscan convents through Spain, drew inspiration from religious images in an attempt to attract the lucrative American market, unsuccessfully. (In Spain a bad painting is called a *pintura de feria*, and a good one, irrespective, a "Murillo.") He died in Seville in 1682, only a few months after he fell from a scaffold while working on a fresco at the church of the Capuchins in Cádiz. Rembrandt himself died poor and enfeebled in later years after his collection of paintings and works of fine art had been sold off at public auctions for a fraction of their value, when his pictures had been seized for debt. Although prolific in his art, his life had been filled with misfortune. He was twice widowed, buried all of his children—three newborns and a fourth child at 27—was widowed twice, sold his house, along with many objects and paintings from his collection, which included his printing press. Moving into a smaller house changed nothing regarding his economy, for he never financially recovered, eventually dying in poverty. He was lowered into a pauper's grave in the Westerkerk in Amsterdam in a numbered "kerkgraf" (a grave owned by the church) on October 4, 1669 (aged 63) at the cost of a meagre 13 florins.

Success matters nothing, or very little. In a very real sense, Gandhi was correct in stating, "Poverty is the worst form of violence." For the greater part of his professional career, after a life of working hard, writing popular novels such as *Animal Farm* (1945) and *Nineteen Eighty-Four* (1949), George Orwell's income had never amounted to more than a few hundred pounds a year. His entire estate was officially assessed for probate at just under 10,000 pounds. Genius comes a cropper when it comes to the creative arts. Who is surprised that such a genius as Vincent van Gogh died sucking-stone poor? At the Van Gogh Museum in Amsterdam I have seen his pencil drawing *Worn Out* (1882), a beleaguered and despairing soul sitting sorrowfully with his head in his hands and thought: *that is you*. According to his brother Theo, Vincent's last words were: "The sadness will last forever."

Beginning in 1885 at age 14, the French painter, draughtsman, and print artist Georges Rouault embarked on an apprenticeship as a glass painter and restorer, which lasted for five years. It has been suggested that his experience in this craft that constituted his mature art was a likely source of the heavy, black contouring and glowing colors, very like the stark, often impressionistic leaded glass illustrations that he saw on church windows commemorating saints, which characterize Rouault's mature painting style. A passionate Christian, he was also a perfectionist, and, at the end of his life, suspecting he would not be able to finish them—he died at age 86 in 1958—he made a conflagration of his pictures, burning 300 of them estimated to be worth today about more than half a billion francs.

George Stubbs, an English painter best known for his paintings of horses, to earn money gave lectures to medical students. Sculptor David Smith worked as a laborer in a car factory. Johannes Wynants was an innkeeper. Claude Lorrain was first trained as a pastry-cook. Renaissance sculptor Agostino do Duccio—the man who was first to work on the block of marble that was later used by Michelangelo for his *David*—was a mercenary soldier. Jacob van Ruisdael, the greatest of the Dutch realist landscape painters, practiced as a surgeon in Amsterdam while continuing to paint. Piet Mondrian, who had a private obsession about painting watercolors of delicate flowers, once contemplated giving up art for a career in horticulture. Pierre Bonnard became a painter only after selling a poster to a champagne maker in 1889. Auguste Renoir worked in a china factory at 13, painting porcelain. As did Jean Watteau, who slept in doorways in Paris, contracting a fatal consumption in the process, in a picture factory, painting skies, skies, skies, for three francs a week and a daily bowl of soup. How many survived toiling away at perfunctory piecework, doing skies, foliage, staffage?

Aert van der Neer, a Dutch landscape painter who specialized in moonlight effects—I consider masterpieces his *Moonlit Landscape with a View of the New Amstel River and Castle Kostver-loren* (1647–49) and his *Winter Landscape with Skaters* (1655)—could not make a living by his brush. He was barely able to support his family by selling the landscapes that were his specialty, none of which at the time were highly valued. In 1659 it seemed necessary to supplement his income by trying to keep a wine tavern in the Kalverstraat, which turned out to be a total failure, and after two years in that business he went broke. Everything went belly-up. He died in Amsterdam in abject poverty, and his art was so little esteemed that the pictures left by him were valued at about five shillings apiece. Abstract painter Serge Poliakoff, who emigrated from Russia in 1919, for many years earned a living in Paris in run-down clubs playing the guitar. Benjamin Marshall turned to writing articles about horse-racing. Camille Pissarro worked as a clerk in his father's general store until he ran away to Venezuela in 1852. And Winslow Homer earned a living as an illustrator—he recorded the Civil War—but only at age 39 could he afford fully to devote himself to painting. As a fledgling artist, he worked repetitively on sheet music covers and other commercial work for two years. By 1857, his freelance career was underway after he turned down an offer to join the staff of *Harper's Weekly*. "From the time I took my nose off that lithographic stone," Homer later declared, "I have had no master, and never shall have any."

It has always been a precarious living, painting, even turning out portraits the way itinerant jobbing daubers did back in the colonial period when portraiture was the most important form of painting, even if as in the early 18th century the rendering of subjects were idealistic, often two dimensional, and not representative of the personality of the sitter. There were to be found well-known and successful portraitists at that time, including John Smibert (1688–1751), Joseph Badger (1708–1765), John Singleton Copley (1738–1815), Ralph Earl (1751–1801), and Charles Willson Peale (1741–1827).

Still, the Starving Artist is an archetype. So too the ignominious fate of much of his work. A Sienese painter named Stefano, the son of Giovanni of Cortona, whom we know by the 18th-century nickname Sassetta, painted one of the largest and most splendid altarpieces of the early Italian Renaissance. Six yards wide and six yards high, painted on both sides like Duccio's *Maestà* in Siena, and made up of 60 images, adorned with a splendid gilt frame over the main altar of the local Franciscan church, it was created from roughly 1437 to 1444 and has always been said to be the high-water mark of early Renaissance painting. But the glory of this paragon, the sheer wonder of the work with its myriad figures and scenes, was too tempting to the greedy, demanding, overreaching and basically soulless collectors of the 19th and 20th centuries, and today its disassembled panels are scattered in twelve museums throughout Europe and the United States.

In the late 18th century, George Romney drudged away in the town of Kendal for five years, making a negligible living by doing commissions at very modest fees, a paltry two guineas for a "half-length," for example. Twenty of Romney's original compositions, including *Lear in the Storm* (undated), *A Landscape with Fingers* (1799), and *A Shandean Piece* (1761–62) were disposed of by lottery at the Kendal Town Hall for the ridiculous sum of 40 pounds. Then there was the fate of the genius Gian Lorenzo Bernini, the leading sculptor of his age, credited with creating the Baroque style of sculpture at the height of his fame, but a man who had portentously prophesied the decline of his reputation; indeed, during his lifetime, an equestrian statue of Louis XIV, completed in 1673, was so disliked that it was altered by Francois Girardon, the French sculptor, into a park ornament.

In 1884 the municipal corporation of the city of Calais invited several artists, Auguste Rodin amongst them, to submit proposals for the project to erect a statue of Eustache de Saint Pierre, eldest of the burghers, his design, which included all six figures rather than just de Saint Pierre. Sculptor Auguste Rodin submitted his proposal and won the invitation, which proved in the end, however, to be controversial. His *Burghers of Calais*—the 12 gaunt original castings, which commemorated an event during the Hundred Years' War, when Calais, a French port on the English Channel surrendered to the English after an 11-month siege—was met not only with a dark, disapproving, and bourgeois public but even dismissed with outright scorn. They felt that it lacked "overtly heroic antique references," which they regarded as integral to all public sculpture.

The public who had a different vision felt that the work failed on several scores. It was not pyramidal in arrangement, and it contained no allegorical figures. It was intended by the sculptor to be placed at ground level, rather than on a pedestal. The burghers, which for Rodin stood for the heroism of self-sacrifice, to the disapproving public were not presented in a positive image of true glory; instead, they displayed "pain, anguish and fatalism." In 1895 the monument was installed in Calais on a large pedestal in front of Parc Richelieu, a public park, which was also contrary to Rodin's wishes, for in his artistic the sculptor wanted contemporary townsfolk, as he explained, to "almost bump into" the figures as a way of feeling solidarity with them. Only later was his vision realized, when the sculpture was moved in front of the newly completed town hall of Calais, where it now rests on a much lower base. Appeasing the public in the matter of art is not by any means a given.

For that matter, Rodin's famous sculpture *The Thinker* (1904) was never erected as he wished, and the statue in Cleveland was not only several times scornfully slubbered over with paint in scornful repudiation of something—who can divine the motives of madness?—but once savaged by a vandal with an axe, and even actually blasted by a bomb! Before dawn on March 24, 1970, a bomb equivalent to about three sticks of dynamite exploded beneath the statue, knocking the figure from—and in the process destroying—the pedestal, turning his lower legs to shrapnel. He landed face down. The directors of the Cleveland Art Museum chose not to replace the statue, strangely enough, but to reinstall it without repairing the damage. The prime motive of the decision, reported Chris Roy in *Art and Design*,

> "was a desire to preserve and honor Rodin's original work which, in turn, might memorialize the turmoil of the Vietnam War years. It's generally agreed that the attack was undertaken by a Cleveland faction of the Weathermen (a.k.a., the Weather Underground) an ultra-radical political group that voiced (and acted upon) its opposition to the Vietnam War and U.S. imperialism in general by bombing government buildings, banks and other targets. A spray-painted message at the base of the toppled statue read 'Off the ruling class.' No one admitted to, or was ever charged, for the crime."

Antonio Correggio's frescoes for the Cathedral Dome in Parma, representing the Assumption and composed of ascending concentric circles of flying figures, were described by one of the canons there as "a hash of frogs' legs." In 1573, Paolo Veronese was called to account by the Inquisition for having brazenly introduced profane subjects—such things as weird dogs (*Boy with a Greyhound*, ca. 1570), and drunken Germans (*The Feast in the House of Levi*, 1573)—into a religious picture. J. M. W. Turner left nearly 300 paintings and nearly 20,000 watercolors to the nation, conditions that have been scandalously disregarded. His pictures have been scattered all the way from Indianapolis to Melbourne, Ottawa to Auckland! Karl Schmidt-Rottluff was expelled from the Prussian Academy in 1933 and in 1941 forbidden to paint at all by the Nazi police. Diego Rivera's mural in Rockefeller Center was replaced by one by Frank Brangwyn on account of a portrait of Lenin rather than for any objection to the style. And hundreds of Camille Pissarro's paintings were used as duckboards in his muddy garden by German invaders in 1870.

The long depressing history of poverty and painters has been documented by everyone from Vasari to Crowe and Cavalcaselle to Morelli to Berenson. Silvestro Lega died blind and utterly impoverished in Florence in 1895. Amadeo Modigliani, born of a wealthy Jewish family that had suddenly fallen on hard times, lived the last 14 years of his life tubercular—he died at 36—and virtually starving in a garret in Paris. Johan Jongkind, who lived in squalor, near Grenoble finally went mad. Jean Honoré Fragonard, living in desperate poverty at the end of his life, was grudgingly given a job in the Museums Service, with thanks to the good offices of painter Jacques David, but he died in Paris almost totally forgotten. George Morland died in prison in 1804 after pathetically producing an enormous amount of scamped work to pay off his debts. What happened was that in 1799 he was arrested for debt and ignominiously jailed, a mitigated confinement—incarcerated "within the rules," meaning that he was allowed to ply his craft within the dim walls—but he spent most of his days there dead drunk, a scapegrace, until 1802 when he was released under the Insolvent Debtors Act, but in precarious health. At the end, he was seized with palsy, lost the use of his left hand, rendering him unable hold his palette. Notwithstanding, he seems to have gone on painting to the last, when he was arrested again for a publican's score, and died in a sponging-house in Eyre Street, Cold Bath Fields, on October 27, 1804.

Honoré Daumier, blind in his old age, was desperately poor. John Michael Wright, painter to Charles II, died penniless. Van Gogh was always insolvent. Completely broke in 1867, Claude Monet left Camille Doncieux, who was pregnant, and went to stay at Sainte-Adresse. (Renoir had to lend him money.) Although she married a doctor, Käthe Kollwitz, whose work is permeated with sympathy for the poor, lived most of her life in the shabbier quarters of Berlin. And it was also in Germany after spending years as a professor of art in Breslau and Berlin that Oskar Schlemmer, dismissed by the Nazis for his so called "degenerate" tendencies, worked for the rest of his life, alone, in a lacquer factory. And the famous exhibition of the *Société anonyme des artistes peintres sculpteurs et graveurs*, as it was called, which opened in April 1874, showing Pablo Picasso, Claude Monet, Pierre-Auguste Renoir, Paul Cézanne, et al. (but not Édouard Manet, who resented his younger colleagues), also showed Alfred Sisley and Armand Guillaumin, who on opening day were destitute.

Paul Gauguin, close to penniless in Tahiti during his last hungry years, was forced to beg for a job as a draftsman in the Public Works Department at six francs a day. It was often next to the knuckle for him, especially in his phantasmagoric final days. In 1895 he wrote to literary critic and poet Charles Morice, "I would have you know I am on the verge of suicide (a ridiculous act, no doubt, but inevitable). I shall make up my mind in the next few months, depending on what replies I get and whether they are accompanied by money. . . . What matters the death of an artist!" An angry malcontent and arguably with good reason, the expressionist painter Chaim Soutine—born Chaim-Iche Solomonovich Sutin, the tenth of eleven children, in the city of Smilaviči in what is now Belarus, in the Chervyen District of Minsk—not only had an intensely hard childhood, but a ruinously poor one, then and later. When France was invaded by German troops on May 10, 1940, Soutine, a Jew, had to escape from the French capital and hide to avoid arrest by the Nazi Gestapo. Fleeing like a hunted parasite from one shabby and unsafe place to another, hiding in thick forests, sleeping in filthy hovels, scrounging around at night for food, he developed a stomach ulcer which, bleeding badly, forced him to leave a safe hiding place to go to Paris for emergency surgery, which, too late, proved ineffective. He died on August 9, 1943, at age 50, of a perforated ulcer.

Soutine's *Carcass of Beef* (1925) has always seemed to me to be a metaphor for the painter's brutal life. He reveled in the subject, which constitutes his most well-known work, having painted 10 works in this series. His carcass paintings were said to inspired by the still-life on the same subject painted by Rembrandt, the Dutch painter's *Slaughtered Ox* (1655), which the lugubrious Soutine discovered while studying the Old Masters in the Louvre, a subject which of course also deeply intrigued Daumier, Delacroix, and especially Francis Bacon. The carcass is hideously suspended by its two rear legs, which, tied by ropes to a wooden crossbeam, is also decapitated and flayed of skin and hair, with its eerie chest cavity stretched open showing the internal organs removed and revealing a mass of flesh, fat, connective tissue, joints, bones, and ribs. It seems a profane simulacrum of the Crucifixion.

Considering the large sums once easily commanded by his pictures—it has been commonly averred that he painted (implying "tossed off") a new canvas a day—Jean-Baptiste Greuze fell on terrible days during the days of the French Revolution. Banks failed, while the artist's savings vanished. He had been in receipt of considerable wealth, which he had dissipated partly by extravagance and bad management, so that during his closing years he had been forced to solicit commissions, which his enfeebled powers no longer enabled him to carry out with success. He had married the greedy extravagant daughter of a bookseller named Mrs. Babuty, a woman devoid of all moral sense. It was a disastrous marriage from all reports. His rapacious wife squandered much of his money on vulgar acquaintances and other men, eventually even embezzling large sums of it. Lampooned in publicly printed cartoons ridiculing her husband for supporting her, cornered, Greuze had to resign his *logement* in the Louvre, until in 1785 a deed of separation enabled him to get rid of her.

Meanwhile, Jacques-Louis David was the new god of the moment. It was in vain that Greuze wrote to the newspapers, desperately calling attention, as of old but in vain, to the moral meaning of his work. He tried to fall in with new ideas. We hear of his receiving 175 francs for a picture that would formerly have brought him thousands of livres. He wore clothes shabby and frayed. Finally, there are the pitiful begging letters that he wrote, one of them asking for an advance on a picture ordered out of charity, another pathetically saying, "I am seventy-five years old, I have not a single order for a picture." From his bed of bitter neglect and dire poverty, he would ask, "Who is king today?" Greuze said to his friend Barthélemy just before he died, "Goodbye. I shall expect you at my funeral. You will be all alone there, like the poor man's dog." Greuze died on March 4, 1805 in great poverty. It was a bleak day, and fully inconsequential, it seemed. The funeral was followed by two persons.

In other instances, grinding toil was only temporary. Henri Rousseau, a musician in the French Army, went to Paris at 25 and first worked as a lawyer's clerk, then as a *douanier*, a minor customs official. Scratching out a living became an obligation for food and shelter. French landscape painter Claude Lorrain worked as a pastry cook until he was 27. Susan Valadon was an acrobat in a Parisian circus at the age of 15, fell, became a model, and gave birth to Utrillo. British painter Gwen John, sister of the painter Augustus John, tried to ferret out a meagre living after settling in Paris in 1904 by posing for other artists and then strangely seeking seclusion for the rest of her life, almost becoming a hermit, in Meudon.

One of the Fauvists, Maurice de Vlaminck got jobs playing the violin, which his musician father had taught him. In 1902 and 1903, he wrote poems, songs, including several mildly pornographic novels illustrated by André Derain—the two of them met on a train after a minor railcar accident in 1900—and they set up a studio together. He painted during the day, doing double-duty as he earned his livelihood by giving violin lessons and performing with various musical bands at night. English semi-abstract painter Graham Sutherland worked as an apprentice at the Midland Railway Works, abandoning a career as a railway engineer to take up painting. Jean Dubuffet, the French painter and sculptor, was born into a family of wholesale wine merchants, part of the wealthy bourgeoisie, and never lost interest in it, starting his own wholesale wine business in

Paris. He moved to Paris in 1918 to study painting at the Académie Julian, becoming close friends with the artists Juan Gris, André Masson, and Fernand Léger. He continued painting, doing a large series of portraits that sold, but he would intermittently turn back to develop his wine business at Bercy. Years later, in an autobiography, he had no qualms about the success of his sideline during the war or the substantial profits he made, buying and selling, during the hated German occupation, breezily supplying wine to the Wehrmacht, the armed forces of the Third Reich.

Money matters, profit and gain. It should not be overlooked either that Bellini, Titian, and Tintoretto all worked for German merchants in Venice. As did Hans Holbein the Younger who arrived in London in 1532 and, after his friend Thomas More resigned from office, found employment from his fellow countrymen under the patronage of the Steelyard, the German business community in London, until 1536 when was appointed court painter to Henry VIII. Titian—Tiziano Vecelli, the Renaissance Italian painter, considered the most important member of the 16th-century Venetian school—was so wealthy, and notorious among his colleagues for his love of money, that Jacopo Bassano in his massive painting *The Purification of the Temple* (1580) at the far right of the canvas satirizes Titian as an avaricious old man greedily hovering over a tableful of purses and bags of coins. Titian amassed a fortune in his lifetime. Charles V paid 100 gold crowns for every portrait of himself.

Peter Paul Rubens, for whom commissions abounded, was fabulously wealthy in his lifetime, enjoying the highest esteem of his contemporaries. Handsome, very sure of himself, Rubens said, "My talents are such that I have never lacked courage to undertake any design, however vast." Like Velázquez, he was a highly respected courtier. Antonio de Corregio was wealthy, in fact—Vasari was wrong—and raised with every advantage. The same could be said of Henri Toulouse-Lautrec, who was descended from the counts of Toulouse and went to fashionable schools. Francesco Solimena, called L'Abate Ciccio, was a prolific Italian painter of the Baroque era in Naples, became a baron, and lived in a palace. Corot was wealthy, both from inheritance and, later, from his success as a painter, although he was subsidized by his prosperous parents until reaching the age of 51.

Edgar Degas, born in Paris of a wealthy family, had a private income that made him independent of sales of his work. There were many others who had the advantages of wealth right from the start: Charles Demuth, Reginald Marsh, Childe Hassam, Robert Motherwell, et al. And in 1812 the somewhat eccentric Girodet, who won the Prix de Rome in 1789, came into an extremely large inheritance. His reaction? He immediately abandoned painting and began to compose long, unreadable poems and screeds on aesthetics, writing in a house completely shuttered against daylight.

Thousands of artists and dabblers were kept alive and from starving during the Thirties working for the WPA (Works Progress Administration) at \$23.60 per week, not bad take-home pay for those precarious times. President Franklin Roosevelt had received a letter from a champion of social art named George Biddle, a muralist, lithographer, and a childhood friend of his from the Groton School, encouraging the government to do something for the many struggling painters in America. As Harry Hopkins, the director of the New Deal programs, put it, "Hell, they've got to eat just like other people." To qualify for a WPA job, a struggling artist had only to prove he was poor, a criterion few frankly had trouble meeting back those days. The federal government hired more than 10,000 artists to create works of art across the country in a wide variety of forms—murals, theater, fine arts, music, writing, design, and more—for schools, hospitals, and a variety of public buildings. Almost all future Abstract Expressionists worked for the WPA, at one time or another. There were many fraudulent commissions, as well—and turmoil. When too many termination notices were received, riots and sit-down strikes often occurred among the artists.

Dutch artist Willem de Kooning, when not standing on a ladder painting houses to make money or doing windows for A. S. Beck, a popular shoe store chain, designed a mural for the Williamsburg Housing Project, but he was fired within a year when it was discovered he was not an American. William Baziotes, a surrealist of sorts, got work teaching art in Queens. Arshile Gorky, who once worked, as did many Armenians, in the Hood Rubber Company in Watertown, Massachusetts, got by living only on donuts in his early years painting in New York. It was Gorky who also painted a mural for the New York World's Fair—as did Philip Guston, who was actually born in Quebec—and who ironically described WPA art as "poor art for poor people." As for Jackson Pollock, he joined Adolph Gottlieb, Mark Rothko, and Ad Reinhardt on the Project's easel division, which required them to produce about one painting per month for allocation to schools, post offices, and various other government buildings. Paintings had to be submitted every four to eight weeks: four weeks for a 16" x 20" canvas, six weeks for a 21" x 36" canvas, three weeks for a watercolor. All easel divisionists had to punch a time clock, report to an office on East 39th Street every morning at 8 a.m. and check out at day's end. Paychecks were withheld for any irregularity.

Artist Jacob Kainen remembers once seeing a hapless, disheveled Pollock, dressed in his ragged pajamas, racing frantically toward the time clock only seconds before the deadline. Even stranger, a few months after the Project began, all the artists were suddenly ordered to stop signing their paintings, the rationale being that bridge builders and bricklayers don't sign their work, so why should painters? There was small room for sentimentality, less for faith. When the Federal Government began phasing out the Project in the early Forties, it disposed of the artwork in its possession as if it were so much scrap metal. Paintings were incinerated, carted away, auctioned off in warehouses—thousands in one Flushing warehouse in 1943—offered for sale by the pound, and even thrown out. One plumber supposedly purchased an entire lot, planning to use the canvases to insulate pipes!

Among the first people to pause and pick through a stack of disposed of canvases, ragged, mildewed, many of them in broken frames, was Herbert Benevy, art collector and owner of the Gramercy Art Frame Shop, a wily fellow. His selection, with all paintings purchased for as little as $3 a canvas, included works by Milton Avery, Alice Neel, Joseph Solman, Mark Rothko, and two by Jackson Pollock.

There have been strange extremes. Vincent van Gogh, who sold virtually none of his work when he was alive, took odd jobs, like working sporadic teaching and working in coal mines. Then there was Rosa Bonheur, who was fatefully bound, in spite of her protestations, to the business that her parents in their wisdom had selected for her—dressmaking—and which they were determined she should adopt. So greatly successful did she later become as a painter—*The Horse Fair*, her greatest picture, first exhibited in 1853, eventually sold for $53,000—that she was able to purchase a country home at Fontainebleau, where she carried out most of her later work. Curiously enough, she adopted male attire, which she constantly wore, except once, when she went to meet her empress to receive the cross of the Legion of Honor. (I have always wondered whether her cross-dressing was a reaction to the direction, so fully distasteful to her, her parents had initially marked out for her.)

Who can know how changes will alter a given life? More to the point, who can bank on the way what one hopes that initial drudgery will set one free to work? I daresay it comes, if it comes at all, like an unpredictable east wind. Without the helpful patronage of an art-loving St. Petersburg lawyer and liberal politician, Maxim Vinaver, who gave him a modest 125 francs a month, Marc Chagall, to take just one example, might have spent the rest of his natural life working as a sign painter.

John Constable worked as a miller—his father's occupation—until he was almost 30. He wasn't recognized as anything like a painter until he was 35, and then only in France. During the Second World War, Thomas Hart Benton was employed as a draftsman for the American Navy. Constantin Brâncuși, born of poor peasants, both worked in the service of a grocer in Slatina and became a domestic in a public house in Craiova, where he remained for several years. Only at the age of 18, when he created a violin by hand with materials he found around his workplace, did his career begin. Francis Bacon in the Twenties earned a modest living as a furniture designer and interior decorator, as did Georges Braque. The first painting of his own that Bacon ever really liked, *Painting 1946*, now hangs in the Museum of Modern Art in New York. It sold for a ridiculous $400. (The artist Edward Gorey once told me he could have bought a Bacon in 1952 for a couple of hundred dollars.)

From 1908 to 1912 Georgia O'Keeffe supported herself in Chicago turning out illustrations of lace and embroidery for an industrial company. Photographer Man Ray, born Emmanuel

Radenski—"the Last of the Red Hot Dadas"—once worked as a map-maker for a map and atlas publisher. Demobbed after World War I, the French surrealist Yves Tanguy for a few days each week in 1922 unloaded vegetables in the Les Halles market, when he stumbled upon a painting by Giorgio de Chirico and was so gobsmacked that he resolved to become a painter himself, in spite of his complete lack of formal training. As a war correspondent for the *New Yorker*, Saul Steinberg worked in the capacity of a reporter, at one point in his hustling about actually covering the Nuremberg trials. In 1958 Frank Stella, with a Princeton BA, supported himself by working as a housepainter. Before working for the WPA, Jackson Pollock, a man whose earnings usually melted like snow on thatch, worked as a $10-a-week janitor joined a crew of laborers who were sent around the city to clean public monuments.

Painter Larry Rivers, supposedly the "Godfather of Pop Art," in his early years supported himself by playing the saxophone with various bands in and around New York City. After studying at the Juilliard School of Music, seemingly destined for a musical career, he came into contact with the New York art world when, during an extended period of severe poverty, he took a job as a delivery boy for an art-supply house, a move that proved fortuitous. "I felt here that I had discovered the delights of art," Rivers later recalled. "My heroes were Picasso and Gonzalez."

Jasper Johns, uneducated, without any prospects, got tired of wandering the streets of New York and briefly began attending Hunter College. After attending a lecture on *Beowulf*, a French class that he admits was over his head, and an art class, he dropped out. Alone, ill from hunger and boredom, he took a job in a small bookshop and did display work for department stores. Soon, he and Robert Rauschenberg, a graphic artist from Texas, both began to earn pocket money by collaborating on free-lance window displays for such posh stores as Tiffany's and Bonwit Teller. Roy Lichtenstein did the same kind of work in Cleveland in the Fifties; he also spent time teaching—at Ohio State, SUNY at Oswego, and Douglass College in New Brunswick, New Jersey. Robert Motherwell also taught school. Sculptor Henry Moore was a full-time teacher in a grammar school in Castleford, England. Another sculptor Herbert Ferber attended evening classes at Beaux-Arts Institute of Design in New York from 1927 to 1930 while at Columbia studying, of all things, dentistry.

Joan Miró, working as a shoe clerk, had a nervous breakdown at the age of 18, and would not physically or mentally improve until his parents were resigned to let him paint. The Belgian surrealist René Magritte, whose mother drowned herself in the Sambre River in Belgium when he was only 14—significantly, when his mother's body was retrieved, her soaked dress was covering her face, an image that has been suggested as the source of several of her son's paintings of people with their faces mysteriously covered and obscured by cloth, including *Les Amants* (1928)—was thus left to his own devices and forced to earn his living working in a wallpaper factory. Anna Mary Robertson, known as Grandma Moses, woman who ran a dairy farm in Eagle Bridge, New York, for most of her life, began painting, at the age of 58, only after her husband had passed away in 1927. Originally, she embroidered pictures from worsted yarn, changing to embroidery in her seventies. She began painting in earnest at age 78. She had an unpretentious view of her work. As a matter of fact, her first solo exhibition, which took place in October 1940, was titled specifically for the show, *What a Farm Wife Painted*. Her painting *Sugaring Off* was sold for $1.2 million in 2006. Jean François Millet, a French artist and one of the founders of the Barbizon school in rural France, by the way, also toiled as a common farmer until, after his father died, he went to Paris in the 1880s, painting portraits in order not to starve. Destitute for much of his life, he often thought of committing suicide and was just as often dissuaded from it by his friend and later biographer, Alfred Sensier.

Many artists who have worked to support their art, taking lesser or menial or even seemingly derisive jobs to do so, have almost willfully considered a secondary job primary. Lucas Cranach, the German Renaissance painter, for example, thrived at owning a book-printing business in Wittenberg as well as an apothecary's shop on the side. The artist George Stubbs, whom we know nowadays as the first-rate British animal painter, ironically, took up what he considered a pedestrian living as a portraitist in the north of England while devoting himself to what was indeed his real passion, *anatomy*.

John James Audubon, after his marriage to Lucy Bakewell in 1808, with his wife's money and a friendly male partner of his opened a general store in Louisville, Kentucky, selling hams, flour, dry goods, etc. "The mercantile business did not suit me," Audubon wrote. "My very first venture on my own, was on the indigo speculation that cost me several hundred pounds, all of which I lost." Whether he turned to business because he considered himself an amateur naturalist in an epoch when most naturalists were wealthy amateurs is another question. He was always drawing birds instead of attending the shop. A gristmill he partly owned in Henderson, Kentucky, went bankrupt in 1819.

Astonishingly, he was also obliged to turn to world of art as a means of livelihood. He did chalk portraits for $20 apiece (about 30 or so of them are still extant) and then moved to Cincinnati, Ohio, where he offered dancing and drawing lessons and took up the craft of taxidermy. In 1822, his wife Lucy, who was from a prosperous family, had to become a governess in order to support the family so that her somewhat feckless husband could work full-time on his project dealing with the birds of America. His classic work, a color-plate book titled *The Birds of America* (1827–39), is considered one of the finest ornithological works ever completed. Audubon is also known for identifying 25 new species.

What is behind the job that takes the brush out of the painter's hand, the pen out of the writer's? Can anything positive be said of it. Is it a displacement activity? A crutch? There is the argument from necessity, of course, and what could be more basic? Giotto had eight children—remarkable, it is said, for their ugliness—and Vermeer 11. The question of vocation is intriguing. Obligation is paramount. As noted earlier, Gerard Manley Hopkins was a priest, as were Calderon, Vivaldi, and Fra Lippo Lippi. Bartolommeo della Porta became a monk. So did Fra Angelico. Bernardo Strozzi, the Genoese painter known as *Il Cappucino* and *Il Prete Genovese*, became a Franciscan friar at the age of 17. Van Gogh also studied for the church and for a while became a missionary in the coal mining district of the Borinage in Belgium. Henry Fuseli's father forced him to become a Zwinglian minister, although he never practiced as a priest. James Jacques Tissot was a Trappist monk for a while. And French painter Henri Michaux also once thought of becoming a monk.

Andrea Pozzo, who became a Jesuit lay brother in 1665 and is often given the courtesy title Padre—known for his grandiose frescoes, by which employed the technique of *quadratura* to create an illusion of three-dimensional space on flat surfaces, he was also a stage designer, architect, and art theoretician—wanted to abandon painting but was made to continue by his superiors. Fra Bartolomeo, the Italian Renaissance painter—his original nickname was Baccio della Porta—spent all his career in Florence until his mid-forties, when he travelled to work in various cities, as far south as Rome. He became a Dominican friar in 1500, incidentally, having earlier fell under the spell of Savonarola (his well-known portrait of Savonarola remains the best-known image of the reformer) and, renouncing painting as a distraction from his religious obligations, remained for whole years without touching a pencil or brush. When eventually he did yield to the solicitations of his friends and superiors to paint again, it was under the strict condition that he would work for the benefit of his order, with his monastery receiving all the produce of his labors.

Do dreams of what we are not somehow tempt us to act against our own better judgements? Register doubt? Pursue other courses? Or even throw the whole thing over? (What, for instance, do we make of that fact that such a gifted Golden Age painter of landscapes as Meindert Hobbema stopped painting in 1668 to take the well-paid position of "wine-gauger" for the Amsterdam licensing board, assessing and collecting local taxes on wine, holding onto this for 40 years until his death? Or that the last 30 years of Marcel Duchamp's life were largely devoted to chess? There is the argument that artists in the many thousand ways possible actually subvert themselves, literally seeking an alternative to the world they suspect or abhor or cannot inhabit. Are diversions a comfort?

Psychologists might argue, for example, that artists thrive best by irritations, that they are goaded on by setback, that, within the many mysteries it presents, art can only persuade those it can seduce to its difficulties. "The stupid believe that to be truthful is easy; only the artist, the great artist, knows how difficult it is," said Willa Cather. Art critic Sir Andrew Marbot advanced a theory as far back as the early 19th century that the creativity of the genius is in fact nothing less than a deviation.

We do know that most great artists, the extraordinary ones especially, demand originality from themselves and, fighting normalcy, consider a daily job a painful deviation from their godly primary activity. Albert Pinkham Ryder, the moody and eccentric allegorist, refused to acquire money, flatly hated it. An uncashed check for more than a thousand dollars was found in his gloomy rooms after he died. ("The artist needs but a roof, a crust of bread, and his easel," he wrote, "and all the rest God gives him in abundance. He must live to paint, not paint to live. He cannot be a good fellow.")

It may be observed as a cardinal notion that artists—in the world, as it were, not of it—tend to find acceptance disgusting and comfort bourgeois—Pierre Bonnard did, so did Francisco Goya— and actually seek repudiation by the world as a final execration of it. It is often terribly bewildering to be popular. Some find it humiliating, finding commercial success the equivalent of kissing the devil's fundament. There are those who, as a palpable way to escape *consequence*, find in drudgery strangely what they need, and in certain cases of hard drinking and drugs, a psychological need to find in such extreme states of anguish and dissolution the very validation of their uniqueness. Just as the expression of mood often usurps the precise recording of nature, the nature of man reacts with a mood of rejection, recalling for me the idea that acceptance alone palls one of Henry David Thoreau's richest—and pessimistic—truisms, "Whatever succeeds with an audience is bad."

To many an artist, his sensibility entangled within the coils of creation, his mind caught within something like the imprisoning structures of a Piranesi *carcere*, success is a failure. The act of completion itself is plaguing, the fact of a particular creation when finished—*as finished*—itself a mortifying dead end.

In his *Notes Toward a Supreme Fiction*, Wallace Stevens ascribes the making of art to our foreignness in the world, and to our desire for a compensatory native world. "From this poem"—it could be any art—"springs: that we live in a place / That is not our own and, much more, not ourselves." Surely artists are, in fact always have been, the first to see and to feel and to know that.

It is perhaps for that reason that we can enter the mind of and come to understand the thoughts of the irrepressible Gulley Jimson, that ill-behaved, lovably scruffy painter and visionary, a poor man, when he says at the end of Joyce Cary's novel *The Horse's Mouth* (1948), "Go love without the help of anything on earth; and that's the real horse meat. A man is more independent that way, when he doesn't expect anything for himself. And it's just possible he may avoid getting in a state."